T0178448

Lecture Notes in Artificial Intelligence 12169

Subseries of Lecture Notes in Computer Science

Ahti-Veikko Pietarinen ·
Peter Chapman · Leonie Bosveld-de Smet ·
Valeria Giardino · James Corter ·
Sven Linker (Eds.)

Diagrammatic Representation and Inference

11th International Conference, Diagrams 2020
Tallinn, Estonia, August 24–28, 2020
Proceedings

 Springer

Editors
Ahti-Veikko Pietarinen [iD]
Tallinn University of Technology
Tallinn, Estonia

Peter Chapman [iD]
Edinburgh Napier University
Edinburgh, UK

Leonie Bosveld-de Smet [iD]
University of Groningen
Groningen, The Netherlands

Valeria Giardino
Université de Lorraine
Nancy, France

James Corter
Columbia University
New York, NY, USA

Sven Linker [iD]
University of Liverpool
Liverpool, UK

ISSN 0302-9743   ISSN 1611-3349   (electronic)
Lecture Notes in Artificial Intelligence
ISBN 978-3-030-54248-1   ISBN 978-3-030-54249-8   (eBook)
https://doi.org/10.1007/978-3-030-54249-8

LNCS Sublibrary: SL7 – Artificial Intelligence

This Springer imprint is published by the registered company Springer Nature Switzerland AG
The registered company address is: Gewerbestrasse 11, 6330 Cham, Switzerland

Preface

The 11th International Conference on the Theory and Application of Diagrams (Diagrams 2020) was originally due to be hosted by the Tallinn University of Technology in August 2020. However, due to the global COVID-19 pandemic, Diagrams for the first time ever took place as a virtual conference during August 2020. The goal of the Diagrams conference series remains to broaden the academic discussion of diagrams.

Submissions to Diagrams 2020 were solicited in the form of long papers, short papers, posters, and Abstracts. The Abstracts category was retained from Diagrams 2018, where it was introduced to encourage participation from authors working in fields where conference publications are not as prestigious as journal publications.

The peer-review process involved all papers and abstracts receiving at least three reviews (at least two for posters) by members of the Program Committee or a nominated sub-reviewer. After reviews were received, authors had the opportunity to submit a rebuttal. The reviews and rebuttals led to a lively discussion involving the Program Committee and the conference chairs to ensure high-quality submissions, covering a broad range of topics, were accepted to the conference. We would like to thank the Program Committee members and the reviewers for their considerable contributions. The robust review process, in which they were so engaged, is a crucial part of delivering a major conference.

In total, 91 submissions were received. Of these, 20 were accepted as long papers. A further 16 were accepted as short papers, 8 as Abstracts, and 22 for poster presentation. Diagrams 2020 sought to expand the research community, and used two special submission tracks on Philosophy and Psychology. These submission tracks had their own Program Committees and calls for papers, and continue to be a successful addition to the conference. There were several satellite events initially planned for Diagrams 2020, including a graduate symposium, the Set Visualization and Reasoning Workshop, and five tutorials covering a range of topics on diagrams. However, in order to allow the organizers to focus on the central scientific program, these satellite events were canceled with great regret.

There are, of course, many people to whom we are indebted for their considerable assistance in making Diagrams 2020 a success. We thank Francesco Bellucci for his role as Workshops and Tutorials Chair; Yacin Hamami for his role as Graduate Symposium Chair; Richard Burns for his help maintaining and producing the Diagrams website; Sven Linker for his role as Proceedings Chair; and Marika Proover for her tireless work as Local Chair. Our institutions, Tallinn University of Technology, Edinburgh Napier University, the University of Groningen, the University of Lorraine, and Columbia University, also provided support for our participants, for which we are grateful. Lastly, we thank the Diagrams Steering Committee for their continual support, advice, and encouragement.

August 2020

Ahti-Veikko Pietarinen
Peter Chapman
Leonie Bosveld de Smet
Valeria Giardino
James Corter

Organization

Program Committee

Mohanad Alqadah	Umm Al Qura University, Saudi Arabia
Francesco Bellucci	University of Bologna, Italy
Andrew Blake	University of Brighton, UK
Leonie Bosveld de Smet	University of Groningen, The Netherlands
Jean-Michel Boucheix	University of Burgundy, France
Michael Burch	University of Stuttgart, Germany
Richard Burns	West Chester University, USA
Jim Burton	University of Brighton, UK
Jessica Carter	University of Southern Denmark, Denmark
Peter Chapman	Edinburgh Napier University, UK
Peter Cheng	University of Sussex, UK
Daniele Chiffi	Tallinn University of Technology, Estonia
James Corter	Columbia University, USA
Gennaro Costagliola	Università di Salerno, Italy
Jennifer Cromley	University of Illinois at Urbana-Champaign, USA
Silvia De Toffoli	Stanford University, USA
Aidan Delaney	Bloomberg, UK
Lorenz Demey	KU Leuven, Belgium
Maria Giulia Dondero	Université de Liège, Belgium
George Englebretsen	Bishop's University, Canada
Jacques Fleuriot	University of Edinburgh, UK
Amy Fox	University of California, San Diego, USA
Valeria Giardino	Archives Henri Poincaré, France
Emily Grosholz	Penn State University, USA
Mateja Jamnik	University of Cambridge, UK
Mikkel Willum Johansen	University of Copenhagen, Denmark
Yasuhiro Katagiri	Future University Hakodate, Japan
John Kulvicki	Dartmouth College, USA
Brendan Larvor	University of Hertfordshire, UK
John Lee	University of Edinburgh, UK
Catherine Legg	Deakin University, Australia
Javier Legris	Universidad de Buenos Aires, Argentina
Jens Lemanski	FernUniversität in Hagen, Germany
Sven Linker	University of Liverpool, UK
Danielle Macbeth	Haverford College, USA
Emmanuel Manalo	Kyoto University, Japan
Kim Marriott	Monash University, Australia
Mark Minas	Universität der Bundeswehr München, Germany

Amirouche Moktefi	Tallinn University of Technology, Estonia
Marco Panza	CNRS, France
Ahti-Veikko Pietarinen	Tallinn University of Technology, Estonia
Helen Purchase	University of Glasgow, UK
Lindsey Richland	University of California, Irvine, USA
Peter Rodgers	University of Kent, UK
Dirk Schlimm	McGill University, Canada
Stephanie Schwartz	Millersville University, USA
Atsushi Shimojima	Doshisha University, Japan
Hans Smessaert	KU Leuven, Belgium
Gem Stapleton	University of Cambridge, UK
Takeshi Sugio	Doshisha University, Japan
Ryo Takemura	Nihon University, Japan
Barbara Tversky	Columbia University and Stanford University, USA
Yuri Uesaka	University of Tokyo, Japan
Jean Van Bendegem	Vrije Universiteit Brussel, Belgium
Petrucio Viana	Federal Fluminense University, Brazil
Reinhard von Hanxleden	Christian-Albrechts-Universität zu Kiel, Germany
Michael Wybrow	Monash University, Australia

Additional Reviewers

De Rosa, Mattia
Domrös, Sören
Gkatzia, Dimitra
Morris, Imogen
Nakagawa, Masanori
Palmer, Jake
Raggi, Daniel
Rentz, Niklas
Schulze, Christoph Daniel
Stockdill, Aaron

Contents

Reasoning with Diagrams

Euler and Venn Diagrams

Empirical Studies and Cognition

Logic and Diagrams

Posters

Diagrams in Mathematics

On "Overspecification" in Medieval Mathematical Diagrams

Gregg De Young[(⊠)]

The American University in Cairo, Cairo, Egypt
gdeyoung@aucegypt.edu

Abstract. In a recent paper [1], Christián Carman advanced a tentative explanation for "overspecification" in medieval mathematical diagrams. Carman argues that the original ("correct") diagrams were corrupted, presumably through incompetent copyists, while preparing the initial copies—often before the tenth consecutive copy. The diagrams then stabilized in an overspecified form and resisted further changes, sometimes for centuries of copies thereafter. I feel hesitant about this hypothesis for several reasons: (1) it assumes that the first Greek diagrams were essentially identical to modern diagrams; (2) pre-modern overspecification is ubiquitous and is rarely reversed; (3) the hypothesis ignores differing traditions of perspective; (4) the informal tests used to support the hypothesis do not precisely mirror the medieval copyist's activity.

Keywords: Medieval mathematical diagrams · Diagrams in Early Greek Mathematics · Overspecification

1 Background

Interest in the diagrams in the classical Greek mathematical treatises [2] received new impetus when Netz [3] pointed out that the diagrams of the Greek mathematical tradition were lettered diagrams and thus differed from diagrams in several other ancient mathematical traditions. These letter labels allowed diagrams to be integrated with the verbal mathematical text in unique ways. He went so far as to argue that these diagrams functioned as a metonym for the verbal text. (As an example, one might consider the Arabic manuscript Kastamonu, Yazma Eser Kütüphanesi, 70, which contains only enunciations and diagrams of the *Elements*.) Saito and Sidoli [4] suggest that diagrams were intended to be redrawn during the course of the mathematical demonstration, contributing a kind of necessity to the verbal argument. Asper [5] further suggested that diagrams and proofs enabled professional mathematicians to distinguish themselves from other intellectuals, such as philosophers and sophists.

Diagrams in medieval copies of ancient mathematical manuscripts derive from this tradition of mathematical discourse. These medieval diagrams often seem unfamiliar to modern readers. Saito [6] identified four characteristics that contribute to this aura of unfamiliarity. The two most frequently encountered are

© Springer Nature Switzerland AG 2020
A.-V. Pietarinen et al. (Eds.): Diagrams 2020, LNAI 12169, pp. 3–9, 2020.
https://doi.org/10.1007/978-3-030-54249-8_1

overspecification, the tendency to draw figures with greater regularity than the mathematical text requires (for example, quadrilaterals appear as squares and parallelograms as rectangles), and an indifference to metrical accuracy (Fig. 1 and Fig. 2). Historians of mathematics have noted the prevalence of overspecification in medieval diagrams [7] and have critiqued the tendency of editors of early Greek mathematics to redraw the medieval diagrams in generalized form, following more contemporary conventions [8].

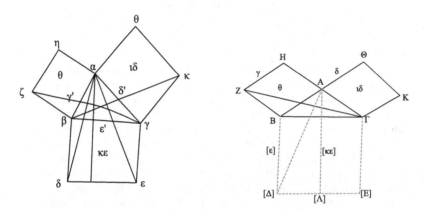

Fig. 1. Byzantine diagrams of *Elements* I, 47. Numerical values show that the right triangles have sides of 3, 4, 5 units. Left: diagram edited from Wien 1015, folio 21a, margin. Neither visually nor numerically overspecified, it ignores metrical accuracy since the squares on the longer side and on the hypotenuse appear equal. Right: diagram edited from Oxford, Bod. Lib., Dorval 301, folio [31a]. The lower portion is obscured, but the upper portion shows an overspecified isosceles right triangle, despite the stated numerical values. Most medieval diagrams of I, 47 are drawn as an isosceles triangle.

The growing appreciation of diagrams among historians has produced critical study of the diagrams in several recent editions of Greek texts [9, 10]. Using medieval diagrams, Decorps-Foulquier [11] investigated the editorial work of Eutocius in preparing his Greek edition of the *Conics* of Apollonius. Sidoli [12] argued that variant diagrams in *On the Sizes and Distances of the Sun and Moon* by Aristarchus show the different ways in which medieval readers understood the text.

More remains to be done to develop the necessary technical tools to edit and study diagrams. DRaFT, a free Java-based software developed by Ken Saito (https://www.greekmath.org/diagrams/diagrams_index.html) offers the capability of collecting and preserving geometrical data from diagrams (including metrical data) for potential use in the editing process. Raynaud [13] has pioneered use of phylogenetics to create stemma based on the diagrams in medieval manuscripts.

2   Was Overspecification Unintentional?

Carman [1] has suggested that overspecification in medieval mathematical diagrams was introduced unintentionally early in the copying process. I am uneasy about this claim. One reason is that it seems to ignore the existence of numerical values attached to geometrical diagrams in some Byzantine Greek manuscripts of Euclid's *Elements* (Fig. 2). Who added these values? We do not know. But they are consistent with the visual overspecification, suggesting that these visual features did not appear by accident in the copying process [14].

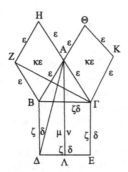

Fig. 2. Diagram of *Elements* I, 47 edited from Firenze, Biblioteca Medicea Laurenziana, ms. Plut.XXVIII 3, folio [14a]. The right triangle is drawn as equilateral, ignoring metrical accuracy. The diagram is overspecified since there is no need that the triangle be isosceles. The Greek alpha-numeric value for the area of the square on each side is 25, while the square on the hypotenuse is 50 (nu). These values suggest that the overspecification was intentional. (The letter mu appears to have been displaced from the point where the perpendicular meets the hypotenuse of the right triangle.)

Moreover, it is difficult to accept that overspecification, as well as indifference to metrical accuracy, occurred only during the production of the first copies of Greek mathematical works and were then preserved essentially unchanged thereafter through centuries of manuscript transmission extending through the medieval period and up to the introduction of print technology [15].

As a counter example, consider the diagram transmission of a mathematical treatise that originated in the medieval period—an Arabic edition of Euclidean geometry, *Taḥrīr Kitāb Uqlīdis*, by Naṣīr al-Dīn al-Ṭūsī. The autograph of this Arabic treatise, completed in 646 AH/AD 1248, is not extant, but the oldest surviving manuscript (British Library, *additum* 23387) is dated 656 AH/AD 1258, well within the author's lifetime. The few years between the original composition and this oldest copy makes it unlikely that extensive changes would have been introduced into the diagrams. Six centuries later, al-Ṭūsī's treatise was printed by lithography (Tehran, 1298 AH/AD 1881), still exhibiting overspecification in its diagrams. The overspecification of the diagram for I, 47 (present from the earliest known copy although occasionally abandoned in specific copies), is

preserved through hundreds of copies over the centuries (Fig. 3), whether reproduced as a freehand sketch or using standard drafting tools.

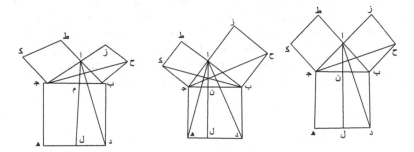

Fig. 3. Diagrams of I, 47 from al-Ṭūsī's *Taḥrīr Uqlīdis.* Left: British Library, *add.*
23387, folio 28a. The earliest known manuscript shows an overspecified isosceles right
triangle since the perpendicular from the right angle bisects the base of the square
on the hypotenuse. (Distortion in the two smaller squares resulted when the copyist
left too little space and the draughtsman attempted to avoid impinging on the text.)
Center: Beyerische Staatsbibliothek, arab 2697 (copied 1142AH/AD 1729), folio 20a,
is an unusual example of a diagram without overspecification. Right: the diagram in
Tehran lithograph (1298 AH/AD 1881), page [27] is overspecified with an isosceles
right triangle.

3   Reservations Concerning Carman's Testing

Carman has conducted several tests of his hypothesis. In these tests, university students were asked to copy mathematical diagrams. The first was given a
"correct" generalized diagram to copy. Each successive student then copied the
copy of the previous student. These tests generally reproduced the appearance
of overspecification after only a few copies of the original diagram. On one level,
this testing process was not dissimilar to what medieval European university
students would have experienced in copying their own textbooks [16].

Carman's assumption that the original mathematical diagrams must have
appeared more-or-less like the generalized diagrams in modern mathematics
textbooks appears to me a debatable point. It presupposes that there is a single
"correct" convention for constructing diagrams—the typical generalized diagram
we would expect to find in a modern textbook. Diagrams failing to conform to
this convention are judged to be somehow "wrong" or defective.

Moreover, this "experimental" testing does not seem to me to mimic completely the medieval copyist's situation. In the test, only one student copied
from the "original," while the others copied from the copy of another student,
usually without access to any other preceding copy. The historical situation was
probably more complex. We know that some medieval translators and copyists

tried to obtain several manuscripts in order to achieve the best text. Presumably they would also compare text diagrams. Thābit ibn Qurra, a mathematician who revised the Arabic translation of the *Elements* attributed to Isḥāq ibn Ḥunayn reports several differences between the Arabic text and Greek manuscripts available to him.

Furthermore, a medieval copyist was not asked to copy an isolated diagram. Rather, he was presented a diagram within the context of a mathematical text and the two were intimately connected. Carman's student "copyists," on the other hand, were presented with a mathematical diagram—usually a complex diagram representing a three-dimensional situation—apparently divorced from textual or mathematical context. Thus arguments based on these experimental results seem to me not to carry convincing force.

We have few documentary sources describing the actual practice of copying manuscripts in Hellenistic and Roman periods. We know somewhat more about the conditions of working in medieval scriptoria associated with monastic houses, but the large majority of work in these institutions was religious rather than mathematical. For a general guide to books and their preparation in the premodern period, see [17,18]. There is a similar dearth of written evidence concerning copying of mathematical manuscripts in the Islamicate world. We must reply primarily on the evidence of the manuscripts themselves. Manuals in Arabic containing instructions for drawing geometric figures, ostensibly directed toward craftsmen, exist from the medieval period but few have been edited, translated, or studied in detail [19]. There also survive exemplars of drawing instruments such as compasses [20] although there has been no detailed study of their production and use.

4   Can We Ignore Conventions of Perspective?

The mathematical text must be understood in order to know what is important in the diagram and what is not important, as well as to decide what techniques

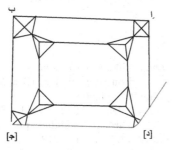 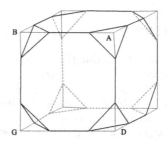

Fig. 4. Left: Truncated octohedron from a medieval Arabic extension of the *Elements* (edited from Hyderabad, Andhra Pradesh Government Oriental Manuscipts and Research Library, *riyāḍī* 496 (dated 1003 AH/AD 1593), p. 446). Right: Truncated octohedron following modern perspective conventions (edited from [22], p. 179).

will convey the intended meaning accurately. When Chinese copyists attempted to create figures describing European technical devises, they often produced inaccurate portrayals because they did not understand the artistic conventions of the Europeans [21]. Medieval perspective can sometimes be considerably different from modern conventions (Fig. 4). This problem has been discussed in [22]. Therefore, judgements about "errors" in diagram construction need to be made contextually and in relation to the textual content.

5   Conclusion

I have outlined several reasons why I found Carman's tentative hypothesis unsatisfying. However overspecification may have arisen, its widespread persistence through centuries of medieval transmission show that further historical studies of medieval mathematical diagrams are required. In one of our many conversations about diagrams, Ken Saito noted that one could perhaps consider the overspecification of the isosceles triangle in *Elements* I, 47 in the tradition of the discussion of the duplication of the square in the famous passage in Plato's *Meno*. And taken in isolation from other diagrams, this idea has a certain intellectual appeal. But it clearly would explain only a small minority of the medieval examples of diagram overspecification. I think that a great deal more historical research needs to be done before we can feel confident that we understand the intellectual and cultural factors that produced overspecification in these diagrams.

I am also concerned that Carman's hypothesis could be used to justify an editor's decision to redraw medieval mathematical diagrams, arguing that overspecification represents a divergence from the "true" form of the diagram. In this case, we would find ourselves back in the diagrammatic tradition of Heiberg or Busard [23], who noted in his editorial remarks for his edition of the so-called Adelard II version of Euclid, "We have silently corrected wrong letters in the figures by using the letters in the text" (page 92). My own view is that we should concur with Jardin and Jardin [24], that editors should retain the medieval diagram forms, and when it is necessary to reconstruct the diagrams to make them more accessible to modern readers, this should always be clearly stated.

References

1. Carman, C.: Accounting for overspecification and indifference to visual accuracy in manuscript diagrams: a tentative explanation based on transmission. Hist. Math. **45**, 217–236 (2018). https://doi.org/10.1016/j.hm.2018.05.001
2. Sidoli, N.: Research on ancient Greek mathematical sciences, 1998–2012. In: Sidoli, N., Van Brummelen, G. (eds.) From Alexandria, Through Baghdad, pp. 25–50. Springer, Heidelberg (2014). https://doi.org/10.1007/978-3-642-36736-6_3
3. Netz, R.: The Shaping of Deduction in Greek Mathematics: A Study in Cognitive History. Cambridge University Press, Cambridge (1999)
4. Sidoli, N., Saito, K.: The role of geometrical construction in Theodosius's Spherics. Arch. Hist. Exact Sci. **63**, 581–609 (2009). https://doi.org/10.1007/s00407-009-0045-2

5. Asper, M.: Mathematik, Milieu, Text. Sudhoffs Arch. **87**, 1–31 (2003)
6. Saito, K.: Traditions of the diagram, traditions of the text: a case study. Synthese **186**, 7–20 (2012). https://doi.org/10.1007/s11229-012-0073-3
7. Saito, K.: A preliminary study in the critical assessment of diagrams in Greek mathematical works. SCIAMVS **7**, 81–144 (2006)
8. Saito, K., Sidoli, N.: Diagrams and arguments in ancient Greek mathematics: lessons drawn from comparisons of the manuscript diagrams with those in modern critical editions. In: Chemla, K. (ed.) History of Mathematical Proof in Ancient Traditions, pp. 135–162. Cambridge University Press, Cambridge (2012)
9. Netz, R.: The Works of Archimedes, Volume I: The Two Books on the Sphere and the Cylinder. Cambridge University Press, Cambridge (2004)
10. De Young, G.: Editing a collection of diagrams ascibed to al-Ḥajjāj: an initial case study. SCIAMVS **15**, 171–238 (2014)
11. Decorps-Foulquier, M.: Sur les figures du traité des Coniques d'Apollonius de Pergé édité par Eutocius d'Ascalon. Revue d'histoire des mathématiques **5**, 61–82 (1998)
12. Sidoli, N.: What we can learn from a diagram: the case of Aristarchus's on the sizes and distances of the sun and the moon. Ann. Sci. **63**, 581–609 (2007). https://doi.org/10.1080/00033790701336841
13. Raynaud, D.: Building the stemma codicum from geometric diagrams. Arch. Hist. Exact Sci. **68**(2), 207–239 (2013). https://doi.org/10.1007/s00407-013-0134-0
14. De Young, G.: Diagram numbers in medieval manuscripts of Euclid's elements. Humanistica **7**, 27–33 (2012). https://doi.org/10.1400/212774
15. De Young, G.: Diagrams in the Arabic Euclidean tradition: a preliminary assessment. Hist. Math. **32**, 129–179 (2005). https://doi.org/10.1016/j.hm.2004.04.003
16. Grant, E.: Foundations of Modern Science in the Middle Ages. Cambridge University Press, New York (1996)
17. Avrin, L.: Scribes, Script, and Books: The Book Arts from Antiquity to the Renaissance. American Library Association, Chicago (2010)
18. Pedersen, J., French, G.: Scribes and books. In: Hillenbrand, R. (ed.) The Arabic Book, pp. 37–53. Princeton University Press, Princeton (1984)
19. Aghayani-Chavoshi, J. (ed. and trans.): Ketâb al-nejârat (Sur ce qui est indispensable aux artisans dans les constructions géométriques). Institut Français de Recherche en Iran, Tehran (2010)
20. Sezgin, F., Neubauer, E.: Katalog der Instrumentsammlung des Institutes für Geschichte der Arabisch-Islamischen Wissenschaften. Institut für Geschichte der Arabisch-Islamischen Wissenschaften, Frankfurt am Main (2010)
21. Hall, B.: The didactic and the elegant: some thoughts on scientific and technological illustrations in the middle ages and Renaissance. In: Baigrie, B. (ed.) Picturing Knowledge: Historical and Philosophical Problems Concerning the Use of Art in Science, pp. 3–39. University of Toronto Press, Toronto (1996)
22. De Young, G.: Book XVI: a medieval Arabic addendum to Euclid's elements. SCIAMVS **9**, 133–209 (2008)
23. Busard, H., Folkerts, M.: Robert of Chester's (?) Redaction of Euclid's Elements, the so-called Adelard II Version: Volume II. Birkhäuser Verlag, Basel (1992)
24. Jardine, B., Jardine, N.: Critical editing of early-modern astronomical diagrams. J. Hist. Astron. **41**, 393–414 (2010). https://doi.org/10.1177/002182861004100307

Transductive Reconstruction of Hippocrates' Dynamical Geometrical Diagrams

Sandra Visokolskis[1](✉) ⓘ, Evelyn Vargas[2] ⓘ, and Gonzalo Carrión[3] ⓘ

[1] National University of Cordoba, Córdoba, Argentina
sandraviso@gmail.com
[2] National University of La Plata/CONICET, La Plata, Argentina
[3] National University of Villa Maria, Villa María, Argentina

Abstract. This paper analyzes the problem of producing diagrams of mathematical explanations that are not necessarily conclusive, instead of diagrammatic proofs. In order to do so, we focus on a case study, namely, the investigation that Hippocrates of Chios carried out in the fifth century B.C., concerning the square of the circle by means of lunules. More specifically, we analyze the discussion regarding two versions that Simplicius presented about the first quadrature, one developed by Alexander of Aphrodisias and the other by Eudemus of Rhodes. Our purpose is to address the relevance of the perspicuity of proof in diagrammatic terms. Classical historiography has regarded the Hippocratic explanation of the allegedly failed quadrature of the circle as not being axiomatic, or able to produce a conclusive demonstration of his results -on the grounds of having analyzed only some cases of lunules and not the totality that allows giving general results-. Therefore, we propose to analyze his argumentation from an abductive point of view. In this sense, taking as a starting point Jens Høyrup's approach of Hippocrates proof as 'reasoned procedures' that are 'explanations', we develop this perspective in terms of transduction, a variant of C.S. Peirce's concepts of abduction. Transduction is dominated by a cluster of non-deductive activities and skills such as: iconic visual inferences, analogies, metaphors, inductive generalizations, among others, all contributing to the construction of one or more hypotheses that explain the emergence of some creative insight, in response to a problem that motivates and drives the creative process.

Keywords: Diagrammatic proof · Mathematical explanation · Transduction

1 Introduction

A large number of classic historians of ancient mathematics agree on considering Hippocrates of Chios (ca. 470-ca. 410 BC) as one of the great Greek thinkers regarding the measurement of the circle, proportionality, incommensurability and the relations between straight and curvilinear figures[1]. In contrast, his results, which were reported

---

[1] Thus: "the most important figure to consider" [22, p. 40]; "the most important name from the point of view of [the progress in the elements down to Plato's time]" [14, p. 182]; "one good

© Springer Nature Switzerland AG 2020
A.-V. Pietarinen et al. (Eds.): Diagrams 2020, LNAI 12169, pp. 10–25, 2020.
https://doi.org/10.1007/978-3-030-54249-8_2

by pivotal figures in both the history of mathematics and philosophy -such as Eudemus, Simplicius, Aristotle, and Proclus, among others-, were devastated by his critics. Among other reasons, the presumed affirmative answer that Hippocrates gave to the problem of the squaring of the circle made him the center of controversies even at times much later than his.

This article seeks to describe Hippocrates's first quadrature diagrammatically, by means of lunules, from the point of view of abductive arguments, and, in turn, expanding this conception through the notion of transductive inference [2, 3]. Transductive methodology seeks to elucidate the diagrammatic processes that aims at explaining a mathematical problem to solve, rather than, to grant absolute certainty converting the argument into a demonstration in the strict sense of the word. Thus, transductions entail the purpose of explaining the reasons why the ideas solve a problem, while remaining at the level of argumentative plausibility, instead of generating an answer to the how and what of a problem, which would lead to its conclusive justification.

2 Transductive Approach to Mathematical Diagrammatical Explanations

As to the use of diagram in mathematics, it is important to distinguish between external visual representations and internal mental imagery in order to determine and individualize the abstract character of mathematical entities. Such entities, unlike diagrams, lack all kind of materiality. Consequently, diagrammatic icons can give them some tangible dimension on which to work. They provide a material embodiment for the mathematical reasoning, a concrete means through which they could achieve an absent "spatial and temporal cohesion that enables [their] manipulability. (…) Even abstract entities need to have a natural dimension to give us knowledge" [24, p. 169].

The following questions arises naturally: as diagrams provide entities and mathematical reasoning with operative materiality, what epistemic character can be assigned to them? Are they mere auxiliary elements that accompany and facilitate the thread of reasoning? Or, in addition to this clearly recognized role, do they fulfill a different, even superior function? If so, what would such functions be? How could we characterize this added and emergent role apart from their merely secondary and tangential use? In addition, it might be the case that not all situations should be analyzed under the same magnifying glass but we should rather think of types of diagrams according to different functions. Now, if diagrams add a material dimension to ideas and mental images, and contribute by creating simulation scenarios, where does the certainty of such resources come from? These important questions have to be postpone for another occasion. We will examine a less ambitious but nonetheless significant question: in addition to the search for certainty, what other epistemic values are expected as requirements for a valid mathematical argumentation, whether diagrammatic, linguistic or mixed? For this purpose, we will focus on the notion of mathematical explanation, by introducing some aspects of Peirce's notion of abductive reasoning. Thus, we will analyze the relevance

---

fifth-century BCE example of a thinker most of whose work related to, or used, one or other branch of mathematics" [27, pp. 294–295]; "a geometer of great distinction" [28, p. 147]; "the first of whom we have any record who did [write a book on elements]" [32, p. 54].

of explanations in mathematics as an alternative to the view that considers certainty as the predominant epistemic value in mathematical contexts. While deduction is usually understood as the predominant style in mathematical work, other types of reasoning also intervene in creative discovery processes. Peirce insisted that the only reasoning that introduced novelty was abduction [30, §5.172], which was also responsible for both hypothesis formation and adoption. According to Peirce, deduction is progressive, and allows to represent predictions from causes to effects; abduction, on the other hand, is employed to provide an explanation in terms of the cause that produces a certain effect, and consequently, in a regressive progression or retrojection. In his late writings, Peirce seemed to attribute the task of hypothesis formation to an "instinct to guess right" [30, §2.3], which would leave out the inferential nature of this first creative stage he emphasized in his previous work. We will adopt a conciliatory reading for this extensively discussed discrepancy in Peirce's writing and distinguish two stages in abductive reasoning: one, related exclusively to the formation of hypotheses, as merely instinctive, and, a second stage corresponding to the selection and adoption of one of such hypotheses.

If this two-stage reading is plausible, we may also examine whether the first stage, that is, the creation of hypotheses, is not inferential, and therefore, deprived of voluntary and controlled acts of reasoning. The alternative view of the first stage introduces the notion of "transduction" [2, 3]. More specifically, transduction consists in the generally non-instinctive formation of hypotheses. Despite of being implicit for the most part, some inferential elements of an associative type that characterize transduction constitute an important contribution to the creative process that leads to the formation of innovative and original hypotheses. However, what would these associative elements that intervene in the formation of hypotheses be, and in what way would they constitute transductive inferences? David Hume gives us the key to an answer. Indeed, Hume characterizes associations as 'principles', which also fulfill a central role in representing 'the cement of the mind' and 'all operations of the mind must largely depend on them' [20, pp. 152–154]. Moreover, he produces a typology of them: "the qualities, from which this associations arises, and by which the mind is after this manner convey's from one idea to another, are three, viz. *resemblance, contiguity* in time or place, and *cause and effect*" [21, 1.1.4.1]. However, of these three, similarity stands out:

> Of all relations, that of resemblance is in this respect the most efficacious; and that because it not only causes an association of ideas, but also of dispositions, and makes us conceive the one idea by an act or operation of the mind, similar to that by which we conceive the other [21, 1.4.2.32].

Similarity will be one of the most important relationships in terms of its scope in the unification of ideas: "The first [quality of a philosophical relation] is *resemblance*: and this is a relation, without which no philosophical relation can exist" [21, 1.1.5.3]. According to Hume, similarity, when it is accompanied by the other associative principles, i.e. through these relationships, elevates the mind from one idea to another, or before the occurrence of an idea 'they naturally introduce the other', thus allowing for the elaboration of a complex mechanism of associations that, acting together, contributes to the elaboration of knowledge: "I have often observ's, that, besides cause and effect,

the two relations of resemblance and contiguity, are to be consider's as associating principles of thought, and as capable of conveying the imagination from one idea to another"
[21, 1.3.9.2]. This is also linked with the capture of the 'effects' that these associations
produce, which, contribute greatly given their generally unconscious and unintended
nature, and reveals a surreptitious way of operating: 'This evident, that the association
of ideas operates in so silent and imperceptible a manner, that we scarce sensible of
it, and discover it more by its effects than by any immediate feeling of perception"
[21, 2.1.9.4; 6, pp. 94–102]. Finally, it is worth mentioning the relationship that Hume
establishes between abstract ideas and their pictorial representations: "abstract ideas are
therefore in themselves individual; however, they may become general in their representation. The image in the mind is only that of a particular object, tho' the application
of it in our reasoning be the same, as if it were universal" [21, 1.1.7.6]. For Hume our
abstract ideas are not mere copies, and, since every idea is but a weakened impression
and that the impressions are presented to the mind determined according to their degrees
of quantity and quality, ideas must also be determined accordingly. Consequently, "[t]his
determination to show that pictorial properties together with principles of association
are sufficient to allow images to be deployed in reasoning in a way that allows them to
represent a unique general content" [33, p. 129].

These features concerning the notion of association according to Hume, are especially relevant for the description of transductive inferences. In effect, just as Hume
highlighted the role of similarities in the association of ideas, transduction is a type of
reasoning that begins with a similarity, and, therefore, this constitutes the pillar from
which the entire structure that constitutes the creative process of hypothesis formation
is based. More specifically, given a problem A to solve, in this case a mathematical
one, this generates a cognitive imbalance until a solution that restores order is reached.
It is possible to obtain solutions to a problem that do not require any type of heuristics, ingenium or special operational skills. In such a case, however, we would hardly
frame the resolution process as a creative one. In order to achieve an innovation in its
resolution, it is expected to overcome the difficulties and obstacles of a disruptive resolution effort, thus providing an unexpected and surprising insight against any other
traditionally expected result. As mentioned above, Peirce takes this state of surprise as
an indication of a discovery that requires an abductive explanation. How was such a
creative insight produced and what does it contribute? Our transductive interpretation
indicates that the emergence of insight constitutes a process of association of ideas that
manifests itself through a similarity: given problem A, a problem or situation B arises
iconically represented. Being B similar to A in a certain aspect/s M, its explanation helps
to solve A through a result C_A, which is analogically inferred from a solution C_B of
B, already known and familiar to the problem solving agent. Thus, the first step of the
transductive process is constituted by the apprehension of the similarity that triggered
the creative insight. The second step of transduction is represented by the task of analytical deepening on the reasons for the similarity between A and B, in order to be able to
extrapolate properties M of B that are also shared by A, and apply them analogously to
A from a known solution C_B of B. Therefore, transduction's second stage is summed up
in the detection and explicitness of the analogical process of transferring characteristics
of C_B to the formation of the C_A hypothesis, which may eventually lead to a plausible

solution of *A*. In this step, associations of contiguity are in place, that is, the second type mentioned by Hume. Finally, the third transductive step delves into the causes of the effect of having postulated C_A as a plausible solution of *A*, the third associative type that Hume provides. It is in this instance that it is explained why hypothesis C_A is *adopted*, thus constituting what Peirce would call abductive *reasoning* proper. As made clear above, there are many more inferential mechanisms -of associative nature-, beyond a mere instinctive act of guessing the answer, which Peirce seems to admit. A question arises: is this proposal of hypothesis C_A only a particular solution without general aspirations? Given the associative nature of this process, does it only achieve a conjecture that does not cover all the cases that exhibit the particular choice of the diagrammatic icon *B*? How confident can we be of having obtained certainty and conclusiveness from a similarity as that between *B* and *A*? It is clear that the notion of transduction, based on a Peircean notion of abduction, introduces an entire discussion that confronts the use of specific and concrete diagrams with particular reasonings seeking for generality. However, one may still wonder whether this contrast between the particular and the general is legitimate. Diagrams, the use of similarities, the construction of analogies, and the production of abductive explanations, all these constitute the transductive scenario that combines clearly particular aspects with generality ambitions.

Historically, diagrams have been extensively used in mathematical practice. However, its epistemic role was a matter of controversy. According to a widely accepted view, their use was limited to discovery, and consequently, its role in proving was neglected. Visual representations such as diagrams could only accompany the process of reasoning proper. This negative attitude toward diagrammatic thinking can be found in the early modern period. Leibniz's view in the *New Essays* illustrates the traditional attitude to diagrams in several respects [26, pp. 360–361]. Firstly, Leibniz rightly holds that geometrical demonstrations are not about the particular figure. Otherwise, we would confuse the iconic representation and the concept of the figure [26, pp. 261–262]; while the force of the proof is independent of the particular figure, the geometer is using [26, p. 360]. By examining the particular figure we come to understand the relevant properties involved in the concept of the figure and focus our attention on them but the proof itself consists of universal propositions, that is, the definitions, axioms and previously proved theorems [26, pp. 360–361]. Only by the discursive expression of the relevant information, the epistemological significance of the proof can be displayed. As Leibniz points out, what is at stake is the certainty of the conclusion of the demonstration, which cannot depend on particular figures[2]. The thinking process that leads to the conclusion must be reliable or truth conductive so that the result is a rationally justified true belief, but according to Leibniz this cannot be achieved through the diagrams alone. The passage from one image to another by imaginative associations has to be distinguished from the conceptual content involved in the relational notion of similarity that only the intellect can analyze. In other words, diagrams are not reliable. They cannot justify the conclusion[3]. "Blind" or symbolic representation, on the other hand, can conclude general and

---

[2] According to Leibniz's theory of cognition, images are confused representations of the geometrical object. However, Leibniz does not reject the role of visualization in reasoning, as it is attested by his project to develop a General Characteristics. See, for example [26, p. 73].

[3] See [26, p. 11]. For ampliative abstraction and analysis in Leibniz, see [13].

necessary conclusions in a reliable way by making explicit the conceptual connections. Leibniz both ascribes an auxiliary role to the geometrical diagrams and puts into question their reliability[4]. He also mentions the case of some geometers who presented Euclidean geometry without including any figures but only text [26, p. 361], implying that figures may be helpful but replaceable. As he points out in his account of Euclidean proof, there are cases in which the ecthesis and manipulation of the original figure are not necessary [26, p. 476].

Leibniz's attitude can be contrasted with Peirce's view. As it is well known, Peirce sustained that all necessary reasoning is diagrammatic. Moreover, mathematics is the science of necessary reasoning [31, pp. 206–207]. Consequently, the American pragmatist has to provide a way to account for the fact that diagrammatic representations are particular while representing something general since the conclusions are general. Diagrams are iconic representations, that is, it is the nature of a Peircean diagram to represent something general [31, p. 303][5]. Proofs are designed in order to increase our knowledge, by extracting information from what we already know. As already mentioned above, for Peirce the only ampliative form of reasoning is abduction [31, p. 205]. Abductive inference introduces novelty and is also a process of reasoning from some particular observation to adopting a hypothesis [30, §5.189]. Now mathematical reasoning may be abductive [31, p. 287][6]. Moreover, mathematics is the science that deals with hypothetical state of things [30, §4.233][7]. The introduction and manipulation of diagrams in a geometrical proof can be described as abductive reasoning [31, p. 303]. But some of his remarks concerning abduction such as the element of surprise might suggest that this inference is not reasoning proper since reasoning proper involves rational control [31, p. 249] and the process by which the hypothesis is achieved does not seem to be deliberate reasoning. However, the process of *adopting* the conjectural explanation is under rational control. Experimenting on the diagram in a mathematical proof suggests a conjectural proposition by resemblance [31, pp. 106–107]. The object of the reasoning is not the diagram itself but the interpreter of the icon *sees* something general in the sense that the interpreting sign of the icon involves a new general feature. The icon itself does not assert any thing [31, p. 307]. It does not display any other information but what is conveyed in the object it represents. But the process of *selecting* the relevant feature by observing the icon consists in discovering a general description that can be applied to all the relevant cases; given the "complete analogy" between the relations among the parts of the diagram and those of the object, unnoticed relations in the object can be discovered by observing the diagram [30, §3.363][8]. The icon becomes significant by being interpreted by a formal hypothesis [30, §2.422fn]. Diagrammatic thinking is not replaceable since interpreting a diagram involves both observation and generalization[9].

---

[4] That is, its ability to "express" the relationships of the object that is being represented.

[5] For an analysis of the relevance of iconic understanding for representing structural articulation and normativity, see [25].

[6] For some important implications regarding Peirce's diagrams as abductive hypotheses, see [19].

[7] Note Peirce's reference to the surprising discovery of new relations involved in the hypothesis: [30, §5.567].

[8] For the relevance of this feature for reasoning, see [5].

[9] For an account of Peirce's view on the epistemic virtues of a mathematician, see [8].

However, Peirce's account of the interpreting process depends on accepting his triadic semiotics. More importantly for our present purposes, Peircean formation of hypotheses pertains to the realm of discovery in mathematics, while the selection of hypotheses constitutes an act of a justifying the generalization process symbolically.

In what follows, the case study that we address in Sect. 3 deals with the way in which Hippocrates of Chios explains a procedure to make the squaring of the circle possible. We will argue that certainty is not the key epistemic value of the Hippocratic argument, representing an opposite view to the Leibnitian rationalist emphasis on complete certainty as a criterion for mathematical results. Therefore, he would presumably adopt an approach closer to Hume or Peirce in this regard. Thus, the case study will show, how Hippocrates of Chios proceeded mathematically following a style that also contrasts to the dialecticians, like Zeno [10, pp. 252–258], Protagoras [10, p. 266], or Democritus [22, p. 56 n. 49], who criticized the use of techniques that did not guarantee precision and rigor in mathematics.

As we will see below, Knorr holds that Hippocrates resorted to many results, presumably active at the time, due to the discovery of the incommensurability of magnitudes. In this respect, Knorr does not accept that the geometric work was in a state of paralysis because of this discovery, but that "heuristic and informal procedures are the rule, not the exception" [22, p. 41]. Thus, according to Knorr, Hippocrates, as well as other fifth- and fourth-century geometers, insisted on the use of not entirely legitimate strategies, despite the proven reasons against them. These geometers "proceeded with their studies of similar figures as if they were still unaware of the foundational consequences of the existence of incommensurable lines" [22, p. 41]. However, it may be worth examining whether this 'foundational' style was not yet in force and widely expanded in his time, just as it would be in Plato's time, for example, and that his strategies had room for other reasons that are not only oriented to the search for mathematical certainty, but to the processes of understanding the ideas at stake. We will proceed to develop the aforementioned case study in the following section.

3 Hippocrates' Lunules as a Plausible Solution to the Quadrature of the Circle: Mathematical and Diagrammatic Transductive Interpretations

3.1 Reduction from Quadratures to Triangulizations

In the search for the solution to the quadrature of the circle, Hippocrates of Chios had presumably analyzed several cases, trying to encompass all possible situations that included a general solution of the problem. The cases to examine had to do with the different ways of *reducing* the problem of squaring a circle, to that of triangulating it by means of lunules[10]. This means that, instead of finding a square whose area coincides with the area of the given circle, the goal is to obtain a right triangle (i.e. with one of its angles, being a right angle) of an equal area to that of the circle. If we achieve the latter, then, we would arrive at the completion of the solution through the following reasoning:

---

[10] A lunule is a plane figure contained by a convex and a concave circular arc.

given a circle A, if the circle is triangulable (by triangle B, i.e. if area(A) = area(B)), and B is squareable (i.e. there exists a square S such that area(B) = area(S)), then area(A) = area(S), and circle A would be squared. In diagrammatic terms, *reasoning α* is formed by two premises ($\bigcirc$ −−→ $\triangle$, $\triangle$ −−→□) and a conclusion ($\bigcirc$ −−→□). It should be noted that the second premise (all triangle is quadrable) indicates a result that apparently was easily justified, as it is the case with every rectilinear figure. Precisely the core of the whole problem of the quadrature of the circle consists in making straight figures compatible with other curvilinear ones.

As to the notion of 'reduction', we know from Eutocius that, in relation to the problem of duplication of the cube, "Hippocrates of Chios (…) turned one puzzle into another one, no less of a puzzle" [11, pp. 88–90], replacing the original problem for the one of finding two mean proportionals in continued proportion. In this respect, Wilbur Richard Knorr adds: "Hippocrates appears to have adopted a similar strategy in the investigation of the circle quadrature" [23, pp. 23–24]. On the other hand, Aristotle in *Prior Analytics* II.25.69a 30–34 exemplifies the definition of "reduction" (*apagogé*) by means of the Hippocratic case in question here:

> For example, suppose D means 'being squared', E a rectilineal figure, F a circle; then if between E and F there is only one intermediate term, namely that the circle together with (certain) lunules is equal to a rectilineal figure, we should be near to knowing [how to square the circle itself] [16, p. 33].

Once Hippocrates reduced the problem, the first transductive step begins, which consists in the production of an association by similarity that shows how to reduce a given circle to a right triangle. This leads to equating lunules with right triangles, as well as all the alternatives of lunules that were possible to build, rather than in a single case. In this regard, Simplicius cites, in his *Commentary on Aristotle's Physics*, two different sources allegedly dealing with Hippocrates' quadratures of lunules: (1) Alexander of Aphrodisias, offering two different cases in his own *Commentary to Aristotle*, and (2) Eudemus of Rhodes, describing in his *History of Geometry* more cases (four), apparently covering the generality of the alternatives in order to explain that *all* types of lunules are squaraeble. The only case we will analyze here is the one for which "the exterior arc of the lune be equal to a semicircle" (in the other two cases it is given that it is greater or less than it). This is the case, as we will see, where "the lune [is] on the side of [a] square" [1, p. 69].

The case we will develop is also the first of the two that Alexander examines. Both Alexander and Eudemus agree on the result but disagree on the procedure that leads to it. It should be noted that we would use Alexander's version (Fig. 1(a)) as we consider it more perspicuous[11] than Eudemus' version, since it would allow us to give a better transductive diagrammatic description of the problem.

From a historiographic point of view, there are two perspectives in relation to the description of this problem, although it is common to describe it through the Eudemus' version, which Simplicius himself attributes to Hippocrates, raising doubts about Alexander's version, his Aristotle commentator competitor. On the one hand, one of

---

[11] In relation to the notion of perspicuity, see [4].

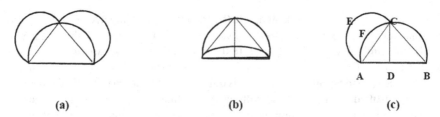

       (a)   (b)   (c)

Fig. 1. Three different diagrams for Hippocrates' first quadrature by means of lunules.

these trends is advocated by Simplicius, who chooses to attribute to Eudemus the correct version that Hippocrates allegedly carried out, considering Alexander's version as less sophisticated. As Heath states:

> The four [cases which Simplicius] quotes textually from Eudemus, (…) which therefore may with certainty be taken to be the only cases included in the genuine work of Hippocrates himself. (…) It would seem that [the cases from Alexander must] somehow wrongly ascribed to Hippocrates (…) it does give the same result (…) though the figures used are different[12] [16, p. 35].

Conversely, in [14], the same historian offers a different diagram (Fig. 1(c)), which is shared by Høyrup [18], following Allman [1], based on Bretschneider [7], although he also claims that his interpretation supports Eudemus' version. The second trend, on the other hand, uses Alexander's version. Authors such as Friberg [12] and Knorr [23] describe it, but Knorr does not take a stance in favor of either version, and simply expose both. In comparison to the version of Fig. 1 that we will develop below, the advantage of the diagram used by Høyrup and Allman (Fig. 1(c)) is that it exhibits what the final triangle that has the same area with the lunule is. On the other hand, it requires specifying a midpoint between the ends of the base segment, and designating letters to make correlative indications between the text (rhetoric) and the graph, which makes it more cumbersome when giving a diagrammatic demonstration.

Conversely, Alexander's version avoids the latter and, diagrammatically, his demonstration is clearer and more perspicuous, although graphically he does not show the triangle with an area half of the original, which is the one that finally equals the lunule in area.

In turn, Høyrup's interpretation begins with a straight line AB, describes a semicircle on it, and then lets the sides of a triangle be inscribed in it. Instead, Alexander starts with the same straight line, constructs a half-square on it, and then a semicircle is applied to all the three sides of the triangle. This avoids having to demonstrate or use a known result, which states that the produced angle when inscribing a triangle in it is straight. This does not happen in Alexander's version. We develop our version in the next section.

---

[12] See Fig. 1(b).

3.2 Equality of Areas Between a Lunule and a Right Triangle: Mathematical Proof and Diagrammatic Explanation

In this section we will show how a specific case of lunule, -the one that is described about the side of a square inscribed in the given circle-, has an area equal to a triangle. The demonstration process takes place in ten steps, each of which is accompanied by a corresponding diagram. The set of the ten diagrams associated with each step of the demonstrative argument are presented in Fig. 2. Each step indicates which previous results are assumed to be known beforehand, in the manner of *elements* required to carry out the detailed explanation of the equality sought between the lunule and the triangle.

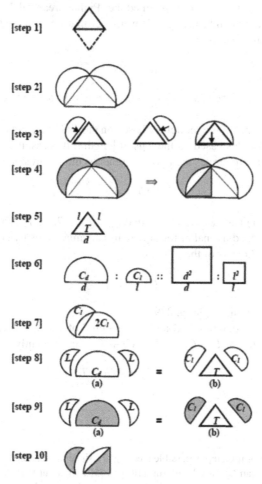

Fig. 2. Diagrammatic proof of Hippocrates' first quadrature.

Step 1. We start by giving a half square, which is also an isosceles right triangle.

Step 2. Three semicircles are applied to the respective sides of the triangle.

Step 3. We can notice that the semicircle applied to the diagonal of the triangle (the base) is a larger one, which also has the triangle inscribed in it.

Step 4. Two lunules are formed. Both have the same area. We will denote with L the area of each of the two lunules, and with T the area of the given right triangle. This seeks to demonstrate that $2L = T$. It will eventually prove that $L = \frac{1}{2}T$, that is, the area of a lunule is equal to the area of a right triangle, that which is half part of the original right triangle[13].

Step 5. Let d be the length of the diameter of the central semicircle, of the diagonal of the square, and also of the hypotenuse of the original right triangle. Let l be the length of each leg from this right triangle. It is assumed the 'Pythagorean rule' to be valid, which is applied to the original right triangle. It turns out that $d^2 = l^2 + l^2 = 2l^2$, which results in the following equation:

$$d^2 = 2l^2 \tag{1}$$

Equality (1) makes use of the additivity of areas: if equals be added to equals, the wholes are equal[14].

Step 6. Let C_d be the area of the semicircle based on the diameter, and C_l the corresponding area of the semicircles based on the legs of length l. It is assumed that Hippocrates knows that circles or semicircles are to one another as the squares on their diameters[15]:

$$C_d : C_l :: d^2 : l^2 \tag{2}$$

Step 7. Combining (1) and (2), we obtain that $C_d : C_l :: 2l^2 : l^2$. This means that the semicircle based on the diagonal of the square has an area that is twice the area of each semicircle based on the legs of the triangle:

$$C_d = 2 C_l \tag{3}$$

Eudemus makes this point in [34, p. 239].

Step 8. The equality of diagrams (a) and (b) in step 8 of Fig. 2 is formed. In terms of areas, this means that: $L + L + C_d = C_l + C_l + T$, or equivalently

$$2L + C_d = 2C_l + T \tag{4}$$

---

[13] The second diagram of this step is possible (see Fig. 2), since the diagonal line can be bisected and a perpendicular can be raised. Høyrup [18, p. 165] points out that Proclus [32, p. 220f] narrates that Oinopides can construct with ruler and compass a similar perpendicular on a line from a point outside it.

[14] This result will appear in Euclid's *Elements*, as a common notion that here is applied to the diagonal of the square. See [15, p. 155].

[15] This result later appeared as Proposition 2 in Book XII of Euclid's *Elements*. See [15, p. 371].

Step 9. Expressions (3) and (4) combined, bring as a consequence that

$$2L = T \tag{5}$$

Geometrically, this is because by removing the shared region of both modes (a) and (b) at the combined diagram in step 9 of Fig. 2 (i.e. the larger semicircle in (a) or the two smaller semicircles in (b)), we obtain that the isosceles triangle in (b) is equal to the two lunules in (a).

Step 10. Looking now at the left quadrant of the large semicircle, and inside it, at the half-triangle of the given original one, due to result (5) above, this in turn results in an area equal to the corresponding lunule, i.e. $L = \frac{1}{2}T$. Therefore, this shows that the lune is triangulable. However, since every triangle is squarable, it concludes that the lune too is squarable.

Figure 2 expresses this proof in an entire diagrammatic transductive style, and it differs from the static way in which Høyrup, following Allman schematizes such proof. Although his version refers directly to the text of Eudemus provided by Simplicius, and not to Alexander's version, he does not make it compatible with the dynamic style with which he usually presents the geometric results of the mathematical texts of Mesopotamia [17].

In sum, we have tried to standardize this typical diachronic style of the Old Babylonian texts that Høyrup designs, but which in this case did not apply in his [18] when describing the Hippocratic procedure. We believe that it makes sense to rebuild Hippocrates' style transductively, given the insightful version offered by Alexander. Moreover, this could also be done with the Eudemus version, with the exceptions of the case, as we did say *ut supra.*

3.3 Transductive Interpretation of the Process

First transductive step: when reducing the problem $\bigcirc -\,-\,-\!\rightarrow \square$ to the problem $\bigcirc -\,-\,-\!\rightarrow \triangle$, this leads to demonstrate that the right triangle B is equivalent to the lunule M in area. This is the similarity that transduction refers to, being in this case an identity of areas. This demonstration is key as it demands all the mathematical work needed to solve the problem and is also part of this step. All that remains are *logical arguments* and *associative descriptions*, which, at this stage, require progressing on the consequences of resembling a lunule to a triangle.

Second transductive step: from the similarity between the lunule M and the right triangle B, in this step, the effects of the equality of areas are examined, i.e., what consequences it brings having shown that B and M are similar in area. The mathematical demonstration provided in the previous step conceals an analogy, that is, we go beyond the similarity between B and M, and draw consequences from the comparison. If we focus on the property of B being squarable, we may wonder if such property of B may be analogically extrapolated to M. Assuming that this is the case , it is represented by *reasoning* δ, composed by two premises ($\mathbb{C} \text{---} \rightarrow \varDelta$, $\varDelta \text{---} \rightarrow \square$) and the conclusion: $\mathbb{C} \text{---} \rightarrow \square$. The analogy shows the quadrability of the lunule from the quadrability of the triangle. This occurs due to a previously noted similarity between M and B, which describes the equality of areas.

Third transductive step: at this stage we seek to acquire an understanding of the resulting consequences, and then proceeding to finally carry out the abductive formation of the hypothesis, which, as we can see, is not merely instinctive, but implies finding the causes of the similarity (achieved in the first step) and its analogical effects (second step). The explanation of reasoning α (see Sect. 3.1), - that is why we go from the problem of inferring $\bigcirc \text{---} \rightarrow \square$ to that of inferring $\bigcirc \text{---} \rightarrow \varDelta$-, lies in the choice of the lunules as a link between $\bigcirc$ and $\varDelta$. This explanation is provided by reasoning β, which takes the lunule $\mathbb{C}$ as a middle term between $\bigcirc$ and $\varDelta$. Thus, the combined β and α reasonings show that the lunule is also the middle term between $\bigcirc$ and $\square$, that is, γ reasoning. It does not explain how (i.e., how the mathematical proof that $\mathbb{C}$ is similar to $\varDelta$ is carried out), but only explains why.

This is the reason to offer an explanation, which can eventually become a demonstration. In this regard, Netz [29, p. 275] insists that the Hippocrates' text as described by Eudemus is not concerned with mathematical proofs but only 'shows' the results. Høyrup adds that by "shows" he may very well mean to "explain", i.e. what we call the transductive way of obtaining results. When it comes to non-conclusive results, such as those obtained by Hippocrates -as he does not work exhaustively with all cases of existing lunules-, we are in the presence of a plausible explanation that does not always become a justification providing certainty to the entire development carried out. In this respect, commenting on Høyrup's perspective on ancient mathematical procedures (as the ones from Paleobabylon), Karine Chemla notes that these only "intend to guarantee an *understanding* of the reasons why the operations should be carried out (…) [and do not place] the exclusive focus on the function of proof as yielding *certainty* [that] would leave out these sources as irrelevant for the history of proof" [9, p. 41]. As discussed in Sect. 2, if the purpose is the search for complete certainty, as Leibniz demanded for geometry, then the kind of explanation as the one given in the case study is not complete: the process of explanation is not necessarily truth-conductive, and therefore, would not be reliable. On the other hand, from Peirce's perspective, the physical images employed in diagrammatic reasoning, for example, when showing that the area of a given circle is equal to that of a lunule is "not what the reasoning is concerned with" [31, p. 207]. That is, the reasoning itself is diagrammatic and offers an answer to the problem to be solved. In summary, the combination of the three types of associations allows us to configure a transductive diagrammatic argumentation that not only facilitates the understanding of the result, but also produces a plausible explanation of it. Figure 3 below summarizes the complete diagrammatic transductive process.

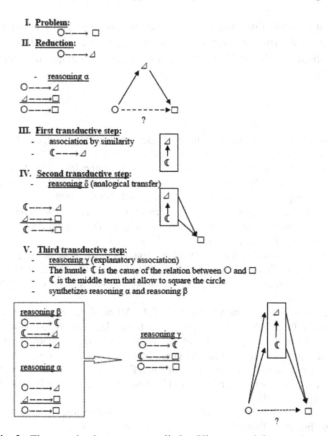

Fig. 3. The transductive process applied to Hippocrates' first quadrature.

4   Conclusion

The case study presented above attempts to reflect a paradigmatic situation concerning diagrammatic inferences: solving a problem -in this case, unsuccessfully attempting to square the circle- is not just to give a proof of a result that guarantees its certainty in the way a valid theorem does, since its conclusion is considered a necessary truth, which supposedly reflects a pure necessity. After we have been led to a conclusion, we also need to know why that was as if it was. We need to understand the facts we have uncovered. We can be led to see that a certain solution is correct, but more importantly, once we see how the proof goes, we can understand why. Finding something problematic in a specific case study is the first step towards an explanation of the phenomenon implicit there. This kind of understanding by transductive processes, and even more so, when they are diagrammatic, is a methodological tool to elicit implicit knowledge.

In order to grasp the argument as a whole, it is not always enough to know that a result is correct and that its demonstration is rigorous and accurate, being able to track and survey the steps of its proof: we should see it through all at once. On a transductive approach, the core phenomena of the proof lies in knowing why it must be true, why it is compelling, the feeling of having got it, of being aware of the ideas behind it. This insightful experience, i.e. the ability to reconstruct in our minds the argument perspicuously by looking at it diagrammatically is a major moment in grasping mathematical results.

References

1. Allman, G.J.: Greek Geometry from Thales to Euclid. Hodges, Figgis & Co., Dublin/Longmans, Green & Co., London (1889)
2. Visokolskis, S.: El fenómeno de la transducción en la matemática. Metáforas, analogías y cognición. In: Pochulu, M., Abrate, R., Visokolskis, S. (eds.) La metáfora en la educación. Descripción e implicaciones, pp. 37–53. Eduvim, Villa María (2009)
3. Visokolskis, S.: La noción de análisis como descubrimiento en la historia de la matemática. Propuesta de un modelo de descubrimiento creativo. Ph.D. doctoral dissertation. National University of Cordoba, Cordoba, Argentina (2016)
4. Visokolskis, S., Carrión, G.: Creative insights: dual cognitive processes in perspicuous diagrams. In: Sato, Y., Shams, Z. (eds.) SetVR 2018, Proceedings of International Workshop on Set Visualization and Reasoning, vol. 2116, pp. 28–43. CEUR Workshop Proceedings, Edinburgh (2018)
5. Vargas, E.: Perception as inference. In: Hull, K.A., Atkins, R.K. (eds.) Peirce on Perception and Reasoning. From Icons to Logic, pp. 14–42. Routledge, New York-London (2017)
6. Carrión, G.: Imaginación y acción humana en David Hume y Adam Smith: Supuestos gnoseológico-antropológicos en la configuración de la ciencia económica moderna. Ph.D. doctoral dissertation. Catholic University of Santa Fe, Santa Fe, Argentina (2015)
7. Bretschneider, C.A.: Die Geometrie und die Geometer vor Euklides: Ein Historischer Versuch. Teubner, Leipzig (1870)
8. Campos, D.: Imagination, concentration, and generalization: peirce on the reasoning abilities of the mathematician. Trans. Charles S. Peirce Soc. **45**(2), 135–156 (2009)
9. Chemla, K.: Historiography and history of mathematical proof: a research programme. In: Chemla, K. (ed.) The History of Mathematical Proof in Ancient Traditions, pp. 1–68. Cambridge University Press, Cambridge (2012)
10. Diels, H., Kranz, W.: Die Fragmente der Vorsokratiker, 6th edn. Weidmanna, Berlin (1951)
11. Eutocius: In Archimedem Commentaria. In: Heiberg, J.L. (ed.) Archimedes Opera, vol 3. Teubner, Stuttgart (1972)
12. Friberg, J.: Amazing Traces of a Babylonian Origin in Greek Mathematics. World Scientific Publishing, New Jersey (2007)
13. Grosholz, E.: Leibniz, Locke, and Cassirer: Abstraction, and Analysis. Stud. Leibnitiana **45**(1), 97–108 (2013)
14. Heath, T.L.: A History of Greek Mathematics, Vol. I: From Thales to Euclid. Clarendon Press, Oxford (1921)
15. Heath, T.L.: The Thirteen Books of Euclid's Elements, 2nd edn. (revised with additions), vol. I. Dover Publications, New York (1956)
16. Heath, T.L.: Mathematics in Aristotle. Thoemmes Press, Bristol (1998)
17. Høyrup, J.: Lengths, Widths, Surfaces: A Portrait of Old Babylonian Algebra and Its Kin. Springer, New York (2002). https://doi.org/10.1007/978-1-4757-3685-4
18. Høyrup, J.: Hippocrates of Chios. His elements and his lunes. A critique of circular reasoning. AIMS Math. **5**(1), 158–184 (2019)
19. Hull, K.A.: The iconic peirce: geometry, spatial intuition and visual imagination. In: Hull, K.A., Atkins, R.K. (eds.) Peirce on Perception and Reasoning. From Icons to Logic, pp. 147–173. Routledge, New York-London (2017)

20. Hume, D.: Resumen del Tratado de la Naturaleza Humana/Abstract of a Treatise on Human Nature. In: Tasset, J.L. (ed.) Libros de Er, Barcelona (1999)
21. Hume, D.: A treatise on human nature, Vol. I & II. In: Fate Norton, D., Norton, M.J. (eds.) The Clarendon Edition of the Works of David Hume, Oxford (2011)
22. Knorr, W.R.: The Evolution of the Euclidean Elements. A Study of the Theory of Incommensurable Magnitudes and Its Significance for Early Greek Geometry. D. Reidel Publishing Company, Dordrecht/Boston (1975)
23. Knorr, W.R.: The Ancient Tradition of Geometric Problems. Birhäuser, Boston (1986)
24. Knuutila, T.: Not just underlying structures: towards a semiotic approach to scientific representation and modeling. In: Bergman, M., Paavola, S., Pietarinen, A.-V. (eds.) Ideas in Action. Proceedings of the Applying Peirce Conference, pp. 163–172. Nordic Pragmatism Network, Helsinki (2010)
25. Legg, C.: The problem of the essential icon. Am. Philos. Q. **45**(3), 207–232 (2008)
26. Leibniz, G.W.: Sämtliche Schriften und Briefe, Sechte Reiche, Sechter Band, Nouveaux Essais. Akademie-Verlag, Berlin (1990)
27. Lloyd, G.E.R.: The pluralism of Greek 'mathematics'. In: Chemla, K. (ed.) The History of Mathematical Proof in Ancient Traditions, pp. 294–310. Cambridge University Press, Cambridge (2012)
28. Mueller, I.: Aristotle and the quadrature of the circle. In: Kretzmann, N. (ed.) Infinity and Continuity in Ancient and Medieval Thought, pp. 146–164. Cornell University Press, Ithaca/London (1982)
29. Netz, R.: Eudemus of Rhodes, Hippocrates of Chios and the earliest form of a Greek mathematical text. Centaurus **46**, 243–286 (2004)
30. Peirce, C.S.: Collected papers of Charles Sanders Peirce, Vol. 1–8. In: Weiss, P., Hartshorne, C., Burks, A.W. (eds.) Harvard University Press, Cambridge (1932–1958)
31. Peirce, C.S.: The essential peirce, Vol. 2: selected philosophical writings (1893–1913). In: Houser, N., Kloesel, C. (eds.) Selected Philosophical Writings (1893–1913). Indiana University Press, Indianapolis (1998)
32. Proclus: A commentary on the first book of Euclid's elements. In: Morrow, G.R. (ed.) Princeton University Press, Princeton (1970)
33. Sedivy, S.: Hume, images, and abstraction. Hume Stud. **21**(1), 117–134 (1995)
34. Thomas, I. (ed.): Selections Illustrating the History of Greek Mathematics, 2 Vol. Heinemann, London/Putnam, New York (1939)

Counting Mathematical Diagrams
with Machine Learning

Henrik Kragh Sørensen[✉] and Mikkel Willum Johansen

Section for History and Philosophy of Science, Department of Science Education,
University of Copenhagen, Øster Voldgade 3, 1350 Copenhagen K, Denmark
{henrik.kragh,mwj}@ind.ku.dk

Abstract. The role and use of diagrams in mathematical research has recently attracted increasing attention within the philosophy of mathematics, leading to a number of in-depth case studies of how diagrams are used in mathematical practice. Though highly interesting, the study of diagrams still largely lack *quantitative* investigations which can provide vital background information regarding variations e.g. in the frequency or type of diagrams used in mathematics publication over time.

A first attempt at providing such quantitative background information has recently been conducted [9], making it clear that the manual labour required to identify and code diagrams constitutes a major limiting factor in large-scale investigations of diagram-use in mathematics.

In order to overcome this limiting factor, we have developed a machine learning tool that is able to identify and count mathematical diagrams in large corpora of mathematics texts. In this paper we report on our experiences with this first attempt to bring machine learning tools to the aid of philosophy of mathematics. We describe how we developed the tool, the choices we made along the way, and how reliable the tool is in identifying mathematical diagrams in corpora outside of its training set. On the basis of these experiences we discuss how machine learning tools can be used to inform philosophical discussions, and we provide some ideas to new and valuable research questions that these novel tools may help answer.

Keywords: Mathematical diagrams · Machine learning · Philosophy of mathematical practice · Digital humanities · Regional convoluted neural networks

1 Introduction

Historians and philosophers of mathematics are developing an ever-increasing interest in the role that diagrams play in mathematical reasoning and research practice [2–6]. This line of research has been highly successfull in unearthing the multi-faceted and complex roles which diagrams play in mathematics; and yet the philosophical study of mathematical diagrams still largely lacks quantitative data providing vital background information for the qualitative investigation of

© Springer Nature Switzerland AG 2020
A.-V. Pietarinen et al. (Eds.): Diagrams 2020, LNAI 12169, pp. 26–33, 2020.
https://doi.org/10.1007/978-3-030-54249-8_3

selected cases. Recently, a quantitative approach has led to new insights into the development in the use of diagrams over the twentieth century [9]. Among their findings is an apparent 'valley' in the use of diagrams, which seems to coincide with the rise of Bourbaki-style formalistic styles in mathematics during the mid-20th century [8,9].

Despite their obvious interest to the historian and the philosopher, even those quantitative studies are based on a sample from only three journals and only include volumes in five year intervals. Judging from these investigations, the major limiting factor in large-scale quantitative investigations of diagrams seems to be the huge amounts of manual labour required to identify and code diagrams by hand. Thus, to substantiate and expand the quantitative approach, an automated procedure is required to count (and subsequently classify and analyse) diagrams in mathematical texts. To this end, recent developments in machine learning may be able to lend a hand to the historian and the philosopher of mathematical practice.

In this paper, we report on our construction of a machine learning system for automated detection of mathematical diagrams. Without providing the system with any definition of a mathematical diagram, we trained an object detector by feeding it instances of diagrams from a (relatively) small set of mathematical papers. Upon iterated training, our detector was able to predict diagrams outside its training base with a (to us) surprising accuracy and precision.

We open the paper by describing how we trained the system, and we report basic measurements of its accuracy. In the final section of the paper, we discuss how an automatic diagram detector may contribute to our philosophical and historical understanding of mathematics. There, we argue that the existence of such a system opens a variety of new philosophical research questions concerning the role and diversity of mathematical diagrams which it has hitherto not been feasible to pursue.

2 Methods

Any object detector involves a number of crucial choices of which model (and implementation) to use and how to build a good training set for the task at hand. We chose to build our diagram detector on one of the well-known existing models of object detectors based on regional convoluted neural networks, known as *Fast R-CNN* [7], implemented under the *keras*-framework and publicly available [1]. And we chose to build our training set from diagrams found in the volumes of the *Journal für die reine und angewandte Mathematik*, colloquially known as *Crelle's Journal* after its first editor. The volumes of Crelle's Journal published from its inception in 1826 until 1998 are available at the SUB Göttinger Digital-isierungszentrum, providing us with more than 130,000 pages of mathematical text spanning the twentieth century and more. What we will refer to as *the object detector* or *the model* is thus the implementation of the framework *plus* a given very large matrix of weights (approximately 100 MB) which represent the parameters of the model.

It is a real feat of the training process that we need not give a single exhaustive definition of a mathematical diagram as such a definition is incredibly difficult to come up with. The standard definitions include aspects such as 1. being essentially two-dimensional [10], and possibly, 2. being intended to provide certain types of cognitive aid in mathematical reasoning [8]. Mathematical practice, however, does not follow such rules consistently. Matrices are, for instance, generally not considered to be diagrams although they are two-dimensional, whereas Dynkin diagrams are considered to be diagrams even in cases where they are one-dimensional. For pragmatic reasons we combined these criteria in our code-book and considered (roughly speaking) a diagram to be a two-dimensional representation generally considered to be a diagram by mathematicians.

As is always the case with supervised training in machine learning, the quality of the detector is dependent on the quality of the training set. And thus, the practice-near definition of mathematical diagrams features into our detector through the code-books which were used in tagging the training set.

During the training, the detector went through a number of iterations, refining models through exposure to both *true positives* and *false positives* (see Fig. 1). Training by true positives provides the detector with input of (ideally) varied examples of what counts as a mathematical diagram. This is provided by human tagging of diagrams in selected parts of the corpus. For the various iterations we picked out subsets of the corpus X_i, picked out all the pages on which diagrams were found, and identified the rectangles bounding the diagrams P_i. To balance the identification of diagrams by ruling out false positives (here called *background*), we implemented a bootstrapping mechanism sometimes referred to as *negative mining*: If we let the model perform predictions on all pages in X_i for which there is no true positive identified in P_i, we know that any box identified as a diagram is a *false positive*. These boxes collected as N_i can then be fed into the training of the next model as background. Thus, the training of a model builds upon the weights of the previous model and sets of boxes of true and false positives.

After we obtained Model 3, results were sufficiently good that we could apply a different method of training, which is a variant of the process known as *active learning*, where predictions made by the model are fed to an *oracle* (a human) who will classify them as true or false positives. Running model 3 on the entire corpus from Crelle's Journal (all 130,000 pages) provided predictions of 8,700 boxes which were inspected, labeled and corrected where needed by a human agent. Together with the previously tagged true positives, these provided the training set for Model 4, which is the present culmination of our training process.

3   Results

The model was implemented under Linux Ubuntu 18.04, building on `python` and `TensorFlow` and run on a computer with an `AMD Phenom(tm) II X3 720` CPU and an NVIDIA `GeForce GTX 750 Ti` GPU. Run-time was a real bottleneck, both in training new iterations of the model and in running predictions on large

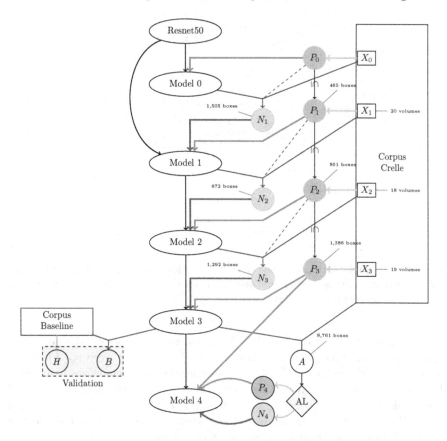

Fig. 1. Illustration of the process of training and validating the models. Boxes are corpora, ellipses are models, circles are sets of boxes (either green true positives or red false positives), diamond is active learning, yellow indicates human interaction, blue indicates prediction. H is hand-tagged, and the comparison of B and H amounts to the validation process discussed below. (Color figure online)

corpora of texts. As the system is small and somewhat dated, this could be mitigated by using more modern and larger hardware.

When we ran predictions by Model 3 on the remaining corpus from Crelle's Journal which was not used in training Model 3, we were quite surprised at the accuracy of true positives and true negatives; in other words, the detector was surprisingly efficient in predicting diagrams precisely when they were indeed present (see Fig. 2).

However, we also encountered all the kinds of mistakes that we would expect: false positives, false negatives, and wrong partitionings. We found various types of false positives, i.e. predictions which do not correspond to diagrams. These included identifying library stamps or indented multiline formula but also some kinds of matrices and continued fractions which could rightly be considered

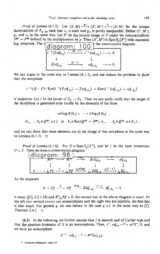

Fig. 2. One example of running the detector (model 3) on the entire corpus from Crelle's Journal, i.e. those papers not used in training the model. For this particular page, it correctly identified two true positives.

diagrams on many definitions [10]. We also found various types of false negatives, in particular some triangular commutative diagrams which were not identified as diagrams by the detector. Another special kind of false negatives came from tableaux pages with many diagrams, especially when the bounding rectangles of different diagrams would overlap; this is thought to be a side-effect of the model chosen. Furthermore, we found instances, where the detector would identify sub-rectangles of a diagram as independent diagrams.

After training our models, and to assess their quality, we ran the detector against a baseline of 677 hand-tagged articles from three journals (*Bulletin of the AMS, Acta Mathematica* and *Annals of Mathematics*) which are outside the training set and were tagged for another project [9]. These articles spanned 23,500 pages and contained a total of 5,271 diagrams. Different measures exist for evaluating this type of machine classification, and the best choice of measure should be based on the concerns of the application. To measure the performance of our detector on such an asymmetric set (many more negatives than positives, higher price of false negatives than of false positives), we chose to balance recall (R) and precision (P) through the F1-score:

$$F1 = \frac{2 \times R \times P}{R + P}, \quad \text{where} \quad R = \frac{TP}{TP + FN} \text{ and } P = \frac{TP}{TP + FP}. \quad (1)$$

If no true positives are found in an article, the F1-score is undefined for that article. As can be seen from the equations, R measures how many positives are picked up and classified correctly, whereas P measures the degree to which those diagrams are identified are indeed true diagrams.

The F1-score for Model 4 against the entire baseline corpus was found to be 0.90777, which is significantly improved from 0.7198 for Model 3. This is a very

On some accounts continued fractions would be considered diagrams.

On some accounts matrices would be considered diagrams.

Sometimes it would also mis-classify horizontal lines as diagrams.

And more frequently, space between lines were mis-classified as diagrams.

Fig. 3. Examples of false positives and wrong partitionings produced by running the detector (model 3) on the corpus from Crelle's Journal against which it was not trained.

Here it picked out only one of the two commutative diagrams; triangular ones are less frequent and sometimes missed.

Some specific diagrams would also sometimes be missed, in particular on pages with overlapping diagram boxes.

Fig. 4. Examples of false negatives produced by the detector (model 3) on the corpus from Crelle's Journal against which it was not trained.

good score for training Model 4 on a relatively small set of tagged images and testing the model against a corpus from different mathematical and typographical traditions. It also shows that Model 4 has succeeded in eliminating many of the false predictions made by Model 3.

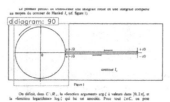

Not capturing the entire diagram; in particular 1-dimensional 'appendices' sometimes allude the detector.

Sometimes, it would pick out both the entire diagram and a part of it.

Fig. 5. Examples of wrong partitioning from running the detector (model 3) on the corpus of Crelle's Journal on which it was not trained.

4 Discussion

Our efforts to build a mathematical diagram detector have been successful to such a degree that we now have a tool that can provide large-scale quantitative background for historical and philosophical investigations of the use of diagrams in mathematics. This background is important for several different reasons. With the detector (and its subsequent improvements) it is possible to build large corpora of diagrams spanning many journals, periods, and sub-disciplines. This will allow a more grounded approach to the investigation of the function of diagrams as large samples that better represent the diversity in the types and uses of diagrams, can easily be accessed.

Furthermore, mathematicians do not only use diagrams (and other representations) as a way to convey mathematical content. Diagrams and other representations also play a major role in the heuristic phases of the mathematical work practice and during idea and concept development. Consequently, changes in the frequency and type of the diagrams being published not only reflects aesthetic and stylistic preferences, but may also indicate underlying changes in cognitive style and epistemic values among the practitioners. The precise understanding of the changes in diagram use over time or between different sub-disciplines of mathematics is thus not only of interest in and by itself, but may also be used to identify specifically interesting periods or publications for further historical or philosophical investigation of the role of diagrams.

Finally, the fact that it is at all possible to build and train a model capable of detecting mathematical diagrams is, in itself, an interesting philosophical result. As pointed out above, it is quite easy to point to many different examples of mathematical diagrams, but difficult to give clear definitions of the concept in terms of necessary and sufficient conditions. Despite this difficulty, the detector is largely capable of mirroring human judgement concerning weather or not something is a diagram (and some of the 'mistakes' made by earlier iterations of the detector even reflect the inconsistencies of the concept as when it classified a continued fraction as a diagram). Although a full explanation of the concept is beyond us, it simply seems that the prototypes embedded in the examples which we provided to the detector are strong enough to allow a reasonably clear concept to form from its actions.

Acknowledgement. The images from Crelle's Journal i Figs. 2, 3, 4 and 5 are used with permission of Walter de Gruyter and Company; permission conveyed through Copyright Clearance Center, Inc.

References

1. Bardool, K., et al.: Keras-frcnn (2019). https://github.com/kbardool/keras-frcnn
2. Carter, J.: Diagrams and proofs in analysis. Int. Stud. Philos. Sci. **24**(1), 1–14 (2010). https://doi.org/10.1080/02698590903467085
3. Carter, J.: Graph-algebras: faithful representations and mediating objects in mathematics. Endeavour **42**(2–3), 180–188 (2018). https://doi.org/10.1016/j.endeavour.2018.07.006
4. De Toffoli, S.: 'Chasing' the diagram: the use of visualizations in algebraic reasoning. Rev. Symb. Log. **10**(1), 158–186 (2017). https://doi.org/10.1017/S1755020316000277
5. De Toffoli, S., Giardino, V.: Forms and roles of diagrams in knot theory. Erkenntnis **79**(4), 829–842 (2013). https://doi.org/10.1007/s10670-013-9568-7
6. Giaquinto, M.: Crossing curves: a limit to the use of diagrams in proofs. Philos. Math. **19**(3), 281–307 (2011). https://doi.org/10.1093/philmat/nkr023
7. Girshick, R.: Fast R-CNN. In: International Conference on Computer Vision (ICCV), pp. 1440–1448 (2015)
8. Johansen, M.W., Misfeldt, M., Pallavicini, J.L.: A typology of mathematical diagrams. In: Chapman, P., Stapleton, G., Moktefi, A., Perez-Kriz, S., Bellucci, F. (eds.) Diagrams 2018. LNCS (LNAI), vol. 10871, pp. 105–119. Springer, Cham (2018). https://doi.org/10.1007/978-3-319-91376-6_13
9. Johansen, M.W., Pallavicini, J.L.: Beyond the valley of formalism: trends and changes in mathematicians' publication practices 1885–2015 (2020, manuscript)
10. Larkin, J.H., Simon, H.A.: Why a diagram is (sometimes) worth ten thousand words. Cogn. Sci. **11**(1), 65–100 (1987). https://doi.org/10.1111/j.1551-6708.1987.tb00863.x

Modes of Continuity in Diagram for Intermediate Value Theorem

Piotr Błaszczyk$^{(\boxtimes)}$ and Marlena Fila

Institute of Mathematics, Pedagogical University of Cracow,
Podchorazych 2, Cracow, Poland
{piotr.blaszczyk,marlena.fila}@up.krakow.pl
https://matematyka.up.krakow.pl/

Abstract. In the ongoing debate over the role of a diagram in the proof of the Intermediate Value Theorem (IVT), Brown's [4] takes a clear position: a diagram does constitute proof of IVT. Giaquinto's [5] points out that a real continuous but nowhere differentiable function lacks a curve, therefore diagrammatic evidence must be restricted to smooth functions. By applying newly-shaped concepts such as *pencil-continuity* and *crossing x-axis* to rational and real maps, $f : Q \mapsto Q$, $f : R \mapsto R$, he comes to the conclusion that the same diagram can represent either a false or true statement, depending on the interpretation in terms of the domain of f.

We analyze Brown's and Giaquinto's arguments in mathematical, philosophical and historical contexts. Our basic observation is the equivalence of IVT and the Dedekind Cut Principle. While Brown does not address the foundational issues at all, Giaquinto seeks to characterize them by the non-mathematical concept of 'desideratum'. As for philosophy, contrary to Giaquinto, we show that the diagram itself constitutes the mathematical context rather than needs an interpretation; yet, contrary to Brown, diagram for IVT does not prove anything, since it represents the axiom (completeness) of real numbers. We adopt a historical perspective to show that both Brown's and Giaquito's arguments involve concepts that take us back to the pre-Bolzano era of non-analytic proofs of IVT.

Keywords: Intermediate Value Theorem · Dedekind Cut Principle · Continuous function · $\varepsilon\delta$-continuity · Pencil continuity · Completeness · Real numbers · Hypereals · Real closed fields

1 Intermediate Value Theorem

Here is the standard wording of the Intermediate Value Theorem (IVT): If continuous function f changes its sign in an interval of real numbers $[a, b]$, then

The first author is supported by the National Science Centre, Poland grant 018/31/B/HS1/03896. The second author is supported by the National Science Centre, Poland grant 2019/33/N/HS1/02045.

A.-V. Pietarinen et al. (Eds.): Diagrams 2020, LNAI 12169, pp. 34–49, 2020.
https://doi.org/10.1007/978-3-030-54249-8_4

there exists an argument c in (a, b) such that $f(c) = 0$. In symbols,

$$f : [a, b] \mapsto R, f(a) \cdot f(b) < 0 \Rightarrow \exists c \in (a, b)[f(c) = 0]. \tag{1}$$

Usually, IVT is included in calculus textbooks, therefore the domain of f is implicit. We make it explicit: f is a real continuous function.

The classic proof emulates the proof developed by Bolzano in [3]. Assume that $f(a) < 0 < f(b)$. Put $S = \{x \in [a, b] : f(x) < 0\}$. The set S is not empty, since $a \in S$; it is also bounded above by b. Therefore, we can apply the least upper bound principle (LUB). Let

$$c = \sup S. \tag{2}$$

There are three possibilities: $f(c) < 0$, $f(c) = 0$, $f(c) > 0$. If $f(c) < 0$, then due to the assumed continuity of f, the sign of $f(c)$ is preserved on some neighborhood of c, that is:

$$(\exists \delta)(\forall x)[x \in (c - \delta, c + \delta) \Rightarrow f(x) < 0]. \tag{3}$$

From (3), it follows that there is x such that $c < x$ and $f(x) < 0$. This contradicts (2). The case $f(c) > 0$ is treated similarly. Hence, $f(c) = 0$.

Therefore, this proof relies on two different concepts of continuity: definition (2) appeals to the continuity (completeness) of the order of real numbers, formula (3) follows from the assumed continuity of f. In fact, [3] provides the first ever definition of the LUB principle and the first ever $\varepsilon\delta$ characterization of the continuous function. Since that time, IVT is associated with concepts rather than diagrams. In Sect. 6, we provide textual evidence showing how Bolzano transformed the diagram for IVT into an analytic framework. Briefly: (1) he turned the intuitive concept of curve into the intuitive concept of function, (2) he turned the intuitive concept of continuity into (2a) the definition of continuous function, and (2b) the continuity of the real number line.

In Sect. 5, we show that IVT is equivalent to the completeness of real numbers in the form of the Dedekind cut principle (DC). Viewed from the perspective $IVT \Leftrightarrow DC$, the diagram for IVT represents something fundamental, non-provable, in the sense that we do not prove axioms. With that knowledge, we proceed to verify the arguments developed in [4] and [5].

2   Brown on Diagram for IVT

2.1   Brown's 'Running Line'

Brown begins with the same proof. The rest of his argument is this:[1] "Consider now visual evidence for the theorem. Just look at the picture (Fig. 1). We have a continuous line running from below to above x-axis. Clearly, it must cross that axis in doing so. Thus understood, it is indeed a 'trivial' and 'obvious' truth" ([4], p. 163).

---

[1] Attached is the diagram he refers to. It is marked as Fig. 1 in [4].

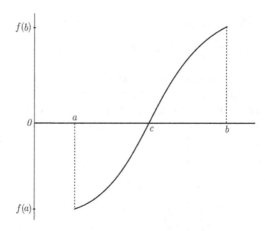

Fig. 1. Brown's diagram for IVT, [4], p. 163.

Brown assumes the framework of real analysis, therefore the x- and y-axes are to represent the line of real numbers. Nevertheless, he pays no attention to how his diagram relates to the assumed continuity of f. Since the f-line "runs from below to above", it represents a movement, rather than the graph of f. Implicitly, an intuitive continuity of movement substitutes the unspecified continuity of the f-line. Indeed, Brown also considers a two-function version of IVT, i.e.

$$f, g : [a, b] \mapsto R, f(a) < g(a), f(b) > g(b) \Rightarrow \exists c \in (a, b)[f(c) = g(c)]. \quad (4)$$

Then, he alludes to "two hikers, one at the 'top, the other at the bottom, both setting out at noon on the same day. Obviously, they eventually meet somewhere on the path" ([4], p. 164).

This story, Brown claims, both illustrates and proves (4). However, in Fig. 1, nothing runs from below to above. Or, if we allow running lines, can lines other than f also run?

The diagram is a synchronic composition of building blocks, however, through letters a, b, and the convention of reading from left to right, Brown already implies his diachronic running line interpretation: f runs from the point $(a, f(a))$ to $(b, f(b))$. However, the diagram could also be read as follows: 'Simply look at the picture (Fig. 1). We have a continuous line running from a to b. Clearly, it must cross the f-line in doing so'. Here, the "continuous line" stands for the line of real numbers. It is the line of real numbers which runs, whereas the f-line stays still. Indeed, viewed form the perspective of the equivalence $IVT \Leftrightarrow DC$, it is as acceptable an interpretation of Fig. 1 as the one advocated by Brown.

2.2 *Logic* of Brown's diagram

Brown's original diagram depicts point c, where $f(c) = 0$. Yet, is it straightforward evidence or a kind of inference? Phrases such as "visual evidence for the theorem" and "obvious truth" suggest the first option. Here is the most clear declaration in support of it: "Using the picture alone, we can be certain of this result—if we can be certain of anything" ([4], p. 164).

But if there is no inference, no assumptions and no conclusions, IVT should be paraphrased such as a conjunction rather than the implication, namely:

$$f : [a,b] \mapsto R, f(a) \cdot f(b) < 0, \exists c \in (a,b)[f(c) = 0]. \tag{5}$$

On the other hand, Brown also suggests that "pictures prove". The sequence of letters a, b, and c sets up a kind of logical dependence: they are not alphabetically arranged from left to right, which implies that the appearance of a, b precedes the appearance of c. But, if Fig. 1 stands for a proof, what thesis does it justify?

Again, the diagram is divided into assumptions and conclusions, although by an interpretation.

All in all, Brown's position on the role of a diagram for IVT is ambiguous: it wavers between evidence and inference, illustration and justification, formula (1) and (5), finally, between the proof and the thesis to be proved. This is most likely due to the fact that Fig. 1 is subject to interpretations.

3   Conceptualizing Diagram

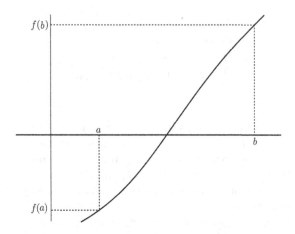

Fig. 2. Diagram for IVT

Figure 2 is our diagram for IVT. It consists of three *continuous* elements, x-axis, y-axis, f-line, and four points, $a, b, f(a), f(b)$. Dotted lines are not essential, they merely illustrate the concept of the function: $f(a), f(b)$ are the values of f at the points a, b respectively. Contrary to Fig. 1, we do not name a supposed intersection point of x-axis and f-line. In our perspective, it represents a crossing of two concepts: the continuity of the line segment $[a, b]$, and the continuity of f-line.

Mathematics provides two conceptual frameworks to analyze Fig. 2: analysis and topology. Within the first, the f-line is interpreted as a continuous real function. Hence, the background space is the Cartesian plane $R \times R$. This idea can be generalized to a Cartesian plane $F \times F$, where F is an ordered field.

Technical concepts enable to characterize both the continuity of f and the continuity of axes. As for the f-line, it could be $\varepsilon\delta$- or sequential-continuity; these concepts make sense in any ordered field. They are equivalent in an Archimedean field, but may differ in a non-Archimedean field. As for the continuity of real numbers, there are more than thirty equivalent versions of completeness. Some of them have adequate graphical representations. In fact, since IVT is equivalent to the completeness of real numbers, Fig. 1 or 2 may play the role of the graphical representation of the continuity of the real number line.

The negation of these two kinds of continuity allows to identify a discontinuity of function, or a gap in a line.

When the background space of the diagram is switched from R to an ordered field, technical concepts support our intuition.

In Table 1, we tally the analytical and intuitive (graphical) concepts characterizing Fig. 2. The term *graphical*, as applied in this context, was introduced by Marcus Giaquinto in a table reproduced below as Table 3. The idea of concepts characterizing diagrams is also due to Giaquinto.

Table 1. Analytical vs graphical.

Analytical	Graphical
Function	Curve
$(F, <)$	x-axis, y-axis
$F \times F$	Background space

The topological framework enables to view the f-line as a graph of f, that is the set $G_f = \{(x, f(x)) \in R^2 : x \in [a, b]\}$. Then, the continuity of f means that the set G_f is a topological continuum, that is, a connected and compact set (see [8], p. 168). Accordingly, gaps in G_f, in R, or in a background space are interpreted in terms of disconnected space; in fact, topology identifies many kinds of disconnected sets.

From a topological perspective, all continuous real functions defined on a line segment are continua. Due to the concept of the derivative, the analytic perspective introduces the concept of the smoothness of function: it is a property measured by the number of continuous derivatives. This idea inspires the interpretation that an f-line on a diagram represents a function which has a continuous first derivative f'.

In Table 2, we tally the topological and graphical concepts characterizing Fig. 2.

In the debate on the role of diagrams in mathematics, the background space is supposed to be a sheet of paper, a computer screen or another *continuous*

Table 2. Topological vs graphical.

Topological	Graphical
Graph of function	Curve
(X, τ_x) topological space	x-axis
(Y, τ_y) topological space	y-axis
$X \times Y$ with product topology	Background space

medium – *continuous* from a viewer's perspective. Since we interpret the background space as $F \times F$, this perceptual *continuity* is guaranteed by the fact that elements of an ordered field F are densely ordered. Nevertheless, in a branch of mathematics called digital geometry (DG), the computer screen is represented by the grid $N \times N$, i.e. the Cartesian product of the set of natural numbers. DG seeks for efficient algorithms to represent common geometrical objects on a disconnected space (see [7]). It takes into account both the physics of the background space and a person's perceptual abilities. Yet, our study, as are [4] and [5], is purely theoretical.

4   Giaquinto on IVT Diagram

4.1   Interpreting the Diagram

While Brown sticks to the position of diagrammatic evidence, Giaquinto adopts a perspective of diagrammatic inference. He seeks to show how one may get from a single graph such as Fig. 2 to IVT.[2] Since the theorem involves concepts defined within the framework of calculus, he introduces their graphical counterparts; these newly-shaped concepts are designed to analyze the diagram from the viewer's perspective. They are listed in Table 3 (see [5], p. 305).

Table 3. Analytical vs graphical by Giaquinto.

Analytical	Graphical
Function	Curve
$\varepsilon\delta$-continuity	Pencil-continuity
Has a zero value	Crosses x-axis
Differentiable	No zig-zags

According to Giaquinto, the alleged diagrammatic argument for IVT consists of three basic steps (see [5], pp. 297–298):

---

[2] Diagram for IVT as presented in [5], p. 283, is rather an illustration of the so-called Darboux property. However, we will not be discussing the difference.

(a) "Any function f $\varepsilon\delta$ continuous on $[a,b]$ with $f(a) < 0 < f(b)$ has a pencil continuous curve from below the x-axis to above".

(b) "Any pencil continuous curve from below the x-axis to above [...] crosses the x-axis".

(c) "For any function f whose curve crosses the x-axis between the points representing a and b, $f(c) = 0$ for some number c between a and b".

While steps (a) and (c) link the analytical and graphical concepts, premise (b) "is taken from the graph" and is not disputed.

An inference starting from a specific f-line which aims at a general conclusion, i.e. concerning a continuous function f, requires a generalization technique. Giaquinto claims that a generalization from Fig. 2 to IVT is not reliable because premises (a) and (c) can be challenged. Here are his arguments.

(Ad a) Firstly, the diagram does not represent the general case, since there are $\varepsilon\delta$-continuous functions that have no curves. These are continuous, nowhere differentiable functions, e.g. the Weierstrass *monster* function; they cannot be *visualized* and cannot be represented on a diagram.

Secondly, since Giaquinto defines pencil-continuity by "no perceptible gap in the curve", this concept does not coincide with the $\varepsilon\delta$-continuity. That difference can be exemplified by a function on rational numbers $f : Q \mapsto Q$ defined by:

$$f(x) = \begin{cases} 1, & \text{if } x^2 < 2 \text{ or } x < 0, \\ -1, & \text{if } x^2 > 2 \text{ and } x > 0. \end{cases}$$

Figure 3 illustrates it. The function f is $\varepsilon\delta$-continuous but is not pencil-continuous.

The gap in the x-axis represented on the Fig. 3 can be characterized by the sets $A = \{x \in Q : x^2 < 2 \text{ or } x < 0\}$ and $B = \{x \in Q_+ : x^2 > 2\}$. The pair (A, B) is the so-called Dedekind gap in the line $(Q, <)$.

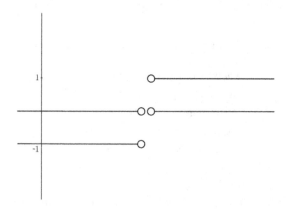

Fig. 3. Function which is $\varepsilon\delta$-continuous, while not pencil-continuous.

Giaquinto's original example is a function defined by

$$g(x) = \begin{cases} x - 2, & \text{if } x^2 < 2 \text{ or } x < 0, \\ x - 1, & \text{if } x^2 > 2 \text{ and } x > 0. \end{cases}$$

He represents the x-axis by a *continuous* line, while the gap (A, B) is represented by the diagonal of a unit square (see [5], p. 299, Fig. 7). Thus, Giaquinto illustrates a gap in the curve, while characterizes the gap in the x-axis analytically.

(Ad c) Since "the curve crosses if and only if it appears to cross", there are $\varepsilon\delta$-continuous functions that have curves which appear to cross the x-axis, but there is no c between a and b such that $f(c) = 0$.[3] Giaquinto exemplifies such case by a parabola $f : Q \mapsto Q$ defined by $f(x) = x^2 - 2$. Figure 4 illustrates it.

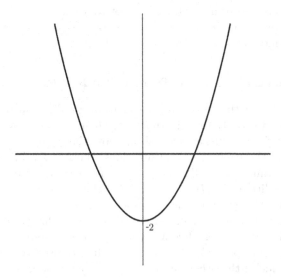

Fig. 4. Diagram representing parabola $x^2 - 2$ with no specified domain.

Examples illustrated by Fig. 3 and 4 are designed to show that the same diagram is subject to various interpretations. Figure 3 is to represent an intuitively discontinuous function which is $\varepsilon\delta$-continuous. Figure 4 may represent, as Giaquinto claims, a false or true version of IVT: "As a continuous function on the rationals and the corresponding function on the reals may have exactly the same diagram, the IVT cannot be read off the diagram" ([5], p. 301).

However, what makes the diagram for IVT subject to interpretation? Giaquinto does not pose this question. Our guess is as follows: when the f-line is viewed as a function, x-axis appears to be its domain. Then the modern

---

[3] Note, while negations of technical concepts are unequivocal, we can not decide what does it mean that *the curve does not cross*. Is it *it does not appear to cross*, or *it appears to not cross*?.

understanding of function opens x-axis to various interpretations; there is only one restriction: a newly established framework enables to reconstruct the concept of continuous function.

This perspective shows that interpretation of a diagram depends on the historical context, but also on individual resources. Hence, Descartes' and Bolzano's views of f-line could differ (they, in fact, differed); nowadays, a pupil's, a student's, or a scholar's view of a f-line can also differ. In Sect. 6, we show that although Bolzano introduced the concept of function, he did not provide the definition. Yet, due to this concept, he could differentiate between a general continuous function and a polynomial. In [3], he sought to prove IVT for real polynomials, whereas IVT for continuous functions played the role of lemma in his paper. Within the framework of diagrammatic reasoning, he could not explicate a difference between f-line and *polynomial*-line. Moreover, the $\varepsilon\delta$-continuity he introduced is applied to a function, but not to a curve.

In the next section, we show how a set of concepts at the viewer's disposal can determine a modern interpretation of the diagram.

4.2   When Background Space Turns to Be $R \times R$

Giaquinto's doubts whether one can get from a single diagram to IVT built on possible interpretations of the x-axis. However, when one assumes, as for instance Brown does, that f-line represents a real function, the role of Fig. 3 and 4 fades. It appears that in the context of real functions, there is no difference between pencil- and $\varepsilon\delta$-continuity, as well as between f-line "crossing the x-axis" and the mathematical condition $(\exists c)[f(c) = 0]$. As for the concept of curve, it means nothing more than the graph of smooth function f.[4]

Giaquinto suggests there is some empirical content in his *graphical* concepts, as he writes: "A curve is pencil-continuous just when there is no perceptible gap in the curve" ([5], p. 298); "One graphical line crosses another when each has parts either side of the other and there is a perceptible meeting place" ([5], p. 298); "the curve crosses if and only if it appears to cross" ([5], p. 300). In fact, concepts such as "perceptible gap", "perceptible meeting place", "appears to cross" are not founded on any empirical data. The rationale for his *graphical* concepts comes from mathematics, since only mathematical examples motivate every pair of concepts in Table 3.

Why then does Giaquinto introduce *graphical* concepts which prove to be useless when applied to real functions? His reply could be this: "the analytical concepts of the IVT are essentially non-perceptual" ([5], p. 305). However, even if non-perceptual, technical concepts affect the individual perception of the diagram.

To elaborate. In regard to the function represented by Fig. 4, Giaquinto writes: "The curve for $x^2 - 2$ in the rationals is the same as the curve for $x^2 - 2$ in the reals. **This is because every real is a limit point of rationals.** This

---

[4] Here, we adopt the following definition: a real function f is smooth when it has a continuous first derivative f'.

entails that for every point P with one or both co-ordinates irrational, there are points arbitrarily close to P with both co-ordinates rational. So no gaps can appear by removing irrational points from the curve for $x^2 - 2$ in the reals. [...] **The IVT is essentially about the reals**; it is not true in the rationals. As a continuous function on the rationals and the corresponding function on the reals **may have exactly the same diagram**, the IVT cannot be read off the diagram, as this example shows" ([5], p. 301, emphasizes added).

Firstly, in every Archimedean field $(F, +, \cdot, 0, 1, <)$, every element $a \in F$ can be presented as a limit of rational points.

Secondly, IVT is not essentially about the domain of f; it also concerns the kind of f. IVT$_{x^2-2}$ is true not only in the field of reals, but also in the field of real algebraic numbers (which is *bigger* than Q and *smaller* that R), as well as in the field of hyperreals (which is bigger than R). In fact, IVT$_{polynomial}$ is true in the field of real algebraic numbers and in the field of hyperreals. Generally, IVT$_{polynomial}$ is true in every real closed field (see [6], ch. 6).[5]

The third note regards the claim that the diagram does not change when we switch the background space from R to Q. While it is true in regard to polynomials, it is not in regard to the so-called transcendental functions, e.g., trigonometric functions, e^x, $\log x$. It is because these functions take irrational values for rational arguments (see [9], ch. 2.) In other words, when we change the range of $\sin x$ from real to rational numbers, the diagram of $\sin x$ will simply disappear.

To sum up, on a diagram, we cannot represent the differences between real, rational, or real algebraic numbers: every ordered field is represented by the same kind of drawn line. But we also cannot represent the differences between polynomial- and non-polynomial lines. Therefore, Fig. 4 can represent a true statement in the context of real functions, but also in the context of polynomials on a real closed field.

5   IVT Is Completeness of Real Numbers

In this section, we briefly discuss the basics of the theory of ordered fields to show that IVT is equivalent to the completeness of real numbers.

5.1   Dedekind's Gaps vs 'Perceptible Gaps'

Throughout [5], Giaquinto refers to the intuitive meaning of gap. In this section, we present its mathematical definition, and show how we can interpret it in regard to diagrams.

Definition 1. *A pair of non-empty sets (A, B) is a Dedekind cut of a totally ordered set $(X, <)$ iff: (1) $A \cup B = X$, (2) $(\forall x \in A)(\forall y \in B)(x < y)$.*

---

[5] In this section, we adopt the following convention: IVT$_{polynomial}$ means that in the formula (1) we take f to be a polynomial function from $[a, b]$ to an ordered field F. Accordingly, IVT$_{x^2-2}$ stands for $x^2 - 2 : [a, b] \mapsto F$, $a^2 < 2 < b^2$, etc.

From the perspective of the proximity region of the sets A and B, there are four kinds of cuts, as represented on the Fig. 5, where the black dot stands for the greatest element in A, or the least element in B, and the blank dot stands for A with no greatest element, or B with no least element. When no cut of $(X, <)$ is of the (1)-kind, the order $<$ is dense. The (2)-kind cuts are called gaps. Dedekind discovered that cuts of that kind in the line $(Q, <)$ can be defined within the arithmetic of rational numbers, i.e., with no reference to irrational numbers.

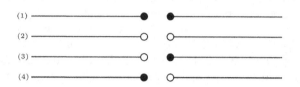

Fig. 5. Possible Dedekind cuts in a totally ordered set.

Definition 2. *A commutative field* $(F, +, \cdot, 0, 1)$ *together with a total order* $<$ *is an ordered field when the sums and products are compatible with the order, that is*

$$x < y \Rightarrow x + z < y + z, \quad x < y, 0 < z \Rightarrow xz < yz.$$

The standard examples of an ordered field are rational numbers $(Q, +, \cdot, 0, 1, <)$ and real numbers $(R, +, \cdot, 0, 1, <)$. Fields which are *between* these extremities are called Archimedean fields. Figuratively speaking, the field of fractions is the *smallest* ordered field, the field or real numbers is the *biggest* Archimedean field, i.e., any ordered field includes the field of fractions, any field extension of real numbers is a non-Archimedean field.

Here are some equivalent forms of the Archimedean axiom:[6]

(A1) $(\forall x \in F)(\exists n \in N)(n > x)$.
(A2) $(\forall x, y \in F)(\exists q \in Q)(x < y \Rightarrow x < q < y)$.
(A3) For any Dedekind cut (A, B) of $(F, <)$ obtains

$$(\forall n \in N)(\exists a \in A)(\exists b \in B)(b - a < \tfrac{1}{n}).$$

The order of any ordered field is dense. It follows from this fact: if $x < y$, then $x < \frac{x+y}{2} < y$. This fact may justify the claim that drawn lines designed to represent an ordered field look the same.

Although an Archimedean field may have gaps, that is, (2)-kind Dedekind cuts, the axiom A3 enables to interpret them as so small that they can not be spotted. That is why we claim that the difference between real, rational and real algebraic numbers cannot be represented by drawn lines.

---

[6] Here, and throughout this paper, the symbol N stands for the set of natural numbers.

It is known that Euclid's straightedge and compass constructions are possible on a Cartesian plane $F \times F$, where F is an ordered field closed under the square root operation. Fields of that kind can be Archimedean or non-Archimedean. Supposing F is both Archimedean and closed under the square root operation, a Euclidean plane can have gaps, meaning the field F has (2)-kind Dedekind cuts. Yet, we can also characterize this kind of space as disconnected. As a result, a Euclidean plane can be a proper subset of the real plane $R \times R$. Nevertheless, when F is both non-Archimedean and closed under the square root operation, gaps in the plane $F \times F$ are *huge* (this can be made into a precise characteristic).

5.2   Axioms vs 'Desiderata'

Giaquinto writes: "I concede that the IVT is not merely a consequence of Dedekind Completeness. The IVT may also be regarded as a desideratum for an account of the real numbers" ([5], p. 302).

In this section, we show that IVT is another version of the completeness of real numbers.

Definition 3. *The field of real numbers is an ordered field* $(F, +, \cdot, 0, 1, <)$, *in which every Dedekind cut* (L, U) *of* $(F, <)$ *satisfies the condition*

$$(\exists x \in F)(\forall y \in L)(\forall z \in U)(y \leq x \leq z). \tag{C1}$$

Constructions of real numbers, e.g., the one that identifies real numbers with cuts of the line of rational numbers $(Q, <)$ due to Dedekind, show that there exists at least one field of real numbers. On the other hand, the categoricity theorem states that any two ordered fields satisfying axiom (C1) are isomorphic. In other words, any ordered field satisfying (C1) is isomorphic to the field of real numbers. Below, we present two other equivalent versions of (C1):

(C2) If $A \subset F$ is a nonempty set which is bounded above, then there exists $a \in F$ such that $a = \sup A$.

(C3) The field is Archimedean and every Cauchy (fundamental) sequence $(a_n) \subset F$ has a limit in F.

Any equivalent form of C1 usually gets the name of continuity or completeness, and the real number system is called the continuous or complete ordered field. The version C2 has already been applied in Sect. 1 of this paper – it is the Least Upper Bound principle. C3 is a combination of the Archimedean axiom and the so-called Cauchy completeness (CC): whereas the A3 version of the Archimedean axiom guarantees each Dedekind cut is *small*, by CC, every such a gap is *filled up* with the limit point of a sequence (a_n).

Since the order of an ordered field $(F, +, \cdot, 0, 1, <)$ is dense, there are no (1)-kind cuts in $(F, <)$. Assuming (A, B) is a Dedekind cut, C1 states that there are no (2)-kind cuts in $(F, <)$: the number z, as it occurs in C1, is the biggest element in A, or the least element in B. Therefore, Fig. 6 illustrates C1.

Theorem 1. *IVT is equivalent to C1.*

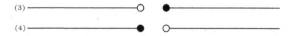

Fig. 6. Possible Dedekind cuts in the line of real numbers.

Proof. In Sect. 1, we have already reminded the classic proof that C1 implies IVT. As for the second part, to reach a contradiction, assume that C1 does not hold. Hence, there is a (2)-kind cut (A, B) in $(F, <)$. The function f defined by

$$f(x) = \begin{cases} 1, & \text{if } x \in A, \\ -1, & \text{if } x \in B. \end{cases}$$

is $\varepsilon\delta$-continuous. Indeed, since there is no biggest element in A, for each $x \in A$ we can find a positive number δ such that the line segment $(x - \delta, x + \delta)$ is a subset of A. Then, for every y in $(x - \delta, x + \delta)$, we have $f(y) = 1$. Similarly,

$$(\forall x \in B)(\exists \delta > 0)(\forall y)[y \in (x - \delta, x + \delta) \Rightarrow f(y) = -1].$$

Take $a \in A$, $b \in B$. On the segment $[a, b]$, the function f changes its sign, however, there is no c, such that $f(c) = 0$. Figure 3 illustrates that kind of continuous function.

From the perspective of the equivalence $IVT \Leftrightarrow C1$, Fig. 2 and 6 represent the same foundational characteristics of real numbers. However, while we understand the sentence $IVT \Leftrightarrow C1$, can we grasp any relationship between these figures?

Strictly speaking, Fig. 2 and 6 do not prove, as they represent axioms. But even as axioms, they need an explanation in technical terms. As for Fig. 2, these are the concepts of real numbers and continuous function. As for Fig. 6, these are concepts of an ordered field and a Dedekind cut. Yet, we find no room here for any cognitive arguments.

5.3   Mathematical vs Cognitive Motives

In regard to real numbers Giaquinto writes: "the main motive for extending the rationals to the reals is to maintain our cognitive predispositions about space, so that real analysis can incorporate and extend geometry rather than overthrow it" ([5], p. 303). However, neither Dedekind's 1872 *Stetigkeit und irrationale Zahlen*, nor Cantor's 1872 *Über die Ausdehnung eines Satzes aus der Theorie der trigonometrischen Reihen* include any cognitive motivations. Dedekind only sought for foundations for the calculus. Cantor sought to explain the concept of derivative P' of a point set P.

6   Bolzano's 1817 *Rein Analytischer Beweis*

Figure 7 represents the logical structure of [3]. Bolzano aims to show the Intermediate Value Theorem for polynomials, IVT_p. On the one hand, the proof applies the theorem that polynomial is a continuous function, *con of poly*, and on the other hand, the Intermediate Value Theorem for continuous function, IVT$_f$. Both of these results apply the definition of continuous function, *df of cont*; the first directly, the other *via* the so-called sign preserving property, SPP, as explained by formula (3) in our paper. The proof of IVT$_f$ employs the Least Upper Bound principle, LUB. Bolzano proves it by Cauchy Completeness, CC. He also seeks to prove *CC*. Throughout the paper, he implicitly refers to two forms of the Archimedean axiom.

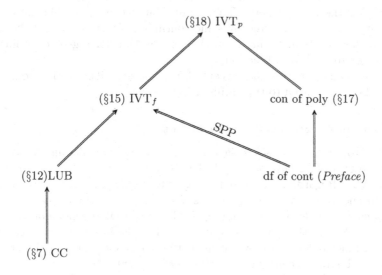

Fig. 7. Plan of Bolzano's *Rein analytischer Beweis*.

Hypothetically, it was possible to prove IVT$_p$ by applying the concept of continuous function straight to a polynomial with no reference to the concept of function.[7] Whether applied to a function or a polynomial, the analytic form of continuity was, at the time, a new idea.

6.1   Function vs Line

Bolzano considers two versions of IVT: for a geometric line and for a function. The first is stated as such: "every continuous line [*kontinuierliche Linie*] of simple curvature of which the ordinates are first positive and then negative (or conversely), must necessarily intersect the abscissae-line somewhere at a point lying between those ordinates" ([10], p. 254). The version for the function is as follows: "If two functions of x, fx and φx, vary according to the law of continuity [*nach dem Gesetze der Stetigkeit*] either for all values of x or for all those

---

[7] In fact, that is what Birkhoff and Mac Lane did in their proof of the Fundamental Theorem of Algebra 150 years after Bolzano; see [1], ch. 4 and [2], p. 19.

lying between α and β, and furthermore if $f\alpha < \varphi\alpha$ and $f\beta > \varphi\beta$, then there is always a certain value of x between α and β for which $fx = \varphi x$" ([10], p. 273). Bolzano provides also a version for one function, namely: "between any two values, which give results of opposite sign, there lies at least one real root" ([10], p. 276).

The paper includes neither a definition of the geometric line, nor a definition of function. Moreover, it does not explain what the continuity of line means.

Now, Bolzano declares that the truth of geometric version of IVT "lies in nothing other than that general truth, as a result of which every continuous function" has the IVT property. This claim, however, assumes that every continuous line can be represented by some continuous function. In fact, he never addressed this question. In any case, that is how IVT for a geometric line has been reduced to IVT for a function.

In modern mathematics, the concept of function prevails, and the geometrical aspect of IVT is reduced to the graph of function.

6.2   Continuous Function vs Movement

In *Preface* to *Rein analytischer Beweis*, Bolzano provides detailed analysis of previous proofs of IVT developed by Euler, Gauss and others. In fact, these were proofs of IVT$_p$. Regarding the proof relying on the concept of movement, Bolzano alludes to one given by Lagrange in his *Traité de la résolution des équations numériques de tous les degrés*. Lagrange's theorem related a polynomial of the form $P - Q$. Yet, in the crucial step, it referred to the intuition of a race: when a quicker runner outruns a slower runner, they must meet at some point. This is a point x, Lagrande concludes, in which $(P - Q)(x) = 0$.

For Bolzano, the proof based on the concept of movement "does not prove the proposition itself, but instead must first be proved by it" ([10], p. 256). In this context, he provides a definition of continuity (*Stetigkeit*) of function, namely "function fx varies according to the law of continuity for all values of x inside or outside certain limits means only that, if x is any such value the difference $f(x + \omega) - fx$ can be made smaller than any given quantity, provided ω can be taken as small as we please [...] or $f(x + \omega) = fx + \Omega$" ([10], p. 256).

In this way, continuous motion was replaced by continuous function. Due to this substitution, Bolzano managed to introduce a kind of algebra of movements: assuming functions f, g represent movements, terms $f + g$, or $f - g$ have clear mathematical meaning, even if the concept of function is not defined.

7   Summary

Both Brown and Giaquinto seek to analyze IVT by an intuitive concept of curve. Brown also refers to the concept of movement, while Giaquinto employs a set of graphical concepts. Through these concepts, they develop a philosophy of diagrams which takes us to back to the pre-Bolzano era. Yet, since Bolzano transformed the diagram for IVT into an analytic framework, there is no way back to the era of visual and mechanical intuitions.

References

1. Birkhoff, G., MacLane, S.: A Survey of Modern Algebra, 4th edn. Macmillan, New York (1977)
2. Błaszczyk, P.: A purely algebraic proof of the fundamental theorem of algebra. Ann. Univ. Paedagogicae Cracoviensis **8**, 6–22 (2016). http://didacticammath.up.krakow.pl//article/view/3638/3268
3. Bolzano, B.: Rein analytischer Beweis das Lehrsatzes, daß zwischen je zwei Werthen, die ein entgegengesetzes Resultat gewähren, wenigsten eine reelle Wurzel der Gleichung Liege. Gottlieb Hasse, Prague (1817)
4. Brown, J.R.: Proofs and pictures. Br. J. Philos. Sci. **48**(2), 161–180 (1997). https://doi.org/10.1093/bjps/48.2.161
5. Giaquinto, M.: Crossing curves: a limit to the use of diagrams in proofs. Philos. Math. **19**(3), 281–307 (2011). https://doi.org/10.1093/philmat/nkr023
6. Jacobson, N.: Lectures in Abstract Algebra, vol. III. Von Nostrand, Princeton (1975)
7. Klette, R., Rosenfeld, A.: Digital Geometry: Geometric Methods for Digital Picture Analysis. Elsevier Inc., Amsterdam (2004)
8. Kuratowski, K., Engelking, R.: Introduction to Set Theory and Topology. International Series of Monographs in Natural Philosophy. Pergamon Press, New York (1972). https://books.google.pl/books?id=kusD7PHoUS4C
9. Niven, I.: Irrational Numbers. Mathematical Association of America, New York (1956)
10. Russ, S.: The Mathematical Works of Bernard Bolzano. Oxford University Press, Oxford (2004)

Modes of Diagrammatic Reasoning
in Euclid's *Elements*

Piotr Błaszczyk[ID] and Anna Petiurenko[(⊠)][ID]

Institute of Mathematics, Pedagogical University of Cracow,
Podchorazych 2, Cracow, Poland
{piotr.blaszczyk,anna.petiurenko}@up.krakow.pl
https://matematyka.up.krakow.pl/

Abstract. The standard attitude to Euclid's diagrams is focused on
assumptions hidden behind intersecting lines. We adopt an alternative
perspective and study the diagrams in terms of a balance between the
visual and theoretical components involved in a proposition. We consider
theoretical components to consist of definitions, *Postulates*, *Common
Notions*, and references to previous propositions. The residuum makes
the visual part of the proof. Through analysis of propositions I.6, I.13,
and II.1–4, we show that such residuum actually exists. We argue that
it is related to a primitive *lesser-greater* relation between figures, or an
undefined relation of the concatenation of figures.

We also identify a tendency in the *Elements* to eliminate visual aspects
in order to achieve generality founded on theoretical grounds alone. Our
analysis spans between two versions of the Pythagorean theorem, i.e.,
I.47 and VI.31. We study the diagrams in Books I through VI in terms
of how visual elements are being replaced in favor of theoretical components. That process is crowned by proposition VI.31. None of its parts
build on the accompanying diagram. Moreover, it concerns objects that
are not represented on the diagram at all. In fact, this pattern applies
to most propositions of Book VI. Therefore, we treat VI.31 as a model
example of Euclidean methodology, not as an exception.

Keywords: Euclid's diagram · Visual components of proposition ·
Concatenation of figures · Generality · Pythagorean theorem

1   Two Main Topics Concerning Euclid's Diagram

There are two components of Euclid's proposition: the text and the lettered
diagram. The Greek text is linearly ordered – sentence follows sentence, from
left to right, and from top to bottom. Diagrams consist of straight lines and
circles. The capital letters on the diagrams are located next to points; they
name the ends of line segments, intersections of lines, or random points.

The fact that crossing lines determine points is sometimes considered to be a
tacit assumption of Euclid's system; see e.g. [7], pp. 29–31. On the contrary, [10],
or [6], argue that it is information which is drawn from the diagrams. We adopt

© Springer Nature Switzerland AG 2020
A.-V. Pietarinen et al. (Eds.): Diagrams 2020, LNAI 12169, pp. 50–65, 2020.
https://doi.org/10.1007/978-3-030-54249-8_5

yet another position and take it to be a hallmark of the ancient Greek tradition. Accordingly, the intersection of lines is represented on a diagram rather than read off from diagrams.[1]

The text of the proposition is a schematic composition made up of six parts: *protasis* (stating the relations among geometrical objects by means of abstract and technical terms), *ekthesis* (identifying objects of *protasis* with lettered objects), *diorisomos* (reformulating *protasis* in terms of lettered objects), *kataskeuē* (a construction part which introduces auxiliary lines exploited in the proof that follows), *apodeixis* (proof, which usually proves the *diorisomos'* claim), *sumperasma* (reiterating *diorisomos*). References to axioms, definitions, and previous propositions are made via the technical terms and phrases in *prostasis*.

It is usually assumed that Euclid's propositions state general results, despite the fact that their *apodeixis* parts refer to specific diagrams. Reviel Netz puts it in a more decisive way: "Greek proofs prove general results", "Greek mathematical proofs are about specific objects in specific diagrams" ([11], p. 241). General results based on specific diagrams seem paradoxical and encourage philosophical speculations, which could be phrased in the form of the following questions: (1) How is it possible to generalize from a single diagram? (2) Are Euclid's proofs about specific diagrams?

(Ad 1) We adopt a perspective to organize Euclid's propositions into hierarchical structures designed to solve specific problems. This allows to realize that although Euclid seeks to prove general results, he has no appropriate means to these ends. To elaborate, in [2] we present proposition II.14 of the *Elements* as the culmination of Euclid's theory of equal figures. The proposition aims "To construct a square equal to a given rectilinear figure".[2] Although the accompanying diagram depicts a quadrilateral, the *ekthesis* reiterates the general claim: "Let A be the given rectilinear figure". Yet, the *apodeixis* shows how to square a quadrilateral rather than a "rectilinear figure". Still, propositions that contribute to II.14, specifically I.45, provide constructions that could be easily generalized by the so-called Pascalian induction, that is, a technique introduced in the early modern era.

There are, of course, propositions that provide general results based on individual diagrams alone; I.32 is a model example. That kind of generalization could be explained by non-degenerative conditions and lemmas, as applied in the area method. The method provides foundations for automated theorem proving in synthetic geometry (see [3,4,9]). Viewed from that perspective, Euclid's propositions can be presented as a process of introducing and eliminating points alone,

---

[1] It can be shown that this *tacit assumption* hypothesis rests on a dogma started in the early modern era which states that lines consist of points.

[2] All English translations of the *Elements* after [5]. Sometimes we slightly modify Fitzpatrick's version by skipping interpolations, most importantly, the words related to *addition* or *sum*. Still, these amendments are easy to verify, as this edition is available on the Internet, and also provides the Greek text of the classic Heiberg edition.

with no reference to lines. However, the area method is not widely known, so any account of Euclid's diagrams based on this method needs an individual study.

(Ad 2) Since all Euclid's propositions have an accompanying diagram, in philosophical interpretations of the *Elements* there is a trend to assume that a kind of diagrammatic reasoning is an essential component of Euclidean *logic*. On the contrary, we identify a tendency in the *Elements* to eliminate visual aspects in order to achieve generality founded on theoretical grounds alone. In this paper, we study diagrams in the *Elements*, Books I through VI, in terms of how visual elements are being replaced in favor of theoretical components. This process is crowned by proposition VI.31. None of its parts build on the accompanying diagram. Moreover, it concerns objects that are not represented on the diagram at all. Yet the result is as general as it can be: the *apodeixis* really proves the claim of the *prostatis*.

2   From *Elements* I.47 to VI.31

Our analysis spans between two versions of the Pythagorean theorem, namely I.47 and VI.31; see Fig. 1. The crux of I.47 consists of the two equalities:

$$sq(BG) = parallelogram\ BL, \quad sq(HC) = parallelogram\ CL \qquad (1)$$

where the term $sq(BG)$ stands for Euclid's phrase "square BG". Here equalities are justified by the theory of equal figures, as explained in [2]. They clearly constitute a theoretical component of the proof. Indeed, the starting point of this theory is the equality in terms of congruence. Yet, the theory is designed to justify the equalities of non-congruent figures. In this sense, it counters visual evidence: we are driven to consider some figures to be equal, although we see them as unequal (i.e., non-congruent).

The conclusion of the proof, namely "the whole square BDEC is equal to the two squares GB, HC", needs a premise

$$BL, LC = BCED. \qquad (2)$$

Formula (2) is a model example of what we call visual evidence. While in (1) the equalities are justified by the theory, in (2), the equality is based on the diagram alone. In fact, such a premise does not occur in I.47; Euclid simply skips this step in his proof. Yet, visual evidences of this kind are explicit in the first propositions of Book II, and will be studied in the next section.

The *diorismos* of VI.31 states: "Let ABC be a right-angled triangle having the angle BAC a right-angle. I say that the figure on BC is equal to the similar, and similarly described, figures on BA and AC".

To compare I.47 and VI.31, let us assume that the figures on the sides of the triangle *ABC* are squares (to this end, we modified the original diagram VI.31). In I.47, the accompanying diagram represents parts of the square *BCED* equal to $sq(BG)$ and $sq(HC)$, respectively, namely rectangles *BL* and *LC*. In VI.31, on the contrary, the squares on *AB* and *BC*, $sq(AB)$, $sq(AC)$, are not represented

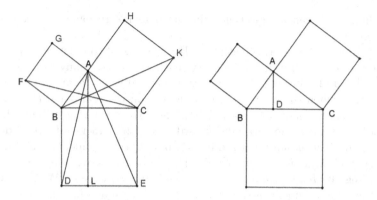

Fig. 1. Euclid's two versions of the Pythagorean theorem: *Elements* I.47 and VI.31.

by any parts of the square on BC, $sq(BC)$. Nonetheless, we can represent the relationship between these squares by the formula

$$sq(AB) + sq(AC) = sq(BC).$$

The sign $+$ finds no diagrammatic counterpart; in fact, there is no reference to the addition in the enunciation of proposition VI.31. Yet, it is understandable on a theoretical level.

Before we dig into the details of VI.31 in Sect. 5, let us analyze purely visual components of Euclid's proofs.

3   Modes of Diagrammatic Reasoning

3.1   Visual Evidence vs Intersecting Lines

The standard attitude toward Euclid's diagrams is focused on a *tacit assumption* hidden behind intersecting circles, especially on the diagram accompanying proposition I.1. Yet, in proposition I.2, the intersection of the straight line and circle is assumed, and in I.10, the intersection of two straight lines is assumed. From the ancient Greek perspective, these three cases are no different. Nevertheless, modern doubts concerning the *tacit assumption* view them differently. It is because Euclid's diagrams are interpreted on a Cartesian plane, and there is also a crucial difference between the circle-circle and straight line-straight line cases (see [7], pp. 144–145).

Moreover, doubts concerning the circle-circle intersection point are motivated by circles on the Cartesian plane of rational numbers $Q \times Q$: the first with the center at $(0,0)$, the second, with the center at $(0,1)$, both having the radius 1. Their (real) intersection point $(\frac{1}{2}, \frac{\sqrt{3}}{2})$ does not exist on the plane $Q \times Q$. Thus, on the one hand it is implied, that we can see circles that seem to be intersecting, and on the other hand, due to the analytic argument, we know that the coordinates of their intersection point are both not rational. The conclusion is: diagrams can deceive.

This argument, however, is deceptive. For the sake of completeness, it should also include a demonstration to the effect that there are as many rational points on the circles under investigation that one can really see them. In fact, it can be shown that when these circles are considered on the real plane $R \times R$, then the sets of their rational points are dense, thus, they are *visible*. Nevertheless, that proof is by no means straightforward (see [12]). All in all, while doubts concerning the *tacit assumption* are based on analytic arguments, we also need another analytic argument to be certain that we really see what we seem to see.

Regarding the *tacit assumption*, Marcus Giaquinto writes: "We should also concede that the argument of the verbal text fails to show that the existence of an intersection point follows logically from Euclid's explicitly stated theoretical apparatus (his postulates, common notions, and definitions" ([6], p. 284). Then he argues that the information regarding the intersecting lines is drawn from the diagram. On the contrary, we take the intersecting lines hypotheses to be the hallmark of the ancient Greek tradition, on par with the *tacit assumption* of modern mathematics stating that in the end, all mathematical objects are point sets. In any textbook or monograph on real analysis, foundations for the course consist of axioms for real numbers. However, due to further developments, suddenly, we realize that curves, surfaces, solids, and other investigated objects are point sets. Although it could be surprising from the local perspective of a given book, it is not that strange from the perspective of the global foundations of modern mathematics. The same, we believe, applies to the ancient assumption concerning intersecting lines. In fact, Euclid's *tacit assumption* is not as *tacit*, since every intersection of lines is represented on diagrams by lettered points, and these letters are then used in the *apodeixis* section of propositions.

Instead of intersecting lines as the main topic of diagrammatic reasoning, we adopt an alternative perspective of studying diagrams, in terms of a balance between the visual and theoretical components involved in a proposition. By theoretical components we mean definitions, *Postulates*, *Common Notions* and references to previous propositions. The residuum is considered the visual part of the proof. Yet, since the *tacit assumption* is beyond the scope of our interest, the question is whether there is anything left on the visual side of a proof. To this end let us take a closer look at Euclid's proposition I.13. It is relevant proposition since it is applied in I.32 – the seal of Euclid's system.

3.2   Implicit Visual Evidence

In I.13, the line of arguments is this; see Fig. 2. Since the following equalities of angles obtain

$$CBE, EBD = CBA, ABE, EBD, \tag{3}$$

$$DBA, CBA = EBD, EBA, ABC, \tag{4}$$

then, by the transitivity of equality, we have

$$CBE, EBD = DBA, CBA. \tag{5}$$

However, there is no demonstration whatsoever but visual evidence that

$$CBA,\ ABE,\ EBD = EBD,\ EBA,\ ABC. \tag{6}$$

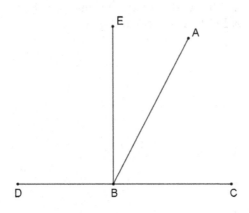

Fig. 2. *Elements* I.13.

The equalitites (3) to (5) have their textual counterparts. As for the first one, it is the following phrase: "CBE, EBD is equal to three CBA, ABE, EBD". The third one is the phrase: "CBE, EBD is also equal to DBA, ABC". Contrarily, no part of I.13 represents the equality (6), therefore, we consider it to be implicit visual evidence. In propositions II.1–4, similar equalities are explicitly included in the proofs. Yet, I.13 also includes a conclusion: "since DBA is equal to the two DBE, EBA" which is based on the diagram alone.

Arguably, Eqs. (3) to (6) represent concatenations rather than sums. We put concatenation on the visual side of proof, while including addition in the theoretical side. A kind of addition occurs in Common Notions 2 (CN2), however, it justifies equality rather than introduces addition. The axiom reads "And if equal things are added (προστεθῇ) to equal things then the wholes are equal". In fact, it is applied in I.13, namely: "since DBA is equal to the two DBE, EBA, let ABC have been added to both. Thus, the DBA, ABC is equal to the three DBE, EBA, ABC." We formalize it as follows

$$DBA = DBE,\ EBA \rightarrow DBA,\ ABC = DBE, EBA, ABC.$$

Herein, the first occurrence of the equality is justified by visual evidence, the second – by CN2.

We identify another kind of addition, namely *synthesis*, as founded on the proportion theory. By analyzing VI.31, we further develop our distinction between concatenation and addition.

3.3 Pure Visual Evidence

Here is the text of proposition II.1, starting with the *diorismos*[3]:

Diorismos "Let A, BC be the two straight-lines, and let BC, be cut, at random, at points D, E. I say that the rectangle contained by A, BC is equal to the rectangles contained by A, BD, by A, DE, and, finally, by A, EC."

Kataskeuē "[...] let BG be made equal A [...]."

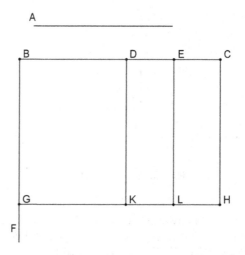

Fig. 3. *Elements* II.1.

"[1] So BH is equal to BK, DK, EH. [2] And BH is by A, BC. For it is contained by GB and BC, and BG is equal to A. [3] And BK (is) by A and BD. For it is contained by GB, BD, and BG is equal to A. [4] And DL is by A and DE. For DK, that is to say BG, is equal to A. [5] Similarly, EH (is) also by A, EC. [6] Thus, by A and BC is equal to by A and BD, by A and DE, and, finally, by A and EC."

Now, we present this proposition in a more schematic form. In what follows, symbol $A \times BC$ stands for the phrase "the rectangle contained by A, BC", while $BH \,\pi\, GB \times BC$ stands for the phrase "BH is contained by GB and BC". We do not use the term $BH = GB \times BC$ on purpose. Since 1975, there has been an ongoing debate on the meaning of Book II, as summarized in [1]. The term $BH = GB \times BC$ would determine the so-called *geometrical algebra* interpretation. However, throughout Book II, the equality between rectangles "contained by" and the figures represented on the diagrams are subject to some strict rules, which rather contest that interpretation (Fig. 3).

Diorismos

$$A \times BC = A \times BD, \; A \times DE, \; A \times EC$$

---

[3] Numbering of sentences and names of parts of the proposition added.

Kataskeuē BG = A
Apodeixis

$$BH = BK, DK, EH$$
$$BH \, \pi \, GB \times BC, \ BG = A \rightarrow BH \, \pi \, A \times BC$$
$$\underline{BK \, \pi \, GB \times BD, \ BG = A \rightarrow BK \, \pi \, A \times BD}$$
$$DK = BG = A \rightarrow DL \, \pi \, A \times DE$$
$$\rightarrow EH \, \pi \, A \times EC$$
$$\rightarrow A \times BC = A \times BD, \ A \times DE, \ A \times EC.$$

The formula in red interprets sentence [1]. It is the starting point of the argument and it represents a pure visual evidence. The rectangles mentioned in the *diorismos* are not represented on the diagram. Euclid's argument is based on the implicit substitution rule revealed in the (underlined) formulas which interpret sentences [3]: it turns the visible figure $GB \times BD$ into the invisible $A \times BD$.

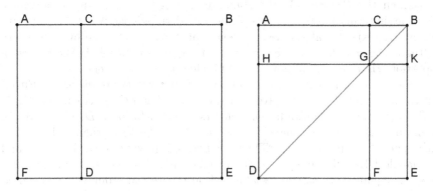

Fig. 4. *Elements* II.13 (left) and II.4 (right).

Below is an analogous scheme for II.3, see Fig. 4; the term BC^2 stands for the phrase "square on BC". Herein, the term $AB \times BC$ represents a non-depicted figure. Again, the formula in red represents pure visual evidence.
Diorismos

$$AB \times BC = AC \times CB, \ BC^2$$

Apodeixis

$$AE = AD, CE$$
$$AE \, \pi \, AB \times BE, \ BE = BC \rightarrow AE \, \pi \, AB \times BC$$
$$DC = CB \rightarrow AD \, \pi \, AC \times CB$$
$$DB = CB^2 \rightarrow AB \times BC = AC \times CB, \ BC^2.$$

Finally, we present a scheme for II.4, see Fig. 4. In this proposition, the visual evidence proceeds the final conclusion.

Diorismos
$$AB^2 = AC^2, CB^2, 2AC \times CB$$

Apodeixis.

$$CGKG = CB^2$$
$$HF = HG^2 = AC^2 \to HF, KC = AC^2, CB^2$$
$$GC = CB \to AG = AC \times CB$$
$$AG = GE \to GE = AC \times CB$$
$$\to AG, GE = 2AC \times CB$$
$$HF = AC^2, CK = CB^2 \to HF, CK, AG, GE =$$
$$= AC^2, BC^2, 2AC \times CB$$
$$HF, CK, AG, CE = ADEB = AB^2 \to AB^2 = AC^2, CB^2, 2AC \times CB.$$

4   Combining Visual and Theoretical Components

Throughout the *Elements*, Euclid compares line segments, triangles, polygons, and angles in terms of *lesser-greater*. From a modern perspective, it is a primitive relation. By textual analysis, we can show that it is characterized by transitivity and the trichotomy law. In the next section, we expose its role in the theory of proportion. Here, we reveal how it is entangled in visual evidence.

Proposition I.6 is a model example of *reductio ad absurdum* proof. Euclid aims to show that $AB = AC$, given the angles at B and C are equal; see Fig. 5. On the one hand, the contradiction consists of a conclusion $\triangle DBC = \triangle ACB$, and on the other hand, a visual evidence that $\triangle DBC$ is lesser than $\triangle ACB$. The crucial part of the proof reads: "Thus, the base DC is equal to the base AB, and the triangle DBC will be equal to the triangle ACB, the lesser to the greater". Thus, the equality of triangles established on theoretical grounds is confronted with visual evidence

$$\triangle DBC = \triangle ACB, \quad \triangle DBC < \triangle ACB. \tag{7}$$

As a characteristics of *lesser-greater* relation, one and only one of the following conditions holds

$$\triangle DBC > \triangle ACB, \triangle DBC = \triangle ACB, \triangle DBC < \triangle ACB. \tag{8}$$

Since there are no rules in the *Elements* which allow to decide whether one triangle is greater than another, we claim that $\triangle DBC < \triangle ACB$ is determined on purely visual grounds. Finally, Euclid's argument, specifically (7) and (8), combines visual and theoretical components.

Kenneth Manders presents an analysis of proposition I.6, stating that it is "read off from the diagram" that $\triangle DBC$ is "a proper part" of the $\triangle ACB$. Here, "read off" means a kind of inference. As far as it is to interpret Euclid, it is a highly speculative argument since there is no inference regarding the inequality of triangles as well as the very term "part" does not occur in the proposition; see ([10], p. 110).

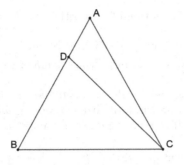

Fig. 5. *Elements*, I.6.

4.1   *Elements*, Book V

The theory of proportions, as developed in Book V, is founded on definitions 5 and 7. Proportion is a relation between two pairs of geometric figures (magnitudes) of the same kind (triangles being of one kind, line segments of another kind, *etc.*). Magnitudes of the same kind form an ordered additive semi-group $\mathfrak{M} = (M, +, <)$ characterized by the five axioms given below.

(E1) $(\forall a, b \in M)(\exists n \in \mathbb{N})(na > b)$.
(E2) $(\forall a, b \in M)(\exists c \in M)(a > b \Rightarrow a = b + c)$.
(E3) $(\forall a, b, c \in M)(a > b \Rightarrow a + c > b + c)$.
(E4) $(\forall a \in M)(\forall n \in \mathbb{N})(\exists b \in M)(nb = a)$.
(E5) $(\forall a, b, c \in M)(\exists d \in M)(a : b :: c : d)$, where $na = \underbrace{a + a + \ldots + a}_{n-times}$.

The term na stands for, in Euclid's words, *multiple of the magnitude* represented by a. We interpret the addition of magnitudes (of the same kind) as a primitive notion. One can show that it is a commutative and associative operation. To be clear, the occurrence of the very word *add* in translations is usually an interpolation. In the Greek text, the addition of magnitudes A and B is represented by the term A, B. It is, thus, a concatenation. Therefore, the above axioms interpret *Elements*.

Axiom E1 interprets definition 4, the so-called Archimedean axiom. It is applied in Book V once: in the proof of proposition V.8. E4 is implicitly applied in proposition V.5. This axiom is not essential, as it can be derived from the four remaining axioms. E5 represents the so-called fourth proportional. In Book V, it is applied in proposition V.5. It is also a building block of the exhaustion method, as developed in Book XII. Axioms E2 and E3 can be identified all throughout Book V.

We interpret Euclid's definition of proportion by the following formula:

$$a : b :: c : d \Leftrightarrow_{df} (\forall m, n \in \mathbb{N})[(na >_1 mb \Rightarrow nc >_2 md)$$
$$\wedge (na = mb \rightarrow nc = md) \wedge (na <_1 mb \Rightarrow nc <_2 md)];$$

the assumption regarding magnitudes a, b, on the one hand, and c, d, on the other, being of the same kind is formalized by $a, b \in \mathfrak{M}_1 = (M_1, +, <_1)$, and $c, d \in \mathfrak{M}_2 = (M_2, +, <_2)$. The term $a : b :: c : d$ stands for 'as a is to b, so is c to d'.

Definition 7, i.e., a relation *greater than* between pairs of magnitudes we interpret as follows:

$$a : b \succ c : d \Leftrightarrow_{df} (\exists m, n \in \mathbb{N})[(na >_1 mb) \wedge (nc \leq_2 md)].$$

Here are four propositions of Book V, which we will refer to in what follows. Although they are stylized on algebra, the only purpose of this modern attire is to reveal similarities between proportions and the arithmetic of fractions. Equality as it occurs in V.9, stands for equal figures.

V.9 $a : c :: b : c \Rightarrow a = b$.
V.12 $a : b :: c : d, \ a : b :: e : f \Rightarrow a : b :: (a + c + f) : (b + d + f)$.
V.16 $a : b :: c : d \Rightarrow a : c :: b : d$.
V.24 $a : c :: d : f, \ b : c :: e : f \Rightarrow (a + b) : c :: (d + e) : f$.

When $a : b :: c : d$ is replaced with $\frac{a}{b} = \frac{c}{d}$, the above propositions will turn into simple rules of the arithmetic of fractions.

4.2 Starting Point of Book VI

In Book VI, Euclid refers explicitly to definition V.5 once: in the proof of proposition VI.1. Its diagram represents rectangles and triangles; see Fig. 6. In regard to triangles, it reads: "Let ABC and ACD be triangles, [...] of the same height AC. I say that as base BC is to base CD, so triangle ABC is to triangle ACD".

Although definition V.5 requires to compare nBC and mCD for every pair n, m, Euclid considers a very specific case, namely segments $3BC$, $3CD$; the accompanying diagram clearly represents this case. Thus, the proof is by no means general. Nonetheless, we are to compare, on the one hand, lines $3BC$, $3CD$, and on the other hand, triangles $\triangle AHC$, $\triangle ACL$. By the *kataskeuē*, $HC = 3BC$, $CL = 3CD$, by the theory of equal figures, $\triangle AHC = 3\triangle ABC$, $\triangle ACL = 3\triangle ACD$. Now, the crucial part of the proof reads: "And if base HC is equal to base CL then triangle AHC is also equal to triangle ACL. And if base HC exceeds base CL then triangle AHC also exceeds triangle ACL. And if less, less."

The only way to verify the inference highlighted in red is to apply the same argument as in proposition I.6. Yet, from this moment on, the train of propositions driving to VI.31 runs smoothly in a way similar to modern theories: by referencing propositions of Book V and some basic rules of geometry. In the next section, we present its two fundamental steps.

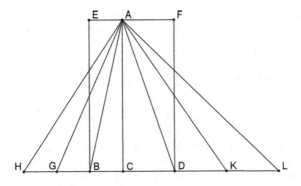

Fig. 6. *Elements*, VI.1.

4.3   Combining Proportions and Geometry

The claim of VI.19 in modern geometry is phrased as follows: Areas of similar triangles are to each other as the square of the similarity scale. Euclid's version is a bit mysterious as it reads: "Similar triangles are to one another in the double ratio of corresponding sides." What is the "double ratio"?

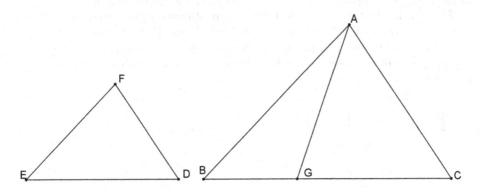

Fig. 7. *Elements*, VI.19.

Let triangles, as presented on Fig. 7, be similar, $\triangle ACB \sim \triangle FDE$. In VI.19, Euclid aims to show that

$$\triangle ACB : \triangle FDE :: BC : BG. \tag{9}$$

Point G represented on the diagram is introduced only in the *apodeixes*; it is constructed in such a way that the proportion $BC : EF :: EF : BG$ obtains. The rest of the proof is as follows. Due to some tricks and references to VI.15, Euclid shows the equality of triangles $\triangle FDE = \triangle AGB$. Then, by VI.1 he easily states the proportion (9).

By similarity of triangles, proportions $AB : DE :: BC : EF$ and $BC : EF :: EF : BG$ obtains. Supposing that $AB : DE = BC : EF = \frac{a}{b}$, we get the following "proportions":

$$BC : BG = (BC : EF)(EF : BG) = \frac{a}{b}\frac{a}{b}.$$

Thus, $\triangle ACB : \triangle FDE = \frac{a}{b}\frac{a}{b}$ represents the square of the similarity scale. However, Euclid's theory does not allow for objects such as $(BC : EF)(EF : BG)$. Yet, there is more. Even within Euclid's system, VI.19 could be stated simply in the form (9). However, the schematic composition of propositions does not allow for any symbols in the *protasis*, which is why he had to coin a specific name, namely "double ratio".

5   Towards Synthesis

5.1   Ratio of Similar Polygons

In VI.20, Euclid seeks to generalize VI.19 to polygons through the triangulation technique. The proposition reads: "Similar polygons can be divided into equal numbers of similar triangles corresponding to the wholes, and one polygon has to the polygon a duplicate ratio with respect to a corresponding side."

Like in II.14, the *apodeixis* treats of pentagons rather than polygons. Nonetheless, the *ekthesis* still states "Let ABCDE and FGHKL be similar polygons." The technique of triangulation suggested by the accompanying diagram – see Fig. 8 – allows to generalize the pentagon case to any polygon by Pascalian induction.

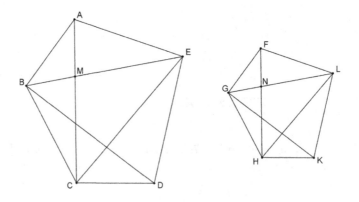

Fig. 8. *Elements*, VI.20.

As for the second part, the similarity scale can be represented by each of the following fractions $AB : GF$, or $BE : GL$, or $CE : HL$. Simplifying the results of proposition VI.19, we represent the square of similarity scale by products $(BE : GL)(BE : GL)$, or $(CE : HL)(CE : HL)$. As a result, by VI.19, we have,

$$\triangle AEB : \triangle FLG :: (BE : GL)(BE : GL),$$
$$\triangle BEC : \triangle GLH :: (BE : GL)(BE : GL),$$
$$\triangle EDC : \triangle LKH :: (CE : HL)(CE : HL).$$

Since $CE : HL = BE : GL$, by V.12, it follows that

$$(\triangle AEB, \triangle BEC, \triangle EDC) : (\triangle FLG, \triangle GLH, \triangle LKH) :: (BE : GL)^2.$$

Finally, since $AB : GF = BE : GL$, we have

$$pentagon(AEDCB) : pentagon(FLKHG) = (AB : GF)(AB : GF).$$

Here, $(AB : GF)(AB : GF)$ represents "double ratio" of similarity scale of the pentagons $AEDCB$ and $FLKHG$.

5.2 Geometry of Ideas

Here are the decisive parts of proposition VI.31.

Protasis "In right-angled triangles, the figure (εἶδος) on the side subtending the right-angle is equal to the similar, and similarly described, figures (εἴδεσι) on the sides surrounding the right-angle."

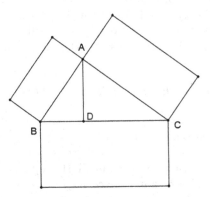

Fig. 9. *Elements*, VI.31.

Diorismos "Let ABC be a right-angled triangle having the angle BAC a right-angle. I say that the figure on BC is equal to the similar, and similarly described, figures on BA and AC."

Kataskeuē "Let the perpendicular AD have been drawn."

Note, there is no crucial difference between the *protasis* and *diorismos* parts: the latter simply adopts notation, yet still treats figures in general. The *kataskeuē* introduces the letter D, which enables to represent the square of similarity scale of the discussed figures. Speaking of figures, Euclid applies the word idea (εἶδος) more generally than polygon, albeit due to the propositions he relies on, the result has to be restrained to polygons alone (Fig. 9).

Let F_{BC}, F_{AB}, F_{AC} stand for figures on BC, AB, AC, respectively. Now, the proof (slightly modified) runs as follows:

$$F_{AB} : F_{BC} :: BD : BC$$
$$F_{AC} : F_{BC} :: DC : BC \xrightarrow[V.24]{} (F_{AB}, F_{AC}) : F_{BC} :: (BD, DC) : BC$$
$$BC = BD, DC \rightarrow (F_{AB}, F_{AC}) : F_{BC} :: BC : BC$$
$$\xrightarrow[V.16,9]{} F_{AB}, F_{AC} = F_{BC}.$$

One may consider the equality $BC = BD, DC$ to be based on visual evidence. Yet, the crucial result, namely the equality $F_{AB}, F_{AC} = F_{BC}$ is based on purely theoretical grounds, namely propositions V.9 and V.16. Moreover, the proof of I.47 is based on a partition of the square $BCED$ into rectangles BLD and CEL; the equality $BCED = BLD, CEL$ is easily represented on the diagram. In VI.31, figures F_{AB}, F_{AC} cannot be represented by any parts of the figure F_{BC}. Nevertheless, we can represent the relationship between these figures by the formula

$$F_{AB} + F_{AC} = F_{BC}. \tag{10}$$

The sign $+$ finds no diagrammatic counterpart; in fact, there is no reference to addition in the enunciation of proposition VI.31. It is, however, understood within the proportion theory, specifically through proposition V.24. It reads: "the first and the fifth, added together (συντεθέν), AG, will also have the same ratio to the second C that the third and the sixth, DH, has to the fourth F." That is, in symbols:

$$AB : C :: DE : F, \ BG : C :: EH : F \rightarrow AG : C :: DH : F.$$

Throughout the whole Book V, magnitudes are represented by line segments. Then, for example, when point B lies on the segment AG between A and G, it is visually obvious that $AB, BG = AG$. Nevertheless, the proof of V.24 aims to apply to any kind of magnitudes. Indeed, in VI.31 it applies to any kind of figure, that is, to εἶδος. Although we cannot place F_{AB} next to F_{AC}, such as segment AB being placed next to BG, or rectangle BL being placed next to rectangle BL (see Fig. 1), through purely theoretical cognition we can grasp that the equality obtains $F_{AB} + F_{AC} = F_{BC}$.

6   Final Remarks

The so-called *tacit assumption* of the Euclid system, hidden behind intersecting lines, is by no means the most fundamental premise of diagrammatic reasoning. From the ancient Greek perspective, it is not *tacit*, since every intersection of lines is represented on the diagrams by lettered points. From a modern perspective, it is no longer hidden, as it has explicit mathematical counterparts. In synthetic geometry, it is the Pasch axiom. In analytic geometry, it is the requirement that when Euclid's straightedge and compass constructions are to be done on a Cartesian plane $F \times F$, F has to be an ordered field closed under the square root operation (see [8], ch. VII).

The phenomena we identified as visual evidence in Euclid's proofs find no obvious counterparts in modern mathematics. First, modern mathematics interprets concatenation as addition. Yet, in Euclid's system, there is a long way from concatenation to addition. Second, visual evidence, as related to the *lesser-greater* relation, finds no obvious counterpart, since in modern synthetic geometry, the relation is defined rather than introduced as a primitive notion, moreover, it is not applied to figures, but to line segments only. Looking for modern counterparts of Euclid's visual evidence, we should consider axioms for algebra, for example $a + b = b + a$, or the axiom for an ordered field called the compatibility of order with addition, i.e., if $a < b$, then $a + c < b + c$. Whatever they may be, what they interpret in mathematics could be considered pre-mathematics from our modern perspective, that is, arguments based on visual evidence.

References

1. Blåsjö, V.: In defence of geometrical algebra. Arch. Hist. Exact Sci. **70**(3), 325–359 (2015). https://doi.org/10.1007/s00407-015-0169-5
2. Błaszczyk, P.: From Euclid's Elements to the methodology of mathematics. Two ways of viewing mathematical theory. Ann. Univ. Paedagogicae Cracoviensis **10**, 5–15 (2018). https://didacticammath.up.krakow.pl/article/view/6613
3. Błaszczyk, P., Petiurenko, A.: Euclid's theory of proportion revised. Ann. Univ. Paedagogicae Cracoviensis **11**, 37–61 (2019). https://didacticammath.up.krakow.pl/index.php/aupcsdmp/article/view/6901
4. Chou, S., Gao, X., Zhang, J.: Machine Proofs in Geometry. World Scientific, Singapore (1994)
5. Fitzpatrick, R., Heiberg, J.: Eculid's Elements. University of Texas at Austin, Institute for Fusion Studies Department of Physics (2007). https://books.google.pl/books?id=7HDWIOoBZUAC
6. Giaquinto, M.: Crossing curves: a limit to the use of diagrams in proofs. Philos. Math. **19**(3), 281–307 (2011). https://doi.org/10.1093/philmat/nkr023
7. Hartshorne, R.: Geometry: Euclid and and Beyond. Springer, New York (2000). https://doi.org/10.1007/978-0-387-22676-7
8. Hilbert, D.: Grundlagen Der Geometrie. Teubner, Leipzig (1903)
9. Janičic, P., Narboux, J., Quaresma, P.: The area method. J. Autom. Reason. **48**(4), 489–532 (2012)
10. Manders, K.: The Euclidean diagram. In: Mancosu, P. (ed.) The Philosophy of Mathematical Practice, pp. 80–133. Oxford University Press, Oxford (2008)
11. Netz, R.: The Shaping of Deduction in Greek Mathematics. Cambridge University Press, Cambridge (1999)
12. Tan, L.: The group of rational points on the unit circle. Math. Mag. **69**(3), 163–171 (1996). http://www.jstor.org/stable/2691462

A Mentalist Look at Gaussian Clock Arithmetic

Dany Jaspers[(✉)]

KU Leuven, Warmoesberg 26, 1000 Brussels, Belgium
dany.jaspers@kuleuven.be

1 Introduction

The present paper takes as its starting point the most common metaphors used in natural language and the thought system behind it to approach the number sequence in a spatial and temporal context. The latter context being less dependent on completely external causal triggering, its cyclical perspective on number will be adopted as the cognitively more realistic option and presented in the well-known format of a Gaussian system of arithmetic commonly called *clock arithmetic*. The duodecimality that is typical of analog clocks will be argued to provide an optimal cognitive base, while a hexadic clock is argued to be the cognitive minimum. On the basis of naturalness considerations formulated in terms of degrees of symmetry, the geometrical patterns on multiplication clocks turn out to show relief and different degrees of symmetry and homogeneity depending on the choice of base. It is the homogeneity restriction, to be worked out below, which is the novelty on the mathematical side. On the basis of such considerations, base 10, the decimal system, can be shown to be a less symmetrical arrangement than base 12, notwithstanding its success thanks to the morphology of the human hands.

2 Clock Arithmetic

In our human conception of number, the spatial and temporal types of experience underlying conceptualizations seem to be different. In the context of spatial objects, our sense of number is primarily rectilinear. Very often, the axis is vertical, as in *adding up, subtracting, over/under 50* [2,10], and the corresponding metaphor *more is up, less is down* [6,8]. In other instances, the axis is viewed as horizontal, witness the number line [4] or the left-right ordering of the number sequence on a ruler.

In the less tangible yet arguably more revealing context of the passage of time, however, number is not conceived of as rectilinear, but as curved, cyclical and recurrent. Thanks to recursion, the geometry of the infinite number sequence can be visually represented in the form of a circle. This property is reflected in notation systems with a fixed base which recycle a finite set of symbols as numbers go up. Such features are aptly captured in a system of arithmetic for the

© Springer Nature Switzerland AG 2020
A.-V. Pietarinen et al. (Eds.): Diagrams 2020, LNAI 12169, pp. 66–73, 2020.
https://doi.org/10.1007/978-3-030-54249-8_6

integers first developed by Carl Friedrich Gauss [5] and often referred to as *clock arithmetic*. Using its circular design, arithmetical operations such as the times tables can be represented as insightful and didactically most useful diagrams on an analog clock. Illustrative examples for the times tables of multiplicands 0 (or 12) up to 7 are provided in Table 1 and Table 2. ≡ is the modulo symbol and it precedes the clock number which the product maps into. Looking at the times table for 7, for instance, $2 \times 7 = 14$. The latter number is not itself on the clock diagram, but we know it is 2 units beyond 12, hence at point 2 on the clock. Therefore the corresponding diagram arrow starts at 2 and ends in 2. (Ignore the use of the blue arrows for the time being, it will become relevant later.) In the modulo system as developed, all multiplications of higher numbers comply with the patterns of arrows on the clocks. Other bases than 12 can also be used and continuously extending the base results in beautiful animations [9].

The mapping of the times tables on the clock is visually insightful and didactically useful. It shows clearly how much surprising symmetry there is in the number system and how what is true for low numbers is automatically true for all higher ones. The representations for the times tables of odd numbers on the 12-clock display not just left-right bilateral symmetry, but also top-bottom symmetry through the 3–9 axis, a property which neatly sets them off from the even number tables on the 12-clock, which have no top-bottom symmetry, only bilateral symmetry. Having top-bottom symmetry on top of left-right bilateral symmetry implies that if one has the initial quarter of the clock arrows for the odd numbers and mirrors them down to the right bottom quarter and then mirrors the right part to the left, the whole clock is as it should be. One quarter (0, 1, 2, 3) suffices, the rest is more of the same.

3   Duodecimality

Do the usual duodecimality of an analog clock and the varying reflection symmetries generated by times tables on it require an explanation beyond a cultural-historical one? In particular, is there merit in the hypothesis that it is cognitively motivated and hence not accidental? An indication that the latter avenue might be worth exploring is that this cognitive preference for duodecimality is also found in the structure of the chromatic scale in music. Even though one could argue that in that realm too, the preference is based on a cultural-historical choice, there is little doubt that it also rests on perceptual (auditory) cognitive foundations involving consonance and dissonance. We therefore tentatively suggest the idea of a homology between the most *natural* intuitive base 12 in mathematics and the duodecimality of the chromatic scale. This parallel, if real, would amount to a recycling of part of the perception-based architecture of the chromatic scale in the conceptual realm of mathematics. Such a relationship between perceptual structures and conceptual ones is not implausible. Jaspers (2012) [7] illustrates a comparable relationship between features of colour perception on the one hand and logical concepts and colour terms on the other. Certain constraints on colour perception reappear in the realm of logical notions and colour terms in the form of a bifurcation between ordinary natural language concepts (such as *and*, *or*, and *nor* in the propositional calculus, *red*, *green*, *blue* for colour words) and less natural, but scientifically most useful ones (such as *nand* and *iff* in logic, *cyan* and *magenta* among colour terms).

In the realm of numbers, duodecimality represents an optimal cognitive balance between keeping the number of the base within bounds in order not to overload declarative memory and extending it enough not to increase recursive configurationality (number of digits of the number) too fast and explosively. Yet, similar to what holds for logical concepts, freedom from stimulus control in the conceptual realm has the consequence that naturalness and optimal cognitive balance can be consciously violated and therefore any other choice of base ("modulo n") can be made, even if with a measurable decrease in naturalness in many cases (formalizable in terms of a reduction of diagrammatic symmetries). The freedom to explore any base has been the source of many new and interesting questions ("What happens if I choose a prime as modulus?", etc.) and has opened new avenues for mathematics far beyond what ordinary concept formation and the bounds of everyday language could provide, a standard situation when humans decide to take their everyday intuitive thinking and talking to careful analytic pieces in order to create novel, consciously constructed concepts better suited for scientific purposes.

Table 1. Times Table Clocks with multiplier-product arrows (multiplicand in black)

0/12	1	2	3
0x 12 = 0	0x 1 = 0	0x 2 = 0	0x 3 = 0
1 x 12 = 12 ≡ 0	1x 1 = 1	1x 2 = 2	1x 3 = 3
2 x 12 = 24 ≡ 0	2x 1 = 2	2x 2 = 4	2x 3 = 6
3 x 12 = 36 ≡0	3x 1 = 3	3x 2 = 6	3x 3 = 9
4 x 12 = 48 ≡ 0	4x 1 = 4	4x 2 = 8	4x 3 = 12 ≡ 0
5 x 12 = 60 ≡ 0	5x 1 = 5	5x 2 = 10	5x 3 = 15 ≡ 3
6 x 12 = 72 ≡ 0	6x 1 = 6	6x 2 = 12 ≡ 0	6x 3 = 18 ≡ 6
7 x 12 = 84 ≡ 0	7x 1 = 7	7x 2 = 14 ≡ 2	7x 3 = 21 ≡ 9
8 x 12 = 96 ≡ 0	8x 1 = 8	8x 2 = 16 ≡ 4	8x 3 = 24 ≡ 0
9 x 12 = 108 ≡ 0	9x 1 = 9	9x 2 = 18 ≡ 6	9x 3 = 27 ≡ 3
10 x 12 = 120 ≡ 0	10x 1 = 10	10x 2 = 20 ≡ 8	10x 3 = 30 ≡ 6
11 x 12 = 132 ≡ 0	11x 1 = 11	11x 2 = 22 ≡ 10	11x 3 = 33 ≡ 9
12 x 12 = 144 ≡ 0	12x 1 = 12 ≡ 0	12x 2 = 24 ≡ 0	12x 3 = 36 ≡ 0

Table 2. Times Table Clocks with multiplier-product arrows (multiplicand in black)

4	5	6	7
0x 4 = 0	0x 5 = 0	0x 6 = 0	0x 7 = 0
1 x 4 = 4	1x 5 = 5	1x 6 = 6	1x 7 = 7
2 x 4 = 8	2x 5 = 10	2x 6 = 12 ≡ 0	2x 7 = 14 ≡ 2
3 x 4 = 12 ≡0	3x 5 = 15 ≡ 3	3x 6 = 18 ≡ 6	3x 7 = 21 ≡ 9
4 x 4 = 16 ≡ 4	4x 5 = 20 ≡ 8	4x 6 = 24 ≡ 0	4x 7 = 28 ≡ 4
5 x 4 = 20 ≡ 8	5x 5 = 25 ≡ 1	5x 6 = 30 ≡ 6	5x 7 = 35 ≡ 11
6 x 4 = 24 ≡ 0	6x 5 = 30 ≡ 6	6x 6 = 36 ≡ 0	6x 7 = 42 ≡ 6
7 x 4 = 28 ≡ 4	7x 5 = 35 ≡ 11	7x 6 = 42 ≡ 6	7x 7 = 49 ≡ 1
8 x 4 = 32 ≡ 8	8x 5 = 40 ≡ 4	8x 6 = 48 ≡ 0	8x 7 = 56 ≡ 8
9 x 4 = 36 ≡ 0	9x 5 = 45 ≡ 9	9x 6 = 54 ≡ 6	9x 7 = 63 ≡ 3
10 x 4 = 40 ≡ 4	10x 5 = 50 ≡ 2	10x 6 = 60 ≡ 0	10x 7 = 70 ≡ 10
11 x 4 = 44 ≡ 8	11x 5 = 55 ≡ 7	11x 6 = 66 ≡ 6	11x 7 = 77 ≡ 5
12 x 4 = 48 ≡ 0	12x 5 = 60 ≡ 0	12x 6 = 72 ≡ 0	12x 7 = 84 ≡ 0

4   A Hexadic Group

Note that the times tables for clock opposites (1 and 7, 2 and 8, 3 and 9, 4 and 10, 5 and 11) are systematically related in that the multiplier-product arrows for even multipliers remain the same, whereas the arrows for odd multipliers go to the opposite position on the clock: compare the reciprocal blue arrows for odd multipliers on the 7-clock in Table 2 to the reflexive red arrows for the corresponding odd multipliers on the 1-clock in Table 1. This relationship suggests that while base 12 may be optimal, it is not minimal: a further reduction of the multiplier-product clocks to base 6 is possible, resulting in a unification of the clocks for 1 and 7, for 2 and 8, and so on (Table 3).

This smaller hexadic base is more economical. It requires only 6 diagrams, primes are now all 0-adjacent, neatly in the two only co-prime positions relative to 6, the number of integer values of the foundational cycle. The foundational numbers are reduced to 1, 2, 3 and (initially implicit) 0, with their additive inverses −0 (≡0), −1 (≡5), −2 (≡4), −3 (≡3) to complete the arguably innate pattern. This reduction to 1, 2, 3 (and 0) tallies well with the experimental results on the nature of the number sense and the claims about the foundational role of these few low numbers made by Stanislas Dehaene (1997) [3].

The hexadic geometrical representations clearly bring out a property which 12-clock opposites like 1 and 7, or 2 and 8, etc. share. Nevertheless, they do so at the cost of hiding a difference between them, namely that the paths

Table 3. Base-6 Times Tables with multiplier-product arrows

0, 6 and 12	1 and 7	2 and 8
3 and 9	4 and 10	5 and 11

traversed to obtain the identical arrows have different lengths. The latter difference (and many others) stands out in the base-12-tables above, where clock opposites clearly show the trajectory-difference between them in the form of different arrows for multiplier 1 (and for the other odd multipliers). Larger bases than 12 keep increasing the number of separated out categories, postponing the point of cyclic recursion. The resulting patterns thereby become ever more elaborate, including different kinds of epicycloids (cardioids, nephroids, etc.) (see [9]). But most interestingly, the schematic layout of the base 12 multiplication clocks remains recognizable in corresponding tables with much higher bases, such as 120 (Bausili 2017) [1], for instance.

5   Why Is a Clock of Six the Cognitive Minimum?

Given that it is known that one is free to choose any base one likes, it seems logical to object to the claim that a clock of six based on 0, 1, 2 and 3 would be the cognitive minimum by pointing out that if you just work with base-2, i.e. 0 and 1, that also works fine - it gives you Jouvet & Leibnitz's binary code - and it is even more minimal than a clock of six.

The answer to that objection is that everybody agrees that primes are the atomic building blocks of the multiplicative number system - given that the identity card of all numbers is their prime factorisation -, so that alongside 0 and 1 one needs at least, and in the minimal set-up at most, the two foundational primes 2 and 3 as separate multiplicative atoms of the basic cognitive set-up. That is why a base lower than the 6-clock is not eligible, because the 6-clock is the minimal bilaterally symmetrical group set-up that has the two foundational primes 2 and 3 as homogenous independent atoms, at the same time as the only primes that are not 6n-adjacent (=adjacent to 0 on the 6-clock), i.e. not in co-prime position relative to 6. By *homogenous* I mean *not being related to a number which has different factors in terms of divisibility by 1, 2 and 3*. Since 2 has factors 1 and 2 and 3 has factors 1 and 3, a set-up in which they are related violates homogeneity. In base 5, for instance, the additive inverse relation relates 2 and 3 so that they are not independent. Since they are not homogenous, the base 5 set-up violates homogeneity. And in base 4, there is an additive inverse relation between 1 and 3, although they too are no homogenous pair.

The homogeneity requirement entails that odd bases are all out as natural bases because they invariably unite both odd and even numbers in every single clock position, so that the number set that any number on the clock represents is internally non-homogeneous.

In terms of homogeneity, the 12-clock is more optimal than the 6-clock, since it does not only have homogenous number sets in each clock position and systematically homogenous additive inverse relations, but the elements of the number sets of all clock opponents also have the same factors in terms of divisibility by 1, 2 and 3. In a hexadic set-up, opponent pairs violate this requirement: the clock opponents 6 and 3, for instance, differ in that 6 is divisible by 1, 2 and 3, while 3 is not divisible by 2, but only by 1 and 3. So while the hexadic set-up does not violate additive inverse homogeneity, it does violate clock opponent homogeneity. Base 12 has all of internal homogeneity, additive inverse homogeneity and clock opponent homogeneity. Indeed, 1, its clock opponent 7, the numbers in its additive inverse position -1 ($\equiv 11$ on the clock) and the numbers in the additive inverse position of 7 ($\equiv 5$) are all divisible by 1, but not by 2 or 3; 2, 8, 10 and 4 are all divisible by 1 and 2, not by 3; 3 and 9 are divisible by 1 and 3, not by 2; and 6 and 12, finally, are both divisible by 1, 2 and 3. It is not hard to explain why the least divisible clock numbers in terms of divisibility by 1, 2 and 3, namely 1, 5, 7 and 11, are adjacent to the most divisible numbers 6 and 12 ($\equiv 0$). The latter (including the number zero itself) are divisible by all three of 1, 2 and 3. It follows from this that to reach a number divisible by two from positions 6 and 0 on the clock, you have to move 2 positions away in either direction; and to reach a number divisible by three from 6 or 0, you have to move 3 positions away in either direction. The logical consequence is that the numbers adjacent to 0 and 6 are only divisible by 1, not by 2 or 3.

It is a well-known fact that a change in the choice of base (say 10, or anything else different from 6n) yields different co-primes, i.e. elements that do not share another factor than 1 with the base number, in casu with 10. On a 10-clock, the co-primes are 1, 9, 3 and 7. It is easy to see that this arrangement violates the three constraints of internal, additive inverse and clock opponent homogeneity. Internal homogeneity is violated for instance in that 6 is divisible by 1, 2 and

3, while another number in the same clock position, 16, is divisible by 1 and 2, not 3 (plenty of other examples can be given). Additive inverse homogeneity is violated in that, among many other examples, 1 (or 11, 21, ...) is divisible by 1 but not by 2 or 3, while the number 9 located in the additive inverse clock position of 1, is divisible by both 1 and 3. And clock opponent homogeneity is violated in that, for instance, 5 is divisible by 1 but not by 2 or 3, while its clock opponent 10 is divisible by both 1 and 2, and not by 3.

Now, why one would conclude that a base that observes the three homogeneity requirements is the most optimal one? Why is it more likely that base 12 is the one that the other bases are either discovered from (namely the rest of base 6n) or constructed from (namely all other bases) by relaxation of constraints than the other way around? The answer that suggests itself is that the existence of a base with a larger set of constraints (and symmetries) is statistically more unlikely and surprising. The more unlikely it is, the harder we feel it becomes to explain it away as completely accidental. Its unlikely existence makes us conclude: what are the odds that this can occur without a strict causal mechanism? The latter is at least statable in terms of the three mathematical homogeneity constraints (if my description of them is accurate) and it is possibly even attributable to recycling of a deeper perceptual substrate coming from a realm where constraints are more rigid and less violable than in the realm of concepts.

Note further that the claim that 10 is a less than optimal choice of base can also be made plausible from another angle. However successful decimality has been thanks to our 10 fingers, which serve as our bodily in-built abacus, it is unlikely that evolution could have foreseen the current secondary function of our fingers as tallying instruments and fashioned our hands with that distant perspective in mind. One may speculate that if by evolutionary accident we had been polydactils with six fingers on each hand (as some people *are*, of course), our hands would have been better in sync with our mental number faculty. Yet, having 10 fingers for tallying can inversely also be viewed as an example of what the Dutch soccer player Johan Cruyff famously called: "Elk nadeel hep se voordeel" ("every disadvantage has its advantage"): indeed, finger decimality may well have been a mathematically beneficial accident, demonstrating by mind-external means that choice of base is not restricted to the minimal or most optimal varieties lodged in the mind.

As regards primes, finally, our claim is that actual primes beyond the foundational ones 2 and 3 are really prime because they are all co-primes of 6n. All that needs to be done to size the set of co-primes of 6n down to that of the actual primes, is to knock out multiples of co-primes. Such an anchoring and solid reason for why all primes other than 2 and 3 are adjacent to 6n is much wanted anyway. In other words, the proposal amounts to postulating that prime numbers (beyond 2 and 3) are prime because they are all co-primes of the cognitively minimal base number (6), and hence also of 12 ($\equiv 6$), the base number of the most optimally symmetrical and homogenous cognitive group setup for number, and of other multiples of 6. All other choices of base are then to be treated as less natural, *constructed* conceptual modifications of that basic natural set-up via constraint relaxation. Indeed, if number has the structure of a group, it follows that there *has* to be a base. And if a base is an inherent element of the basic cognitive set-up of number, it makes sense to say that one such base is likely to be the original one (6) and one the most optimal one in terms of memory considerations, symmetry and homogeneity (12). All base-choices that can be made, are a function of the basic one that comes with the definition of what a group is. And they show a relief pattern in terms of homogeneity and symmetry that throws up base 12 as the most optimal choice.

6   Conclusion

On the whole, the main argument of this squib is that Gauss's clock arithmetic was not only revolutionary in unlocking the potential of modular arithmetic in general. It also forces one to confront the cognitively interesting question why among the infinitely many modulus-choices in principle accessible to the human conceptual capacity, there is at least a prototypicality preference for duodecimality. Is that a purely cultural predilection or is it attributable to deeper aspects of mathematics and/or the human mind? By comparing decimal and duodecimal multiplication diagrams in terms of symmetry/opposition and by comparing clocks for multiplication and the perceptual chromatic scale clock, a plausible case can be made that the latter view has most to go for it.

References

1. Bausili, B.: Visualizing Math in Tableau: Multiplication Circles (2017). https://interworks.com/blog/bbausili/2017/05/01/visualizing-math-tableau-multiplication-circles/
2. Corver, N., Zwarts, J.: Prepositional numerals. Lingua **116**(6), 811–836 (2006)
3. Dehaene, S.: The Number Sense: How the Mind Creates Mathematics. Oxford University Press, New York (1997)
4. Dehaene, S.S.B., Giraux, P.: The mental representation of parity and number magnitude. J. Exp. Psychol. **122**(3), 371–396 (1993). https://doi.org/10.1037//0096-3445.122.3.371
5. Gauss, C.: Disquisitiones Arithmeticae. Yale University Press, New Haven (1965–1801)
6. Grade, S., Lefèvre, N., Pesenti, M.: Influence of left-right vs. up-down gaze observation on random number generation. Exp. Psychol. **60**(2), 122–130 (2013)
7. Jaspers, D.: Logic and colour. Logica Universalis **6**, 227–248 (2012). https://doi.org/10.1007/s11787-012-0044-y
8. Lakoff, G., Johnson, M.: Metaphors We Live By. University of Chicago Press, Chicago (1980)
9. Mathologer: Times tables, mandelbrot and the heart of mathematics (2015). https://www.youtube.com/watch?v=qhbuKbxJsk8
10. Nouwen, R.: A remark on conceptual metaphor and scalarity. MS (2018)

A Diagram of Choice: The Curious Case of Wallis's Attempted Proof of the Parallel Postulate and the Axiom of Choice

Valérie Lynn Therrien[(✉)]

Philosophy Department, McGill University, Montréal, Canada
valerie.l.therrien@mail.mcgill.ca
http://www.valerielynntherrien.com

Abstract. Wallis's attempted proof of Euclid's Parallel Postulate is an important but oft neglected event leading to the discovery of non-Euclidean geometries. Our aim here is to show Wallis's own reliance on three non-constructive diagrammatic inferences that are not (fully) explicit in his own supplement to Euclid's axioms. Namely, there is *i-* an implicit assumption concerning the possibility of motion; *ii-* an implicit assumption about the continuous nature of space and time; and *iii-* an explicit assumption about the existence of similar triangles which conceals an appeal to a combinatoric principle of reasoning that is tantamount to appealing to the Axiom of Choice.

Keywords: Euclidean geometry · Parallel Postulate · Diagrammatic proof · Axiom of Choice · Axiomatic systems · John Wallis

1 Introduction

Wallis's attempted proof of Euclid's Parallel Postulate is an important but oft neglected event leading to the discovery of non-Euclidean geometries. Falling short of an actual proof of the Parallel Postulate, Wallis nevertheless proved the equivalence of the Parallel Postulate with the existence of similar figures (Wallis's Postulate). Wallis's attempted proof was notably criticized for being non-constructive, and 'more metaphysical than mathematical'. Our aim here is to show Wallis's own reliance on three non-constructive diagrammatic inferences that are not (fully) explicit in his own supplement to Euclid's axioms. Namely, there is *i-* an implicit assumption concerning motion in the construction space; *ii-* an implicit assumption about the continuous nature of space and time; and *iii-* an explicit assumption about the existence of similar triangles which conceals an

This paper was inspired by the unpublished lecture notes of Michael Hallett as well as his interest in the proposed thesis of this paper. As such, we extend special thanks to Prof. Hallett and duly note that Sect. 3 and 4 rely heavily on shared insights.

© Springer Nature Switzerland AG 2020
A.-V. Pietarinen et al. (Eds.): Diagrams 2020, LNAI 12169, pp. 74–90, 2020.
https://doi.org/10.1007/978-3-030-54249-8_7

appeal to a combinatorial principle of reasoning strikingly similar to the Axiom of Choice – both in reasoning and in the contemporary critique they engendered. Though oft neglected, Wallis's attempted proof is an important step leading to the discovery of non-Euclidean geometries, by providing a springboard for conceiving of the Parallel Postulate not as a statement about a property of straight lines, but about a property of the space in which they are embedded in.

2   Situating Wallis's Attempted Proof of the Parallel Postulate

Before proceeding to the amphitheatre of Wallis's attempted proof of the Parallel Postulate, it is incumbent upon on us to first set the stage. As such, we will briefly survey 1- the evolution of Euclidean axiomatics that Wallis's proof (as well as the axiom he introduced for this very purpose) inscribes itself within; then 2- the prevalent use of kinetic reasoning by his contemporaries; as well as 3- the changing standards of proof in the Early Modern period which influenced his approach; and, finally, 4- Wallis's particular approach to proving the Fifth Postulate.

2.1   On the Development of Euclidean Axiomatics

For centuries, Euclid's *Elements* was the model of scientific and deductive reasoning. Indeed, the influence of the *Elements* on European thought is second only to the Bible. Since Antiquity, the *Elements* have been translated, edited and commented on hundreds of times. However, Euclid's system was also challenged. Missing arguments were uncovered and additional axioms were added to fill in those gaps. Moreover, as axioms were not then taken to be unprovable assertions, many mathematicians undertook the task of proving Euclid's axioms from more basic statements. As such, some axioms were removed entirely, whilst others were reworded. In other instances, new axioms were added to extend geometrical results beyond the ones achieved in Antiquity [2]. From the Middle Ages (mostly by Arab scholars) to the *translatio studiorum*, then onwards to the Early Modern period (particularly by French and Italian scholars), through to the XIXth c., hundreds of editions provided their own principles upon which to ground Euclidean geometry. Well over 350 different new axioms were created to this effect. The XVIIth c. was particularly rich in such developments [2]. John Wallis's 1663 attempted proof inscribes itself well within this history.[1] His proof was an attempt to prove the Parallel Postulate from the four preceding axioms

---

[1] John Wallis (1616–1703) was appointed to the Savilian Chair of geometry at the University of Oxford by Oliver Cromwell in 1649. It was Henry Savile, his predecessor, who had famously remarked that "On the most beautiful body of Geometry there are two moles, two blemishes, and, so far as I know, no more", the chief blemish being the Parallel Postulate [3]. The incumbent of this chair was obligated to give a lecture every year on classical geometry. Wallis is most known for a decades long feud with Hobbes, as well as for making headlines in 1685 for calculating the square root of a 53 digit number entirely in his head during a bout of insomnia, and remembering the 27 digit result entirely from memory the next morning [11].

in the *Elements*, and his own novel axiom: **Proposition VIII** which postulates the existence of similar figures of arbitrary size [8].

2.2   On Kinetic Reasoning in the Early Modern Period

For XVIIth c. mathematicians and scientists alike, mathematical diagrams were more than simple heuristic aides to demonstration: not only could information be conveyed by scientists *via* a diagram, but brute information could be extracted directly from the diagram [7]. In diagrammatic reasoning, a kinetic epistemic action naturally accompanies a visual epistemic action – that is, the information that we 'see' in the diagram is just as much in the physical image as it is in the physical image *as it is moved* by our imagination. Not only do we 'see' how the proof unfolds in a given case, but we 'see' how the proof holds under permissible changes (that is, how it holds for all possible constructions). Of course, kinetic diagrammatic reasoning goes back at least to Euclid, for whom motion had to be implicitly assumed to account for superposition arguments.

As we will see, it is primarily this type of kinetic reasoning that Wallis's diagrammatic proof of the Parallel Postulate rested on. In this respect, Wallis is in excellent company.[2] Indeed, the Early Modern period was rife with diagrams of moving points and sliding lines. This situation may be partly explained by two notable features of XVIIth c. mathematics: 1- it continued the tradition of hierarchizing geometrical knowledge as more certain than arithmetical/algebraic knowledge; and 2- the majority of mathematical output took place as so-called 'mixed' mathematics (that is, the mathematics of optics, of astronomy, *etc.*). Thus, not only diagrammatic reasoning but kinetic reasoning especially play a large inferential role throughout all of XVIIth c. science. This role was not relegated to that of mere visual representation of some piece of knowledge acquired either *a priori* or *a posteriori*. Rather, mathematical diagrams were a **source** *par excellence* of mathematical and scientific knowledge [7].

2.3   On the Changing Standards of Proof in the Early Modern Period

However, the aforementioned primacy of geometry over arithmetic was slowly but surely being contested. Indeed, the XVI–XVIIth c. bore witness to a growing dissatisfaction amongst mathematicians with complex Archimedean proofs, and to a growing recognition that the methodology leading to proof is not perforce the actual methods of the mathematician that lead to discovery [8]: "But this, their Art of Invention, they seem very studiously to have concealed: contenting themselves to demonstrate by Apagogical Demonstrations, (or reducing to

---

[2] Indeed, kinetic diagrammatic reasoning *via* the contiguously developping field of kinematics was indispensable to the development of the calculus. For our purposes, Isaac Barrow's work on the infinitesimal derivation of tangent lines – disseminated in a series of lectures at Cambridge in the mid-1660s – is particularly relevant due to the limit 'characteristic triangle' similar to the triangle inscribed by the tangent, the x axis and any line perpendicular to the x axis [4].

Absurdity, if denied,) without shewing us the method, by which they first found out those Propositions, which they thus demonstrate by other ways" (Wallis 1685, cited in [8]). This change in the aspirational constraints placed on the ideal proof provided Wallis with ample motivation to apply a more direct style of proof to the Savilian 'blemish' on Euclidean geometry.

Notably, Wallis was an early adopter of the new analytic method which was accompanied by a profound change in the concept of number. The growth of this approach led to a need for reclassification of the branches of mathematics as well as to define a purported *Mathesis universalis* that could ground all of these branches. Since the Ancients, geometry had been foundationally prior to arithmetic. With Descartes's analytic approach to geometry, a more precise and elegant procedure was now available, one that reduced geometrical concepts such as magnitudes to algebraic equations. Thus, in Wallis's own conception of such a *Mathesis Universalis*, it is algebra (and, ultimately, arithmetic) which are to be situated as foundationally prior to geometry, for "the objects of arithmetic are of a higher and more abstract nature than those of geometry" [8].

What then to make of Wallis's proof of the Parallel Postulate, which relies so heavily on diagrammatic reasoning and which (superficially) makes little appeal to the algebraic approach? As we shall see, his proof relies heavily on the endless *possibility* of constructing similar triangles – similar triangles which need not be *constructed* in a given instance, as such a possibility is guaranteed by both the nature of the geometric continuum, as well as the infinite nature of the arithmetical processes which underlie the algebraic approach to geometry. Furthermore, the source of the growing power of the analytic approach lies precisely in its ability to rigorously capture information that is gleaned from kinetic reasoning.

2.4 On Wallis's Approach to Proving the Parallel Postulate

Wallis studied seriously the works of the medieval Arab scholars, especially Nasīr al-Dīn al-Tūsī's 1298 works on the Parallel Postulate.[3] While he rejected al-Tūsī's proof, it was the starting point of his own attempt to prove Euclid's Fifth Postulate from Euclid's first four Postulates. Like al-Tūsī, Wallis considers the Parallel Postulate in the Proclusian sense – that is, as the converse of **I, 17**:

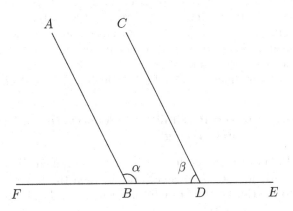

Fig. 1. If $\alpha + \beta = 180°$, then lines AB and CD are parallel (equivalent to the Parallel Postulate).

---

[3] In fact, Wallis commissioned a translation into Latin and was the first to publish the work independently of Clavius's *Commentary on Euclid* (1574) [2].

"In any triangle the sum of any two angles is less than two right angles". Thus, where the Parallel Postulate is equivalent to its inverse which states that if a straight line falling on two straight lines makes the interior angles equal to 180°, then the latter two straight lines are parallel (see Fig. 1)[4], Wallis aims to show this by proving the converse of **I, 17** – that is, by showing that if the angles sum to less than two right angles, then there exists a corresponding triangle.

In this way, the task of proving the Fifth Postulate is reduced to the task of proving the possibility of constructing triangles of arbitrary size, out of two given angles. Wallis intends to show this by proving the possibility of constructing the desired triangle out of a similar triangle constructed specifically for this purpose. Crucially, the litmus test of any purported proof of the Parallel Postulate would have had to been in the way it accounts for the fact that the *desired* triangle is potentially infinite in area. Indeed, the chief difficulty and main source of contention of the Fifth Postulate is precisely the limit case where the sum of the interior angles produced by laying a straight line along a pair of straight lines which incline towards each other is equal to $179.\overline{99}°$. The aim is to prove that the two lines *will* eventually meet, rather than converge endlessly and eternally.

3   On the First Part of Wallis's Proof and Its Implicit Assumptions

For ease of understanding – as well as to gain a better grasp not only of Wallis's method, but also his underlying assumptions – we will proceed by dividing Wallis's argument into two distinct parts. In the first part, Wallis's aim is to show the possibility of constructing a triangle **similar** to the *desired* triangle. Then, in the second part, the goal is to show the possibility of constructing the *desired* triangle **similar** to the previously constructed one. Once the desired triangle is obtained, the converse of **I, 17** has been proven and, thus, the Parallel Postulate along with it. Here, we will review the first part of his proof and examine its implicit assumptions about the nature of space, time and motion. These implicit assumptions were the flash-point for Wallis's detractors, as his proof doubled down on the same nagging doubts concerning the same implicit assumptions about motion, space and time which had also plagued Euclid's *Elements*.

3.1   On the Possibility of Constructing a Triangle Similar to the Desired Triangle

To summarize the first part of the argument: if two straight lines (cut by a third) incline towards each other, then the line with the smaller angle relative to the third can be **moved** in such a way that it crosses the other. The point of

---

[4] See also **I, 27** for an equivalent formulation. By contrast, the **Fifth Postulate** states that *"if a straight line falling on two straight lines makes the interior angles on the same side less than two right angles, the two straight lines, if produced indefinitely, meet on that side on which are the angles less than the two right angle"* [6].

intersection then describes a triangle whose sides are each a segment of one of these three lines. In this way, a triangle **similar** to the *desired* one is constructed. This is completed in eight steps (see Fig. 2):

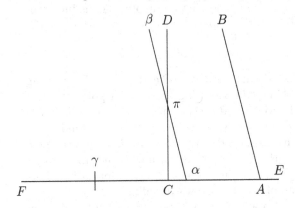

Fig. 2. Wallis's Figure 6

1. Assume two lines AB and CD, cut by a third line EF, incline towards each other at less than two right angles (180°), then each of the exterior angles is greater than the opposite interior angle.
2. Either $\angle BAC < \angle DCF$, or $\angle DCF < \angle BAC$. Otherwise, the lines would be parallel, which would contradict the assumption.

3. By assumption, let $\angle BAC < \angle DCF$. The remainder of the argument applies equally to the alternate case.
4. By Wallis's **Lemma VI**, if the line AB moves to the position of C, then it will lie outside (that is, entirely to the left) of line CD. Let this new line be denoted $\alpha\beta$.
5. Therefore, at some point in its movement, $\alpha\beta$ must have crossed CD at least one point in time.
6. Two cases:
   A) $\alpha\beta$ crosses line CD at several points in space (other than C), at sequential points in time.
   B) Line $\alpha\beta$ crosses line CD all at once (that is, at one single point in time). But then $\angle \beta\alpha F = \angle DCF$ i.e., lines $\alpha\beta$ and CD are parallel, which contradicts our assumption.
   By disjunctive syllogism, line $\alpha\beta$ cuts CD at least one point in time.
7. Choose just such a point of intersection, and let this point be denoted π.
8. We can now construct $\triangle \pi\alpha C$.

3.2   On the Implicit Assumptions of Wallis's Diagrammatic Proof

For heuristic purposes, we pause here Wallis's proof in order to unpack the implicit assumptions involved in this proof up until now. This will help us understand the qualms his contemporaries had with both parts of the proof. As well, once the perennial flaws are out of the way, we will be able to discuss without distractions the more novel analogy we wish to make with the reasoning at the heart of the second part of the proof and the one at the heart of the controversial Axiom of Choice. In the first part of the proof we have just seen, Wallis's reasoning is based on two implicit assumptions. Roughly, they are both assumptions about the temporal space in which the objects are embedded. The first concerns assumptions about the possibility as well as the nature of **motion** in the context of a diagrammatic proof. The second concerns assumptions about the **continuity** of both the space and the time in which his geometrical objects are constructed and set into motion. Here, the diagram hoodwinks us into considering that only a single type of motion, space and time are *natural* to the Euclidean space into which it is embedded.

On the Implicit Assumptions About Motion. Clearly, both the crossing argument and the construction of the triangle using the posited point of intersection rely strongly on **parallel motion**. More specifically, they rely on *i*- the very *possibility* of parallel motion[5]; and on *ii*- the *preservation* of the fundamental characteristics of the figure that is moved. Crucially, in this case, the angle of intersection, directionality, length of the line, curvature of the line, are all assumed to be preserved throughout the duration of the transformation. Furthermore, the possible extensions of the lines towards infinity so vital to the second part of the argument are also assumed to move along with the lines in such a way that their fundamental properties are also preserved. Equally important is what is excluded: the possibility that motion may be accompanied by a distortion in any or all of the figures's fundamental characteristics.

The specific kind of parallel motion assumed by Wallis[6] appears completely natural. We *see* the line $\alpha\beta$ move seamlessly along the shortest path (line AF) to point C. We do not envisage that the line $\alpha\beta$ could grow or shorten, could get 'stuck' in one point due to some internal or external perturbation and begin to curve as the rest of the line is dragged through the parallel motion, *etc.* One might be puzzled at the possibility of motion in the static image – how does the line move? Surely one can draw lines and add figures to an image, but how does one 'drag' the line using a compass and a ruler? Certainly, one can simply draw a line parallel to the original one at the desired location where it crosses CD at point π, but one can never witness the line actually moving seamlessly.[7] Yet, the kinetic reasoning one must supplement to the diagram is limpid. Once given the diagram and the instructions, our intellect augments the diagram by sliding the line $\alpha\beta$ until it meets CD using the simplest, most simultaneously ideal and 'natural' movement available to our intellect.

Still, as natural as the possibility of parallel motion appears, its role in geometrical proofs has long been questioned. Indeed, Wallis himself criticized

---

[5] For it is not at all given that parallel motion is possible on an idealized plane ostensibly frozen in both space and time.

[6] And, indeed, by Euclid himself, though he was somewhat more parsimonious in his deployment of this technique. It is tempting to analyze the few usages of motion in Euclid's *Elements* as an unsavoury fail-safe when no constructive method could be ascertained to deliver the Proposition in a more agreeable manner.

[7] At least, not in the XVIIth century. Nowadays, it is quite easy to compile a kinematic diagram showing exactly this type of parallel motion on the idealized plane.

Euclid's reliance on diagrammatic inferences not explicitly contained in his axioms or definitions and his proof aimed at redressing such issues. Thus, Wallis came fully prepared in 1663 to defend specifically his use of parallel motion, as well as to answer to his detractors, by appealing directly to Euclid's own methods.[8] For Wallis, this exact kind of motion was already assumed in the **Third Postulate**.[9] Furthermore, he asserted that this kind of motion is precisely the same as the one assumed by Euclid in his superposition argument in **I, 4**.[10]

On the Implicit Assumptions About the Continuity of Space and Time. The aforementioned implicit assumption about parallel motion itself relies on important assumptions concerning the continuity of the space the figure is embedded in, as well as the continuity of the time in which the appropriate motion (and constructions) occur. By assumption, this space – along with the unfurling time-frame – is **uniform** and **continuous** in all of its characteristics. That is, any properties inherent to the nature of this idealized space and time that might act as constraints (or pressures) on the possible constructions, as well as the possible transformations which may be operated on the constructed figure, are applied uniformly and continuously. It is assumed that the line $\alpha\beta$, when in motion, will not 'jump' past line CD without crossing it. What is excluded here is i- the possibility of *discrete motion* that could result from a discrete

---

[8] "One should not object here that Euclid himself in his proofs never appears to have applied the *movement of a straight line* and never mentioned this in the postulates, since just as in the explanation of the sphere, he uses *the movement of a circle*, in the explanation of a cone, he uses the movement of a triangle, in the explanation of a cylinder, he uses the movement of a rectangle, he could have used, if necessary, the movement of a straight line in his proofs. From time to time *Archimedes, Apollonius,* and other geometers do this. Indeed, Euclid himself uses the movement of two straight lines where the angle between them does not alter, and indeed very close to the beginning, in that he proves Proposition 4 [i.e., I, 4] by a covering argument, and that assumption is necessary to the covering. And in my Lemma, I use the notion of *movement* in exactly the same way. In addition, the same is assumed in the third postulate (namely, *to describe a circle with any given centre and radius*), since one assumes (in the drawing of the circle) that the circular surface is described by the moving around of the radius (while one of its endpoints remains fixed at the centre). I mention this in order that I do not give the impression of having neglected the *Euclidean* rigour in proofs and that I have brought in new postulates (other than those admitted by *Euclid* himself)" [12].

[9] In Euclid's **Third Postulate**, the construction of a circle of any center and radius is allowed, since any such circle may be drawn by moving the radius around the centre. The length and curvature of the radius are assumed to not incur any distortions through this motion. However, Euclid falls slightly short of postulating the actual existence of infinitely many circles of arbitrary size. The **Third Postulate** remains a construction postulate, not an existence postulate. As we shall see, Wallis will also attempt to justify the explicit assumption at the center of the second part of his proof through appeal to this Postulate.

[10] *Pace* Wallis, the argument there could be achieved by a different kind of motion: lifting the figure from the plane and repositioning it, or by folding the plane, *etc.*

conception of space (and time)[11]; as well as *ii*- the possibility of *local perturbations* in space (or time) that could lead the line $\alpha\beta$ to somehow circumnavigate the line CD, or cross CD but with distortions of its fundamental properties.

Without this implicit assumption, parallel motion of the kind assumed by Wallis would simply not be possible. The medium in which diagrams are presented hoodwinks us into only seeing the possibility of the simplest and most ideal version of the kind of parallel motion, the kind of space and the kind of time that we personally experience on a daily basis.[12] Disentangling the Parallel Postulate from its implicit assumptions was an important and crucial step towards the discovery of non-Euclidean geometry. A modern continuity principle is required even for Euclid's claim that a point exists at the intersection of two lines. Yet, in pre-non-Euclidean geometry, the continuity principle that permeates diagrammatic reasoning must remain implicit: where the space of a diagram appears to be a continuous one, continuity is 'shown' through the very possibility of constructing a continuous line on a continuous piece of paper. It is 'shown' through the very conditions of possibility of the diagram. That reality may not be as it appears is not a direct mathematical question: an explicit assumption of continuity simply does not make sense for a science of continuous magnitudes – though it certainly makes tremendous sense for the science of various kinds of spaces. The clarity, novelty and force of Wallis's argument was such that these hidden assumptions could be scrutinized much more closely.

---

[11] For instance, like the depiction of space and time presented in Zeno's fourth paradox of motion, the Stadium argument. Our only source for Zeno's Stadium argument is due to Aristotle. Due to the difficulty in interpretating this paradox, it is usually presented alongside two simple diagrams. It is perhaps notable that, while these diagrams *are* genuine heuristic aides to understanding the paradox, so difficult is the task of 'visualizing' the diagrams discretely (that is, of 'visualizing' these diagrams outside the assumption that space and time are both continuous) that seldom does the paradox strike us on our first, second, or even third time encountering it.

[12] Consider a Poincaré disk model where line CD cuts straight through the center. As the line $\alpha\beta$ moves closer to the center and approaches some point π where it might cross CD, one or both of its nodes would appear to get 'left behind' due to the potentially infinite distances they must travel compared to the segment of the line closest to the center (where the deviation from the Euclidean planar model is lesser). Such a space is continuous, but it is not uniform: here, the first part of Wallis's argument is not just fallacious, it is simply not possible. Yet, even when looking at a diagram of a non-Euclidean space represented on a Euclidean plane, it is very difficult for us to *see* how the hyperbolic parallel motion of line $\alpha\beta$ behaves. In our world, as in our diagrams, objects moving along the shortest path from one point to another move smoothly, without morphing, disappearing and reappearing, *etc.* The intellectual knowledge that our experience of the world may not be as it appears does little to lift the nearly insurmountable obstacle presented by our senses.

4   On the Second Part of Wallis's Proof and Its Explicit Assumption

As we have seen, Wallis's proof improved little on the long-standing gaps in Euclid's *Elements* with respect to the implicit assumptions about motion, space and time. Though he makes explicit and elevates his own reliance on parallel motion (which remained wholly implicit in Euclid), the sheer possibility as well as the exclusive nature of this motion remained implicit. Still, by making this reliance explicit, this assumption was fully brought to light and enabled the assumptions about the nature of space and time to sour in this light as well. Furthermore, as we have noted, in the first part of Wallis's proof, the concept of geometric construction is somewhat stretched. There, Wallis willed the 'construction' of a triangle through the mental operation of 'moving' a given line until it intersects another.[13] In the second part of his proof, Wallis stretches the concept of geometrical construction to its limit by claiming that, since the Euclidean plane admits of the existence of a dense infinity of **similar** triangles, the *desired* triangle need not be constructed at all, *for it already exists.*

4.1   On the Possibility of Constructing the Desired Triangle Out of the Similar Triangle

To summarize the second part of the argument: to the triangle previously described in Sect. 3.1, there exists a **similar** triangle of larger size with base AC and with sides lying along the extensions of lines AB and CD. Therefore, it is proved that the two lines converge and meet at the point prescribed by the extension of the two original lines. *Ergo*, the Parallel Postulate is also proved. Thus, Wallis's argument requires three additional steps (see Fig. 3):

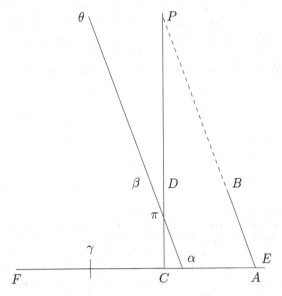

Fig. 3. Wallis's Figure 7, modified to extend line $\alpha\beta$ to $\alpha\theta$

---

[13] Curiously, the first part of Wallis's proof can be entirely dispensed with in favour of a Euclidean construction. As such, we have not belaboured this point. Nevertheless, this explicit kinetic reasoning is highly informative as to the implicit kinetic reasoning we conjecture is at play in the second part of his proof.

9. By **Proposition VIII**, to any arbitrarily chosen figure, there exists similar figures of arbitrary size. Thus, applying **Proposition VIII** to $\triangle \pi \alpha C$, then there must exist a similar triangle with base AC. Let this triangle be denoted $\triangle PAC$.

10. Clearly, by our original assumption $\angle ACD < \angle BAC$. Now, by our assumption of similarity, $\angle \alpha C \pi = \angle ACD$ and $\angle \pi \alpha C = \angle BAC$. So, still by our assumption of similarity, $\angle C \pi \alpha = \angle CPA$.

11. Since P lies both on the extension of CD and the extension of AB, then if CD and AB are indefinitely extended, they will meet. □

4.2   On the Explicit Assumptions of Wallis's Diagrammatic Proof

In proving the possibility of 'constructing' the *desired* triangle out of the triangle constructed in the first part of his argument so as to be **similar** to the *desired* one, Wallis laid out a crucial explicit assumption:

Proposition VIII "*To any arbitrarily chosen figure, there is always another similar to it and of arbitrary size*" [12].

Wallis's Proposition VIII boldly states that the existence of arbitrary similar triangles is independent of their geometrical constructibility. Yet, this is tantamount to saying that the desired triangle does not need to be *actually* constructed: **it already exists**. All that was needed was to construct in the first part of his argument a similar triangle to the desired one, and the desired triangle would follow immediately from Wallis's novel **Proposition VIII**.

Wallis argued that his principle is in complete continuity with Euclid's method, and is furthermore implicit in the aforementioned **Third Postulate**.[14] In Wallis's estimation, his new axiom merely extended the reach of Euclid's

---

[14] See note 9. "Indeed, since magnitudes can always be divided and multiplied without restriction, this seems to follow from the nature of relationships between magnitudes, namely that every figure can always be reduced or increased without restriction while retaining its own form. In fact all geometers have made this assumption (without expressing it or even remarking on it), among them Euclid. For when he requires that a circle with given centre and radius can always be described, he assumes that there is a circle of arbitrary size or with arbitrary radius, and when he assumes that something is possible, then he requires that one can carry this out. To be sure, it would be no automatic requirement that, without the necessary knowledge being set out, one should be able to draw a similar figure to a given one according to a given measure. But [given this demand] one can just as well assume that this can be carried out for an arbitrary figure as for a circle" [12].

Third Postulate to encompass *all* figures.[15] Granted then that a triangle of arbitrary size **similar** to the given triangle was by *petitio principii* constructible, the equivalent Parallel Postulate could easily be 'proven'. Nevertheless, *pace* Wallis's claims that his methodology is Euclidean through and through, it is clear that the argument shifts gears with **Proposition VIII**. While the *desired* triangle is here obtained within the frame of the diagram, the limit case that constitutes the litmus test of an adequate proof of the converse of **I, 17** is merely gestured at:

> "In preparing to prove a theorem (this is certainly much less relevant in the solution of a problem by construction), it might be that one assumes that things can be carried out and actually are carried out, whose geometrical constructibility has not yet been shown. (...) And nevertheless the proofs of the theorems work just as well as if the geometrical construction were indeed fully known" [12].

So then how did Wallis arrive at **certain** knowledge of his **Proposition VIII** if not through construction? Given the unnecessary reliance on parallel motion to 'construct' a triangle similar to the desired one in the first part of his proof, we posit that this knowledge was gleaned through **kinetic reasoning**. With Fig. 3, we are invited to consider the extension of our previous line CD to line CP, with P being the arbitrarily distant apex of the desired triangle. We *see* how moving anew the unlimited extension of line $\alpha\beta$ to $\alpha\theta$ back towards line AB *continuously* inscribes in its wake an infinitely dense field of triangles similar to $\triangle\pi\alpha C$. This **movement** ostensibly actualizes a saturated infinity of potential

---

[15] Yet Wallis's explicit assumption entails more than does Euclid's **Third Postulate**. For all circles are by definition similar in the desired respect. The ability to construct a given circle entails the ability to construct a similar circle of arbitrary size. It follows from the ability to construct any circle – barring, of course, certain physical constraints placed on the construction of compasses. On the other hand, triangles vary widely in the desired respect. The ability to construct a given triangle does not immediately entail the ability to construct a **similar** triangle of *arbitrary* size. Euclid shows how to construct specific triangles only twice: 1- in **I, 1**, Euclid shows how to construct equilateral triangles of arbitrary size by inscribing them within constructed circles; and 2- in **I, XXII**, Euclid shows how to construct a triangle out of three given lengths – yet his method again relies on the ability to construct arbitrary circles, *given* here that we are also given the exact length of all three sides. It is then far from clear that Euclid believed the construction of similar triangles of arbitrary size to be anything close to a fundamental principle.

similar triangle, until the line $\alpha\theta$ coincides with line AB and then halts, forming $\triangle PAC$ – this, no matter how indefinitely far point P is from point C.[16]

Wallis's alternative postulate for Euclidean geometry was roundly criticized not only for being blatantly non-constructive, but also for being 'more meta-physical than mathematical'.[17] This non-constructive *existence postulate* was not only far from contemporary beliefs about the nature and ontological sta-tus of mathematical objects, but far from the usual methods and constraints of mathematicians that were considered as desirable, certain and rigorous. Indeed, up until the XIXth century, mathematics was constructive – or, at the very least, aspired and considered itself to be *constructive*. It is only in hindsight that ves-tiges of non-constructive arguments have been traced back as far as Euclid [3, 9]. Still, in the XVIIth century, **Proposition VIII** was controversial. What Wallis *wanted* was to **choose** the desired triangle from the collection of all the similar triangles to $\triangle\pi\alpha C$. But what he *needed* was a Euclidean proof that all of the postulated similar triangles are **constructible** using Euclidean methods.

Wallis's explicit assumption was the fatal flaw of his proof: for the existence of similar triangles is, as we now know, itself equivalent to the Parallel Postulate. Indeed, as Saccheri later pointed out, postulating the existence of non-congruent similar figures is equivalent to unconditionally assuming his "hypothesis of the right angle".[18] If a given triangle's angles do not sum up to two right angles, then the angle-angle-angle congruence will not be preserved when diminishing or enlarging it – even through parallel motion. In hyperbolic and elliptic geometry, any two similar triangles are perforce congruent [10]. Thusly, Wallis's failed dia-grammatic proof of the Parallel Postulate set geometry into motion away from a science of continuous magnitudes and towards a science of space.

5   A Diagram of Choice: Wallis's Diagrammatic Reasoning and the Axiom of Choice

Nevertheless, even granted the existence of some continuous space saturated with similar figures and permitted the possibility of parallel motion which pre-serves the properties of the figure being moved, it is unclear how we always arrive at the desired triangle with **absolute certainty**. In terms of motion, if

---

[16] The way that **Proposition VIII** is set up, Wallis does not *need* to invoke motion in the second part of his argument. But consider again Fig. 3. It differs from Wallis's own Figure 7 solely by the extension of line $\alpha\beta$ to $\alpha\theta$. It is immediately clear that the only way that $\triangle PAC$ could be constructed in a manner that would still concord with at least Wallis's own construal of Euclidean methodology, is through motion. In doing so, it is also immediately clear how a dense infinity of similar triangles to $\triangle\pi\alpha C$ appears to be *given* by the diagram. Nevertheless, Wallis's argument still requires him to 'choose' the desired triangle from the uncountably infinite collection of all the similar triangles to $\triangle\alpha C\pi$. Positing that line $\alpha\theta$ 'scans' the space and halts when it coincides with line AB does the trick nicely.

[17] Wallis's existence postulate was furthermore deeply rooted in his theory of magni-tudes and proportions which he derived partly from Aristotle's *Categories*.

[18] That is, that quadrilaterals with two sides perpendicular to the other two are rect-angles (*c.f.*, Euclid's Definition X), itself equivalent to the Parallel Postulate [6].

$\triangle PAC''$ is larger than $\triangle PAC'$ by some infinitesimally small margin, when does line $\alpha\theta$ halt? Furthermore, suppose $\angle\pi\alpha C$ is smaller than a right angle by some infinitesimally small margin (such that point P lies indefinitely far away), does the motion definitely halt? That is, does our litmus triangle exist? Have we not just pushed back the problem of infinity that laid at the heart of the historical uncertainty surrounding the Parallel Postulate? We now turn our sights to another controversial axiom – the Axiom of Choice – and the intriguing historical and methodological parallels to be found therewith.

The Axiom of Choice has been touted as "probably the most interesting and, in spite of its late appearance, the most discussed axiom of mathematics, second only to Euclid's Axiom of Parallels which was introduced more than two thousand years ago" [5]. According to Moore, vestiges of the Axiom of Choice can be found already in Euclid's *Elements* [9].[19] Yet, when made explicit, this implicit assumption became one of modern mathematics biggest controversies, and contributed to a cleaving between classical and constructive mathematics. Just as Wallis devised his **Proposition VIII** specifically for the purpose of proving the Parallel Postulate, Zermelo first formulated his 'postulate of choice' as a means to secure a proof of Cantor's Well-Ordering Principle. Furthermore, just as **Proposition VIII** turned out to be equivalent to the Parallel Postulate, so did the Axiom of Choice turn out to be equivalent to the Well-Ordering Theorem. As Zermelo formulated his set theoretic axiom in 1904, given any family $\mathscr{F}$ of non-empty sets, a single element from each member of $\mathscr{F}$ can be selected *via* a choice function f on $\mathscr{F}$, and the output collected to form a new set. Applied to a finite collection, the Axiom of Choice is but a trivial matter of combinatorics and "seems humdrum, almost self-evident" [1].[20] Yet it is the case of an infinite collection where similar troubles to that of Wallis's proof appear.[21]

Consider again the triangle PAC. It seems humdrum, almost self-evident that one can just finitely extend CD and $\alpha\beta$ and simply re-draw $\alpha\theta$ to any position where it crosses the extension of CD on or above point P. The function f that 'halts' the procedure and picks out the coordinates of any similar triangle $\geq \triangle PAC$ can simply be defined through these coordinates. Thus, to answer our first question ('when exactly does the line $\alpha\theta$ halt?'): it doesn't matter, so long

---

[19] It is even the very basis of the Euclidean method which consists in proving a generalization by choosing an arbitrary but definite object, and then showing that the argument holds for that object [9].

[20] Indeed, Zermelo himself stated that "[t]his logical principle cannot, to be sure, be reduced to a still simpler one, but is applied without hesitation everywhere in mathematical deduction" [13].

[21] If the set S is finite (or consists of a countable infinity of positive integers), the existence of such a choice function follows through induction from the precepts of basic logic and of set formation; it is the case of an infinite set S (whether countable like $\mathbb{Z}$ or $\mathbb{Q}$, or uncountable like $\mathbb{R}$) where the rule for $f(A)$ may be un-determinable – thus rendering the Axiom of Choice necessary [1,9].

as it halts. Once any sufficiently large similar triangle is picked out, however arbitrarily, the choice function f can be defined in reference to it, however arbitrarily.[22] But what happens when the extension could *never* fit on any diagram? For instance, suppose base AC is continuously lengthened as line $\alpha\theta$ is moved. Here, an answer to the question 'does the line $\alpha\theta$ always halt?' is not answerable through diagrammatic reasoning without appeal to a potentially arbitrary choice principle combined with a spatio-temporal continuity principle[23]

On a much more heightened scale, so it was with Zermelo's (accepted) proof of the Well-Ordering Theorem. The choice function f that simultaneously picks out the elements of $\mathbb{R}$ required to establish a well-ordering cannot be defined. Zermelo's solution was also an *existence postulate*: the choice function **already exists**, regardless of whether we can construct it. The proof stirred up immense controversy as it could not in the slightest heuristically facilitate any insight or understanding as to what a well-ordering of $\mathbb{R}$ would resemble. At the heart of the debate, was the Axiom of Choice. When Zermelo made explicit this step that is indeed implicit but nevertheless used seemingly everywhere, cognitive difficulties arose: notably, if S is an infinite set (other than a set of positive integers) *how* does the function f pick out the elements in each subset A in the absence of a concrete rule specifying the mechanism underpinning the 'choice'? From a constructive point of view, in the absence of a rule specifying the method of constructing $f(A)$ (and, thus, its output), how is $f(A)$ (and, thus, the 'generated' set) a valid mathematical object [1, 9, 13]?[24].

---

[22] Here, the nature of the geometrical continuum hides the uncountable infinity of similar triangles that must be scanned before arriving at the end point. This is a seeming paradox, which traces its roots back to Zeno's Dichotomy paradox of motion (or, Achilles and the Tortoise). Thus, this is only a problem if we require that the line scan all the points contained in the line segment $\pi P''$ and halt *exactly* at the first available moment. But Achilles is not asked to plant flags at all the half-way points, he is merely asked to cross the finish line. *Any* similar $\triangle \geq \triangle PAC$ will do.

[23] Finite similar triangles may indefinitely be produced, but none of those are our litmus case. The litmus case is a similar triangle potentially infinite in area – the biggest possible one. As such, what we are primarily concerned with is the inability to halt on the triangle that lies 'beyond' all finite iterations of similar triangles and thus define even an arbitrary choice function f for this litmus case. For instance, suppose that the universe is continuous, finitely wide, but infinitely tall. Suppose that $\angle\pi\alpha C$ is arbitrarily close to $180°$, and that base AC is the open interval bounded by the limits of the width of the universe. Does the line $\alpha\theta$ *always* halt as it approaches the limit? Here, flags need to be planted, for there is no finish line to cross. After any flagged similar triangle there is an uncountable infinity of larger similar triangles. The choice function f for $\triangle PAC$ cannot simply be defined retroactively.

[24] A classic illustration of this cognitive problem is Russell's example of an infinite set of pairs of shoes and an infinite set of pairs of socks: while constructing a rule behind a choice function f on the (countably) infinite set of pairs of shoes is unproblematic (choose the right one), establishing any kind of a possible rule behind the 'choice' function f on the (uncountably) infinite set of pairs of socks is completely arbitrary.

Essentially, a basic version of this cognitive step is presented in Wallis's attempted diagrammatic proof of the Parallel Postulate. Consider a diagram populated by *all* the possible **similar** triangles to some given triangle. It would be entirely blackened. Granted then the existence of any similar triangle of arbitrary size, one simply has to 'choose' the desired $\triangle PAC$ from this uncountably infinite collection. Wallis's Figure 7 (see Fig. 3) is then a diagram of choice. Furthermore, as "there is always another similar to it and of arbitrary size" [12], one is not limited by the limits of the diagram – the diagram merely helps us to see the humdrum-ness of the statement in a finite context. But when the desired triangle happens to be one of infinite area, or when *exactly* $\triangle PAC$ is demanded, or when the spatio-temporal constraints are fine-tuned, then the principle simply does not provide a concrete mechanism to construct it. It may only be metaphysically 'chosen' *via* a non-constructive existence fiat. Just as diagrammatic reasoning conceals the assumptions about motion, space and time, so it seems to 'give' us the existence of a unique parallel line going through a given point along with a saturated infinity of similar figures. Diagrammatic reasoning is simply not the right heuristic tool for fathoming the full implications of geometric infinity.

6   Conclusion

Both Proposition VIII and the Axiom of Choice serve to highlight the important distinction between existence postulates and construction postulates. As well, both Wallis and Zermelo assume the possibility of openly adopting postulates that are implicitly used. Furthermore, both with Zermelo's Axiom of Choice and Wallis's Proposition VIII, the main qualm was a methodological one, concerning its non-constructive nature and, thus, whether the object picked out could be further used in proof. However, the debate about the Axiom of Choice considered whether an object picked out using the axiom could properly be said to be a mathematical object at all, whereas Wallis's use of this reasoning escaped such stronger metaphysical considerations. Wherein the increasing complexification of XIXth c. mathematics as well as the foundational crisis ultimately rendered XXth c. mathematicians amenable to non-constructive methods, Wallis's contemporaries could not accept his Proposition VIII as a viable axiom of geometry. Indeed, for an Early Modern mathematician known for his opposition to the use of *reductio ad absurdum* in proofs, Wallis's lapse into the realm of non-constructive proofs is somewhat jarring. While Wallis may have been vindicated in the end for his reliance on a choice principle to obtain the desired similar triangle, he was nevertheless not vindicated for his implicit assumptions about space, time and motion.

References

1. Bell, J.L.: The Axiom of Choice. College Publications, London (2009)
2. Saccheri, G.: Introduction and notes. In: De Risi, V. (ed.) Euclid Vindicated from Every Blemish, Halsted, G.B., and Allegri, L. (trs.). Birkhäuser, Basel [1733] (2014)
3. De Risi, V.: The development of euclidean axiomatics: the systems of principles and the foundations of mathematics in editions of the elements in the early modern age. Arch. Hist. Exact Sci. **70**(6), 591–676 (2016)
4. Edwards, C.H.: The Historical Development of the Calculus. Springer, New York (1979). https://doi.org/10.1007/978-1-4612-6230-5
5. Fraenkel, A., Bar-Hillel, Y., Levy, A.: Foundations of Set Theory, 2nd edn. Elsevier, Amsterdam (1973)
6. Heath, T.L.: The Thirteen Books of Euclid's Elements, Three Volumes, 2nd edn. Cambridge University Press, Cambridge (1925)
7. Heeffer, A.: Using invariances in geometrical diagrams: Della Porta, Kepler and Descartes on refraction. In: Borrelli, A., Hon, G., Zik, Y. (eds.) The Optics of Giambattista Della Porta (ca. 1535–1615): A Reassessment. A, vol. 44, pp. 145–168. Springer, Cham (2017). https://doi.org/10.1007/978-3-319-50215-1_7
8. Mancosu, P.: Philosophy of Mathematics and Mathematical Practice in the Seventeenth Century. Oxford University Press, New York (1996)
9. Moore, G.H.: Zermelo's Axiom of Choice: Its Origins, Development and Influence. Studies in the History of Mathematics and Physical Sciences, vol. 8. Springer, New York (1982). https://doi.org/10.1007/978-1-4613-9478-5
10. Saccheri, G.: Euclid Vindicated from Every Blemish. Risi, V. (ed.), Halsted, G.B., and Allegri, L. (trs.). Birkhäuser, Basel [1733] (2014)
11. Wallis: Two Extracts of the Journall of the Phil. Soc. of Oxford; One Containing a Paper, Communicated March 31, 1685, by the Reuerend Dr Wallis, President of That Soc. concerning the Strength of Memory when Applied with due Attention: The Other, Dated Dec. 15th, 1685, Describing a Large Stone Voided by Way of Urine. Phil. Trans. (1683–1775) **15**, 1269–1271 (1685)
12. Wallis, J.: De Postulato Quinto et Definitione Quinta. Lib. 6. Euclidis; Disceptatio Geometrica. In: Wallis J. (ed.) De Algebra Tractatus; Historicus & Practicus. Cumvariis Appendicibus; Partim prius editis anglice, partim nunc primum editis. Operum Mathematicorum Volumen alterum, pp. 665–678. Theatrum Sheldonianum, Oxoniae [1663] (1693)
13. Zermelo, E.: Bewis, dass jede Menge wohlgeordnet warden kann (1904). In: van Heijenoort, J. (ed.) From Frege to Gödel. A Source Book in Mathematical Logic, 1897–1931. pp. 139–141. Harvard University Press, Cambridge (1967)

Diagram Design, Principles,
and Classification

A Sketch of a Theory and Modelling Notation for Elucidating the Structure of Representations

Peter C.-H. Cheng[(⊠)] [iD]

Department of Informatics, University of Sussex, Brighton, UK
p.c.h.cheng@sussex.ac.uk

Abstract. A structural theory of visual representations and an accompanying modelling notation are outlined. The theory identifies three types of fundamental representational components, specified as cognitive schemas, that span internal mental and external physical aspects of representations. The structure of diverse and complex example representations are analyzed. Twenty-three requirements that a general theory of representations must address are presented. The new theory satisfies the large majority of them. The theory and notation may provide a basis for future methods to predict the efficacy of representations.

Keywords: Representations · Structural theory · Compositional analysis · Diagrams · Notations · Cognitive explanation

1 Introduction

This sentence that your eyes are running over is a representation. Figures 1, 2 and 3, which are explained in Sect. 2, are other representations. The set of numbers that index the section and subsection headings here is yet another. All these examples are different, but they are but a small sample of the vast diversity of existing visual representations. What do all representations have in common that makes them representations? How do they differ as representations irrespective of the domains they encode? Being able to answer these questions will allow us to study representations more systematically than is possible currently, and in the future to ask hard questions such as: How can we choose representations to suit individuals with different levels of domain knowledge and experience of representations, for specific problems, in particular domains [24]? How can we systematically invent novel representations [7]?

The nature of representations is an enduring and important subject for study. Classifications and taxonomies of representations have been proposed [10, 11, 18]. Accounts of representations have been given in terms of formal attributes using formal languages [1, 13, 20, 23, 27, 28], cognitive properties [4, 8, 14, 17, 19, 23, 30], graphical or perceptual attributes [2, 8, 9, 29], and properties of information [5, 10, 21, 32, 33]. For sake of illustration each reference has been exclusively cited in just one of the informal categories above, but many of them span multiple categories. See [3] for a meta-taxonomy of representation classifications.

© Springer Nature Switzerland AG 2020
A.-V. Pietarinen et al. (Eds.): Diagrams 2020, LNAI 12169, pp. 93–109, 2020.
https://doi.org/10.1007/978-3-030-54249-8_8

Fig. 1. Simple representations: (a) original smiley; (b) painting sold (c) "look there"; (d) set A; (e) modern emoticon; (f) litmus paper; (g) fuel gauge, (h) intersection of two sets.

Despite the numerous accounts of representations, none appears sufficient to address even the first set of challenging questions posed in the first paragraph. None have the scope to systematically analyze any representation, for any domain, and at any level of user competence. Thus, the first aim of this paper is to specify a set of characteristics for a general and operationalizable theory of representations; a set of stringent requirements that an adequate theory must satisfy (Sect. 3). The second aim of the paper is to outline a cognitive theory with an accompanying modelling notation for the analysis of notations and visual representations (Sect. 4). The theory posits three fundamental representational components from which all representations are built. An demonstration of the utility of the theory and notation is provided (Sect. 4) by using them to analyze the structure of the diverse examples of representations to be introduced in the next section. The potential uses and limitations of the theory and notation are discussed at the end (Sect. 6).

2 Sample Representations

Here are some representations to serve as ongoing examples in the following sections.

$$x_{1,2} = -b \pm \frac{\sqrt{b^2 + 4ac}}{2a}$$

Fig. 2. Solutions to the quadratic equation.

Simplest Representations. Figure 1 shows some elementary representations. Figure 1a is a smiley from early in the history of email before the idea of a meta-comment on some text was extended to a whole range of emoticons (Fig. 1e). Figure 1b is a red dot on the frame of a painting in an art gallery indicating that it has been sold. Figure 1c was printed on a flier to capture peoples' attention. Figure 1d is one set from a Venn diagram. Figure 1f is a piece of litmus paper whose purple end registers a pH of 9. Figure 1g is a fuel gauge whose segments show that the tank is 4/10ths full. Figure 1h is an intersection of a two set Venn diagram.

Equation Representation. Figure 2 is the formula for the roots of the quadratic equation. It is primarily a sentential representation, a linear concatenation of symbols, that encodes mathematical meaning through the chosen symbols and syntactic rules. Note that it has multiple occurrences of some variables and that it encodes two solutions.

Thermodynamics Graph. Figure 3 is a "monster" representation that engineers use to understand how the Second Law of thermodynamics determines the efficiency of steam engines [12, 25]. It is a graph with axes for entropy, s, temperature, T, and pressure, P. Under different conditions water will be liquid, vapour or a mixture of the two. The bell curve, or *saturation dome*, marks the transition between these states. Under the saturation dome, the dryness fraction, x, gives the proportion of vapour to liquid. The operation of steam engines (running Rankine cycles) are shown by the dashed rectangles. Each side of the rectangle stands for a thermodynamic process: 1–2 – pressurizing the mixture so it all turns to liquid; 2–3 – heating the water until it is all vapour; 3–4 – heat in the vapour is transformed into mechanical energy by a turbine, which turns the vapour back in to a mixture; 4–1 – further heat is released in a condenser to turn most of the vapour back in to liquid, so the cycle can repeat. From the Second Law we can determine the efficiency of a cycle in two ways. First, the energy put into the water by heating is given by the area under line 2–3 (down to $T = 0$ K) and the heat extracted in the condenser is the area under line 4–1, so the energy produced by the engine is the area of the rectangle, hence the efficiency is that area divided by the total heat input, the area under line 2–3. The second way to compute efficiency is to divide $T_2–T_1$ by T_2, which can be computed by comparing the length of line 1–2 with the altitude of T_2.

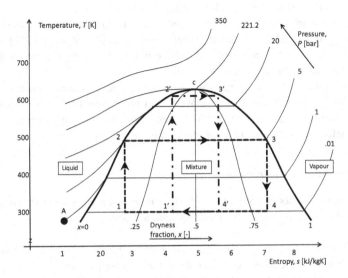

Fig. 3. A monster thermodynamics graph.

3   Criteria for a Theory of Representation Structure

What should a general broad scope theory of representations encompass? Five groups of requirements that a structural theory should address are considered, ranging from fundamental properties of representations to pragmatic concerns about their utility. Some of these are implicit common assumptions or just basic tenets of good science, but where they are explicitly identified in the literature references are given.

3.1 Fundamental Requirements

These aspects are essential things that a theory must encompass, such that in their absence we would not consider the theory to be an account of representations.

R1. Represented world: a representation encodes knowledge about some domain, a *represented world*, including general information about objects, properties, values and relations [22].

R2. Representing world: a representation has graphical parts, including icons and words, that do the encoding of the things from the represented world [22].

R3. Compositional structures: represented and representing worlds are typically rich compositional structures, which are often hierarchical [16].

R4. Semantics: a representation represents, so knowing the encoding relations between the things in the represented and the representing worlds is critical [26].

R5. Syntax: a representation has rules that govern the valid configurations of graphical parts that are potentially meaningful [10].

R6. Supplementary structure. A representation may include graphical parts that are not intended to encode domain information, and not covered by the representation's syntax, but are an integral part of the representing world for practical reasons (e.g., the typeface of this text and locations of the line returns).

3.2 Interpretation Requirements

This set of requirements concerns the rich ways in which a representation may encode meaning, and constraints on such encodings, that a theory must recognize.

R7. Parsimony: the theory should propose a small number of types of components that should be the same across all classes of representations.

R8. Multi-level interpretation: as representations are compositional, their meaning can be interpreted at multiple levels; from domain elements, represented by graphic elements, through to high level general abstractions, represented by complex expressions [1, 6].

R9. Alternative interpretations: representations can support interpretations from different perspectives depending on the user's goals and knowledge [14]: e.g., one may view a representation as a composition of its components, or one may think of mutually interacting constraints among components.

R10. Alternative representations: a domain may be encoded in representations with different structures (e.g., 24 h versus AM/PM time of day formats).

R11. Alternative domains: the same representation may be used to encode quite distinct domains (e.g., mathematics is a domain general representation).

R12. Cognitive theory compatibility: for human users of representations, a theory of representations must be compatible with our knowledge about human cognition in general, including perception, memory, thinking and learning.

R13. Theories about information and knowledge: a theory of representations should be compatible with accounts of the nature of particular kinds of information and knowledge; e.g., Steven's [31] analysis of quantity scales.

3.3 Scope of Theory Requirements

These are requirements about the coverage or scope of a theory of representations.

R14. Representation scope: a theory should cover all types of representations, although, below we focus on static visual notations and diagrams.
R15. Domain scope: a theory should address representations from any domain.
R16. Complexity: a theory should span representations of all degrees of complexity; e.g., from Figs. 1, 2, 3, and beyond.

3.4 Existing Representational Theory Requirements

This single requirement recognizes that much has been discovered about the nature of representations, some empirically verified. So, a theory must either make equivalent predictions about previous findings or be able to interpret such existing accounts.

R17. Embody existing theories. Three illustrative examples: *Locational indexing*: Diagrams are (sometimes) superior to sentential representations, because they use spatial associations to establish relations among elements [16]. *Isomorphism*: prefer representations that use just one distinct symbol in a display to stand for one distinct domain concept (i.e., isomorphic) rather than one-to-many or many-to-one mappings [1, 13, 21, 32]. *Separable dimensions*: favour visual properties that are naturally *separable*, because they depend upon different perceptual processes and so demand less conscious effort to distinguish [33].

3.5 Utility Requirements

This final set considers features expected of a valuable and effective theory.

R18. Explanatory: the theory should provide analysis of representations that predict their likely efficacy and explain why they are so or otherwise.
R19. Design patterns: the theory should identify general patterns of representational structures that serve similar functional roles, because they encode similar types of concepts in equivalent ways.
R20. Precise components: the components of the theory should be well-defined and clearly distinct from each other.
R21. Precise sub-components: similarly, subclasses of components should be well-defined and clearly distinct from each other.
R22. Analysis rules: clear operational rules to guide the analysis of representations should be provided.
R23. Functional components: the theory should readily identify those components of a representation that are core to its function as a representation, in contrast to superfluous decoration or "chart junk".

In what follows, numbers in curly brackets, e.g., {R23}, refer to specific requirements.

4 Structural Theory of Representations and Modelling Notation

The proposed theory draws its inspiration from molecular theory in chemistry that explains the diverse properties of countless substances in terms of structures composed of distinct elements. What are the representational elements – fundamental components – and how are they combined in representational molecules – representational structures {R3}? Three types of fundamental components are proposed {R7}.

4.1 Preliminaries

Before introducing the components, this sub-section gives some terminology.

A *topic* is some part of a larger knowledge domain pertaining to a task on which a user is working with a representation {R1}. The thermodynamic power cycles of a particular type of heat engine is the topic of Fig. 3. Not all the concepts of the topic are necessarily encoded in the representation.

A *display* is the external part of a representation in some physical medium, such as print on paper, pixels on a computer screen, or the raised lines on a tactile graphic {R2}.

A *concept* is an idea, fact, category, property, or value of a property from the topic {R1}. Ideas include things such as laws, classifications schemes, constraints, prototypical and extreme cases, which may be complex and hierarchically structured.

A *schema* is a mental cognitive structure that encodes categorial information as a collection of *slots*, variables, that contain *fillers*, values [26]. The set of slots defines the category and a specific set of fillers instantiates a particular instance of the category. Schemas are widely used in cognitive science to explain how the mind systematically stores and organizes knowledge [26]. Specialized schemas are used for reasoning in domains that combine both propositional and diagrammatic information [6, 15]. The present theory generalizes the idea of such schemas to all representations {R12}.

Graphic-objects and *properties* are visual entities that a viewer of a display takes as separate things or features of the display. Elementary graphic objects are established by our perceptual systems (visual or haptic). Parts of graphic objects may themselves be graphic objects {R7, R8}; e.g., the dryness axis is that part of the P curves that are under the bell curve in Fig. 3. Graphic objects may be composites; e.g., an axis comprises a scale, tick marks and labels. Similarly, different features of a graphical object may represent different concepts {R7, R8}; e.g., the height of a rectangle in Fig. 3 is a temperature difference and its area is an amount of heat. The relative height of the two rectangles, with conscious effort, may be interpreted as a composite graphic object.

4.2 Representational Components

Tokens, *Representation-dimensions* (R-dimensions), and *Representation-schemes* (R-schemes) are the three proposed types of components {R7}. The fundamental function of these components is to encode and associate information about the target domain and about the display. Each is specified as a schema {R9, R12} and are represented, respectively, in the modelling notation by particular shapes, Figs. 4b, c, & d. The tablet shape icon stands for a whole representation; Fig. 4a. Again, the main purpose of all three components is to coordinate {R4} things from the represented world {R1} with things in the representing world {R2}. The form of the component icons reflects this fundamental idea: the top label of each icon names the encoded concept and the bottom label names the encoding graphic object (or property).

Fig. 4. Icons for (a) representations, (b) Tokens, (c) R-dimensions, (d) R-schemes, (e) multiple Tokens, (f) multiple R-dimensions.

A **Token** is a "fixed" component that pairs (A) one concept and (B) one graphic object. It's icon is lozenge shaped, Fig. 4b. Examples include: (i) Figs. 1a–d and their associated concepts; (ii) a letter and its domain variable (e.g., T – *temperature*); (iii) a rectangle and a cycle in Fig. 3; (iv) the whole equation in Fig. 2 and two quadratic equation solutions; (v) in Fig. 1h, the middle zone of the Venn diagram and an intersection.

Concept: 1 object, instance or value
Graphic: 1 graphic object
Function: *semantic, auxiliary, arbitrary*
Explicit: *yes, no*
Tokens: 0 or more
R-dimensions: 0 or more
R-schemes: 0 or more

Fig. 5. Token schema. Slot names in bold. Names of specific fillers in italic.

A Token schema has seven slots (Fig. 5). One pair of slots is for the concept and the graphic object {R4}. Three slots hold Tokens, R-dimensions and R-schemes that are directly associated, children, of the Token. This captures local connections that on the large scale define the overall network structure of components {R3} (see below). The other slots differentiate further features of a token {R21}. The *function* slot specifies the role of the token in the representation. A *semantic* filler means that the Token encodes a domain concept. A Token whose function is to pragmatically aid the interpretation of the representation but is not itself semantic has *auxiliary* as a filler {R6}: e.g., commas grouping triplets of digits in long numbers; the size and position of circles in a Venn diagram (whereas an overlap of circles is semantic). An *arbitrary* filler indicates the Token is neither semantic nor auxiliary, so merely serves a decorative or aesthetic purpose. In an icon for a concept-less Token, the concept label is replaced by a '##' symbol. The *explicit* slot specifies whether a Token's graphic object is physically present in the display or is to be imagined by the user; e.g., envisage a new P curve in Fig. 3 between a pair of printed isobars. In icons for such imagined concepts, a '##' symbol is used in place of a label to denote the absence of a graphic object.

Concept: domain property
Concept-scale: *nominal* (N), *ordinal* (O), *interval* (I), *ratio* (R)
Concept-attributes: e.g., max, min, magnitude range, %
Graphic: graphic property, axis, sub-notation (see text)
Graphic-scale: *nominal* (N), *ordinal* (O), *interval* (I), *ratio* (R)
Graphic-attributes: e.g., graphic range, type (linear, logarithmic)
Scope: *global, local*
Function: *semantic, auxiliary, arbitrary*
Explicit: *yes, no*
R-dimension: 0 or more R-dimensions as sub-dimensions
Tokens: 1 or more

Fig. 6. R-dimension schema. Specific fillers values in italic.

A Representation-dimension (R-dimension) is a component that deals with "variation" in a class of Tokens. It pairs (A) a concept that can take alternative values of one domain property with (B) some means of encoding alternative values {R4}. The R-dimension icon is a trapezium, Fig. 4c. R-dimension examples include: (i) pH values as colours; (ii) metered quantities as numbers of bars on a scale, Fig. 1g; (iii) alternative emotions depicted by different emoticons; (iv) the basic relations between sets encoded by spatial configurations of circles (separate, overlapping (Fig. 1h), embedded); (v) values of some property as a x-coordinate (horizontal) position in a graph; (vi) quantities of energy as areas of rectangles in Fig. 3; (vii) a list of some facts.

The R-dimension schema has eleven slots (Fig. 6). The first three *concept* slots name the concept, specify its type of quantity scale, and give selected attributes of the quantity {R1}. Three matching *graphic* slots do the same for the means of encoding {R2}. For a *concept-scale* or *graphic-scale* slot, the fillers are one of Steven's [31] types of quantities: in the icon the letters following the concept and the graphical object names give the scale type (i.e., replace S in Fig. 4c, with N, O, I, or R). The scale types of the concept and graphical object may differ. Forms of encoding may be graphic properties and also more complex graphic structures, such as an axis of a Cartesian graph or a sub-notation (e.g., a numeration system or an indexing scheme) {R5}.

Three further slots are used to define types of R-dimensions {R21}. The *function* slot is the same as the function slot in the Token schema; for example, position in a simple unordered list is an *auxiliary* R-dimension, because positions merely differentiate Tokens but do not encode a domain concept. The function slot is important because it has a key role in distinguishing sentential from diagrammatic representations (see below). The *explicit* slot specifies whether the R-dimension is physically represented in the display or must be imagined; e.g., *no* fills the slot for the R-dimension standing for areas beneath curves in Fig. 3, because the origin of the T axis is below the s axis scale. The *scope* slot specifies whether the R-dimension covers the whole display or is more localized (e.g., in Fig. 3, T, s, and P are global, whereas x is local). The *Token* slot holds at least one token whose value is encompassed by the R-dimension. The *R-dimensions* slot identifies any subparts of an R-dimension that happen to be specifically meaningful (e.g., the excess revs red zone of a tachometer).

Domain-structure: relations among domain concepts
Graphic-structure: graphical structure
Function: *semantic, auxiliary, arbitrary*
Scope: *global, local*
Explicit: *yes, no*
Tokens: 0 or more
R-dimensions: 2 or more, 1 if also ≥1 Tokens
R-schemes: 0 or more
Organization: specifies relations among components

Fig. 7. R-scheme schema.

A **Representation-scheme (R-scheme)** is a "structural" component that pairs (A) a conceptual structure of the domain with (B) a graphical structure that is more complex than an R-dimension. Examples of R-schemes include: (i) a graph coordinate system (e.g., in Fig. 3 T-s is Cartesian); (ii) a table's grid of rows and columns; (iii) Hindu-Arabic numbers that exploit digit position as power and digit shape as numerosity [33]; (iv) the coordination of labels and zones in a Venn diagram (e.g., Figure 1h); (v) the combination of location and shapes of icons in a map; (vi) multi-dimensional index systems (e.g., Library of Congress book classification scheme).

The R-scheme icon is rectangular, Fig. 4d, and its schema has nine slots (Fig. 7). The *concept-structure* and *graphic-structure* slots name their respective target structures {R4}. Again, the schema has *function, scope* and *explicit* slots that are equivalent to those slots in R-dimensions {R21}. The *Tokens, R-dimensions,* and *R-schemes* slots hold the constituents of the R-scheme. The relations among an R-scheme's components may be complex, so the names in the concept-structure and graphic-structure slots are pointers to descriptions of them (e.g., in the modelling notation or text).

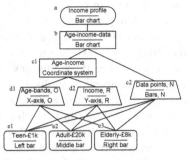

Fig. 8. A sample representation structure.

The *Organization* slot contains a description of how concept structures and graphic structures are related {R4}. A R-scheme cannot contain a single R-dimension alone; it would be an R-dimension. An ordered list is an R-scheme, because it combines a categorical R-dimension to identify different items with an ordinal R-dimension for the priority of the items. The reading directions of text, such as top-to-bottom then right-to-left in traditional Chinese, is an auxiliary function R-scheme.

4.3 Modelling Notation

The modelling notation supports the explication of the relations between Token, R-dimensions and R-schemes through the construction of network diagrams to show their organization {R3}. A tablet icon for the representation tops what is generally a tree-like structure. Below each icon for a schema, further schema icons are drawn for the contents of its Token, R-dimension and R-scheme slots. Imagine a simple a bar chart for income in three age bands: Fig. 8 shows one possible interpretation of its structure. Below the representation icon, Fig. 8 (a), it possesses an R-scheme (b) that is a bar chart assembly for data. The graph has a coordinate system R-scheme (c1) in which data values, drawn from a nominal scale R-dimension (c2), are plotted. The coordinate system has an ordinal scale R-dimension for age-bands (d1) and a ratio scale R-dimension for income (d2). The bars for three cases are the Tokens (e1–e3). Figure 8 may be viewed as a design pattern for this class of representations {R19}.

For compactness in the diagrams, multiple instances of Tokens or R-dimensions of the same kind may be represented with a dashed perimeter, Figs. 4e and 4f, and an expression (replacing *n*) indicates the number of instances. For complex domains, additional information, not defined in the schemas themselves, can be encoded using supplementary notational elements between icons as required (see below).

4.4 Analysis Guidelines

From the experience of analyzing more than a dozen disparate representations, here are ten representation analysis guidelines: a step towards {R22}. (1) Consider a target user with a particular level of knowledge of the domain and a certain degree of experience of the class of representation in question. (2) From the perspective of the target user, catalogue domain concepts noting the levels of abstraction and granularity at which they occur, in particular what concepts are fixed and variable things, and what concepts are relations. (3) Select typical examples of displays appropriate to the competence of the target user. (4) Catalogue all the graphical parts of the display that have semantic and auxiliary functions, plus any other parts that may be arbitrary but important; for instance, because they are likely to be misconceived by target users. (5) Using the two catalogues, define schemas for Tokens, including those at higher levels of abstraction or granularity. (6) From the list of Tokens and the catalogues, specify R-dimensions for sets of similar tokens, paying special attention to *concept-scale* and *graphical-scale* slots of the schemas. Unless a token is solitary and stands for an unvarying concept, it will be an instance of some R-dimension. (7) Identify the R-schemes using two approaches. (a) Propose configurations of R-dimensions, perhaps with anchor Tokens, for the primary conceptual relations of the topic, such as its sets of underpinning laws. (b) Sets of R-dimensions, and Tokens, with strong conventional associations may constitute R-schemes. (8) Alternate between bottom-up composition from Tokens and top-down decomposition from R-schemes {R8}. (9) In a drawing package, construct a model with icons for each schema, whilst iteratively working through steps (1) to (8). (10) Revisit steps (1) and (3) in order to explore alternative interpretations of the representation. Consider the overall coherence and parsimony of the structures in order to judge the plausibility of particular interpretations {R9}.

The next section analyses the representations presented in Sect. 2.

5   Examples Analyzed

The structures of the examples are modelled in fine detail to demonstrate the rigour of the theory and utility of the notation. However, the reader need not track all the technicalities of the analyses in order to follow the discussion of the implications below.

5.1   Icons and Indicator Scales

The representations in Fig. 1 are simple. In the historical context of its first use as a meta-comment on some text, the smiley was just a Token without a R-dimension as no other types of this Token existed. The later coining of related emoticons created an R-dimension. In their typical use, "sold" dots (Fig. 1b) are also Tokens, because alternative colours are not used for "unsold" or "under offer". Figures 1c, d, f, & g have R-dimensions that, respectively, vary across (c) gaze direction and pupil position, (d) sets & labeled circles, (f) pH and colour, and (g) fuel level and number of bars. Figure 1h is a Token with an R-dimension for set relations encoded by degrees of overlapping circles, and in turn is a part of a larger R-scheme for sets and Venn diagrams.

5.2   Equations

Figure 9 is a representation structure model for Fig. 2, assuming a user who is competent in mathematics. The representation icon is located at C1 in the figure's coordinate system. Overall, the model encodes the idea that the equation is a sentential representation based on a linear concatenation of symbols. Nested R-schemes encode successive layers of expressions that includes R-dimensions and Tokens for mathematical operators, variables, numbers and signs. The overall equation consists of a left hand side (LHS) formula, the equals sign, and a right hand side (RHS) formula, which are encoded by a R-scheme (B3), a Token (C3) and another a R-scheme (F3), respectively. The arrow (D3) indicates the nodes below are ordered. The LHS formula is an elementary expression (*Elem exp*) (B3) consisting of a R-dimension for a sign (A4–5) and a R-dimension for a variable or number (*Var/num*) (B4–5), in this case x. An additional R-scheme for two subscripts that identify alternative solutions is anchored to the x Token (B6–C8). The comma between the numbers is an auxiliary Token (B7).

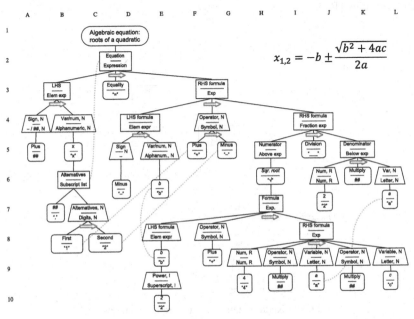

Fig. 9. Representation structure diagram for the equation in Fig. 2 (repeated top right).

The equation's RHS is a formula R-scheme (F3), whose LHS is another elementary expression R-scheme (D4–E6). Unusually, the operator of the RHS formula's is not a Token but a R-dimensions (F4) because it provides options of *plus* or *minus* Tokens (F5, G5). The RHS of the formula is a R-scheme (I4) and notably includes a Token for the square-root that anchors another formula R-scheme (H6). The rest of the decomposition follows in a similar fashion.

Some noteworthy features of the model include: (i) the large number of R-schemes; (ii) ##s note the absence of graphic objects for the multiplication ($\times$) Tokens (e.g., K6); (iii) several concepts are represented multiple times as denoted by the dotted lines.

A key feature of the theory and notation is its ability to support alternative interpretations of a representation {R9}. To illustrate this, Fig. 10 gives a representation structure diagram for algebraic equations that abstracts away from all the detail in Fig. 9. The overall structure is a tree whose leaves are Tokens for variables, numbers, signs (+/−), or operators. Nodes are R-schemes for expressions or R-dimensions for those Tokens. The top level R-scheme (F2) encodes the relation between two formulas encoded as R-schemes (D3, G3). Various graphical devices are used to concisely encode expressions and recursive structure. A pair of *s on a left branch (E3) and on a corresponding right branch (G3) of a node indicates that the structure on the left is repeated on the right (similarly, C4–F5). The loops from the bottom of a R-scheme to its top (C3–4, E3–4) signify the potential for building expressions recursively. The possible relations between the equation's formulas are held in a nominal R-dimension (F3) and one is the chosen Token (F4). The description of the rest of the model is similar to the lower parts of Fig. 9. Overall, the model captures the idea that equations may be described by a generative set of syntactic rules {R5}.

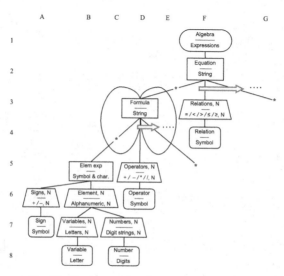

Fig. 10. Representational structure of equations.

5.3 Thermodynamics Graph

Figure 11 is the model for Fig. 3. It assumes a user whose is familiar with both thermodynamics and power cycle property graphs. The primary R-scheme (C2) is a x-y-z graph coordinate system, consisting of ratio scale R-dimensions for variables T, s and P (B3, D3, E3), in to which data point Tokens are plotted from a nominal scale R-dimension (A3). The P z-axis is encoded by the isobar curves. Vast numbers of Tokens for data points are depicted in Fig. 3 (A4) but just two are specifically noted (C4, D4). The saturation curve, bell dome, is a Token (G4) composed of many data points. The thick arrow to that Token specifies that it, and subsequent components, inherit all the structure of the T-s-P R-scheme. The dome (G4) and critical point (D4) are anchor Tokens for two local nominal R-dimensions (C6, J4). The first of these R-dimensions (C6) encodes state transitions and has two Tokens for the liquid (B7) and the vapour boundaries (D7). In turn, these Tokens serve as anchors for a nominal scale R-scheme (C8), which has four tokens for the states themselves (A9–E9). One of those Tokens, the mixture Token (C9) is an anchor for the local ratio scale dryness fraction R-dimension (C10) and its many possible values (BC11).

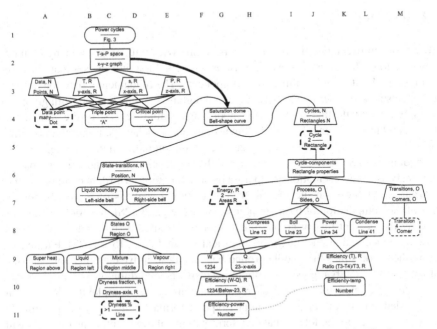

Fig. 11. Representational structure of the thermodynamics graph in Fig. 3.

The second R-scheme (J4), anchored by the saturation dome, encodes the two power cycle Tokens (J5). Two cycles are presented so that efficiencies can be compared. An R-scheme (J6) is attached to both cycles, which has three R-dimensions for quantities of energy (G7), process stages (J7) and transitions between those stages (M7). The process stage R-scheme provides four Tokens (H8–L8). The ordinal scale transitions R-scheme has four Tokens (I8). Areas defined by the energy ratio scale R-dimension (G7) and certain process Tokens definer quantities of power, W (F9), and heat, Q (H9). From these an efficiency ratio scale R-dimension (G10) is defined and Tokens for efficiency are given (G11). Further, from just two of the process Tokens (J8, L8) another efficiency R-dimension (K9) is defined on the basis of temperature differences. The two efficiency values (G11, K10) are equal, shown by the grey dotted line.

Figure 9 is complex because Fig. 3 is complex, but the model reveals interesting things about that complexity. First, Fig. 3 is actually relatively simple as it has only two R-schemes compared to the quadratic solution's nine (Fig. 9). Second, it is a relatively coherent representation: the global coordinate system permeates nearly all aspects of the representation, with all graphical objects interpretable in terms of T, s and P. Further, the second, local, R-scheme is fully embedded within that main coordinate system. The diagram has multiple R-dimensions for specific aspects of the topic but mappings between the concepts and graphic elements is isomorphic. A seeming exception is the efficiency of the cycles, the dotted line between two Tokens (G11–K10). However, they and their R-dimensions refer to two quite different ways to compute thermodynamic efficiency from the Second Law.

6 Discussion

A theory of representational structure has been proposed with an accompanying modelling notation. The theory is novel in various respects. First, it proposes that all representations are built from just three core components. The fundamental function of these components is *representational*: they serve to integrate domain concepts with graphical structures. Second, the theory focuses on modelling the multi-level structure of representations as relations among Tokens, R-dimensions and R-schemes, rather than positing properties of whole representations as has been common in the literature [e.g., 18, 27]. The guidelines in Sect. 4.4 suggest the possibility of developing systematic approaches to the analysis of representations supported by software tools. Third, in contrast to other approaches that focus on the formal or computational analysis of representations in terms of the composition of basic graphic elements [e.g., 20, 28], the components proposed by the present theory are cognitive schemas posited as psychological entities, whose existence and impact might be empirically tested [e.g., 15, 19, 23]. Further, the present theory occupies the middle ground between descriptive classifications and formal accounts, whilst being usable without extensive formal training. Fourth, the scope of the theory is intended to cover all representations of any complexity {R16}, from any knowledge domain {R15}, and in any type of format or display {R14}. Fifth, the theory can be used to model alternative interpretations of representations for users with differing levels of domain knowledge and familiarity in specific graphical formats, rather than providing a single canonical characterization {R9}.

The theory and notation appear to satisfy most of the 23 requirements given in Sect. 3, so it might be superior to previous accounts. A definite assessment demands a systematic review of the previous theories in terms of the requirements. The satisfaction of the requirements by the theory may partially be attributed to the compositional structural approach using just three core cognitive components that are fundamentally defined as things that *represent*.

The examples above suggest that the theory and notation may provide a means to systematically contrast disparate representations across classes of format. For instance, the above examples allowed us to compare the relative complexity of a diagram and sentential representation that are not informationally equivalent (cf., [16]). Although the formula is simpler graphically than the thermodynamics graph, the latter is simpler and more coherent in various ways. (1) It employs just two R-schemes rather than the equation's nine. (2) All of its concepts are explicitly represented, whereas some of the equation's graphic objects are absent from its Tokens. (3) The equation has multiple Tokens for some concepts, whereas the graph is desirably isomorphic {R17}.

The author has applied the theory and notation to over a dozen other representations, with interesting results. For example, revisiting Larkin and Simon's [16] seminal work by modelling their alternative representations for the pulley system problem, reveals that although the depth of the sentential representation's structure is similar to that of the diagram, it is branchier and composed of more R-schemes. This observation might yield a complementary explanation to the benefit of diagrammatic representations: they demand fewer R-schemes than sentential representations. This mirrors the observed contrast between the quadratic solution equation and the thermodynamics graph.

The representation structure diagram reveals the hidden complexity of Fig. 2, of which someone proficient in algebra may no longer be consciously aware. Figure 9 could serve as a guide to an instructor of all the features of the equation that must be explained to learners. Similarly, Fig. 11 might be used to guide instruction on Fig. 3.

Analysis of further representations by others is required to fully evaluate the utility of the theory and notation. In particular, are the three proposed components sufficient and are their slots necessary and sufficient? The "sketch" in the title acknowledges that the theory has only been outlined here: some aspects of the theory and notation need further development. The compatibility of the theory with existing theories about the efficacy of representations must be established {R17}. For example, considerations of isomorphism [13, 21] can be examined through occurrence of repeated Tokens and by the presence of components with concepts but no graphic objects, and vice versa.

Finally, it is noted that the theory and notation may be able to address theoretical implications about the *cognitive cost* in representation choice {23}, or might be used to investigate how alternative representations might impact learning. The relative number of R-dimensions and R-schemes, whether models are simple hierarchies rather than more complex networks, and the extent use of auxiliary R-schemes and R-dimensions are potential avenues for exploration {R6}.

Acknowledgements. My thanks go to members of the Representational Systems lab and Rep2Rep team, and the three anonymous *Diagrams 2020* reviewers. This work was supported by the UK EPSRC: grants EP/R030642/1 and EP/T019034/1.

References

1. Barwise, J., Etchemendy, J.: Heterogenous logic. In: Glasgow, J., Narayanan, N.H., Chandrasekaran, B. (eds.) Diagrammatic Reasoning: Cognitive and Computational Perspectives, pp. 211–234. AAAI Press, Menlo Park (1995)
2. Bertin, J.: Seminology of Graphics: Diagrams, Networks, Maps. University of Wisconsin Press, Wisconsin (1983)
3. Blackwell, A., Engelhardt, Y.: A meta-taxonomy for diagram research. In: Anderson, M., Meyer, B., Olivier, P. (eds.) Diagrammatic Representation and Reasoning, pp. 47–64. Springer, London (2002). https://doi.org/10.1007/978-1-4471-0109-3_3
4. Blackwell, A.F., et al.: Cognitive dimensions of notations: design tools for cognitive technology. In: Beynon, M., Nehaniv, C.L., Dautenhahn, K. (eds.) CT 2001. LNCS (LNAI), vol. 2117, pp. 325–341. Springer, Heidelberg (2001). https://doi.org/10.1007/3-540-44617-6_31
5. Card, S., MacKinlay, J., Shneiderman, B.: Information visualization. In: Card, S., MacKinlay, J., Shneiderman, B. (eds.) Readings in Information Visualization: Using Vision to Think, pp. 1–34. Lawrence Erlbaum Associates, Mahwah (1999)
6. Cheng, P.C.-H.: Networks of law encoding diagrams for understanding science. Eur. J. Psychol. Educ. **14**(2), 167–184 (1999)

7. Cheng, P.C.-H.: What constitutes an effective representation? In: Jamnik, M., Uesaka, Y., Elzer Schwartz, S. (eds.) Diagrams 2016. LNCS (LNAI), vol. 9781, pp. 17–31. Springer, Cham (2016). https://doi.org/10.1007/978-3-319-42333-3_2

8. Cheng, P.C.-H., Lowe, R.K., Scaife, M.: Cognitive science approaches to diagrammatic representations. Artif. Intell. Rev. 15(1–2), 79–94 (2001)

9. Cleveland, W.S., McGill, R.: Graphical perception and graphical methods for analyzing scientific data. Science 229, 828–833 (1985)

10. Engelhardt, J.: Language of Graphics. Amsterdam ILLC, University of Amsterdam (2002)

11. Engelhardt, Y., Richards, C.: A framework for analyzing and designing diagrams and graphics. In: Chapman, P., Stapleton, G., Moktefi, A., Perez-Kriz, S., Bellucci, F. (eds.) Diagrams 2018. LNCS (LNAI), vol. 10871, pp. 201–209. Springer, Cham (2018). https://doi.org/10.1007/978-3-319-91376-6_20

12. Ewing, J.A.: The Steam-Engine and Other Heat-Engines, 4th edn. CUP, Cambridge (1926)

13. Gurr, C.A.: On the isomorphism, or lack of it, of representations. In: Marriott, K., Meyer, B. (eds.) Visual Language Theory, pp. 293–306. Springer, New York (1998). https://doi.org/10.1007/978-1-4612-1676-6_10

14. Hegarty, M.: The cognitive science of visual-spatial displays: implications for design. Top. Cogn. Sci. 3, 446–474 (2011)

15. Koedinger, K.R., Anderson, J.R.: Abstract planning and perceptual chunks: elements of expertise in geometry. Cogn. Sci. 14, 511–550 (1990)

16. Larkin, J.H., Simon, H.A.: Why a diagram is (sometimes) worth ten thousand words. Cogn. Sci. 11, 65–99 (1987)

17. Lohse, G.L.: A cognitive model for understanding graphical perception. Hum.-Comput. Interact. 8, 353–388 (1993)

18. Lohse, G., Biolsi, K., Walker, N., Rueter, H.: A classification of visual representations. Commun. ACM 37(12), 36–49 (1994)

19. Markman, A.B.: Knowledge Representation. Lawrence Erlbaum, Mahwah (1999)

20. Marriott, K., Meyer, B., Wittenburg, K.B.: A survey of visual language specification and recognition. In: Marriott, K., Meyer, B. (eds.) Visual Language Theory, pp. 5–86. Springer, New York (1998). https://doi.org/10.1007/978-1-4612-1676-6_2

21. Moody, D.L.: The "physics" of notations: toward a scientific basis for constructing visual notations in software engineering. IEEE Trans. Softw. Eng. 35(6), 756–779 (2009)

22. Palmer, S.E.: Fundamental aspects of cognitive representation. In: Rosch, E., Lloyd, B.B. (eds.) Cognition and Catergorization, pp. 259–303. Erlbaum, Hillsdale (1978)

23. Peebles, D.J., Cheng, P.C.-H.: Modelling the effect of task and graphical representations on response latencies in a graph-reading task. Hum. Factors 45(1), 28–45 (2003)

24. Raggi, D., Stockdill, A., Jamnik, M., Garcia Garcia, G., Sutherland, Holly E.A., Cheng, P.C.-H.: Inspection and selection of representations. In: Kaliszyk, C., Brady, E., Kohlhase, A., Sacerdoti Coen, C. (eds.) CICM 2019. LNCS (LNAI), vol. 11617, pp. 227–242. Springer, Cham (2019). https://doi.org/10.1007/978-3-030-23250-4_16

25. Rogers, G.F.C., Mayhew, Y.R.: Engineering Thermodynamics, 4th edn. Longman, Harlow (1992)

26. Schank, R.C., Abelson, R.P.: Scripts, Plans, Goals, and Understanding: An Enquiry into Human Knowledge Structures. Erlbaum, Mahwah (1977)

27. Shimojima, A.: Semantic Properties of Diagrams and Their Cognitive Potentials. CSLI Press, Stanford (2015)

28. Shimojima, A., Barker-Plummer, D.: Operations on single feature indicator systems. In: Chapman, P., Stapleton, G., Moktefi, A., Perez-Kriz, S., Bellucci, F. (eds.) Diagrams 2018. LNCS (LNAI), vol. 10871, pp. 296–312. Springer, Cham (2018). https://doi.org/10.1007/978-3-319-91376-6_28

29. Simkin, D., Hastie, R.: An information-processing analysis of graph perception. J. Am. Stat. Assoc. **82**(398), 454–645 (1987)
30. Stenning, K., Oberlander, J.: A cognitive theory of graphical and linguistic reasoning: logic and implementation. Cogn. Sci. **19**(1), 97–140 (1995)
31. Stevens, S.S.: On the theory of scales of measurement. Science **103**(2684), 677–680 (1946)
32. Zhang, J.: A representational analysis of relational information displays. Int. J. Hum Comput Stud. **45**, 59–74 (1996)
33. Zhang, J., Norman, D.A.: A cognitive taxonomy of numeration systems. In: Polson, M. (ed.) Proceedings of the Fifteenth Annual Conference of the Cognitive Science Society, pp. 1098–1103. Lawrence Erlbaum, Hillsdale (1993)

Modality and Uncertainty in Data Visualizations: A Corpus Approach to the Use of Connecting Lines

Verena Elisabeth Lechner$^{(\boxtimes)}$ iD

University of Agder, 4630 Kristiansand, Norway
verena.lechner@uia.no

Abstract. In data visualizations, connecting lines may have various semiotic functions, including the semiotic potential of indicating modality and uncertainty. The goal of this article is to find out how this semiotic potential is realized in current best practices of data visualizations and what conventions exist for the visual manifestations of these functions. This issue is addressed by using a corpus-based approach and a two-level analysis method within a social semiotic framework. First, the article offers a theoretical discussion on how the concepts of modality and uncertainty interrelate. Second, a method for investigating how these concepts are visualized at different levels is presented. Third, a corpus analysis including 163 award-winning data visualizations is presented. The results indicate the existence of certain conventions for visual modality markers, and thus offer new insights relevant for both design theory and practice.

Keywords: Uncertainty · Modality · Social semiotics · Visual variables · Line · Connection · Reliability · Probability

1 Introduction

Data visualization (further abbreviated as *DV*) is a rapidly developing visual means of communication, strongly influenced by the advent of new digital technologies [1]. The amount of accessible data is greater than ever [2] and the forms of representation are constantly being developed further [3]. Consequently, the desire to express a variety of meanings through DV is increasing, and so are the graphical opportunities to do it. Such 'new modes of production bring with them new affordances' [4], which means that the conventions that connect visual expressions to culturally shared meanings are constantly under development. A specific graphical element, namely the line that is used to connect two entities (further referred to as *connecting line*), appears in many different

---

[1] The Peutinger Map, known as the first route map (366-225 BC) [3] and a multiple time-series graph showing planetary movements over time (10th century) [5] are historic visualizations that use connecting lines as their central graphical element.

This work was supported by the Research Council of Norway under Grant number 259536.

A.-V. Pietarinen et al. (Eds.): Diagrams 2020, LNAI 12169, pp. 110–127, 2020.
https://doi.org/10.1007/978-3-030-54249-8_9

visualization types (such as line charts, network diagrams, route maps etc.) and not just since the digital age.[1] However, the possibilities to signify specific meanings with such connecting lines have increased, because the application of transparency, interaction effects, animations etc., has become much easier in the digital era.

In the practice field of DV, *uncertainty* is a much-disputed topic[2]. One reason for that is that many big and complex datasets available today include elements of uncertainty related to confidence, variability, trends etc. [2]. The consequence for DV designers (here used as a collective term for all persons included in the DV production process) is that they have to find ways to visualize this uncertainty. Especially when designing visualizations for lay audiences, depicting uncertainty still remains a challenge, so big that it sometimes is not visualized at all [10].

Modality, as investigated by linguists and semioticians in verbal and visual text, is a concept that to some extent overlaps with uncertainty, as it is discussed in the practice field of DV. However, modality has not been brought into that field so far.

In the following, I will present the different perspectives on modality, both from a functional grammar point of view [following 11] and from a multimodality point of view [following 4 and 12] and relate the concept of modality to the concept of uncertainty. This is done because the linguistic concept of modality is very elaborated, and it is a hypothesis underlying this study, that it is relevant and useful also in the investigation of DVs. Following this theoretical trajectory, a two-level analysis method of modality and uncertainty in DVs will be presented.

This method is applied in the second, analytical part of the article. A corpus analysis of 163 award-winning DVs that include connecting lines, is presented. The focus of analysis is whether and how modality and uncertainty are expressed through connecting lines. Summing up, this article aims for three goals: (1) to clarify the relation between the concepts of modality and uncertainty in the field of DV, (2) to present a two-level method of analysis of modality and uncertainty in this text type, (3) to reveal graphical variations and conventions concerning the expression of modality and uncertainty through connecting lines within a corpus of award-winning DVs.

Corpus-based studies on current digital DVs in general and particularly those focusing on single graphical elements are still rare. Possible reasons for that may be the low availability of ready-to-use corpora and that the methods for accurately and time-effectively analyse such material are still at beginning stages [13–15].

2 Theoretical Perspectives on Modality and Uncertainty

2.1 Modality in Verbal Language

As a discussion capturing the breadth of works around the concept of modality is well outside the scope of this article I shall here only briefly introduce the work of the linguist Michael Halliday, who extended the system of modality with several aspects [16] relevant in this context.

---

[2] This can be stated because uncertainty was subject to many presentations at the IEEE Vis conference 2018 and 2019 [6, 7] as well as by the large number of publications published lately [additionally to the ones already cited in this article [e.g.: 8, 9].

Halliday sees modality as 'the speaker's judgement, or request of the judgement of the listener, on the status of what is being said' [11]. Modality 'construe[s] the region of uncertainty that lies between "yes" and "no"' [11] and is therefore an 'expression of indeterminacy' [11]. His system of modality – as applied on the clause level – includes four variables: the 'modality type', 'value', 'polarity' and 'orientation' [11]. I will further go deeper into the first two of these variables. The *modality type* 'modalization' [11] is most relevant in the context of DVs because it counts clauses that indicate some degree of a proposition's probability or usuality. Indications of probability, verbally expressed, for example, with adverbs (modal disjuncts) like *certainly, probably* or *possibly,* play an important role in some DVs, where an element of uncertainty is aimed to be communicated. They express a high, median and low *modality value*, respectively, which are the three modal judgement options suggested by Halliday [11]. Demonstrated with an example of Halliday [11]: *It certainly is* expresses a higher probability of this proposition than *It possibly is,* but both lie in between *It is* and *It isn't.*

2.2   Modality in Visual Material

As seen above, Halliday looked at the ways in which single words or word groups can express different degrees of probability. When it comes to modality in visual material, Gunther Kress and Theo van Leeuwen have borrowed the basic concepts from Halliday's functional grammar [12, 16]. The different levels of modality (modality value) are defined on scales of modality markers, such as colour saturation [12]. What constitutes a modality marker and where exactly on the scale the highest or lowest modality value is determined, is dependent on the 'coding orientation' [12]. Coding orientation, as Kress and Van Leeuwen further explain, refers to what counts as real in different social practices. Four types are named: the 'technological', 'sensory', 'abstract' and 'naturalistic coding orientation' [12].

In contexts where the semiotic content is a 'general pattern' or a 'deeper "essence" of what it depicts' [16] (as it often is in DVs), an abstract coding orientation will be applied. In such cases, semiotic reduction is crucial. This means a DV is valued as realistic if the most 'reduced articulation' [16] possible is used. A photo, on the other hand, is, according to Van Leeuwen [16], judged realistic if the colours, the articulation of depth, light and shadow, detail and background etc. are natural. Thus, a naturalistic coding orientation is applied.

By introducing the concept of coding orientation to different types of visual material, the issue of the 'construal and evaluation of the reliability of messages' [4] is focused. This constitutes a different aspect of a statement than probability. Thus, expressions of probability (*it will probably rain tomorrow*) and reliability (*you can believe me when I say that it will rain tomorrow*) have to be considered separately. However, especially in the context of statements realized by DVs, expressions of probability and reliability may be combined (*you can believe me when I say that it will probably rain tomorrow*). Moreover, it should be noted that the exemplary visual analyses carried out by Kress and Van Leeuwen regard the visual representation mainly as a whole [17] and therefore evaluate whether it, in its entirety, represents the 'given "proposition" (…) as true or not' [12]. In contrast to that, Halliday [11] looks at modality expressions on the clause level which means that the modality value of single sentences within a verbal text can vary.

2.3 Relating Modality Theory to the Analysis of Data Visualizations

As Halliday's statement that modality 'construe[s] the region of uncertainty that lies between "yes" and "no"' [11] implies, modality and uncertainty are intertwined. However, uncertainty is not only a research object for linguists and semioticians, but also widely disputed within the practice field of DV. Uncertainty is in that context related to different stages of the DV communication process. As a basis for the production of a DV, the designer has collected data about an aspect of the world that is either certain or uncertain. If the data is uncertain, this is what Dasgupta et al. [18] call data uncertainty. Data uncertainty may be caused by several reasons, like measurement imprecision, incompleteness of data (including missing values, sampling, aggregation), inference (including predictions, modeling and describing past events), disagreement and data incredibility [19].

During the design phase, the designer must decide what level of certainty that is most expedient to signal. The designer can decide to signal a high or low level of probability and reliability – or not to signal modality at all. After that decision, visual techniques for intendedly signalling a certain level of probability and reliability are chosen and applied by the designer. The results can be seen as visual expressions of modality. In most cases, what Dasgupta et al. [18] call *visual uncertainty* correlates with an intention to express a lowered level of probability (based on *data uncertainty*) or reliability. But it can also be a result of an unintended or unconscious application of visual forms that by convention or by earlier experience are associated with uncertainty by readers.

Summing up, *uncertainty* is a wider concept than *modality*, because it includes all factors causing uncertainty on the side of the reader, whether or not intended by the producer. In the present study, I am only interested in the visual expressions of modality that relate to lowered probability or reliability.

This comparative discussion of uncertainty (as discussed in the practice field of DV) and modality (as discussed by linguists and semioticians) allows for applying a more nuanced vocabulary when talking about uncertainty in DVs. It also allows for developing a detailed analysis method of modality in DVs, as presented below. The method is designed to answer the following research questions:

- How is lowered probability and reliability expressed by connecting lines in a corpus of award-winning, digital DVs?
- Does the corpus indicate any clear conventions concerning this issue?

3 A Two-Level Analysis Approach to Modality in Data Visualizations

3.1 Visual Segmentation

I will in the following propose a two-level approach to the investigation of modality in DVs. The two levels, further called *detail* and *global level*, refer to what parts of the DV that are in focus. How this visual segmentation is done, is inspired by Morten Boeriis' [17] dynamic functional rank scale. In *Tekstzoom* [17] he claims that a visual text can have several modality profiles on different text levels, and differentiates between four different text levels. For analysing modality in DVs, I propose that distinguishing between two zoom levels is sufficient.

At the detail level, only single graphical elements, like single lines or points, and the associated words, are considered (see right part of Fig. 1). This unit is comparable to a verbal sentence, as a part of a whole text. Here, we are interested in how these graphical elements – together with associated words – signal a certain level of probability and reliability, related to the detail statement they represent.

At the global level, the whole visualization (which may be integrated into a larger multimodal text including more verbal text or other visualizations) is focused (see left, the black part of Fig. 1). The pertinent question on this level is whether and how the choice of visual style signals that the visualization is a true reflection of an aspect of the world or not. The issue of coding orientation is here central, considering e.g. the effect that a hand drawing might have, compared to a digitally produced DV, regarding reliability. However, it may also be possible to find verbal hints of data uncertainty (expressing lowered probability) that concern not only the detail statement, but also the global statement of the whole DV. These verbal hints may be found within the global level, or in the surrounding co-text, as it might exist e.g. in a news article (see the grey area in Fig. 1).

Such a separation into two text levels allows for the investigation of whether and how single graphical elements, as well as the visual style of the whole visualization, signal modality.

Although this study focuses on the detail level, due to the connecting line constituting the study object, it is important to understand this model as a holistic concept. Boeriis claims that the overall modality of a text is a product of all modality profiles on all levels [17]. In other words, modality expressions on different text levels influence each other. However, how exactly this influence takes place and what effect it has on the overall modality profile is not a focused issue in this study.

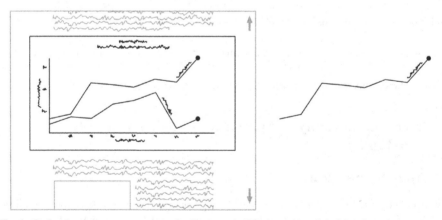

Fig. 1. Left: abstract representation of a line graph (black part = global level) and the co-text (grey) within a website; Right: only the detail level.

3.2 Operationalizing the Theory

Based on the two proposed levels for the DV analysis, Table 1 introduces concrete questions for an analysis of modality in DVs as well as the answer options. It should be understood as an extensible method offer, that may be adjusted to fit also analyses of other semiotic material or other research foci.

Table 1. Questions and answer options for an analysis of modality in DVs.

Nr.	Question	Answer options
Questions on the detail level:		
1	Only focus on the graphical elements that convey the main statement of the DV. If there are more of the same kind, decide for one exemplary unit, comparable to a clause. How could this clause be formulated?	Verbal statement
2	What kind of graphical element(s) represent(s) this statement?	Description of the visual element(s)
3	Which coding orientation needs to be applied when viewing this/these visual element(s)?	Abstract-, naturalistic-, technological-, sensory coding orientation [16] or none of these
4	What do(es) the graphical element(s) look like?	Description of the visual appearance of the visual element(s) in focus, see Table 2
5	Does the visual appearance of the graphical element(s) indicate any form of modality in terms of lowered probability or lowered reliability?	Yes or no
6	If yes, how is this lowered probability and/or lowered reliability signalled visually?	Description of the visual variables used
7	Is it explicitly verbally stated on detail or on global level of the DV, or in the co-text, that data uncertainty is represented within this detail statement of the DV?	Yes or no
8	If it is explicitly verbally stated that data uncertainty is represented, how?	Concrete formulation
9	Based on the former questions, do(es) the graphical element(s), signal modality in terms of lowered reliability?	Yes or no

(continued)

Table 1. (*continued*)

Nr.	Question	Answer options
10	Does the verbal sentence from question 1 need a reformulation, considering modality in terms of lowered probability and reliability, if any of them are expressed? If yes, which?	Verbal statement

Questions on the global level:

Nr.	Question	Answer options
11	What is the overall statement of this DV?	Verbal statement
12	Which coding orientation needs to be applied to the visual expression of the overall statement?	Abstract-, naturalistic-, technological-, sensory coding orientation [16] or none of these
13	Does the choice of visual style signal any sense of modality in terms of lowered reliability?	Yes or no
14	If yes, which modality value is signalled?	High, medium or low modality value
15	If yes, how does it signal a high, medium or low modality value?	Description of the visual clues that underly this decision [based on the descriptions of the coding orientations of 16]
16	Is it explicitly verbally stated on the detail or global level of the DV, or in the co-text, that data uncertainty is represented in the overall statement of the DV?	Yes or no
17	If it is explicitly verbally stated that data uncertainty is represented, how?	Verbal statement

Note. The verbal statements that are the answers to questions 1, 10, and 11 are only meant to serve as proposals. Visual language cannot be directly translated to verbal language or the other way around [12, 20]. However, the formulation of these sentences is considered helpful for investigating the semiotic potentials.

3.3 Description of the Visual Appearance of Connecting Lines

In Table 2, I suggest a set of visual variables and manifestation categories that can be used when focusing on connecting lines on a detail level. They are based on the system of 'visual variables' suggested by Jacques Bertin [21], as well as other scholars [22–27], who developed Bertin's visual variables further or contributed to a nuanced description of the visual appearance of lines. Figure 2 shows some visual examples to each visual variable of Table 2.

Table 2. The visual variables a line can have, and a suggestion of manifestation categories.

Nr.	Variable	Manifestation categories					
1	Position	Left out because dependent on DV specifications like scales, dimension of the DV, screen and window					
2	Orientation						
3	Size						
4	Colour	No variation (single - coloured)		Abrupt variation		Smooth transition	
5	Clarity: crispness	High			Lowered		
6	Clarity: transparency	None			Low, medium or high		
7	Clarity: resolution	High			Lowered		
8	Pattern	Continuous line	Dashed /dotted line	Irregularly dashed/ dotted line	Change between continuous line and dashe / dotted line	Change between continuous line and large interruptions(s)	Change between continuous line, dashed/dotted line and large interruption(s)
9	Shape: forces	One force (straight)	Two forces, curved	Two forces, bent		Three or more forces, curved	Three or more forces, bent
10	Shape: line pressure	Consistent			Inconsistent		
11	Shape: form of extremities	No and direction-signifying extremity			Direction-signifying extremity (like e.g., an arrowhead)		
12	Interaction	Not possible			Possible		
13	Dynamics	Not available			Available, in one or more other visual variables (1-12)		

3.4 How to Identify Visual Indications of Lowered Probability and Reliability

Based on existing literature, we can assume there are three ways to identify visual indications of lowered probability and reliability in DVs. First, some visualization types are specifically developed to represent data uncertainty. Second, users may judge a visual element as an indication of uncertainty based on an analogy to the 'experiential world' [12]. Third, the user judgement may be based on criteria for what is real in the coding orientation applied.

Within the field of statistics, error bars and several newer visualization types, like gradient plots, violin plots or fan plots, are designed for indicating data uncertainty [28]. Also other visualization types can express data uncertainty, as is the case e.g. in various kinds of weather forecasts (see Hullman et al. [29] for other examples). However, in this study, focusing on the semiotic functions of connecting lines, it is most relevant to consider ways to identify signals of lowered probability and reliability on the detail level.

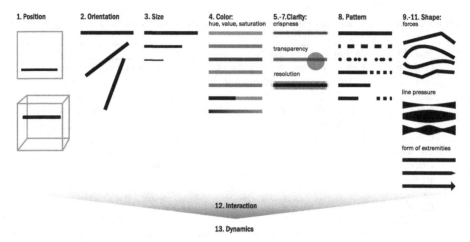

Fig. 2. Some examples to each of the visual variables from Table 2.

A first hint of potentially signalled lowered probability or reliability (referring to question 5 of Table 1) can be found when the line in focus resembles directly or metaphorically what the uncertainty indicates [30]. Analogies to our 'experiential world' [12] can be the reason why certain characteristics intuitively are interpreted as signs of uncertainty. The *sketchiness* of hand-drawn lines may metaphorically signal uncertainty [30], as well as the visual degradation of the line (through blur), since 'the harder it is to see ..., the more uncertain it appears' [31]. Thus, blurry, sketchy, animated lines or lines with a pattern that leads to interruption (e.g., dashed lines) and lines with certain colour characteristics (e.g., low saturation) can indicate uncertainty [30, 31]. Also, if the visual appearance of the line changes along the length, this may be a hint of an indication of uncertainty. To an analyst, these aspects have to be considered, together with the coding orientation in use.

Given that one needs to apply an abstract coding orientation when analysing a line in a DV, the question to ask is: Is this the most 'reduced articulation' to represent the 'general pattern' or 'the deeper "essence" of what it depicts' [16] or not? Depending on the DV type and context, a line with the characteristics of the 3rd column of Table 2 (a straight, single-coloured, continuous, non-transparent etc. line) is counted as using the most reduced articulation. Whenever a more elaborated visual appearance is used, and other reasons behind this specific visual appearance can be ruled out, the line visually signals lowered probability or reliability. Such reasons can be: a) the intention to differentiate between different categories by different kinds of lines (as seen in Fig. 7); b) the intention to create a certain aesthetic effect, or c) the technical production tools favouring that kind of visual appearance.

In order to differentiate between signalled lowered probability and lowered reliability, it is often helpful to observe clues in the verbal text. If the visually depicted modality represents data uncertainty (and therefore lowered probability), the visual signal will normally be accompanied by explicit verbal clues (e.g., *forecast, scenario, 95% confidence*). If that is not the case, and yet, the line visually signals some kind of modality, the analyst can conclude that the line signals lowered reliability. This conclusion can be based on the existence of 'intermodal tension' [32], i.e. that the verbal and the visual modes offer different, incompatible information. Engebretsen also states, that the conventions within 'genres focusing on informativity and fact-oriented learning ... points [sic] toward a rhetoric of clarity and unambiguousness' [32]. Thus, unclarity and polysemy within visualizations have a negative impact on the reliability. In practical analysis, it can be difficult to judge whether incidents of such tension represent an intended use of modality or an unintended visual uncertainty expression.

4 Corpus Analysis

4.1 Data Selection and Database Setup

The method suggested in the previous section was applied to a corpus of 163 DVs. Due to the focus on the connecting line in this study, only the detail level was included in the analysis. The DVs were collected from the winner lists of the 2015, 2016 and 2017 Kantar Information is Beautiful Awards[3] [33] and the Malofiej Awards number 24, 25 and 26[4] [34]. All DVs but one were targeted to the general public and were published in online news media or other channels of public information. All winners with publicly available digital DVs (at the date of data collection) that contained one or more central DVs with one or more connecting line(s) in the leading role of communicating the DV's meaning were selected. The result of this filtering process was 163 single DVs stemming from 105 award-winning websites[5]. To establish a stable data basis for the analysis, over 400 screenshots, PDF documents and screencasts were created and organized in a relational database.

Due to the nature of the World Wide Web, it is impossible to claim that this corpus is a representative sample of the whole population of DVs with the characteristics mentioned above. Thus, the results of this analysis can by no means be used to generate valid statements about the whole population. However, this corpus contains a broad variety of DVs produced during the named timeframe in the western world, and the results of the research based on this material can be seen as a good approximation of how DVs in these countries have been developed in this specific time frame. Moreover, such awards raise publicity, and these DVs are judged by experts as 'best practices' and viewed by a broad audience, including practicioners. Therefore, they are expected to serve as models and to have strong convention forming abilities.

4.2 Method

Each DV was coded according to the method proposed in Section *A two-level analysis approach to modality in data visualizations*, using a detailed coding scheme. The detailed coding scheme contained the same questions and answer options as those in Table 1, with a description of criteria for choosing each option. Before that, an inter-rater reliability

---

[3] This includes projects created between May 2014 and September 2017.

[4] These projects were published between 2015 and 2017.

[5] A full list of all included DVs, the coding instructions and results of the inter-rater reliability study and the final coding scheme can be requested from the author.

study of a random sample of 25 DVs (approx. 15% of the corpus) was performed for the questions that contain judgement variables. This was necessary in order to 'estimate how reliable the categorisation (coding) is' [35], and therefore make sure that the stated questions and offered answer categories are precise and adequate. Two coders (a second coder and me) used the same coding instructions and worked independently. With the answers of both coders, Gwet's AC_1 and Gwet's AC_2 coefficient [36] were calculated. Results showed that for all questions, the coders had either substantial agreement or higher when analysed according to Gwet's benchmarking method [36][6]. This amount of agreement was deemed sufficient and the coding method was generally approved.

However, follow-up discussions between the two raters after the pre-test and also during the start of the single-coded analysis revealed that a few small adjustments of the coding scheme would still improve the rating process. Following an iterative method, these changes were made, resulting in the final coding scheme, that was then applied to the whole corpus. In instances of doubt, the second rater of the inter-rater reliability test was contacted to discuss the final codings. The (single-coded) analysis of the whole corpus then made it possible to generate frequency counts of whether and how modality is signalled in this corpus with connecting lines.

4.3   Analysis Findings

This section presents the results of the analysis on the detail level, using question 1 to 10 in Table 1. Due to the selection criteria for this corpus, the main statement in each DV is represented through graphical lines. For each DV, only one line is focused in the analysis. For all except two of the 163 lines in focus, an abstract coding orientation needs to be applied. For the final two, a naturalistic coding orientation is the most suitable.

As shown in Fig. 3, the connecting line in the focus of 26 (18 + 8) DVs out of 163 are found to indicate modality (lowered probability or lowered reliability). Within 33 (15 + 18) DVs, it is explicitly stated verbally that data uncertainty is represented within the detail statement represented through the focused connecting line. However, in only 18 DVs modality is signalled *both* visually through the connecting line in focus *and* through a corresponding verbal clue for data uncertainty. These 18 lines are therefore considered to signal lowered probability, while the reliability is not reduced. Under the earlier presented assumption that intermodal tension causes lowered reliability, this means that, on the detail level, the focused lines of 23 DVs (8 + 15) are found to be included in an instance of lowered reliability.

68% of the 41 DVs that verbally and/or visually signal modality on the detail level, are either route maps (41%) or line graphs (27%). The high occurrence of these two DV types also reflects the fact that these two types are the most common ones in this corpus (36% route maps, 23% line graphs).

I will now look at what visual variables of the connecting lines signal what kind of modality. When the lines in focus signal lowered probability (based on data uncertainty), different manifestation categories of the visual variable pattern were the most commonly used – especially those with pattern changes (see column three Table 3).

---

[6] The benchmarking method proposed in Gwet (2014: 173–181) was complemented by information given by Gwet in personal mail correspondence on 9–17 July 2019.

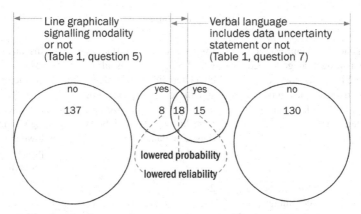

Fig. 3. Distribution of visually and/or verbally signalled modality.

Changes between a continuous line and large interruption(s) and between a continuous line and a dashed/dotted line are used 6 and 5 times respectively. Figure 4 presents an example of the latter. However, also other visual characteristics, namely transparency, lowered crispness, colour variations, inconsistent line pressure, three or more forces (curved) or dynamics in the size are used for that purpose.

Table 3. Distribution of visual characteristics of connecting lines used to signal modality (lowered probability and reliability) and the distribution of the same characteristics being used for other purposes. Note that in some DVs, several visual characteristics are used simultaneously to signal modality. N for each line in this table is 163 connecting lines from 163 DVs.

Visual variable used for signalling either lowered probability (data uncertainty) or reliability (answer to question 6 of Table 1)	Manifestation category used (answer to question 4 of Table 1)	Instances of visual characteristics signalling lowered probability (based on data uncertainty)	Instances of visual characteristics signalling lowered reliability	Instances of visual characteristics used for other purposes than signalling lowered probability or reliability
Pattern	Change between continuous line and dashed/dotted line	5	2	4
Pattern	Change between continuous line and large interruptions(s)	6	–	4

(*continued*)

Table 3. (*continued*)

Visual variable used for signalling either lowered probability (data uncertainty) or reliability (answer to question 6 of Table 1)	Manifestation category used (answer to question 4 of Table 1)	Instances of visual characteristics signalling lowered probability (based on data uncertainty)	Instances of visual characteristics signalling lowered reliability	Instances of visual characteristics used for other purposes than signalling lowered probability or reliability
Pattern	Change between continuous line, dashed/dotted line and large interruption(s)	2	–	–
Pattern	Dashed/dotted line	2	–	9
Pattern	Irregularly dashed/dotted line	–	1	4
Clarity: transparency	Low, medium or high	3	1	35
Clarity: crispness	Lowered	1	–	–
Colour	Abrupt variation	2	–	8
Colour	Smooth transition	1	–	15
Shape: forces	Two forces, curved	–	2	18
Shape: forces	Three or more forces, curved	1	1	47
Shape: line pressure	Inconsistent	3	–	13
Dynamics in size	Yes	1	1	50
Dynamics in orientation	Yes	–	1	16
Dynamics in position	Yes	–	1	15

When we look at how lowered reliability is signalled by the focused connecting lines (see column four Table 3), the results reveal that the visual variable *pattern* does not have such a prominent role. The pattern and the curviness of the lines signal lowered reliability three times. However, dynamics (in size, orientation and position) and transparency are also found once each.

An example of a visualization where curvature signals lowered reliability can be found in *An interactive visualization of every line in Hamilton* [38, see Fig. 5]. Here, the

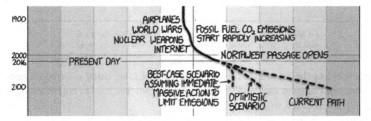

Fig. 4. Screenshot from *A timeline of earth's average temperature*, indicating data uncertainty by pattern change to a dashed line. © Randall Munroe [37]. Distributed under CC BY-NC 2.5.

semiotic motivation behind some connecting lines being curved, while others are straight, is not clear. Because the DV does not use the most reduced articulation possible (while applying an abstract coding orientation), it is rated as expressing lowered reliability.

As shown in Table 3, most of the visual characteristics of lines used to express modality, are not used exclusively for that purpose. Column five shows how many times the visual characteristics highlighted in column three and four are used for other purposes. For instance, in the visualization *The Stories Behind a Line* [39], different categories of transport means are visualized through different dashed/dotted lines (see Fig. 7). Another example of dashed lines not signalling modality is found in *Syrian war explained in 5 min* [40: 5:00, see Fig. 6]. Here, the animated dashes iconically represent moving bombs.

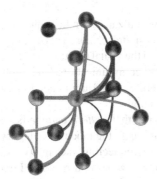

Fig. 5. Screenshot from *An interactive visualization of every line in Hamilton*, where curvature indicates lowered reliability. © Shirley Wu [38]. Reproduced with permission. Photos are blurred for copyright reasons.

Fig. 6. Abstract representation of a film frame of *Syrian war explained in 5 min* [40: 5:00]. The dashes move towards the square field named 'rebels', iconically representing moving bombs.

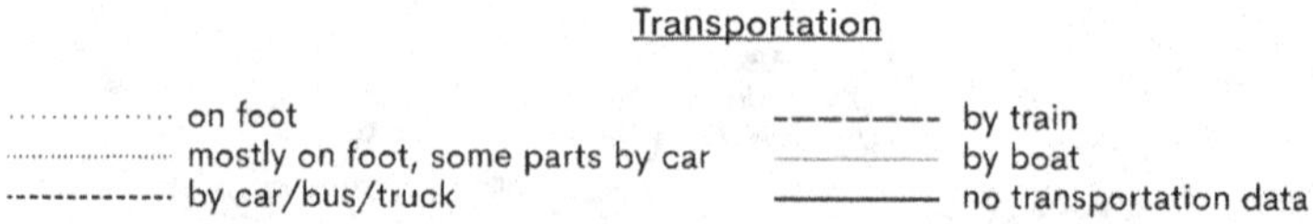

<u>Transportation</u>

············· on foot	‒‒‒‒‒‒‒ by train
················· mostly on foot, some parts by car	‒‒‒‒‒‒ by boat
············ by car/bus/truck	———— no transportation data

Fig. 7. Screenshot of the legend of *The Stories Behind a Line*, using interrupted lines for different categories of transport means. © Federica Fragapane, designed in collaboration with Alex Piacentini [39]. Reproduced with permission.

4.4 Limitations of the Results

Because most of the DVs were only single-coded and some questions contain judgement variables, it has to be kept in mind that my cultural background and previous knowledge might have influenced the interpretation. To counter this, the coding instructions were developed as detailed as possible, strictly followed and the inter-rater reliability study was performed.

Moreover, since only one connecting line was focused on the detail level of each DV, even if sometimes one DV contained more connecting lines, it is possible that the results could have changed if I had chosen to focus on other lines. Therefore, I have been careful when reporting these numbers, to refer only to the connecting lines 'in focus', not to all connecting lines in the material.

4.5 Implications and Conclusion

Within this corpus of 163 DVs, out of the 41 visualizations indicating some kind of modality on the detail level, 23 exhibit cases of intermodal tension. This number indicates that intermodal tension, meaning that the verbal and the visual resources offer conflicting signals, is fairly common in this field of DV-based communication. One implication of this finding is that the potential for DV designers to avoid unintended ambiguity by giving more attention to multimodal coherence is high.

The results further indicate a convention saying that *pattern change* is well suited for visually signalling data uncertainty, corresponding to the modality category *lowered probability*. Why pattern change – in the shaping of connecting lines in DVs – is emerging as a conventionalized signal of modality, may have several reasons. First, it must be assumed that pattern change potentially signals modality based on an analogy to the 'experiential world' [12]. Furthermore, the use of patterns, or larger interruptions, is not expected as a typical line form in any DV type (unlike e.g. curvature, which is common in spline graphs for instance), thus such characteristics are free to use as modality markers. Moreover, it is technically easy with most design tools to apply different patterns to a graphical line (unlike e.g. dynamics). Last, patterns are possible to use also in two-coloured DVs, and they are printable and drawable analogously, which points to a long application history. For signalling *lowered reliability*, however, no such convention was traced, as the results show a more varied and unsystematic use of characteristics indicating this kind of modality.

Summing up, the study reveals that various visual characteristics of connecting lines are used to signal modality in this corpus of award-winning DVs. However, *pattern change* is used more often than any of the other variables found in the corpus. Due to the relatively low number of observations in this corpus, it is impossible to provide practitioners with a simple recipe for what visual clues are most effectively applied to signal modality in DVs. Nonetheless, the results provide an overview of the current practices in using lines for indicating modality, which is helpful for practitioners to make informed design decisions.

5 Further Research

In this article, a method for analysing modality in DVs is presented, based on a body of pre-existing theory and terminology around modality and uncertainty. A newly collected corpus of digital DVs is analysed with the suggested method, offering detailed knowledge about how certain visual characteristics of the graphical line are used for signalling modality. The findings indicate certain conventions regarding the semiotic potential of the graphical line in relation to modality. Such insights are valuable both for designers and scholars in relevant fields, as they contribute to the colouring of some of the white spots on the map over a graphical language still in its making. However, more empirical research is needed in order to draw a more detailed and reliable map over the field of multimodal modality. The findings, as well as the methodology presented in this study, will hopefully be a contribution to this future work.

References

1. Kirk, A.: Data Visualization: A Successful Design Process. Packt Publishing, Birmingham (2012)
2. Bonneau, G.-P., et al.: Overview and state-of-the-art of uncertainty visualization. In: Hansen, C.D., Chen, M., Johnson, C.R., Kaufman, A.E., Hagen, H. (eds.) Scientific Visualization. MV, pp. 3–27. Springer, London (2014). https://doi.org/10.1007/978-1-4471-6497-5_1
3. Friendly, M., Denis, D.F.: Timeline. http://www.datavis.ca/milestones. Accessed 12 Feb 2019
4. Ravelli, L.J., Van Leeuwen, T.: Modality in the digital age. Vis. Commun. 17 (2018). https://doi.org/10.1177/1470357218764436
5. Friendly, M.: A brief history of data visualization. In: Chen, C., Härdle, W., Unwin, A. (eds.) Handbook of Data Visualization. SHCS, pp. 15–56. Springer, Heidelberg (2008). https://doi.org/10.1007/978-3-540-33037-0_2
6. IEEE: VIS 2018 program. http://ieeevis.org/attachments/vis18-program.pdf. Accessed 15 Jan 2019
7. IEEE: VIS 2019 program. http://ieeevis.org/year/2019/info/papers-sessions. Accessed 16 Oct 2019
8. Brodlie, K., Allendes Osorio, R., Lopes, A.: A review of uncertainty in data visualization. In: Dill, J., Earnshaw, R., Kasik, D., Vince, J., Wong, P. (eds.) Expanding the Frontiers of Visual Analytics and Visualization, pp. 81–109. Springer, London (2012). https://doi.org/10.1007/978-1-4471-2804-5_6
9. Kinkeldey, C., MacEachren, A.M., Schiewe, J.: How to assess visual communication of uncertainty? A systematic review of geospatial uncertainty visualisation user studies. Cartogr. J. 51, 372–386 (2014). https://doi.org/10.1179/1743277414Y.0000000099
10. Hullman, J.: Why authors don't visualize uncertainty. IEEE TVCG 26, 130–139 (2020). https://doi.org/10.1109/TVCG.2019.2934287

11. Halliday, M.A.K.: An Introduction to Functional Grammar. 3rd edn. Revised by Matthiessen, C.M.I.M. Arnold, London (2004)
12. Kress, G., Van Leeuwen, T.: Reading Images: The Grammar of Visual Design. 2nd edn. Routledge, Abingdon (2006)
13. Bateman, J., McDonald, D., Hiippala, T., Couto-Vale, D., Costetchi, E.: Systemic functional linguistics and computation. New directions, new challenges. In: The Cambridge Handbook of Systemic Functional Linguistics, pp. 561–586. Cambridge University Press (2019)
14. Kembhavi, A., Salvato, M., Kolve, E., Seo, M., Hajishirzi, H., Farhadi, A.: A diagram is worth a dozen images. In: Leibe, B., Matas, J., Sebe, N., Welling, M. (eds.) ECCV 2016. LNCS, vol. 9908, pp. 235–251. Springer, Cham (2016). https://doi.org/10.1007/978-3-319-46493-0_15
15. Hiippala, T., et al.: AI2D-RST: a multimodal corpus of 1000 primary school science diagrams (Forthcoming)
16. Van Leeuwen, T.: Introducing Social Semiotics. Routledge, Abingdon (2005)
17. Boeriis, M.: Tekstzoom - om en dynamisk funktionel rangstruktur i visuelle tekster. In: Hestbæk Andersen, T., Boeriis, M. (eds.) Nordisk socialsemiotik - multimodale, pædagogiske og sprogvidenskabelige landvindinger, pp. 131–153. University Press of Southern Denmark, Odense (2012)
18. Dasgupta, A., Chen, M., Kosara, R.: Conceptualizing visual uncertainty in parallel coordinates. In: Computer Graphics Forum, pp. 1015–1024. Blackwell, Vienna (2012). https://doi.org/10.1111/j.1467-8659.2012.03094.x
19. Skeels, M., Lee, B., Smith, G., Robertson, G.: Revealing uncertainty for information visualization. In: AVI 2008 Proceedings of the Working Conference on Advanced Visual Interfaces, pp. 376–379. ACM, New York (2008). https://doi.org/10.1145/1385569.1385637
20. Saint-Martin, F.: Semiotics of Visual Language. Indiana University Press, Bloomington (1990)
21. Bertin, J.: Semiology of Graphics: Diagrams, Networks, Maps. ESRI Press, Redlands (2011)
22. DiBiase, D., MacEachren, A.M., Krygier, J.B., Reeves, C.: Animation and the role of map design in scientific visualization. Cartogr. Geogr. Inf. Syst. **19**, 201–214 (1992). https://doi.org/10.1559/152304092783721295
23. Kandinsky, W.: Punkt und Linie zu Fläche: Beitrag zur Analyse der malerischen Elemente. Albert Langen, München (1926)
24. MacEachren, A.M.: How Maps Work: Representation, Visualization, and Design. Guilford Press, New York (1995)
25. Saulnier, A.: La perception du mouvement dans les systèmes de visualisation d'informations. In: Proceedings of the 17th Conference on l'Interaction Homme-Machine, pp. 185–192. ACM, Toulouse (2005). https://doi.org/10.1145/1148550.1148574
26. Weger, G.: Cartographie Volume 1: Sémiologie graphique et conception cartographique. École nationale des science géographiques, Marne la Vallée (1999)
27. Wong, W.: Principles of Form and Design. Wiley, New York (1993)
28. Cairo, A.: The Truthful Art: Data, Charts, and Maps for Communication. New Riders, Thousand Oaks (2016)
29. Hullman, J., Qiao, X., Correll, M., Kale, A., Kay, M.: In pursuit of error: a survey of uncertainty visualization evaluation. IEEE TVCG **25**, 903–913 (2018). https://doi.org/10.1109/TVCG.2018.2864889
30. Boukhelifa, N., Bezerianos, A., Isenberg, T., Fekete, J.-D.: Evaluating sketchy lines for the visualization of qualitative uncertainty. Research Centre Saclay - Île-de-France, Le Chesnay Cedex (2012)
31. Tak, S., Toet, A., van Erp, J.: The perception of visual uncertainty representation by non-experts. IEEE TVCG **20**, 935–943 (2014). https://doi.org/10.1109/TVCG.2013.247

32. Engebretsen, M.: Balancing cohesion and tension in multimodal rhetoric. An interdisciplinary approach to the study of semiotic complexity. Learn. Media Technol. **37**, 145–162 (2012). https://doi.org/10.1080/17439884.2012.655745
33. The Information is Beautiful Awards Ltd.: KANTAR Information is Beautiful Awards. https://www.informationisbeautifulawards.com/. Accessed 31 Mar 2018
34. Malofiej Infographic World Summit: Malofiej Infographic World Summit. https://www.malofiejgraphics.com/awards/. Accessed 05 Nov 2018
35. Brezina, V.: Statistical choices in corpus-based discourse analysis. In: Taylor, C., Marchi, A. (eds.) Corpus Approaches to Discourse: A Critical Review, pp. 259–280. Routledge, Abingdon (2018)
36. Gwet, K.L.: Handbook of Inter-rater Reliability: The Definitive Guide to Measuring the Extent of Agreement Among Raters. 4th edn. Advanced Analytics. LLC, Gaithersburg (2014)
37. Munroe, R.: A timeline of earth's average temperature. https://xkcd.com/1732/. Accessed 24 Apr 2018
38. Wu, S.: An interactive visualization of every line in Hamilton. https://pudding.cool/2017/03/hamilton/index.html. Accessed 29 Oct 2019
39. Fragapane, F.: The stories behind a line. A project in collaboration with Alex Piacentini. http://www.storiesbehindaline.com. Accessed 23 July 2019
40. Fisher, M., Harris, J.: Syrian war explained in 5 minutes. https://www.youtube.com/watch?v=qxzMa7j6LN0. Accessed 20 June 2018

Channel-Theoretic Account of the Semantic Potentials of False Diagrams

Atsushi Shimojima[1]($\boxtimes$) and Dave Barker-Plummer[2]

[1] Faculty of Culture and Information Science, Doshisha University,
1-3 Tatara-Miyakodani, Kyotanabe 610-0394, Japan
`ashimoji@mail.doshisha.ac.jp`
[2] CSLI, Stanford University, Cordura Hall, 210 Panama Street,
Stanford, CA 94305, USA
`dbp@stanford.edu`

Abstract. People make mistakes. Whether because lines are misdrawn, data are mistabulated, or because coffee is spilled on documents, diagrammatic representations may not be entirely correct. Yet experience tells that such diagrams are not entirely useless.

In this paper, we describe a semantic theory of representation, which naturally explains the utility of erroneous diagrams. In particular, the theory captures the possibility of obtaining true pieces of information from erroneous representations in a reliable manner.

We identify two dimensions along which there are choices in how to read a representation. In one dimension, we may read only part of the representation, avoiding the erroneous information. We call this *partial reading*. In the other, we focus on abstract properties of the representation, ignoring errors in the precision of the information represented. We call this *abstract reading*. Along either or both dimensions, true information can be obtained from erroneous diagrams.

The theory is based on Barwise and Seligman's channel theory, and captures these different modes of readings in terms of multiple representation systems in which a diagram carries information about its target. On this theory, one and the same diagram can be accurate in one system and inaccurate in others, and the reader switches systems when they read the diagram in different modes.

1 Introduction

Consider bar charts (Fig. 1b–d), which all represent the sales of a particular book in a certain quarter period. For simplicity, let us assume that books are sold by this publisher in lots of 100, with 1000 being the maximum number sold in any month. We will further assume that each 100 books sold is represented by 1 cm of length of the bar. Note that the lengths of bars in Fig. 1b–d are slightly different chart by chart, expressing different sets of data about the sales of the book in this quarter.

© Springer Nature Switzerland AG 2020
A.-V. Pietarinen et al. (Eds.): Diagrams 2020, LNAI 12169, pp. 128–143, 2020.
https://doi.org/10.1007/978-3-030-54249-8_10

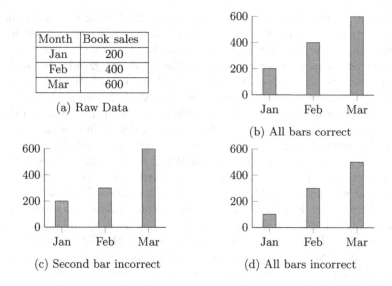

Fig. 1. Correct and incorrect bar charts

Now suppose the actual sales in this period are as shown in Table (Fig. 1a). Then, bar chart Fig. 1b is "true", in the sense that the lengths of all bars are correctly constructed to convey the actual sales amounts in Table (Fig. 1a). Thus, one can obtain a true set of information by interpreting the lengths of these bars according to the pre-defined semantic rules. Reading a true diagram correctly, just like reading a true sentence correctly, one reaches a truth. Call this the "literal way" of reading a diagram.

Interestingly, one can reach a truth by reading a false diagram. Consider bar chart (Fig. 1c). Here, the bar for February is too short, so it is not true in the same sense as Fig. 1c is true, and a literal reading of the chart results in false information. Nevertheless, the lengths of the other two bars are correct, so we could read them to obtain true information about the sales amounts of January and March. With some independent evidence that this chart is reliable about January and March, the failure of the chart with respect to February does not stop us from interpreting the bars for January and March.

There is another way in which one can read off a truth from a false diagram. Consider bar chart (Fig. 1d). This chart has all the bars of incorrect length, they are uniformly too short, and in this respect, every concrete piece of data in the chart is false. Yet, if we are concerned only with sales trends, then we may well read the right-ascending pattern of the bars in this chart to obtain the true information that sales are increasing. The fact that the chart is wrong in the lengths of individual bars does not prevent us from reading off this general trend from chart (Fig. 1d).

Note that this is not a case of the partial reading practice illustrated above. In partial reading, true components of a diagram (e.g., the bars for January and

March) are separable from false components (e.g., the bar for February) and the reader interprets the former to the exclusion of the latter. In contrast, *all* the bars are interpreted in the present case, in spite of the fact that they are all of incorrect length. Yet the abstract information (e.g., the increasing trend) obtained from this false diagram can be true. We call this reading practice "abstract reading".

In this paper, we describe a semantic theory of diagrams that naturally explains these reading practices. As suggested above, there are two major dimensions along which they are classified. There is a partiality dimension: when considering the diagram in its entirety, we are performing a *global* reading, while when considering only part of the diagram it is a *local* reading. There are many different partial readings determined by the particular parts of the complete diagram that are under consideration. In the abstractness dimension, when we consider the absolute lengths of the bars, we are performing a *concrete* reading, and when only the relative lengths of the bars is at issue, we are performing an *abstract* reading. Thus, what we alluded to above as the "literal reading" of a barchart is categorized in this space as a *global, concrete* reading. Our example of a single bar being incorrect illustrates a *local, concrete* reading, while the example in which all bars of incorrect length but trend data is correct would be a *global, abstract* reading. Were we to encounter a bar chart on which a coffee stain obscured the top of the middle bar, we might still be able to conclude that sales in February were at least 300 books. This would be an example of a *local, abstract* reading.

Accounting for these possibilities within a semantic theory is important for at least two reasons. First, they are prevalent. People are engaged in these practices not only with bar charts, but with a wide varieties of diagrams. Even when some dots are placed in wrong positions in a scatter plot, it does not necessarily prevent us from extracting data from other dots (partial reading) nor from reading off the general trend indicated by the overall pattern of the entire dots (abstract reading). Even when a map is not exact with respect to the border between a particular pair of counties, it does not necessarily prevent us from reading off the borders of other pairs of counties (partial reading) nor from reading off the overall spatial arrangement of counties in the region (abstract reading). Even if a subway route map incorrectly connects a particular pair of station symbols, it does not necessarily prevent us from interpreting the connections of other pairs of station symbols (partial reading) nor from estimating the overall connectivity of the subway system (abstract reading). Seemingly non-standard practices of reading off true information from false diagrams are, from this standpoint, quite normal for diagram users.

The second reason why these practices are important is related to this last point. People are repeatedly engaged in these practices. They are not just *ad hoc* tricks that people happen to do and obtain good results by accident. They are measures by which people obtain good results non-accidentally. Otherwise, people would not repeat the processes and they would not have stood out as notable practices. Thus, the information read from false diagrams in these processes are not only possibly true, but must be regularly true. This suggests that the notion of truth, as once and finally applied to a diagram, may be useless for the present purpose. There may be multiple ways in which a diagram can carry information about its target, so that a diagram that is totally inaccurate in one way may serve as a perfectly accurate representation of its target in another channel. As we will see later, no existing semantic theories of diagrams, such as [2, 8, 11], have addressed the general issue of fruitfulness of false diagrams, let alone taking up the above suggestion of multiple channels for a diagram to be evaluated for accuracy.

The semantic theory presented in this paper can incorporate this suggestion quite naturally. It has a notion of *representation systems* that enable different readings of the same diagram. Thus, it accounts for the utility of false diagrams in terms of multiple representation systems in which a diagram may carry information about its target. So, one and the same diagram can be accurate in one system and inaccurate in others, and the reader switches systems when they read the diagram in the literal mode, a partial mode, and an abstract mode.

The notion of representation system in our theory is adopted from Barwise and Seligman's mathematical theory of information channels [1]. Our exposition in this paper is informal and focuses on how that notion is naturally applied in a semantic theory of diagrams (Sect. 2) and how it is productively applied to the understanding of our subject (Sect. 3). We will then specify the merit of our theory in comparison to the related semantic theories of diagrams (Sect. 4). It will turn out that the full explanation of the utility of false diagrams requires a semantic theory, such as ours, founded on the notion of reliability rather than that of truth.

2   General View of Representations

In this section, we present our general view of how a system of representations emerges and how information comes to be carried by a representation in the system. We owe this view largely to Barwise and Seligman's theory of representations [1], coupled with Millikan's theory of reproduction [5]. Some materials in this section originated in a previous paper of ours [9], where we described Barwise and Seligman's theory in more detail.

2.1   Issues

In our view, the use of a diagram involves a set of *target issues* either explicitly or implicitly. This set reflects how we want to conceive of the given situation; it determines which portion of the reality we take as our *target*. In the case of the system of bar charts, there are 3 target issues, corresponding to January, February, and March in a given quarter period, which may be written as:

How many copies of the book are sold in January?
How many copies of the book are sold in February?
How many copies of the book are sold in March?

When the target object or situation is conceived with the help of a set of issues, we have the opportunity to design a representation that answers these issues by carrying relevant information. A bar-chart answers them with the lengths of bars. An alpha-numeric table, such as Fig. 1a, answers them with numerals placed in appropriate cells. Thus, different diagrams can be designed for the same set of target issues. We will later see that the converse is also true: different sets of target issues can be answered by a single diagram.

2.2   Representational Acts

Central to our account is the notion of *representational act*. We borrow terminology from Barwise and Seligman [1] and define a representational act as "the particular spatial-temporal process whereby the representation comes to represent what it does" (p. 236). In our running example, a representational act is an act, possibly conducted by the publisher, that consists of collecting relevant information about the book sales in a particular quarter period, editing the information in the form expressible in a chart, and finally physically printing it on a particular sheet of paper.

We can think of the individual tasks of collecting, editing and printing representations as sub-acts of a larger representational act. The assembly and editing of information may be quite onerous (consider for example, physically surveying a location in order to produce a topographical map). Once the information has been marshaled though, many bar chart tokens can be produced from the same information, perhaps by printing on a laser printer.

To see this situation more clearly, let e_1 and e_2 be the sub-acts of information collection and information editing, respectively, and p_1 and p_2 be two sub-acts producing distinct representational tokens. Then, the representational act c_1 is the sequence $e_1 \circ e_2 \circ p_1$ of sub-acts, while the representational act c_2 is the sequence $e_1 \circ e_2 \circ p_2$. Generally, every act p_i of producing a new chart token based on the information collected and edited in e_1 and e_2 gives rise to a new representational act $c_i = e_1 \circ e_2 \circ p_i$.

Conceived in this way, every individual chart-making act c has a unique chart as its product, and a unique quarter period as the object about which information is assembled and edited. We call the former the *representing object* and the latter the *target* of the act c. We often write "s-c-t" to indicate a representational act c having representing object s and target t. Note that even though each act has a unique target, the same target may be the subject of many chart-making acts.

2.3   Reproduction of Representational Acts

Representational acts, like other acts, are often reproduced. Imagine that the first bar chart produced by representational act c_1 has some desirable properties such as being clear, informative, or easy to produce. These characteristics may prompt the publisher to print several copies of the same bar-chart, say for wider circulation. Act c_2 may be one of these reproductions. The publisher may produce similar bar charts again and again to represent the sales of the book in subsequent quarter periods. Or somebody else, say another publisher in the company, may imitate this publisher's practice and start producing similar charts to represent the sales of a different book.

These acts, say $c_1, \ldots, c_7$, make up a characteristic class of objects, which Millikan calls a *reproductively established family*, [5]. This family is defined by the fact that, except for the original act c_1, every member is a reproduction of some other members of the family, where the reproduction process is a more or less conscious effort to produce another act with a particular desirable property.

Remember that each representational act c comes with a unique representing object and a unique target and hence is written as "s-c-t". So, the family consisting of $c_1, \ldots, c_7$ can be depicted as in Fig. 2, where solid arrows show the direct reproduction relation. Different acts can have the same target, as illustrated by $c_1, \ldots, c_4$ all having t_1 to their right. Still, these acts have different representing objects $s_1, \ldots, s_4$ to their left, meaning that different chart tokens are produced by them to represent the same target t_1, perhaps through successive printing.

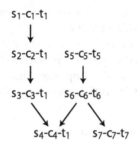

Fig. 2. A family of representational acts that produce bar charts

2.4   Semantic Constraints

As we have indicated, the reproduction of representational acts may be driven by various desirable properties of them. In many cases, however, the most fundamental desirable property is that the representation produced by the act gives accurate answers to the set of target issues that people are concerned with.

In order to have this virtue, an act must be conducted under a certain set of constraints. In the case of bar charts, for example, the actor must be precise in all of the information-collection phase, the information-editing phase, and the final production phase, so that the chart that results contains bars of certain lengths only when the quarter it is concerned with have certain sales amounts for its months. To be specific, it must be conducted so as to satisfy the set of constraints of the following form:

(1) Its representing object has lengths m_1, m_2, and m_3 cm for the first, second, and third bars only if its target has sales amounts $100 \times m_1$, $100 \times m_2$, and $100 \times m_3$ for the first, second, and third months.

For brevity, we write this form of constraints in the following way:

(2) $\langle m_1, m_2, m_3 \rangle \vdash \langle 100 \times m_1, 100 \times m_2, 100 \times m_3 \rangle$

Since m_1, m_2, and m_3 range over integers 0 through 10, this stands for a total of 11^3 constraints.

These constraints are something that every actor in this family of representational acts should try to conform to, since they guarantee that the resulting charts will carry genuine information about the present target issues. Surely, the contents of these constraints are *arbitrary* in their origin—the correspondence of bar lengths and sales amounts did not have to be the multiple of 100 at all. Yet, once people start conforming to these constraints and believe that everybody conforms to them, it provides significant mutual benefit for them to keep conforming to them. They thus become "self-perpetuating" constraints over the representational acts of a group of people. Lewis [4] has developed a general theory of how such a constraint becomes a stabilized character of human conduct.

We call the activities of a group of people producing representations by means of a reproductively established family of acts, a *representational practice*, and we call the set of constraints thus established among a family of representational acts the *semantic constraints* of that practice. The satisfaction of semantic constraints is often one of the most fundamental properties that representational acts in the family should crave to inherit from their predecessors.

2.5   Normality of Representational Acts

It should be clear from the above explanation that semantic constraints on representational acts are more like traffic laws than physical laws. Unlike the absolute limit on faster-than-light travel, it is possible to travel faster than the speed limit. Similarly, actors may fail to respect semantic constraints if the process by which they reproduce representational acts is defective in some way or another. For example, the publisher who successfully produced the accurate bar chart for a certain quarter period may try to repeat the same general process to produce a bar chart for the next quarter, but she may fail to take the necessary care in either the information collection sub-act, the information editing sub-act, or the physical production sub-act. When this happens, the semantic constraints do not necessarily hold of this newly reproduced act. Perhaps, for example, the incorrectness of the bar chart in Fig. 1c is due to incorrect reporting of sales figures by a book store, or that of the chart in Fig. 1d results from the publisher misreading the scale of the chart.

We call a reproductive act *normal* with respect to a set of semantic constraints if its reproductive process constitutes a sufficient cause for it to satisfy them. A reproductive act is called *abnormal* with respect to that set of semantic constraints otherwise. It follows that every normal act satisfies the set of semantic constraints. If the reproduction process of a representational act goes well and sufficient care is taken for all sub-acts, then there is a reason that the reproduced act satisfies those constraints—it satisfies them out of necessity, not just by accident.

It however does not follow that no abnormal act satisfies these constraints. Some abnormal acts may satisfy them by accident. Perhaps the publisher takes insufficient care, is not paying attention to the constraints that they should be trying to maintain, but nonetheless draws a chart with bar lengths $\langle 2, 5, 8 \rangle$ for a target quarter period that has sales of $\langle 200, 500, 800 \rangle$. The act satisfies the constraints by accident, not out of necessity. Such an act would be considered abnormal in our theory.

2.6   Representation Systems

Given three things: a reproductively established family A of representational acts, a set $\vdash$ of semantic constraints on it, and a set N of normal acts relative to this set of semantic constraints, we can determine the information flow from representations and targets.

Take our running example of bar charts. Let c be a member of the reproductive family of those bar charts. The set of semantic constraints on this family is given in (2), and suppose c is normal with respect to this set. Suppose further that the lengths of bars in c's representing object are $\langle 2, 4, 6 \rangle$, as in the bar chart in Fig. 1b. Since c is normal with respect to (2), constraint $\langle 2, 4, 6 \rangle \vdash \langle 200, 400, 600 \rangle$ holds of c. As a consequence, c's target has property $\langle 200, 400, 600 \rangle$, that is, the represented quarter has these book sales for its individual months.

Thus, this triple of a reproductively established family A of representational acts, a set $\vdash$ of semantic constraints on it, and a set N of normal acts relative to this set of semantic constraints can be considered a *system* that supports information flows from representations and targets. We call such a triple a *representation system*.

Given a representation system R, we denote R's family of representational acts with A_R, R's semantic constraints with $\vdash_R$, and R's normal set of representational acts with N_R. We write $\sigma \vdash_R \tau$ to indicate the holding of a semantic constraint from property σ of representational objects to property τ of targets.

Generally, for every member c of A_R, if c is a member of N_R, $\sigma \vdash_R \tau$ is a constraint in $\vdash_R$, and c's representing object has property σ, then it follows that c's target has property τ. When this happens, we say that c's representing object *carries information τ about c's target in representation system R.*

The specification N_R of normal representational acts in a representation system R lets us define accuracy of representation in a rather strict manner. Following Barwise and Seligman [1], we call a representation *accurate* in R if and only if it is produced by a normal representational act in R, that is, by a member of N_R. This definition is strict in that it excludes representations produced by abnormal representational acts even if they happen to satisfy the semantic constraints $\vdash_R$.

3   A Multitude of Representation Systems

This paper set out by asking the following questions. How can people read off true pieces of information from a false diagram? What is the logical ground on which such reading practices yield truths on a regular basis? The view of representation described in the last section provides natural answers to these questions.

3.1   Derivative Semantic Constraints

Figure 3a shows system R_1 of bar charts that we have been using as our running example. The long closed curve demarcates $c_1, \ldots, c_5$ as normal representational acts in this system. The semantic constraints for R_1 are listed in the upper right area.

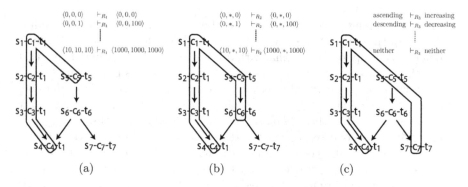

(a)   (b)   (c)

Fig. 3. Three representation systems, R_1–R_3, based on the same family of representational acts

It is well known that diagrams can carry meanings beyond those directly warranted by their basic semantic conventions. For example, a bar chart can mean that the book sales are increasing, decreasing, or neither by having the heads of its bars in an ascending, descending, or neither pattern. These meanings are clearly different from more basic meanings of the bar chart that specify the sales amounts of individual months. A two-dimensional scatter plot can exhibit the degree of correlation of two quantitative variables, which are different from more basic meanings it carries about the values of individual data points on the relevant variables. Extraction of these extra meanings from diagrams have been variously conceived by researchers as "global reading" [7], "macro reading" [13], and "direct translation" [6].

Shimojima [8] investigated this phenomenon in detail, and showed that it extends to a wide variety of diagrams, including line graphs, iconic tables, and connection maps. He also demonstrated that the extra meanings that a diagram carries are due to a meaning relation that holds as a logical consequence of basic semantic conventions. We formalized Shimojima's analysis in [10].

In our present terminology, Shimojima's analysis means that a new set of semantic constraints can hold as a logical consequence of basic semantic constraints. And indeed this is so. The fact that actors strive to maintain a collection of semantic constraints in their representational acts leads, in fact, to them maintaining many additional constraints too.

Consider for example the set of constraints 3, that asserts that the length of the first and third bars in one of our bar charts are in appropriate proportion to the number of sales in the first and third months of the quarter.

(3) The representing object has length m_1, m_3 cm for the first and third bars only if its target has sales amounts $100 \times m_1$ for the first month and $100 \times m_3$ for the third month.

(4) $\langle m_1, *, m_3 \rangle \vdash \langle 100 \times m_1, *, 100 \times m_3 \rangle$.

It is an immediate consequence of the attempt to maintain the basic constraints 1, that these constraints will also be maintained. That is, if a representational act conforms to the set of basic constraints 1, then this act necessarily conforms to the to the set of constraints 3. Consequently, derivative meanings for the representations produced in this practice will necessarily arise. Specifically, this derivative meaning yields the ability to perform a partial reading of the bar chart involving only the first and last bar of that chart, and to thereby extract true information from Fig. 1c.

Abstract readings arise in the same way, because of the maintenance of other constraints that follow from the basic constraints that actors in the representational practice strive to maintain. Consider, for example, the set of constraints 5.

(5) The bars increase/decrease in length from left to right in the representing object only if sales are increasing/decreasing in the target.

(6) *ascending* ⊢ *increasing, descending* ⊢ *decreasing, neither* ⊢ *neither.*

This set of constraints is maintained as a consequence of maintaining the basic semantic constraints, and result in the ability to read trend data from a bar chart.

3.2   Switching Between Representation Systems

Because of the extensive presence of derivative sets of semantic constraints, we can make use of a different set of semantic constraints, either basic or derivative, depending on what target issues we are interested in. For example, if our target issue is how many more books are sold in January than in March, we can make use of set (4) of semantic constraints to read off relevant information from the given bar chart; if our target issue is trend data for the book sales in a quarter, we can make use of set (6).

Remember that we have defined a representation system as the triple of a reproductively established family of representational acts, a set of semantic constraints on it, and a set of normal representational acts relative to this set of semantic constraints. So, the co-existence of multiple sets of semantic constraints on a family of representational acts implies that multiple representation systems are established by that family. Figure 3 compares the original representation system R_1 with the representation systems featuring derivative sets (3) and (6) of semantic constraints. We call these systems R_2 and R_3, respectively.

Figure 3 makes it clear that the switch of the sets of semantic constraints discussed above amounts to a switch of representation systems. While working with the same bar chart, say with s_3 produced by act c_3, we can switch representation systems, from R_1 to R_2 and to R_3 and so on, depending on what target issues we are concerned with. The co-existence of multiple representation systems makes a single diagram a flexible tool to explore different sets of issues.

However, it is one thing that multiple representation systems are made available as derivatives of a basic representation system, and it is another that we can actually utilize those systems. Here, we wish to only point out the former. The latter heavily depends on the user's perceptual and conceptual abilities, and as such, it is the subject of careful empirical investigation in cognitive psychology. The use of system R_3, for example, requires an ability to perceive an increasing or decreasing shape among bars, and an ability to recognize the logical relation between these shapes and sales trends.

3.3   Relativity of Normality

Let us now turn to the sets of normal representational acts in R_1–R_3. For the purpose of answering the main questions in this paper, the crucial fact is that what counts as a normal act is relative to the set of semantic constraints it is assessed against. Compare the sets of semantic constraints for R_1 and R_2. In order for the constraints for R_1 to hold, a representational act must be conducted with a rather high level of care for precision, in the information collection phase for the sales amounts of individual months, in editing the collected data, and in drawing a chart with all bars in exact lengths. Thus, an act performed without sufficient care for these matters would not support the semantic constraints for R_1, for there is a real possibility that it would violate one of the constraints, say by producing a chart with bar lengths $\langle 2, 5, 8 \rangle$ while its target quarter has sales amounts $\langle 200, 400, 800 \rangle$. The representational act is a reproduction of some previous act in family A_{R_1}, yet the reproduction process is not good enough to support the constraints $\vdash_{R_1}$ and is therefore deemed abnormal in system R_1.

Now the same act, performed in exactly the same way, may be good enough when assessed against a different set of semantic constraints. Consider $\vdash_{R_2}$ for example. Even though the level of care for precision taken in this act is not sufficient to prevent the errors in the lengths of all individual bars, sufficient care may be taken for the lengths of the first bar and the third bar. And if a representational act is performed with the latter level of care but not with the former, it is qualified as normal in representation system R_2 but is not so qualified in system R_1. Figures 3a and b illustrate this kind of situation. One and the same act, c_6, is demarcated as normal in Fig. 3b but not in Fig. 3a.

A similar situation holds between systems R_1 and R_3, but for a different kind of reason. Figures 3a and c show act c_7 is normal in system R_3 but not in system R_1. A representative reason for this to occur is that an act, say c_7, is performed with insufficient care with respect to all of the months in the target quarter and all of the bars in the chart, but not with respect to the relative lengths of the bars. Act c_7 thus supports set $\vdash_{R_3}$ of constraints and is qualified as normal in system R_3. Yet, since c_7 uses insufficient care in handling the absolute lengths of the bars it may well produce a chart with bar lengths $\langle 2, 5, 8 \rangle$ while its target quarter has sales amounts $\langle 100, 400, 700 \rangle$. This possibility disqualifies c_7 for a normal act in system R_1. Note that the same possibility also disqualifies c_7 for a normal act in system R_2, for it would mean that the act may produce the first and second bars with incorrect absolute lengths. Figure 3b therefore excludes c_7 from the normality curve.

We saw in Sect. 3.2 that multiple representations systems with different sets of semantic constraints can co-exist on the same family of representational acts. What we have just seen is that those multiple systems can have different sets of normal representational acts, too.

An immediate consequence of this observation is that one and the same diagram can be a perfectly accurate representation of its target in one representation system, while it is an inaccurate representation of the same target in another. If the representational act that produces it is like c_6, the diagram is an inaccurate representation of its target in representation system R_1, since c_6 is abnormal in R_1. But this only means that c_6 is not good enough to support the particular set of semantic constraints in R_1 and that the diagram accordingly carries no information in this particular representation system. In place of these, the act does support the semantic constraints in R_3 and the diagram can carry genuine piece of information in this representation system.

The situations we discussed in the introduction to this paper can be analyzed as the occurrence of such a system switch in diagram reading. Even when a bar chart is inaccurate in the sales amounts of individual months, it does not have to (or even should not) stop us reading off other pieces of information from the chart. There are other representation systems defined on the family of representational acts that produces the chart, and the chart can be a perfectly accurate representation of the target in some of them. Depending on the target issues we are interested in, we can make use of such a system to read of genuine piece of information. Reading off a general trend of sales is one example. Reading off only the sales in January and March is another. We can thus read off truths from a false diagram. And we can do so reliably, since whatever representation systems we take, it guarantees valid information flows of its own kind.

Given physical quantities such as lengths of bars and areas of pies are on continuous scales, it is next to impossible to adjust them exactly to indicate the particular values that the target objects have. Thus, a majority of statistical charts used in everyday life are doomed to be inexact in their bars' lengths, pies' areas, and other important quantities. In this regard, most geographical maps and drawings of physical objects are also inexact. The theory presented in this paper may be applied to explain why we nevertheless can keep using them. In many cases, our target issues are elsewhere than what those quantities may indicate, and dedicated representation systems are established under which those diagrams can usefully our target issues. However, a full account of the phenomenon would require significantly more elaboration.[1]

4 Discussion

We have shown that the view of representation described in Sect. 2 could be used to account for the common practice of extracting true information from false diagrams. In this section, we stop to consider exactly what aspects of this view let us account for the usefulness of false diagrams. We will show that this derives from the move of the semantic theory to incorporate *production processes* of representations in its scope.

As far as we know, every systematic semantic theory of diagram has some notion of truth for diagrams, either explicitly or implicitly. Model-theoretic semantics, applied to diagrams in such work as [2,3], is a quintessential example. It offers a formal definition of what makes a diagram true in a model or structure.

These semantics formally define the "truth-conditions" of a diagram by specifying the range of set-theoretic structures (models) that satisfy it. Although the truth of a diagram is thus relativized to particular structures it is evaluated in, once the structure is fixed, either it is completely true or completely false in it. We call such theories "holistic", since they consider diagrams as a whole.

With this rather straightforward notion of truth, holistic theories do not make any room for extracting information from a false diagram, even though it is one of our common reading practices. And that is to be expected, as this semantic theory is designed to capture something else (typically, the consequence relation among diagrams), not our common reading practices.

Other semantic theories discuss individual *properties* of diagrams, not just whole diagrams, and thus imply more fine-grained notion of truth. In her analysis of Venn diagrams for example, Shin [11] distinguishes multiple "representing facts" that hold in a Venn diagram. For example, the following are two representing facts that can simultaneously hold in a Venn diagram:

(7) the intersecting region of the circles labeled "A" and "B" is shaded.
(8) the complement region of the circle labeled "A" relative to the circle labeled "B" has a symbol "x".

In Shin's system, shaded regions represent emptiness, while the presence of an "x" in a region indicates non-emptiness. If both $A \cap B$ and $A - B$ are in fact empty, then we can say that the Venn diagram is true with respect to representing fact (7), while it is false with respect to representing fact (8). Thus,

---

[1] We thank an anonymous reviewer for drawing attention to the issue of apparent ubiquity of inexact diagrams.

the truth of a diagram can be relativized to individual representing facts that hold in the diagram.

The semantic framework used in Shimojima [8] also posits meaning-carrying properties of diagrams (called "source types") as distinguished from diagram tokens, and the notion of "meaning-carrying relationship" used by Stapleton and her colleagues also captures the same idea, [12]. Thus, these theories also support a notion of truth attributed separately to individual properties of diagrams. Let us call these semantic theories that distinguish meaning-carrying properties of diagrams from diagram tokens "granular theories" for ease of reference. Granular theories of truth allow for a holistic semantics, since a diagram can be considered holistically true if it is true with respect to all of the representing facts in the diagram, but they go beyond it.

With this more fine grained notion of truth, granular theories allow us to extract information from diagrams on an issue-by-issue basis, and therefore enable the extraction of true information from diagrams that would be considered false by a holistic theory. Granular theories allow us to pick a true property of the given diagram (e.g., representing fact (7) above) and interpret it to obtain true information ($A \cap B = \emptyset$) even though the diagram is partially false because of the presence of a false property (representing fact (8) above).

Although a granular theory of diagrams allows us to read true information from a holistically false diagram, it is silent about why a single representation can have both properties that represent true information and those that do not. Yet, we often distinguish some of the former from the latter more or less accurately, and use them to extract true information. This is an indication that some key ingredients are still missing from the existing granular theories for them to do full justice to our reading practice.

For this we turn to another aspect of our theory. The concept of representational act allows us to model the process by which a diagram is produced—including the process of information collection and editing, as well as the physical production of the diagram token. Individual sets of semantic constraints provide individual standards against which the process is assessed for normality, and this serves as the index of accuracy of the diagram for a particular set of target issues. Our concept of *accuracy*, inherited from [1], refers to the character of a diagram determined in this way, with reference to its production process.

From the point of view of a reader seeking to learn true information about some issue from a diagram, we must examine the process by which the diagram was created. We can then evaluate whether that process is *reliable* with respect to our issue, and then extract information from the relevant parts of the diagram. A diagram that is useful to us is one that has been produced by a reliable process (one which involves normal representational acts), with respect to our target issue.

It is a strength of our theory that it models the process by which representations are produced, by making representational acts first-class objects in the theory. In our theory, diagrams are not simply pre-existing artifacts to be used, but are the product of human processes which can themselves be subject to analysis.

Of course, in practice the consumers of representations typically do not have access to the process by which a representation is produced. If we had full knowledge of the complete process then we would likely have direct information about the facts concerning the target issue itself. In real life, other factors stand as proxies for knowledge of the process of production. Does the producer of this representation have access to the target data that it is representing? Does this producer have a track-record of producing accurate representations? Is the producer willing to discuss the methods by which they produced the representation? Among a host of many similar questions. These are questions which generally fall under the category of media-literacy, and are fundamental to our selection of information to be used.

5 Conclusion

In this paper we have presented a semantic theory of diagrammatic representation that has novel desirable features. Our theory begins with a conception of representation systems as emerging from representational practices. These practices are carried out by people, and as such are susceptible to error. The theory therefore must take seriously the possibility of representations which are inaccurate. But, we observe, diagrammatic representations can be inaccurate with respect to some readings, but not with respect to others. That is, it is possible to avoid, or abstract away, inaccurate aspects of the representation and extract true information from such a representation.

The explanation for this ability emerges naturally from the theory. The critical component of the theory is that actors within the representational practice strive to maintain certain constraints that relate the represented object to its representation. Primary among these constraints are those which allow true information to be obtained from representations when read according to established conventions. But the maintenance of a collection of basic constraints can necessarily involve the maintenance of other derivative constraints. Our theory therefore naturally models the common feature of diagrammatic representations known as derivative meaning.

As derivative meanings arise naturally from the theory, so too do the opportunities for partial and abstract readings of the representations. Each set of derived constraints allow us to read the representations in a new way. One and the same representation can be read using different information channels, and these channels allow the extraction of different information from that representation. In particular, some information channels can allow us to read just a part of the diagram, to obtain information about part of the target. Similarly information be obtained at different levels of abstraction.

Consequently, the theory models the possibility of obtaining true information from inaccurate diagrams by recognizing the possibility of information channels that do not consider the parts of the representation that is erroneous (partial reading), or channels which extract abstract information so as to render errors of precision irrelevant (abstract reading). The existence of these channels account for the ability to extract true information from false diagrams.

Finally then, our theory is distinguished from other semantic theories of diagrams by its focus on the reliability of a representation relative to a particular set of target issues rather than in absolute terms. Our theory models the possibility that a diagram may be used to reliably obtain information about one set of issues, but not about another within the same domain.

References

1. Barwise, J., Seligman, J.: Information Flow: The Logic of Distributed Systems. Cambridge Tracts in Theoretical Computer Science. Cambridge University Press, Cambridge (1997). https://doi.org/10.1017/CBO9780511895968
2. Hammer, E.: Logic and Visual Information. CSLI Publications and the European Association for Logic, Language and Information, Stanford (1995)
3. Howse, J., Molina, F., Taylor, J., Kent, S., Gil, J.Y.: Spider diagrams: a diagrammatic reasoning system. J. Vis. Lang. Comput. **12**, 299–324 (2001)
4. Lewis, D.: Languages and language. In: Philosophical Papers, pp. 93–115. Oxford UP, Oxford (1975/1985). Originally published in 1975
5. Millikan, R.G.: Language, Thought, and Other Biological Categories: New Foundation for Realism. The MIT Press, Cambridge (1984)
6. Pinker, S.: A theory of graph comprehension. In: Aritificial Intelligence and the Future of Testing, pp. 73–126. L. Erlbaum Associates, Hilsdale (1990)
7. Ratwani, R.M., Trafton, J.G., Boehm-Davis, D.A.: Thinking graphically: extracting local and global information. In: Proceedings of the Twenty-Fifth Annual Conference of the Cognitive Science Society, pp. 958–963 (2003)
8. Shimojima, A.: Semantic Properties of Diagrams and Their Cognitive Potentials. CSLI Publications, Stanford (2015)
9. Shimojima, A., Barker-Plummer, D.: The Barwise-Seligman model of representation systems: a philosophical explication. In: Dwyer, T., Purchase, H., Delaney, A. (eds.) Diagrams 2014. LNCS (LNAI), vol. 8578, pp. 231–245. Springer, Heidelberg (2014). https://doi.org/10.1007/978-3-662-44043-8_25
10. Shimojima, A., Barker-Plummer, D.: Channel-theoretic account of reification in representation systems. Logique & Analyse (2020, to Appear)
11. Shin, S.J.: The Logical Status of Diagrams. Cambridge University Press, Cambridge (1994)
12. Stapleton, G., Jamnik, M., Shimojima, A.: What makes an effective representation of information: a formal account of observational advantages. J. Log. Lang. Inf. **26**(2), 143–177 (2017). https://doi.org/10.1007/s10849-017-9250-6
13. Tufte, E.R.: Envisioning Information. Graphics Press, Cheshire (1990)

Dissecting Representations

Daniel Raggi[1]([✉]), Aaron Stockdill[1], Mateja Jamnik[1], Grecia Garcia Garcia[2], Holly E. A. Sutherland[2], and Peter C.-H. Cheng[2]

[1] University of Cambridge, Cambridge, UK
{daniel.raggi,aaron.stockdill,mateja.jamnik}@cl.cam.ac.uk
[2] University of Sussex, Sussex, UK
{g.garcia-garcia,h.sutherland,p.c.h.cheng}@sussex.ac.uk

Abstract. Choosing effective representations for a problem and for the person solving it has benefits, including the ability or inability to solve it. We previously devised a novel framework consisting of a language to describe representations and computational methods to analyse them in terms of their formal and cognitive properties. In this paper we demonstrate the application of this framework to a variety of notations including natural languages, formal languages, and diagrams. We show how our framework, and the analysis of representations that it enables, gives us insight into how and why we can select representations which are appropriate for both the task and the user.

Keywords: Knowledge representation · Reasoning · Intelligent systems

1 Introduction

A given problem can be represented in a variety of ways, and the choice of representation determines whether it can be solved at all, as well as influences the performance of problem solvers—either helping or hindering them. It is up to the problem solver to represent the problem appropriately before solving it. Likewise, in a tutoring setting, it is up to the tutor to select an effective representation for a given audience. But *what is an effective representation,* and *how can we tell it apart from a bad representation?*

The quality of a representation is a confluence of many factors [2,4], including whether it expresses the necessary information, makes this accessible, enables useful inferences, and reduces the search space for the problem solver. Many of these factors are user-dependent; some representations may be ideal for expert users, but not for novices, and vice-versa. The ultimate goal of our research is to understand what makes an effective representation, computationally model this analysis, and thus enable the automation of representation selection.

This work was supported by the EPSRC grants EP/R030650/1, EP/R030642/1, EP/T019034/1 and EP/T019603/1. We thank Gem Stapleton for her useful comments.

A.-V. Pietarinen et al. (Eds.): Diagrams 2020, LNAI 12169, pp. 144–152, 2020.
https://doi.org/10.1007/978-3-030-54249-8_11

In previous work we introduced a language [9] for encoding the properties of representational systems, in addition to correspondences between them [11]. The purpose was to calculate an informational measure, which, given a problem, estimates the likelihood that the important information for this problem can be expressed in any given representational system. In subsequent work we implemented algorithms for computing cognitive measures of representations. Calculating these measures requires a richer and more structured language, which we incorporated in our framework. Specifically, we introduced *attributes* which allow us to encode structural information and more detailed descriptions of the representation's components. In this paper we illustrate through examples how to use our language (including its new additions) to describe representations in the framework. Moreover, we demonstrate how the framework can be used for representation selection based on informational and cognitive measures. Our work provides novel and general computational methods for assessing and comparing sentential and diagrammatic representations that are formal and informal, general and specialised; and could thus be used for making AI systems more human-like and adaptable to the user. An Appendix for this paper can be found at https://sites.google.com/site/myrep2rep/publications/dissecting.

2 How to Describe Representations?

The fundamental objects that our framework aims to describe are *representational systems* (RSs). For example, Arithmetic Algebra forms an RS in which expressions are constructed using tokens (e.g., $x, 0, +, =, \leq$) with some grammatical constraints (e.g., $\_ = \_$ needs to be filled with expressions of the same type), and its expressions can be manipulated according to some rules (e.g., $x + 0 \leq y$ can be rewritten as $x \leq y$). Moreover, our framework also describes concrete instances of representations, such as *problem* formulations. For instance, the problem in Arithmetic Algebra: *assuming $0 < x$ and $x \cdot y = 0$, prove $y = 0$.*

2.1 Representational Systems and Problems

We characterise a representational system (RS) by its formal **components**: its *tokens, expressions* (which we capture by *patterns*), *types, tactics*, and *laws*. A component can have *attributes*, specified as a record of features associated with it. We introduced these concepts (excluding attributes) elsewhere [9], so here we only provide a brief explanation: tokens are atomic symbols from which expressions are built. Patterns are abstractions of expressions; and their attributes encode structural information (e.g., how expressions can be nested in one another). Types are a grammatically meaningful classification of expressions (e.g., the type of $\pi + 4$ is real), tactics are the possible manipulations and inferences within the system (e.g., applying the modus ponens rule), and laws are the rules or units of knowledge that enable some manipulations and inferences to be made.

A representational system is a general tool for representing many things, but we are particularly interested in its use for representing *problems*. In this paper we demonstrate how (four) different representations of the same problem can be dissected and evaluated by the tools that our framework provides. We chose to focus our analysis primarily on two RSs. The first (*Bayesian*) is a standard formal notation for conditional probability, and the second (*PS diagrams*) is a novel diagrammatic notation for probability, which has been shown to improve students' problem solving and learning [3].

Problem (Lightbulbs). *There are two lightbulb manufacturers in town. One of them is known to produce defective lightbulbs 30% of the time, whereas for the other one the percentage is 80%. You do not know which one is which. You pick one to buy a lightbulb from, and it turns out to be defective. The same manufacturer gives you a replacement. What is the probability that this one is also defective?*

The problem is presented in English (*NL: Natural Language*), which we do not analyse here, but results for its informational and cognitive measures are shown in Sect. 3. An analysis of the NL formulation can be found in Appendix.

Representation 1 (Bayesian). *Denote the manufacturers as a and b. Let d_1 and d_2 be the events of the first and second lightbulbs being defective, respectively. Clearly, d_2 is conditionally independent of d_1 given the choice of manufacturer.*

$$\text{Assume: } b = \bar{a} \tag{1}$$
$$\Pr(a) = \Pr(b) \tag{2}$$
$$\Pr(d_2 \mid x \cap d_1) = \Pr(d_2 \mid x) \text{ for } x \in \{a, b\} \tag{3}$$
$$\Pr(d_1 \mid a) = \Pr(d_2 \mid a) = 0.3 \tag{4}$$
$$\Pr(d_1 \mid b) = \Pr(d_2 \mid b) = 0.8 \tag{5}$$
$$\text{Calculate: } \Pr(d_2 \mid d_1).$$

Some notable tokens here are Pr, $|$, $\cap$, a, b, d_1, d_2. Some features of these tokens can be encoded by attributes. For instance, we write

$$\text{token } a : \{\text{type} := \texttt{event}, \text{occurrences} := 5\}$$

to indicate that a is a token with type `event`, and that it occurs 5 times in this specific representation. Moreover, we can assign more complex types, such as `event × event → real` to Pr. In our framework this implies that there is a pattern, associated with the token Pr, encoded as follows:

$$\text{pattern patt}(\text{Pr}) : \{\text{type} := \texttt{real}, \text{holes} := [\texttt{event}^2], \text{tokens} := [\,\text{Pr}, |, (,)\,]\}$$

Intuitively, patt(Pr) represents the expressions of the shape $\Pr(\_ \mid \_)$. The declaration above means: first, that these expressions have type `real`; second, that they are formed by plugging in two expressions of type `event` into the *holes*; and third, that they necessarily use each of the tokens Pr, $|$, (, and). In our implementation,[1] every pattern associated with a token (of nontrivial type) is generated automatically, such as for $\cap$, $=$, and $\in$.

---

[1] https://github.com/rep2rep/robin.

Our framework can also encode inferential aspects (use of tactics and laws), which we illustrate by analysing the solution below.

Solution (Bayesian). *Amongst other things, use the law of total probability (LTP), de Finetti's axiom of conditional probability (dF), Bayes' theorem (BT), arithmetic calculation (calc). For conciseness we show only a part of the solution:*

$$\Pr(d_2 \mid d_1) = \Pr(d_2 \cap a \mid d_1) + \Pr(d_2 \cap b \mid d_1) \qquad \text{(by LTP, asm 1)}$$
$$= \Pr(d_2 \mid a \cap d_1)\Pr(a \mid d_1) + \Pr(d_2 \mid b \cap d_1)\Pr(b \mid d_1) \qquad \text{(by dF)}$$
$$\vdots$$
$$= \frac{0.3 \cdot 0.3 + 0.8 \cdot 0.8}{0.3 + 0.8} \approx 0.663 \qquad \text{(by calc)}$$

Every step in this solution can be characterised as an application of the tactic *rewrite*, or an arithmetic calculation. This, and more information (e.g., how many times each tactic is applied) can be encoded by attributes, as follows:

tactic **rewrite** :{occurrences := 18, inference_type := substitution,

law_params := 1, pattern_params := 1}

tactic **calculate** :{occurrences := 1, inference_type := calculation,

law_params := 0, pattern_params := 1}

Foreshadowing what this means in terms of the cognitive cost of using this representation, calculation is in principle a more complex operation, but rewriting has a larger contribution to the breadth of the search space because it can be applied in many ways depending on the laws at hand.

Representation 2 (PS diagrams). *Below, labelled segments represent events and their lengths represent their probability. The ratio that needs to be calculated is that of the thicker line relative to the space between the thick delimiters.*

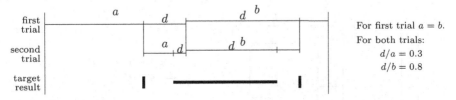

For first trial $a = b$.
For both trials:
$d/a = 0.3$
$d/b = 0.8$

This representation has some important characteristics (segments, delimiters, proportions, etc.) that need to be captured in our description. Amongst others, some tokens are the horizontal segments (thin and thick), the vertical marks (thin and thick) and the vertical lines. Emergent components, such as a segment formed by two colinear segments, relations between components, or values thereof (e.g., length), can be expressed as patterns:

pattern **joint_segments** : {type := segment, holes := [segment^2], ...}

pattern **aligned_segments** : {type := relationship, holes := [segment^2], ...}

pattern **relative_length** : {type := real, holes := [segment^2], ...}

Patterns also allow us to represent emergent *gestalt* items. For instance, the 'segment' in between the 2 target delimiters can be encoded by:

pattern `segment_from_delimiters` :{type := `segment`,

holes := [`delimiter`^{2}], ...}

We proceed to analyse the inferential aspects of this representation by looking at a solution.

Solution (PS diagrams). *The length of the segments labelled d in the second trial must be* $0.3 \cdot 0.3 \cdot x$ *and* $0.8 \cdot 0.8 \cdot x$ *where x is the length of a (and b) in the first trial. Moreover, the length between the target delimiters must be* $0.3 \cdot x + 0.8 \cdot x$. *Thus, the desired ratio is* $\frac{0.3 \cdot 0.3 \cdot x + 0.8 \cdot 0.8 \cdot x}{0.3 \cdot x + 0.8 \cdot x}$. *This yields* ≈ 0.663.

This solution is quite condensed because each inference relies on mere *observations* which are possible as an immediate consequence of having represented the assumptions [10]. Here we assume observations apply to patterns; e.g., observing the relative length is obtaining the real number that represents such relation. We can capture the notion of observation as a tactic:

tactic `observe` :{occurrences := 10, inference_type := observation,

pattern_params := 1, law_params := 1, ...}

Finally, the sequence of observations leads to a ratio that the user still needs to calculate, so we need a calculation tactic similar to the Bayesian RS.

So far we analysed one sentential and one diagrammatic representation. We hope this demonstrates that our language is simple yet expressive. Below, we give alternative representations under consideration, but without analysis.

Representation 3 (Areas). *In the figure, regions represent events, and their relative areas represent the corresponding probabilities. Solution in Appendix.*

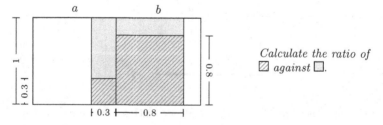

Calculate the ratio of ▨ *against* □.

Representation 4 (Probability trees). *In the rooted tree below, the values of edges represent conditional probabilities and the values of the nodes represent the joint probability of the nodes in the path. Solution in Appendix.*

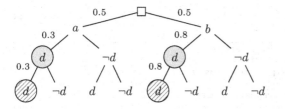

Calculate the ratio of the values of the nodes enclosed in ⊘ against the values of the nodes enclosed in ○.

2.2 Writing RS and Q Descriptions

The example RSs above demonstrate the expressiveness and intuitions behind the components of our framework. But, *what should the end result of analysing representations look like?*

An **RS description** is a collection of meaningful components of an RS: it must include tokens that typically appear in the instances of such an RS, and patterns, laws and tactics that are relevant for using such an RS. Similarly, a **Q description** (Q for *question*) is a collection of meaningful components of a problem representation in some specific RS that the question is posed in. Each component in a Q description must have an *importance* [9] value associated with it, encoding how informative this component is for finding a solution (defined in the interval between 0 for noise and 1 for maximal relevance; we use colours for discretised values). A longer discussion of importance can be found in Appendix.

See Fig. 1 for two RS descriptions, and Fig. 2 for a Q description (organised in a hierarchy of 4 importance values, where purple is the most important).

Bayesian	
types	event, real, formula, proof
tokens	$=$: {type := $\alpha \times \alpha \to$ formula}, Pr : {type := event $\times$ event $\to$ real, $\quad$ tokens := [	.(.)]}, $\cap$: {type := event $\times$ event $\to$ event}, Ω : {type := event}, ...
patterns	equality_chain : {type := proof, $\quad$ holes := [$\alpha^{O(\log n)}$], $\quad$ tokens := [=]}, ...
tactics	rewrite : {inference_type := subst, ...}, calculate : {inference_type := calc, ...}, lemma : {inference_type := match, ...}
laws	LTP, dF, BT, ...

PS diagrams	
types	segment, vertical_guide, delimiter, real
tokens	$outcome_segment : {type := segment}, $target_delimiter : {type := delimiter}, $target_segment : {type := segment}, ...
patterns	joint_segments : {type := segment, $\quad$ holes := [segment^2]}, relative_length : {type := real, $\quad$ holes := [segment^2]}, ...
tactics	observe : {inference_type := obs, ...}, calculate : {inference_type := calc, ...}
laws	MNR, EAS, LADJ, ...

Fig. 1. Snippets of Bayesian and PS diagrams RS descriptions. Note the prefix $ to specify that this is a label for a non-unicode token.

Lightbulbs in NL	
answer type	ratio
types	number,event
tokens	probability : {type := N, occurrences := 1}, % : {type := number → ratio, occurrences := 2}
patterns	sequential_events : {type := relationship, holes := [event²],...}, conditionally_independent_events : {type := relationship, holes := [event²],...}
tokens	30 : {type := number, occurrences := 1}, 80 : {type := number, occurrences := 1}, percentage : {type := N, occurrences := 1}
tokens	lightbulb : {type := N, occurrences := 2}, defective : {type := N, occurrences := 3},...
patterns	SfromNPandVP : {type := S, holes := [NP, VP],...}...

Fig. 2. A section of the Q description of the Lightbulbs problem in NL.

3   Evaluating Representations

We can use RS and Q descriptions to compute important measures: *informational suitability* (presented in [9]), and *cognitive cost*.

The Informational Suitability (IS) of an RS, r, given a problem q is the sum of the strengths of analogical *correspondences* [11] between components that match the source q and the target r, modulated by the importance of said components:

$$\text{IS}(q,r) = \sum_{\langle a,b,s \rangle \in C} s \cdot \text{importance}_q(a). \tag{6}$$

It computes the extent to which an RS can express all the relevant parts of the problem at hand. For the Lightbulb problem with 5 candidate RSs the results are shown below:

RS	Bayes	PS diag.	Areas	Pr-trees	NL
Score	7.9	7.5	7.2	6.6	6.3

The Cognitive Cost encodes the RS's processing cost to the user, and is calculated by computing a set of properties of the representation, all of which can be estimated by values computed from Q descriptions (out of the scope of this paper). These properties are based on established cognitive science concepts [1,6–8,12,13], presented schematically in Fig. 3.

Each of the properties is associated with a cognitive process, and thus a cognitive cost. Moreover, the user is modelled by their expertise [5], which is accounted for in two ways: by flattening importance (to model that a novel user cannot distinguish between important and unimportant properties), and by inflating the cost of higher-level cognitive processes. Given a Q description for a problem q, the costs for each cognitive property p and user u are calculated,

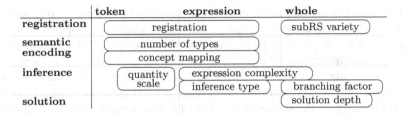

Fig. 3. Cognitive properties organised according to granularity (columns) and cognitive process level (rows).

normalised, and weighted by an expertise factor $c_p(u)$. The values for all p are summed to obtain a total cost.[2]

$$\text{Cost}(q, u) = \sum_p c_p(u) \cdot \text{norm}_p(\text{cost}_p(q, u)). \tag{7}$$

See the rankings of RSs according to their estimated cognitive cost for the Light-bulb problem, for three different users:[3]

			Bayesian			PS diag			Areas			Pr trees			NL		
Expert	Avg.	Novice	1	2	4	4	1	1	2	3	2	5	4	3	3	5	5

The main contributing factor to the differences in rankings between novices and experts comes from the cognitive costs associated with high granularity properties, for example: branching factor and solution depth. Because the weights associated with these costs scale with expertise, a representation like the Bayesian representation is penalised more heavily here for novices than for experts (dropping from first to fourth). Conversely, we see the Areas and PS diagrams representations have relatively low values in these cognitive costs, and as such are less penalised for novice users.

4   Conclusion and Future Work

We demonstrated our computational framework for analysing representations by explicitly constructing RS and Q descriptions for a particular problem and a number of candidate alternative representations. These descriptions serve as input to compute informational and cognitive measures of the suitability and the cost of using a representation by a particular user. Q and RS descriptions need to be built by an expert analyst; this includes decomposing into components,

---

[2] These calculations rely on parameters whose values we gave provisionally based on the literature, but which need to be tuned based on empirical data.

[3] The costs, broken down per cognitive property, can be found in appendix.

assigning importance and attributes to components, setting up correspondences with their strengths, and tuning the parameters of cognitive properties based on empirical data. Current and future work involve operationalising the process of obtaining descriptions and carrying out user studies for parameter tuning.

The generality of our approach makes our framework potentially useful for a variety of endeavours: from multi-representational tutoring systems, to user-sensitive interactive theorem provers. The ability to consider the user allows the framework to be deployed across many domains varying in their level of specialisation. The framework's descriptions are computation-friendly, creating an opportunity for diverse, diagrammatic representations to be evaluated and subsequently implemented in domains where sentential representations dominate.

References

1. Anderson, J.: Spanning seven orders of magnitude: a challenge for cognitive modeling. Cogn. Sci. **26**(1), 85–112 (2002)
2. Blackwell, A.F., et al.: Cognitive dimensions of notations: design tools for cognitive technology. In: Beynon, M., Nehaniv, C.L., Dautenhahn, K. (eds.) CT 2001. LNCS (LNAI), vol. 2117, pp. 325–341. Springer, Heidelberg (2001). https://doi.org/10.1007/3-540-44617-6_31
3. Cheng, P.: Probably good diagrams for learning: representational epistemic recodification of probability theory. Top. Cogn. Sci. **3**(3), 475–498 (2011)
4. Cheng, P.C.-H.: What constitutes an effective representation? In: Jamnik, M., Uesaka, Y., Elzer Schwartz, S. (eds.) Diagrams 2016. LNCS (LNAI), vol. 9781, pp. 17–31. Springer, Cham (2016). https://doi.org/10.1007/978-3-319-42333-3_2
5. Chi, M.: The Nature of Expertise. Lawrence Erlbaum Associates Inc., Hillsdale (1988)
6. Larkin, J., Simon, H.: Why a diagram is (sometimes) worth ten thousand words. Cogn. Sci. **11**(1), 65–100 (1987)
7. Moody, D.: The "physics" of notations: toward a scientific basis for constructing visual notations in software engineering. IEEE Trans. Software Eng. **35**(6), 756–779 (2009)
8. Newell, A.: Unified Theories of Cognition. Harvard University Press, Cambridge (1990)
9. Raggi, D., Stockdill, A., Jamnik, M., Garcia Garcia, G., Sutherland, H.E.A., Cheng, P.C.-H.: Inspection and selection of representations. In: Kaliszyk, C., Brady, E., Kohlhase, A., Sacerdoti Coen, C. (eds.) CICM 2019. LNCS (LNAI), vol. 11617, pp. 227–242. Springer, Cham (2019). https://doi.org/10.1007/978-3-030-23250-4_16
10. Stapleton, G., Jamnik, M., Shimojima, A.: What makes an effective representation of information: a formal account of observational advantages. Logic Lang. Inf. **26**(2), 143–177 (2017)
11. Stockdill, A., et al.: Correspondence-based analogies for choosing problem representations in mathematics and computing education. In: 2020 IEEE Symposium on Visual Languages and Human-Centric Computing (VL/HCC) (2020, in press)
12. Van Someren, M., et al.: Learning with multiple representations. Advances in Learning and Instruction Series, ERIC (1998)
13. Zhang, J.: A representational analysis of numeration systems. Cognition **57**(3), 271–295 (1995)

Towards Data-Driven Multilinear Metro Maps

Soeren Nickel⬤ and Martin Nöllenburg(✉)⬤

Algorithms and Complexity Group, TU Wien, Vienna, Austria
{soeren.nickel,noellenburg}@ac.tuwien.ac.at

Abstract. Traditionally, most schematic metro maps as well as metro map layout algorithms adhere to an *octolinear* layout style with all paths composed of horizontal, vertical, and 45°-diagonal edges. Despite growing interest in more general *multilinear* metro maps, generic algorithms to draw metro maps based on a system of $k \geq 2$ not necessarily equidistant slopes have not been investigated thoroughly. We present and implement an adaptation of the octolinear mixed-integer linear programming approach of Nöllenburg and Wolff (2011) that can draw metro maps schematized to any set $\mathcal{C}$ of arbitrary orientations. We further present a data-driven approach to determine a suitable set $\mathcal{C}$ by either detecting the best rotation of an equidistant orientation system or by clustering the input edge orientations using a k-means algorithm. We demonstrate the new possibilities of our method in a real-world case study.

1 Introduction

Metro maps are ubiquitous schematic network diagrams that aid public transit passengers in orientation and route planning in almost all types of urban public transit systems worldwide. Since Henry Beck's classic schematic London Tube Map of 1933, metro maps have developed a common visual language and adopted similar design principles. Designing professional metro maps is still mostly a manual task today, even if cartographers and graphic designers are supported by digital drawing tools. Algorithms for automated layout of metro maps have received substantial interest in the graph drawing and network visualization communities as well as in cartography and geovisualization over the last 20 years [9,14]. The vast majority of metro map layout algorithms focus on so-called *octolinear* (sometimes also called *octilinear*) metro maps, which are limited to Henry Beck's classical and since then widely adopted 45°-angular grid of line orientations [4]. However, not all metro maps found in practice are strictly octolinear. There is empirical evidence from usability studies that the best set of line orientations for drawing a metro map depends on different aspects of the respective transit network, and it may not always be an octolinear or even an equiangular one [12,13].

In this paper we present an algorithmic approach using global optimization for computing (unlabeled) metro maps in the more flexible *k-linearity* setting,

© Springer Nature Switzerland AG 2020
A.-V. Pietarinen et al. (Eds.): Diagrams 2020, LNAI 12169, pp. 153–161, 2020.
https://doi.org/10.1007/978-3-030-54249-8_12

where each edge in the drawing must be parallel to one of $k \geq 2$ equidistant orientations whose pairwise angles are multiples of $360°/2k$. In this sense, a k-linear map for $k = 4$ corresponds to the traditional octolinear setting. In fact, most octolinear maps use a horizontally aligned orientation system. It is possible though, for some transit networks and city geometries, that a rotation of the orientation system by an angular offset yields a more topographically accurate metro map layout. Hence we also consider such *rotated k-linear maps*. In addition to equiangular k-linear orientation systems, we further study irregular *multilinear* (or *C-oriented*) maps [12], in which the edges are parallel to any given, not necessarily equiangular set C of orientations. There exist a number of metro map layout algorithms (see [9,14,15] for comprehensive surveys) that would technically permit an adaptation to a different underlying angular grid, yet most previous papers optimize layouts in the well-known octolinear setting only and do not discuss extensions to different linearities explicitly. A few algorithms for generic multilinear or k-linear layouts exist [1,2,5,6], but they are aimed at paths or polygons rather than entire metro maps. In the field of graph drawing many algorithms for planar orthogonal network layouts with $k = 2$ as well as for polyline drawings with completely unrestricted slopes are known [3], but they do not generalize to k-linearity and multilinearity.

Contributions. We present two approaches for deriving suitable, data-dependent linearity systems (Sect. 3). Then we adapt the octolinear mixed-integer linear programming (MIP) model of Nöllenburg and Wolff [10] by generalizing their mathematical layout constraints to k-linearity and multilinearity (Sect. 4). The main benefit of this model in comparison to other approaches is that it defines sets of hard and soft constraints and guarantees that the computed layout satisfies all the hard constraints and (globally) optimizes the soft constraints. The trade-off for providing such strong quality guarantees is that computation time is typically higher compared to other methods [15]. By modeling fundamental metro map properties such as strict adherence to the given linearity system and topological correctness as hard constraints, we obtain layouts that satisfy these layout requirements strictly. The soft constraints optimize for line straightness, compactness, and topographicity [11], i.e., low topographical distortion. Our modifications yield a flexible MIP model, whose complexity measured by the number of variables and constraints grows linearly with the number of orientations k. We demonstrate the effect of horizontally aligned and rotated k-linear and multilinear orientation systems in a case study with the metro map of Vienna and evaluate the resulting number of bends and angular distortions for typical small values of $k = 3, 4, 5$ (Sect. 5).

Due to space constraints, some details are omitted; these can be found in [7].

2   Preliminaries

We reuse the notation of Nöllenburg and Wolff [10]. The input is represented as an embedded planar metro graph $G = (V, E)$ with n vertices and m edges. Each

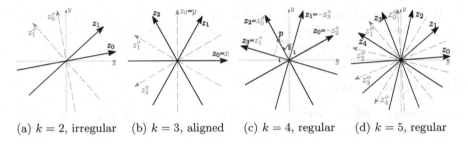

(a) $k = 2$, irregular   (b) $k = 3$, aligned   (c) $k = 4$, regular   (d) $k = 5$, regular

Fig. 1. Coordinate axes for different orientation systems. (c) includes a point with the redundant coordinates $p = (0, 1, \sqrt{2}, 1)$.

vertex $v \in V$ represents a metro station with x- and y-coordinates and each edge $e = (u, v) \in E$ is a segment linking vertices u and v that represents a physical rail connection between them. Finally, $k \geq 2$ is an input parameter that defines the number of available edge orientations in the orientation system $\mathcal{C}$. The set $\mathcal{C}$ and the parameter k can be part of the input or they can be derived automatically from the input geometry, see Sect. 3. Figure 1 shows three examples of orientation systems. Since every orientation can be used in two directions this yields $2k$ available drawing directions. Let $\mathcal{K}$ be this set of $2k$ directions. We note that every edge is assigned exclusively to an outgoing direction of its incident vertices, which implies that the maximum degree Δ of G can be at most $2k$. In turn, Δ gives a lower bound on the required number of orientations.

The general algorithmic metro map layout problem studied in this paper is to find a *$\mathcal{C}$-oriented schematic layout* of G, i.e., a graph layout that preserves the input topology, uses only edge directions parallel to an orientation from $\mathcal{C}$, and optimizes a weighted layout quality function (here composed of line straightness, topographicity, and compactness). If $\mathcal{C}$ corresponds to a k-linear orientation system, we also call the layout *k-linear* instead of $\mathcal{C}$-oriented; otherwise it can alternatively be called *multilinear*.

3   Orientation Systems

A set of edge orientations (or an *orientation system*) $\mathcal{C} = \{c_1, \ldots, c_k\}$ is a set of k angles (expressed in radian), where $0 \leq c_1 < \cdots < c_k < \pi$. We distinguish three different kinds of possible edge orientation sets. An edge orientation set $\mathcal{C}$ is called *regular* (or *equiangular*) if the angles $\{c_1, \ldots c_k\}$ divide the range $[c_1, c_1 + \pi)$ into k parts of equal size π/k, i.e., $c_i - c_{i-1} = \pi/k$ for all $i \in \{2, \ldots, k\}$. Otherwise we call $\mathcal{C}$ *irregular*. A regular orientation system $\mathcal{C}$, in which $c_1 = 0$ is called *aligned*. A classical octolinear layout has the orientation system $\mathcal{C}_o = \{0, \pi/4, \pi/2, 3\pi/4\}$.

Regular (non-aligned) and irregular systems allow us to derive a suitable system $\mathcal{C}$ from the geometric properties of the input data, with the goal to minimize the topographic distortion of the layout compared to the input.

We measure the distortion of $\mathcal{C}$ with respect to a metro graph G by summing up the difference in slope between each edge $e \in E$ (with slope $\gamma_e \pmod{\pi}$) and the angle $c \in \mathcal{C}$ which is closest to γ_e as $\mathrm{dist}_G(\mathcal{C}) = \sum_{e \in E} (\min_{c \in \mathcal{C}} |c - \gamma_e|)$.

3.1   Regular Orientation Systems

Fixing a single angle in a regular orientation system $\mathcal{C}$ fixes all other orientations. It is therefore sufficient to specify the first orientation $c_1 \in \mathcal{C}$. We denote by $\mathcal{C}_{\mathrm{opt}}$ a regular orientation system with minimal distortion, i.e., $\mathrm{dist}_G(\mathcal{C}_{\mathrm{opt}}) \leq \mathrm{dist}_G(\mathcal{C})$ for any k-regular orientation system $\mathcal{C}$. We can show [7] that one can find such an optimal system $\mathcal{C}_{\mathrm{opt}}$, in which at least one $c \in \mathcal{C}_{\mathrm{opt}}$ is parallel to an input edge. Thus we can restrict our search to orientation systems in $\mathfrak{C}(E) = \{\mathcal{C} \mid \exists e \in E : \gamma_e \in \mathcal{C}\}$, i.e., to orientation systems, where at least one orientation coincides with the slope of an edge in E. The set $\mathfrak{C}(E)$ contains $O(|E|)$ elements and we select $\mathcal{C}_{\mathrm{opt}}$ as the one yielding the minimum $\mathrm{dist}_G(\mathcal{C})$ for all $\mathcal{C} \in \mathfrak{C}(E)$.

3.2   Irregular Orientation Systems

In an irregular orientation system $\mathcal{C}$ with k orientations, each orientation can be selected independently. We interpret the orientation system as a clustering of the set $\Gamma = \{\gamma_e \mid e \in E\}$ of all input edge slopes, where each cluster is formed around the closest orientation in $\mathcal{C}$. Our goal is to find a set $\mathcal{C}$ of k orientations (clusters) that minimizes $\mathrm{dist}_G(\mathcal{C})$. To this end we apply the exact 1-dimensional k-means clustering algorithm of Nielsen and Nock [8] to the set Γ. This algorithm has running time $O(n^2 k)$ using a precomputed auxiliary matrix as a look up table.

4   MIP Model

Next we sketch how the MIP model of Nöllenburg and Wolff [10] must be modified in order to compute more general $\mathcal{C}$-oriented metro maps for an arbitrary set $\mathcal{C}$ of k orientations. Hard constraints encode properties of a layout which can not be violated. Soft constraints model the aesthetic quality criteria to be optimized in the layout. The hard constraints of the MIP comprise four aspects: $\mathcal{C}$-oriented coordinate system, assignment of edge directions, combinatorial embedding, and planarity. The soft constraints comprise line straightness, topographicity, and compactness. Each requires a set of linear constraints and a corresponding linear term in the objective function. While almost all constraints require smaller modifications, we focus here only on the coordinate system as the most central change from the octolinear MIP model [10]. For our full MIP model see [7].

Coordinate System. Every vertex u of G has two Cartesian coordinates in the plane $\mathbb{R}^2$, specified as $x(u)$ and $y(u)$. In order to address vertex coordinates in an octolinear system, Nöllenburg and Wolff [10] defined a redundant system of four coordinates. To adapt this system for any number k of orientations, we define a system of k coordinates $z_0, \ldots, z_{k-1}$, which are all real-valued variables in the MIP model and can all be obtained by rotating the x-axis counterclockwise by one of the angles in the orientation system $\mathcal{C} = \{\theta_0, \ldots, \theta_{k-1}\} \subset [0, \pi)$. We define the coordinate $z_i(u)$ using $x(u)$ and $y(u)$ as $z_i(u) = \cos(\theta_i) \cdot x(u) + \sin(\theta_i) \cdot y(u)$.

In order to express that two vertices u, v are collinear on a line with a slope in $\mathcal{C}$, we need the orthogonal orientation z_i^o for each coordinate z_i. Note that while z_i^o can coincide with other coordinates, this is guaranteed only in a regular orientation system with an even number of orientations. In general, this is not the case and hence we define a second set of redundant coordinates, see Figs. 1a, 1b and 1d. Using a rotation by $\pi/2$ we obtain $z_i^o(u) = -\sin(\theta_i) \cdot x(u) + \cos(\theta_i) \cdot y(u)$.

All other constraints of [10] need to be adapted to comply with the newly created coordinate system. For a full description of the modifications see [7].

5   Experiments

We performed experiments on real-world data to compare the computational performance and visual quality of metro maps with different linearity systems. Due to space constraints, we only present the results for the metro network of Vienna. The full experimental evaluation can be found in [7].

5.1   Setup

We generated schematic layouts of the metro network of Vienna ($n = 90$, $m = 96$), using aligned, regular and irregular orientation systems with $k \in \{3, 4, 5\}$ orientations. All layouts were created with two different weight vectors $(f_1, f_2, f_3) = (3, 2, 1)$ and $(10, 5, 1)$ for the objective function[1]. For all layouts we added planarity constraints on demand and concentrated on the overall layout geometry and interchanges without showing the individual stops along the lines.

To judge the quality and performance of a layout, we use several measurements. Firstly, the total number of bends in a layout as a measure of line straightness. Secondly, the MIP allows an edge to be drawn in the direction closest to its input direction (preferred) or one direction offset to the left or right (penalized in the objective function). The sector deviation is a coarse measure of topographicity, counting how many edges are not drawn in their preferred direction. Sector deviation is measured in total and on average per edge. Another measure of topographicity is the angular distortion, i.e., the actual angular difference between input edges and schematized output edges, which is measured on average per edge. Finally, we measure the runtime in seconds.

The experiments were run as single threads on an Intel Xeon E5-2640 v4, 2.40 GHz, with 64 GB of available memory space, using IBM ILOG CPLEX 12.8.

---

[1] f_1 emphasizes line straightness, f_2 the topographicity and f_3 compactness of an optimal layout.

5.2   Results

The performance and quality measurements for the 18 different instances are given in Table 1. Due to space constraints, we show only one representative set of nine layouts for Vienna in Fig. 2 and omit the other nine layouts.

Table 1. Results for the Vienna network. The model parameters are the number of available directions (k) and the orientation system (ori. sys.). The measures are the number of bends, sector deviation total (sec. dev.) and per edge (p.e.), distortion per edge (dist. p.e.) and the runtime in seconds.

Weights		$k =$	3			4			5		
		Ori. sys.	Aligned	Regular	Irregul.	Aligned	Regular	Irregul.	Aligned	Regular	Irregul.
(3, 2, 1)		#bends	**16**	**16**	17	22	24	21	25	25	29
		sec. dev.	27	27	**13**	21	18	17	24	24	21
		↳ p.e.	0.28	0.28	**0.14**	0.22	0.19	0.18	0.25	0.25	0.22
		dist. p.e.	31.47	36.07	15.96	23.18	22.96	16.07	19.45	26.68	**14.46**
		time [s]	308	349	**8**	108	116	299	69	217	113
(10, 5, 1)		#bends	16	16	**15**	19	19	19	25	25	29
		sec. dev.	25	25	**19**	27	27	**19**	24	24	23
		↳ p.e.	0.26	0.26	**0.2**	0.28	0.28	**0.2**	0.25	0.25	0.24
		dist. p.e.	31.18	33.5	17.76	25.19	23.53	16.35	19.45	26.68	**15.01**
		time [s]	53	39	**8**	140	115	41	44	27	51

We refer to specific sets of instances by their number of orientations k or their weights (f_1, f_2, f_3). Our first observation from generalizing the octolinear MIP model [10] is that the model size, i.e., the numbers of constraints and variables, scales linearly with k. So as long as k is a (small) constant, the asymptotics with respect to the graph size remain the same. Yet, in practice, doubling the size of the model may yield a significant slow-down in the solution time.

Next we look at the visual effects of increasing k. The increase in bends can be explained in part by an increase in unavoidable bends. The probability that two consecutive edges in a metro line cannot be drawn in the same direction decreases with increasing k; it could be counteracted by allowing more than three sectors for each edge. Sector deviation increases (under an irregular orientation system), but for aligned and regular systems, no trend emerges. Distortion seems to decrease overall, since the maximally possible angle distortion for each edge decreases. We would expect a greater runtime for an increasing k, however we did not observe this for Vienna.

Next we compare the two different weight vectors. Unsurprisingly, we have a similar or smaller amount of bends, when emphasizing bend minimization by changing $f_1 = 3$ to $f_1 = 10$. This also (slightly) increases the angle distortion. Sector deviation is on average slightly smaller for $(3, 2, 1)$, where choosing the preferred sector is more emphasized relative to the line straightness. The more emphasized setting $(10, 5, 1)$ leads overall to lower runtimes.

Finally we compare the effect of different orientation systems. While the number of bends is comparable for aligned and regular systems, for the irregular system they increase for $k = 5$, which might be specific to Vienna [7]. Sector deviation is again comparable for aligned and regular system but improves in the irregular setting. The same is true and even more pronounced for the distortion.

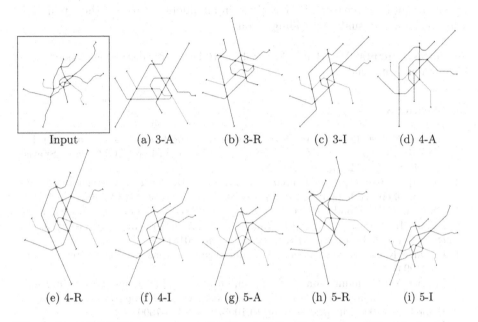

Input   (a) 3-A   (b) 3-R   (c) 3-I   (d) 4-A

(e) 4-R   (f) 4-I   (g) 5-A   (h) 5-R   (i) 5-I

Fig. 2. Layouts of Vienna generated with objective function weights $(f_1, f_2, f_3) = (3, 2, 1)$. For each $k \in \{3, 4, 5\}$ layouts are labeled as created with aligned (k-A), regular (k-R) and irregular (k-I) orientation system.

5.3   Discussion

Our approach of increasing topographicity in metro maps through data-driven selection of orientation systems seems to be promising based on our initial experiments. Choosing an irregular orientation system is a valid option to increase topographicity, even if the irregular set of slopes is unfamiliar.

Looking at the actual metro maps produced by our system, we can see one major caveat of our approach to minimize distortion by deciding the directions based on the input. While for most edges we have a very suitable representative direction in the orientation system, the constraints of the MIP might still force an edge to be drawn in a different sector, thus working against the topographicity. On a positive note, we can see that irregular orientation systems can create metro maps that resemble the input more closely than typical aligned systems.

We can also see that most of the layouts, which are not using an aligned orientation system do not include the horizontal direction. This might be helpful in labeling these metro maps, since it is difficult to place the visually preferred horizontal labels along a horizontal line with clear association to a station.

We conclude by reinforcing that our system should not be understood as a stand-alone method to metro map generation, but rather as an automated tool to help a designer explore the layout space more thoroughly and find a suitable orientation system for a network at low time cost. One approach to choose a suitable linearity k for a given input might be to use the smallest k which generates visually appealing layouts.

Acknowledgments. We thank Maxwell J. Roberts for discussions about non-standard linearity models.

References

1. Buchin, K., Meulemans, W., van Renssen, A., Speckmann, B.: Area-preserving simplification and schematization of polygonal subdivisions. ACM Trans. Spatial Algorithms Syst. **2**(1), 2:1–2:36 (2016)
2. Delling, D., Gemsa, A., Nöllenburg, M., Pajor, T., Rutter, I.: On d-regular schematization of embedded paths. Comput. Geom. Theory Appl. **47**(3A), 381–406 (2014)
3. Duncan, C.A., Goodrich, M.T.: Planar orthogonal and polyline drawing algorithms. In: Tamassia, R. (ed.) Handbook of Graph Drawing and Visualization, chap. 7, pp. 223–246. CRC Press, Boca Raton (2013)
4. Garland, K.: Mr Beck's Underground Map. Capital Transport Publishing, Middlesex (1994)
5. Merrick, D., Gudmundsson, J.: Path simplification for metro map layout. In: Kaufmann, M., Wagner, D. (eds.) GD 2006. LNCS, vol. 4372, pp. 258–269. Springer, Heidelberg (2007). https://doi.org/10.1007/978-3-540-70904-6_26
6. Neyer, G.: Line simplification with restricted orientations. In: Dehne, F., Sack, J.-R., Gupta, A., Tamassia, R. (eds.) WADS 1999. LNCS, vol. 1663, pp. 13–24. Springer, Heidelberg (1999). https://doi.org/10.1007/3-540-48447-7_2
7. Nickel, S., Nöllenburg, M.: Towards data-driven multilinear metro maps. CoRR abs/1904.03039 (2019). https://arxiv.org/abs/1904.03039
8. Nielsen, F., Nock, R.: Optimal interval clustering: application to bregman clustering and statistical mixture learning. IEEE Signal Process. Lett. **21**(10), 1289–1292 (2014)
9. Nöllenburg, M.: A survey on automated metro map layout methods. In: 1st Schematic Mapping Workshop, Essex, UK (2014)
10. Nöllenburg, M., Wolff, A.: Drawing and labeling high-quality metro maps by mixed-integer programming. IEEE Trans. Vis. Comput. Graph. **17**(5), 626–641 (2011)
11. Roberts, M.J.: What's your theory of effective schematic map design? In: 1st Schematic Mapping Workshop, Essex, UK (2014)
12. Roberts, M.J., Gray, H., Lesnik, J.: Preference versus performance: Investigating the dissociation between objective measures and subjective ratings of usability for schematic metro maps and intuitive theories of design. Int. J. Hum. Comput. Stud. **98**, 109–128 (2016)
13. Roberts, M.J., Newton, E.J., Lagattolla, F.D., Hughes, S., Hasler, M.C.: Objective versus subjective measures of paris metro map usability: Investigating traditional octolinear versus all-curves schematics. Int. J. Hum. Comput. Stud. **71**, 363–386 (2013)

14. Wu, H.Y., Niedermann, B., Takahashi, S., Roberts, M.J., Nöllenburg, M.: A survey on transit map layout – from design, machine, and human perspectives. Comput. Graph. Forum **39**(3), 619–646 (2020)
15. Wu, H.Y., Niedermann, B., Takahashi, S., Nöllenburg, M.: A survey on computing schematic network maps: The challenge to interactivity. In: 2nd Schematic Mapping Workshop, Vienna, Austria (2019)

Visualizing Sound, Hearing Diagrams: On the Creative Process of *Syrmos* by Iannis Xenakis

José L. Besada$^{(\boxtimes)}$

Universidad Complutense de Madrid, Madrid, Spain
besadajl@gmail.com

Abstract. A salient feature of Iannis Xenakis' compositional practices was the use of several concepts and techniques borrowed from architectural design and from scientific fields. He sometimes drew complete graphic scores preluding the transcription of his fair copy of conventional musical notation. I discuss the diagrammatical features of Xenakis' graphic score for *Syrmos*: although disparate representations depend on shared image schemata and cross-modal correspondences, their respective compositional logics are dissimilar.

Keywords: Science-based composition · Sketch studies · Cross-modal correspondences · Material anchors · Iannis Xenakis

1 Introduction

In *Syrmos*, a piece for string orchestra for eighteen players, Iannis Xenakis achieved a synthesis between compositional perspectives he developed during the 1950s. He implemented extra-musical ideas in compositional processes mainly borrowed from architectural design, mathematics, and physics. When playing *Syrmos*, the musicians and the conductor are supposed to read a score with standard notation on their respective music stands. A first and diagrammatic version of *Syrmos* is kept in the composer's archives. It was written on graph paper in order to transcribe the data it contains as accurately as possible. Among its numerous pages, one of them displays a kind of hyperbolic envelope surrounded by a seemingly unpatterned cluster made of little crosses (see Fig. 1).

Henceforth, I will only focus on this page, as a paradigmatic case in which both graphical elements, line segments and dots, are confronted. I will prove that, although both elements are immersed in the same diagrammatical space and share therefore common features, their underlying compositional logics are quite different. For that purpose, I will summon arguments from the fields of

This work has been funded by the research program "Atracción de Talento Investigador" 2019-T2/HUM-14477, financed by the Comunidad de Madrid. I thank Mâkhi Xenakis for allowing me to reproduce some of his father's compositional sketches.

A.-V. Pietarinen et al. (Eds.): Diagrams 2020, LNAI 12169, pp. 162–166, 2020.
https://doi.org/10.1007/978-3-030-54249-8_13

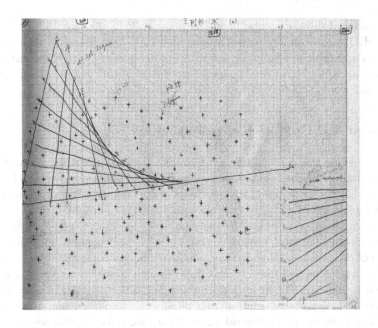

Fig. 1. Graphic score for *Syrmos*, bars 255–259 ©Iannis Xenakis Family.

experimental psychology—mainly based on studies of cross-modality [3,8]—and cognitive linguistics—particularly those coming from image schemata of the conceptual metaphor theory [7] and from the conceptual blending theory [4].

2   Music, Notation, and Cross-modality

We can imagine any Western musician quickly grasping the kind of information that Xenakis was providing on the graph paper. After all, the implicit axes of his diagrammatic notation are consistent with those of the standard musical notation. Both the symbolic and the graphic systems of representation share image schemata: PITCH RELATIONSHIPS ARE RELATIONSHIPS IN VERTICAL SPACE and TIME FLOWS FROM LEFT TO RIGHT. This strong relationship is not however an equivalence: pitches across the staves are not uniformly distributed; also, the rhythmic notation is sequential but rarely spatially proportional.

The aforementioned image schemata are not universal. For instance, research on time conceptualizations has shown a lack of universalism of the left-to-right image schema [5]. Concerning pitches, a large variety of conceptualizations spreads across different cultures. In spite of this diversity, empiric research points to some cross-modal correspondence: individuals subjected to verbal expressions or visual representations of pitches tend to provide responses which are consistent with the Western image schema from other cultural frames [1,2].

Xenakis was not the first composer putting forward a proportional representation of pitches and durations. His choice is aligned with notational needs based on technological developments, from the piano rolls of the late 19th century to current MIDI protocols [9]. Nevertheless, Xenakis' approach in *Syrmos* was not devised as a graphical system for interpreting his music. Quite the contrary, he explored and exploited a visual space in order to facilitate several compositional choices that were further rewritten with a conventional notation.

3   Linear vs. Dotted Representations

One year before the composition of *Syrmos*, Xenakis published a short article summarizing the main extra-musical influences that had proven to have an impact on his creative mind. He described three main categories, namely the "numbers parable", the "space parable", and the "gas parable"[1].

In the paragraph devoted to the space parable [10, p. 17], Xenakis highlighted that, "[i]n music, the most sensitive straight line is the constant and continuous variation of pitch"—i.e. the *glissando*[2]—as an elemental constituent for "building sonorous surfaces (or volumes)". This link between geometry and sound reveals a blended conception of music that enabled Xenakis to somehow ductilize the image schemata for managing time and pitches. He exploited massive *glissandi* for the first time in his orchestral piece *Metastaseis*; the sketch for one of its passages is equivalent to some architectural drafts he designed when working with Le Corbusier [11, pp. 3, 6–7]. The choice of the hyperbolic envelope for *Syrmos* in Fig. 1 follows the same logic. In doing so, the cross-hatching pattern became a material anchor for conceptual blends [6], because Xenakis projected the two-dimensional image schema onto a preexistent visual form.

In the paragraphs devoted to the gas parable [10, p. 18–19], Xenakis made the "punctual sounds" match with gas molecules. Instead of focusing on the "individual movement of sounds", he was interested in unfolding "mass effects" via the laws of gas kinetics. This time, the recurrent expression "sound clouds" in Xenakis' writings is the key to grasp his blended conception, as an attempt to aurally interpret the scatterplots—*nuages de points* in French—in statistics. Xenakis had already written three instrumental pieces guided by statistical laws—*Pithoprakta*, *Achorripsis*, and *Analogique A*—before *Syrmos*. A comparison between somme charts in his essay on *Analogique A* [11, p. 101] and a sketch

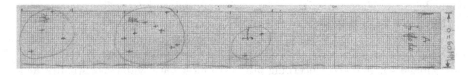

Fig. 2. Detail of a sketch for distributing "punctual sounds" in *Syrmos*   ©Iannis Xenakis Family.

---

[1] All translations are mine.

[2] String players obtain *glissandi* by sliding a finger of the left hand along the pressed string while the right hand normally bows.

for *Syrmos* (see Fig. 2) proves the recycling of previous ideas for managing the musical "density"—i.e. the number of events per unit of time. It seems that Xenakis freely distributed his crosses—standing for *pizzicati* and *col legno*[3]—on the graph paper: consequently, they should not be regarded as material anchors.

4 Overview

Through the case study I have provided, three important features of the compositional practices related to diagrammatic extramusical sources have been detected. First, cross-domain correspondences and the habit of Western musical notation tend to root the adoption of privileged image schemata for managing pitch and time. These schemata may facilitate new conceptual mappings with other fields during composition. Secondly, these schemata can host both prescriptive patterned figures—acting as material anchors—and stimulate prospective ideations, via dissimilar cognitive strategies. Third, composers sometimes develop auxiliary technology in order to mitigate some cognitive effort related to their tasks. It is the case for instance of a pitch ruler made by Xenakis (see Fig. 3) for the transcription from his graphic score to the conventional one.

Fig. 3. Pitch ruler made by Xenakis for *Syrmos* ©Iannis Xenakis Family.

References

1. Athanasopoulos, G., Antović, M.: Conceptual integration of sound and image: a model of perceptual modalities. Musicae Scientiae **22**(1), 72–87 (2018)
2. Eitan, Z., Timmers, R.: Beethoven's last piano sonata and those who follow crocodiles: cross-domain mappings of auditory pitch in a musical context. Cognition **114**(3), 405–422 (2010)
3. Evans, K.K., Treisman, A.: Natural cross-modal mappings between visual and auditory features. J. Vis. **10**(1), 1–12 (2010)
4. Fauconnier, G., Turner, M.: The Way We Think. Conceptual Blending and the Mind's Hidden Complexities. Basic Books, New York (2002)
5. Fuhrman, O., Boroditsky, L.: Cross-cultural differences in mental representations of time: evidence from an implicit nonlinguistic task. Cogn. Sci. **34**(8), 1430–1451 (2010)
6. Hutchins, E.: Material anchors for conceptual blends. J. Pragmat. **37**, 1555–1577 (2005)

---

[3] A *pizzicato* is obtained by plucking a string; *col legno* is a technique in which the bow is reversed for hitting with its wooden part.

7. Johnson, M.: The Body in the Mind: The Bodily Basis of Meaning, Imagination, and Reason. University of Chicago, Chicago (1987)
8. Spence, C.: Crossmodal correspondences: a tutorial review. Atten. Percept. Psychophys. **73**(4), 971–95 (2011)
9. Weibel, P.: The road to UPIC: from graphic notation to graphic user interface. In: Weibel, P., Brümmer, L., Kanach, S. (eds.) From Xenakis's UPIC to Graphic Notation Today, pp. 486–523. Hatje Cantz, Berlin (2020)
10. Xenakis, I.: Musique. Architecture. Casterman, Tournai (1976)
11. Xenakis, I.: Formalized Music: Thought and Mathematics in Composition (revised edition). Pendragon, Stuyvesant (1992)

String Diagrams for Assembly Planning

Jade Master[1] , Evan Patterson[2] , Shahin Yousfi[3],
and Arquimedes Canedo[3(✉)]

[1] University of California Riverside, Riverside, CA 92507, USA
jmast003@ucr.edu
[2] Stanford University, 450 Serra Mall, Stanford, CA 94305, USA
evan@epatters.org
[3] Siemens Corporate Technology, 755 College Rd E, Princeton, NJ 08540, USA
arquimedes.canedo@siemens.com

Abstract. Assembly planning is a difficult problem for companies. Many disciplines such as design, planning, scheduling, and manufacturing execution need to be carefully engineered and coordinated to create successful product assembly plans. Recent research in the field of *design for assembly* has proposed new methodologies to design product structures in such a way that their assembly is easier. However, present assembly planning approaches lack the engineering tool support to capture all the constraints associated to assembly planning in a unified manner. This paper proposes COMPOSITIONALPLANNING, a string diagram based framework for assembly planning. In the proposed framework, string diagrams and their compositional properties serve as the foundation for an engineering tool where CAD designs interact with planning and scheduling algorithms to automatically create high-quality assembly plans. These assembly plans are then executed in simulation to measure their performance and to visualize their key build characteristics. We demonstrate the versatility of this approach in the LEGO assembly domain. We developed two reference LEGO CAD models that are processed by COMPOSITIONALPLANNING's algorithmic pipeline. We compare sequential and parallel assembly plans in a Minecraft simulation and show that the time-to-build performance can be optimized by our algorithms.

Keywords: String diagrams · Assembly planning · Category theory

1 Introduction

Today, mass customization of products such as automobiles and consumer electronics is forcing companies to provide a very large product variety to address the diverse customer requirements. Digital manufacturing technologies make it possible to accommodate mass customization during product design and manufacturing. For example, parametric designs in computer aided design (CAD) software allow for the specification of configurable products, and computer aided manufacturing (CAM) algorithms allow for the fabrication of products on different machines. Unfortunately, there is very limited engineering tool support for

---

All authors contributed equally to this work while at Siemens.

© Springer Nature Switzerland AG 2020
A.-V. Pietarinen et al. (Eds.): Diagrams 2020, LNAI 12169, pp. 167–183, 2020.
https://doi.org/10.1007/978-3-030-54249-8_14

product assembly planning. Although some companies use *design for assembly* (DfA) [19] and *design for manufacturing and assembly* (DfMA) [13] methodologies that attempt to develop product structures that facilitate their assembly, their implementation is ad-hoc. Therefore, assembly planning is a task that is loosely coupled to the rest of the digital manufacturing pipeline. The objective of this paper is to open new avenues for *interoperable* assembly planning that is tightly coupled to the upstream design activities, and the downstream assembly tasks.

String diagrams are a powerful graphical calculus for reasoning in category theory [27]. String diagrams have also proven useful in many other domains. They have been shown to provide a mathematically sound graphical language in domains including linguistics [9], systems engineering [6], and computer science [20]. Generally, string diagrams represent processes which require and produce resources. Assembly planning is the discipline of understanding how to optimally chain assembly processes together to craft a whole product from separate parts [15]. Thus, string diagrams are a natural tool for formulating assembly planning problems and constructing their solutions.

To demonstrate this thesis we show that string diagrams can be used to build construction schedules for various LEGO models. From each LEGO 3D CAD file we generate a *connectivity graph* where the nodes represent LEGO pieces and the edges indicate that they are connected in the final model. Given a hierarchical clustering of this connectivity graph, we generate a *construction plan* represented by string diagrams which is hierarchical, compositional, and interpretable. Using the formalism of string diagrams, complex sub-assemblies can be *black boxed* into larger string diagrams. Having this hierarchical structure allows us to manipulate or adapt our plan at a desired level of abstraction. Furthermore, there is a categorical formalism that enables schedules to be generated from these string diagrams. We use topological sorting, Girvan-Newman, and Leiden algorithms to generate assembly plans and schedules with different properties. Finally, we use Minecraft [3] as a simulator to validate the resulting schedules and measure their time-to-build performance.

In this paper, we demonstrate the versatility of this approach with a framework, COMPOSITIONALPLANNING, that provides a new way of talking about assembly planning. Our category theoretic interpretation provides a flexible mathematical foundation that allows for an end-to-end demonstration from CAD design to assembly simulation. The contributions of this paper are the following:

- we show how string diagrams are an intuitive yet mathematically sound language to represent an assembly planning domain.
- as large string diagrams can be tedious and cumbersome for humans to work with, our framework automates the creation of large string diagrams and thus eliminates the overhead traditionally associated with them.
- a novel algorithm that converts string diagrams to *expressions* that result in highly parallel assembly plans.
- a Minecraft based simulation environment modification or "mod" to execute LEGO assembly plans.

– we publish the CompositonalPlanning framework as a Julia [4] package for others to reproduce and build upon our work[1].

2 Related Work

Assembly planning problems and approaches have been widely investigated. A comprehensive survey of them can be found in [15]. In [30], a survey of assembly design and planning systems is presented. In particular, the *Assembly Sequence Planning* (ASP) problem that we target in this paper is an NP-hard problem. ASP's goal is to find a collision-free sequence of assembly operations that put together individual parts given the geometry of the final product and the relative positions of parts in the final product. ASP is considered a combinatorial problem and therefore representations of the space of possible sequences has been an active area of research [17]. While various representations ranging from AND-OR graphs [11] to Petri nets [24] have been proposed, we are the first to study ASP under a category theoretic framework. In this paper, we show that category theory provides both an *explicit* and an *implicit* representation on assembly sequences. On the one hand, string diagrams provide an explicit ASP representation of partial and full assemblies. On the other hand, expressions provide us mathematical soundness and rigor as they implicitly encode precedence assembly relationships.

Although this paper focuses on LEGO and Minecraft models, the CompositionalPlanning framework can be easily adapted to other domains. In 3D CAD modeling, for example, parts are composed into assemblies in a similar way to how LEGO pieces compose into LEGO models. The specification of the parts themselves and their composition of assemblies is defined in a CAD file that is analogous to a LEGO 3D CAD file. Therefore, the first step would be to create a custom parser for a specific CAD file format to extract a connectivity graph from the information about parts and their composition. Given that there are many CAD file formats in the market today [8], the scalability of CompositionalPlanning in the CAD domain is dependent on the availability of custom parsers.

Related work in automated assembly planning illustrates how this field is highly fragmented. Most researchers develop custom assembly planning solutions that work for specific products and processes. In [21], the authors present a system to address the assembly planning of multi-variant products in modular production systems. The product requirements and their feasible assembly orders are modeled in a directed graph referred to as the *Augmented Assembly Priority Plan* (AAPP). The AAPP encodes how two initial subassemblies are joined together to form a new subassembly through a value adding task such as "assembly" or "screwing". From the authors' description, the AAPP can be mapped as a string diagram to leverage the planning capabilities of our CompositionalPlanning framework. Similarly, the authors in [23] present a system to generate *assembly precedence graphs* from CAD files. Similar to our results,

---

[1] CompositionalPlanning - https://github.com/CompositionalPlanning/.

they show that an assembly precedence graph contains all the valid sequences of an assembly. Their assembly precedence graphs correspond to our connectivity graph, and their assembly sequences correspond to our plans and schedules. There are two important differences compared to our work: (a) their means of user-interaction and visualization are spreadsheets instead of graphs, and (b) their implementation is based on a proprietary CAD software.

3   Categorical Assembly Planning Framework

Our COMPOSITIONALPLANNING framework, shown in Fig. 1, consists of five reusable software components. The first step is to infer a connectivity graph from the CAD model that describes how the different parts come together in terms of their geometry (e.g., orientation) and assembly operations (e.g., snap, glue, weld, insert). This step is necessary because most CAD models list quantities of all parts and detailed structural functions in relation to a finished product, and this information does not directly map to their assembly.

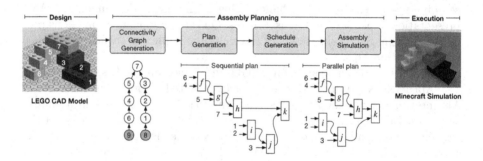

Fig. 1. COMPOSITIONALPLANNING framework pipeline.

The second step consists of plan generation [14] – described by different string diagrams – that have different properties of order and parallelism. These plans, although expressed by different expressions of string diagrams, generate the same LEGO model as they: (i) bring an initial world to a goal world using a set of assembly operators, and (ii) minimally impose ordering constraints.

The third step generates a schedule using a plan and a detailed knowledge of the execution environment (e.g., number of workers, machines). The job of the schedule generation [14] is to impose further ordering constraints on the assembly operator application to achieve a robust (e.g., against failures) and time-efficient execution of the assembly task (e.g., time-to-assembly).

The fourth and final step consists of executing the schedule in a simulator to visualize the assembly task, and to generate performance metrics. Although this paper focuses on LEGO CAD models as an input, and Minecraft simulations as an output, our components are domain agnostic, and they can be easily adapted for use in other domains.

3.1   Connectivity Diagram Generation from CAD

COMPOSITIONALPLANNING parses the text-based LDraw files [2] and automatically builds the connectivity diagram. Every LEGO model has a unique connectivity diagram that describes how the pieces are connected to each other. LDraw files [2] describe all the bricks in the model by type (e.g., 2×2, 2×4), color, center coordinates (x, y, z), and a 3×3 rotation matrix. This LDraw file represents the bill of materials (BOM) of the LEGO model and does not contain any information about the connectivity of the bricks. Therefore, the first step is to parse this information from the LDraw file f and generate a list of LegoObjects. The second step is to create a directed graph and add a node for every object in the LegoObjects list. Note that these nodes are not yet connected by edges.

Vertical stacking is the most common operation with LEGO bricks as shown in the example in Fig. 1. Therefore, the third step in our framework is to infer the vertical connectivity in the LEGO CAD model. In LDraw's coordinate system $-y$ is "up". Therefore, two bricks are connected if: (a) the top face of one brick has the same y coordinate as the other brick's down face ($a.top\_ycoord() ==$ $b.bottom\_ycoord()$); (b) and their boxes (defined by (x, z) center coordinates and the brick's *width* and *length*) intersect ($(abs(a.x - b.x) * 2 < (a.length + b.length))$ and $(abs(a.z - b.z) * 2 < (a.width + b.width))$). For every connected pair of objects we create an edge from a to b in the connectivity diagram. Other less common operations such as horizontal stacking, and operations involving other LEGO pieces such as pegs are left for future work. However, the connectivity inference would follow a similar principle as the one described above.

The fourth step consists of grounding all nodes in the connectivity diagram that do not have any predecessors. Having explicit ground nodes helps the processing of the connectivity diagram by the following algorithms. As an illustrative example consider the LEGO model and its connectivity diagram shown in Fig. 1. It consists of seven bricks sequentially numbered from (1), ..., (7). In addition, our algorithm also includes the "ground" nodes to facilitate the model construction using the base build plate. In this example, the ground nodes (9) and (8) connected to (6) and (1), respectively.

Extending our framework beyond LEGO would require new parsers to read CAD file formats, and new inference algorithms to derive the connectivity between parts.

3.2   String Diagrams

String diagrams are diagrams where resources are represented by strings (wires) and processes are represented by boxes. For example a process which snaps a peg into a hole is represented by

String diagrams can be composed in sequence

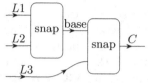

indicating that the processes must be performed in sequence. String diagrams can also be composed in parallel

indicating that the order in which the tasks are performed does not matter. String diagrams also have algebraic expressions called morphisms. For example, the first example has a corresponding algebraic expression given by

$$\text{snap}\colon L1 \otimes L2 \to \text{base}$$

Note that this expression is both functional and typed. This makes COMPOSITIONALPLANNING an efficient and type-safe framework. In a similar way, the expressions which string diagrams represent can be composed in sequence and parallel using the two operations

$$(f\colon x \to y, g\colon y \to z) \mapsto f \cdot g \colon x \to z \tag{1}$$

$$(f\colon x \to y, f'\colon x' \to y') \mapsto f \otimes f' \colon x \otimes x' \to y \otimes y' \tag{2}$$

Rather complicated expressions can be built using these operations, e.g., see the string diagrams in Fig. 4. A natural question to ask is when two expressions correspond to the same string diagram. The answer to this question is essential to understanding how planning domain dependencies represented in string diagrams can be algebraically manipulated. It turns out that if the algebraic expressions satisfy the right set of axioms, then the way that a string diagram is drawn is independent of the expression it generates. A structure of algebraic expressions satisfying these axioms is a well-known structure in category theory called a symmetric monoidal category. In [18] it is shown that string diagrams unambiguously represent morphisms in a given symmetric monoidal category. The following theorem ensures the soundness of string diagrams in the LEGO assembly domain.

Theorem 1. *Let $G = (E, V)$ be a simple graph whose nodes V represent pieces of a LEGO model and whose edges E indicate a connection in the completed structure. Then, there is a symmetric monoidal category where:*

- *an object is finite tensor product $X_1 \otimes X_2 \ldots X_n$ of subsets of V i.e. all possible tensors of subassemblies.*
- *A morphism $f\colon X_1 \otimes X_2 \ldots \otimes X_n \to Y_1 \otimes Y_2 \ldots Y_n$ is a construction plan which turns the subassemblies $X_1 \otimes X_2 \ldots \otimes X_n$ into the subassemblies $Y_1 \otimes Y_2 \ldots \otimes Y_n$ using only the joins allowed by the edges of G.*

- *The composite $g \cdot f$ represents the construction plan where f and g are performed in sequence.*
- *The tensor product $g \otimes f$ represents the construction plan where f and g are performed in parallel.*

Proof. Symmetric monoidal categories can be freely generated from the data of a Petri net. In "On the Category of Petri Net Computations", Sassone showed that for a Petri net P, there is a strict symmetric monoidal category $\mathcal{Q}[P]$ whose objects are finite strings of places in your Petri net and whose morphisms correspond to *strongly concatenable processes* [26]. These are sequences of events which can occur using the transitions of your Petri net in sequence and in parallel.

Recall that a Petri net is a tuple (T, P, s, t) where

- T is a finite set of events which can occur,
- P is a finite set of available resources,
- $s \colon T \to P^{\oplus}$ is a function from events to multisets of resources indicating which resources are required for each event and,
- $t \colon T \to P^{\oplus}$ is a function from events to multisets of resources indicating which resources are produced by each event.

To construct the desired symmetric monoidal category, we set T equal to $\mathcal{P}(E)$, the set of subets of edges in G and set P equal to $\mathcal{P}(V)$ the set of subsets of nodes in G i.e. all possible sub-assemblies of the LEGO model. Define $s \colon \mathcal{P}(E) \to \mathcal{P}(V)^{\oplus}$ by the rule

$$\{(x_1, y_1), (x_2, y_2), \ldots (x_n, y_n)\} \mapsto \{x_1, x_2, \ldots, x_n\} + \{y_1, y_2, \ldots, y_n\}.$$

where $+$ indicates the occurrence of both subsets in the multiset $\mathcal{P}(V)^{\oplus}$. Define $t \colon \mathcal{P}(E) \to \mathcal{P}(V)^{\oplus}$ by the rule

$$\{(x_1, y_1), (x_2, y_2), \ldots (x_n, y_n)\} \mapsto \{x_1, x_2, \ldots, x_n\} \cup \{y_1, y_2, \ldots, y_n\}.$$

The symmetric monoidal category in the theorem statement is obtained by taking the category of strongly concatenable processes on this Petri net.

The next section describes how the string diagrams of these symmetric monoidal categories can be leveraged to produce construction plans.

3.3 Planning

A LEGO CAD model and its connectivity graph describe an object in its final, assembled state, but not how to assemble it. A *plan* consists of step-by-step instructions on how to assemble the atomic parts (LEGO bricks) into the desired object. In general, there are many possible plans for assembling the same object, corresponding to different ways of forming intermediate sub-assemblies.

For us, plans are string diagrams. In such a diagram, the strings represent sub-assemblies and the boxes represent operations of joining together sub-assemblies to make a larger sub-assembly. Formally, a sub-assembly is a subset of the atomic parts, interpreted as being assembled. Each join operation takes two disjoint sub-assemblies A and B as inputs and produces a single output, the union $A \cup B$. A plan is a string diagram that takes all the singleton sets (sub-assemblies consisting of a single part) as inputs and produces as output the set of all parts (full assembly). Although every plan is valid at this level of description, not every plan will be physically feasible.

As proof of concept, we implemented two simple algorithms for assembly planning. In the *sequential algorithm*, we topologically order the edges of the connectivity graph. That is, we first topologically order the nodes, where a topological ordering is any total ordering consistent with the directed edges. Then we lexicographically order the edges, viewed as ordered pairs of nodes. For each edge, taken in this order, we join the two sub-assemblies containing the source and target, if they are distinct; otherwise, we do nothing. We continue in this way until all the edges have been exhausted, at which point the object is fully assembled. When the connectivity graph is a path graph, the sequential plan is the obvious plan that joins the parts together one-at-a-time.

In the *parallel algorithm*, we create more opportunities for parallelism by partitioning the connectivity graph into components, making plans on each component, and then treating these plans as black boxes in a higher-level plan. This meta-algorithm has several knobs to tune, and it can be applied recursively. To partition the graph, we can apply any community detection algorithm that finds non-overlapping communities. In our experiments, we use the Girvan-Newman algorithm [16] and a variant of the Louvain method [7], the Leiden algorithm [28]. We perform only one level of partitioning and we do sequential planning within each partition and also to assemble the resulting sub-plans. The use of community detection to find opportunities for parallelism is a heuristic, but works well in our experiments.

3.4   Scheduling

A plan, in the form of a string diagram, says what steps to perform and how the steps depend on each other. A *schedule* extends the information in a plan by assigning the steps a definite order; formally, a schedule is any linear extension of the topological ordering of the operations (boxes) in the plan. For simplicity, we take a resource-agnostic view of scheduling, in which the number of workers is unknown at the time of planning and scheduling. The aim in scheduling is therefore to maximize the opportunities for parallelism, given the constraints imposed by the plan [25].

Our scheduling algorithms have two major phases. First, we create a syntactic expression representing the plan. In general, a single string diagram can be represented by many different expressions; we construct one of them. We then linearize the expression, using a simple recursive algorithm, to obtain a schedule.

A small example will illustrate the relationship between string diagrams and syntactic expressions. Consider the string diagram shown in Fig. 2, the composite of f and g in parallel with composite of h and k. We can represent this diagram by either of the expressions $(f \cdot g) \otimes (h \cdot k)$ (read "f then g, and h then k") and $(f \otimes h) \cdot (g \otimes k)$ (read "f and h, then g and k").

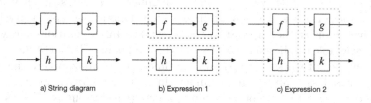

a) String diagram   b) Expression 1   c) Expression 2

Fig. 2. Relationship between string diagrams and syntactic expressions

We have developed an algorithm to find an expression for any string diagram representing a morphism in a symmetric monoidal category. As the algorithm is fairly elaborate, we will not digress to present it carefully, except to say that it is inspired by existing algorithms that recognize in a DAG, or reduce a DAG to, a series-parallel digraph [22,29].

The second phase of scheduling is more straightforward. Having formed an expression for the plan, we schedule the plan by recursively linearizing the expression tree. Given a composition $f \cdot g$, we simply concatenate the schedules for f and g. Given a product $f \otimes g$, we *interleave* the schedules for f and g, meaning that we take the first element of the f-schedule, then the first element of the g-schedule, then the second element of the f-schedule, and so on, until the both schedules have been exhausted. For example, both of the above expressions $(f \cdot g) \otimes (h \cdot k)$ and $(f \otimes h) \cdot (g \otimes k)$ yield the same schedule (f, h, g, k). Note that the ordering of the monoidal products affects the schedule, so that $f \otimes g$ yields a different schedule than $g \otimes f$. This procedure can be seen as a special case of an existing algorithm for optimally scheduling series-parallel digraphs [10].

3.5   Simulation

Minecraft is an immensely popular 3D open-world video game where players can build their own structures [12]. The game world and most of its elements are made of different kinds of blocks. These blocks can be used to create structures of any complexity. This versatility makes Minecraft a good fit to represent the CAD model and to simulate their assembly process. It has already proven to be a well-suited simulation tool in other robotics domains [5]. To execute the schedule generated by our framework we extended Minecraft by a new mod. With this "mod" we can simulate the whole assembly process of the CAD model described by the schedule. The simulation not only provides us with a comprehensible visual representation of the process, but also allows us to quantify execution time and worker occupancy of different schedules.

Our open source Minecraft "mod" executes the assembly operations in the correct order as dictated by the generated schedule. The geometric CAD information is encoded in the connectivity diagram and it is parsed by our mod. Each

LEGO brick is represented by a single or multiple Minecraft blocks. The schedule and the operations specified in it determine which and how many bricks can be connected to each other per step. In addition to the precedence constraints encoded in the schedule, we can define a number of *workers*. Each worker is allowed to perform a single operation per step. Operations are dispatched to workers in the order they appear in the schedule. Only operations for which a worker is available can be executed. Hence, the level of parallelism of the schedule and the number of workers determine the time it takes to complete the assembly. Disjoint sub-assemblies are assembled in their own area respectively until they are connected to each other forming a new (sub-)assembly. The assembly process is finished when all of the schedule's operations have been completed by the available workers.

4   Results

To validate the COMPOSITIONALPLANNING's pipeline we designed the two LEGO CAD models shown in Fig. 3(a–b). The design objective was to have two LEGO models of around 100 bricks each with a rich set of features and a few human-intuitive sub-assemblies to validate our approach. The Columns model (Fig. 3(a)) is inspired by roman temples and consists of 77 bricks. This model consists of four column sub-assemblies, each composed of 12 vertically stacked 2×2 bricks each. The roof sub-assembly consists of two pairs of support beams, each arranged in a stair configuration supporting a flat roof. The House model (Fig. 3(b)) consists of 86 bricks. The house foundation sub-assembly consists of eight 4×10 green bricks and supports the house sub-assembly and an electric pole. The house sub-assembly consists of four non-identical walls. We designed each wall using different compositions of bricks (i.e., 1×1, 1×8, 1×10, $1 \times 2 \times 2$, etc.) that result in different connectivity features as highlighted by the different shades of brown. The front wall has a square window and a door. The two side walls have two windows each while the back wall is solid. The four walls support a two layer roof. The pole sub-assembly consists of eleven 1×1 bricks, and one 1×6 brick on top.

4.1   Connectivity Diagrams

The generated connectivity diagrams for the two CAD models are shown in Fig. 3(c–d). The Columns model was designed with regularity and symmetry in mind. These features are explicit in its connectivity diagram in Fig. 3(c) with the four long strands representing the columns, and the dense layer on top representing the roof. On the other hand, the House model was designed with asymmetry and irregularity in mind. These features are clearly visible in its connectivity diagram in Fig. 3(d). In the House connectivity diagram, the walls are irregular and asymmetric with gaps representing the windows and the door. The pole is represented by the long strand.

Typically, LEGO models come with assembly instructions, or *build instructions* [1]. These instructions are, most likely, made for human enjoyment and

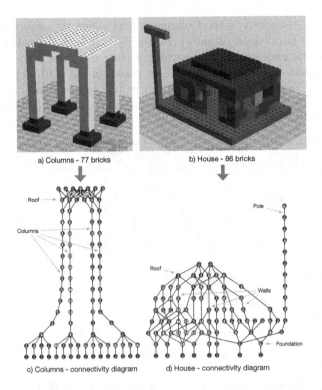

Fig. 3. LEGO CAD models and their inferred connectivity diagrams. (Color figure online)

therefore must be intuitive. One natural way to organize these instructions is by sub-assemblies such that humans can relate to the structure they are constructing (e.g., a house). In some cases, these sub-assemblies are obvious. For example, the column and roof sub-assemblies in the Columns connectivity diagram (Fig. 3(c)) are easily distinguishable and therefore can be decomposed into a reasonable build plan. However, there are other cases when these sub-assemblies are not obvious. For example, decomposing the interlinked wall sub-assembly in the House model (Fig. 3(d)) into a reasonable plan is not trivial. For both examples, our plan generation pipeline on string diagrams can be used to generate sequential and highly parallel assembly plans.

4.2   Plan Generation

In this paper, the quality of an assembly plan is determined in terms of how many operations can be executed in parallel, rather than on maximizing human enjoyment. For each LEGO CAD model, we generate two schedules. A sequential schedule is generated by topologically sorting the connectivity diagram, and a parallel schedule is generated with the algorithms introduced in Sect. 3.3. Figure 4 shows the sequential schedules generated for the Columns and the House models.

The column symmetry in the Columns model allows the sequential schedule to expose some parallelism as shown in Fig. 4(a). If several workers are available, this natural parallelism can be exploited to reduce the time-to-build. The sequential schedule for the House model, as shown in Fig. 4(b), exposes very little parallelism due to the asymmetry and irregularity in the model. These two examples help us illustrate the inherent limitations of sequential schedules.

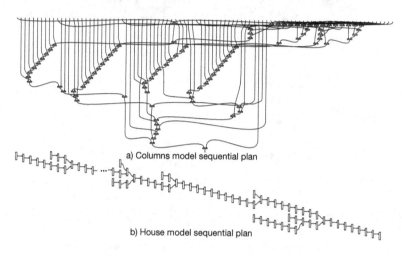

a) Columns model sequential plan

b) House model sequential plan

Fig. 4. Sequential plans generated for the two LEGO CAD models.

Using the parallel plan generation algorithms described in Sect. 3.3, our framework exposes higher levels of parallelism as shown in Fig. 5. Here, the black boxes corresponding to a partitioning of the connectivity diagram are shown by the labeled black boxes. The number in each black box represents the number of bricks within the black box sub-plan. The execution schedules are derived from these parallel plans. Even in the case of a purely sequential plan of the black boxes (represented by the width of the black boxes), it can be observed that the amount of parallelism is higher compared to the sequential schedules in Fig. 4. In particular, the House model's parallel plan in Fig. 5(b) exposes much higher parallelism when compared to the its sequential plan in Fig. 4(b) consisting of a stairs configuration with minimum parallelism.

4.3   Simulated Schedule Execution

The schedule and the number of workers determines how many operations can be executed in parallel. This parallelism can be visualized in the simulation when multiple sub-assemblies are constructed at the same time. Figure 6 shows a time-lapse of the parallel assembly process for the Columns and House models

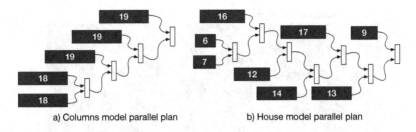

a) Columns model parallel plan   b) House model parallel plan

Fig. 5. Parallel plans generated for the two LEGO CAD models. The width of the black boxes represent a sub-plan (i.e., a stairs configuration).

with an unlimited number of workers. The top row shows the assembly process at an early stage after a few blocks were already added. Note the parallel construction areas of the assemblies highlighted by the red squares. Furthermore, the main construction area where pieces and sub-assemblies will eventually be connected to each other can be recognized. Sub-assemblies that are connected to the ground are not constructed in separate construction areas but at their final position in the main construction area. This prevents excessive shifting of assemblies. While all the sub-assemblies are easily distinguishable for the Columns model, the House's main construction area already consists of three sub-assemblies which can be recognized by the three separate walls on top of the House's base. These construction areas are based on the black boxes of the plans and their representation in the corresponding schedule. The (sub-)schedule for a black box may contain some level of parallelism like the Columns model. Besides the parallel assembly of the columns the derived schedule allows for a parallel assembly of the roof in three separate construction areas. The middle row shows the half completed assemblies. The structures are more advanced, and some sub-assemblies have already been connected to other assemblies. The bottom row shows the fully assembled Columns and House LEGO models.

To assess the quality of the generated plans we simulate the assembly process for the sequential and the parallel schedules for both models. The simulation is run with a varying number of workers – 1, 2, 4, 8 and 16. For each configuration we measured the total number of steps it takes to build the assembly and the average occupancy ratio of the workers. Table 1 summarizes the results. Our baselines are simulations run with a single worker. While pieces can be snapped to the ground or to an already existing assembly, two single pieces can also be combined to a new sub-assembly. In the latter case we must first connect a LEGO brick to the ground and this occupies a worker for a time step. For this reason, the time-to-built for the parallel schedule with a single worker is higher than the one for the sequential schedule. Unsurprisingly, the parallel schedule with more than one worker always requires fewer steps to complete the assembly while maintaining a higher occupancy rate than its sequential counterpart. The performance difference between the sequential and parallel schedules for the Columns model is rather small because of its architecture. Its sequential plan (Fig. 4(a)) already exposes some parallelism. However, our parallel schedule is

Fig. 6. Time-lapse of the execution of parallel plans. Black box sub-assemblies are built simultaneously on different construction areas highlighted by the red squares. (Color figure online)

Table 1. Execution time and worker occupancy for different schedules with varying number of workers.

Schedule	Workers	Columns model		House model	
		Steps	Occupancy	Steps	Occupancy
Sequential	1	92	1.00	93	1.00
	2	50	0.92	75	0.62
	4	33	0.70	69	0.34
	8	25	0.46	65	0.18
	16	23	0.25	65	0.09
Parallel	1	95	1.00	98	1.00
	2	50	0.95	55	0.89
	4	30	0.79	36	0.68
	8	19	0.63	26	0.47
	16	17	0.35	21	0.29

able to exploit additional opportunities and provides slightly better performance over the sequential schedule.

For the House model on the other hand, the parallel schedule yields significantly faster assembly times with an increasing number of workers; up to 3 times with 16 workers. Additionally, the workers are used to a higher capacity and the occupancy ratio deteriorates at a slower rate as the number of workers increases. This model shows that our algorithms are able to identify and exploit non-obvious parallelism in less regular and symmetric models.

5   Conclusion and Future Work

In this paper, we studied the use of string diagrams for assembly planning and developed a framework to demonstrate this approach in the LEGO domain. This new perspective gives us multiple advantages. First, it provides us with a powerful graphical calculus for reasoning about the assembly planning domain in category theory. Second, this formalism allows string diagrams to be easily manipulated within a programming framework to generate plans and schedules. This allows us to seamlessly interconnect the different disciplines involved in assembly planning. Third, with a novel hierarchical planning approach using black boxes, we demonstrated that the resulting plans expose high-degrees of parallelism that result in efficient assembly. Our COMPOSITIONALPLANNING framework has several limitations that prescribe future research. (i) As a proof of concept, we focused on the most popular LEGO assembly operations. Since our framework is domain agnostic, extending to other domains is an important direction for future work. (ii) We implemented three planning and one scheduling algorithm. Implementing other algorithms will help us validate the full potential of string diagrams for assembly planning. (iii) The planning algorithms yield different string diagrams. Developing new algorithms to *morph* a string diagram to another with different properties (e.g., more parallelism) is a challenging but very interesting research direction.

References

1. Building instructions (2019). www.lego.com/en-us/service/buildinginstructions
2. Ldraw.org standards: File format 1.0.2 (2019). www.ldraw.org/article/218.html
3. Minecraft Java Edition. [digital] (2019). www.minecraft.net/en-us/download
4. The Julia Programming Language (2020). https://julialang.org/
5. Aluru, K.C., Tellex, S., Oberlin, J., MacGlashan, J.: Minecraft as an experimental world for AI in robotics. In: 2015 AAAI Fall Symposium Series (2015)
6. Baez, J.C., Erbele, J.: Categories in control. Theory Appl. Categ. **30**(24), 836–881 (2015). Available at arXiv:1405.6881
7. Blondel, V.D., Guillaume, J.L., Lambiotte, R., Lefebvre, E.: Fast unfolding of communities in large networks. J. Stat. Mech: Theory Exp. **2008**(10), P10008 (2008)
8. Cheney, D., Fischer, B.: Measuring the PMI Modeling Capability in CAD Systems: Report 1 - Combined Test Case Verification. Technical report 15–997, NIST, November 2015

9. Coecke, B., Sadrzadeh, M., Clark, S.: Mathematical foundations for a compositional distributional model of meaning (2010). Available at arXiv:1003.4394
10. Cordasco, G., Rosenberg, A.L.: On scheduling series-parallel DAGs to maximize AREA. Int. J. Found. Comput. Sci. **25**(05), 597–621 (2014)
11. De Mello, L.H., Sanderson, A.C.: And/or graph representation of assembly plans. IEEE Trans. Robot. Autom. **6**(2), 188–199 (1990)
12. Duncan, S.C.: Minecraft, beyond construction and survival. Well Played **1**(1), 1–22 (2011). Available at dl.acm.org/citation.cfm?id=2207096.2207097
13. Favi, C., Germani, M., Mandolini, M.: Design for manufacturing and assembly vs. design to cost: toward a multi-objective approach for decision-making strategies during conceptual design of complex products. Procedia CIRP **50**, 275–280 (2016)
14. Fox, B., Kempf, K.: Opportunistic scheduling for robotic assembly. In: Proceedings of 1985 IEEE International Conference on Robotics and Automation, vol. 2, pp. 880–889, March 1985
15. Ghandi, S., Masehian, E.: Review and taxonomies of assembly and disassembly path planning problems and approaches. Comput. Aided Des. **67**(C), 58–86 (2015)
16. Girvan, M., Newman, M.E.: Community structure in social and biological networks. Proc. Natl. Acad. Sci. **99**(12), 7821–7826 (2002)
17. Jiménez, P.: Survey on assembly sequencing: a combinatorial and geometrical perspective. J. Intell. Manuf. **24**(2), 235–250 (2013). Available at doi.org/10.1007/s10845-011-0578-5
18. Joyal, A., Street, R.: The geometry of tensor calculus, i. Adv. Math. **88**(1), 55–112 (1991). Available at www.sciencedirect.com/000187089190003P
19. Kretschmer, R., Pfouga, A., Rulhoff, S., Stjepandi, J.: Knowledge-based design for assembly in agile manufacturing by using data mining methods. Adv. Eng. Inform. **33**(C), 285–299 (2017)
20. Master, J.: Generalized petri nets (2019). Available at arXiv:1904.09091
21. Michniewicz, J., Reinhart, G., Boschert, S.: Cad-based automated assembly planning for variable products in modular production systems. Procedia CIRP **44**, 44–49 (2016). 6th CIRP Conference on Assembly Technologies and Systems (CATS)
22. Mitchell, M.: Creating minimal vertex series-parallel graphs from directed acyclic graphs. In: Proceedings of the 2004 Australasian Symposium on Information Visualisation, pp. 133–139 (2004)
23. Pintzos, G., Triantafyllou, C., Papakostas, N., Mourtzis, D., Chryssolouris, G.: Assembly precedence diagram generation through assembly tiers determination. Int. J. Comput. Integr. Manuf. **29**, 1045–1057 (2016)
24. Rosell, J.: Assembly and task planning using petri nets: a survey. Proc. Inst. Mech. Eng. Part B J. Eng. Manuf. **218**(8), 987–994 (2004)
25. Rosenberg, A.L.: Scheduling DAGs opportunistically: the dream and the reality circa 2016. In: Dutot, P.-F., Trystram, D. (eds.) Euro-Par 2016. LNCS, vol. 9833, pp. 22–33. Springer, Cham (2016). https://doi.org/10.1007/978-3-319-43659-3_2
26. Sassone, V.: On the category of Petri net computations. In: Mosses, P.D., Nielsen, M., Schwartzbach, M.I. (eds.) CAAP 1995. LNCS, vol. 915, pp. 334–348. Springer, Heidelberg (1995). https://doi.org/10.1007/3-540-59293-8_205
27. Selinger, P.: A Survey of Graphical Languages for Monoidal Categories. In: Coecke, B. (ed.) New Structures for Physics. Lecture Notes in Physics, vol. 813. Springer, Heidelberg (2010). https://doi.org/10.1007/978-3-642-12821-9_4. Available at arXiv:0908.3347
28. Traag, V.A., Waltman, L., van Eck, N.J.: From Louvain to Leiden: guaranteeing well-connected communities. Sci. Rep. **9**, 1–12 (2019)

29. Valdes, J., Tarjan, R.E., Lawler, E.L.: The recognition of series parallel digraphs. SIAM J. Comput. **11**(2), 298–313 (1982)
30. Zha, X., Lim, S., Fok, S.: Integrated intelligent design and assembly planning: a survey. Int. J. Adv. Manuf. Technol. **14**(9), 664–685 (1998)

Reasoning with Diagrams

An Alternative Reformulation of the Transformation Rules in the Beta Part of Peirce's Existential Graphs

Shigeyuki Atarashi[(✉)] [ID]

Department of Philosophy, Doshisha University, 601 Imadegawa-Karasuma,
Kyoto 602-8580, Japan
satarash@mail.doshisha.ac.jp

Abstract. The aim of this paper is to reformulate the transformation rules presented by Peirce in the Beta part of Existential Graphs, in a different way from the rules systemized by Roberts and Shin. Existential Graphs provides an iconic system of logic. In other words, it visualizes logical reasonings by using diagrammatic representations. Specifically, a *graph* represents a situation occurring in a certain universe of discourse. In addition, Peirce introduced a *line of identity* and a *cut*. The former is a thick line that affirms the identity of two particulars signified by its two ends. The latter is a closed curve that is drawn with a thin line. By enclosing a graph entirely by a cut, the content represented by the graph is denied. Peirce forbid a line of identity from crossing a cut, yet both Roberts and Shin presumed that a line of identity can cross a cut. Hence, this paper eliminates that presumption completely and shows an alternative reformulation of the transformation rules in the Beta part of Existential Graphs.

Keywords: Existential Graphs · Graph · Line of identity · Cut · Transformation rule

1 Introduction

Existential Graphs, developed by Charles Sanders Peirce, provides a diagrammatic system of logic. Peirce used the term *graphs* to refer to diagrammatic representations of states of affairs in a discourse of universe [2, 4.421]. Existential Graphs expresses deductive reasonings diagrammatically by transforming given graphs into other graphs in accordance with certain rules.

Unfortunately, Peirce's original descriptions of the transformation rules are complicated. In *The Existential Graphs of Charles S. Peirce*, Roberts made them much more understandable [3, 56–60]. Later, in *The Iconic Logic of Peirce's Graphs*, Shin acknowledged that Roberts' reconstruction of the transformation rules eliminated some confusion from Peirce's explanations of them [4, 135–139].

© Springer Nature Switzerland AG 2020
A.-V. Pietarinen et al. (Eds.): Diagrams 2020, LNAI 12169, pp. 187–201, 2020.
https://doi.org/10.1007/978-3-030-54249-8_15

Shin also pointed out, however, that Roberts' reformulation for them involved new difficulties [4, 135–139]. Hence, Shin attempted to overcome those difficulties and provide a new, more effective and systematic reformulation of the transformation rules. Shin's reformulation was successful [4, 139–150], yet it did not completely conform to Peirce's original ideas of Existential Graphs. Therefore, in this paper, I propose another symmetrical arrangement of the transformation rules as an alternative reformulation along the lines of Peirce's conceptions of Existential Graphs.

2   No Crossing of Cuts

For the Beta part of Existential Graphs, Peirce introduced three kinds of diagrammatic devices: *spots*, *lines of identity*, and *cuts*. A spot corresponds to a predicate in a classical first-order predicate language [2, 4.438]. A line of identity is a thick line segment and "a graph asserting the numerical identity of the individuals denoted by its two extremities" [2, 4.444]. Each end of a line of identity designates a different indefinite individual, and the line of identity affirms that the two individuals are identical with each other. Finally, a cut is a closed curve drawn with a thin line, which has "the effect of denying the entire graph in its area" [2, 4.402]. Peirce also called the area enclosed by a cut its *close* [2, 4.437]. Thus, enclosing a graph entirely by a cut denies the content of the state of affairs signified by the graph.

Peirce declared that "[t]wo cuts cannot intersect one another" [2, 4.399]; and that no graph crosses a cut [2, 4.414]. Hence, we can attach no interpretation to a graph that crosses a cut. Shin also excluded a cut "crossing a predicate symbol" [4, 41]. In other words, we cannot place a spot in such a manner that a cut crosses it. From this standpoint, it is natural that no line of identity should cross a cut. In fact, Peirce clearly wrote that "a line of identity is a partial graph; and as a graph it cannot cross a sep" [2, 4.499]. Note that Peirce used the term *sep* instead of *cut* elsewhere [2, 4.437]. Thus, as long as a line of identity is a graph, it never crosses a sep or a cut either into its close or out of its close.

Nevertheless, Roberts and Shin both presumed that a line of identity can cross a cut. For example, concerning the graph in Fig. 1, Roberts would insist that "we have a line of identity crossing a cut" [3, 50]. This graph means that something exists that is not ugly. Concerning the structure of the graph, Roberts wrote that "there are, in a sense, two lines of identity: one outside the cut, and one inside the cut" [3, 50]. This way of understanding would fit Peirce's notion of a line of identity, but Roberts did not adopt it. Instead, according to Roberts, "it is quite natural and inconsequential to speak of a line of identity as crossing a cut, as Peirce did himself" [3, 50n].

In contrast, Peirce argued that "it will be well to avoid the idea of a graph's being cut through by a sep, and confine ourselves to the effect of joining dots on the sep to dots outside and inside of it" [2, 4.449]. This remark indicates what follows; in Fig. 1, the line of identity outside the cut couples a point outside with the intersectional point on the cut, and the line of identity inside the cut couples

Fig. 1. No crossing of cuts.

a point inside with the same intersectional point. At first sight, it might seem that Peirce did "not bother to explain" that "the part of a line of identity that crosses is not a graph" in 4.458 and 4.459 [3, 50n]. As cited above, however, in 4.499, Peirce emphasized that a line of identity does not cross a cut; and, in 4.501, Peirce still wrote in such words as "[t]he connexion or disconnexion of a line of identity outside a sep with a marked or an unmarked point on the sep" and "the junction or disjunction of a line of identity inside the sep with a point upon the sep" [2, 4.501]. Thus, it is evident that Peirce held fast to the notion that no line of identity crosses a cut.

3   Use of Dots

From the viewpoint that no line of identity crosses a cut, Peirce formulated the rules for transforming graphs in the Beta part of Existential Graphs. Roberts read Peirce's statements about the transformation rules in a manner contrary to Peirce's indication, so it follows that Roberts failed to fully grasp Peirce's original aims. For instance, Peirce permitted lengthening a line of identity from the outside of a cut to a point on it under certain conditions [2, 4.505]. We may thus change the first graph in Fig. 2 into the second one. Though Roberts himself also introduced a rule for such a transformation, he thought that Peirce lost sight of a necessary requirement for the transformation: "no crossing of cuts results from this addition" [3, 57]. Nevertheless, Peirce admitted this only as the lengthening of a line of identity to "a vacant point" on a cut, and he never overlooked the constraint on it [2, 4.505], as I will discuss in Sect. 4.

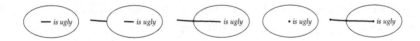

Fig. 2. Usage of dots.

In addition, Roberts classified the rule for this transformation into the rule of iteration [3, 57], while Peirce did not [2, 4.505]. Shin wrote the following about Peirce's rule of iteration: "[t]he main idea of the iteration rule is that when certain conditions are satisfied, we are allowed to copy (i.e., reiterate) a certain part of a graph" [4, 136]. In short, the rule of iteration enables us to make replicas of a graph if certain prerequisites are met. Then, what kind of graph is iterated in the above transformation? Is it a portion of a line of identity? It is unclear why the transformation is a consequence of the rule of iteration.

Shin examined the difficulties of Roberts' system in details and presented a new reformulation of the transformation rules. Shin's system is more comprehensive than that of Roberts and explicitly deals with some graph transformations that Roberts did not explicate. For example, $\exists x Fx \vee \exists x Gx$ and $\exists x(Fx \vee Gx)$ are equivalent in any logical system of classical first-order predicate language, and Shin distinctly demonstrated that two graphs corresponding to those propositions are mutually transformable. Shin's attempt was a successful elaboration of Roberts' system on the foundation of the notion that lines of identity cross cuts. Therefore, we must be able to define the transformation rules for lines of identity via an alternative reformulation in conformity with the principle that no line of identity crosses a cut.

As seen above, Peirce used dots to prevent lines of identity from crossing cuts. For example, in Fig. 1, the thick line is not a single line of identity but a series of two lines of identity, one lying outside the cut, and the other lying inside. These lines of identity abut each other at a point on the cut. We can place a dot at the intersection to make the meeting more explicit, as seen for the third graph in Fig. 2. Peirce stated that "[p]oints on a sep shall be considered to lie outside the close of the sep" [2, 4.450]. Thus, in the third graph, the dot on the cut is actually outside it.

Peirce used the term *hook* for the blank of a spot [2, 4.441]. For instance, in the first graph in Fig. 2, *is ugly* is a predicate with one argument in a classical first-order predicate language, and it is a spot with one hook in terms of the Beta part of Existential Graphs. Peirce offered a usage of dots to fill the hooks of a spot [2, 4.441]. Thus, we can fill the hook of *is ugly* with a dot instead of a line of identity with a loose end, giving the fourth graph in Fig. 2. According to Peirce, a dot is "a separate sign of an indesignate individual existing in the universe and belonging to some determinate category, usually that of "things"" [2, 4.441]. Hence, the fourth graph denies that there is something that is ugly. A line of identity plays a role of linking one dot to another dot. In the third graph in Fig. 2, the line of identity outside the cut links the point of its loose end to the dot on the cut, and we can place a dot at the loose end. Thus, the proposed system substitutes the last (rightmost) graph in Fig. 2 for the graph in Fig. 1. This paper refers to a dot at a loose end, a dot on a cut, and a dot at a hook as a *loose-end dot*, a *cut dot*, and a *hook dot*, respectively.

4   Alternative Reformulation of Transformation Rules

The function of a line of identity as a graph is to link two dots and assert the numerical identity of two individuals denoted by them. Erasure of a line of identity means removing such a line linking two dots, while insertion of a line of identity means linking two dots by it. If a diagrammatic representation is evenly enclosed, then it is enclosed by any finite even number of cuts, including zero; if oddly enclosed, then it is enclosed by any finite odd number of cuts [2, 4.505]. Thus, erasure or insertion is performed in a close that is evenly or oddly enclosed. Here, I consider how many cases exist when erasing or inserting a line of identity in one and the same close. A line of identity is related to two dots, of which there are three kinds, giving six combinations of dots: (1) loose-end dot—loose-end dot; (2) loose-end dot—cut dot; (3) loose-end dot—hook dot; (4) cut dot—cut dot; (5) cut dot—hook dot; (6) hook dot—hook dot. In addition, there are two kinds of closes: (A) evenly enclosed close; (B) oddly enclosed close. Hence, we have 6 × 2 cases for both erasure and insertion of a line of identity, as enumerated in Table 1.

How many cases exist when erasing a line of identity linking two dots in different closes or inserting such a line of identity? In the proposed system, no line of identity crosses a cut, and a dot outside a cut thus cannot be immediately linked to a dot inside the cut by a single line of identity. Here, we only have to consider a line of identity within a cut by which a dot on the cut is linked to a dot within the cut, because a dot on a cut lies outside the close of the cut and in a different close from any dot inside the cut. This gives three combinations of dots: (i) cut dot—loose-end dot; (ii) cut dot—cut dot; (iii) cut dot—hook dot. So, there are 3 × 2 combinations for both erasure and insertion of a line of identity, as listed in Table 2.

Table 1. In same close.		Table 2. In different closes.	
1 Erasure		**3 Erasure**	
(A) Evenly enclosed close	(1)(2)(3)(4)(5)(6)	(A) Evenly enclosed close	(i)(ii)(iii)
(B) Oddly enclosed close	(1)(2)(3)(4)(5)(6)	(B) Oddly enclosed close	(i)(ii)(iii)
2 Insertion		**4 Insertion**	
(A) Evenly enclosed close	(1)(2)(3)(4)(5)(6)	(A) Evenly enclosed close	(i)(ii)(iii)
(B) Oddly enclosed close	(1)(2)(3)(4)(5)(6)	(B) Oddly enclosed close	(i)(ii)(iii)

Regarding which of these combinations to select, Peirce stipulated the following rule for erasing or inserting a line of identity:

(a) This rule pemits any ligature, where evenly enclosed, to be severed, and (b) any two ligatures, oddly enclosed in the same seps, to be joined. (c) It permits a branch with a loose end to be added to or (d) retracted from any line of identity.
(e) It permits any ligature, where evenly enclosed, to be severed from the inside of the sep immediately enclosing that evenly enclosed portion of it, and (f) to be extended to a vacant point of any sep in the same enclosure. (g) It permits any ligature to be joined to the inside of the sep immediately enclosing that oddly enclosed portion of it, and (h) to be retracted from the outside of any sep in the same enclosure on which the ligature has an extremity. ((a), (b), ..., added.) [2, 4.505]

This quotation consists of eight sentences. Because a ligature in the proposed system is composed of lines of identity abutting one another at a dot on a cut, sentence (a) indicates that every evenly enclosed line of identity may be removed. It might seem to cover both 1(A)(1)–(6) in Table 1 and 3(A)(i)–(iii) in Table 2. For example, in the first graph in Fig. 3, the line of identity in the close of the inner cut is enclosed by two cuts and immediately by the inner cut. According to sentence (e), the line of identity can be removed to give the second graph. This illustrates that sentence (e) permits erasing lines of identity in 3(A)(i)–(iii) rather than in 1(A)(1)–(6). This paper calls the transformation rule for the former a *disjoin* and the latter a *disconnection*.

Similar consideration applies to sentences (b) and (g). In the third graph in Fig. 3, the dot on the second cut from the outside is enclosed by only the outermost cut. If that dot is linked to the dot on the outermost cut by a line of identity, then the line of identity is enclosed by one cut and immediately by the outermost cut, as the last graph in Fig. 3 shows. Likewise, in the fourth graph in Fig. 3, the hook dot of G is enclosed by three cuts. If that dot is linked to the dot on the third cut from the outside by a line of identity, then the line of identity is enclosed by three cuts and immediately by the third cut, as the last graph in Fig. 3 shows. Therefore, sentence (g) allows inserting lines of identity designated by 4(B)(i)–(iii) in Table 2. This paper calls the corresponding transformation rule a *join*. Furthermore, insertion of lines of identity in 2(B)(1)–(6) in Table 1 is permitted by sentence (b), for which the transformation rule is called a *connection*.

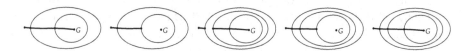

Fig. 3. Disjoin and join.

Sentences (c) and (d) refer to a branch, which is a graph "signifying the identity of the three individuals" [2, 4.446]. In a branch, a line of identity goes separately from the middle of another line of identity. The proposed system places a dot not only at each of the three extremities of a branch but also at its fork, as the first graph in Fig. 4 shows. On the basis of sentence (c), in an evenly or oddly enclosed close, a line of identity can be lengthened with a loose-end dot from a cut dot, a hook dot, or another loose-end dot. Hence, in Fig. 4, the second graph is transformable into the third one, and the last graph is transformable into the fourth one. Because the lengthening of the lines of identity in the latter case uses a *connection* and a *join*, we need only consider the former case, which corresponds to 2(A)(1)–(3) in Table 1 and 4(A)(i) in Table 2. This paper calls the rule for that case a *joint*. In Fig. 4, sentence (d) allows changing the third graph into the second one, or the fourth graph into the last one, where the former transformation uses a *disconnection* and a *disjoin*. Then I introduce a *disjoint* as a new rule for the latter transformation, which covers 1(B)(1)–(3) and 3(B)(i).

In sentence (f), a "vacant" dot on a cut is one from which no line of identity is lengthened towards the outside or inside of the cut. Sentence (f) enables

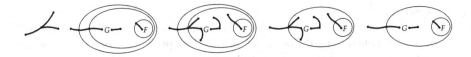

Fig. 4. Joint and disjoint.

linking a dot to a vacant dot on a cut by a line of identity in the same evenly enclosed close in which the cut lies. This, however, involves linking a loose-end dot to a vacant dot, which is accomplished by a *joint*. Hence, in the proposed system, sentence (*f*) is considered to focus particularly upon 2(A)(4)–(5). The rule for these cases is called an *extension*, and it allows transforming the first graph in Fig. 5 into the second one, or the third one into the last one. Sentence (*h*) mentions the content that is contrary to that of sentence (*f*). The rule for the transformation indicated by sentence (*h*) is called a *retraction*. In Fig. 5, this is exemplified by deleting the outermost cut from each of the four graphs and passing from the right-hand graph to the left-hand one in each of the two pairs, thus illustrating 1(B)(4)–(5).

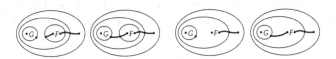

Fig. 5. Extension and retraction.

This research has revealed that Peirce's original statements about the erasure and insertion of a line of identity symmetrically covered all the necessary rules. The scrutiny proves that Peirce's formulation of the transformation rules for lines of identity was based upon the principle that no line of identity crosses a cut. Hence, I can reformulate the rules in the following way:

(1) **Disconnection**
    If the close of a cut is evenly enclosed and two dots in the close proper to the cut are linked by a line of identity in the same close, then the line of identity can be removed.

(2) **Connection**
    If the close of a cut is oddly enclosed, then two dots in the close proper to the cut can be linked by a line of identity in the same close.

(3) **Disjoin**
    If the close of a cut is evenly enclosed and a dot on the cut is linked to a dot in the close proper to the cut by a line of identity in the same close, then the line of identity can be removed.

(4) **Join**
    If the close of a cut is oddly enclosed, then a dot on the cut can be linked to a dot in the close proper to the cut by a line of identity in the same close.

(5) **Disjoint**

If the close of a cut is oddly enclosed and a line of identity with a loose-end dot is lengthened inward from a dot in the close proper to the cut, including a dot on that cut, then the line of identity can be removed.

(6) **Joint**

If the close of a cut is evenly enclosed, then a line of identity with a loose-end dot can be lengthened inward from a dot in the close proper to the cut, including a dot on that cut.

(7) **Retraction**

If the close of a cut is oddly enclosed and a line of identity is lengthened from a hook dot or a cut dot in the close proper to the cut, including a dot on that cut, to a vacant dot on a cut in the same close, then the line of identity can be removed.

(8) **Extension**

If the close of a cut is evenly enclosed, then a line of identity can be lengthened from a hook dot or a cut dot in the close proper to the cut, including dot on that cut, to a vacant dot on a cut in the same close.

Finally, without adding or deleting a line of identity, any graph can be scribed in an oddly enclosed close or removed in an evenly enclosed close. I call the rule for the former and latter transformations simply *insertion* and *erasure*, respectively.

5   Rule of Iteration and Deiteration

The rule of iteration or deiteration permits inserting a replica of a given graph or erasing an iterated graph in a designated close under certain conditions. Peirce provided the rule in the following way: "[a]nywhere within all the seps that enclose a replica of a graph, that graph may be iterated with identical ligations, or being iterated, may be deiterated" [2, 4.505]. For example, in the first graph in Fig. 6, G lies in the annulus between the middle and the innermost cuts. By *iteration*, G can be repeated anywhere within the two cuts. For instance, as the second graph in Fig. 6 shows, a replica of G with its hook dot can be placed next to G. On the other hand, such an iteration cannot be performed in the annulus between the outermost and the middle cuts, as the graph iterated in such a way is not within the middle cut.

Peirce referred to "identical ligations" in the statement cited above. He noted that "[t]he operation of iteration consists in the insertion of a new replica of a graph which there is already a replica, the new replica having each hook ligated to every hook of a graph-replica to which the corresponding hook of the old replica is ligated" [2, 4.506]. Peirce used the term *replica* or *graph-replica* to refer to a diagrammatic expression scribed as a token of a graph. What is already scribed as a replica of G in the first graph in Fig. 6 is an old one, and what is added in the second graph is a new one. In the first graph in Fig. 6, the hook dot of the old replica of G is linked to the dot on the middle cut by the line of identity inside, and that cut dot is linked to the hook dot of the replica of F by the line of identity outside. To complete the iteration in the second graph, it is necessary that the hook dot of the new replica of G contacts that of the replica of F through a series of lines of identity. Hence, the hook dot of the new replica of G is linked to the dot on the middle cut by a line of identity, thereby obtaining the linkage between the hook dot of the new replica of G and that of the replica of F in the last graph in Fig. 6.

Fig. 6. Iteration.

Indeed, an *iteration* enables proceeding from the first graph in Fig. 7 through the second one to the third. Such a transformation is feasible, however, without appealing to *iteration*: an *insertion* permits transforming the first graph into the second one; from there, the third graph can be modified by an *extension* and a *join*.

Deiteration is the converse of *iteration*. Peirce explained it in the following way: "[t]he operation of deiteration consists in erasing a replica which might have illatively resulted from an operation of iteration, and of retracting outwards the ligatures left loose by such erasure until they are within the same seps as the corresponding ligature of the replica of which the erased replica might have been the iteration" [2, 4.506]. In applying *deiteration* to the third graph in Fig. 7, first of all, we erase the iterated replica of G in the close of the innermost cut in that graph, thus changing it into the last graph. In that graph, *deiteration* means the outward retraction of the line of identity with a loose-end dot in the close of the innermost cut. Because the hook dot of the original replica of G is linked to the dot on the middle cut by the line of identity in the annulus between the middle and the innermost cuts, that retraction must be performed to that cut dot at two steps; at the first step, the line of identity linking the hook dot of the erased replica of G to the dot on the innermost cut is removed; at the second step, the line of identity linking the dot on the innermost cut to the dot on the middle cut is removed. Thus, we obtain the first graph in Fig. 7. Though a *deiteration* allows turning the last graph in Fig. 6 into the first one, the transformation can also use a *disjoin* and an *erasure*, without using a *deitertation*.

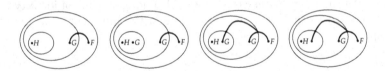

Fig. 7. Deiteration.

6   Applications of Transformation Rules

The proposed system provides an alternative reformulation of the transformation rules in the Beta part of Peirce's Existential Graphs. How can this system handle the graph transformations demonstrated in Shin's book? According to Shin, "[w]e may extend a loose end of an LI inwards through cut(s)" [4, 140], where "LI" denotes a line of identity. In the first graph in Fig. 8, for example, the line of identity has a loose end in the annulus between the outer and the inner cuts. This may be lengthened into the close of the inner cut, as the second graph shows. In that graph, two loose ends in the inner close cannot be linked by a line of identity, for "[w]e may join two loose ends of identity lines (a) in an O-area" [4, 140]. Here, an "O-area" is an oddly enclosed close, but those two loose ends are enclosed by two cuts, prohibiting them from being linked by a line of identity.

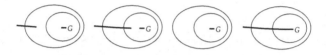

Fig. 8. Shin's transformations.

On the other hand, for the third graph in Fig. 8, Shin's system allows lengthening the loose end of the line of identity from G outward to the outside of the outer cut [4, 140]. As a result, we obtain the last graph. Shin added three conditions to this transformation. Such a lengthening is possible "unless there is another LI (A) which is attached to the same predicates, (B) whose scope is bigger than the LI we are interested in extending, and (C) whose outermost part is in an O-area" [4, 140]. If, for instance, in the third graph in Fig. 8, G has another line of identity with a loose end that is lengthened outward to the annulus between the outer and the inner cuts, then we cannot lengthen the loose end of the shorter line of identity. We are thus banned from transforming the first graph in Fig. 9 into the second one. Let G denote the predicate $Loves(x, y)$. Then, the former graph affirms $\forall y \exists x Loves(x, y)$, and the latter graph corresponds to $\exists x \forall y Loves(x, y)$. As Shin pointed out, $\exists x \forall y Loves(x, y)$ can never be derived from $\forall y \exists x Loves(x, y)$ in any logical system of classical first-order predicate language [4, 144]. Rather, the latter follows from the former, and the second graph in Fig. 9 is transformable into the first one. Shin gave such a transformation by the following rule: it permits us to "retract a loose end of an LI inwards (ii) from an E-area to an E-area" [4, 140]. In the second graph, the loose end of the left-hand line of identity of G lies outside the outer cut, which is enclosed by no cut: it is in an evenly enclosed close. Therefore, the line of identity can be retracted inward to the evenly enclosed close of the inner cut, thus giving the first graph.

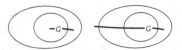

Fig. 9. $\forall y \exists x \, Loves(x, y)$ & $\exists x \forall y \, Loves(x, y)$.

The proposed system can deal with these transformations in a more consistent manner with no additional restrictions. It turns the first graph in Fig. 8 into the first one in Fig. 10 while obeying the principle that no line of identity crosses a cut and using loose-end dots, cut dots, and hook dots. The first graph in Fig. 10 means $\forall x \exists y (x = y) \rightarrow \exists z Gz$, as Burch presents the interpretation that a line of identity linking two dots asserts $\exists x \exists y (x = y)$ in the paper entitled "The fine structure of Peircean ligatures and lines of identity" [1, 40–63]. In that graph the inner loose-end dot of the line of identity in the annulus between the outer and the inner cuts may be linked to a dot on the inner cut by a line of identity via a *connection*. This gives the second graph in Fig. 10, which means $\forall x \exists y (x = y) \rightarrow \exists z Gz$. A *joint* permits lengthening a new line of identity with a loose-end dot inward from the dot on the inner cut, as the third graph shows, which means $\exists x \exists y (x = y) \wedge \exists z Gz$. On the other hand, in that graph, no rule allows linking the loose-end dot in the close of the inner cut to the hook dot of G.

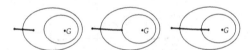

Fig. 10. Extension and joint.

Similarly, the third and the last graphs in Fig. 8 are changed into the first and the second graphs in Fig. 11, respectively. For the first graph in Fig. 11, however, the proposed system does not have any rule for linking a dot on the inner cut to the hook dot of G in its close by a line of identity. How, then, do we transform that graph into the second graph in Fig. 11 in this system? Peirce introduced the rule of *biclosure* [2, 4.508], which allows enclosing any graph by a *double cut* and withdrawing it from about any graph enclosed by it [2, 4.508]. Here, a double cut is a pair of two cuts such that one is within the other and the annulus between them does not contain any graph [2, 4.508]. In the first graph in Fig. 11, the two cuts enclosing G constitute a double cut. By a *biclosure*, we may withdraw it, thus giving the third graph. Then, a *joint* enables lengthening a line of identity with a loose-end dot from the hook dot of G in that graph, which leads to the last graph. And, a *biclosure* transforms the last graph into the second one. Note again that a double cut has no graph in its annulus. For a *biclosure*, therefore, we must scribe a double cut in such a manner that neither a loose-end dot nor a hook dot of an already scribed line of identity occurs in its annulus, nor does the line of identity stop at a dot on the inner cut of it. The proposed system thus places dots at the intersections of a line of identity and the two cuts of a double cut, as the second graph in Fig. 11 shows.

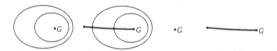

Fig. 11. Biclosure.

Shin's system can change the third graph in Fig. 8 into the last one. No system, however, permits transforming the first graph in Fig. 9 into the last one. Therefore, Shin imposed three constraints on lengthening a line of identity with a loose-end dot outward from an evenly enclosed close to an evenly enclosed close. In contrast, the system proposed here expresses the two graphs in Fig. 9 as shown in Fig. 12; and, in the first graph in Fig. 12, which means $\forall y \exists x G x y$, this system never allows lengthening a line of identity with a loose-end dot outward from the hook dot of G to the close outside the outer cut. Nevertheless, the second graph, which means $\exists x \forall y G x y$, is transformable into the first one. Then, how does this system convert the former graph into the latter?

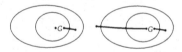

Fig. 12. $\forall y \exists x Loves(x, y)$ & $\exists x \forall y Loves(x, y)$.

In the second graph in Fig. 12, a *disjoin* permits removing the line of identity linking the dot on the inner cut to the hook dot of G. This manipulation produces the first graph in Fig. 13, which means $\forall z \exists w(z = w) \rightarrow \forall y \exists x G x y$. In that graph, a *retraction* can remove the line of identity linking the dot on the inner cut to the dot on the outer cut, thus giving the last graph in Fig. 13, which means $\exists z \exists w(z = w) \wedge \forall y \exists x G x y$. Finally, a *disconnection* allows removing the line of identity linking the loose-end dot outside the outer cut to the dot on that cut, thus giving the first graph in Fig. 12.

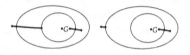

Fig. 13. Transformation of $\exists x \forall y Loves(x, y)$ into $\forall y \exists x Loves(x, y)$.

7   Transformations of Graphs

In any logical system of classical first-order predicate language, we may derive $\exists x F x \vee \exists x G x$ from $\exists x (F x \vee G x)$. Shin's system represents the former by the last graph in Fig. 14 and the latter by the first one. According to Shin, "[w]e may *disjoin* an identity line in an E-area" [4, 140]. We thus remove a portion of the line of identity outside the outer cut in the first graph, giving the second graph. As we have seen, in that graph, we retract each of the two lines of identity having their loose ends in the outermost close enclosed by no cut to the innermost close enclosed by two cuts. As a result, we obtain the last graph.

Fig. 14. Shin's transformations.

Those operations depend on the presumption that lines of identity can cross cuts. In contrast, the proposed system takes a different route from the first graph in Fig. 14 to the last one. Specially, it uses dots to express the former graph as the first one in Fig. 15. Applying a *disjoin* to that graph twice, we get the second graph, which means $\forall z \exists w (z = w) \rightarrow (\exists x F x \vee \exists x G x)$. Two applications of a *retraction* turn it into the third graph, which means $\exists z \exists w (z = w) \wedge (\exists x F x \vee \exists x G x)$. Finally, by a *disconnection*, we remove the line of identity outside the outermost cut in that graph, thus giving the last graph in Fig. 15, which corresponds to the last one in Fig. 14.

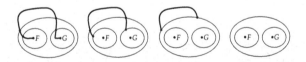

Fig. 15. Transformation of $\exists x (F x \vee G x)$ into $\exists x F x \vee \exists x G x$.

In the last graph in Fig. 15, we lengthen a line of identity with a loose-end dot from each of the hook dots of F and G by a *joint*, thus giving the first graph in Fig. 16, which means $\exists x F x \vee \exists x G x$. In that graph, by a *biclosure*, a double cut is scribed in the close of the left-hand inner cut in such a manner that the loose-end dot of the line of identity from F lies on the outer cut of the double cut. The similar transformation can be performed in the close of the right-hand inner cut in that graph, thus giving the second graph in Fig. 16, means $\neg\neg\exists x F x \vee \neg\neg\exists x G x$. There, an *insertion* permits scribing in the proper close to the left-hand third cut from the outside the graph where G is enclosed by a cut and its hook dot is linked to a dot on the cut by a line of identity. Similarly, an *insertion* permits scribing in the proper close to the right-hand third cut from the outside the graph where F is enclosed by a cut and its hook dot is linked to a dot on the cut by a line of identity. Thus, we arrive at the last graph in Fig. 16, which means $(\exists x F x \vee \forall x G x) \vee (\forall x F x \vee \exists x G x)$.

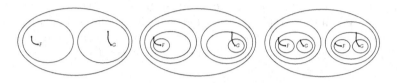

Fig. 16. Transformation of $\exists x F x \vee \exists x G x$ into $\exists x (F x \vee G x)$.

In each of the left- and the right-hand sides of the last graph in Fig. 16, by an *extension*, we may lengthen a line of identity from the dot on the third cut from the outside to a vacant dot on the same third cut. This gives the first graph in Fig. 17, which means $(\exists x F x \vee \forall x G x) \vee (\forall x F x \vee \exists x G x)$. Then, in each of the left- and right-hand sides of that graph, a *join* can be used. This introduces a line of identity to link the dot on the third cut from which no line of identity is lengthened inward to the dot on the fourth cut from which the line of identity is lengthened inward to the hook dot of G or F. As a result, one and the same graph occurs twice repeatedly in the same close of the outermost cut, as the second graph in Fig. 17 shows, which means $\exists x (F x \vee G x) \vee \exists x (F x \vee G x)$. Therefore, we may remove one of them by a *deiteration*. In the last graph in Fig. 17, which means $\neg \neg \exists x (F x \vee G x)$, because there is no graph in the annulus between the first and the second cuts from the outside, the pair of them forms a double cut, and a *biclosure* allows removing it. Consequently, we obtain the first graph in Fig. 15.

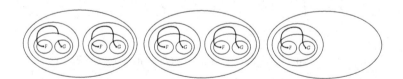

Fig. 17. Transformation of $\exists x F x \vee \exists x G x$ into $\exists x (F x \vee G x)$.

8   Conclusion

This investigation has revealed that one of the fundamental conceptions in Peirce's Existential Graphs, that no line of identity can cross a cut, more effectively confers a symmetrical configuration of the transformation rules in the

Table 3. Transformation rules.

Erasure	Insertion
Simple erasure	Simple insertion
Disconnection	Connection
Disjoin	Join
Disjoint	Joint
Retraction	Extention
Deiteration	Iteration
Biclosure	Biclosure

Beta part of Existential Graphs. This involves two kinds of operations, namely, *erasure* and *insertion*. Table 3 briefly summarizes these operations.

In Table 3, *simple erasure* and *simple insertion* mean deleting and adding a graph, respectively, without deforming any line of identity. Basically, we are prohibited from inserting a graph in an evenly enclosed close or erasing a graph in an oddly enclosed close. The subsequent rules—*disconnection* and *connection*, *disjoin* and *join*, *disjoint* and *joint*, *retraction* and *extension*—enumerate all the necessary transformation rules for erasing or inserting lines of identity. They completely excludes the rules for (a) erasing a line of identity linking two hook dots in one and the same oddly enclosed close (1(B)(6) in Table 1); (b) inserting a line of identity linking two hook dots in one and the same evenly enclosed close (2(A)(6) in Table 1), (c) erasing a line of identity linking a dot on a cut whose close is oddly enclosed to a hook dot or a cut dot in the close proper to the cut (3(B)(ii)–(iii) in Table 2) (d) inserting a line of identity linking a dot on a cut whose close is evenly enclosed to a hook dot or a cut dot in the close proper to the cut (4(B)(ii)–(iii) in Table 2). Finally, the rules for *biclosure* are of two kinds: one for erasing a double cut, and the other for inserting it.

This proposal suggests that the proposed system of the Beta part of Existential Graphs is equivalent to a classical first-order predicate logic with no free variable. The equivalence remains to be proved formally.

References

1. Burch, R.W.: The fine ftructure of Peircean ligatures and lines of identity. Semiotica **186**, 21–68 (2011)
2. Charles Sanders Peirce: Collected Papers of Charles Sanders Peirce. The Belknap Press of Harvard University Press, Cambridge, MA (1974)
3. Roberts, D.D.: The Existential Graphs of Charles S. Peirce. Mouton, The Hague (1973)
4. Shin, S.-J.: The Iconic Logic of Peirce's Graphs. A Bradford Book, Cambridge (2003)

Observational Advantages and Occurrence Referentiality

Francesco Bellucci[1]([✉]) and Jim Burton[2]

[1] Department of Philosophy and Communication, University of Bologna, Via Azzo Gardino 23, 40122 Bologna, Italy
francesco.bellucci4@unibo.it
[2] CSIUS, University of Brighton, Brighton BN2 2GJ, UK
j.burton@brighton.ac.uk

Abstract. Logical diagrams are known to have certain advantages over sentential notations for particular reasoning tasks: using a diagram may make logical consequences directly evident, when these consequences are "hidden" in an equivalently expressive sentential language. This phenomenon is known as a "free ride" or "observational advantage". Where does this advantage come from, and why? We answer this question by distinguishing two general kinds of logical languages: occurrence-referential languages, in which sameness of reference (for sentential and predicate variables) is determined by the sameness of variable occurrence, and type-referential languages, in which sameness of variable type determines sameness of reference. We explain that it is the occurrence-referential nature of some languages that explains for their observational advantage over equivalently expressive type-referential languages.

Keywords: Euler diagrams · Observational advantages · Type · Token · Occurrence

1 Introduction

That certain notations have the capacity to yield more information than is necessary for their construction is a well-known phenomenon. It was called a "free ride" by Shimojima (1996a, 1996b), who pointed to many examples including those found in maps, tabular data, and logical languages. In particular, the occurrence of free rides in logical languages has provided one motivation for the use and promotion of heterogeneous (mixed sentential and diagrammatic) and purely diagrammatic logics. The notion of free ride has recently been generalized to that of *observational advantage* (Stapleton et al. 2017, 2018), and it has been argued that logical diagrams have observational advantages over sentential logics, giving them the potential to be a more accessible and reliable vehicle for expressing and drawing inferences from precise information, at least for certain tasks. Aspects of this broad hypothesis have been empirically confirmed (see, for instance, Alharbi et al. 2017).

Our aim in this paper is to set out an explanation of *why* certain logical notations are observationally advantageous over others. What is the salient and common property of

© Springer Nature Switzerland AG 2020
A.-V. Pietarinen et al. (Eds.): Diagrams 2020, LNAI 12169, pp. 202–215, 2020.
https://doi.org/10.1007/978-3-030-54249-8_16

those notations that have observational advantages? It would be tempting to answer this question by saying that diagrams are observational advantageous over non-diagrammatic languages, and that it is precisely the property of "being a diagram" that explains the presence of observational advantages. Unfortunately, this strategy is unviable, in the first place, because we do not have a satisfactory definition of "diagram" that would capture all and only those notations that we would intuitively consider diagrammatic. In the second place, the strategy is unviable because, as it will be shown below, notations exist which we would intuitively consider diagrammatic that do not display observational advantages.

This paper is about observational advantages in standard Euler diagrams, a notation intuitively characterized as diagrammatic which is known to be observationally advantageous over equally expressive languages. By examining research that addresses the mechanics of observational advantages in Euler diagrams, we consider the best current explanation of *how* they arise. We answer the question of *why* Euler diagrams are observationally advantageous over others by forging a distinction of our own between two distinct ways in which a logical language may refer: we distinguish between "type-referential" notations, in which sameness of reference depends on sameness of symbol type, and "occurrence-referential" notations, in which sameness of reference depends on sameness of symbol occurrence. It will be our argument that observational advantages in Euler diagrams depend on occurrence-referentiality.[1]

The paper is divided as follows: in Sect. 2 we look at recent work on the mechanics of observational advantages, including the concept of "meaning-carrying relationships". In Sect. 3 we discuss the notions of type, token, and occurrence, and in Sect. 4 we use this discussion to introduce our main distinction, that between type-referential and occurrence-referential notations. In Sect. 5 we show that Euler diagrams are observationally advantageous over first order logic because they display multiple meaning-carrying relationships, and we argue that this is so, in turn, because they are occurrence-referential. In Sect. 6 we turn to observational disadvantages. Here we show that Euler diagrams are observationally disadvantageous ("overspecific") over first order logic because they display multiple meaning-carrying relationships, and we argue that this is so, again, because they are occurrence-referential. In Sect. 7 we suggest that a parallel distinction between type- and occurrence-referential languages exists with respect to identity, whose systematic investigation lies outside the scope of the present work.

2 Observational Advantages and Meaning-Carrying Relationships

That Euler diagrams have the capacity to yield more information than is necessary for their construction is a well-known phenomenon with its own history (Bellucci et al. 2014; Moktefi 2015). This phenomenon, originally labelled "free ride" by Shimojima, has recently been generalized to that of "observational advantage" (Stapleton et al. 2017, 2018). Roughly, the contrast upon which the theory of observational advantages is based is between *inferring* a statement from a given representation of information and *observing* that statement without inferring it. It is said that a given representation

---

[1] Howse et al. (2002) applied the type/token distinction to logical diagrams but in that work the distinction is between drawn diagrams (tokens) and abstract syntax (types).

of information is observationally advantageous over another if the former allows us to observe something that must be inferred from the latter. For example, take the premises of a syllogism in Barbara, as expressed in the standard language of first order logic:

1) $\forall x\,(Ax \supset Bx)$
2) $\forall x\,(Bx \supset Cx)$

These premises can be "copulated" by means of the conjunction operator so as to produce a single statement forming a composite premise:

3) $\forall x\,(Ax \supset Bx)\,\&\,\forall x\,(Bx \supset Cx)$

Having written down the premises, either singularly or in conjunction, we still need to apply some general rule of inference in order to obtain the conclusion:

4) $\forall x\,(Ax \supset Cx)$

(4) is *inferable* from (1) and (2) taken together, i.e. from (3), but is not *observable* in either (1) and (2) singularly or in (3).

Now consider the same syllogism as represented in Euler diagrams. The premises are represented in Fig. 1, where the fact that a circle is wholly enclosed in another circle means that a class is wholly contained in another class. Thus, in order to represent that "All A are B" we draw the circle A inside the circle B, and in order to represent that "All B are C" we draw the circle B inside the circle C. However, as soon as we have drawn the diagram of the premises, the diagram of the conclusion is drawn as well: the circle A is in fact inside the circle C, and this means that "All A are C". The conclusion of the syllogism is not inferred from the premises by means of inference rules; rather, it is *observed* in the diagram of the premises. The diagram of the premises is at the same time the diagram of the conclusion.

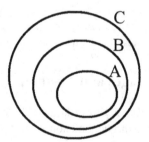

Fig. 1. Euler diagram

Despite this state of affairs being frequently commented upon, few authors have attempted to explain *why* this might be so. Stapleton et al. (2017) attempt to do so by making appeal to the notion of *meaning-carrying relationship* (MCR). An MCR is a relation on the syntax of an expression that carries semantic content, i.e. one which can be evaluated to either "true" or "false". For example, in (1) the fact that "Ax" is at the immediate left of "⊃" and that "Bx" is at its immediate right is an MCR, because it carries semantic content: it means that the open formula at the immediate left of "⊃" is the antecedent and the open formula at its immediate right is the consequent of a conditional sentence whose truth-conditions are given by the usual truth-table for the material conditional. By contrast, the fact that in (3) "Ax" is at the left (but not at the *immediate* left) of the second occurrence of "⊃" is not an MCR: this fact is, indeed, a fact about the symbols contained in the formula, but it does not have semantic content, i.e. it cannot be evaluated to true or false.[2]

Circle A in Fig. 1 has multiple MCRs. It is included in circle B, and this has a semantic content ("All A are B"). It is also included in circle C, which also has semantic content ("All A are C"). Given the conventions of Euler diagrams, circle A would have MCRs with any other circle that could be drawn according to the conventions of the system. Thus, in the Euler diagram in Fig. 2, circle A is not only included in circles B and C, but also disjoint from circles D, E and F.

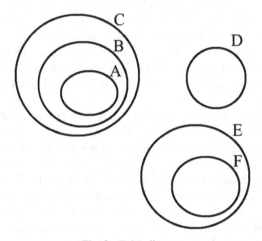

Fig. 2. Euler diagram

Euler diagrams are observationally advantageous over first order logic because each circle in an Euler diagram has multiple MCRs, i.e. has an MCR with any other circle that is part of the same (unitary) diagram, while each predicate variable in a first order logic formula does not have MCRs with any other predicate variable that is part of the same

---

[2] Another way of saying this is as follows. Whether a statement is simple (atomic) or composite (molecular), the relation of the syntax that carries semantic content, i.e. the MCR, always concerns the components of the statement which are in the scope of the main operator, i.e. the operator that has the widest binding. So "Ax" has no meaning-carrying relationship with the second occurrence of "⊃" because they are not the components of the statement which are operands of "&". These are "∀x (Ax ⊃ Bx)" and "∀x (Bx ⊃ Cx)". As we suggest below, this scope limitation for the occurrence of an MCR does not hold for Euler diagrams, because in this system the scope of any information expressed is always the entire unitary diagram.

formula. Having established the notion of MCR Stapleton et al. (2017) go on to formalise observational advantages and disadvantages as relations between sets of expressions in different logical notations. Our question, on the other hand, is *why* do circles in Euler diagrams have multiple MCRs when this is not the case for predicate variable in first order logic?

3   Types, Tokens, and Occurrences

The distinction between "type" and "token" expressions is a well-known distinction in philosophy and linguistic theory. Consider the following sentence:

(5)   war is war

(5) may be said to contain either two or three words according to two different senses of the word "word". In one sense, (5) contains three word tokens ("war", "is", and "war"). In another sense, it contains two word types ("war" and "is"). A type is a general, abstract, and unique kind of entity; a token a concrete and individual one. When an editor asks an author to write a paper of 10.000 words, what she means is 10.000 word tokens. When a corpus linguist says that Dante's *Divina Commedia* contains 12.831 words, what she means is 12.831 word types. The distinction derives from Peirce, who was the first to draw it and to provide the terminology which is still current today (Peirce 1932–1958, 2.243–246, 4.537).

However useful the type/token distinction may have proven to be, it is insufficient for the purposes of even some simple linguistic analyses. Here is an example of its insufficiency, adapted from Wetzel (1993). Let us assume that the type/token distinction is exhaustive, i.e. that a simple or composite expression is either an expression type or an expression token. Let us further assume that (5) is a sentence type. The sentence consists of three words. Are these three word types or three word tokens? The sentence cannot consist of three word tokens, because we have assumed it to be a sentence type and thus an abstract entity, while tokens are concrete entities: an abstract entity cannot in itself be regarded as being made of concrete entities. Nor can (5) consist of three word types, because there are only two word types of which it might consist.

The problem is solved by recognizing a third level of linguistic analysis, which is the *occurrence* of an expression in some linguistic context. Assuming (5) to be a sentence type, we may say that the word type "war" occurs twice in (5), and is instantiated or betokened twice in every token of that sentence. The two occurrences of the word type "war" in (5) are differentiated by saying that one of them is "the first occurrence of 'war' in (5)", the other "the second occurrence of 'war' in (5)". A parallel differentiation can be made for the two occurrences of the word token "war" in every token of (5). The notion of occurrence solves the problem exemplified in the preceding paragraph: as a sentence type, (5) contains *one* type of the word "war" (and not *two* of them), and two *occurrences* of it (and not two *tokens* of it).

4 Type and Occurrence Referentiality

Extending a suggestion by John Etchemendy to Keith Stenning,[3] in this section we use the notions of "type" and "occurrence of a type" in order to distinguish between two main families of logical languages. Etchemendy and Stenning were discussing the phenomenon in general. In this work we focus on the referentiality of notation for sentences, predicates and classes. The relevance of this qualification will be addressed in Sect. 7.

We call a language in which the sameness of sentences and predicates (including classes) is represented by the sameness of the variable type "type-referential": in a type-referential notation, each occurrence of a variable type refers to one and the same sentence or predicate (including classes). We call a language in which the sameness of sentences and predicates (including classes) is represented by the sameness of the variable occurrences "occurrence-referential": in an occurrence-referential notation, each occurrence of a variable type refers to a distinct sentence or predicate (including classes).

Let us make some examples. In sentence (6) there are three sentential variable types, "P", "Q" and "R". Since in the first conjunct of (6) "Q" figures as the consequent of a conditional whose antecedent is "P" while in the second conjunct it figures as the antecedent of another, distinct conditional whose consequent is "R", and since the conditional operator is a *binary* operator, in order for "Q" to be in two distinct relations, one to the sentential variable "P" and another to the sentential variable "R", it has to *occur twice*. In each of its two occurrences in (6), "Q" remains the same variable type. In our terminology, the sentential language in which (6) is written is type-referential. Similarly with the predicate logic sentence (7), where the occurrences of the predicate variables "P", "Q" and "R" each instantiate their respective types. Both the language of (6) and that of (7) are type-referential in that in these languages each occurrence of a variable type is interpreted as referring to the same sentence (as in (6)) or predicate (as in (7)) as any other occurrence of the same variable type.

(6) $(P \supset Q) \,\&\, (Q \supset R)$
(7) $\forall x\,(Px \supset Qx) \,\&\, \forall x\,(Qx \supset Rx)$

Type-referentiality is not a feature of linear languages only. Figure 3 is a Beta graph equivalent in information to (7). In the usual transliteration it says "it is not the case that something is P and not Q and it is not the case that something is Q and not R". Just as with (7), there are here three predicate variable types. Multiple occurrences of

---

[3] "Etchemendy (personal communication) uses this framework to derive a common distinguishing characteristic he calls type vs. token referentiality. In type referential systems (a paradigm case would be formal languages), repetition of a symbol of the same type (say of the term x or the name "John") determines sameness of reference by each occurrence of the symbol. Obviously there are complexities such as anaphora and ambiguity overlaid on natural languages, but their design is fundamentally type referential. Diagrams, in contrast are token referential. Sameness of reference is determined by identity of symbol token. If two tokens of the same type of symbol occur in a single diagram, they refer to distinct entities of the same type (e.g. two different towns on a map)" (Stenning 2000: 134). With the distinction between token and occurrence in hand we re-frame the Etchemendy/Stenning distinction in terms of occurrence-referentiality.

a given variable type may appear, and must, if we are to say several things about the predicate in question; so, in Fig. 3 the predicate variable type "Q" occurs twice, once in the partial graph at the left and once in the partial graph at the right. Like the foregoing linear examples, Beta graphs are type-referential.

Fig. 3. Beta graphs

The notion of type-referentiality would seem somewhat trivial if all languages were of this sort. But this is not so. Consider the Euler diagram in Fig. 4, which provides equivalent information to the first order logic sentence (7) and the Beta graph in Fig. 3. The type of symbol used in this language for the representation of a class is the closed curve, or circle. Now, each occurrence of this type in a formula refers to a *distinct* class: in Fig. 4 there are three occurrences of the circle type, and each refers to a distinct class. Labels are used to facilitate differentiation, but are not an integral part of the language: we could refer to each occurrence of the circle by means of topological descriptions. The important thing about the Eulerian language is that each occurrence of the circle type is the representation of a class which is distinct or distinguishable from any other class represented by other occurrences of the same type. Indeed, it would violate the rules of the notation to label two occurrences of the circle in the same way, because the convention about distinctness of referentiality would be in contradiction with the sameness of the labels. Thanks to this feature of the syntax, unlike in the languages we have considered above, in Euler diagrams we are able to assert two things about the class Q whilst only mentioning it once.

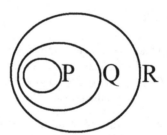

Fig. 4. Euler diagram.

Our discussion has focused so far on the relations, which are MCRs, between represented classes, their disjointness, proper subsumption, and so on. We can be more general: the MCRs in question are between those parts of a class that are represented; in diagrammatic terms, the *zones* of the diagram. If the information used to construct Fig. 5 were equivalent to the set theoretic expressions "A ⊆ B" and "B ∩ C = ∅", then the observational advantage is not only that "A ∩ C = ∅", but also includes "(B−A) ∩ C = ∅". In other words, each zone displays an MCR with any other zone. This, as we shall see, is due to the occurrence-referential nature of the system.

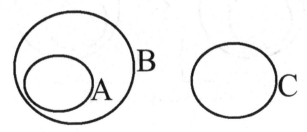

Fig. 5. Euler diagram.

5 Occurrence Referentiality and Observational Advantages

We are now in the position to explain why we think that it is the occurrence-referential nature of Euler diagrams that allows multiple MCRs, which in turn, as shown by Stapleton et al. (2017), is what explains Euler diagrams' observational advantages. Consider again the Euler diagram in Fig. 4 and the first order logic sentence equivalent to it, (7). Figure 4 and (7) express the same information. According to the conventions of Euler diagrams, the topological relation of inclusion between two labeled circles expresses that any element of the class represented by the enclosed circle is an element of the class represented by the enclosing one. Since in Fig. 4 the circle P is included in the circle Q, we can say that this relation of inclusion corresponds to the sub-formula "$\forall x\,(Px \supset Qx)$" of (7); likewise, since the circle Q is included in the circle R, we can say that this relation of inclusion corresponds to the sub-formula "$\forall x\,(Qx \supset Rx)$" of (7). Each of the two conjuncts of (7) displays an MCR that has a corresponding MCR in Fig. 4. Now, Fig. 4 displays a further MCR not displayed by (7): in Fig. 4 the circle P is included in the circle R, which would correspond to the first order logic formula "$\forall x\,(Px \supset Rx)$". But this latter formula is not observable in, only inferable from, (7); therefore, Fig. 4 is observationally advantageous with respect to (7).

Such an observational advantage depends on the language of Fig. 4's being occurrence-referential. To see this let us imagine a non-unitary version of Euler diagrams, in which the two conjuncts of (7) are represented by distinct unitary diagrams which are joined by a conjunction operator (see Fig. 6).

The language is precisely that of standard unitary Euler diagrams, with in addition the possibility of joining unitary Euler diagrams into "conjunctive" or "disjunctive" non-unitary Euler diagrams. To do so, a special convention for conjunction or disjunction is introduced (the symbol between boundary rectangles). Now, as soon as the possibility of constructing "conjunctive" and "disjunctive" non-unitary Euler diagrams is opened, the language ceases to be occurrence-referential and becomes type-referential: for example, in Fig. 6 circle Q occurs twice, once in the left hand side unitary diagram and once in the right hand side unitary diagram, without however ceasing to refer to one and the same

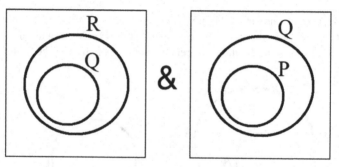

Fig. 6. Non-unitary Euler diagram.

class. Precisely because of this, the system does not display the kind of observational advantages that unitary Euler diagrams do; we are not able to observe in Fig. 6 that "$\forall x$ (Px ⊃ Rx)" as we do in Fig. 4.

The presence in Fig. 4 of an MCR that is not displayed by (7), namely that the circle P is included in the circle R, which would correspond to information conveyed by the first order logic formula "$\forall x$ (Px ⊃ Rx)", is due to the fact that in Fig. 4 one single occurrence of circle Q is *at once* in a certain relation to circle P and in a certain relation to circle R. If the occurrence of circle Q is "split" over two separate unitary diagrams, the relation between circle Q and circle P and that between circle Q and circle R are also "split" over two separate unitary diagrams, with the result that the relation between class P and class R is not observable anymore. The possibility of imagining non-unitary Euler diagrams, which are type-referential and which are not as observationally advantageous as unitary ones, shows that it is the occurrence-referential nature of the system that is responsible for its observational advantages over first order logic.

To see this more clearly, let us ask in what manner the conjunction symbol "&" is rendered in Euler diagrams. To do this, it is instructive to consider a comparison made in Stapleton et al. (2017) between expressions of five different languages each of which represents the same information (Fig. 7).

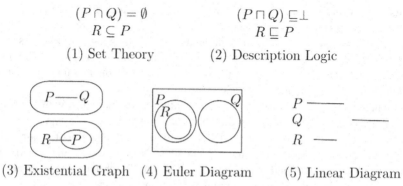

Fig. 7. Language comparison from Stapleton et al. (2017)

The Euler diagram in Fig. 7.4, contains the same information as the two sentences in Fig. 7.1 combined. Set theory does not contain an operator for conjunction. Suppose we add a copulative operator, "&", to the language of set theory. We can then restate the information contained in Fig. 7.1 in a form more comparable to Fig. 7.4:

(8) $P \cap Q = \varnothing \; \& \; R \subseteq P$

The two separate set theoretic sentences in Fig. 7.1 display a single MCR each, where the sentence in (8) displays three MCRs. These can be so described: (a) the fact that "$P \cap Q = \varnothing$" occurs at the left of "&" and that "$R \subseteq P$" occurs at its right is an MCR: it means that both expressions are conjunctively asserted; (b) the fact that "$P \cap Q$" occurs at the left of "=" and that "$\varnothing$" occurs at its right is an MCR: it means that the set expressed by the left hand side is empty; (c) the fact that "R" occurs at the left of "$\subseteq$" and that "P" occurs at its right is an MCR: it means that R is a subset of P. Despite containing multiple MCRs, the expression in (8) contains far fewer MCRs than the corresponding Euler diagram in Fig. 7.4, which makes this latter observationally advantageous over the former. What we want to call attention to, however, is a special fact about one of the MRCs that both Fig. 7.4 and (8) do display. In Fig. 7.4, MCR (b) is represented by the disjointness of the circles P and Q; MCR (c) is represented by the inclusion of circle R in circle P. We have thus been able to identify two of the relations between the labeled circles displayed in Fig. 7.4 with two of the MCRs displayed in (8). But what about MCR (a)? There is no specific relation holding between the circles in Fig. 7.4 that represents what "&" represents in (8), i.e. there is no specific relation between the circles in Fig. 7.4 that corresponds to MCR (a) in (8). It is the occurrence-referential nature of Euler diagrams that as it were *embodies the conjunction operator*.

The same is true of Fig. 4 and (7). Since we assume Fig. 4 and (7) to be equivalent in the information expressed, one might reasonably ask what is it that plays the role of the "&" of (7) in Fig. 4. The conjunction is part of the information expressed by (7), and thus, given equivalence in expressed information, also of the information expressed by Fig. 4. The question then becomes, is there any single element or piece of syntax in the language of Fig. 4 that "stands for" the conjunction symbol of (7)? The notion of occurrence referentiality answers this question. In Fig. 4 no specific element plays the role that "&" plays in (7). What fulfills the function of combining the sub-formulas that in (7) appear as conjuncts is *the very fact that the notation is occurrence-referential*. In (7) the symbol type "Q" occurs twice, but each occurrence refers to the same predicate. By contrast, in Fig. 4 the circle type that is labeled "Q" occurs only once and it is precisely this single occurrence of the type that is able to represent that it is the same class Q which has a certain relation to the class represented by circle P and a certain relation to the class represented by the circle R. As soon as a unitary Euler diagram is turned into a conjunction of unitary Euler diagrams, i.e. into a conjunctive non-unitary Euler diagram, the conjunction operator that was implicit in the unitary diagram becomes explicit, but the occurrence-referential nature of the language is lost.

The occurrence-referential nature of Euler diagrams embodies the conjunction operator. The fact described in Stapleton et al. (2017) that the elements of a single Euler diagram display multiple MCRs is due to the fact that this notation is occurrence-referential; since the symbol of a particular class, the circle, can only occur once in a unitary Euler diagram, it has at once MCRs to any other circle occurring in it. In a type-referential language a conjunction operator is always needed, while in an occurrence-referential language the conjunction operator is embodied in the syntax of the system.

6 Occurrence Referentiality and Observational Disadvantages

Euler diagrams are not only observationally advantageous over equally expressive languages. They are also observationally *dis*advantageous, in the sense that sometimes the information that is observable in an Euler diagram is not inferable from the information that was necessary to construct it. This phenomenon is known as "over-specificity" (Shimojima 1996a, 1996b). Consider the following first order logic sentences:

9) $\forall x\,(Ax \supset Bx)$
10) $\sim \exists x\,(Ax\,\&\,Cx)$
11) $\forall x\,(Ax \supset Bx)\,\&\,\sim \exists x\,(Ax\,\&\,Cx)$

The information which each of (9) and (10) conveys can be separately expressed by two distinct unitary Euler diagrams. The conjunction of (9) and (10), namely (11), can be expressed in a non-unitary, conjunctive Euler diagram, such as the one in Fig. 8. But while unitary Euler diagrams can separately represent (9) and (10), no unitary Euler diagram can represent (11) without also representing pieces of information that is not contained in (11). Suppose we express (9) by the unitary Euler diagram in the left-hand side of Fig. 8. Then, in order to represent the remaining part of the information contained in (11), i.e. (10), in the same unitary diagram, we should place circle C outside circle A. Now there are three possibilities here: C may be disjoint from B, it may partly overlap with B, or it may be contained in B. The information conveyed by (10) implies none of them. But while in first order logic it is possible to write down the information that A and C are disjoint without implying anything as to the relations between C and B, this is not possible in unitary Euler diagrams. The information corresponding to (11) can only be represented by a non-unitary, disjunctive Euler diagram (Fig. 9).

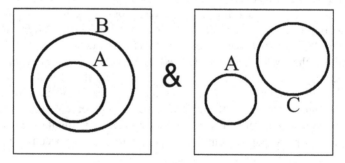

Fig. 8. Non-unitary Euler diagram.

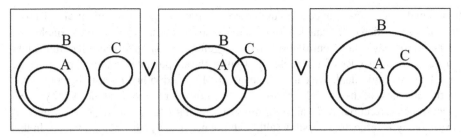

Fig. 9. Non-unitary Euler diagram.

The source of this phenomenon is the fact that, unlike what happens in some other equally expressive languages like first order logic, each circle in a unitary Euler diagram has at once MCRs to any other circle that occurs in the same unitary diagram. As soon as circle C is added to the Euler diagram expressing (9), it must be so drawn as to be in some MCR to circle B, even though the corresponding sentence (10) did not convey that information. Since the multiplicity of MCRs is due to the occurrence-referential nature of the system – non-unitary Euler diagrams only differ from unitary ones by being type-referential rather than occurrence-referential – it is the occurrence-referential nature of the system that provides the most basic explanation of both observational advantages and disadvantages.

Unitary Euler diagrams are over-specific: there is no way in this system to represent certain information without making some other, consequential or unconsequential information observable in it. When the information observed is consequential, we have an observational advantage; when it is inconsequential, we have an observational disadvantage. Both are caused by the simultaneous presence of multiple MCRs in a single unitary diagram, which in turn is due to the occurrence-referential nature of this language.

7 Occurrence Referentiality and Identity

In what precedes we have focused on the distinction between type-referential and occurrence-referential languages with respect to the representation of sentences, predicates, and classes. Languages can however differ as to whether they are type-referential or occurrence-referential with respect to the representation of individuals. Consider again the Beta graph in Fig. 3 above. We saw that with respect to the predicate variables this language is type-referential: in Fig. 3 the predicate variable type "Q" occurs twice, once in the partial graph at the left and once in the partial graph at the right, and both occurrences refer to the same predicate. Under this respect, Beta graphs do not differ from first order logic. However, Beta graphs differ markedly from first order logic with respect to the representation of individuals. In Fig. 3 there are two "lines of identity", i.e. thick lines connecting the predicate variables. Each of these counts as a distinct occurrence of the "line of identity" type: in Beta graphs, there is only one line type, each occurrence of which denotes a possibly (although not necessarily) distinct individual. In first order logic, by contrast, there is an infinite supply of distinct variable types (x, y, z, ...), and every occurrence of the same type (in the scope of the same quantifier) denotes the same individual. This circumstance gives us a reason to draw a further distinction: we call those languages in which individual identity is represented by the sameness of the variable type "type referential at the identity level" (or type-referential-I): in a type-referential-I language, each occurrence of a variable type (within the scope of its quantifier) refers to one and the same individual. We call a language in which individual identity is represented by the sameness of the variable occurrences "occurrence referential at the identity level" (occurrence-referential-I): in an occurrence-referential-I language, each occurrence of a variable type refers to a possibly (although not necessarily) distinct individual. In this sense, Beta graphs are type-referential but occurrence-referential-I.

This gives us the opportunity to mention another distinction which should not be conflated with the type-/occurrence-referential-I distinction. A notation for identity and quantification is susceptible of an inclusive or exclusive interpretation. Under the inclusive interpretation, difference of variables type or occurrence does not assure difference of individuals denoted. This is the case of standard first order logic, which is type-referential-I (difference of variable type does not assure difference of individuals denoted), and of Beta graphs, which is occurrence-referential-I (difference of variable occurrence does not assure difference of individuals denoted). Under the exclusive interpretation, difference of variables type or occurrence assures difference of individuals denoted. This is the case of Spider diagrams (Howse et al. 2005), which is occurrence-referential-I (difference of variable occurrence assures difference of individuals denoted) and of Wittgenstein's notation for quantification and identity (Rogers and Wehmeier 2012), which is type-referential-I (difference of variable types assures difference of individuals denoted). The systematic investigation of this second sort of referentiality (at the identity level) remains outside the scope of the present work.

8   Conclusion

Unitary Euler diagrams are occurrence-referential in the sense specified. We saw above that languages exist, like Peirce's Existential Graphs or the non-unitary version of Euler diagrams, which we would intuitively regard as diagrammatic and which however fail to be occurrence-referential. On the other hand, we believe we have shown that occurrence referentiality accounts for observational properties which are usually found in diagrams, and which are certainly found in Euler diagrams. This should suggest that while occurrence referentiality should by no means be identified with "iconicity" (or "diagrammaticity"), yet there certainly is a close connection between occurrence-referentiality and iconicity. The depth and breadth of this connection will be the subject or our future research.[4]

References

Alharbi, E., Howse, J., Stapleton, G., Hamie, A., Touloumis, A.: Visual logics help people: an evaluation of diagrammatic, textual and symbolic notations. In: IEEE Symposium on Visual Languages and Human-Centric Computing 2017. IEEE, December 2017

---

[4] This work was supported by the UK Research Council under the project The Applied Semiotics of Visual Modelling (EP/R043949/1). Many thanks to Gem Stapleton, Atsushi Shimojima, and Ahti-Veikko Pietarinen for useful feedback.

Bellucci, F.; Pietarinen, A.-V., Moktefi, A.: Diagrammatic autarchy. Linear diagrams in the 17th and 18th centuries. In: Burton, J., Choudhury, L. (eds.) Proceedings of the International Workshop on Diagrams and Cognition. CEUR Workshop Proceedings, vol. 1132, pp. 23–30 (2014)

Howse, J., Molina, F., Shin, S.-J., Taylor, J.: On diagram tokens and types. In: Hegarty, M., Meyer, B., Narayanan, N.H. (eds.) Diagrams 2002. LNCS (LNAI), vol. 2317, pp. 146–160. Springer, Heidelberg (2002). https://doi.org/10.1007/3-540-46037-3_18

Howse, J., Stapleton, G., Taylor, J.: Spider diagrams. LMS J. Comput. Math. **8**, 145–194 (2005)

Moktefi, A.: Is Euler's circle a symbol or an icon? Sign Syst. Stud. **43**, 597–615 (2015)

Rogers, B., Wehmeier, K.: Tractarian first-order logic. Identity and the n-operator. Rev. Symb. Log. **5**, 538–573 (2012)

Shimojima, A.: On the efficacy of representation. Ph.D. thesis, Indiana University (1996a)

Shimojima, A.: Operational constraint in diagrammatic reasoning. In: Allwein, G., Barwise, J. (eds.). Logical Reasoning with Diagrams, 27–48. Oxford University Press, Oxford (1996b)

Stapleton, G., Jamnik, M., Shimojima, A.: What makes an effective representation of information: a formal account of observational advantages. J. Logic Lang. Inform. **26**, 143–177 (2017)

Stapleton, G., Shimojima, A., Jamnik, M.: The observational advantages of Euler diagrams with existential import. In: Chapman, P., Stapleton, G., Moktefi, A., Perez-Kriz, S., Bellucci, F. (eds.) Diagrams 2018. LNCS (LNAI), vol. 10871, pp. 313–329. Springer, Cham (2018). https://doi. org/10.1007/978-3-319-91376-6_29

Stenning, K.: Distinctions with differences: comparing criteria for distinguishing diagrammatic from sentential systems. In: Anderson, M., Cheng, P., Haarslev, V. (eds.) Diagrams 2000. LNCS (LNAI), vol. 1889, pp. 132–148. Springer, Heidelberg (2000). https://doi.org/10.1007/3-540-44590-0_15

Wetzel, L.: What are occurrences of expressions? J. Philos. Logic **22**, 215–219 (1993)

The Diagram Problem

Piotr Kozak[(⊠)]

University of Bialystok, Białystok, Poland
piotr.kozak1@gmail.com

Abstract. The goal of the paper is to argue against the claim that thoughts can be modelled as having a diagram-like structure. The argument has a form of the so-called Diagram Puzzle, according to which the same features make diagrams cognitively reliable (and desirable) and unreliable (and non-desirable). I argue that to solve the Puzzle we have to accept the instrumental interpretation of diagrams, according to which diagrams are instruments of reasoning comparable to calculators. Instrumental view on the nature of diagrams leads to the problem of content determination: the claim that instruments can determine thoughts' content, entails that, for example, a calculation carried out with fingers has a different content that the same calculation carried out with abacus. If instruments do not determine content, they can be seen as instruments that reveal the content of thoughts, but they do not change the thoughts content. I argue that diagrams are epiphenomenal which means that they cannot influence the thought's content. Therefore, we can think with the help of diagrams, but it does not follow that thoughts have a diagram-like nature.

1 Diagrams in Mind

One of the causes of the increase of the interest in diagrams is the fact that the latter seem to be one of the most promising models of interpretation of what is thinking and what are thought processes. Let us call it a diagrammatic approach to thinking. The approach, represented most notably by Peirce, is based on two assumptions. Firstly, it seems reasonable to assume that some forms of higher order thought processes can be modelled in terms of operations conducted with diagrammatic representations, such as flowcharts or graphs. It means that diagrams can be used as tools for conducting some reasoning processes [21].

Secondly, it is believed [4, 7, 25] that understanding the nature of diagrammatic representations may be decisive to understand the nature of how (mental) representations work. The general idea is that the way humans encode information is based on a structural resemblance between the mental representation and the represented object, which both describes the nature of humans mental representations, as well as diagrammatic representations.

The diagrammatic approach to the nature of thinking can be defined as a conjunction of two claims. Firstly, thoughts possess a structure that is diagrammatic or diagrammatic-like, which means that transitions between thoughts are similar to transitions between diagrams. Thus the logic of thinking t is similar to the logic of diagrams. Secondly,

© Springer Nature Switzerland AG 2020
A.-V. Pietarinen et al. (Eds.): Diagrams 2020, LNAI 12169, pp. 216–224, 2020.
https://doi.org/10.1007/978-3-030-54249-8_17

that certain features of vehicle of representation are responsible for the cognitive value of diagrammatic thinking. For example, thanks to its particular and accessible form, diagrams are cognitively more useful than other forms of representation, and are a source of a genuine, diagrammatic knowledge.

In the paper I argue that the promises are not supported by the way we think about the features of diagrams and diagrams' functions. I present the so-called Diagram Puzzle and I argue that if we want to save the idea of cognitive usefulness of diagrams, then we have to accept the claim that they can play only on auxiliary role. That, however, leads to the claim that diagrams are epiphenomenal in the processes of thinking.

2   Cognitive Merits of Diagrams

Although there is no general consensus on how to form a precise definition of a diagram [20, 23, 27], diagrammatic representations may be interpreted, generally, as spatial representations of abstract pieces of information that enable us to infer the features of the things represented by inspection of the spatial features of a representation. Diagrams consist in providing one-to-one mapping of information that is stored in spatial form at the particular locus of a relevant diagram, including information about relations with the adjacent loci [16]. Accordingly, diagrammatic reasoning may be described in terms of a reasoning process based on manipulation and inspection of diagrams.

The cognitive value of diagrams has been explicated in two entangled ways: by a reference to the diagrams' cognitive accessibility, among others to the informative richness of diagrams, and by a reference to the particularity of diagrams which is a property that limits possible interpretations of a relevant concept and helps to discover new interpretations of the concept. Both ways seem to point out features that make diagrams, a genuine form of representation: diagrams are more informative and more specific than non-diagrammatic, especially symbolic, representations.

2.1   Diagrams' Cognitive Accessibility

In the number of studies, including classical examples of the 'tic-tac-toe problem' Zhang's [29] or the 'pulley problem' Larkin and Simons' [16], it has been demonstrated how effective, in comparison to the sentential representations, diagrammatic representations support solving different cognitive tasks.

It is commonly held that the ease of obtaining information from the diagram follows, on the one hand, from the informative structure of the diagram, on the other, from psychological capacities of the subject. The structural interpretation could be put in terms of 'informative richness', respectively, 'perceptual enhancement' of diagrams. It means that we can locate a specific information on a diagram easily, for every diagrammatic representation is a spatially indexed set of predicates describing the features of an object and the relations between those features. The spatial organisation of indices reflects the logical relations between the elements of the set. The ability to represent, next to logical properties, spatial – topological and geometrical – features simultaneously on one and the same vehicle makes diagrams *informatively rich*. As a consequence, diagrams allow us to grasp more pieces of information at once than a relevant symbolic representation

– the pieces of information we do not have to be aware of before the act of a diagram construction [13, 14]. An alternative way to express the informative richness is based on the observation that representing logical relations in virtue of spatial organisation of indices enables us to perceive certain relations directly. It means that the process of acquiring information is perceptually enhanced by the way the information is organised. As Larkin and Simon [16] put it: "the great utility of the diagram arises from *perceptual enhancement*, the fact that it makes explicit the relative positions of the equilibrium points, so that the conclusions can be read off with the help of simple, direct perceptual operations".

The psychological interpretation of the diagrams' cognitive accessibility is based on a claim that diagrammatic reasoning helps to use our cognitive capacities of coding information more effectively. It could be argued, either that since diagrams are not mediated in symbolic representations, they allow us to make inferences directly with the help of perceptual system [3, 28]; or that understanding diagrams seems to be a capacity that connects and coordinates various cognitive systems in order to enhance our inferential powers. Using diagrams involves the conceptual system, the visuo-spatial system, and the motor system [5, 6, 11].

2.2 Particularity of Diagrams

The particular nature of diagrams is the most vivid in the case of the use of diagrams in mathematics. Although in the philosophy of mathematics the most important point of concern is the issue of so called diagrammatic proofs, for the purposes of this text, particularly interesting is a cognitive role of diagrams in knowledge acquisition. It is claimed, on the one hand, that we can gain knowledge in virtue of inspection of diagram's features representing features of mathematical objects and theorems. On the other, that we can gain knowledge in virtue of transformation of a visual form of a mathematical object. The inference by transformation is based on a manipulation of the topological and geometrical properties of a diagram in order to achieve a desired conclusion.

It is argued that the usefulness of diagrams in mathematics follows from the fact that a particular and perceptual form of a diagram directs the mind towards the correct solution of genitive tasks. A particular form of a diagram means that, for example, a diagram of a triangle is always a diagram of a particular triangle – a right triangle, an equilateral triangle, etc. First, diagrams limit the number of possible interpretations of a concept and possible transformation of the geometrical object, leading to the correct interpretation of the latter, helping to discover a proof strategy. Second, the inspection and transformation of diagrams' features has a non-linear character. It means that they are not determined in advance, for example, in virtue of the symbolic content of a relevant concept. Third, a particular form of diagrams allows 'aspect shifting', that is, it enables us to see elements of the diagrams in different ways, for example, it enables us to see a "single expression as an instance of two distinct forms" [8].

It may is claimed [2, 24, 26] that particular and perceptual nature of diagrams is the source of an 'diagrammatic' form of inference which, on the one hand, indicates the difference between diagrammatic and symbolic representation systems, and on the other, explains why we can automatically read off a conclusion from a representation of premises. While the symbolic reasoning is based on manipulation and interpretation of abstract symbols, the diagrammatic form of inference is based on the fact, that we directly and non-deductively see the conclusion. For the conclusion is already there, in a specific form of premises. What would be an active inference from premises to conclusion in a symbolic representations system, comes along as a 'free ride' in particular diagrammatic systems [16, 22].

3 The Diagram Puzzle

The examples mentioned above seem to clearly illustrate the claim that diagrams, thanks to their inherit merits, are indispensable in some acts of reasoning and problem solving. Granted, there is little doubt that diagrams facilitate efficient reasoning. Yet, after a closer look, one might still doubt whether it suffices to justify the claim that they can serve as models of thoughts.

Notice that here I do not contest the claim that diagrams are essential in many cognitive processes. Certainly I do not claim that diagrams are superfluous for the process of thinking, that is, that they are mere illustrations of the thoughts. The point is that diagrams can serve as tools for thinking, and be frequently used for many cognitive purposes, no one argues against that. The point of controversy is an issue whether or not diagrams play only an *auxiliary* role, being a sort of an aid for the thought process, where the nature of the latter is completely different than the nature of the instrument that was used to think with. If the answer to this question were positive, then diagrams would be replaceable in the process of thinking. In other words, even if we agree that diagrams are tools for reasoning, we do not have to commit ourselves to the view that diagrams are basic units in our cognition. For diagrams can merely accompany the process of thinking, while not being bearers of thoughts.

This controversy is well illustrated by the example of diagrammatic reasoning in mathematics. Let us go back to the features listed above, that were to be responsible for the cognitive usefulness of diagrams. Firstly, it has been claimed that every diagram is a particular object, for example, a diagram of a triangle is a diagram of an equilateral triangle or an obtuse angled triangle, etc. It means that a diagrammatic representation of a mathematical object represents the mathematical concepts as having properties that, though are not ruled out by the content of the concept, are not demanded by it, as well. In comparison, verbal description of the concept's content is discrete, that is, they contain no more information than it is needed. Diagrams, on the other hand, are indiscrete by nature, representing a concept in a particular way. For example, any diagram of a triangle represents the triangle as being isosceles or equilateral, even if neither property is required by the concept $\triangle ABC$. However, the consequence of particularity of diagrams is that they cannot be representative for a wider class of objects and cannot be used to express some predicate over a universally quantified variable, and thus cannot justify general propositions. Putting it more precisely, using a diagram to infer about a wider class of objects we risk an unwarranted generalisation [9, 15].

Secondly, a consequence of informative richness of diagrams is that every diagram conveys more information than it is needed to represent certain concept, a certain proposition, or what is needed for a proof. For example, every diagram conveys an information on the thickness of lines representing a certain line segment, a colour of the diagram, or brings to light imperfections regarding the shape of a line or a curve. The danger here is a possibility to draw conclusions from accidental features, strictly speaking, the lack of possibility to distinguish essential from nonessential features we can or cannot draw conclusions from [1].

Thirdly, it may be generally stated that thanks to their perceptual form, diagrams are deceptive. First of all, a drawing may be simply inaccurate or imprecise. The well-known 'infinite chocolate bar trick' is an example of how the lack of precision of representation may deceive us.

And here goes the Diagram Puzzle. On the one hand, it might be said that if diagrams were deprived of their features, such as particularity and cognitive accessibility, there would be no many important scientific discoveries, particularly, most probably there would be no Euclidian geometry at all [17, 18]. On the other, in virtue of the possessing the very same features of diagrams which were to be responsible for their cognitive value, it is contested that they play any important cognitive role at all, except serving merely heuristic and pedagogical tools. Speaking precisely, it is claimed, both, that diagrams, because of their particular and perceptual nature, are cognitively indispensable, and at the same time that they cannot be a source of justified beliefs and provide justifications.

However, in show the apparent nature of the Puzzle, it is important to understand the reason one doubts in the cognitive role of diagrams. A traditional way is to argue that because of the features of diagrams, such as their particular, over-informative, and imprecise nature, diagrams seem to be unreliable, and therefore they can play only an instrumental and inferior role. Particularly, diagrams possess certain features that make it impossible for them to be a basis of a mathematical practice, especially it is impossible for diagrams to serve as a proof for mathematical theorems. Yet, firstly, it does not explain why at the same time we claim that the very same features of diagrams are responsible for cognitive effectiveness of the latter. Secondly, if one claims that diagrams are unreliable, and therefore they can play only an instrumental role, then, in principle, it would be possible that if we perfected the diagrammatic logic, for example by means of formalising diagrams, the latter could be a full-fledged form of a proof in mathematics. And still, despite of a rapid development in formalisation of diagrams, we are relatively far from achieving that last goal.

Another way to think about the cognitive role of diagrams is to argue that diagrams are in the first place *tools* for reasoning [10, 12, 19], and *that* is the reason why they may be unreliable. In other words, diagrams can be viewed as scientific instruments like scales and microscopes. Notice that if it is the case that diagrams play an auxiliary role of a tool in reasoning, then their effectiveness depends on their goal, that is, it depends on what one wants to prove. In contrast, if it were the case that thinking consists in manipulating diagrams, then the diagrams should serve different goals in a similar fashion, regardless the subject one is thinking about. For example, we measure the mass with the help of the scales, but it depends on the object of measurement what kind of the 'scales' one has to use. If one wants to measure the mass of potatoes, one has to use a different measurement device than in the case of measuring the mass of the Sun, since the subject of the measurement influences the matter of efficiency of the measurement tool. However, thinking about the mass of potatoes and thinking about the mass of the Sun is conducted in the same medium of thought and expresses the same operation of measurement mapping the mass of the object onto a relevant scale. For we think not with the *help* of thoughts, but *in* thoughts, and therefore it does not matter, what we are thinking about.

And obviously, using diagrams is like measuring the mass of potatoes with the help of the scales. It means that the usefulness of diagrams depends on what we are trying to prove. As a consequence, they serve well for some purposes, while for others they do not. That is the basis of the well-known claim that although diagrams can play a facilitating and instrumental role in mathematics, they cannot serve as a proof, cannot determine steps in a deductive reasoning, or take a propositional form. In other words, it is not the case that diagrams are imperfect and fallible, and that is the cause of theirs auxiliary role. It is rather the case that diagrams can play only an auxiliary role, and therefore they may seem as if they were either effective or fallible.

The second approach to diagrams explains well, why we interpret the very same features of diagrams, simultaneously, as the causes and the barriers of their cognitive effectiveness, depending on the purpose of the tool's use. In the same way the mass of a hammer may be an advantage, if one wants to nail a picture to the wall, and a disadvantage, if one wants to use a hammer to knock an egg.

4 Instrumentality and Epiphenomenality

However, if we agree that diagrams can play only an instrumental role in thinking, then it follows that, although they may have a significant psychological role in making some reasoning more comprehensible, they are epiphenomenal. It means that images may accompany thought acts but cannot affect the content of thoughts. Diagrams can prompt some thoughts but do not influence the thoughts logical mechanism. Diagrammatic reasoning is only a matter of using a different notation of thoughts' content and not a matter of a different content of thoughts. As an illustration, the equation $22 \times 23 = x$ can be solved with the Japanese multiplication method or with a grid multiplication method, affecting the effectiveness of problem solving, but the content of the equation remains the same.

Therefore, although we do perform certain cognitive tasks in virtue of manipulation of diagrams, the objection may be that the former cannot be performed without referring to other, more basic, assumingly verbal or propositional in nature, mechanisms and representations. According to the objection, the true nature of thinking is based on a manipulation of non-diagrammatic representations. Diagrams, like a steam whistle in a locomotive, accompany the acts of thoughts, but they are only epiphenomena of the latter, that is, they contribute nothing to the logical mechanisms of thought. In short, one may claim that diagrams are *parasitic* upon other forms of representations. In other words, diagrams may be tools for thoughts, that is, we can think *with the help* of diagrams, but it does not follow that we think in or with diagrams. For the nature of thinking is conceptually and metaphysically different from the nature of the tool we use to express our thoughts.

The argument for the epiphenomenality of diagrams may take a form of an argument of content determination. Notice that if manipulation of diagrams were to be able to be an instantiation of some diagrammatic way of thinking, then diagrams has able to determine the content of thoughts. For example, if one argues that one thinks in some kind of a language-like system, then one claims that the semantic and syntactic features of the system determine the content of one's thoughts. However, accepting both, the view that diagrams determine thoughts content and that diagrams have an instrumental nature, leads to nonsensical conclusions. If we agree that diagrams play an instrumental role in the thought acts, then it means that they are a means to an end. If the latter claim is true, then diagrams are replaceable by any other functionally equivalent tool in the same way as we can sometimes replace a hammer and nails with a glue or an adhesive tape. If, however, we would like to argue that the tool we use to think with determines the content of thought, then we have to agree that different tools determine the thoughts content in different ways. It means that relatively to the tool we use, we can have a different thought content. This claim does not seem to be counterintuitive in an obvious way. For example, if my thought$_1$ that $2 + 2 = 4$ was caused by the fact that the numerals were randomly generated, and my thought$_2$ that $2 + 2 = 4$ was caused by the fact that I have mastered the skill to count, then the content of thought$_1$ and thought$_2$ would be different. The content of the thought$_1$ could be, for example, that if one presses a button on a stochastic device, then it says that $2 + 2 = 4$. The content of the thought$_2$ could be, for example, that if one adds two objects together, then one gets four objects, whatever these objects are.

The claim that the kind of a tool determines the content of thoughts leads, however, to a nonsensical consequence. It would follow, for example, that adding with the help of fingers $2 + 2 = 4$, and adding in the mind $2 + 2 = 4$ lead to two different thoughts, which is an absurd. In the case of thought$_1$ and thought$_2$, what matters is not the tool we have used, but a different logical function – either a stochastic one, or a sum function. Thus, diagrams cannot determine the content of thoughts.

Let me clarify this point. What the argument shows is that diagrammatic representations may be an effective tool to make the content explicit. They can draw attention to properties of an object which has not been noticed. Diagrams may influence a viewer by prompting a different way of seeing an object. Though, they do not determine the thoughts content. They can make some thoughts more clear and can point out some features of the thought content that we were not previously aware of, but they cannot change the thoughts content. In the same way, a calculator is a perfect tool to make explicit what is a result of complicated calculations but it does not determine the result. It can make evident results of some complicated calculations, but it cannot change the result of the calculation. If it did so, it would be a broken calculator. Diagrams are like calculators – they can make some pieces of content more visible, but do not affect the content. Even if diagrams provide heuristic tools and discovery strategies for certain thoughts, it does not mean that they determine content of thoughts.

Acknowledgment. This work was supported by the research grant "What is Thinking with Images?", SONATA 10, granted by the National Science Centre, Poland, on the basis of the decision No. 2015/19/D/HS1/02426.

References

1. Ayer, A.: Language, Truth and Logic. V. Gollancz, London (1936)
2. Barwise, J., Shimojima, A.: Surrogate reasoning. Cogn. Stud. Bull. Jpn. Cogn. Sci. Soc. **4**(2), 7–27 (1995)
3. Bauer, M.I., Johnson-Laird, P.N.: How diagrams can improve reasoning. Psychol. Sci. **4**, 372–378 (1993)
4. Bechtel, W.: Mental Mechanisms: Philosophical Perspectives on Cognitive Neuroscience. Lawrence Erlbaum Associates, New York (2008)
5. Beilock, S.L., Goldin-Meadow, S.: Gesture changes thought by grounding it in action. Psychol. Sci. **21**, 1605–1610 (2010)
6. Bordwell, D.: Poetics of Cinema. Routledge, New York (2008)
7. Cummins, R.: Representations, Targets, and Attitudes. MIT Press, Cambridge (1996)
8. Giaquinto, M.: Visual Thinking in Mathematics: An Epistemological Study. OUP, Oxford (2007)
9. Giaquinto, M.: Crossing curves: a limit to the use of diagrams in proofs. Philosophia Mathematica **19**, 281–307 (2011)
10. Giardino, V.: A practice-based approach to diagrams. In: Moktefi, A., Shin, S.-J. (eds.) Visual Reasoning with Diagrams, pp. 135–151. Birkhäuser, Basel (2013). https://doi.org/10.1007/ 978-3-0348-0600-8_8
11. Giardino, V.: Diagramming: connecting cognitive systems to improve reasoning. In: Benedek, A., Nyiri, K. (eds.) The Power of the Image: Emotion, Expression, Explanation, pp. 23–34. Peter Lang, Frankfurt (2014)
12. Giardino, V., Moktefi, A., Mols, S., Van Bendegem, J.P.: Introduction: from practice to results in mathematics and logic. Philosophia Scientiæ **16**(1), 5–11 (2012)
13. Kirsh, D.: Thinking with external representations. Artif. Intell. Simul. Behav. **25**, 441–454 (2010)
14. Kitcher, P., Varzi, A.: Some pictures are worth 2[aleph]0 sentences. Philosophy **75**(3), 377–381 (2010)
15. Kulpa, Z.: Main problems of diagrammatic reasoning. Part I: the generalization problem. Found. Sci. **14**(1–2), 75–96 (2009)
16. Larkin, J.H., Simon, H.A.: Why a diagram is (sometimes) worth ten thousand words. Cogn. Sci. **11**, 65–99 (1987)
17. Macbeth, D.: Diagrammatic reasoning in Euclid's elements. In: Van Kerkhove, B., De Vuyst, J., Van Bendegem, J.P. (eds.) Philosophical Perspectives on Mathematical Practice, pp. 235–267. College Publications, London (2010)
18. Manders, K.: The euclidean diagram. In: Mancosu, P. (ed.) The Philosophy of Mathematical Practice, pp. 80–133. OUP, Oxford (2008)
19. Moktefi, A.: Diagrams as scientific instruments. In: Benedek, A., Veszelszki, A. (eds.) Visual, Virtual, Veridical, Visual Learning, vol. 7, pp. 81–89. Peter Lang Verlag, Frankfurt (2017)
20. Pietarinen, A.-V.: Is there a general diagram concept? In: Krämer, S., Ljundberg, C. (eds.) Thinking with Diagrams: The Semiotic Basis of Human Cognition, pp. 121–137. Mouton de Gruyter, Berlin (2016)
21. Sato, Y., Mineshima, K.: How diagrams can support syllogistic reasoning: an experimental study. J. Logic Lang. Inform. **24**(4), 409–455 (2015). https://doi.org/10.1007/s10849-015-9225-4
22. Shimojima, A.: Operational constraints in diagrammatic reasoning. In: Barwise, J., Allwein, G. (eds.) Logical Reasoning with Diagrams, pp. 27–48. OUP, Oxford (1996)
23. Shimojima, A.: The graphic-linguistic distinction: Exploring alternatives. In: Blackwell, A. (ed.) Thinking with Diagrams, pp. 5–27. Kluwer Academic, Dordrecht (2001)

24. Shin, S.-J.: The Iconic Logic of Peirce's Graphs. MIT Press, Cambridge (2002)
25. Sloman, A.: Diagrams in the mind? In: Anderson, M., Meyer, B., Olivier, P. (eds.) Diagrams, pp. 7–28. Springer, London (2002). https://doi.org/10.1007/978-1-4471-0109-3_1
26. Stenning, K.: Seeing Reason: Image and Language in Learning to Think. OUP, Oxford (2002)
27. Stjernfelt, F.: Diagrammatology: An Investigation on the Borderlines of Phenomenology, Ontology and Semiotics. Springer, Dordrecht (2007). https://doi.org/10.1007/978-1-4020-5652-9
28. Ware, C.: Information Visualization. Perception for Design. Morgan Kaufmann, Burlington (2000)
29. Zhang, J.: The nature of external representations in problem solving. Cogn. Sci. **21**, 179–217 (1997)

The Blot

Ahti-Veikko Pietarinen[1,2(✉)], Francesco Bellucci[3], Angelina Bobrova[4],
Nathan Haydon[1], and Mohammad Shafiei[5]

[1] Tallinn University of Technology, Tallinn, Estonia
{ahti-veikko.pietarinen,nathan.haydon}@taltech.ee
[2] HSE University, Moscow, Russia
[3] Department of Philosophy and Communication, University of Bologna, Via Azzo Gardino 23,
40122 Bologna, Italy
francesco.bellucci4@unibo.it
[4] Moscow University for the Humanities, Moscow, Russia
angelina.bobrova@gmail.com
[5] Shahid Beheshti University, Tehran, Iran
m.shafiyi@gmail.com

Abstract. The blot is a sign in Peirce's diagrammatic syntax of existential graphs that has hitherto been neglected in the literature on logical graphs. It is needed in order to trigger the cut-as-negation to come out from the scroll, namely from the implicational sign of a positive implicational (paradisiacal) logic. Since the cut-as-negation presupposes the blot and the scroll, what does the blot represent? On the one hand, it stands for constant absurdity, but on the other hand, Peirce takes it to be an affirmative sign. This paper explores the blot and its logical and conceptual properties from the multiple perspectives of notation, rules of transformation, icons, and scriptibility of graphs. It explains the apparent conflict in the blot's meaning in its capacity of giving rise to the pseudo-graph that exploits positive character of absurdity. In effect, the blot is the mirror image of the sheet of assertion, not its complementation. On the sheet, it acts as a non-juxtaposable singularity.

Keywords: Blot · Pseudo-graph · Scroll · Existential graphs · Absurdity · Scriptibility

1 Introduction

The blot is a constant logical sign (the pseudograph) in Peirce's diagrammatic syntax of existential graphs. Studies of its nature and even the very existence have hitherto been neglected in the literature on logical graphs (with the sole exception of Roberts 1973, p. 36). The blot is needed in order to trigger the cut-as-negation to come out from the

A.-V. Pietarinen—The paper was prepared within the framework of the HSE University Basic Research Program and funded by the Russian Academic Excellence Project '5-100'.
N. Haydon—Research supported by the ESF funded Estonian IT Academy research measure (project 2014-2020.4.05.19-0001).

© Springer Nature Switzerland AG 2020
A.-V. Pietarinen et al. (Eds.): Diagrams 2020, LNAI 12169, pp. 225–238, 2020.
https://doi.org/10.1007/978-3-030-54249-8_18

scroll, namely from the implicational sign of a positive implicational (what Peirce calls *paradisiacal*) logic. Since the cut-as-negation presupposes the blot and the scroll, what does the blot represent? On the one hand, it stands for constant absurdity, but on the other hand, Peirce takes it to be an affirmative sign. Either way, it is a pseudo-graph because it ought to be an "expression to which the interpreter shall be free to give any propositional meaning he pleases" (R 492, 1903). A pseudo-graph represents no possible or conceivable state of the universe.

This paper explores the blot and its logical and conceptual properties from the multiple perspectives of diagrammatic notation, rules of transformation, icons, and scriptibility of graphs. It explains the apparent conflict in the blot's meaning by its capacity of giving rise to the pseudo-graph that exploits the positive character of absurdity. In effect, the blot is the mirror image of the sheet of assertion, not its complementation. On the sheet, it acts as a non-juxtaposable singularity.

2 Peirce on the Blot

The blot was a new addition to Peirce's theory of existential graphs introduced during his preparation of the 1903 Lowell Lectures. In the unpublished "Logical Tracts. No. 1" (R 491) he described it (without yet naming it as the blot) as a pseudograph which "is a construction out of elements like those of graphs, but which, owing to the way in which these are put together, has no meaning as a diagram of the system to which it belongs". The need for it arises from the need of depicting absurdity in graphs in some suitably quasi-diagrammatic fashion. Substitute a pseudo-graph "What is false is true" in place of c in Fig. 4, and it may be read, "If b is true the false is true". This, Peirce states, "reduces b to absurdity, and is equivalent to a denial of b". He proposes to simplify the scribing of these graphs by making the inner enclosure "indefinitely small, or be suppressed; so that Fig. 2 denies b; and generally, a single enclosure has the effect of denying the whole graph which it contains". Hence, Peirce tells, "Fig. 3 asserts that b is true and c false; while Fig. 4 denies this, that is, asserts that either b is false or c is true, or, in other words, that if b is true, so is c" (*ibid*).[1]

Fig. 2   *Fig. 3*   *Fig. 4*

In a long follow-up treatise also produced during 1903, entitled "Logical Tracts. No. 2" (R 492), Peirce explains the procedure by introducing "alogoid" conditional propositions, namely those that express "If anything, then everything":

> Whichever method of expressing conditionals be used, it will sometimes be desirable to place in one of the compartments a proposition either absurd or well-understood between the graphist and his interpreter to be false, which may be called an *alogoid* proposition (I prefer this form, because *alogous* might be wanted to mean logically absurd). If we say that two propositions which will always be true or false together are *equivalent*, then any alogoid proposition is equivalent to "If anything, then everything". For logic has no purpose

---

[1] The caption numberings in quotations preserve those in Peirce's original writings.

unless some consequence is false; and therefore this must be well-understood between the graphist and his interpreter.

Alogoid propositions are expressed by blackening the respective compartment within which the alogoid proposition is located:

> In order to express an alogoid proposition, therefore, we need only an expression to which the interpreter shall be free to give any propositional meaning he pleases. Such an expression, introduced into our system of graphs, will not be a graph because it does not represent any possible state of the universe. I shall call it *the pseudograph*; for, however it be written, it remains the same in its equivalence. Since it is the assertion of all propositions, nothing can be added to it; and therefore it may be represented by blackening the whole compartment within which it is placed. Let this convention be adopted. The compartment so blackened may then be made very small or thin. Thus ... Fig. 8 and Fig. 9 will express "If *a* is true, everything is true"; that is, "*a* is not true".

Fig. 8   Fig. 9   Fig. 10   Fig. 11

In practice, Fig. 10 would naturally be drawn in place of either Fig. 8 or Fig. 9. Following this practice, Fig. 11 will in either system be another way of writing the pseudograph. (*ibid.*)

Peirce soon formulates this idea as a specific convention of existential graphs:

Convention No. 10. *The* pseudograph, *or expression in this system of a proposition implying that every proposition is true, may be drawn as a black spot entirely filling the close in which it is.* Since the size of signs has no significance, the blackened close may be drawn invisibly small. Thus Fig. 33 as in Fig. 34, or even as in Fig. 35, Fig. 36, or lastly as in Fig. 37.

Fig. 33   Fig. 34   Fig. 35   Fig. 36   Fig. 37

Interpretational Corollary 1. *A scroll with its contents having the pseudograph in the inner close is equivalent to the precise denial of the contents of the outer close.* (*ibid.*)

In the lecture notes related to this convention, Peirce had characterised the writing of the pseudograph on the sheet of assertion as "equivalent to burning up the sheet, since the sheet only exists, as such, in the minds of the graphist and the interpreter, and *that* by virtue of the agreement which the writing of the pseudograph destroys". He notes that it is nevertheless "useful to write the pseudograph in the inner close of a graph" (R 450). For example, the graph

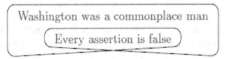

says "If Washington was a commonplace man, then every assertion is false",[2] which is the same as to say that "Washington was not a commonplace man". Convention 10 tells that filling up a close leaves no room in it, which means that the pseudograph is inserted in the close. To deny that Washington was a commonplace man, Peirce scribes the corresponding graph as follows:

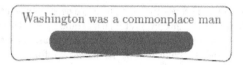

Since the size of a sep (the inner loop) is not a significant feature, Peirce scribes this equivalently as

"Making the loop infinitesimal", Peirce continues, "we shall understand a sep as denying what is written in its close" (R 450). In the related 1903 text "Syllabus of Logic" (R 478) Peirce described the "filling up of any entire area with whatever writing material (ink, chalk, etc.)" to amount to "*obliterating* that area". Notice that it is the area that is obliterated, not the loop itself. It follows from the obliteration as a corollary that, "[s]ince an obliterated area may be made indefinitely small, a single cut will have the effect of denying the entire graph in its area. For to say that if a given proposition is true, everything is true, is equivalent to denying that proposition" (R 478).

The pseudograph is the sign of nothing. Yet is asserts that "everything is true" (R 455). Peirce explains: "Were every graph asserted to be true, there would be nothing that could be added to that assertion", and that accordingly, "our expression for it may very appropriately consist in completely filling up the area on which it is asserted" (*ibid.*). Here (and this happens during his second Lowell Lecture), Peirce introduces the term "blot" for the first time: "Such filling up of an area may be termed a *blot*". We can learn from his notes that there are thus "two peculiar graphs": the *blank place* "which asserts only what is already well understood between us to be true, and the *blot* which asserts something well understood to be false" (*ibid.*). In addition, in the Alpha graphs one then only needs "two signs which are not graphs." First, "the putting of two graph-replicas upon the same area," where (recall that a blank is a graph), includes "the scribing of a single graph as a special case". Peirce rightly takes the idea that "scribing a graph is a transformation of a graph already accepted" to be a "very useful one" (*ibid.*). Second, the other sign is the *scroll*.

There are only a few further occasions in which Peirce revisits the blot and provides some further analyses and explanations of it. The idea of the blot surfaces in R 693 (1904) and in the related glossary of graphs in terms of *oppleted* graphs: "An area is said to be *oppleted*, or *opplete*, when it is virtually quite filled up, all graphs having replicas upon it. This is represented by completely blackening it. An enclosure whose area is

---

[2] The consequent should be "…then every assertion is true". The meaning of the "red blot" as "…then every assertion is false" comes from an earlier lecture draft (R 450), which Peirce soon in his next draft (R 455) corrects to the original meaning of the blot as in Convention 10.

opplete is equivalent to a blank". The last couple of definitions (33–40) in the glossary of 40 technical terms relate to this filling up of areas:

> An area so affected is said to be *opplete* (33) or to be *oppleted* (34) (from *oppléere*, to stuff up). Or we may prefer to say that it is the *annulus* (35), or annular space, comprising all that area except that occupied by the replica that effects the *oppletion* (36) that is *oppleted* (37). Or again, we may say that the enclosure in the area of which the *opplent* (38) replica occurs is *opplete* (39). Connected with this conception is that of a vacant *enclosure* (40), which is an enclosure whose area is entirely blank. (R S-26)

Another occasion is found among the many copy-texts and segments prepared for his 1906 "Prolegomena" paper but not included in the published version (R S-30, "Copy T"):

> [T]he Scroll affords me no other means of denying any Graph, say A, than by scribing that if A be true, everything is true. Now since it is impossible by any addition to increase Everything, this I can suitably express by completely filling with a blot the Inner Close of a Scroll that carries only A (and the Blank) in its Outer Close, so that there shall be no more room in that Inner Close for anything else.
>
> I can then make this blackened Inner Close as small as I please, at least, so long as I can still see it there, whether with my outer eye or in my mind's eye (Horatio). Can I not make it quite invisibly small, even to my mind's eye? "No", you will say, "for then it would not be scribed at all". You are right. Yet since confession will be good for my soul, and since it will be well for you to learn how like walking on smooth ice this business of reasoning about logic is,—so much so that I have often remarked that nobody commits what is called a "logical fallacy", or hardly ever does so, except logicians; and they are slumping into such stuff continually,—it is my duty to say that this error of assuming that, because the blackened Inner Close can be made indefinitely small, therefore it can be struck out entirely, like an infinitesimal. That led me to say that a Cut around a graph-instance has the effect of denying it. I retract: it only does so if the Cut encloses also a blot, however small, to represent iconically the blackened Inner Close. I was partly misled by the fact that in the Conditional *de inesse* the Cut may be considered as denying the contents of its Area. That is true, so long as the entire Scroll is on the Place. But that does not prove that a single Cut, without an Inner Close, has this effect. On the contrary, a single Cut, enclosing only A and a blank, merely says: "If A", or "If A, then" and there stops. If what? You ask. It does not say. "Then something follows", perhaps; but there is no assertion at all. This can be proved, too. For if we scribe on the Phemic Sheet the Graph expressing "If A is true, Something is true", we shall have a Scroll with A alone in the Outer Close, and with nothing but a Blank in the Inner Close. Now this Blank is an Iterate of the Blank-instance that is always present on the Phemic Sheet; and this may, according to the rule, be deiterated by removing the Blank in the inner close. This will do, what the blot would not; namely, it will cause the collapse of the Inner Close, and thus leaves A in a single cut. We thus see that a Graph, A, enclosed in a single Cut that contains nothing else but a Blank has no signification that is not implied in the proposition, "If A is true, Something is true".

This long passage from "Copy T" deserves a comment, in part because its reading of the single cut differs from the standard presentation (i.e. as simple negation) in existential graphs. The conditional is used in denying a graph, A, by scribing that "If A be true, everything is true". The consequent cannot be represented in Alpha graphs, because in

Alpha graphs there is no way to assert "everything". In Beta (first-order) graphs, on the other hand, there is no way of quantifying over assertions. Peirce's solution is to have the whole area of the inner close of the scroll saturated by the blot, which conveys the idea that nothing else can be added to that area (Fig. 1). The "blotted area" signifies that what is placed in it "is true", but since nothing else can be added to the blotted area, nothing else in it is true, namely everything in it is true. Now "everything in it" amounts to "everything", since no further specification needs to be given. The filling of the area of the inner close of the scroll is therefore an *icon* of the assertion "everything is true".

Fig. 1.   Fig. 2.

Peirce then explains that the "blotted inner close" of a scroll can be made infinitesimally small (Fig. 2) though it never completely disappears (it leaves two opposite turning points on the boundary, and so is not the "unknotted knot" in the sense of knot theory). The reason, he explains, is that a single cut (here taken in the sense of a simple closed boundary curve with no intersection points, that is, as the "trivial knot") does not signify negation; negation can only be signified by a "blotted cut" (a scroll with a blotted inner close, however small). To show the difference between the single cut and the blotted cut he imagines a scroll like in Fig. 3:

Fig. 3.   Fig. 4.

The inner close of the scroll in Fig. 3 contains a blank, which may be considered as the result of an iteration of the blank that lies outside of the scroll, which here as always may be the blank of the sheet. This is the new thought that Peirce develops in "Copy T": The sheet means "Something is true," and so does any portion of it that is the result of an application of the rule of iteration. The graph in Fig. 3 therefore means "If A, something is true." But since it is iterated, the blank in the inner close of that scroll can also be de-iterated. What would be the result of such de-iteration? Peirce says that this will do something that the blot does not do: "it will cause the collapse of the Inner Close, and thus leaves A in a single cut" (R S-30). The de-iteration of the blank from the inner close of the scroll does not turn the graph in Fig. 3 into that of Fig. 1. It causes the *collapse* of the inner close, turning Fig. 3 into Fig. 4, that is, into the single cut. But then the single cut does not signify negation. It only signifies what the graph in Fig. 3 signifies before the de-iteration, namely "If A, then something is true." This, Peirce suggests, amounts to the truncated statements "If A…" or "If A, then…" These are not complete assertions but non-well-formed, deformed parts that violate the grammar of the diagrammatic syntax. They do not mean the same as the negation of A, which is properly represented by the graphs as depicted in Figs. 1 and 2.

We may then restate the argument above in "Copy T" as follows. The primary notational function of the oval is to group propositions together. That is, it is a *collectional sign* like parentheses are in a non-diagrammatic syntax (R 430, 1902; R 670, 1911; Bellucci and Pietarinen 2016a, 2016b). In a system whose primitive operations are those of *conjunction* and *conditional*, collectional signs are only needed to distinguish the antecedents of the conditionals from their consequents (for conjunction is associative). The collectional oval is only needed in Alpha graphs in this role. In a scroll, the outer loop marks the area of the antecedent and the inner cut marks the area of the consequent. Thus the meaning of the graph in Fig. 4 is simply "If A, then...", because since there is no inner cut there is no consequent.

The meaning of the single cut is *purely collectional*. In a complete scroll, with the blot (the pseudograph or absurdum) appearing in the inner close, the meaning of negation is *added to* the collectional meaning of the cut, and this results in a sign of negation (the blotted cut). In other words, Peirce realised around 1906 that negation is represented in existential graphs by the blotted cut, and that the single cut simply functions as a collectional sign devoid of truth-functional meaning.

3   Positive and Negative Absurdity

We are not done yet. If there is a difference between a single cut and a blotted cut, however small or invisible this blot may be, what justifies using them interchangeably in the diagrammatic system, one of whose aims is to make the differences observable? Further analysis is needed in order to clarify the meaning of absurdity and accordingly the iconic generation of the cut.

First of all, the notion of absurdity is supposed to be a basis for that of negation; thus it itself has to be formed in a positive manner. When the system has only positive forms, that is, contains no notion of falsity, and no sign for negation, either, how can one express that a proposition, A, is false? Peirce's answer was to go on to assert, "If A is true, then everything is true". Such conditionals have no negation as a constituent. But notice that to say that "A is true only if everything is true" is also a rather strong *refutation* of the possibility of A being the case. Thus, to form negative propositions is to assign a sign for the proposition "Everything is true". This is what the blot does. Does it need to fill up the entire area then? As any instance of a graph in an area means its presence everywhere on that area (graphs can be scribed at any position in an area, i.e. all those positions are isotopy-equivalent), both the graphs in Figs. 5 and 6 equally express that absurdity implies P.

Fig. 5.   Fig. 6.

The blot as shown in Fig. 6 is the preferred notation, however, for one should distinguish between the blot and the scroll with both areas filled with black. Also, the blot should not be confused with a cut filled with black stuff. The blot with radiating, blurred boundaries is, we propose, to be preferred as the notation for it. This is consistent with Peirce's Convention 10, since we fill the inner close *with* a blot. A blot is *in* the inner close, it is not the filled inner close itself. The loop around the blot is not part of the blot. Roberts (1973, p. 36) describes the pseudo-graph to be "a cut entirely filled in, or blackened", but this is not the best possible choice of words.

The sign for negation, namely the scroll with a blot in its inner close, may be considered as a simple oval, the cut, since "the blackened close may be drawn invisibly small". The justification of this is not to be derived from the behavior of the permissive, deductive rules of transformation, since there is no cut in such language as yet. The blackened inner close remains on the boundary. However, if the aim of this language is to sustain diagrammatic syntax and the virtues of the iconization of reasoning (Bellucci and Pietarinen 2017), we should be wary of *apropos* conventions and remain mindful of the genealogy of the cut. What is it that justifies the equation between the cut and the scroll with a blot in its inner close? A further look at the notion of absurdity may be helpful here.

The definition of "negation of P" as "P implies absurdity" was known to Peirce since his 1885 "Algebra of Logic" paper. In the context of the further development of algebra into graphs, we find reasons for defining negation as a shorthand for $P \rightarrow \bot$ becoming increasingly clear precisely when Peirce is moving on to an interpretation of absurdity as "Everything is true." This "positive" characterization of absurdity is one of Peirce's profound insights into negation. If the negation of P is to be understood as P implying any absurdity, this "negative" sense of absurdity, namely absurdity understood as any false (or necessarily false) proposition, introduces no real insight into the embryonic development of the idea of negation. In some sense, it *presupposes* negation, while at the same time being that from which negation is developed.

However, in order to explore all possible iconic possibilities we have to consider other conceptions of absurdity. An alternative to absurdity (taken as a proposition) is the statement "There is no truth" or "Nothing is true". How can we state "Nothing is true" in existential graphs? We have the sheet of assertion, which represents the truth. When nothing is scribed on any position on the sheet, the blank asserts "Something is true". As the sheet is the place for truths, perhaps we can show that there is no place for truth by "closing off" the sheet of assertion or some parts of it. There are two problems: how can one denote the collapse of the sheet of assertion? As soon as that is somehow done, one would be *asserting* that "Nothing is true". But we also need that as a proposition to be used in other graphs. Therefore, we need to separate the scopes and then collapse one of them. According to the rule of the scroll, the scroll with blank outer and inner closes can be scribed and erased around any graph. Thus any part of the sheet of assertion enclosed within such a scroll would mean the same as it did before. The graph ⟨⊙⟩ says "If something is true then something is true".

Now since the inner close is the place of truth, if we were to completely obliterate it, it would diagrammatise the state in which there is no place for truth. This would result in the proposition, "If something is true then nothing is true". The following sequence is intended to show how a proposition "If P then something is true" morphs into the proposition "If P then nothing is true" by obliterating the inner close (Fig. 7):

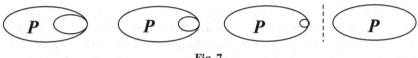

Fig. 7.

As far as the inner close exists and thus possesses a blank area, however small, the graph still means "If P then something is true". But when the inner close is completely dissolved, the meaning changes to "If P then nothing is true". Hence there is an equivocation in the above sequence; it does not display a meaning-preserving process of transformations.

Now we have a graph for "If P then nothing is true" but not a graph for "Nothing is true". But "Nothing is true" is equivalent to "If something is true, then nothing is true". Therefore the cut with a blank area is read "Nothing is true". Provided that "If P, then nothing is true" is synonymous with the negation of P, then a cut with P in its scope means not-P, as does the scroll with P in the outer close and the blot in the inner close, which states "If P, then everything is true".

To show something of the nature of absurdity by closing off some scopes is a realization of what Peirce had termed "unscriptibility" of some graphs in another slightly earlier and unpublished work of his (R 501, 1901; Ma and Pietarinen 2019). We propose to endow absurdity with this meaning. Both the blot and the collapsed inner close partake of the character of unscriptibility. Nothing is scriptible in a collapsed close: no space exists in a collapsed close at all. Nothing is scriptible in a close with the blot, either, since everything is already scribed in that blackened area. Miniaturising the inner close would not affect the character of unscriptiblity, since even if it were to dissolve into the boundary, the character of unscriptibility will be preserved. Therefore, although the sequence of graphs in Fig. 7 is not a meaning-preserving transformation, the one in Fig. 8 is:[3]

Fig. 8.

There are now two ways to introduce the cut. In the first, absurdity is "Everything is true", in the other it is "Nothing is true". Peirce's preference lies with the former,

---

[3] In Peirce's hand, a similar sequence looked like this (R 455(s)):

Peirce intended this to show that "the impossibility [that exists within the inloop] destroys the cut and all it contains" (*ibid.*). By this, Peirce is preparing ground for his decidability operations for the Alpha system (Roberts 1997).

since it *analyses* falsity and negation without assuming it. The proposition "Everything is true" will do that work well. Absurdity should be of the nature of affirmation, not denial. "Everything is true" is absurdity as an affirmative, "There is no truth" as a denial. Indeed "affirmation is psychically the simpler", confirms Peirce, and "I therefore make the blot an affirmation". That is, he makes the absurdity an affirmation and then equates it with the blot, namely "Everything is true".

Taking absurdity as "Everything is true" has some other conceptual and formal advantages that we briefly list. (1) It explains *ex falso*: If everything is true then P also is true. There is no need for an axiom or a rule and no need to appeal to proofs by disjunctive syllogisms, which are known to be circular. (2) The Law of Excluded Middle (LEM) and the elimination of double cut are laws not inherent in the nature of negation, which is a desirable feature intuitionistically (Peirce came close to intuitionistic logic in many related senses).[4] (3) The double cut rule is to be derived, if justified, from more primitive, observational considerations. If the cut were defined as reversing its area, then the double cut rule would be immediate by symmetry. But symmetry, though advantageous in calculus, is an unfavorable guideline when the purpose is logical analysis (CP 4.375).

On the other hand, although the absurdities "Everything is true" and "There is no truth" are semantically equivalent, the latter is gotten from the former: rules like the elimination of double cut are not eligible at this level of analysis. From "Everything is true" it follows that "It is true that there is no truth". But from "There is no truth" it follows, for example, that "It is wrong that something is wrong", which means that everything is true. However, we need an extra move here. Thus from negative absurdity we cannot directly derive the positive absurdity (its justification would need another rule or an axiom, such as LEM). But from positive absurdity other facets of absurdity follow.

Another candidate for the meaning of absurdity is *unassertibility*: It is irrational to assert absurdity. Or, one may say that absurdity is whatever is rationally unassertible. How can we scribe such absurdity in graphs? How can we assert the unassertible? A meaningless sign or nothing would not do because they express nothing; we want to express absurdity when its assertion is rationally forbidden. It is not meaningless activity: it just has a meaning that is to be avoided at all costs. One has a right to be irrational, but penalties will be visited upon one who chooses to be so. Asserting the unassertible is possible but risky. In existential graphs, three candidates could be thought of: (1) to close off a loop by collapsing an area so that no space remains for any assertion, (2) to fill the area so that no assertion can fit there, (3) to police an area by flagging it, such as a cross mark ×, that forbids any assertion in that area. The last option is not that promising as one has to use an *ad hoc* mark for unassertibility, yielding little iconic harvest. The first two resort to diagrammatic unscriptibility to effect unassertibility. Peirce's option was the second. Maybe something can be reaped from (1), too, as it preserves diagrammatic results and features no further conventions.

---

[4] See Oostra (2010) on Alpha System with the scroll that agrees with propositional intuitionistic logic. In this case, new graph for disjunction needs to be introduced as in intuitionistic logic, logical connectives are not interdefinable. How such modifications demonstrate the potential insights of Peirce's EGs has been discussed in Shafiei (2019). Moreover, Ma and Pietarinen (2018) have offered an EGs version for intuitionistic logic analyzing the nature of deep inference.

Considering the pragmatistic office of existential graphs, yet another conception for the absurdity may be proposed. In comparison to the pragmatistic motto "do not block the way of enquiry", we might say in existential graphs, and in logic as such, we have the principle: "do not block the way of inference". The way of inference would be blocked when we have a graph from which no consequences follow or a graph that cannot be antecedently motivated, i.e. that cannot be taken to be the consequence of an inference. This situation is exactly that of absurdity. Therefore, in order to show absurdity we show a case when inference is blocked. The smallest part of inference, an illation, is diagrammatized by the scroll. To obliterate the inner close would prevent the consequence being asserted. Therefore, if we put P in the outer close and close off the inner close it means "From P nothing follows" (not even itself), and this amounts to taking P as an expression of absurdity. The case has been discussed above. On the other hand, placing P in the inner close and closing off the outer oval, which results in a cut enclosing P, means that P follows from nothing, or that P is true under no assumptions. This equally amounts to taking P as absurd. Notice that here we are not saying "P is true under *any* assumption" which would be to consider P as a logical truth; rather we say "P is true under *no* assumption". In order to iconize the former one should leave the outer close, i.e. the place of assumption, blank and receptive for any graph; for the latter case one should totally close down the place of assumption, which is to dissolve the outer close in the boundaries of the inner close. Such new analysis now leads to a different type of a generation of the cut, but results in the same meaning as the previous ones did. In this new respect, the cut is the inner close of the scroll in whose boundaries the outer oval has been dissolved. (Peirce had a similar argument in another "Copy Text" of R S-30 not quoted in the previous section.) Notice that this case states that "Under no assumption P is true", which is different from "Under the assumption of nothing, P is true", for it is the place of assumptions that is obliterated instead of being filled with nothingness or absurdity.

4   The Blot and the Sheet of Assertion

This returns us back to some basic questions about notation. Why can a blank scroll be made to appear and disappear on the sheet? The sheet is a tautology and the blank scroll does not make any transformations of it. The sheet embraces all tautologies and true propositions that may ever be scribed on it.

There is one more element in the genealogy of negation to be pointed out. As briefly mentioned, Peirce proposes the original element of reasoning to be *paradisiacal* (R 493, c.1899; R 669, 1911): only the scroll is presented on the sheet. This positive, proto-reasoning operates without the presence of falsity or negation. Anything implies any-thing. Take one-valued logic (Hamblin 1967) or positive implicational logic as similarly paradisiacal proposals. There is not even any juxtaposition and hence no conjunction in positive implicational logic. In existential graphs, proto-reasoning has a paradisiacal scroll, in which the inner scroll may be blackened to contain all possible assertions, so that nothing could be added to it. Paradisiacal reasoning is in a highly unstable state, however, since "it will soon be recognized that not every assertion is true; and that once recognized, as soon as one notices that if a certain thing were true, every assertion would be true, one at once rejects the antecedent that lead to that absurd consequence" (R 669; Pietarinen 2015, p. 920). Any small perturbation and the blackened area atrophies to the first, primordial cut; a serpent appears in the paradise of pure reason.

Since the blot has the power of tipping the sheet off the equilibrium, the result is a scroll that promulgates cuts endowed with the meaning of negation. The blot is strictly speaking then not part of the logical vocabulary of the theory at all. It operates prior to the formation of logical systems (such as classical or some non-standard Alpha, Beta, etc.). The blot generates falsity and loses its signification and power (which are now hidden) in the process. Contrast this with the sheet of assertion. The blot has an opposite behavior to that of the sheet: white–black, blank–filled, scriptible–non-scriptible (see Ma and Pietarinen 2019). This area signifies the space of all possible consequences, which means that "non-scriptibility" is not identical to falsity or negation, and scriptibility is not identical to that of truth. These are Peirce's proposed generalisations of values (R 501). Likewise, the blot is not a logical complementation of the sheet. Both areas are positive. One more confirmation of this affirmative nature of the blot is found in a fragment of Peirce's late letter to J. Kehler 1911:

The simplest part of speech which this syntax contemplates, which, as scribed, I shall term a blot is itself an assertion. Ought it to be an affirmation or a denial? A denial is logically the simpler, because it implies merely that the utterer recognizes, however vaguely, some discrepancy between the fact and the speech, while an affirmation implies that he has examined all the implications of the latter and finds no discrepancy with the fact. This is a circumstance to be borne in mind; but since the denial implies recognition of the affirmation, while the affirmation is so far from implying recognition of the denial, that one might imagine a paradisaic state of innocence in which men never had the idea of falsity, and yet might reason, we must admit that affirmation is psychically the simpler. Now I think that upon this point we must prefer psychical to logical simplicity. I therefore make the blot an affirmation. (RL 376, 1911)

Strictly the blot is not placed on the sheet at all and thus is not to be asserted. Rather it is a mirror image of the sheet of assertion: assertible/non-assertible. The blot may appear to the field of vision from within the sheet, but it does so only when confined to the areas of the scroll. The sheet alone has no blots in it. What is more, any juxtaposition of a graph with the blot would result in an annihilation of that graph, including any blank graph such as the sheet. On the dark side of the sheet, there are no juxtapositions.[5]

Zaitsev and Grigoriev (2011) have proposed a generalisation of logical values beyond a Cartesian divide of them as either epistemological or ontological. Something of this sort is happening at Peirce's paradisiacal level of existential graphs. Zaitsev and Shramko (2013) call the truth-values from the ontological perspective "referential", and the truth-values treated as characteristic of statements involved in reasoning "inferential", which "means that a sentence is *taken as* (i.e., considered) true (and thus accepted) or false (and thus rejected)" (Zaitsev and Shramko 2013, p. 1302). A combination of two sets of truth-values has one of them interpreted referentially by $2^T = \{T, F\}$ and the other inferentially by $2^1 = \{1, 0\}$. In Peirce's case, this project should be read as a way (may

---

[5] When things are unscriptible, it is even not clear whether deduction works as the right mode of reasoning in that dark realm (Peirce once talked about the mode of reasoning of "correction", which is not "deduction" when all propositions are unscriptible (Ma and Pietarinen 2019).

not be the only one) to clarify how the initial paradisiacal logic, which is implicational without juxtaposition, operates. These values are initially limited to two singletons {T} and {1}, since the paradisiacal state of mind is not acquainted with falsity. Now the value {1} may be assigned to the sheet while the value {T} may be assigned to the blot. These values are not juxtaposable, although the areas to which they are assigned are not unrelated: Something that is considered as true {1} is objectively true {T}. The consequence reminds one of stereotypical thinking in which agents' objective truth is aligned with anything they are about to observe. Paradisiacal scroll relates these two values, stating that anything that is scribed and *considered* true implies anything that has to be *objectively* true. The scroll is the connection between the white and the black sheet. The border of the scroll is the place where two types of truth meet, and can be treated as the limit case of {T, 1}.

5 Conclusion

This paper surveyed Peirce's notion of "blot" and explained some of its main characteristics: logical notation, two kinds of absurdities, paradisiacal logic of the scroll, obliterating loops, and the relation of the blot to the rules of transformations. A few ways forward along the last point may be added. As it stands, negation in existential graphs is often treated as an ordinary graph-instance where the other inference/transformation rules still apply (such as iteration and de-iteration, or modus ponens and modus tollens). This is fine if negation is meant as a type of complement or inversion of truth-values, but in the case of absurdity a pragmatic elucidation would have to go further, because absurdity suggests that the rules themselves, including both the permissive transformations and the conventions, begin to break down. This is where the notion of absurdity begins to have a deeper meaning, and it is here that the blot gives us a valuable way forward. One interesting feature of the blot is that because of its nature of being non-vacant, completely occupied area, adding a scroll (or scribing a scroll on top of the blot as it were) does nothing to the graph. What this means is that the ordinary dualities and symmetries start to degrade. Maybe the idea of deduction has to go over the board, too. What would be interesting is to trace this effect to the origins of the inference rules to see at which stage, when retrogressing towards our proto-logical paradise, the rules themselves start to degrade.

References

Bellucci, F., Pietarinen, A.-V.: Existential graphs as an instrument of logical analysis: Part I. Alpha. Rev. Symb. Log. **9**, 209–237 (2016a)

Bellucci, F., Pietarinen, A.-V.: From Mitchell to Carus. Fourteen years of logical graphs in the making. Trans. Charles S. Peirce Soc. **52**, 539–575 (2016b)

Bellucci, F., Pietarinen, A.-V.: Two dogmas of diagrammatic reasoning: a view from existential graphs. In: Hull, K., Atkins, R. (eds.) Peirce on Perception and Reasoning: From Icons to Logic, pp. 174–195. Routledge, London (2017)

Hamblin, C.L.: One-valued logic. Philos. Q. **17**, 38–45 (1967)

Ma, M., Pietarinen, A.-V.: Peirce's Logic of Dragon Head, manuscript (2019)

Ma, M., Pietarinen, A.-V.: A graphical deep inference system for intuitionistic logic. Logique Analyse **245**, 73–114 (2018)

Oostra, A.: Los gráficos alfa de Peirce aplicados a la lógica intuicionista. Cuadernos de Sistemática Peirceana **2**, 25–60 (2010)

Peirce, C.S.: On the algebra of logic: a contribution to the philosophy of notation. Am. J. Math. **7**(2), 180–196 (1885)

Peirce, C.S.: Charles Sanders Peirce Papers (MS Am 1632). Houghton Library, Harvard University. Catalogued in Robin, Richard S. 1967. Annotated Catalogue of the Papers of Charles S. Peirce. University of Massachusetts Press, Amherst (1967)

Peirce, C.S.: Collected Papers of Charles Sanders Peirce. (8 vols. Hartshorne, Charles; Weiss, P., eds., vols. 1–6; Burks, A.W., ed. vols. 7–8.). Harvard University Press. Mass (1931–1958)

Peirce, C.S.: Prolegomena to an apology for pragmaticism. Monist **16**, 492–546 (1906)

Peirce, C.S.: Logic of the future: Peirce's writings on existential graphs. In: Pietarinen, A.-V. (ed.) vol. 1–3. Mouton De Gruyter, Berlin (2020)

Pietarinen, A.-V.: Two papers on existential graphs by Charles Peirce. Synthese **192**, 881–922 (2015)

Roberts, D.D.: The Existential Graphs of Charles S. Peirce. The Hague, Mouton (1973)

Roberts, D.D.: A decision method for existential graphs. In: Houser, N., Roberts, D., Evra, J.V. (eds.) Studies in the Logic of Charles Sanders Peirce. Indiana University Press, Bloomingtom (1997)

Shafiei, M.: Peirce's existential graphs as a contribution to transcendental logic. In: Shafiei, M., Pietarinen, A.-V. (eds.) Peirce and Husserl: Mutual Insights on Logic, Mathematics and Cognition. LEUS, vol. 46, pp. 97–122. Springer, Cham (2019). https://doi.org/10.1007/978-3-030-25800-9_6

Zaitsev, D.V., Grigoriev, O.M.: Two kinds of truth – one logic. In: Logical Investigations, vol. 17, pp. 121–139 (2011)

Zaitsev, D., Shramko, Y.: Bi-facial truth: a case for generalized truth values. Stud. Logica **101**(6), 1299–1318 (2013)

Two Implications and Dual-Process Theories of Reasoning

Angelina Bobrova[1] and Ahti-Veikko Pietarinen[2,3(✉)]

[1] Russian State University for the Humanities, Moscow, Russia
angelina.bobrova@gmail.com
[2] Tallinn University of Technology, Tallinn, Estonia
ahti.pietarinen@gmail.com
[3] HSE University, Moscow, Russia

Abstract. Dual-process theories of reasoning assume a fundamental difference between two cognitive systems: fast and intuitive System 1, and slow and rational System 2, grounded on rules of logical inference. Peirce's diagrammatic logic challenges the dichotomy. Both systems are based on similar inferential connections, but the former draws its conclusions as modelled in positive implicational fragment of the latter. This logical connection between two systems explains empirical results from Wason's card selection task without appeal to confirmation bias.

Keywords: Logic · Cognition · Dual-processes · Diagrammatic logic · Peirce's graphs · Positive implication · Wason card selection task

1 Introduction

Ability to reason is one of the great questions in the evolution of the genus *homo*. Contemporary studies in the cognitive science have mostly attempted to explain the emergence of this ability within psychology, generally categorized under two headings: *dual-process theories* [2,5] and *single-system conceptions* [3,6,15]. Formal logic was taken to have at best a supportive function. Yet normativity of logic suggests that psychological theories of reasoning supervene on logical ones.

Under the dual approach, logic and psychology are closely related. We argue that both systems of reasoning (System 1 and System 2) are based on similar inferential connections, but drawing conclusions in the former (S1) needs to be modelled in a positive implicational fragment of the latter (S2). Two kinds of implications are involved in a logical modelling of the two processes: primitive (the scroll) and ordinary (material). The absence of negation in the former explains why inferences can be fast and why they seem intuitive. The distinction draws from Peirce's theory of diagrammatic reasoning, especially his Existential

Supported by #20-011-00227 A of Russian Foundation for Basic Research (Bobrova) and the HSE University Basic Research Program funded by the Russian Academic Excellence Project '5-100' (Pietarinen).

A.-V. Pietarinen et al. (Eds.): Diagrams 2020, LNAI 12169, pp. 239–243, 2020.
https://doi.org/10.1007/978-3-030-54249-8_19

Graphs (EG) and the "paradisiacal" conception of the evolution of logical notations. From this vantage point, empirical results from Wason's card selection task can be explained without appealing to confirmation bias.

2 Two Systems of Reasoning and Existential Graphs

Dual-process theories date back to James [4], rising to prominence much later [2,14]. Broadened to decision theory by e.g. [5], they contrast spontaneous with deliberate reasoning. It is common to see S1 responsible for fast, associative and effortless reasoning, in contradistinction to S2 that produces rule-based, rational and criticized consequences of thoughts, with increased cognitive effort expended on tracing those consequences. It is also commonly maintained that in ordinary circumstances, S1 has an appeal as an easier one leading to effective solutions and short-cuts characteristic of human reasoning. It is only when S1 fails us that S2 may interject to correct subject's inferential performances.

Evidence for the presence of two systems of cognition draws from numerous experimental results, most famously the Wason card selection task [16]:

– A subject sees four cards. Two cards have their letter sides up; the other two the have their number faces up. It is common knowledge that each card has a letter on the one side and a number on the other. Participants are then asked to answer the question: Which cards they should turn over to prove the rule "If on one side of the card there is an E, then on the other side there is a 2".

This experiment assumes the schemata of Modus Ponens and Modus Tollens. "If an E, then a 2" means not that only an E is paired with this number. The results have been taken to show that a vast majority of subjects ignore the 'not only' condition (the correct answer is E and 7). A negative version of the selection task has then been taken to reinforce this standard lesson: when the rule "If on one side of the card there is an E, then on the other side there is a 2" is modified to "If on one side of the card there is an E, then on the other side there is not a 2", and rest of the conditions are left unaltered, participants who are asked to prove the latter do significantly better.

We propose an analysis of this situation by the *diagrammatic logic of EG*. In it, we see that (1) both systems rely on general logical schemata of reasoning, and (2) certain differences exist in how the consequences are drawn, which suffices to logically explain the differences in subjects' responses in the two versions (positive and negative) of the task.

EG is a graphical method of logic that covers a range of logics from propositional, first-order, modal and other non-classical ones [7,9,13]. Graphs are propositional expressions "of any possible state of the universe" (CP 4.395) presented or scribed on the *sheet of assertion* (as e.g. the two graphs of Fig. 1). Diagrammatic transformations show how one graph, as a "moving-picture of thought", is turned into another along the logical consequence relation. Such 'moving pictures' govern reasoning by what Peirce calls *guiding principle of reasoning*; it "determines us, from given premisses, to draw one inference rather than another" (CP 5.367).

Figure 1: (A (B))   (A (B)

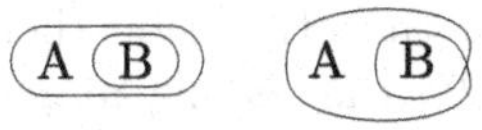

As an interpretation of implication, guiding principle may be modelled either as two nested ovals (Fig. 1, left) or as "the scroll" composed of one continuous line or two closed lines one inside the other (Fig. 1, right). Antecedent is in the outer compartment, consequent in the inner. Implication is the basic logical sign and introduces negation by generating the oval. The oval is the result of the evolution of logic from the fundamental notation of the scroll: "a certain development of reasoning was possible before ... the concept of falsity had ever been framed" (R 669, 1910; [11, p. 920]). Such a state of affairs is termed *paradisiacal* (R 669). In it, assertions take the form "If X be true, then every assertion is true." Once the idea of incompatibility is introduced and it is clear that X might be not true, a simple oval (negation) appears (see [12]).

The process of evolution of a fundamental logical conception of negation enables us to distinguish two kinds of implications, *viz.* paradisiacal (the scroll) and *de inesse* (two ovals one within the other). Both have the same structure as regards the guiding principle. But presuppositions of the two implications differ. Material implication evolves from the paradisiacal one. The presence of the latter ascertains that reasoning can proceed even in negation-free and falsity-free situations.

3   Wason's Card Selection Task and Two Implications

Indeed human reasoning is prone to default on negation-free situations. It is the scroll that provides general premise-conclusion schemata. We propose this to explain both the theoretical connection and the difference between S1 and S2.

The results of the selection task are thus to be interpreted as follows: when participants choose their cards, they tend to admit reasoning grounded on what they observe, and for such reasons refrain in such default state from proceeding to look for alternative solutions. Humans are prone to invoke paradisiacal, proto-implication, divested of falsity and negation. Peirce's assertion that "affirmation is psychically the simpler" (R L 386) is consistent with empirical data that suggests infants below c.14 months of age are unable to conceptualise negation, contradiction, or even that of absence. Difficulties include grammar acquisition and production and comprehension of illocutionary forces [1]. Yet logical reasoning is present, carried out with positive instances only. A derivative nature of hypotheticals indicate that the presence of falsity is easily suppressed from one's awareness.

Processes of refutation are less naturally exhibited in human reason than those of confirmation. Negation is a polar phenomenon, and for negation to make itself manifest, certain further, *boundary* conceptions are needed, and to maintain them in one's mental images of diagrammatic thought is non-trivial and costly. Geometrically, at least two areas must be simultaneously present, something that exists and something that exhibits a mere possibility. For such reasons, S1 tends to take precedence in reasoning. But if the rule "If on the one side of the card there is an E, then on the other side there is not a 2" readily conveys a negative concept "not a 2", the setting markedly differs in meaning from the positive token of the standard version of the test, and correct conclusions more expediently drawn. In both cases, subjects imagine the sign of implication, but in the latter task the higher success rates are triggered by subjects' recognition that "not every assertion is true".

This hypothesis can be experimentally tested and it applies to single-process theories of reasoning as well. A popular explanation of the selection task serves as an illustration: "Affirmative rule makes no prediction on the letter to be found on the hidden side of the 2 card, but the negative version of the rule does: an E on the hidden side of the 2 card would falsify the negated rule" [15, p.43]. Why does only the negative version trigger the prediction? This further question has remained unanswered. Our hypothesis offers an explanation: the affirmative rule does not make it evident that "not every assertion is true". But the negative rule does just that.

4   Conclusion

Selection tasks are not textbook cases of confirmation bias. Subject's ignorance of a relevant piece of information is not a bias but crucial part of logical reasoning at the level of the paradisiacal implication, and predicted by Peirce's theory of EG. As the language of the positive implicational fragment has a particularly clear diagrammatic structure, it could moreover be one of the future candidates for models of general and common-sense reasoning.

References

1. Clark, H., Clark, E.: Psychology and Language. Hartcourt, New York (1997)
2. Evans, J.S.B.T., Over, D.E.: Rationality and Reasoning. Psychology Press, Hove (1996)
3. Gigerenzer, G., Regier, T.: How do we tell an association from a rule? Comment on sloman 1996. Psychol. Bull. **119**(1), 23–26 (1996)
4. James, W.: The Principles of Psychology. Dover, New York (1950/1890)
5. Kahneman, D.: Thinking, Fast and Slow. Farrar, Straus & Giroux, New York (2011)
6. Keren, G., Schul, Y.: Two is not always better than one: a critical evaluation of two-system theories. Perspect. Psychol. Sci. **4**(6), 533–550 (2009)
7. Ma, M., Pietarinen, A.-V.: Proof analysis of Peirce's alpha system of graphs. Stud. Logica. **105**(3), 625–647 (2017)
8. Peirce, C.S. Collected Papers, vols. 1–8. Harvard UP, Cambridge (1931–1958). Cited as CP
9. Peirce, C.S. Logic of the future. Writings on existential graphs. In: Pietarinen, A.-V. (ed.) Three volumes. Mouton De Gruyter, Berlin (2019–2020)
10. Pietarinen, A.-V.: What do epistemic logic and cognitive science have to do with each other? Cogn. Syst. Res. **4**(3), 169–190 (2003)

11. Pietarinen, A.-V.: Two papers on existential graphs by Charles Peirce. Synthese **192**(4), 881–922 (2015)
12. Pietarinen, A.-V. et al.: The Blot. In: Pietarinen, A.-V. (ed.) Diagrams 2020. LNAI, vol. 12169, pp. 225–238. Springer, Hiedelberg (2020)
13. Roberts, D.D.: The Existential Graphs of C. S. Peirce. The Hague, Mouton (1973)
14. Sloman, S.A.: The empirical case for two systems of reasoning. Psychol. Bull. **119**(1), 3–22 (1996)
15. Sperber, D., Mercier, H.: The Enigma of Reason. Harvard UP, Cambridge (2017)
16. Wason, P.C.: Reasoning about a Rule. Q. J. Exp. Psychol. **20**, 273–281 (1968)

Euler and Venn Diagrams

Well-Matchedness in Euler and Linear Diagrams

Gem Stapleton[1,2]($\boxtimes$) (iD), Peter Rodgers[2] (iD), Anestis Touloumis[3] (iD), and Andrew Blake[3] (iD)

[1] University of Cambridge, Cambridge, UK
ges55@cam.ac.uk
[2] University of Kent, Canterbury, UK
{g.stapleton,p.j.rodgers}@kent.ac.uk
[3] Centre for Secure, Intelligent and Usable Systems, University of Brighton, Brighton, UK
{a.touloumis,a.l.blake}@brighton.ac.uk

Abstract. A key feature of diagrams is well-matchedness, referred to as iconicity in philosophy. A well-matched diagram has a structural resemblance to its semantics and is believed to be an effective representation. In this paper, we view well-matchedness as a feature of diagrams' meaning carriers – syntactic relationships that convey meaning. Each meaning carrier may or may not structurally resemble, i.e. be well-matched to, its semantics. This paper provides the first empirical study that evaluates the impact of well-matched meaning carriers on effectiveness in Euler diagrams and linear diagrams. There are two key take-away messages: using only well-matched meaning carriers led to the best task performance and using both well-matched and non-well-matched meaning carriers in a single diagram should be approached with caution.

Keywords: Well-matched · Iconicity · Diagrams · Visualization · Sets

1 Introduction

The notion of well-matchedness encapsulates the property of a diagram's syntactic relations corresponding, structurally, to its semantics [4,10]. A highly related notion is the concept of iconicity: Peirce took iconicity to embody the structural resemblance of a syntactic entity (a sign) to its semantics (object) [13]. In this paper, we demonstrate that well-matchedness is a property of meaning carriers [15]. This paper presents empirical studies that evaluate the impact of well-matched meaning carriers on effectiveness in Euler diagrams and linear diagrams, with the study designs embodying this fine-grained view of well-matchedness. The studies use stimuli that vary the use of meaning carriers to convey information within diagrams to test the impact of well-matchedness on task performance.

Section 2 illustrates the key ideas of meaning carriers and well-matchedness and makes the first contribution of this paper: identifying well-matchedness as a

© Springer Nature Switzerland AG 2020
A.-V. Pietarinen et al. (Eds.): Diagrams 2020, LNAI 12169, pp. 247–263, 2020.
https://doi.org/10.1007/978-3-030-54249-8_20

property of meaning carriers, not global properties of diagrams. Section 3 evaluates well-matchedness in Euler diagrams, presenting the hypotheses to be tested, the design of the empirical study, the methods used to analyse the collected data and the results. Section 4 covers linear diagrams, proceeding in the same manner as Sect. 3. We conclude in Sect. 5. Supporting material can be found at www. eulerdiagrams.com/wellmatched.

2 Well-Matchedness and Meaning Carriers

A fundamental aspect of any notation, diagrammatic or otherwise, is how it combines basic syntactic elements to form meaningful expressions. A meaning carrier is a relationship between syntactic elements that conveys either true or false information [15]. A key goal is to provide general theories about the relative cognitive effectiveness of competing diagram choices through understanding meaning carriers and their role in cognition. Meaning carriers allow us to identify information that is explicitly conveyed by a representation of information: this explicit information is defined to be observable from the representation [15]. It is also vital to understand meaning carriers when exploring well-matchedness: if a meaning carrier resembles the semantics it conveys then it is considered to be well-matched. Well-matchedness is a property of some meaning carriers but not others, distinguishing it from the notion of observability, and is hypothesised to help explain the relative cognitive benefits of competing diagram choices.

2.1 Meaning Carriers

Euler and linear diagrams both exploit spatial relationships between curves and, respectively, lines to convey information about sets. Each of these notations can be augmented with shading [6, 7] to convey information in a syntactically different way. We are only focusing on subset or disjointness relationships between pairs of sets and, therefore, are only concerned with the meaning carriers identified below. In general, other meaning carriers arise.

Meaning Carriers in Euler Diagrams. Figure 1 contains four diagrams that show information about the countries visited by people. We focus on part of the information conveyed: *everyone who visited Ukraine also visited Romania.* This is subset information: the set of people who visited Ukraine is a subset of those who visited Romania. In the leftmost diagram, only spatial relationships between circles convey information: the inclusion of one circle inside another is a meaning carrier, since it conveys information about the relationship between the corresponding sets. The first and second diagram in Fig. 1 both place Ukraine inside Romania, expressing the subset-style statement spatially using circles.

The third and fourth diagrams do not exploit an equivalent spatial relationship: Ukraine is not inside Romania. To convey the subset information, the region inside the former but outside the latter is shaded (shading identifies set emptiness). Shading can be viewed as an annotation that the corresponding set is empty: it is fundamentally different to spatial relations between circles when

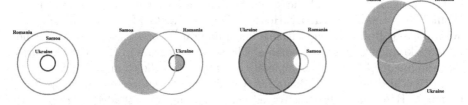

Fig. 1. Euler diagrams with varying meaning carriers: subset information.

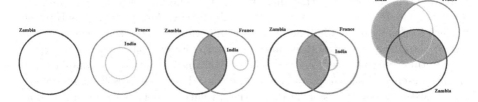

Fig. 2. Euler diagrams with varying meaning carriers: disjointness information.

Fig. 3. Linear diagrams with varying meaning carriers: subset information.

Fig. 4. Linear diagrams with varying meaning carriers: disjointness information.

used to convey information. In the third diagram, therefore, the placement of shading inside parts of the Ukraine circle ensures that the diagram expresses that everyone who visited Ukraine also visited Romania. Similar reasoning can be applied to the fourth diagram.

Regarding disjointness relations, using Fig. 2 we focus on the statement *no one visited both India and Zambia*. In the first and second diagram, the non-overlapping nature of the India and Zambia circles is a meaning carrier expressing this information. By contrast, the third and fourth Euler diagram express the disjointness information by shading the region inside both India and Zambia.

Meaning Carriers in Linear Diagrams. In Fig. 3, the linear diagrams convey the same information as the Euler diagrams in Fig. 1. In the first linear diagram, only spatial relations between lines convey information: if the x-coordinates of one line are entirely subsumed by those of another line then the set represented by the former is a subset of the latter. So, one line being completely overlapped by another is a meaning carrier. Hence, since (the line for) Ukraine is completely overlapped by Romania, the leftmost linear diagram expresses that everyone who visited Ukraine also visited Romania. The second diagram in Fig. 3 also ensures that the line for Ukraine is completely overlapped by the Romania line.

In the third and fourth diagrams, Ukraine is not completely overlapped by Romania. Here, meaning is conveyed using shading: in a shaded overlap[1], the represented set is empty. Thus, to express one set is a subset of another, we can shade the overlaps that include a line for the former but not the latter. In the third diagram, the overlap that includes the Ukraine line but not the Romania line is shaded. In the fourth linear diagram, the two overlaps that include Ukraine but not Romania are shaded. So both these diagrams express that everyone who visited Ukraine also visited Romania. As with the Euler diagram case, to extract the information that everyone who visited Ukraine also visited Romania relies on the presence of shading, not simply the spatial relationships between lines.

Regarding the expression of disjointness relations between sets, linear diagrams exploit either spatial relations between lines or shading. Using Fig. 4, we again consider the statement *nobody visited both India and Zambia*. In the first two diagrams of Fig. 4, the non-overlapping nature of the India and Zambia lines is a meaning carrier expressing this information. By contrast, the third and fourth linear diagram express the disjointness information by shading the overlaps that contain lines for both India and Zambia.

2.2   Well-Matchedness of Meaning Carriers

Recall that a meaning carrier is well-matched to its semantics if there is a structural resemblance between the way in which the meaning carrier expresses information and the information being expressed. Well-matchedness is a property of meaning carriers, not a global property of diagrams. To study well-matcheness in general, not just for Euler and linear diagrams, we need to identify the meaning carriers that are present in diagrams and whether they are well-matched. This fine-grained view of well-matchedness is potentially important for our continued study of the efficacy of diagrams.

Well-Matchedness in Euler Diagrams. Spatial meaning carriers arising from circles are well-matched. In the subset case, the inclusion of circle A inside B matches the meaning that all of set A is included in set B. Likewise, the disjoint interiors of two non-overlapping circles, C and D, matches the meaning that the two represented sets are disjoint. That is, in Euler diagrams, meaning carriers arising from circles are well-matched to their semantics. By contrast, there is no structural resemblance of shading to its meaning: the presence of a syntactic device – shading – is being used to express the absence of elements. Thus, meaning carriers arising from the use of shading are not well-matched.

---

[1] Overlapping lines represent set intersections with distinct overlaps are separated by vertical grid lines. The first diagram in Fig. 3 has three overlaps, with the first one representing the intersection of the three sets since all three lines appear.

Returning to Figs. 1 and 2, we can see that in both cases the leftmost diagrams only exploit well-matched meaning carriers, the middle two diagrams blend well-matched and non-well-matched meaning carriers and the rightmost diagram only uses non-well-matched meaning carriers.

Well-Matchedness in Linear Diagrams. Spatial meaning carriers arising from lines are also well-matched. In the subset case, line A being completely overlapped by line B matches the meaning that all of set A is included in set B. This is because the semantics are derived from the x-coordinates occupied by the line A forming a subset of those for the line B. So, the subset of x-coordinates at the syntactic level matches the subset of elements at the semantic level. Likewise, the non-overlapping nature of two lines, C and D, matches the meaning that the two represented sets are disjoint. That is, in linear diagrams, spatial meaning carriers arising from lines are well-matched to their semantics, just as for Euler diagrams. Again, there is no structural resemblance of shading to its meaning: shading is not well-matched. Returning to Figs. 3 and 4, we can see that in both cases the leftmost diagrams only exploit well-matched meaning carriers, the middle two diagrams blend well-matched and non-well-matched meaning carriers and the rightmost diagram only uses non-well-matched meaning carriers.

2.3 Research Questions

The specific research questions addressed for these two notations are:

(RQ1) Do diagrams with only well-matched meaning carriers significantly improve performance over diagrams with some non-well-matched meaning carriers?

(RQ2) Do diagrams whose meaning carriers are well-matched to *the information to be extracted in a given task* significantly improve performance over diagrams that are *not* well-matched to *the information to be extracted*?

Answers will shed new light on the role of the well-matchedness of meaning carriers in Euler and linear diagrams and will inform the design of visual modes of communication: if well-matched meaning carriers yield demonstrable performance benefits then we should favour visualization methods that exhibit them. Moreover, if non-well-matched meaning carriers negatively impact performance then they should be avoided.

3 Evaluating Well-Matchedness in Euler Diagrams

To begin our study of well-matchedness, we will derive hypotheses concerning its role in Euler diagrams and its potential impact on cognition, measured via task performance. For our purposes, a representation is judged to support more effective information extraction than another if there is a significant accuracy or speed benefit. The evaluation of Euler diagrams was run in alongside the study on linear diagrams, presented in Sect. 4: data were collected concurrently.

3.1 Hypotheses

The above discourse on the role of meaning carriers in conveying information and their potential to be well-matched leads to our first hypothesis:

[H1] to identify a piece of information from a diagram that is conveyed *using a well-matched meaning carrier* is *significantly easier* than identifying it *using a non-well-matched meaning carrier.*

This suggests that, in each of Figs. 1 and 2, the two diagrams on the left will support significantly more accurate or, else, significantly faster time performance than the two diagrams on the right. What other differences between the diagrams in these figures might we expect to establish, empirically, if the well-matchedness of meaning carriers is a fundamental property that impacts task performance? To get a more precise handle on this we appeal to the theory of boundary segregation [5], which states that colour hue is favoured over shape when segregating boundaries, and the Gestalt Principles of Perceptual Organisation, in particular the principle of good continuation [17].

Suppose we wish to extract the information that *everyone who visited Ukraine also visited Romania* and that *no one visited both India and Zambia* from the diagrams in Figs. 1 and 2 respectively. In each of the diagrams, their circles can be visually segregated from each other, primarily because of their distinguishing hues as colour[2] is more salient than form [5]. In addition, in each of the leftmost diagrams, the visual salience of the circles is further promoted: since no pair of circles have intersections between their boundaries, each circle exhibits the principle of good continuation. In the remaining diagrams, visual segregation is impaired because at least one pair of circles exhibit changes in good continuation at the points where circles intersect. Indeed, these changes in good continuation arise precisely because a non-well-matched meaning carrier is used and they promote the visual saliency of the intersection. These insights support [H1] and suggest that the leftmost diagram is more effective than the second diagram in each figure, leading to another hypothesis:

[H2] to identify a piece of information from a diagram that *only has well-matched meaning carriers* is *significantly easier* than identifying it from a diagram that *blends well-matched and non-well-matched meaning carriers, and expresses the desired information in a well-matched way.*

We suggest as the number of changes in good continuation increases (due to the use of non-well-matched meaning carriers), the less salient the circles become and the more difficult the task may get. However, we must also consider the crucial role of shading. That is, to understand the role of meaning carriers in information extraction, we need to understand the relative salience of circles and shaded regions. Since the same colour hue is used throughout for the shading, we posit that no one shaded region is more prominent than another, but the

---

[2] The discussion in this section is assuming the viewer of the representations is not impeded by colourblindness.

circles are more readily distinguishable due to their varying hues. Hence, the most salient information in an Euler diagram may arise from its well-matched meaning carriers. This further supports [H1] since it distinguishes the second and third diagrams in each of our figures: the second diagram uses a well-matched meaning carrier to convey the required information whereas the third diagram does not. Moreover, the third diagram uses a well-matched meaning carrier to express different information, which we speculate will act as a distraction from the task of identifying that *everyone who visited Ukraine also visited Romania* in Fig. 1 and that *no one visited both India and Zambia* in Fig. 2. It is known that, in general, syntax which causes a distraction from the target syntax required for the task can lead to reduced performance [9]. Applying this to Euler diagrams, the saliency of the well-matched meaning carrier in the third diagram of each figure inhibits the identification of the target, non-well-matched, syntax that must be interpreted to extract the aforementioned statements. By contrast, in the fourth diagram, there are no (salient) well-matched meaning carriers to distract form the task of identifying the required information. We obtain a third hypothesis:

[H3] to identify a piece of information from a diagram that *uses only non-well-matched meaning carriers* is *significantly easier* than identifying it from a diagram that *uses both well-matched and non-well-matched meaning carriers and expresses the desired information using a non-well-matched meaning carrier.*

To summarise, combining [H1], [H2], and [H3], we expect the diagrams to be ranked, in terms of their ability to support the extraction of the stated information, as: the leftmost diagram is most effective ([H1] and [H2]), followed by the second diagram ([H2]), then the fourth ([H1] and [H3]) and, finally, the third diagram ([H1] and [H3]).

3.2 Methods

We recruited participants using the Prolific Academic crowdsourcing platform. Participants were asked to perform 8 tasks, presented in the *performance phase* of the study which was preceded by a *training phase*. Each task was a multiple choice question with five options, exactly one of which was the correct answer. There were two *preference phase* questions, one for subset-style statements and one for disjointness-style statements. The performance phase and preference phase each included additional questions to establish whether participants were paying attention. This is standard technique when crowdsourcing [8]. Data from inattentive participants – i.e. those who fail to answer at least one attention checking question correctly – are not included in any statistical analysis.

The study adopted a within group design. The participants would be asked, in the performance phase, a multiple choice question and were required to identify which of five options was correct. Two options were subset-style statements, two were disjointness-style statements and the fifth option was 'none of the above'.

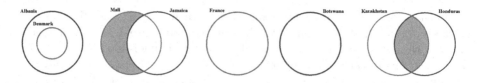

Fig. 5. The first four training Euler diagrams.

There were four tasks for subset-style statements and four for disjointness-style statements. All diagrams included in the paper to illustrate the study design are scaled for space reasons (typically to 30%). For the study materials, see www.eulerdiagrams.com/wellmatched.

Training Phase. Participants were shown diagrams similar to, but distinct from, those used in the other two phases. The first four training diagrams each displayed two sets. Of these, the first two conveyed subset information and the second two conveyed disjointness information. The fourth and fifth diagrams each used three sets, the first focusing on subset training and the second on disjointness. Figure 5 shows the first four training diagrams, covering the use of spatial relations between circles and shaded regions as meaning carriers for subset and disjointness information. The training diagrams were presented in a fixed order.

Performance Phase. This phase included four subset-style tasks and four disjointness-style tasks alongside one question to check for attentiveness. Figure 6 shows a subset task where the answer is well-matched (correct answer: option 4) alongside the performance-phase attention checker. The options for the attention checker indicated which option to pick and, for the remaining options, used country names that did not appear in the diagram. The four tasks associated with each task type covered the following treatments:

- Well-Matched (WM): the diagram only exploits well-matched meaning carriers (spatial relationships between circles).
- Well-Matched to the Answer (WMA): the diagram exploits a well-matched meaning carrier to convey the correct answer, but also uses a non-well-matched meaning carrier (shading) to convey other information.
- Not Well-Matched to the Answer (NWMA): the diagram exploits a non-well-matched meaning carrier to convey the correct answer, but also uses a well-matched meaning carrier to convey other information.
- Not Well-Matched (NWM): the diagram only exploits non-well-matched meaning carriers.

Based on our hypotheses, we would expect our treatments to be ranked as WM > WMA > NWM > NWMA, where > means more accurate or faster.

The four Euler diagrams for the subset-style task conveyed the same information, up to label swapping, and varied only by their use of spatial relationships between circles and shading. Similarly, this was the only variation in the diagrams used for the disjointness tasks. Figures 7 and 8 show all of the diagrams

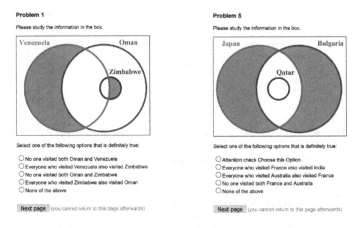

Fig. 6. Task presentation (left) and an attention checker (right).

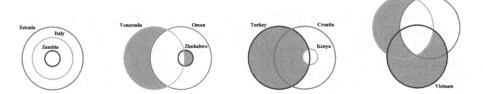

Fig. 7. The four Euler diagrams used for subset tasks.

used in the study. In each case, the diagrams are ordered (from left to right): WM, WMA, NWMA, NWM. No pair of diagrams shared a country name and, within each diagram, each country name started with a different first letter to reduce the potential for misreading. The colours assigned to the circles were derived from ColorBrewer to ensure they were perceptually distinct and suitable for categorised data [11].

Regarding the five options, the first four included two subset-style statements and two disjointness-style statements. The three incorrect options, excluding 'none of the above', had the sets involved randomly selected whilst ensuring that the options were not true. Regarding the correct answer, it would not be sensible to always place it in the same position (eliminating answer position as a variance across treatments): it would be easy to spot that the correct answer was always in, say, position 2. Table 1 indicates the positions of the correct answers for each statement style and treatment. In addition, we indicate the sets involved in the correct answer, abbreviating their names to first letters only and expressing the statement in mathematical notation (note the answers were always written as 'Everyone ...' and 'No one ...' statements). For each participant, the order of the tasks was randomly generated, except that the attention checker always appeared after the fourth performance-phase task.

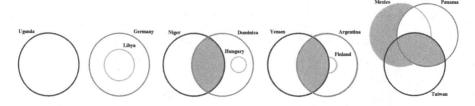

Fig. 8. The four Euler diagrams used for disjointness tasks.

Table 1. Answer positions for each question.

Treatment	Subset				Disjoint			
	WM	WMA	NWMA	NWM	WM	WMA	NWMA	NWM
Answer position	1	4	2	3	4	1	3	2
Answer	$Z \subseteq E$	$Z \subseteq O$	$V \subseteq P$	$T \subseteq C$	$L \cap U = \emptyset$	$H \cap N = \emptyset$	$F \cap Y = \emptyset$	$M \cap T = \emptyset$

Preference Phase. Participants were presented with two preference questions, asking them to rank four diagrams according to which most effectively conveyed a specified subset and, respectively, a disjointness statement. For the subset-style statement, the diagrams in Fig. 1 were used and the statement was *Everyone who visited Ukraine also visited Romania*. For the disjointness-style statements, the diagrams in Fig. 2 were used and the statement was *No one visited both India and Zambia*. The diagrams used in the preference phase were identical to the eight diagrams in the main study, except that the labelling differed. The diagrams were presented in a random order, generated for each participant, to reduce any potential ordering effect. Equal rankings were permitted and participants were asked to explain their ranking. The subset question included an attention check, with participants being asked to choose a specified option from a dropdown list.

Statistical Methods. We collected accuracy and time data as indicators of performance, with accuracy viewed as more important than time: one treatment is judged to be more effective than another if users can perform tasks significantly more accurately with it or, if no significant accuracy difference exists, performance is significantly quicker when correct answers are provided. We employed a generalized estimating equations model [12] to analyse the accuracy and time data. For the preference analysis, we analysed data that related to the most preferred treatment. A local odds ratios GEE model [16] estimated the probability of each treatment being most preferred. The treatments were then compared pairwise, using the ratio of their associated probabilities. For the accuracy, time and preference data, it was not appropriate to apply commonly used parametric or non-parametric statistical method (e.g. ANOVA and Kruskal–Walis tests) because the data violated the normality assumption and the responses for each individual are expected to be correlated, and so not independent. The models and statistical output can be found at www.eulerdiagrams.com/wellmatched.

3.3 Euler Diagram Results

We report on the results of our evaluation of well-matchedness in Euler diagrams; the two studies (the other on linear diagrams) were run in parallel, with Prolific Academic participants being randomly exposed to either Euler or linear diagrams. We set pre-screening criteria: the first language had to be English, they had to have an approval rating of at least 98%, and have completed at least five studies on the Prolific platform. In addition, we only permitted the study to be taken on a desktop device, excluding the use of mobiles and tablets. Each participant was paid £2.06 and told that we expected the study to take 15 min, with a maximum time allowed of 56 min (set by Prolific).

The pilot revealed that some questions had unexpectedly low accuracy rates. This led us to improve the training material at the beginning of the study, with additional explanation on the meaning of shading and new pages explaining the task answers. We also assigned a letter to each diagram in the preference phase and asked participants to use these letters when making comments, so that we could more accurately match their remarks to the diagrams. Lastly, we rectified an incorrect positioning of the correct answer to question 8. When gathering data for a second pilot, there was a technical issue, resulting in partial data being collected. Therefore, we ran a third pilot which still revealed low accuracy rates for some questions. Having already added material to the training given, it was felt that these low accuracy rates could be a feature of the treatments being evaluated, so we proceeded with the main data collection. The pre-screening criteria were carried forward with the additional criterion that no pilot participant could take part. As is standard, no participant could take part more than once.

We recruited 126 participants with the following distribution: 101 successfully completed, 0 were inattentive, and 25 failed to complete the study. Of the 101 participants who completed, 70 identified as female and 31 as male. Ages ranged from 18 to 69, with a mean of 34. Results are declared significant if $p \leq 0.05$. Note that we do not apply Bonferroni corrections. Some researchers routinely do so but corrections should only be applied when certain conditions are met [3][3].

Accuracy Analysis. The mean accuracy rate overall was 61.39% with the treatment rates being: 86.63% for WM, 60.89% for WMA, 45.54% for NWMA, and 52.48% for NWM. These rates are indicative of performance differences but we must be mindful that the statistical methods employed do not compare them. When conducting our analysis, we found that there was no significant interaction between the treatment and the task type ($p = 0.174$), so we report on an analysis excluding the associated interaction term from the model. From this we derived

---

[3] The goal of [3] is to provide advice, to researchers whose studies involve multiple testing, on when to use corrections: "[Bonferroni corrections] should not be used routinely and should be considered if: (1) a single test of the 'universal null hypothesis' (Ho) that all tests are not significant is required, (2) it is imperative to avoid a type I error, and (3) a large number of tests are carried out without preplanned hypotheses". None of these considerations apply in our case.

the following ranking of treatments:

$$accuracy\ ranking\colon WM > WMA > NWM > NWMA.$$

This matches our hypothesised ranking. For space reasons, we omit the p-values, which ranged from 0.0499 to <0.0001.

Time Analysis. The mean time taken overall was 30.34 s with the treatment means being: 21.79 s for WM, 30.03 s for WMA, 34.28 s for NWMA, and 35.24 s for NWM. For correct answers only, the overall mean was 26.16 s, with the treatment means being: 20.29 s for WM, 26.42 s for WMA, 30.94 s for NWMA, and 31.39 s for NWM. Again, these rates are indicative of performance differences but the statistical methods employed do not compare them. When conducting our analysis, there was a significant interaction between the treatment and the task type ($p = 0.0108$), so we report on an analysis broken down task type:

$$time\ ranking\ for\ subset\colon WM > WMA = NWMA = NWM.$$
$$time\ ranking\ for\ disjoint\colon WM = WMA > NWMA = NWM.$$

This ranking is the partially consistent with our hypothesised ranking. In the significant cases, the subset p-values ranged from 0.0001 to <0.0001 and for the disjoint analysis all were less than 0.0001.

Preference Analysis. From the data provided by participants, we found an overwhelming preference for well-matched Euler diagrams, which were top-ranked 190 times. The other treatments were ranked top as follows: 17 times for WMA, 3 times for NWMA, and 11 times for NWM; recall joint rankings were permitted. When fitting our statistical model, we found that preference did not depend on task type ($p = 0.4715$) and, so, our results are based on a simplified model from which we obtained the following ranking:

$$preference\ ranking\colon WM > WMA = NWMA = NWM.$$

For space reasons, we omit the associated p-values, with those below the 5% threshold ranging from 0.0215 to <0.0001. Comments made by participants often indicated that shading was confusing and highlighted their perceived simplicity of the diagrams that used only spatial relations between circles. Generally, the participants' comments supported the exploitation of spatial relationships between circles over shading.

Discussion. For Euler diagrams, we can answer RQ1 and RQ2 affirmatively. Given that we view accuracy as the most important indicator of relative performance, our data also support [H1] to [H3]. In summary, the well-matchedness of meaning carriers does significantly impact task performance. It is particularly interesting that, when tasks required information to be obtained from non-well-matched meaning carriers, the presence of well-matched meaning carriers led to significantly worse accuracy performance than when there were no well-matched meaning carriers at all.

4   Evaluating Well-Matchedness in Linear Diagrams

The design of the linear diagrams study matched that of the Euler diagram study. The only difference was due to the notation. The linear diagrams used in the performance phase are equivalent to those in Figs. 3 and 4, relabelled similarly to the Euler diagram study (see Figs. 1 and 7 as well as Figs. 2 and 8). The diagrams in Figs. 3 and 4 were used in the preference phase.

4.1   Hypotheses

We immediately carry forward [H1] to the linear diagram case, since it is regarded that well-matched meaning carriers are more effective. We must further explore linear diagrams when considering [H2] and [H3] since lines do not intersect as circles do, a core feature of our earlier deliberations. We again focus on the extraction of the information that *everyone who visited Ukraine also visited Romania* and that *no one visited both India and Zambia*, this time from Figs. 3 and 4. The observation that colour hue is favoured over shape (in this case, lines) holds for linear diagrams. However, whilst the lines never intersect each other they sometimes have line breaks, where more than one line segment represents a set. The Gestalt principle of similarity tells us that people will group together visual objects that share characteristics seeing them as 'belonging together'. This suggests that using varying colours for the lines could outweigh potential performance degradation arising from line breaks. Current empirical research into the impact of the number of line segments in task performance is, however, inconsistent [1,14] and requires further investigation. Thus, there is no clear evidence that a hypothesised ranking of diagrams should be based on the presence of line breaks, which is a feature not directly related to well-matchedness.

Therefore, we focus our attention on the use of shading. As with Euler diagrams, the use of one colour for shading compared to varying hues for the lines renders the well-matched meaning carriers more salient than the non-well-matched meaning carriers. Further, the same reasoning as in the Euler diagrams' case can be applied to the use of non-well-matched meaning carriers to convey the required information in a diagram that also uses well-matched meaning carriers. Hence, we also carry forward [H2] and [H3] to the linear diagram case.

4.2   Linear Diagram Results

Regarding the pilots for the linear diagram study, they ran concurrently with the Euler diagram study. The adaptations and errors identified were reported in Sect. 3. For the main study on linear diagrams, we recruited a total of 146 participants with the following distribution: 104 successfully completed, 3 were classified as inattentive, and 39 failed to complete. Of the 104 participants, 69 identified as female and 35 as male. Ages ranged from 18 to 67 (mean: 33).

Accuracy Analysis. The accuracy rate overall was 63.22% with treatment rates: 84.13% for WM, 64.42% for WMA, 50.48% for NWMA, and 53.85% for

NWM. When conducting our analysis, we found that there was no significant interaction between the treatment and the task type ($p = 0.5921$), so we report on an analysis excluding the interaction term from the model. We derived the following:

$$accuracy\ ranking : WM > WMA > NWMA = NWM.$$

This ranking is the same as our hypothesised ranking, except that NWMA and NWM are not distinguished. The p-values below the 5% threshold ranged from 0.0180 to <0.0001.

Time Analysis. The mean time taken overall was 27.79 s with the treatment means being: 21.30 s for WM, 27.47 s for WMA, 32.52 s for NWMA, and 29.87 s for NWM. For correct answers only, the overall mean was 25.64 s, with the treatments means being: 19.72 s for WM, 27.00 s for WMA, 32.00 s for NWMA, and 27.31 s for NWM. When conducting our analysis, there was a significant interaction between the treatment and the task type ($p < 0.0001$), so we report on an analysis broken down task type:

$$time\ ranking\ for\ subset: WM > WMA = NWMA = NWM.$$
$$time\ ranking\ for\ disjoint: WM > WMA = NWMA = NWM.$$

This ranking is the partially consistent with our hypothesised ranking. In the significant subset cases, the below-threshold p-values ranged from 0.0002 to <0.0001 and for the disjoint cases they were between 0.0315 and 0.0002.

Preference Analysis. From the data provided by participants, we found an overwhelming preference for well-matched linear diagrams, which were top-ranked 187 times. The other treatments were ranked top as follows: 11 times for WMA, 7 times for NWMA, and 7 times for NWM. As with Euler diagrams, we found that preference did not depend on task type ($p = 0.0631$), so our results are based on a simplified model from which we obtained the following ranking:

$$preference\ ranking: WM > WMA = NWMA = NWM.$$

For space reasons, we omit the associated p-values, with those below the 5% threshold all <0.0001.

Participants' comments again indicated that shading was confusing. In addition, comments alluded to the clarity of diagrams when spatial relationships between lines were used. A minor theme through the comments centred on line breaks, with some participants feeling that broken lines were problematic (when multiple line segments are used to represent a set). These comments are consistent with prior work, which suggests people perceive linear diagrams with more line segments as being more cluttered [2].

Discussion. For linear diagrams, we also answer RQ1 and RQ2 affirmatively. However, our data supported [H1] and [H2] but not [H3]. We speculate about why this is different to the Euler diagram case. In linear diagrams, when extracting information about a number of sets, it is always possible to ignore the lines that represent any other sets. This is because the lines are laid out in parallel, with their relative x-coordinates conveying semantics, and they never intersect each other. In our study, only two lines and any present shading needed to be considered to correctly perform the task. In both the NWMA and NWM cases, the two lines involved in the task are in a non-well-matched relationship. This leads us to speculate that an irrelevant third set is not a distraction in linear diagrams. Hence, there is no distinguishing feature – from the perspective of well-matchedness – between the NWMA and NWM cases, providing a plausible reason as to why [H3] is not supported. Furthermore, this reasoning does not contradict [H1] or [H2]. In the case of [H1], we are comparing WM and WMA with NWMA and NWM: in the former two cases, the two lines are both well-matched and in the latter two they are both non-well-matched. For [H2], in each diagram the two relevant lines are well-matched, but in the WM case there is no distracting shading unlike the WMA case (e.g., in Fig. 4, part of the Zambia line occupies a shaded overlap in the WMA case but not in the WM case).

We contrast the discussion above with the Euler diagram case. In most Euler diagrams the circles intersect, which causes points of discontinuation, to form regions. To compare two sets in Euler diagrams remains straightforward if the two corresponding circles are in a (salient) well-matched relationship. However, the presence of the third (well-matched) circle in the NWMA case renders the task more difficult: the third circle is not easily ignored, unlike linear diagrams, due to the intersecting nature of the circles. Intersecting circles form an atomic component (single unit) unlike the separate lines in a linear diagram. Thus, we posit that the intersecting nature of the circles in Euler diagrams makes ignoring a third, irrelevant, circle, non-trivial. Hence, the discussions here may suggest reasons why [H3] was supported for Euler diagrams but not for linear diagrams.

5   Conclusion

A major goal of the Diagrams community is to better understand features of diagrams that make them effective. Through our examination of meaning carriers, we have exposed their potential importance in this context. By viewing meaning carriers as being well-matched, or otherwise, we have begun to explore the role of well-matchedness in Euler and linear diagrams. Our results suggest that extracting information from well-matched meaning carriers is significantly easier (as measured by accuracy) than in non-well-matched cases. A particularly striking result arose with Euler diagrams: when tasks required information to be obtained from non-well-matched meaning carriers, the presence of well-matched meaning carriers led to significantly worse accuracy performance than when there were no well-matched meaning carriers at all. By contrast, blending well-matched and non-well-matched meaning carriers in linear diagrams did not expose the same behaviour. This difference between notations is embodied in [H3] being supported for Euler diagrams but not for linear diagrams.

There are two key take-away messages: using only well-matched meaning carriers led to the best performance and using both well-matched and non-well-matched meaning carriers in a single diagram is sometimes problematic. In the latter case, it is necessary to consider how the syntax of the diagrams gives rise to meaning carriers and their role in information representation and potential ability to distract from the task at hand.

There is ample scope for further work. Specifically for Euler and linear diagrams, there is the potential for eye-tracking studies to either support or refute our speculation concerning why we had different results for [H3]. Evaluations are needed for a richer variety of meaning carriers and tasks and also to explore how participant familiarity with the notations impacts the results. Meaning carriers and well-matchedness should be further explored in other diagrammatic notations. One such example arises from the semantics assigned to Euler and linear diagrams. Extending their semantics so that regions have existential import means that regions represent non-empty sets. Under these semantics, new meaning carriers arise, such as the intersection between two circles representing a non-empty set. Understanding whether our results generalise are important for our continued exploration of the benefits of diagrammatic communication.

Acknowledgement. Gem Stapleton is partially supported by EPSRC grant EP/T019603/1.

References

1. Alqadah, M.: The impact of clutter on the comprehension of set visualizations. Ph.D. thesis, University of Brighton (2017)
2. Alqadah, M., Stapleton, G., Howse, J., Chapman, P.: The perception of clutter in linear diagrams. In: Jamnik, M., Uesaka, Y., Elzer Schwartz, S. (eds.) Diagrams 2016. LNCS (LNAI), vol. 9781, pp. 250–257. Springer, Cham (2016). https://doi.org/10.1007/978-3-319-42333-3_20
3. Armstrong, R.: When to use the Bonferroni correction. Ophthalmic Physiol. Opt. **34**(5), 502–508 (2014)
4. Barwise, J., Etchemendy, J.: Visualization in mathematics, chap. Visual information and valid reasoning, pp. 8–23. Mathematical Association of America (1990)
5. Callaghan, C.: Interference and dominance in texture segregation: hue, geometric form and line orienation. Percept. Psychophys. **4**(46), 299–311 (1989)
6. Chapman, P., Stapleton, G., Rodgers, P.: PaL diagrams: a linear diagram-based visual language. J. Vis. Lang. Comput. **25**(6), 945–954 (2014)
7. Chapman, P., Stapleton, G., Rodgers, P., Micallef, L., Blake, A.: Visualizing sets: an empirical comparison of diagram types. In: Dwyer, T., Purchase, H., Delaney, A. (eds.) Diagrams 2014. LNCS (LNAI), vol. 8578, pp. 146–160. Springer, Heidelberg (2014). https://doi.org/10.1007/978-3-662-44043-8_18
8. Chen, J., Menezes, N., Bradley, A., North, T.: Opportunities for crowdsourcing research on Amazon Mechanical Turk. Hum. Factors **5**(3) (2011)
9. Duncan, J., Humphreys, G.: Visual search and stimulus similarity. Psychol. Rev. **96**(3), 433 (1989)
10. Gurr, C.: Aligning syntax and semantics in formalisations of visual languages. In: IEEE Symposium on Human-Centric Computing Languages and Environments, pp. 60–61. IEEE (2001)
11. Harrower, M., Brewer, C.: ColorBrewer.org: an online tool for selecting colour schemes for maps. Cartogr. J. **40**(1), 27–37 (2003). Accessed November 2013

12. Liang, K.Y., Zeger, S.L.: Longitudinal data analysis using generalized linear models. Biometrika **73**, 13–22 (1986)
13. Peirce, C.: Collected Papers, vol. 4. Harvard University Press, Cambridge (1933)
14. Rodgers, P., Stapleton, G., Chapman, P.: Visualizing sets with linear diagrams. ACM Trans. Comput. Hum. Interact. **22**(6) (2015). Article 27, 28 pages
15. Stapleton, G., Jamnik, M., Shimojima, A.: What makes an effective representation of information: a formal account of observational advantages. J. Logic Lang. Inf. **26**(2), 143–177 (2017)
16. Touloumis, A., Agresti, A., Kateri, M.: Generalized estimating equations for multinomial responses using a local odds ratios parameterization. Biometrics **69**(3), 633–640 (2013)
17. Wagemans, J., Elder, J., Kubovy, M., Palmer, S., Peterson, M., Singh, M.: A century of gestalt psychology in visual perception: I. Perceptual grouping and figure-ground organisation. Psychol. Bull. **138**(6), 1172–1217 (2012)

Intuitionistic Euler-Venn Diagrams

Sven Linker[(✉)]

University of Liverpool, Liverpool, UK
s.linker@liverpool.ac.uk

Abstract. We present an intuitionistic interpretation of Euler-Venn diagrams with respect to Heyting algebras. In contrast to classical Euler-Venn diagrams, we treat shaded and missing zones differently, to have diagrammatic representations of conjunction, disjunction and intuitionistic implication. Furthermore, we need to add new syntactic elements to express these concepts. We present a cut-free sequent calculus for this language, and prove it to be sound and complete. Furthermore, we show that the rules of cut, weakening and contraction are admissible.

Keywords: Intuitionistic logic · Euler-Venn diagrams · Proof theory

1 Introduction

Most visualisations for logical systems, like Peirce's Existential Graphs [6] and the Venn systems of Shin [16], are dedicated to some form of classical reasoning. However, for example, within Computer Science, constructive reasoning in the form of intuitionistic logic is very important as well, due to the Curry-Howard correspondence of constructive proofs and programs, or, similarly, of formulas and types. That is, each formula corresponds to a unique type, and a proof of the formula corresponds to the execution of a function of this type. Hence, a visualisation of intuitionistic logic would be beneficial not only from the perspective of formal logic, but also for visualising program types and their relations.

Typical semantics of intuitionistic logic are given in the form of Heyting algebras, a slight generalisation of Boolean algebras, and an important subclass of Heyting algebras is induced by topologies: the set of open sets of a topology forms a Heyting algebra. In particular, it is well known that intuitionistic formulas are valid, if and only if, they are valid on this subclass of Heyting algebras [15]. Hence, for a visualisation, a formalism that uses topological relations to reflect logical properties seems to be a natural choice. Due to these reasons, we will study how such a formal system of diagrams, Euler-Venn diagrams, can be used to visualise constructive reasoning based on intuitionistic logic.

Euler-Venn circles are known to be a well-suited visualisation of classical propositional logic. In previous work [9], we have presented a proof system in the style of sequent calculus [5] to reason with Euler-Venn diagrams. There, we

This work was supported by EPSRC Research Programme EP/N007565/1 *Science of Sensor Systems Software*.

© Springer Nature Switzerland AG 2020
A.-V. Pietarinen et al. (Eds.): Diagrams 2020, LNAI 12169, pp. 264–280, 2020.
https://doi.org/10.1007/978-3-030-54249-8_21

speculated that, similar to sentential languages, restricting the rules and sequents in the system would allow for intuitionistic reasoning with Euler-Venn diagrams. However, further investigation showed that such a simple change is not sufficient, due to the typical use of the syntax elements of Euler-Venn diagrams.

Consider for example the diagrams in Fig. 1. In the classical interpretation, these diagrams are equivalent: the shaded zone in Fig. 1a denotes that the situation that a is true and b is false is prohibited, which is exactly what the omission of the zone included in the contour a, but not in b in Fig. 1b signifies as well.

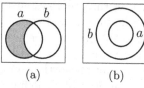

(a)   (b)

Fig. 1. Euler-Venn diagrams

That is, shading a zone and omitting it is equivalent in classical Euler-Venn diagrams. Additionally, we can interpret these two diagrams in two ways: Fig. 1a may intuitively be read as $\neg(a \wedge \neg b)$: we do not allow for the valuations satisfying a, but not b. Figure 1b, however, is more naturally read as $a \rightarrow b$: whenever a valuation satisfies a, it also satisfies b. While classically, these two statements are indeed equivalent, they are generally not equivalent in an intuitionistic interpretation (see the examples in Sect. 2). Hence, we want to treat missing zones and shaded zones differently. Since typically, proof systems for Euler diagrams allow to transform missing zones into shaded zones [7,9,17], this implies a stronger deviation from our sequent calculus rules than anticipated.

We want to emphasise a constructive approach to reasoning. In particular, instead of emphasising a *negative* property by prohibiting interpretations of the diagrams, we will treat shading as a *positive* denotation. While this would not make a difference in a classical system, negation in intuitionistic systems is much weaker, and hence not suited as a basic element for the semantics of a language.

In this paper, we present an intuitionistic interpretation of Euler-Venn diagrams that takes the preceeding considerations into account. To that end, we will distinguish between *pure Venn*, *pure Euler* and *Euler-Venn* diagrams, and present semantics of these diagrams based on Heyting algebras. Pure Venn diagrams are diagrams similar to Fig. 1a, containing all possible zones of a set of contours, and shadings of some of the zones. Pure Euler diagrams only represent topological relations, for example, whether a contour is inside of another. In particular, they do not allow for any shading of zones. Hence, Fig. 1b could be seen as a pure Euler diagram. However, we will need to distinguish pure Euler diagrams from diagrams using both topological relations and (possibly) shaded zones, called general Euler-Venn diagrams. To achieve such a distinction, we draw contours with dotted lines in pure Euler diagrams, With this convention, Fig. 1b is a general Euler-Venn diagram, and not a pure Euler diagram.

Subsequently, we present a proof system in the style of sequent calculus, which we prove to be sound and complete. Furthermore, we show that the structural rules of weakening, contraction and cut are admissible. Due to space limitations, we refer for most of the proofs to the extended version of this paper [10].

Related Work. For existential graphs, there exist several visual reasoning systems for non-classical variants. For example, Bellucci et al. defined *assertive graphs* [1], including a system based on rules for iteration and deletion of graphs, among others. This logical language reflects intuitionistic logic, but the rules manipulate only single graphs, while sequent calculus systems manipulate sequents of diagrams. Ma and Pietarinen presented a graphical system for intuitionistic logic [12] and proved its equivalence with Gentzen's single succedent sequent calculus for intuitionistic logic. To that end, they translate the graphs into sentential formulas. They also extended their approach to existential graphs with quasi-Boolean algebras as their semantics [11]. Legris pointed out that structural rules of sequent calculi can be seen as special instances of rules in the proof systems for existential graphs, to analyse substructural logics [8]. de Freitas and Viana presented a calculus to reason about intuitionistic equations [4]. However, we are not aware of any intuitionistic reasoning system using Euler-Venn diagrams. Following this introduction, we briefly recall the foundations of intuitionistic logic and its semantics in terms of Heyting algebras in Sect. 2. In Sect. 3, we define the system of Euler-Venn diagrams, followed by the graphical sequent calculus system, as well as soundness and completeness proofs, in Sect. 4. Finally, we discuss our system and conclude the paper in Sect. 5.

2   Intuitionistic Logic

In this section, we give a very brief overview of the aspects of intuitionistic logic we will use. We present the underlying semantical model: Heyting algebras.

Definition 1 (Heyting Algebra). *A* Heyting algebra $\mathcal{H} = (H, \sqcup, \sqcap, \mapsto, 0, 1)$ *is a bounded, distributive lattice, where* $\sqcup$ *is the join,* $\sqcap$ *the meet,* 0 *the bottom and* 1 *the top element of the lattice. Observe that such a bounded lattice possesses a natural partial order* $\leq$ *on its elements. The binary operation* $\mapsto$*, the implication, is defined by* $u \sqcap s \leq t$ *if, and only if,* $u \leq s \mapsto t$*. That is,* $s \mapsto t$ *is the join of all elements* u *such that* $u \sqcap s \leq t$*. We will use the abbreviation* $-s$ *for* $s \mapsto 0$*. Furthermore, we set* $\bigsqcap_{i \in \emptyset} s_i = 1$ *and* $\bigsqcup_{i \in \emptyset} s_i = 0$ *for any* s_i*.*

We collect a few basic properties of Heyting algebras that we need in the following. Proofs can be found, e.g., in the work of Rasiowa and Sikorski [15].

Lemma 1 (Properties of Heyting Algebras). *Let* $\mathcal{H}$ *be a Heyting algebra. Then for all elements* s*,* t *and* u*, we have*

$$s \sqcap (s \mapsto t) \leq t \ (1) \qquad (s \mapsto t) \sqcap t = t \ (2) \qquad s \mapsto (t \mapsto u) = (s \sqcap t) \mapsto u \ (3)$$

As an example, consider the set $H = \{0, a, b, 1\}$, totally ordered by $0 < b < a < 1$, and where $s \sqcap t = \min\{s, t\}$ and $s \sqcup t = \max\{s, t\}$ for $s, t \in H$. Then, we have $a \mapsto b = b$, since b is the maximal element x such that $x \sqcap a \leq b$. However, we also have $-b = b \mapsto 0 = 0$, and hence $-(a \sqcap -b) = -(a \sqcap 0) = -0 = 1$. So in this Heyting algebra $a \mapsto b$ is not the same as $-(a \sqcap -b)$.

As a different, more topological example, consider the Heyting algebra whose elements are the open subsets of the reals, as defined by the standard topology, and where the meet and join are given by the set-theoretic union and intersection operators. The bottom element is the empty set $0 = \emptyset$, the top element is $1 = \mathbb{R}$, and the implication operation is defined as $a \mapsto b = \mathsf{Int}(\bar{a} \cup b)$, where $\bar{a}$ denotes the complement of a and Int the interior operator. This implies that the negation operation corresponds to $-a = \mathsf{Int}(\bar{a})$. Now consider $a = (-1,1)$, the open interval between -1 and 1. Then $a \sqcup -a = (-1,1) \cup \mathsf{Int}(\bar{a}) = (-1,1) \cup \mathsf{Int}((-\infty, -1] \cup [1, \infty)) = (-1,1) \cup (-\infty, -1) \cup (1, \infty) = \mathbb{R} \setminus \{-1, 1\} \neq \mathbb{R}$. So, this is an example where $a \sqcup -a \neq 1$.

The syntax of propositional intuitionistic logic is similar to classical Boolean logic, with the difference that the operators are not interdefinable. Hence, the signs for conjunction, disjunction, and implication are all necessary as distinct symbols, and cannot be treated as abbreviations. We will assume a fixed, countable set of propositional variables Vars.

Definition 2 (Syntax). *Intuitionistic formulas are given by the following EBNF*

$$\varphi: \ = \bot \mid a \mid \varphi \wedge \varphi \mid \varphi \vee \varphi \mid \varphi \to \varphi \ , where \ a \in \mathsf{Vars} \ .$$

We let $\top \equiv \bot \to \bot$. The semantics of a formula is based on valuations, associating each variable with an element of a given Heyting algebra.

Definition 3 (Semantics). *Let $\mathcal{H}$ be a Heyting algebra and $\nu: \mathsf{Vars} \to H$ a valuation, mapping variables to elements of $\mathcal{H}$. We lift valuations to formulas.*

$$\nu(\bot) = 0 \qquad\qquad \nu(\varphi \wedge \psi) = \nu(\varphi) \sqcap \nu(\psi)$$
$$\nu(\varphi \vee \psi) = \nu(\varphi) \sqcup \nu(\psi) \qquad\qquad \nu(\varphi \to \psi) = \nu(\varphi) \mapsto \nu(\psi)$$

A formula φ holds in $\mathcal{H}$, if $\nu(\varphi) = 1$. If φ holds for every valuation of $\mathcal{H}$, we write $\mathcal{H} \models \varphi$. If $\mathcal{H} \models \varphi$ for every Heyting algebra $\mathcal{H}$, we say that φ is valid.

3   Euler-Venn Diagrams

In this section, we present the syntax and semantics of Euler-Venn diagrams with an intuitionistic interpretation. Generally, a diagram can be *unitary* or *compound*. A unitary diagram consists of a set of *contours* dividing the space enclosed by a bounding rectangle into different *zones*. Zones may also be shaded. Depending on how the contours may be arranged, and whether zones may be shaded, we distinguish between *Venn* diagrams, *Euler* diagrams, and *Euler-Venn* diagrams. Compound diagrams are constructed recursively. Since the structure of compound diagrams is the same, regardless of the type of unitary diagrams, we present their syntax first.

Definition 4 (Compound Diagrams). *A compound diagram is created according to the following syntax, $D:: = d \mid D \wedge D \mid D \vee D \mid D \to D$, where d is a unitary diagram.*

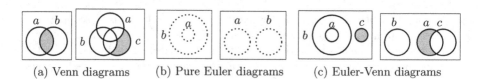

(a) Venn diagrams   (b) Pure Euler diagrams   (c) Euler-Venn diagrams

Fig. 2. Examples of Euler-Venn diagrams

Definition 5 (Compound Diagram Semantics). *The semantics of compound diagrams for a Heyting algebra $\mathcal{H}$ and a valuation ν is given as follows.*

$$\nu(D_1 \wedge D_2) = \nu(D_1) \sqcap \nu(D_2)$$
$$\nu(D_1 \rightarrow D_2) = \nu(D_1) \mapsto \nu(D_2)$$
$$\nu(D_1 \vee D_2) = \nu(D_1) \sqcup \nu(D_2)$$

where D_1, D_2 are compound diagrams. If $\nu(D) = 1$, for all intuitionistic models $\mathcal{H}$ and valuations ν then we call D valid.

Observe that we did not give the semantics for unitary diagrams in the previous definition. First we present notations that are used for all types of diagrams alike. Formally, a *zone* for a finite set of contours $L \subset \mathsf{Vars}$ is a tuple $(\mathsf{in}, \mathsf{out})$, where in and out are disjoint subsets of L such that $\mathsf{in} \cup \mathsf{out} = L$. We will also write $\mathsf{in}(z)$ and $\mathsf{out}(z)$ to refer to the corresponding sets of contours in z. The set of all possible zones for a given set of contours is denoted by $\mathsf{Venn}(L)$.

Venn Diagrams. A *Venn diagram* is a diagram where all possible zones for a set of contours are visible. For example, Fig. 2a shows two unitary Venn diagrams, one with the contours a and b, and the other with contours a, b, and c. Formally, a Venn diagram is of the shape $d = (L, \mathsf{Venn}(L), Z^*)$, where Z^* is the set of shaded zones and $Z^* \subseteq \mathsf{Venn}(L)$. Hence the only diagrammatic elements that may carry meaning are the presence of contours, and whether a zone is shaded. For a given diagram d, we denote the set of shaded zones also by $Z^*(d)$. We allow for the diagrams $\bot = (\emptyset, \{(\emptyset, \emptyset)\}, \emptyset)$ and $\top = (\emptyset, \{(\emptyset, \emptyset)\}, \{(\emptyset, \emptyset)\})$. A *literal* is a Venn diagram for a single contour, with exactly one shaded zone. If the zone $(\emptyset, \{c\})$ is shaded in a literal, then we call it *the negative literal for* c, otherwise it is *the positive literal for* c (see Fig. 3). Furthermore, if d is the positive literal for c, then we call the negative literal for c the *dual of* d (and vice versa). Observe that our notion of literals deviates from the original definition of Stapleton and Masthoff [17] and from our previous work [9]. The main difference between our presentation and classical Venn diagrams is the interpretation of shaded zones.

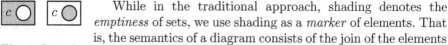

Fig. 3. Literals

While in the traditional approach, shading denotes the *emptiness* of sets, we use shading as a *marker* of elements. That is, the semantics of a diagram consists of the join of the elements denoted by the shaded zones. This is more in line with a constructivist approach: instead of relying on a negative aspect (emptiness), we construct the semantics out of their building blocks (the shaded zones).

Definition 6 (Zone Semantics). *Let $\mathcal{H}$ be a Heyting algebra, ν a valuation, and z a zone. The* semantics *of z is given by $\nu(z) = \bigsqcap_{c \in \mathsf{in}(z)} \nu(c) \sqcap \bigsqcap_{c \in \mathsf{out}(z)} -\nu(c)$.*

We can now define the semantics of a Venn diagram in general.

Definition 7 (Venn Diagram Semantics). *For a Venn diagram d, a Heyting algebra $\mathcal{H}$ and a valuation ν, the semantics of d are given by $\nu(d) = \bigsqcup_{z \in Z^*(d)} \nu(z)$.*

Note that we have $\nu(\top) = 1$ and $\nu(\bot) = 0$, for any valuation ν. Furthermore, for a unitary diagram without shaded zones, i.e. $d = (L, \mathsf{Venn}(L), \emptyset)$, we have $\nu(d) = 0$. However, the semantics already diverge from the classical case for a fully shaded diagram with one contour: if $d = (\{a\}, \mathsf{Venn}(\{a\}), \mathsf{Venn}(\{a\}))$, then $\nu(d) = \nu(a) \sqcup -\nu(a)$, which in general is not equal to 1. This semantics has one consequence in particular: a zone can be decomposed into an equivalent compound diagram, and any Venn diagram into a disjunctive normal form.

Lemma 2. *Let z be a zone for the contours L. Then the semantics of the compound diagram $d_z = \bigwedge_{c \in \mathsf{in}(z)} \boxed{c\ \mathbf{O}} \wedge \bigwedge_{c \in \mathsf{out}(z)} \boxed{c\ \mathbf{O}}$ equals the semantics of z, i.e. $\nu(d_z) = \nu(z)$. For a Venn diagram d, we have $\nu(d) = \nu(\bigvee_{z \in Z^*(d)} d_z)$.*

In particular, this implies that we cannot draw a unitary Venn diagram that expresses intuitionistic implication.

Lemma 3. *Let a and b be propositional variables. Then there is no unitary Venn diagram d such that $\nu(d) = \nu(a \to b)$ for all models and valuations.*

Observe however that we can trivially define a *compound* diagram $\boxed{a\ \mathbf{O}} \to \boxed{b\ \mathbf{O}}$.

Pure Euler Diagrams. We need additional syntax if we want to express intuitionistic implication diagrammatically. This new syntax needs to be directed (since $a \to b$ is different to $b \to a$). Observe that our notion of zones already contains an asymmetry that we can understand as a direction: we distinguish between contours the zone is inside of, and contours it is outside of. So, we may treat a zone as *directed from the "in"-contours to the "out"-contours.* Furthermore, a *missing zone* expresses topological information. Following these considerations, we allow for missing zones in the diagrams. Consequently, we will now discuss pure Euler diagrams. In contrast to Venn diagrams, the semantics of a pure Euler diagram is the meet of the semantics of its missing zones.

Definition 8 (Pure Euler Diagrams). *A pure Euler diagram is a structure $d = (L, Z)$, where L is the set of contours and $Z \subseteq \mathsf{Venn}(L)$ the set of visible zones of d. Furthermore, the set $\mathsf{MZ}(d) = \mathsf{Venn}(L) \setminus Z$ is the set of missing zones of d. The missing zone semantics of a zone z is given by $\nu_\mathsf{m}(z) = \left(\bigsqcap_{c \in \mathsf{in}(z)} \nu(c)\right) \mapsto \left(\bigsqcup_{c \in \mathsf{out}(z)} \nu(c)\right)$. Then, for a pure Euler diagram d, we have $\nu(d) = \bigsqcap_{z \in \mathsf{MZ}(d)} \nu_\mathsf{m}(z)$.*

In contrast to Venn diagrams, pure Euler diagrams do not allow for *any* shading. To distinguish pure Euler diagrams from Venn diagrams (and Euler-Venn diagrams, see below), we draw them with dotted contours. Even with this additional syntax, we are not able to express *every* implication. A simple example would be $a \rightarrow a$, since we cannot have a zone $(\{a\}, \{a\})$. However, for this particular example, we do not lose expressivity, since $a \rightarrow a \equiv \top$ for all a. But we have a diagram equivalent to $a \rightarrow b$, as shown in the left diagram of Fig. 2b. The right diagram in Fig. 2b denotes $(a \sqcap b) \mapsto 0$, which is $-(a \sqcap b)$. Observe that in contrast to Venn diagrams without shaded zones, a pure Euler diagram without missing zones denotes 1, i.e., for $d = (L, \mathsf{Venn}(L))$, we have $\nu(d) = \nu(\top) = 1$. Furthermore, the diagram without any contours and zones denotes 0, since $\nu((\emptyset, \emptyset)) = \nu_{\mathsf{m}}((\emptyset, \emptyset)) = \bigsqcap_{c \in \emptyset} \nu(c) \mapsto \bigsqcup_{c \in \emptyset} \nu(c) = 1 \mapsto 0 = 0$. In the following, we will need to identify zones that are divided by a contour c abstractly.

Definition 9 (Adjacent Zone). *Let $z = (\mathsf{in}, \mathsf{out})$ be a zone for the contours in L and $c \in L$. The zone adjacent to z at c, denoted by $\overline{z}^c$ is $(\mathsf{in} \cup \{c\}, \mathsf{out} \setminus \{c\})$, if $c \in \mathsf{out}$ and $(\mathsf{in} \setminus \{c\}, \mathsf{out} \cup \{c\})$ if $c \in \mathsf{in}$.*

Now we can define a way to remove contours from a pure Euler diagram d. This contrasts to our previous work, where we allowed that the diagram to be reduced contains shading [9].

Definition 10 (Reduction). *Let $d = (L, Z)$ be a pure Euler diagram and $c \in L$. The reduction of a zone $z = (\mathsf{in}, \mathsf{out})$ is $z \setminus c = (\mathsf{in} \setminus \{c\}, \mathsf{out} \setminus \{c\})$. The reduction of d by c is defined as $d \setminus c = (L \setminus \{c\}, Z \setminus c)$, where $Z \setminus c = \{z \setminus c \mid z \in Z\}$.*

Lemma 4 (Properties of Reduction). *We have $z \setminus c = \overline{z}^c \setminus c$. Furthermore, for each $z' \in \mathsf{MZ}(d \setminus c)$ and z with $z \setminus c = z'$, we have $z \in \mathsf{MZ}(d)$. In particular, both $z \in \mathsf{MZ}(d)$ and $\overline{z}^c \in \mathsf{MZ}(d)$.*

If each missing zone in a pure Euler diagram d has a missing adjacent zone, then the reduction of d by any contour is contained in the semantics of d. In particular, the meet of all reductions equals the semantics of d. This will allow us to show soundness of some rules of the sequent calculus in Sect. 4.

Lemma 5. *Let $d = (L, Z)$ be a pure Euler diagram, where for each $z \in \mathsf{MZ}(d)$, there is a contour $\ell \in L$ such that $\overline{z}^{\ell} \in \mathsf{MZ}(d)$. Furthermore, let $L' = \{c \mid \mathsf{MZ}(d \setminus c) \neq \emptyset\}$. Then $\bigsqcap_{c \in L'} \nu(d \setminus c) = \nu(d)$.*

As an example, consider diagram d_C^* of Fig. 4. Intuitively, this diagram

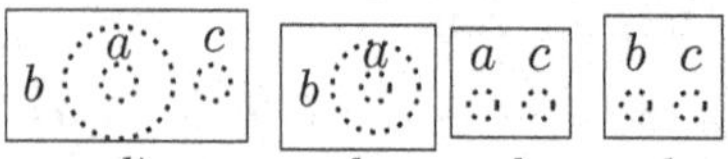

d_C^* d_c d_b d_a

Fig. 4. Example of a reduction.

contains the information that contour c is disjoint from both a and b, and that a is contained in b. Now, if the diagram satisfies the precondition of the previous lemma, then we can reduce d_C^* to diagrams reflecting exactly these properties. The set of missing zones of d_C^* is $\mathsf{MZ}(d_C^*) = \{(\{a\}, \{b, c\}), (\{a, c\}, \{b\}), (\{b, c\}, \{a\}), (\{a, b, c\}, \emptyset)\}$, and indeed, each of these missing zones has at least one adjacent missing zone. For example, if $z = (\{a\}, \{b, c\})$, then $\overline{z}^c = (\{a, c\}, \{b\})$. So, d_C^* can be reduced according to the lemma. The set of visible zones is $Z(d_C^*) =$

$\{(\emptyset, \{a, b, c\}), (\{c\}, \{a, b\}), (\{b\}, \{a, c\}), (\{a, b\}, \{c\})\}$. Reducing this diagram by the contour c yields the set $Z(d_c) = \{(\emptyset, \{a, b\}), (\{b\}, \{a\}), (\{a, b\}, \emptyset)\}$, which is visualised in Fig. 4 as the pure Euler diagram d_c. Similarly, it can be checked that reducing d_C^* by b indeed yields d_b, and respectively for d_a. By Lemma 5, the conjunction of these three diagrams is equivalent to the original diagram d_C^*.

Euler-Venn Diagrams. In this section, we combine pure Euler diagrams with shading. Our main idea is as follows: we treat the information given by a pure Euler diagram as a condition for the construction of the combinations of atomic propositions denoted by the shading. That is, whenever we have constructions as indicated by the spatial relations of contours in a diagram d, we also have a construction of the elements denoted by the shaded zones of the diagram. Since we use the syntactic elements of pure Euler diagrams and Venn diagrams, we will subsequently call such diagrams *Euler-Venn diagrams*. Figure 2c shows two Euler-Venn diagrams that omit some of the possible zones and contain shading.

The abstract syntax of Euler-Venn diagrams is similar to Venn diagrams. A diagram is a tuple $d = (L, Z, Z^*)$ consisting of a set of contours L, a set of visible zones Z over L, and a set of shaded zones $Z^* \subseteq Z$. We will often need to refer to the pure Euler or Venn aspects of an Euler-Venn diagram separately. Hence, we introduce some additional notation. For an Euler-Venn diagram $d = (L, Z, Z^*)$ we will write $\mathsf{Venn}(d) = (L, \mathsf{Venn}(L), Z^*)$ for the Venn diagram with the same set of shaded zones as d, and $\mathsf{Euler}(d) = (L, Z)$ for the pure Euler diagram with the same set of visible zones as d. Similarly to pure Venn and Euler diagrams, we will refer to the missing zones of d by $\mathsf{MZ}(d)$ and to its shaded zones by $Z^*(d)$.

Definition 11 (Euler-Venn Diagram Semantics). *The semantics of a unitary* Euler-Venn diagram *for a valuation ν is $\nu(d) = \nu(\mathsf{Euler}(d)) \mapsto \nu(\mathsf{Venn}(d))$.*

Observe that with this definition, the semantics for the case $\mathsf{MZ}(d) = \emptyset$ and $Z^*(d) \neq \emptyset$ yields $\nu(d) = 1 \mapsto \bigsqcup_{z \in Z^*(d)} \nu(z) = \bigsqcup_{z \in Z^*(d)} \nu(z)$. Furthermore, we get $\nu(\bot) = 1 \mapsto 0 = 0$ and $\nu(\top) = 1 \mapsto 1 = 1$. The language of compound Euler-Venn diagrams can be seen as a subset of intuitionistic logic. In particular, we can translate every diagram into a formula, which we call its *canonical formula*. This translation is very similar to the translation of spider diagrams into monadic first-order logic with equality [18].

Definition 12 (Canonical Formula). *The* canonical formula *of any diagram is given by the following recursive definition. We start with the definition of the canonical formula of shaded and missing zones.*

$$\chi^z(z) = \bigwedge_{c \in \mathsf{in}(z)} c \wedge \bigwedge_{c \in \mathsf{out}(z)} -c \qquad \chi^m(z) = \bigwedge_{c \in \mathsf{in}(z)} c \rightarrow \bigvee_{c \in \mathsf{out}(z)} c$$

For a pure Euler diagram d_e, a Venn diagram d_v, an Euler-Venn diagram d and compound diagrams D and E, the canonical formula is given as

$$\chi(d_e) = \bigwedge_{z \in \mathsf{MZ}(d_e)} \chi^m(z) \qquad \chi(d_v) = \bigvee_{z \in Z^*(d_v)} \chi^z(z)$$

$$\chi(d) = \chi(\mathsf{Euler}(d)) \rightarrow \chi(\mathsf{Venn}(d)) \qquad \chi(D \otimes E) = \chi(D) \otimes \chi(E) \quad, \otimes \in \{\wedge, \vee, \rightarrow\}$$

Remark 1. Observe that according to Definition 12, we get $\chi(\boxed{c\ \mathbf{o}}) = c \wedge \top$ and $\chi(\boxed{c\ \mathbf{o}}) = \top \wedge -c$. However, for simplicity, we will assume that the canonical formula construction omits superfluous occurences of $\top$ and $\bot$. Hence, $\chi(\boxed{c\ \mathbf{o}}) = c$ and $\chi(\boxed{c\ \mathbf{o}}) = -c$. Similarly, e.g., $\chi^m((\emptyset, L)) = \bigvee_{c \in L} c$.

4   Sequent Calculus

Sequent calculus, as defined by Gentzen [5] is based on *sequents*, which are composed by rule applications. In the following, we will define a multi-succedent version of sequent calculus for Euler-Venn diagrams called EDim, inspired by the work of Dragalin [3], but following the modern presentation of Negri and von Plato [13].

Definition 13 (Sequent). *A sequent $\Gamma \Rightarrow \Delta$ consists of multisets Γ and Δ of Euler-Venn diagrams, where Γ (Δ) is the* antecedent *(succedent, respectively).*

If Γ (Δ) is the empty multiset, we write $\Rightarrow \Delta$ ($\Gamma \Rightarrow$, respectively). Axioms are sequents of the form $p, \Gamma \Rightarrow \Delta, p$ where p is a positive literal. A sequent $D_1, \ldots, D_k \Rightarrow E_1, \ldots, E_l$ is valid, if, and only if, $\nu(D_1) \sqcap \ldots \sqcap \nu(D_k) \leq \nu(E_1) \sqcup \ldots \sqcup \nu(E_l)$ for all valuations ν in all Heyting algebras. We will often abbreviate $\nu(D_1) \sqcap \ldots \sqcap \nu(D_k)$ by $\nu(\Gamma)$ and $\nu(E_1) \sqcup \ldots \sqcup \nu(E_l)$ by $\nu(\Delta)$.

A *deduction* for a sequent $\Gamma \Rightarrow \Delta$ is a tree, where the root is labelled by $\Gamma \Rightarrow \Delta$, and the children of each node are labelled according to the rules defined below. If the validity of the premises of a rule imply the validity of its conclusion, we call the rule *sound*. A deduction where the leaves are labelled with axioms, or instances of $L\bot$ and $R\top$, is called a *proof* for $\Gamma \Rightarrow \Delta$. We will write $\vdash \Gamma \Rightarrow \Delta$ to denote the existence of a proof for $\Gamma \Rightarrow \Delta$. In all rules, we call the diagram in the conclusion that is being composed the *principal diagram*. For example, in $L\wedge$, the principal diagram is $D \wedge E$, and in the rule Ls it is d. For a given proof of $\Gamma \Rightarrow \Delta$, its *height* is the highest number of successive proof rule applications [13]. We will write $\vdash_n \Gamma \Rightarrow \Delta$ if $\Gamma \Rightarrow \Delta$ is provable with a proof of height at most n.

We now turn to define and explain the rules of EDim. The rules to treat compound diagrams, shown in Fig. 5, are directly taken from sequent calculus for intuitionistic logic and can be proven sound by adapting the proofs by Ono [14].

Lemma 6 (Soundness). *The rules for sentential operators are sound.*

Remark 2. If we take the placeholders D, E and F as formulas according to Definition 2 and both Γ and Δ as multisets of such formulas, then the rules of Fig. 5 together with axioms $p, \Gamma \Rightarrow \Delta, p$ form the sentential sequent calculus G3im [13]. Provability in G3im is equivalent to provability in Gentzen's system LJ. The system LJ is sound and complete [14]. Hence, G3im is sound and complete as well. Furthermore, the structural rules of weakening, contraction and cut are admissible [13]. Observe that we treat $L\bot$ as a *rule*, and not as an axiom.

$$\frac{D,E,\Gamma \Rightarrow \Delta}{D \wedge E,\Gamma \Rightarrow \Delta}\,L\wedge \qquad \frac{D,\Gamma \Rightarrow \Delta \quad E,\Gamma \Rightarrow \Delta}{D \vee E,\Gamma \Rightarrow \Delta}\,L\vee \qquad \frac{\Gamma, D \to E \Rightarrow D \quad E,\Gamma \Rightarrow \Delta}{D \to E,\Gamma \Rightarrow \Delta}\,L\to$$

$$\frac{\Gamma \Rightarrow \Delta, D \quad \Gamma \Rightarrow \Delta, E}{\Gamma \Rightarrow \Delta, D \wedge E}\,R\wedge \qquad \frac{\Gamma \Rightarrow \Delta, D, E}{\Gamma \Rightarrow \Delta, D \vee E}\,R\vee \qquad \frac{D,\Gamma \Rightarrow E}{\Gamma \Rightarrow \Delta, D \to E}\,R\to$$

$$\frac{}{\Gamma, \bot \Rightarrow \Delta}\,L\bot$$

Fig. 5. Proof rules for sentential operators

Rules for Venn Diagrams. The rules in Fig. 6a let us reduce negative to positive literals. Observe that we may introduce arbitrary sets of formulas into the succedent. Rule $R\top$ lets us finish a proof similarly to $L\bot$. Let d, d_1 and d_2 be Venn diagrams with the same contours such that $|Z^*(d)| > 1$, and $Z^*(d) = Z^*(d_1) \cup Z^*(d_2)$. Then the rules Ls and Rs in Fig. 6b *separate* d into d_1 and d_2. These rules are closely related to the *Combine* equivalence rule for Spider diagrams [7]. For a Venn diagram d with $Z^*(d) = \{z\}$, where $z = (\{n_1,\dots,n_k\}, \{o_1,\dots,o_l\})$, the rules $Ldec$ and $Rdec$ of Fig. 6b *decompose* the single zone z.

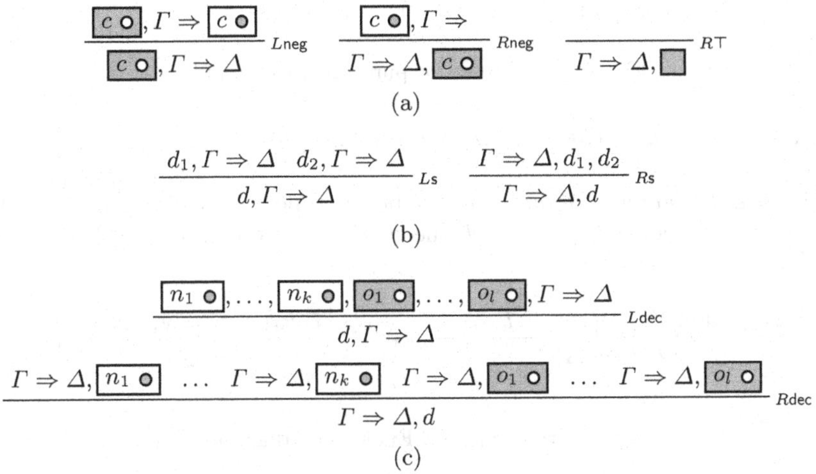

(a)

$$\frac{d_1,\Gamma \Rightarrow \Delta \quad d_2,\Gamma \Rightarrow \Delta}{d,\Gamma \Rightarrow \Delta}\,Ls \qquad \frac{\Gamma \Rightarrow \Delta, d_1, d_2}{\Gamma \Rightarrow \Delta, d}\,Rs$$

(b)

(c)

Fig. 6. Rules for Unitary Venn diagrams

Lemma 7. *The rules shown in Fig. 6 are sound.*

Rules for Pure Euler Diagrams. Now let $d = (L, Z)$ be a pure Euler diagram, where for each $z \in \mathsf{MZ}(d)$ there is a contour $\ell \in L$, such that $\overline{z}^{\ell} \in \mathsf{MZ}(d)$. Furthermore, let $\{c_1,\dots,c_k\} \subseteq L$ be the maximal set of contours such that $\mathsf{MZ}(d \setminus c_i) \neq \emptyset$ for every $i \leq k$. Then we can *reduce* d according to the rules Lr

and Rr shown in Fig. 7a. Let $d = (L, Z)$ be a pure Euler diagram with more than one missing zone, i.e., $|\mathsf{MZ}(d)| > 1$, and let $d_1 = (L, Z_1)$ and $d_2 = (L, Z_2)$ be two pure Euler diagrams such that $Z_1 \cap Z_2 = Z$. Then the rules LMZ and RMZ of Fig. 7b *separate* the diagram z at its missing zones. If d is a pure Euler diagram with a single missing zone, i.e. $\mathsf{MZ}(d) = \{z\}$ and $z = (\{n_1, \dots, n_k\}, \{o_1, \dots, o_\ell\})$, then the rules of Fig. 7c decompose z into literals.

$$\frac{d \setminus c_1, \dots, d \setminus c_k, \Gamma \Rightarrow \Delta}{d, \Gamma \Rightarrow \Delta} \; Lr \qquad \frac{\Gamma \Rightarrow \Delta, d \setminus c_1 \;\; \dots \;\; \Gamma \Rightarrow \Delta, d \setminus c_k}{\Gamma \Rightarrow \Delta, d} \; Rr$$

(a)

$$\frac{d_1, d_2, \Gamma \Rightarrow \Delta}{d, \Gamma \Rightarrow \Delta} \; LMZ \qquad \frac{\Gamma \Rightarrow \Delta, d_1 \;\; \Gamma \Rightarrow \Delta, d_2}{\Gamma \Rightarrow \Delta, d} \; RMZ$$

(b)

$$\frac{d, \Gamma \Rightarrow \boxed{n_1 \; \bullet} \;\; \dots \;\; d, \Gamma \Rightarrow \boxed{n_k \; \bullet} \;\; \boxed{o_1 \; \bullet}, \Gamma \Rightarrow \Delta \;\; \dots \;\; \boxed{o_\ell \; \bullet}, \Gamma \Rightarrow \Delta}{d, \Gamma \Rightarrow \Delta} \; L\mathsf{ldec}$$

$$\frac{\Gamma, \boxed{n_1 \; \bullet}, \dots, \boxed{n_k \; \bullet} \Rightarrow \boxed{o_1 \; \bullet}, \dots, \boxed{o_\ell \; \bullet}}{\Gamma \Rightarrow \Delta, d} \; R\mathsf{ldec}$$

(c)

Fig. 7. Proof rules for pure Euler diagrams

Lemma 8. *The rules shown in Fig. 7 are sound.*

Rules for Euler-Venn Diagrams. Let d be an Euler-Venn diagram. Then the rules $L\mathsf{det}$ and $R\mathsf{det}$ of Fig. 8 *detach* the spatial relations from the shading.

$$\frac{d, \Gamma \Rightarrow \mathsf{Euler}(d) \quad \mathsf{Venn}(d), \Gamma \Rightarrow \Delta}{d, \Gamma \Rightarrow \Delta} \; L\mathsf{det} \qquad \frac{\mathsf{Euler}(d), \Gamma \Rightarrow \mathsf{Venn}(d)}{\Gamma \Rightarrow \Delta, d} \; R\mathsf{det}$$

Fig. 8. Proof rules for Euler-Venn diagrams

Lemma 9. *The rules shown in Fig. 8 are sound.*

By an induction on the height of proofs, we get the soundness theorem for EDim, using Lemma 6, 7, 8, and 9.

Theorem 1 (Soundness). *If $\Gamma \Rightarrow \Delta$ is provable in* EDim, *then $\Gamma \Rightarrow \Delta$ is valid.*

A rule is *height-preserving invertible*, if whenever we have a proof of height n for its conclusion, its premises are provable with a proof of at most height n.

Lemma 10 (Inversions)

1. *All of the rules $L\wedge$, $R\wedge$, $L\vee$, $R\vee$ Ldec, Rdec, Ls, Rs, Lr, Rr, LMZ, and RMZ are height-preserving invertible.*
2. *If $\vdash_n d, \Gamma \Rightarrow \Delta$ for an Euler-Venn diagram d, then also $\vdash_n \mathsf{Venn}(d), \Gamma \Rightarrow \Delta$.*
3. *If $\vdash_n d, \Gamma \Rightarrow \Delta$ for a pure Euler diagram with one missing zone $z = (\{n_1, \ldots, n_k\}, \{o_1, \ldots, o_l\})$, then also $\vdash_n \boxed{o_i\ \mathbf{\circ}}, \Gamma \Rightarrow \Delta$ for all $1 \leq i \leq l$.*

Invertibility is used in the following lemma, where we connect provability of a sequent $\Gamma \Rightarrow \Delta$ within EDim with the provability of the sequent $\chi(\Gamma) \Rightarrow \chi(\Delta)$ consisting of the canonical formulas of the antecedent and the succedent.

Lemma 11. *Let $\Gamma \Rightarrow \Delta$ be a sequent of compound diagrams. Then $\Gamma \Rightarrow \Delta$ is provable in EDim if, and only if, $\chi(\Gamma) \Rightarrow \chi(\Delta)$ is provable in G3im.*

Proof. Let $\Gamma \Rightarrow \Delta$ be provable in EDim. By Theorem 1, the sequent is valid, and hence the sequent $\chi(\Gamma) \Rightarrow \chi(\Delta)$ is valid as well. Since G3im is complete (cf. Remark 2), the sequent is provable in G3im.

For the other direction, we proceed by induction on the height n of the proof of $\chi(\Gamma) \Rightarrow \chi(\Delta)$. If $n = 0$, then $\chi(\Gamma) \Rightarrow \chi(\Delta)$ is an axiom $p, \Gamma' \Rightarrow \Delta', p$ or an instance of $L\bot$. In the first case, since the only diagram D with $\chi(D) = p$ is a positive literal, $\Gamma \Rightarrow \Delta$ is an axiom as well. The second case is trivial.

The induction step is mostly straightforward. We partially present one of the cases, and refer to the extended version for the full proof [10]. If the last rule is $R \rightarrow$ then the sequent is of the form $\chi(\Gamma) \Rightarrow \chi(\Delta'), \chi(D)$, where D is either a compound diagram $D = E \rightarrow F$, a pure Euler diagram $D = d_e$ with a single missing zone, an Euler-Venn diagram with missing zones and shaded zones $D = d$, a single negative literal for a contour c, or $D = \top$. The first case is straightforward. For the case where d is an Euler-Venn diagram, we have $\chi(d) = \mathsf{Euler}(d) \rightarrow \mathsf{Venn}(d)$. and hence the premiss of the last step is $\chi(\mathsf{Euler}(d)), \chi(\Gamma) \Rightarrow \chi(\mathsf{Venn}(d))$. By the induction hypothesis, we get that $\mathsf{Euler}(d), \Gamma \Rightarrow \mathsf{Venn}(d)$ is provable, and by applying Rdet, $\Gamma \Rightarrow \Delta, d$ as well. Now assume that the principal diagram is a pure Euler diagram d_e with a single missing zone $z = (\{n_1, \ldots, n_k\}, \{o_1, \ldots, o_l\})$. Hence, the premiss of the last step in G3im is $\bigwedge_{1 \leq i \leq k} n_i, \chi(\Gamma) \Rightarrow \bigvee_{1 \leq i \leq l} o_i$. Since both $L\wedge$ and $R\vee$ are height-preserving invertible, the sequent $n_1, \ldots, n_k, \chi(\Gamma) \Rightarrow o_1, \ldots, o_l$ is provable with height less than n. Since the canonical formula is only atomic for diagram literals, we have that $\boxed{n_1\ \mathbf{\circ}}, \ldots, \boxed{n_k\ \mathbf{\circ}}, \Gamma \Rightarrow \boxed{o_1\ \mathbf{\circ}}, \ldots, \boxed{o_l\ \mathbf{\circ}}$ is provable by the induction hypothesis, and hence by applying Rldec also $\Gamma \Rightarrow \Delta, d_e$. The other cases are proven using suited applications of Rneg and R$\top$. $\square$

Since every valid sequent is derivable in G3im, we get the completeness result for EDim directly from Lemma 11.

Theorem 2 (Completeness). *If $\Gamma \Rightarrow \Delta$ is valid, then $\Gamma \Rightarrow \Delta$ is provable.*

We show that some rules are admissible. To that end, we define the *weight* of diagrams, to order them by the number of their syntactic elements.

Definition 14. *The weight $\omega(d)$ of a diagram is defined inductively. The base cases are given by* $\omega(\perp) = 0$, $\omega(\boxed{c\ \mathbf{o}}) = 0$, *and* $\omega(\boxed{c\ \mathbf{o}}) = 1$. *Otherwise we set*

$$
\omega(d) = \begin{cases}
|Z^*(d)| + 1 & \text{, if d is a Venn diagram} \\
|MZ(d)| + 1 & \text{, if d is a pure Euler diagram} \\
\omega(\mathsf{Euler}(d)) + \omega(\mathsf{Venn}(d)) + 1 & \text{, if d is an Euler-Venn diagram} \\
\omega(d_1) + \omega(d_2) + 1 & \text{, if $d = d_1 \otimes d_2$ for $\otimes \in \{\wedge, \vee, \rightarrow\}$}
\end{cases}
$$

Lemma 12 (Structural Rules)

(1) For any diagram D, the sequent $D, \Gamma \Rightarrow \Delta, D$ is provable in EDim.
(2) Weakening:
   i) If $\vdash_n \Gamma \Rightarrow \Delta$, then also $\vdash_n D, \Gamma \Rightarrow \Delta$.
   ii) If $\vdash_n \Gamma \Rightarrow \Delta$, then also $\vdash_n \Gamma \Rightarrow \Delta, D$.
(3) Contraction:
   i) If $\vdash_n D, D, \Gamma \Rightarrow \Delta$, then also $\vdash_n D, \Gamma \Rightarrow \Delta$.
   ii) If $\vdash_n \Gamma \Rightarrow \Delta, D, D$, then also $\vdash_n \Gamma \Rightarrow \Delta, D$.
(4) Cut: If $\vdash \Gamma \Rightarrow D, \Delta$ and $\vdash D, \Gamma' \Rightarrow \Delta'$, then $\vdash \Gamma, \Gamma' \Rightarrow \Delta, \Delta'$.

Proof. (1) can be proven by a straightforward induction on the weight of D. Items (2), and (3) can be proven by induction on the height of the proofs using Lemma 10 and arguments similar to Negri and von Plato [13]. For (4), we use soundness and completeness of EDim. If both sequents are provable, they are also valid, by soundness. So choose an arbitrary valuation ν. Then $\nu(\Gamma) \leq \nu(D) \sqcup \nu(\Delta)$ and $\nu(D) \sqcap \nu(\Gamma') \leq \nu(\Delta')$. Now we have $\nu(\Gamma) \sqcap \nu(\Gamma') \leq (\nu(D) \sqcup \nu(\Delta)) \sqcap \nu(\Gamma') = (\nu(D) \sqcap \nu(\Gamma')) \sqcup (\nu(\Delta) \sqcap \nu(\Gamma')) \leq \nu(\Delta') \sqcup (\nu(\Delta) \sqcap \nu(\Gamma')) \leq \nu(\Delta') \sqcup \nu(\Delta)$. This is due to the first premiss, distributivity, the second premiss and the fact $a \sqcap b \leq a$. Since ν was arbitrary, $\Gamma, \Gamma' \Rightarrow \Delta, \Delta'$ is valid, and due to completeness, $\Gamma, \Gamma' \Rightarrow \Delta, \Delta'$ is provable. □

Remark 3. It is also possible to prove cut admissibility with a purely syntactic argument by adapting the inductive proof for the system G3im [13].

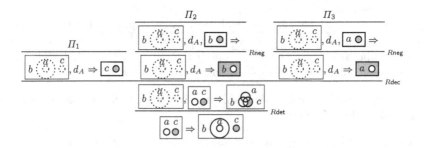

Fig. 9. Proof using Euler-Venn diagrams

A derivation that uses all three types of diagrams can be found in Fig. 9. We explain parts of the proof from bottom to top. The last applied rule detaches the pure Euler part from the Venn part of the succedent, so that we can then decompose the single shaded zone into literals. This splits the proof into three branches, which we treat in the sub-derivations Π_1, Π_2 and Π_3, respectively (see Fig. 11). For reasons of brevity, we use the abbrevations for diagrams as shown in Fig. 10.

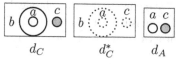

$$d_C \qquad d_C^* \qquad d_A$$

Fig. 10. Diagram abbreviations

Now, the two right proof branches contain a negative literal in the succedent, which we move to the antecedent with an application of Rneg. Then, all three proof branches proceed similarly: we reduce the pure Euler diagram d_C^* into smaller diagrams, as explained in Sect. 3. Π_1 proceeds by detaching the Euler and Venn aspects of the diagram d_A, which immediately closes the left branch, due to Lemma 12 (1). The right branch ends in an axiom after decomposing the single shaded zone in the antecedent. Within Π_2 there is a similar structure, denoted by the derivation Π_1', where the antecedent contains slightly different diagrams, but the application of rules is similar. The other branches proceed similarly. This example shows how the reduction rules lead to smaller diagrams, and how the rules of Lemma 12 may reduce the size of the proofs, here in the form of the generalised axioms.

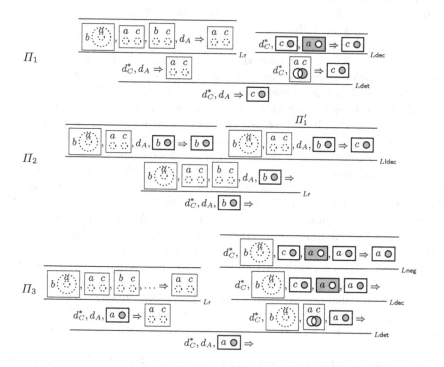

Fig. 11. Auxiliary derivations for Fig. 9

5   Conclusion

In this paper, we presented an intuitionistic interpretation of Euler-Venn diagrams, based on a semantics of Heyting algebras. We then defined a cut-free sequent calculus EDim, which we have proven to be sound and complete with respect to this semantics. Furthermore, we have shown that the structural rules of contraction, weakening and cut are admissible. We deviated from classical Euler-Venn diagrams in two ways: we did not treat missing zones and shaded zones as equivalent, and we introduced the new syntactic element of dotted contours.

The first deviation is due to the basic restrictions of intuitionistic reasoning. More specifically, intuitionistic implication cannot be treated as an abbreviation of the other operators. To have a syntax explicitly for implications, we need to increase the number of distinct syntactic elements of Euler-Venn diagrams. Hence, distinguishing these two elements is a natural choice. Of course, it can be argued that shading should be used to reflect implications. However, we think that since the representation of missing zones (or rather their absence) introduces a direction into the diagram, in the form of inclusions, this choice is justified.

The introduction of dotted diagrams is more debatable. Arguably, the need for distinguishing pure Euler diagrams arises, since we interpret the missing zones of Euler-Venn diagrams as a precondition for the construction of the elements denoted by the shaded zones. That is, in the constructive interpretation of intuitionistic reasoning, an Euler-Venn diagram means that, given a construction as indicated by the missing zones, we have another construction for the assertions given by the shaded zones. Hence, there is an additional implication within the semantics of Euler-Venn diagrams, as can also be seen in the rules of EDim to detach the pure Euler from the Venn aspects of a diagram. These rules behave similarly to the rules for implication in sentential intuitionistic sequent calculus.

However, the introduction of new syntactic elements is necessary, due to the independence of the operators. Compare for example the intuitionistic systems based on Existential Graphs (EGs). While the operations in classical EGs are denoted by juxtaposition and cuts, reflecting conjunction and negation, respectively, the assertive graphs [1] explicitly introduce notation for disjunction, and also treat the "scroll" as a distinct element. Similarly, the intuitionistic EGs [12] include the notion of n-scrolls for each $n > 0$. We think that our system stretches the idea of Euler-Venn diagrams quite far. In particular, logics that need even more independent operators, for example substructural logics, may not be well-matched for such a diagrammatic system. While it may be possible to define such an interpretation, the necessary syntax is far from obvious, if we want to keep the diagrammatic structure of Euler-Venn diagrams. Of course, it is always possible to add new operators to the compound part of the system, but we think that such an addition misses the point of a diagrammatic reasoning system.

Still, there are future directions this work can be taken into. For example, our sequent calculus resembles sentential sequent calculus, while typical Euler-Venn reasoning systems work by adding syntax to single diagrams, and then removing unnecessary parts [2]. It is interesting to see, if we can define such a system for intuitionistic Euler-Venn diagrams. We assume that for the rules to introduce and remove contours, or to copy contours, the reduction of a pure Euler diagram (cf. Definition 10 and Lemma 5) will play a significant role.

References

1. Bellucci, F., Chiffi, D., Pietarinen, A.V.: Assertive graphs. J. Appl. Non-Class. Log. **28**(1), 72–91 (2018)
2. Burton, J., Stapleton, G., Howse, J.: Completeness proof strategies for euler diagram logics. In: Euler Diagrams 2012, vol. 854, pp. 2–16. CEUR (2012)
3. Dragalin, A.G.: Mathematical Intuitionism. Introduction to Proof Theory, Translations of Mathematical Monographs, vol. 67. American Mathematical Society (1988)
4. de Freitas, R., Viana, P.: A graph calculus for proving intuitionistic relation algebraic equations. In: Cox, P., Plimmer, B., Rodgers, P. (eds.) Diagrams 2012. LNCS (LNAI), vol. 7352, pp. 324–326. Springer, Heidelberg (2012). https://doi.org/10.1007/978-3-642-31223-6_40
5. Gentzen, G.: Untersuchungen über das logische Schließen I. Math. Z. **39**, 176–210 (1935)
6. Hammer, E.: Peircean graphs for propositional logic. In: Allwein, G., Barwise, J. (eds.) Logical Reasoning with Diagrams, pp. 129–147. Oxford University Press, Oxford (1996)
7. Howse, J., Stapleton, G., Taylor, J.: Spider diagrams. LMS J. Comput. Math. **8**, 145–194 (2005)
8. Legris, J.: Existential graphs as a basis for structural reasoning. In: Chapman, P., Stapleton, G., Moktefi, A., Perez-Kriz, S., Bellucci, F. (eds.) Diagrams 2018. LNCS (LNAI), vol. 10871, pp. 590–597. Springer, Cham (2018). https://doi.org/10.1007/978-3-319-91376-6_53
9. Linker, S.: Sequent calculus for euler diagrams. In: Chapman, P., Stapleton, G., Moktefi, A., Perez-Kriz, S., Bellucci, F. (eds.) Diagrams 2018. LNCS (LNAI), vol. 10871, pp. 399–407. Springer, Cham (2018). https://doi.org/10.1007/978-3-319-91376-6_37
10. Linker, S.: Intuitionistic Euler-Venn-diagrams (extended) (2020). https://arxiv.org/abs/2002.02929
11. Ma, M., Pietarinen, A.-V.: A weakening of alpha graphs: quasi-boolean algebras. In: Chapman, P., Stapleton, G., Moktefi, A., Perez-Kriz, S., Bellucci, F. (eds.) Diagrams 2018. LNCS (LNAI), vol. 10871, pp. 549–564. Springer, Cham (2018). https://doi.org/10.1007/978-3-319-91376-6_50
12. Ma, M., Pietarinen, A.V.: A graphical deep inference system for intuitionistic logic. Log. Anal. **245**, 73–114 (2019)
13. Negri, S., von Plato, J.: Structural Proof Theory. Cambridge University Press, Cambridge (2001)
14. Ono, H.: Proof Theory and Algebra in Logic. Short Textbooks in Logic. Springer, Singapore (2019)
15. Rasiowa, H., Sikorski, R.: The Mathematics of Metamathematics. Panstwowe Wydawnictwo Naukowe, Warszaw (1963)
16. Shin, S.J.: The logical Status of Diagrams. Cambridge University Press, Cambridge (1995)

17. Stapleton, G., Masthoff, J.: Incorporating negation into visual logics: a case study using Euler diagrams. In: VLC 2007, pp. 187–194. Knowledge Systems Institute (2007)
18. Stapleton, G., Howse, J., Taylor, J., Thompson, S.: The expressiveness of spider diagrams. J. Log. Comput. **14**(6), 857–880 (2004)

Schopenhauer Diagrams for Conceptual Analysis

Michał Dobrzański[1] and Jens Lemanski[2(✉)]

[1] Institute of Philosophy, University of Warsaw, Warsaw, Poland
michaldobrzanski@uw.edu.pl
[2] Institute of Philosophy, University of Hagen, Hagen, Germany
jenslemanski@gmail.com

Abstract. In his *Berlin Lectures* of the 1820s, the German philosopher Arthur Schopenhauer (1788–1860) used spatial logic diagrams for philosophy of language. These logic diagrams were applied to many areas of semantics and pragmatics, such as theories of concept formation, concept development, translation theory, clarification of conceptual disputes, etc. In this paper we first introduce the basic principles of Schopenhauer's philosophy of language and his diagrammatic method. Since Schopenhauer often gives little information about how the individual diagrams are to be understood, we then make the attempt to reconstruct, specify and further develop one diagram type for the field of conceptual analysis.

Keywords: Spatial logic diagrams · Linguistic abstraction · Bundle theory

1 Introduction

It is only in recent years that it has become known that in his so-called *Berlin Lectures* of the 1820s [1] the German philosopher Arthur Schopenhauer made intensive use of logic diagrams in an original and novel way. One of Schopenhauer's original ideas was to use diagrams not only for logic and eristics, but also for semantics and conceptual analysis.

We would like to present and elaborate on this idea in the present paper. For this purpose, we will first introduce the basic principles of Schopenhauer's theory of language in Sect. 2, illustrating them with some of his logic diagrams for conceptual analysis. Since Schopenhauer himself gives only a few sentences about the use of these diagrams, we will reconstruct and develop one type of diagram in Sect. 3 and explain the basic principles presented in Sect. 2 with the help of this reconstruction.

To avoid misunderstandings, it should be noted that we do not claim that Schopenhauer diagrams are better than other visual systems, such as conceptual graphs [2], concept diagrams [3] etc., which are currently used in semantics. Although the *Berlin Lectures'* diagrams show similarities with Euler, Kant, Venn and Peirce diagrams, we will avoid comparisons with other diagram systems as far as possible and therefore use

© Springer Nature Switzerland AG 2020
A.-V. Pietarinen et al. (Eds.): Diagrams 2020, LNAI 12169, pp. 281–288, 2020.
https://doi.org/10.1007/978-3-030-54249-8_22

the neutral term "Schopenhauer diagrams" here. In addition, we will leave out many topics, theses and problems of Schopenhauer's theory of language[1], but—if possible—we will refer to existing literature in several places.

2 Schopenhauer's Theory of Language

In this section, we give an overview of Schopenhauer's theory of language taken from the *Lectures on the Entire Philosophy*, Chapter 3, which is entitled *Of the Abstract Representation, or Thinking: which Chapter contains Logic*. In §§1–6 we will focus on Schopenhauer's theory of representation and concepts, in §§7–10 on his logic and in §§11–14 on some visualizations of concepts.

§1. Definition of Concepts. Schopenhauer distinguishes two classes of objects that can be perceived by the subject, which he calls representations: (1) intuitive representations that are recognized by the external senses and (2) abstract representations recognized by reason alone ([1], 118) that are free of temporal-spatial determinations. For Schopenhauer, the representations of class (2) are concepts. As products of reason, they have a close connection with language, which is described as one of the "main expressions of reason" in man ([1], 240f.). Concepts are the actual material of human thinking, or, in other words, thinking and reasoning is described only as the "realization of concepts" (Vergegenwärtigung der Begriffe; [1], 243).

§2. Concreta and Abstracta. Schopenhauer divides concepts into *concreta* and *abstracta*. *Concreta* are "abstracted directly from intuitive representations". In contrast, *abstracta* are formed by omitting some properties of other concepts. Examples of *concreta* are concepts such as blue, dog, house, whereas *abstracta* is used for concepts such as quality, artwork, friendship ([1]; 252). Despite this distinction, Schopenhauer points out that, strictly speaking, all concepts are abstract and the distinction between *abstracta* and *concreta* is only useful to clarify the relation of concepts to each other, but not the relation of concepts to intuition.

§3. Generality of Concepts. Similar to Euler ([7], L. CI), Schopenhauer also denies the possibility of singular propositions (*propositio singularis*). He claims that "a concept is always general, even if there is only one thing that is thought by it; and only a singular intuition that gives it content (Gehalt), is a proof of it", since "the concept is always an abstractum, a thought, but never a single individual thing". This is true even for proper names such as "Socrates", since it is also possible to denote more than one object with it ([1], 276f.).

§4. Origin of Concepts. According to Schopenhauer, reason produces concepts by abstracting from the many properties of objects that are given in intuitive representation. Thus, a concept "does not contain everything" that is given or contained in its intuitive basis. On the other hand, "innumerable intuitive objects" can be thought of with the help of a concept ([1], 249). However, Schopenhauer emphasizes the dependence of concepts on intuition: "the whole world of reflection [...] rests on the intuitive one as its basis of cognition" ([1], 252).

---

[1] For these topics, see [4–6].

§5. Empirical Criterion of Meaning. He also claims that each concept can be described as distinct and meaningful if and only if, in the course of concept analysis, its properties can ultimately be substantiated with clear intuition ([1], 254f.). Thus, *abstracta* must be broken down to *concreta*, and *concreta* must refer to given objects in intuitive representations. This goes along with his rejection of *a priori* concepts and his criticism of innatism ([1], 235). This empirical criterion of meaning thereby also forms the basis for his criticism of scholasticism ([1], 255), rationalism ([1], 254) and idealism ([1], 236f., 495).

§6. Incommensurability of Language and Thought. Furthermore, he seems to claim the separation of conceptual thought processes from language, despite the close connection of concepts to words. Words are described as merely sensory "sign[s] of concept[s]" ([1], 243). They are, however, necessary in order to remember concepts willingly (willkürlich) and to be able to perform intersubjectively perceptible thought operations with them. Thus it is not possible to communicate a concept for which there is no word ([1], 244). At the same time there is no isomorphism between language and thinking. Schopenhauer makes it clear in numerous written passages that one should not equate language analysis with concept analysis: It would be wrong "if the argument that signs are necessary for concepts was used to justify the assumption that we would actually operate with the signs alone when thinking and talking, and that they completely represent the concepts" ([1], 247). This is still based on Schopenhauer's strict separation of two types of representation—the intuitive (temporal-spatial) and the abstract. Words belong to the first, since they are just sensory perceptible signs of abstract thoughts. Schopenhauer, by the way, sees his "sharp separation of concepts from intuitive representation, i.e. things" as an important contribution to the history of logic ([1], 357).

§7. Definition of Logic. According to Schopenhauer, logic is "the general knowledge of the peculiar way of proceeding of reason, gained through the self-observation of reason and abstraction of all content, expressed in the form of rules" ([1], 362). It is further described as the discipline that deals with the analysis (of the operations) of concepts, i.e. thinking and reasoning, or "the pure science of reason", which mainly teaches how one may "operate" with concepts ([1], 368). Logic need not necessarily have anything to do with language; however, both language and logic have in common that they must use signs to represent thoughts. Since language and logic have different rules and since language is only understood as a system of sensory perceivable signs for the evocation of concepts, it is possible that other signs could also be used for both purposes, for example: diagrams.

§8. Extension and Intension. Schopenhauer introduces his circle diagrams by claiming that concepts have a "sphere" (Sphäre) or a "circumference" (Umfang). Because of the sphere and the circumference, concepts are limited and bounded. Thus, expressions such as "boundary", "circumference" and "sphere" refer to a limited set of objects (intuitive or abstract) that are thought of in a concept ([1], 257)—nowadays we would usually call this the extension of a concept. Furthermore, Schopenhauer also speaks about the content (Inhalt) of concepts in order to denote the given properties (Merkmale) of a represented object—this could be understood as the intension of a concept. In Schopenhauer's words: The circumference is equal to what can be thought "through" a concept, and the content with what can be thought "in" a concept ([1], 258).

§9. Law of Reciprocity. The relationship between extension and intension is stated in the law of reciprocity. According to Schopenhauer, the circumference of the sphere of a concept is in an "inverse relationship" to its content ([1], 258). In other words: The more extension a concept has, the less intension it has and vice versa. This law, which was made popular by Kantian logic, and especially the problems with the notion of intension, are discussed in great detail by Hauswald [8].

§10. Bundle-Theory. What Schopenhauer seems to mean by content (intension) is a bundle of concrete properties associated with a concept. One can deduce this from the law of reciprocity: the wider the sphere of a concept is or the more universally a concept is applicable to different objects, the smaller the bundle of concrete properties that describe the various objects. This is supported by the statement that the concept that has the biggest content is the one in which we think the "most properties" ([1], 271). Content, as a bundle of properties, is thus one of the features that can be illustrated by specific types of diagrams.

§11. Conceptual Spheres. For Schopenhauer, conceptual spheres are the actual substance of logic—a discipline of reason that deals with the correct "cognition of the relationships of conceptual spheres to one another" ([1], 364). With that Schopenhauer anticipates what many current authors also explain: that these relations, and indeed all possible ones, can be represented by diagrams in the form of circles and that there is a kind of isomorphic relation between circle diagrams and conceptual spheres (i.e. human thoughts!). Where this isomorphism comes from cannot be explained by Schopenhauer; however, he acknowledges that this is "an extremely fortunate occurrence" and states that it was made popular by Gottfried Ploucquet (in square form), Johann Heinrich Lambert (in line form) and Leonhard Euler (in circle form) ([1], 269). Circles symbolize conceptual spheres and not words, since Schopenhauer always consistently speaks of "conceptual spheres" (see [1], 269 ff.). It should be noted that words must nevertheless be used in the diagrams to designate the concepts that are actually to be examined with them. It seems, then, that Schopenhauer's diagrams should primarily be understood as the study of human thought that takes place in concepts and is a process largely independent of language. However, language is needed to demonstrate it.

§12. Circle-Inclusion. But how should the diagrams be read? Schopenhauer is curt. On one hand he explicitly states that the "relative size of the spheres", i.e. the size of one sphere in relation to another, refers "not to the size of the content of the concept, but to the size of the circumference" ([1], 271). On the other hand, a number of diagrams can be found in the *Lectures* where the size of the circle seems to be irrelevant. Even though this needs further analysis, it can at least be assumed that it is necessary that two circles have different sizes if one conceptual sphere is completely contained in another. For example: The concept `triangle` (Dreieck) has more concrete properties than the concept `figure` (Figur) but a figure comprises more objects than just triangles, thus the narrower conceptual sphere of `triangle` is completely included in the wider sphere of figure. The same applies to the concept bird (Vogel) in the concept animal (Thier), as Fig. 1 illustrates.

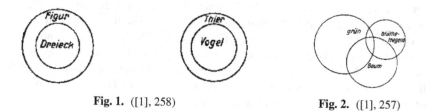

Fig. 1. ([1], 258)   **Fig. 2.** ([1], 257)

§13. Circle-Exclusion. However, in other situations Schopenhauer seems to treat the above stated rule more loosely, depending on what he intends to demonstrate with the diagram. For example: the size of two circles does not play a role if two concepts have nothing in common and are mutually exclusive. The spheres of concepts such as stone and animal have no common extension. This means, that there is no object in intuitive representation which can be both, a stone and an animal. Therefore, two circles with arbitrary sizes have to be drawn in the diagram, and both show neither an intersection nor an inclusion ([1], 274). The same applies e.g. to triangle and bird in Fig. 1.

§14. Circle-Intersection. Schopenhauer also depicts concepts that "mutually contain each other". In this case, the content (not the circumference) of one results directly from the content of the other (see [1], 273). In summary, it can be assumed that in the diagrams the relationship of the conceptual contents (intension) is represented by the spatial relationship of the circles to each other, while the size of the circles only sometimes might represent the conceptual circumference (extension). In Fig. 2, for example, we see three concepts denoted by the words green (grün), tree (Baum) and flower-bearing (blüthetragend), whose mutual containment is represented only by the spatial relations of the circles.

3   Schopenhauer Diagrams

Figure 2 is a good example of how Schopenhauer finds new applications for logic diagrams in the *Berlin Lectures*. In this case, the circle diagram is applied to conceptual analysis but only explained with a few sentences in the text. However, we are not concerned here with interpretation of these few sentences, but with the reconstruction, specification and development of Schopenhauer's diagrammatic ideas in semantics. As a case study, we take Fig. 2 as a paradigm and reconstruct in §§15–18 a diagram with two concepts from the intuitive representation. In §§19–25, we end with a reconstruction of diagrams with three and more concepts.

§15. First Two Definite Concepts. Let us imagine that in our intuitive representation we find a certain object that we occupy with the concept tree. Since it has been abstracted directly from the intuitive representation (§2), the concept is a *concretum* which has a definite sphere (§§8, 11) and is illustrated by a circle. Furthermore, we have found criteria through our intuitive representation that allow us to say what belongs to the tree and what does not. Thus, we can also refer to the indefinite concept non-tree which is located outside the circle of tree but inside a square frame F. Both diagrammatic objects, the circle and the frame together form diagram D1. But let us now assume that we find in the intuitive representation another object called table that intuitively has similarities to and differences from the first object mentioned. For table and non-table we can therefore draw a similar diagram D1*. Let us further assume that both objects of intuitive representation have a common property which we call green. In this case, we can now make an addition for D1 and D1* and draw a further conceptual sphere which is marked with the word green.

§16. Diagrammatic Representation. But where exactly is the conceptual sphere of green in D1 or D1*? Since both objects intuitively have at least one thing in common—green—but also have differences, green cannot be congruent with tree in D1 or with table in D1*. Circle-Inclusion (§12) is therefore not possible. However, since green is assigned to both concepts, otherwise the similarity of the property would not be intuitively given, green must have an intersection with tree or table. Thus, Circle-Exclusion (§13) is also excluded. This means that a part of green is contained in the region of tree and a part of green in the region of non-tree, and this region of non-tree will also contain table somewhere. So the relationship of green to tree and table is that they mutually contain each other. The result of this consideration is that green divides the sphere given in D1 and D1* respectively, i.e. D2 and D2*. We see in D2 and D2* that the indefinite concept is located outside both circles and thus negates the two definite concepts. However, the intuitive representation given in D1 and D1* now appears to be separated: the circle, which in D1 and D1* denoted one object with many properties, has now been divided into two regions. This raises the question of which region of a diagram such as D2 or D2* is closest to intuitive representation.

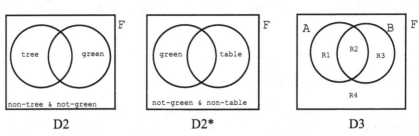

D2   D2*   D3

§17. Syntax of D3. In diagram D3, we separate the syntax of the diagrams from the semantics and therefore assign the concepts in D2 and D2* the variables A and B. Within the diagrammatic frame (F), D3 shows two circles (A, B), which together form four areas that can be called regions (R1, R2, R3, R4). Connections of regions can form diagrammatic objects, such as {R1, R2} = A or {R2, R3} = B. Similar to [9], the distinction between diagrammatic objects and regions results in several options for describing D3 such as: {R1} depicts the abstraction of B from A, $A \backslash B$. {R2} depicts the intersection of A and B: $A \cap B$. {R3} depicts the abstraction of A from B: $B \backslash A$. {R1, R2, R3} depicts the union of A and B: $A \cup B$.

§18. Semantics of D1 or D2. D2 and D2* display two circles, four regions and a diagrammatic frame in the same setting as D3. Thus, we can substitute `tree`, `green` or `table` with `A` or `B`. For example, we take D2: {R1} depicts the abstraction of `green` from `tree`: tree\green. {R2} depicts the intersection of `tree` and `green`: tree ∩ green. {R3} depicts the abstraction of `tree` from `green`: green\tree. {R1, R2, R3} depicts the union of `tree` and `green`: tree∪green. {R4} depicts the negation of `tree` and `green`: F\(tree ∪ green).

§19. n-term Diagrams. Schopenhauer himself has also designed diagrams for n-terms, which produce large conceptual clusters by circle intersection and exclusion. As an example, one could take the concepts `tree` and `table`, which according to §15 are different objects (tree △ table), but both can have the property `green`. A unification of D2 and D2* would then be D4.

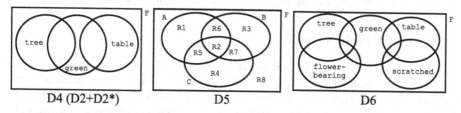

D4 (D2+D2*)   D5   D6

§20. Regions of D5. But if there is no exclusion for three concepts, we arrive at D5: {R1}: $A\backslash(B \cup C)$; {R2}: $(A \cap B \cap C)$; {R3}: $B\backslash(A \cup C)$; {R4}: $C\backslash(A \cup B)$; {R5}: $(A \cap C)\backslash B$; {R6}: $(A \cap B)\backslash C$; {R7}: $(B \cap C)\backslash A$; {R8}: $F\backslash(A \cup B \cup C)$.

§21. Semantics for D5. We now adopt the semantics of D2, so that `A` denotes the concept `tree` and `B` the concept `green`. Let us now assume that the object of intuitive representation of §15 also has the property of bearing a `flower`. We now use the concept `flower-bearing` for `C` and thus arrive at a semantics for the respective regions in which, for example, {R5} denotes an object to which the concepts `green`, `flower-bearing` apply, {R6} on the other hand, designates objects with the properties `tree` and `green`. Thus, D5 gives the syntax for Fig. 2.

§22. Bundle of Intersections. According to the arguments of §§2–4, *concreta* are concepts that have no or as few conceptual abstractions as possible. In the case of D5, one can see from the eight regions shown above that {R2} is the *concreta* and can only represent an objectual abstraction: the concept is a pure bundle (§10) of intersections $(A \cap B \cap C)$, which does not have any conceptual abstraction. All other regions, however, show abstractions of at least one diagrammatic object.

§23. Convex and Concave Concepts. The degree of abstraction of a concept can be measured by how many convex and concave boundaries it has. If D5 is broken down into individual regions, a total of four levels can be seen: (1) {R2} is a *concretum* since it has only concave boundaries; (2) {R5}, {R6} and {R7} have two concave and one convex boundary and are therefore *1st level-abstracta*; i.e. they are a conceptual abstraction of {R2}, but more concrete than regions of higher levels; (3) {R1}, {R3} and {R4} have one concave and two convex boundaries and are thus *2nd level-abstracta*; i.e. they are conceptual abstraction of a concept of a lower level. (4) {R8} has only convex boundaries and is therefore the *highest level-abstractum.*

§24. Conceptual Clusters. Through the exact interpretation of D4 and D5 we are now able to create and read more complex diagrams with Intersections and Exclusions. As an example, we take D4 (D2 + D2*) and add two more concepts: first, flower-bearing (similar to Fig. 2) and, second, a new one such as scratched. One possible diagram with 5 conceptual spheres and 14 regions may be D6 including 2 *concreta* (1.flower-bearing ∩ green ∩ tree; 2. green ∩ table ∩ scratched), 6 *1st level-abstracta* (1.flower-bearing ∩ green; 2. flower-bearing ∩ tree; 3. tree ∩ green; 4. green ∩ scratched; 5. green ∩ table; 6. scratched ∩ table), and 5 *2nd level-abstracta* and 1 *highest level abstracta.* Due to the lack of space, we have only given the positive relations (intersections) in this description of the regions. Furthermore, we stop at this point with the prospect of what more complex Schopenhauer diagrams look like.

4 Summary and Outlook

In Sect. 2 we have presented Schopenhauer's main principles of his theory of language. In Sect. 3 a reconstruction, specification and further development esp. of Fig. 2 (D5) was carried out. In this context, we were able to explain many of the principles listed in Sect. 2 again with the help of Schopenhauer diagrams. However, this does not mean that research on Schopenhauer diagrams for conceptual analysis is by any means complete. Many of Schopenhauer's principles, topics and theses have not been addressed or sufficiently explained here, e.g. the principle of Circle-Inclusion from §12, Schopenhauer's theory of language development, the theory of translation, and many more.

References

1. Schopenhauer, A.: Philosophische Vorlesungen (Sämtliche Werke IX). In: Deussen, P., Mockrauer, F. (eds.) Piper & Co., München (1913)
2. Dau, F.: Formal logic with conceptual graphs. In: Hitzler, P., Scharfe, H. (eds.) Conceptual Structures in Practice, pp. 17–45. Taylor & Francis, London (2009)
3. Stapleton, G., Howse, J., Chapman, P., Delaney, A., Burton, J., Oliver, I.: Formalizing concept diagrams. In: 19th International Conference on Distributed Multimedia Systems, Visual Languages and Computing, Knowledge Systems Institute, pp. 182–187 (2013)
4. Dobrzański, M.: Begriff und Methode bei Arthur Schopenhauer. Königshausen & Neumann, Würzburg (2017)
5. Dobrzański, M.: Problems in reconstructing Schopenhauer's theory of meaning. with reference to his influence on Wittgenstein. In: Lemanski, J. (ed.) Language, Logic, and Mathematics in Schopenhauer, pp. 25–46. Birkhäuser, Basel (2020)
6. Lemanski, J.: Logik und Eristische Dialektik. In: Schubbe, D., Koßler, M. (eds.) Schopenhauer-Handbuch: Leben – Werk – Wirkung, 2nd ed. pp. 160–169. Metzler, Stuttgart (2018)
7. Euler, L.: Letters of Euler to a German Princess, on Different Subjects in Physics and Philosophy, vol. I. Murray, London (1795)
8. Hauswald, R.: Umfangslogik und analytisches Urteil bei Kant. Kant-Studien **101**, 283–308 (2010)
9. Demey, L.: From Euler diagrams in Schopenhauer to Aristotelian diagrams in logical geometry. In: Lemanski, J. (ed.) Language, Logic, and Mathematics in Schopenhauer, pp. 181–206. Birkhäuser, Basel (2020)

Euler Diagrams for Defeasible Reasoning

Ryo Takemura(✉)

Nihon University, Tokyo, Japan
takemura.ryo@nihon-u.ac.jp

Abstract. We investigate Euler diagrammatic systems for defeasible reasoning by extending the usual systems for Euler and Venn diagrams corresponding to standard classical logic. To achieve this, we use the generalized quantifier "most" to formalize defeasible reasoning, as proposed by Schlechta (1995), where defeasible knowledge is represented as "Most A are B" and axioms for "most" are defined. We introduce an Euler diagrammatic system for defeasible reasoning by introducing circle mA that represents "most A" for each circle A. We show that our Euler diagrammatic system is a diagrammatic representation of the symbolic system of the generalized quantifier "most". Furthermore, we investigate skeptical and credulous strategies in defeasible reasoning with our Euler diagrams.

1 Introduction

Among various diagrams applied in logical reasoning, Euler and Venn diagrams are the most traditional and basic, and various logical systems based on them have been developed so far. These diagrammatic systems are characterized, using symbolic logic via correspondences and translations between diagrammatic systems and well-established symbolic logical systems. For example, Shin's Venn-II [14] of a Venn diagrammatic system was shown to be equivalent to monadic first-order classical logic; Spider diagrams were shown to be equivalent to monadic first-order classical logic with equality in [15,16]; Second-order spider diagrams were shown to be as expressive as monadic second-order classical logic in [1]; an Euler diagrammatic system of [9,20] was shown to correspond, at the proof level, to the syllogistic fragment of minimal logic without disjunction.

Standard logic such as classical, intuitionistic, and minimal logic has been formalized to model reasoning with ideal truth or knowledge in mathematics and they universally hold true without exception. Thus, once we obtain a conclusion or knowledge with standard logical reasoning, it remains true and can never be defeated even if we obtain additional knowledge later. Thus, reasoning based on standard logic is considered *monotonic*.

In contrast, ordinary reasoning is used for uncertain knowledge with insufficient information, which allows for exceptions. Thus, conclusions or knowledge obtained from our ordinary reasoning can be defeated by additional knowledge, thereby making such reasoning *nonmonotonic*. Thus, if standard classical logic

© Springer Nature Switzerland AG 2020
A.-V. Pietarinen et al. (Eds.): Diagrams 2020, LNAI 12169, pp. 289–304, 2020.
https://doi.org/10.1007/978-3-030-54249-8_23

is used to formalize defeasible or nonmonotonic reasoning, it may produce contradiction (cf. the following Example 1). Hence, various logical systems such as Reiter's default logic [10], defeasible inheritance network [5], and circumscription that differ from standard monotonic logic have been closely examined. See, for example [2,3], for defeasible or nonmonotonic reasoning.

In this article, we investigate an Euler diagrammatic system to provide a model for defeasible reasoning by extending the usual systems of Euler and Venn diagrams corresponding to standard classical logical systems. To achieve this, we use the generalized quantifier "most", as proposed in [12]. In contrast to the universal knowledge such as "All A are B" that is used in standard logic, uncertain and defeasible knowledge is expressed as "Most A are B" with the generalized quantifier "most", and a logical system for defeasible reasoning has been introduced in [12]. Additionally, natural set-theoretical semantics extended from the usual semantics of standard logic has been introduced, and the completeness theorem has been established in [12]. We apply the generalized quantifier "most" to Euler diagrams, and we introduce circle mA representing "most A" inside every circle A. In this manner, we extend the typical Euler and Venn diagrammatic systems, so that they can be applied as models of defeasible reasoning.

In the following part of the paper, we first review defeasible reasoning based on the defeasible inheritance network of [5], and investigate the corresponding Euler diagrammatic representation in Sect. 2. Then, we define an Euler diagrammatic system for defeasible reasoning in Sect. 3. In Sect. 4, we review the symbolic system of the generalized quantifier of [12], and investigate a translation from the system of the generalized quantifier into our Euler diagrammatic system. In Sect. 5, we further investigate skeptical and credulous strategies in defeasible reasoning using our Euler diagrams.

2 Defeasible Reasoning

We begin by examining the so-called Tweety example using a graphical representation.

Example 1 (Tweety). Assume first that we know "Tweety (denoted by t) is a bird (B)" and "Birds fly (F)". This knowledge can be graphically represented as follows.

$$t \longrightarrow B \longrightarrow F$$

By the transitivity of $\rightarrow$-edge, we can infer $t \rightarrow F$, i.e., "Tweety flies".

Then, assume that we further obtain the following knowledge. "Tweety is a penguin (P)", "Penguins are birds", and "Penguins do not fly". The above graph is augmented with this new knowledge in the following manner, where the negative statement "Penguins do not fly" is represented as $P \nrightarrow F$.

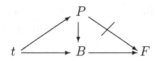

Then, from edges $t \to P$ and $P \nrightarrow F$, we can infer $t \nrightarrow F$, i.e., "Tweety does not fly". However, in the usual classical logic framework, the previously obtained knowledge, i.e., "Tweety flies" remains true even after new knowledge has been introduced; therefore, we obtain both "Tweety flies" and "Tweety does not fly" resulting in a contradiction.

Defeasible inheritance network [5,6], DI-net for short, is a formalization of the above informal graphical representation: a DI-net is a labeled finite directed acyclic graph having the following four types of edges:

- $A \Rightarrow B$, called a strict edge, means "all A are B", i.e., $\forall x(A(x) \Rightarrow B(x))$;
- $A \not\Rightarrow B$, called strict negative edge, means "all A are not B" or "no A are B", i.e., $\forall x(A(x) \Rightarrow \neg B(x))$;
- $A \to B$, called defeasible edge, means "most A are B", "typical A are B" or, "it is most natural to suppose that A are B".
- $A \nrightarrow B$, called defeasible negative edge, means "most A are not B", "typical A are not B" or, "it is most natural to suppose that A are not B".

The Tweety example can be represented by a DI-net as follows.

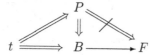

In the framework of DI-net, to avoid the previous contradiction in the Tweety example, various criteria such as specificity have been discussed. Specific to the Tweety example, the knowledge $t \to F$ (obtained from $t \Rightarrow B \to F$) is defeasible; however, the knowledge $t \nrightarrow F$ (obtained from $t \Rightarrow P \nrightarrow F$) obtained after the introduction of new knowledge is strict (definite). Therefore, maintaining the new knowledge $t \nrightarrow F$ and rejecting $t \to F$ is natural. More generally, to determine the edge of $A \nrightarrow B$ and $A \to B$ that should be retained, a more subtle and complicated discussion is needed.

In the graphical representation of DI-net, identifying the part of the given graph that represents contradiction or conflict is not intuitive but rather conventional. This is because, in general, the expressive power of graphical representation is rather high, and we can easily express information on contradiction and indeterminacy without special devices by using graphical representation. In contrast to the graphical representation of DI-net, basic Euler diagrams that only comprise circles and points can neither express information on contradiction (cf. [4,13] for example) nor indeterminacy. Hence, their expressive power is limited, but they contain cognitive clarity. On top of such basic Euler diagrams, information on indeterminacy can be expressed by introducing linking (i.e., disjunction) between points and between diagrams (cf. [14]). In this article, we consider basic Euler diagrams comprising circles and points, as well as linking between points. Then, for our basic Euler diagrams, we introduce, for each circle A, a circle named mA representing "most A". Using Euler diagrams in this manner, we can express the above Tweety example as shown in Fig. 1.

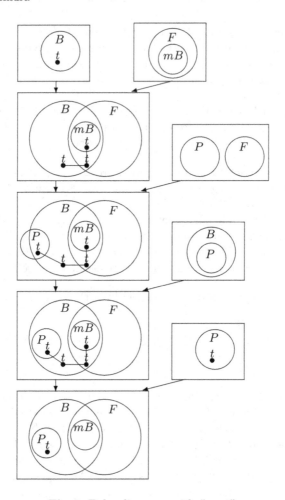

Fig. 1. Euler diagrams with "most"

In Fig. 1, each circle labeled X represents a set of entities that satisfy property X, and the point labeled t represents the entity Tweety. At the first step to unify two diagrams representing "Tweety is a bird" and "Most birds fly", (1) we first place circle mB meaning "most birds" inside circle B after the unification, since most birds are of course birds; (2) then, we place circle F in such a manner that it overlaps with B without any implication of a specific relationship (inside or outside) between F and B following the Venn diagrammatic convention; (3) subsequently, we place point t at the all possible regions inside B and link all of them. The linking represents the disjunctive information on t. In the above proof, the order in which the premises are unified is indifferent, and we obtain the same conclusion in any order.

As discussed in Example 1, using standard classical logic, we obtain a contradiction. By contrast, it is obvious at a glance with Euler diagrams that we cannot conclude "Tweety flies", and there is no contradiction. Furthermore, compared with a graphical DI-net, because of geometrical constraint of circles in Euler diagrams, the information $t \to F$ disappears, and we can easily read off "Tweety does not fly". Let us compare DI-net and our Euler diagrams in more detail. On the one hand, with DI-net, a conflict exists between two paths: $t \Rightarrow P \not\Rightarrow F$ and $t \Rightarrow B \to F$. On the other hand, with Euler diagrams, "Tweety does not fly" ($t \not\Rightarrow F$) definitely holds true. However, regarding $t \Rightarrow B \to F$, Tweety may or may not be a typical bird even though "Tweety is a bird", and hence, Tweety may or may not fly even though "Most birds fly". Thus, these two paths in DI-net are not in conflict from the viewpoint of Euler diagrams.

In this article, we investigate the Euler diagrammatic representation of defeasible reasoning by introducing a representation of the generalized quantifier "most". Sato and Mineshima [11] presented an empirical study of the generalized quantifier "most" using Euler diagrams. In their system, areas of regions play an essential role, and "Most A are B" is represented by drawing the majority of circle A inside circle B as in the following diagram $\mathcal{D}_1$. Thus, the following $\mathcal{D}_2$ does not represent "Most A are B".

 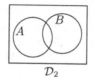

$\mathcal{D}_1$ $\mathcal{D}_2$

By contrast, in our proposed approach, we do not pay attention to the area of regions; however, we introduce circle mA to directly represent "most A" and hence, our framework is essentially topological.

Remark 1. In fact, the interpretation of a defeasible edge $A \to B$ is different in DI-net and our Euler diagrams. In DI-net, $A \to B$ can be read as "It is most natural to suppose that A are B", where the scope of the generalized quantifier "most" is "A are B" as a whole. The transitivity of $\to$ holds with this interpretation. However, in our Euler diagrams, as well as in the system of the generalized quantifier "most" [12], $A \to B$ is read as "Most A are B", where the scope of "most" is A. Therefore, in this interpretation, the transitivity does not hold: "Most A are B" and "Most B are C" does not generally imply "Most A are C". However, this difference does not matter for the above Tweety example, where the transitivity of $\to$ does not play an essential role.

3   Euler Diagrams with "most"

In this section, we define an Euler diagrammatic system by introducing circle mA representing "most A". Various Euler diagrammatic systems based on different concepts exist, for example [4,7,8,17]; however any of these systems are applicable for our discussion provided the inference rule of unification of diagrams is defined.

Definition 1 (Euler diagrams with "most"). An Euler diagram is a plane with a finite number of simple closed curves (simply called circles) labeled as $A, B, C, \ldots$, as well as $mA, mB, mC, \ldots$, constant points labeled as $a, b, c, \ldots$, and existential points labeled as $x, y, z, \ldots$.

Constant points and existential points in different regions that have the same name are linked by a line.

No two circles share a name.

When both the circles A and mA appear in a single diagram, mA should appear inside circle A.

A rectangle is used to represent the plane in a diagram, and Euler diagrams are denoted by $\mathcal{D}, \mathcal{E}, \mathcal{D}_1, \mathcal{D}_2, \ldots$.

Each circle represents a set of entities, each constant point represents an entity, and each existential point represents the existence of some entity (cf. [19]). Linking between points represents disjunctive information (cf. [14]). To maintain the simplicity and the cognitive clarity of basic Euler diagrams, we assume the contradiction is not expressible in a single diagram. Thus, to avoid expressing the contradiction "Most A are not A" with A being nonempty, we impose the condition that circle mA should appear inside circle A when both mA and A appear in a single diagram. Cf. the semantics of "most" in Sect. 4.

Based on the above definition of Euler diagrams, inference rules of Euler diagrammatic systems such as [4,7,8,17] are extended by introducing the following axiom.

Definition 2 (Axiom for "most"). The following form of diagram is an axiom for every A:

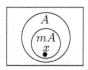

The axiom represents the true sentence "Most A are A". Furthermore, following [12], we assume that some entity exists when we consider "most A" (in other words, we do not consider "most A" when the set A is empty) and hence, we place existential point x in the above axiom. Note that our axiom implies the so-called existential import, i.e., an entity always exists that satisfies A for any A.

4   Generalized Quantifier "most"

In this section, we review the semantics of the generalized quantifier "most" given in [12], which also provides the semantics of our Euler diagrammatic system. Then, we investigate the translation from the system of the generalized quantifier "most", which is also called GQ-system, into our Euler diagrammatic system.

A formula of GQ-system has the following forms:

$$A(t_1, \ldots, t_n) \mid \varphi \wedge \psi \mid \varphi \vee \psi \mid \varphi \Rightarrow \psi \mid \neg\varphi \mid \forall x\varphi(x) \mid \exists x\varphi(x) \mid \nabla x\varphi(x) : \psi(x)$$

Here, we denote predicate symbols by $A, B, C, \ldots$; first-order constants by $a, b, c, \ldots$; variables by $x, y, z, \ldots$; first-order terms by $t_1, \ldots, t_n$; formulas by $\varphi, \psi, \sigma, \ldots$.

∇ is the generalized quantifier "most", and $\nabla x\varphi(x) : \psi(x)$ means "Most φ are ψ." In [12], for a technical reason, the dual quantifier $\Diamond$ of ∇ is also introduced as $\Diamond x\varphi(x) : \psi(x) \equiv \neg\nabla x\varphi(x) : \neg\psi(x)$, which does not play a role in the discussion that follows.

In usual set-theoretical semantics, the denotation of a formula φ is the set of entities for which φ holds. Then, the denotation of $\nabla x\varphi(x)$ i.e., "most φ" is given in terms of a weaker notion of the algebraic *filter*.

Definition 3 ($\mathcal{N}$-system). Let X be a set. $\mathcal{N}(X) \subseteq \mathcal{P}(X)$, where $\mathcal{P}(X)$ is the powerset of X, is called an $\mathcal{N}$-system over X if it satisfies the following conditions:

1. $X \in \mathcal{N}(X)$
2. If $\alpha \in \mathcal{N}(X)$ and $\alpha \subseteq \beta$, then $\beta \in \mathcal{N}(X)$.
3. If $\alpha, \beta \in \mathcal{N}(X)$, then $\alpha \cap \beta \neq \emptyset$ if $X \neq \emptyset$.

Condition (3) is weaker than that defining the usual notion of *filter*, where $\alpha \cap \beta \in \mathcal{N}(X)$ is imposed.

Definition 4 (Model). A model is $\mathcal{M} =< \mathcal{N}(\alpha), \alpha \subseteq M >$, where M is the domain of the model, and $\mathcal{N}(\alpha)$ is an $\mathcal{N}$-system over α for every $\alpha \subseteq M$ with $\alpha \neq \emptyset$.

Intuitively, $\nabla x\varphi(x)$ is true in a model $\mathcal{M}$ if and only if there exists $\alpha \in \mathcal{N}(M)$ such that $\varphi(m)$ is true for all $m \in \alpha$.

Definition 5 (Satisfiability). The satisfiability of the usual first-order formulas is defined as usual. Then that of the $\nabla x\varphi(x) : \psi(x)$ is defined as follows:

$\mathcal{M} \models \nabla x\varphi(x) : \psi(x)$ if and only if there exists $\alpha \in \mathcal{N}(\{m \mid \mathcal{M} \models \varphi(m)\})$ such that for all $m \in \alpha$, $\mathcal{M} \models \psi(m)$.

GQ-system is the usual system of the first-order logic augmented with the following axioms for "most".

Definition 6 (GQ-system). The inference rules of GQ-system comprise the usual rules for the first-order logic with the following axioms.

A1. $\exists x\varphi(x)$
A2. $\forall x(\varphi(x) \Leftrightarrow \sigma(x))$ *and* $\nabla x\varphi(x) : \psi(x)$ *imply* $\nabla x\sigma(x) : \psi(x)$
A3. $\nabla x\varphi(x) : \psi(x)$ *and* $\forall x(\varphi(x) \wedge \psi(x) \Rightarrow \sigma(x))$ *imply* $\nabla x\varphi(x) : \sigma(x)$
A4. $\nabla x\varphi(x) : \psi(x)$ *implies* $\neg\nabla x\varphi(x) : \neg\psi(x)$
A5-1. $\forall x(\varphi(x) \Rightarrow \psi(x))$ *implies* $\nabla x\varphi(x) : \psi(x)$
A5-2. $\nabla x\varphi(x) : \psi(x)$ *implies* $\exists x(\varphi(x) \wedge \psi(x))$

A1 is the existential import, which is not imposed in [12]. Although A5-2 originally takes the following form in [12]: $\nabla x \varphi(x) : \psi(x) \Rightarrow (\exists x \varphi(x) \Rightarrow \exists x(\varphi(x) \wedge \psi(x)))$, we do not need the condition $\exists x \varphi(x)$ because of the existential import A1. (Similarly for A4.)

A3 can be divided into the following two axioms, which are more appropriate for our discussion below.

Lemma 1. A3 *is equivalent to the following pair of* A3-1 *and* A3-2.

A3-1. $\nabla x \varphi(x) : \psi(x)$ *and* $\forall x(\psi(x) \Rightarrow \sigma(x))$ *imply* $\nabla x \varphi(x) : \sigma(x)$
A3-2. $\nabla x \varphi(x) : \psi(x)$ *implies* $\nabla x \varphi(x) : (\varphi(x) \wedge \psi(x))$

Proof. We first show that A3-1 and A3-2 are derived by using A3. To show A3-1 is derived, assume $\nabla x \varphi(x) : \psi(x)$ and $\forall x(\psi(x) \Rightarrow \sigma(x))$. From $\forall x(\psi(x) \Rightarrow \sigma(x))$, we obtain $\forall x(\varphi(x) \wedge \psi(x) \Rightarrow \sigma(x))$, which implies $\nabla x \varphi(x) : \sigma(x)$ by A3 together with the assumption $\nabla x \varphi(x) : \psi(x)$. To show A3-2 is derived, assume $\nabla x \varphi(x) : \psi(x)$. Then, together with a tautology $\forall x(\varphi(x) \wedge \psi(x) \Rightarrow \varphi(x) \wedge \psi(x))$, we obtain $\nabla x \varphi(x) : (\varphi(x) \wedge \psi(x))$ by A3.

We next show that A3 is derived by using A3-1 and A3-2. Assume $\nabla x \varphi(x) : \psi(x)$ and $\forall x(\varphi(x) \wedge \psi(x) \Rightarrow \sigma(x))$. From $\nabla x \varphi(x) : \psi(x)$, we obtain $\nabla x \varphi(x) : (\varphi(x) \wedge \psi(x))$ by A3-2, which implies $\nabla x \varphi(x) : \sigma(x)$ by A3-1 together with the other assumption $\forall x(\varphi(x) \wedge \psi(x) \Rightarrow \sigma(x))$. ∎

We show that our Euler diagrammatic system is a diagrammatic representation of a subsystem of GQ-system by restricting the language of GQ-system. To show this, a concrete system of Euler diagrams must be set, and hence, we investigate a translation from a fragment of GQ-system into our Euler diagrammatic system based on [9,20], whose inference rules comprises only of the unification rule for two diagrams and the deletion rule for diagrammatic objects.

We restrict the formulas of GQ-system to the following syllogistic forms.

Definition 7 (Syllogistic GQ-formulas). Syllogistic GQ-formulas are GQ-formulas of the following forms, where A, B, A_i are unary predicate symbols.

$B(a);$ $\neg B(a);$ $\forall x(A(x) \Rightarrow B(x));$ $\forall x(A(x) \Rightarrow \neg B(x))$;
$\exists x(A_1(x) \wedge \cdots \wedge A_n(x));$ $\nabla x A(x) : B(x);$ $\nabla x A(x) : \neg B(x).$

We concentrate on the syllogistic fragment of GQ-system, that is, we consider the logical consequence between syllogistic GQ-formulas. Then, the syllogistic fragment of GQ-system is represented by our Euler diagrammatic system. Next, we discuss the translation from the syllogistic fragment of GQ-system into our Euler diagrammatic system. Because the correspondence of the part with first-order logic and our Euler diagrammatic system was established in [9,20], we concentrate on the part of the generalized quantifier "most".

We first define the translation from the syllogistic GQ-formulas into our Euler diagrams. In [9,20], each Euler diagram is specified in terms of its inclusion and exclusion relations holding between points and circles, and each Euler diagram is regarded symbolically as the set of inclusion and exclusion relations that hold in the diagram. Thus, we describe the translation from the GQ-formulas into the inclusion and exclusion relations between a point and a circle, as well as between two circles.

Definition 8. The translation from the syllogistic GQ-formulas into the inclusion and exclusion relations that hold for Euler diagrams is defined as follows.

- $B(t)$, where t is a constant or a variable, is translated into:

- $\neg B(t)$ is translated into:

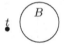

- $\forall x(A(x) \Rightarrow B(x))$ is translated into:

- $\forall x(A(x) \Rightarrow \neg B(x))$ is translated into:

- $\nabla x A(x) : B(x)$ is translated into:

- $\nabla x A(x) : \neg B(x)$ is translated into:

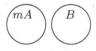

- $\exists x(A_1(x) \wedge \cdots \wedge A_n(x))$ is translated into the part of a diagram, where point x is located at the intersection region of circles $A_1, \ldots, A_n$.

Based on the translation from the syllogistic GQ-formulas into our Euler diagrams, as defined above, we show that the translation of the GQ-axioms are provable in our Euler diagrammatic system.

Proposition 1 (Translation of GQ-axioms). *Translations of GQ-axioms in the syllogistic fragment are provable with Euler diagrams.*

Proof.

A1. $\exists x A(x)$ is obtained from the axiom for "most" of our Euler diagrammatic system by deleting the circle mA.

A2. $\forall x(A(x) \Leftrightarrow C(x))$ *and* $\nabla x A(x) : B(x)$ *implies* $\nabla x C(x) : B(x)$
This axiom is trivial because $\forall x(A(x) \Leftrightarrow C(x))$ means that circles A and C, as well as mA and mC, are the same.

A3-1. $\nabla x A(x) : B(x)$ *and* $\forall x(B(x) \Rightarrow C(x))$ *imply* $\nabla x A(x) : C(x)$

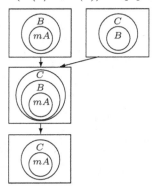

A3-2. $\nabla x A(x) : B(x)$ *implies* $\nabla x A(x) : (A(x) \wedge B(x))$

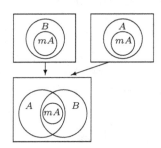

Here, the top-right diagram is obtained from the axiom for "most" by deleting point x. Although the formula $\nabla x A(x) : (A(x) \wedge B(x))$ is not syllogistic, we regard it as the pair of formulas $\nabla x A(x) : B(x)$ and $\nabla x A(x) : C(x)$ that are not semantically equivalent, but this does not matter for our syntactic translation.

A4. $\nabla x A(x) : B(x)$ *implies* $\neg \nabla x A(x) : \neg B(x)$
This axiom is equivalent to: $\nabla x A(x) : B(x)$ *and* $\nabla x A(x) : \neg B(x)$ *implies the contradiction*, which holds in our Euler diagrammatic system:

and are the contradiction, that is, they cannot be expressed in a single diagram, by Definition 1.

A5-1. $\forall x(A(x) \Rightarrow B(x))$ *implies* $\nabla x A(x) : B(x)$

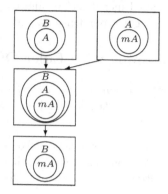

Here, the top-right diagram is obtained from the axiom for "most" by deleting point x.

A5-2. $\nabla x A(x) : B(x)$ *implies* $\exists x(A(x) \wedge B(x))$

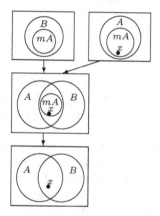

Conversely, by defining a translation of Euler diagrams into GQ-formulas, the translation of the axiom for "most" of Euler diagrammatic system is also provable in GQ-system. Let us examine the following axiom for "most".

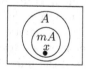

This diagram is specified by the following three relations: x *is inside* A, mA *is inside* A, and x *is inside* mA. The first two of them correspond to the following formulas: $\exists x A(x)$, which is the axiom **A1** of GQ-system, and $\nabla x A(x) : A(x)$, which is obtained from the tautology $\forall x(A(x) \Rightarrow A(x))$ by **A5-1**. Although there is no formula expressing x *is inside* mA in GQ-system, the above translation is sufficient because we restrict our language to the syllogistic fragment, where sentences of the form x *is inside* mA neither appear in the premises nor the conclusion in question.

However, the linking, i.e., disjunction in Euler diagrams destroys the simple correspondence between our Euler diagrams and GQ-formulas. Hence, we leave an investigation on the full correspondence for future work.

5   Defeasible Reasoning with Euler Diagrams

In this section, we further examine another well-known example called the Nixon diamond and investigate skeptical and credulous strategies in defeasible reasoning.

Example 2 (Nixon diamond). Assume that "Nixon (n) is both Republican (R) and Quaker (Q)", "Most Republicans are not Pacifists (P)", and "Most Quakers are Pacifists". This knowledge is represented by DI-net as follows.

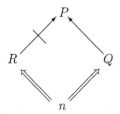

In our Euler diagrams, by unifying the given knowledge, we obtain the following diagram $\mathcal{D}$ in Fig. 2, which corresponds to the above DI-net. As seen in diagram $\mathcal{D}$, the position of n is not uniquely determined, and hence, Nixon may or may not be a Pacifist.

Thus far, our framework essentially represents *standard logic* with the generalized quantifier "most", and we derive the most general diagram, where all possibilities with respect to the position of a point are retained with linking thereof. In the literature of defeasible reasoning studies, this reasoning strategy is called the *skeptical strategy*. Another strategy may also be investigated in which a point is regarded as typical and one of the positions thereof is fixed among the appropriate regions of "most" if no exceptional information appears. This strategy is called the *credulous strategy*. To implement the credulous strategy in our Euler diagrammatic framework, we have two options:

1. Link-elimination rule: From a given diagram, we can choose a point labeled by t located in a region of "most" mA, and delete all other points labeled by t as well as links associated with those points.
2. Point fixing unification rule: When there are several possibilities for the location of the point t in an application of the unification rule for two diagrams, we choose one of the possible locations that is in a region of "most" mA, and we place t in that chosen location.

By appropriately applying (1) Link-elimination rule after each application of the usual unification rule, option (2) Point fixing unification rule can be simulated. Hence, we investigate (1).

At the proof construction level, the following options are available.

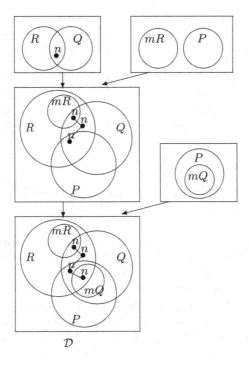

Fig. 2. Nixon example

1-1. We apply Link-elimination rule only at the end of a proof.

1-2. We apply Link-elimination rule anywhere in a proof.

If we allow the application of Link-elimination rule anywhere (1-2), we may be led into a contradiction even if the given knowledge is consistent. For example, assume that we have the additional knowledge "Most Republicans are not Quakers" in Example 2. Then, in the immediately preceding diagram of $\mathcal{D}$ in Fig. 2, if we fix point n to that located in mR (cf. the following diagram $\mathcal{D}_2$), we may be led to the contradiction to unify "Most R are not Q," although the given knowledge is consistent as a whole. Thus it seems appropriate to restrict applications of Link-elimination rule to the final step of a proof (1-1).

By applying Link-elimination rule to diagram $\mathcal{D}$ in Fig. 2, we obtain one of the following two diagrams $\mathcal{D}_1$ and $\mathcal{D}_2$, where we can conclude "Nixon is a Pacifist" from $\mathcal{D}_1$, and "Nixon is not a Pacifist" from $\mathcal{D}_2$.

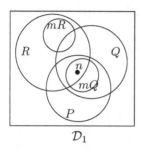 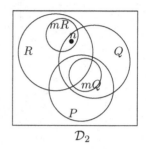

$\mathcal{D}_1$ $\mathcal{D}_2$

In view of DI-net, this illustrates the problem of how we read DI-net, which is formally defined through the notion of the *extension* of a path in a DI-net, cf. [5,6].

Our strategy of applying Link-elimination rule only at the final step of a proof accords with the notion of *normal proof*, as defined in [18], where a normal proof is described as consisting of the construction of a maximal diagram with unifying given premises, and following extraction of a conclusion from the unified diagram. As discussed in [18], from a cognitive standpoint, a maximal diagram may not be comprehensible or manageable due to its complexity. This also applies to our strategy, where the linking of points usually makes a diagram complex. Thus, from a cognitive viewpoint, (2) Point fixing unification rule may be more appropriate and effective wherein we fix the position of a point arbitrarily at every step of unifying diagrams without retaining all possibilities.

6   Conclusion

By using the generalized quantifier "most" in [12], we introduced an Euler diagrammatic system for defeasible reasoning. Our system was obtained by introducing the circle mA representing "most A" inside the circle A for every A and hence, applied uniformly to any well-established Euler and Venn diagrammatic systems. We showed that our Euler diagrammatic system is a diagrammatic representation of the syllogistic fragment of the system of the generalized quantifier "most" by defining a translation based on [9,20]. We further investigated skeptical and credulous strategies, which have been discussed in the literature on defeasible reasoning studies, in our Euler diagrammatic system. The credulous strategy can be implemented using Link-elimination rule in our Euler diagrammatic system.

The trade-off between the expressive power and the cognitive clarity of diagrams is often noted. In general, to increase their expressive power by introducing various conventional devices, the cognitive clarity of the diagrams decrease. The expressive power of a graphical representation such as DI-net is generally high, and information on contradiction and indeterminacy can be expressed in a single graph. Thus, to read a given graph, it is required that the paths that are in conflict and the nodes that are reachable must be formally defined by using, for example, the notion of the *extension* of a path in [5,6]. By contrast, although the expressive power of our basic Euler diagrams is limited, they have cognitive clarity. In our basic Euler diagrams, the conflict in DI-net can be classified into two groups. One relates to the usual contradiction in the sense of the standard logic, and it cannot be expressible using our Euler diagrams because of the geometrical constraints regarding circles. The other conflict stems from indeterminacy, that is, there exists two possibilities to be or not to be, and it is not a contradiction and can be expressed by linking between points in our Euler diagrams.

References

1. Chapman, P., Stapleton, G., Delaney, A.: On the expressiveness of second-order spider diagrams. J. Vis. Lang. Comput. **24**(5), 327–349 (2013)
2. Gabbay, D.M., Hogger, C.J., Robinson, J.A., Nute, D. (eds.): Handbook of Logic in Artificial Intelligence and Logic Programming Volume 3: Nonmonotonic Reasoning and Uncertain Reasoning. Oxford University Press, Oxford (1994)
3. Gabbay, D.M., Woods, J. (eds.): Handbook of the History of Logic Volume 8: The Many Valued and Nonmonotonic Turn in Logic. Elsevier, Amsterdam (2007)
4. Hammer, E., Shin, S.: Euler's visual logic. Hist. Philos. Log. **19**, 1–29 (1998)
5. Horty, J.F.: Some direct theories of nonmonotonic inheritance. In: Gabbay, D., Hogger, C., Robinson, J.A. (eds.) Handbook of Logic in Artificial Intelligence and Logic Programming, vol. 3, pp. 111–187. Oxford University Press, Oxford (1994)
6. Horty, J.F., Thomason, R.H., Touretzky, D.S.: A skeptical theory of inheritance in nonmonotonic semantic networks. Artif. Intell. **42**(2–3), 311–348 (1990)
7. Howse, J., Stapleton, G., Taylor, J.: Spider diagrams. LMS J. Comput. Math. **8**, 145–194 (2005)
8. Mineshima, K., Okada, M., Takemura, R.: A diagrammatic inference system with Euler circles. J. Logic Lang. Inform. **21**(3), 365–391 (2012)
9. Mineshima, K., Okada, M., Takemura, R.: Two types of diagrammatic inference systems: natural deduction style and resolution style. In: Goel, A.K., Jamnik, M., Narayanan, N.H. (eds.) Diagrams 2010. LNCS (LNAI), vol. 6170, pp. 99–114. Springer, Heidelberg (2010). https://doi.org/10.1007/978-3-642-14600-8_12
10. Reiter, R.: A logic for default reasoning. Artif. Intell. **13**(1–2), 81–132 (1980)
11. Sato, Y., Mineshima, K.: Human reasoning with proportional quantifiers and its support by diagrams. In: Jamnik, M., Uesaka, Y., Elzer Schwartz, S. (eds.) Diagrams 2016. LNCS (LNAI), vol. 9781, pp. 123–138. Springer, Cham (2016). https://doi.org/10.1007/978-3-319-42333-3_10
12. Schlechta, K.: Defaults as generalized quantifiers. J. Log. Comput. **5**(4), 473–494 (1995)
13. Shimojima, A.: Semantic Properties of Diagrams and Their Cognitive Potentials. CSLI Publications, Stanford (2015)
14. Shin, S.-J.: The Logical Status of Diagrams. Cambridge University Press, Cambridge (1994)
15. Stapleton, G., Howse, J., Taylor, J., Thompson, S.: The expressiveness of spider diagrams. J. Log. Comput. **14**(6), 857–880 (2004)
16. Stapleton, G., Taylor, J., Thompson, S., Howse, J.: The expressiveness of spider diagrams augmented with constants. J. Vis. Lang. Comput. **20**(1), 30–49 (2009)

17. Swoboda, N., Allwein, G.: Heterogeneous reasoning with Euler/Venn diagrams containing named constants and FOL. Electron. Notes Theor. Comput. Sci. **134**, 153–187 (2005)
18. Takemura, R.: Towards a proof theory for heterogeneous logic combining sentences and diagrams. In: Chapman, P., Stapleton, G., Moktefi, A., Perez-Kriz, S., Bellucci, F. (eds.) Diagrams 2018. LNCS (LNAI), vol. 10871, pp. 607–623. Springer, Cham (2018). https://doi.org/10.1007/978-3-319-91376-6_55
19. Takemura, R.: Completeness of an Euler diagrammatic system with constant and existential points. J. Hum. Sci. Nihon Univ. **19**(1–2), 23–40 (2013)
20. Takemura, R.: Proof theory for reasoning with Euler diagrams: a logic translation and normalization. Stud. Log. **101**(1), 157–191 (2013)

Empirical Studies and Cognition

Event Unit Analysis: A Methodology for Anticipating Processing Demands of Complex Animated Diagrams

Richard Lowe[1,2(✉)] and Jean-Michel Boucheix[1]

[1] Université Bourgogne Franche-Comté (LEAD-CNRS), Dijon, France
r.k.lowe@curtin.edu.ac
[2] Curtin University, Perth, Australia

Abstract. The addition of explicit, faithfully represented dynamics to diagrams that depict complex behaviours may negatively affect viewers' information processing and prejudice their comprehension of the referent subject matter. This presentation introduces a methodological tool for identifying and characterizing likely sources of the negative consequences that can arise from an animated diagram's dynamics. *Event Unit Analysis* offers a systematic way to document these sources so that they can be minimized by implementing changes in how animations are designed. This analytical methodology underlies the development of a novel animation design approach that significantly improves viewer comprehension over that obtained using conventionally designed animations. The origins of event unit analysis in the theoretical framework of the Animation Processing Model and its development as a tool for analyzing increasingly sophisticated dynamics are described. Its potential breadth of its application and opportunities for further elaboration are illustrated through two contrasting types of content.

Keywords: Animated diagrams · Dynamics · Analysis · Comprehension · Design

1 Introduction

Before the advent of digital technology, animated diagrams were a relative rarity. This was not only because the production of such animations was a slow, labour intensive, highly specialized and costly endeavor but also because of the various barriers that existed to their dissemination. However, the situation is now very different due to the ready availability of sophisticated graphics processing technologies and the ubiquity of internet access. It is therefore not surprising that traditional static diagrams are increasingly accompanied by their supposedly superior animated counterparts. This trend reflects a widespread conviction that diagrams will be more effective if they are animated rather than static, especially if they are to represent dynamic subject matter (but see [1]). Animated diagrams allow the subject matter's dynamics to be represented directly (not just indirectly, as is the only option with static diagrams [2]). In contrast to what is required

© Springer Nature Switzerland AG 2020
A.-V. Pietarinen et al. (Eds.): Diagrams 2020, LNAI 12169, pp. 307–322, 2020.
https://doi.org/10.1007/978-3-030-54249-8_24

for static depictions, viewers of an animation are not obliged to infer the referent subject matter's dynamics. Because an animated diagram provides an explicit (rather than implicit) portrayal of dynamics, it relieves viewers from having to perform the potentially error-prone 'mental animation' processes that are required to interpret a corresponding static depiction [3]. However, research has shown that despite this potential advantage over static diagrams, animations actually pose their own distinctive information processing challenges for viewers [4]. Ironically, these challenges can arise from the very same dynamics that are supposed to make animations intrinsically superior to static diagrams.

The dynamics-related processing problems viewers can encounter tend to be particularly severe for conventionally-designed animations that faithfully depict the dynamics of complex subject matter (in contrast to the animations targeted in [1]). If dynamics can seriously compromise viewer processing, it is important that animated diagrams are designed to minimize their potentially negative consequences. An essential first step in devising such designs is to identify and characterize likely sources of such problems. However, this is not a trivial task because these sources can be subtle and elusive. This paper presents a methodological tool that provides a systematic approach for analyzing complex dynamic subject matter in order to expose possible dynamics-related processing challenges. *Event Unit Analysis* is a methodology that can be used to help devise novel animation design approaches that support more effective viewer processing. In the next section, we consider the nature of animated diagrams (in particular, those depicting complex subject matter) and discuss how their dynamics may impede proper processing of the presented information.

2 Animation Dynamics and Processing

A common feature of conventionally-designed animated diagrams that portray complex systems is the presence of substantial simultaneous activity. Typically, the animated display simultaneously depicts a varied assortment of system components, with each of these components being engaged in its own individual set of behaviours. Because they are diagrammatic portrayals, these components are represented by abstract graphic entities rather than by veridical depictions. In contrast, the dynamics associated with these components are almost always represented with a high degree of realism that faithfully reflects the behaviours present in the referent content. We use the term 'Comprehensive' to characterize such conventional animation designs. The behaviours that are presented in animations can be broadly classified into three main types [4]: *transitions* (change in the presence of an entity, i.e., appearance or disappearance), *motions* (change in the position of an entity, i.e., rotations between positions or translations between locations), and *transformations* (change in the form of an entity, i.e., shape, size, colour, etc.). In some animations, just one of these behaviour types may be exhibited whereas in others, different types may occur within a given animation (sometimes even with respect to a single graphic entity).

Much of our previous research has investigated how viewers process a conventionally-designed animated diagram portraying the inner workings of a traditional upright piano (e.g., [5, 6]). Figure 1a shows a frame taken from that research material, with the mechanism's components identified in Fig. 1b. This comprehensive piano animation illustrates how several varied instances of a specific type of behaviour (motions) can occur simultaneously across multiple components of a system. When the piano key is depressed, a set of events is initiated that ultimately causes the corresponding hammer to strike a string and thereby produce a musical note.

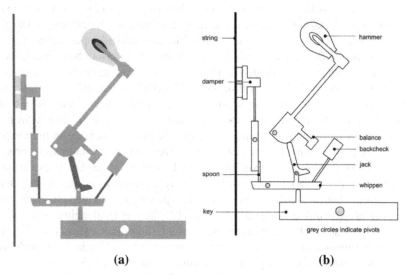

Fig. 1. (a) Frame from conventionally-designed ('Comprehensive') version of piano animation. (b) Identification of piano mechanism components.

Despite its sophisticated functionality, the piano mechanism consists essentially of a range of simple levers that transmit action throughout the system by rotating about their respective pivots. In common with most mechanical devices, the only type of dynamics involved in this entire system is *motion*; there are no transitions (entities are not added or removed) or transformations (entities do not undergo any intrinsic change). The behaviours exhibited during the piano mechanism's operation take place in a coordinated way across the system. These dynamic changes occur simultaneously or in a rapid cascade and involve multiple components. This means that on any occasion during the animation's time course, the viewer is faced with a varied array of graphic entities performing different actions in locations that are spread throughout the display area. For example, when the key is depressed, the key-head moves clockwise, the whippen anticlockwise (while carrying the jack upwards with it), the damper clockwise, and the hammer anticlockwise. In addition, each of these movements occurs to a different extent – the hammer's movement is greatest, that of the jack is least, and the other entities move to intermediate extents between these extremes.

2.1 Processing Challenges

For viewers to have any chance of comprehending how the piano mechanism functions as a whole, at the very least they would need to keep track of all these varied and widely dispersed behaviours. However, that is only part of the story. They would also have to follow the flow of causality throughout the system and determine the dynamic interrelationships between the mechanism's different subsystems that allow it to function as required. An example of such interrelationships can be found with the reciprocal action of the damper relative to the hammer that (i) un-damps the string so it is free to vibrate just before the hammer strikes it and (ii) damps out the string's vibration when the note is to finish sounding. Similar contingent relationships occur for other components of the piano system and these alter during the time course of the mechanism's operational cycle. All in all, this animation confronts viewers with a rich set of multifarious behaviours, each of which makes an indispensable contribution to the referent system's overall functionality.

As theorized in the Animation Processing Model [7] a crucially important initial task for a viewer attempting to comprehend the referent subject matter is to extract all of the functionally relevant information offered by the animation. The APM posits that comprehension of the subject matter depicted in a comprehensive animation (e.g., understanding how a piano mechanism works) involves the viewer's internal construction of a high quality mental model from the externally presented display. If extraction of functionally relevant information from this display is deficient, mental model quality (and thus comprehension) will be compromised. A perception-oriented characterization of what is involved in this task suggests that is likely to be very challenging, especially for domain novices who lack background knowledge about how pianos work. The challenges arise from the mismatch between (i) how a conventionally-designed comprehensive version of the piano animation presents its information and (ii) the capacities of the human information processing system (particularly with respect to how it deals with dynamic visual stimuli).

Human visual perception of detailed information is handled by foveal vision while more general aspects, such as the broader visual context, are allocated to peripheral vision [8]. Foveal processing plays a crucial role in a viewer's extraction of functionally relevant information from an animation. It relies on a series of short, highly localized eye fixations, each of which take a finites amount of processing time and encompasses a very limited area only. Characterization of a multi-entity visual display results from the cumulative effect of these successive individual fixations. Because the scope of each of these fixations is small relative to the total visual field, this processing needs to be highly selective. In the transient context of complex dynamic displays with substantial simultaneity (such as the comprehensive piano animation), this constraint can be problematic. The trouble is that while the viewer is fixating on one specific small region of the total display in order to collect information about (say) a particular entity and its behaviour, important things are also happening in other regions of the display that are not being fixated. An unfortunate consequence of foveal vision therefore is that simultaneously occurring events occurring outside of the current fixation area largely escape the viewer's notice and so are not internalized for further processing. The net effect is that viewers can miss out on much of the information necessary for building a high quality mental model of the referent subject matter. Our empirical investigations of learning from the comprehensive piano animation confirm that the quality of mental models developed is indeed severely compromised (e.g., [9]).

2.2 Event Unit Analysis

In recent years, researchers in the fields of educational psychology and multimedia learning have been particularly active in seeking ways to improve the instructional effectiveness of animations. They have investigated various types of interventions intended to support better learner processing of conventionally-designed comprehensive animations [10]. These approaches included the provision of user-control over an animation's presentation regime with respect to playing speed, direction, continuity, etc., segmentation of the animation's time course into smaller temporal chunks separated by pauses, visual cueing of important information using techniques such as colour coding and highlighting, and the addition of ancillary learning activities to be undertaken by learners as they studied the animated presentation. In an effort to improve comprehension of the piano mechanism, we applied a range of these approaches to the comprehensive animated version of this subject matter. However, in common with the findings of other researchers who tried such interventions across many different types of content, there was little or no improvement in performance scores. In the case of the piano animation, we interpreted these less-than-impressive results as indicating that our participants had been unable to build high quality mental models of the mechanism's functionality.

In an effort to characterize possible reasons for the lack of success of these interventions, we considered how it might be possible to expose the processing challenges that were not being effectively ameliorated. We hypothesized that the simultaneous spatially distributed presentation of multiple entities exhibiting a variety of behaviours could be a major contributor to these challenges. It seemed that in order to better understand the processing implications of this situation, it needed to be systematically documented and unpacked. To tackle this issue, we invoked a fundamental aspect of the Animation Processing Model – the concept of an *event unit*. An event unit is a notional composite consisting of an entity and its associated behaviour. A distinctive feature of the APM approach to characterizing an animation is that it does not treat an entity in isolation from its dynamics. Application of findings from research on visual perception (e.g., [11]) to animation processing suggests that dynamics exert a powerful influence on how viewers process an animation's constituent entities. Rather than being an independent attribute with respect to processing, an entity's dynamics (i.e., its spatiotemporal characteristics) seem to be intimately bound up with its other properties (i.e., its visuospatial characteristics). For example, in the piano animation, we attribute viewers' tendency to notice the hammer but neglect the jack not only to their differences in appearance (size, distinctiveness of shape, etc.), but also to differences in the extent of their respective movements.

Event unit analysis provides a systematic method for setting out the situation with dynamic subject matter that exhibits a substantial degree of simultaneity. It should be noted that this technique targets the dynamic subject matter *itself*, not a particular representation of that content. Figure 2 illustrates how we initially applied this diagrammatic approach to our comprehensive piano mechanism animation. Each entity row of the diagram represents a particular series of event units that contribute to the overall operation of the mechanism (with segments denoting individual event units for the entity concerned). For example, the damper entity first swings away from the string, then pauses (a null event unit since dynamics are absent), and finally swings back to the string. The

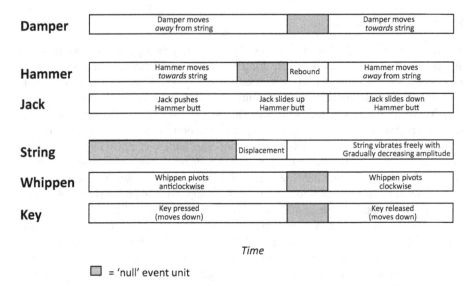

Time

☐ = 'null' event unit

Fig. 2. Event unit analysis for piano mechanism operation (initial version). The time course of the mechanism's operation can be divided into three successive stages – (1) Strike, (2) Rebound, and (3) Reset.

horizontal time axis specifies the duration of each of these event units within an operational cycle. Because this analysis assumes depiction via a comprehensive animation, the relative durations of the event units faithfully reflect that of the referent mechanism itself. For example, the duration of the hammer's rebound is much briefer than the time it takes to reach the string after a key press.

A most revealing aspect of this analysis is the way it sets out how different event units coincide in time (i.e., the degree of simultaneity that a viewer must cope with). An APM-based interpretation of such analysis suggests that higher levels of simultaneity in a display would tend to impair viewer extraction of functionally relevant information. This is because of the increased competition for the viewer's visual attention associated with the co-presence of multiple event units.

Circumstances during the time course of a comprehensive animation where substantial competition for attention is likely to exist can be identified by examining the event unit analysis shown in Fig. 2. For example, simultaneity is greater at the beginning of the mechanism's operation (Stage 1, 'Strike') than midway through (Stage 2, 'Rebound'). This indicated by the degree of coincidence amongst event units (if we exclude null event units from consideration). Our research results indicate that viewers are most successful in extracting information about the initial hammer event unit but far less successful in characterizing some others (especially the jack). This finding is consistent with the hammer winning the competition for attention by a large margin when it and the jack move simultaneously. However, to fully appreciate what is at work here, we need to consider not only the event unit analysis diagram, but also the visuospatial and spatiotemporal characteristics of the individual event units it documents. In particular, the combined effect of the hammer's large size, distinctive shape and extensive movement make it far more perceptually salient than its accompanying components so it out-competes them for the viewer's limited visual attention. With the jack, the situation is reversed. The fact that it is a tiny, visually unremarkable entity that moves only slightly helps to explain why viewers tend to extract very little information about this component.

Some care is required in interpreting the likely implications of this event unit analysis. If we ignore the null event units (i.e., those for which nothing happens), the simultaneity decreases somewhat after the initial operational phase, from five coincident event units down to just three. So, any competition for attention that occurs is between fewer event units. Despite what might be expected, viewers actually do worse in characterizing this second Rebound stage of the mechanism's operation. Most of our viewers completely missed what was happening then. Part of the explanation may be that this intermediate stage is very brief indeed compared with the initial and final stages. Consequently, there is simply insufficient time available to process the presented information adequately. Further, the relatively small movement of the rebounding hammer and the inconspicuousness of the jack suggest that a perceptual salience effect may increase the likelihood of these aspects being overlooked.

2.3 Design Response to an Event Unit Analysis

The event unit analysis discussed above is no more than an initial attempt to provide a systematic way of identifying and characterizing what processing challenges viewers may face with a comprehensive animation containing substantial simultaneity. Despite its limitations (which we discuss in more detail later), this tool helped us to ask some fundamental questions about conventionally designed animated diagrams. One of these concerned an unchallenged design assumption about how these animations should represent their subject matter. We noted earlier that, as is the case for static diagrams, it is standard practice for animated diagrams to use highly abstracted depictions (simple lines, geometric shapes, etc.) to represent the referent entities. In effect, this abstraction is equivalent to performing major manipulations on the *visuospatial* properties of the original referent and so constitutes a massive departure from reality. However, there is no corresponding level of manipulation applied to the *spatiotemporal* properties. Rather, the dynamics of entities depicted in such animated diagrams tend to closely mirror those of the original referents. In other words, there is a high degree of behavioural realism (c.f. [12]).

This inconsistency in the level of manipulation of visuospatial and spatiotemporal properties deserves close consideration. Extensive *visuospatial* manipulation is such an entrenched part of diagrammatic practice that its utility is rarely questioned. It has long been accepted as an effective way of making the subject matter more tractable to viewers. A notable example is the use of simple symbols and regularized layouts in electronic circuit diagrams. The question then arises as to why when dynamics are introduced into a diagram, it is not equally acceptable to implement a similar level of *spatiotemporal* manipulation. One probable reason is that this would negate the presumed advantage of animated over static diagrams, that is, the capacity to represent a referent's behaviours directly, explicitly, and accurately. Nevertheless, one is entitled to wonder why viewers who are so adept in dealing with extensive visuospatial manipulation would be unable to handle even a modest level of spatiotemporal manipulation.

We have seen that an animation's dynamics can be a two-edged sword, especially when a substantial degree of simultaneity is involved. Is it possible that some reduction in this simultaneity could benefit viewers by reducing wasteful competition for visual attention, thus allowing deeper, better processing of more of the information that needs to be internalized? Using the event unit analysis shown in Fig. 2 as our starting point, we devised a highly unconventional approach to animation design that was intended to test this possibility. A primary aim of the design was to reduce the level of simultaneity identified by the event unit analysis and so decrease competition for attention. Termed a 'Composition Approach', this design regime abandoned the slavish adherence to behavioural realism that characterizes conventional comprehensive animations. Instead of faithfully mirroring the referent's true dynamics by presenting multiple event units simultaneously, a staged approach was used. Our goal was to better align the animation's *external* presentation of information with the viewer's *internal* processing activities that are posited by the APM. The rationale for the graduated staging of information exposure was that some temporal spacing-out of event unit presentation should decrease competition for attention and thus reduce the likelihood that the viewer would miss crucial information. This approach was implemented through a design in which functionally interacting event units were progressively exposed in a pairwise fashion. This presentation regime followed a sequence that was carefully constructed to be consistent with the progress of causal chains throughout the mechanism. In one sense, this manipulation involved a quite drastic departure from the referent's actual dynamics and thus had the potential to severely disrupt comprehension. However, the sequencing was carefully designed to facilitate the progressive, cumulative, hierarchical internal composition processes hypothesized by the APM to be necessary for building high quality mental models. Subsequent empirical testing of the composition approach against the conventionally designed piano animation confirmed that it indeed resulted in somewhat improved mental models [13]. This result suggested that this initial version of event unit analysis did provide some useful insights about how to design more effective animated diagrams.

3   Elaborating and Refining Event Unit Analysis

Despite the statistically significant improvements in mental model quality obtained by using a composition approach to animation design, the overall scores for this indicator of comprehension were nevertheless comparatively modest (around 50%). Clearly there were still considerable deficiencies in viewer understanding of the depicted subject matter, despite the animation's increased net effectiveness. Participant responses indicated that several specific aspects of piano mechanism's operation remained poorly understood. Unfortunately, these aspects were also ones of crucial importance to a piano's functionality. The jack is a particularly illuminating case in point. It plays a vital but subtle role in ensuring that the hammer is able to repeat its striking action reliably, at the required speed, and in a musically-appropriate way.

In an effort to identify reasons why comprehension of aspects such as the jack's behaviours showed little improvement from a comprehensive to a compositional design, further consideration was given to the event unit analysis. A number of observations were made. First, the jack is the only lever in the system that does not have a stationary pivot point. Instead, its pivot is attached to the whippen so that the jack rides with the whippen producing a composite motion that is intrinsically more complex than that of its neighbours. Second, the functionality of the jack varies across the time course of the piano's operation. To begin with, it produces a short, sharp impact that kicks the butt of the hammer so that the hammer's head is projected forcefully toward the string. Next, when the hammer first rebounds slightly from the string so its balance is caught by the backcheck, the jack's job is very different. In this case, its tip slides a little way along the curved surface of the hammer butt and fulfills an escapement function. Finally, when the mechanism resets, the jack's tip completes the journey back to its starting position by travelling along the rest of the hammer butt. By returning to this initial configuration, the jack is again readied to perform its role in the strike stage of the mechanism's operation. Compared with the behaviour of the mechanism's other components, the jack's dynamics are relatively complex and varied. In addition, it is the least perceptually salient of all the mechanism's components. These factors likely contributed to the persistently poor results for the jack (despite the use of a compositional animation design).

Revisiting our original event unit analysis (Fig. 2), we concluded that too little consideration had been given to the distinctive nature of the jack's visuospatial and spatiotemporal attributes. This can be appreciated by comparing the jack with another more typical component, such as the damper. As already indicated, the jack would have a considerably lower perceptual salience than the damper due to its size, shape and behaviour. This makes it less likely to receive viewer attention. However, even if the jack was to receive similar attention to the damper, its dynamics pose an additional processing challenge. The action of the damper during the (final) reset stage of operation is just the reverse of its action in the (initial) strike stage. These two actions could therefore be parsimoniously represented in the viewer's knowledge structure by a single event unit that runs forward for the strike stage and backwards during reset. However, the jack event units cannot be condensed in this manner and so must each be analyzed and internally represented on an individual basis. This suggest that the perceptual and cognitive processing required for the jack is likely more involved than for other components. Considered together with its low perceptual salience, it is perhaps unsurprising that viewers' processing of the jack event units remained inadequate.

We are currently investigating an expanded, finer-grained approach to event unit analysis that is designed to capture these process-related aspects more effectively. Our goal is to develop a principled and systematic basis for further refining the composition approach to animation design so that it takes more account of variations in the level of processing challenge posed by different types of event units. This more refined approach is exemplified by a re-consideration of the way the jack's dynamics were treated in the original event unit analysis. Rather than using just the single jack entity as the basis for analysis as was done originally, in the revised analysis it is characterized in terms of three separate event units. The rationale for this adjustment is that although there is only *one entity* involved, that single entity performs *three distinct behaviours*, each of which imposes its own processing demands.

We consider that such modification makes the revised event unit analysis more sensitive to the range of processing challenges that may be faced by viewers. Better detection of such potential challenges can allow additional improvements in animation design to be made that further support effective viewer processing. For example, adjustments to the degree of spatiotemporal manipulation applied could be made to ameliorate the excessive processing demands that would otherwise be imposed by certain event units. In the case of the jack, one response could be to depart from the uniformly applied pairwise presentation used in the original compositional design. In that approach, two different entities (with their dynamics) were presented at a time, regardless of the characteristics of the entities involved. A modified compositional design based on our revised approach to event unit analysis is being tested to determine its effectiveness relative to the original composition approach in terms of mental model quality.

In the next section, we discuss the need for further refinement of event unit analysis so it is better suited to the typical characteristics of biological subject matter (which are very different from those of the piano mechanism example) [14]. The biological example we consider is a pentapedal type of kangaroo locomotion commonly called 'punting' [15]. This unhurried gait is quite distinct from the kangaroo's much more energetic hopping motion and is typically used when the animal is grazing. Although there are some similarities to the piano example (e.g., they both involve cyclical dynamics), there are also several important differences that should be addressed.

3.1 Event Unit Analysis for a Biological System

In common with most biological systems, the dynamic changes exhibited during kangaroo punting involve not only motions but also extensive co-occurring transformations. Combinations of these two different types of dynamics are not typically found in mechanical systems such as the piano. From a perceptual perspective, the situation facing the viewer of a piano animation contains considerably less indeterminacy and variability than is present in a kangaroo punting animation. To appreciate the implications of that difference, consider someone who is unfamiliar with this type of kangaroo movement and has no expertise in the science of animal locomotion. Suppose such a person is set the task of developing a broad understanding of kangaroo punting solely by studying a conventionally-designed (behaviorally realistic) animation of this activity. This animation has no accompanying explanatory text or narration so its visual portrayal is the viewer's sole source of task-relevant information. The expected outcome is that the viewer will able to specify the key set of coordinated events involved in progressing the kangaroo during punting. In particular, this will entail knowing that the tail and fore-limbs form a tripod for supporting the body while the hind limbs are lifted off the ground and swung through to a new forward position. It is relatively straightforward for viewers to understand punting at this very general level, *provided* they have first internalized all the relevant information. However, actually obtaining this information from a conventionally-designed animation is far from straightforward for the type of viewer we are considering.

Without specialist background knowledge to provide top-down guidance for information extraction, such a viewer is largely dependent on bottom-up, perceptually-based processing of the display (c.f. [16]. Bottom-up extraction of the necessary information is demanding because of the challenges that the animation's veridical dynamics pose to visual perception. As with the conventionally-designed piano animation, these challenges are partly due to multiple behaviours that both take place simultaneously and are spread across the animation's display area. For example, the crucial relational information that needs to be extracted in order to determine the support function of the tail plus fore-limbs is widely separated in the display and so cannot be captured within the limited scope of a single foveal fixation. As already noted, this can severely prejudice proper information extraction because the information presented in behaviourally realistic animations is necessarily transitory. While foveal attention is being directed to events occurring in one of the two regions concerned (e.g., with respect to the fore-limbs), the finite time required to process information in that area precludes foveal processing of what is happening simultaneously in the second distant area (e.g., with respect to the tail).

Because it depicts a biological rather than mechanical system, a conventional animation of kangaroo punting introduces further aspects over and above this simultaneity-related issue that likely make it even more perceptually demanding than the piano animation. One of these is the absence of clear visual boundaries to mark where one entity ends and another begins. Because the internal structure of a kangaroo is not shown in the animation, viewers must infer where such inter-entity boundaries should be located. The resulting indeterminacy as to what constitutes an entity makes proper characterization of event units (as an entity plus its dynamics) more uncertain. This is potentially problematic in terms of the Animation Processing Model which posits event units as the fundamental raw material that viewers use for internal knowledge construction. A second additional issue likely to interfere with effective processing of such an animation is the co-presence of motion and transformation dynamics. Entities depicted in the corresponding piano animation are rigid and so exhibit only motion behaviour – their shapes remain unchanged as they perform various movements across space. This is not the case with the kangaroo animation because at the same time as its entities change their locations, their overall shapes are also changing (Fig. 3). In the next section, the likely perceptual impact of these differences will be considered along with its implications for mental model building.

Fig. 3. Initial state and early stage of kangaroo punting cycle. Note that the front legs both swing forward as a whole (motion) and change their shape (transformation). [17] gives a detailed account of how event unit analysis is implemented for this example.

3.2 Decomposition, Motion and Transformation

One of the original motivations for devising event unit analysis was to provide a basis for decomposing the array of simultaneous dynamic information presented in conventionally designed animations. Our research had indicated that a serious impediment to viewer processing was their inability to break down such animations appropriately in order to properly characterize functionally important event units. Considering the results of event unit analysis in light of the APM suggested that it may be too much to expect viewers to carry out such decomposition unaided. The compositional design that was developed as a consequence largely removed the need for viewers to perform this problematic decomposition activity. In effect, the pairwise sequence of event units used in our compositional animation offered viewers an accurately 'pre-decomposed' form of information presentation. This meant that their finite processing resources could then be mostly devoted to composition of event units into the superordinate order knowledge structures necessary for building high quality mental models. However, as already noted, this indiscriminate application of pairwise event unit scheduling proved not to be effective in all cases. It had little impact where entities such as the jack were concerned because of the more challenging processing involved. A somewhat analogous situation exists with kangaroo punting, but in this case one that is rather more extreme.

We have already noted that whereas the piano mechanism involves only motion dynamics, with kangaroo punting both motion and transformation occur simultaneously, essentially across all aspects of locomotion. Recent fundamental research [17] has revealed that viewers presented with animations displaying simultaneous motion and transformation tend to extract information about only one or other of these types of dynamics. That is, they satisfactorily process *either* the paths taken by entities *or* changes in the form of those entities but not both. Applying this finding to the case of viewers watching a conventional animation of kangaroo punting, it seems reasonable to expect that something similar may occur. This would be extremely problematic for processing, particularly when information needs to be extracted about the dynamics of entities that are widely separated in the display but closely related in a functional sense (as with the joint tripod support role of the fore-limbs and the tail in punting). The problem of viewers probably missing information about the non-fixated aspect of the tripod arrangement is further exacerbated by the fact that a proper appreciation of how this configuration is generated requires the viewer to extract information not only about the changes made in the positions of the fore-limbs and the tail, but also about the shape changes they undergo in order for this to take place. In a comprehensive animation of kangaroo punting, the two related sets of changes involved in this fore-limbs/tail example are of course embedded in a broader dynamic context. These other concurrent motions and transformations in the rest of the animal's body provide additional competition for the viewer's attention that likely further compromise effective information extraction (and hence mental model construction).

3.3 Extending and Implementing Event Unit Analysis

The kangaroo example is currently being used to further develop event unit analysis so it can help reveal the additional processing challenges posed when animations contain both motions and transformations. To this end, the analysis approach has been expanded so that it now assigns two rows to each entity – one for motion and one for transformation. As already noted, for a conventional animation of subject matter in which these two types of behaviour co-occur, viewer attention (and hence information extraction) would likely tend to favour one of them to the exclusion of the other. Assigning an extra 'transformation' row to each entity makes such potential problems readily apparent. However, some practical issues need to be addressed in order to implement this extended form of analysis effectively. The ultimate utility of event unit analysis as a tool for probing potential problems that may occur with animations of complex biological subject matter depends on how well it is able to characterize that content. An important part of this characterization is the determination of appropriate boundaries between different individual entities and events (i.e., where one entity or event ends and another begins).

Boundary determination is an on-going background activity that we all perform routinely during our everyday dealings with the world around us. The capacity to perform this visuospatial and spatiotemporal partitioning of our environment has been attributed to our recognition of discontinuities that signal the presence of inter-entity or inter-event boundaries [18]. More specifically, a boundary between two neighboring event units occurs where it is no longer possible for the viewer to predict (from the pre-existing trend exhibited by the first event unit) what will happen next. This form of boundary demarcation is equally applicable for motions, transformations, and transitions. Recognition of event boundaries is assumed to be based on one's extensive accumulated experience with our everyday surroundings – what it looks like and how it behaves. The effectiveness of event unit analysis also relies on proper determination of the boundaries that exist between entities and between events. However, in the types of cases we have considered here, the determining of appropriate boundaries cannot rest merely on the type of generally applicable knowledge that we invoke during our daily lives. Rather, specialist knowledge of the subject matter is required that allows boundaries to be recognized on the basis of discontinuities that are of functional relevance to the domain concerned. Consequently, non-experts cannot be expected to divide specialist dynamic content correctly into event units. For example, proper segmentation of the kangaroo's continuous body into separate *entities* with respect to the roles they play in punting relies on having a sophisticated understanding of both its underlying anatomy (skeleton, muscles, etc.) and the biomechanics of its locomotion. A similar level of advanced knowledge is needed to determine the boundaries that allow the kangaroo's complete punting cycle to be broken down into the individual *events* that contribute to this form of locomotion (and to distinguish motion contributions from transformation ones). The expanded version of event unit analysis as applied to biological systems includes explicit specification of the subject matter's component entities based on expert knowledge of functionally relevant boundaries.

Traditionally, much of the ultimate responsibility for the way animated diagrams end up presenting their subject matter has rested with the depiction's designer (typically a professional animator). Of course, that designer would first have been supplied with reference material (often including static diagrams and perhaps a video) provided by the person commissioning the animation. Almost without exception, when such designers are left to their own devices, they follow the conventional path of generating a behaviourally realistic animation of the content. When a subject matter expert checks the result, the dominant concern is with the overall accuracy of the depiction – especially, how faithfully it portrays the content's dynamics. Once any shortcomings in the draft animations have been corrected, the material is given approval for release. Unfortunately, as explained above, animations depicting complex subject matter that are designed using this conventional approach are likely to be relatively ineffective for viewers who are not experts in the depicted domain.

Compared with this conventional approach to design, developing animations on the basis of an event unit analysis demands much greater involvement on the part of the subject matter expert and far more collaboration with the designer. This is particularly the case for the type of biological content discussed here. Most designers are simply not equipped with the knowledge required to identify and characterize the entities and events that will be the basis for the analysis. Instead, this aspect of the work needs to be directed by someone who knows the content inside out so that boundaries can be determined on the basis of the specific functionality involved, rather than according to intuition and everyday background knowledge. An event unit analysis provides a mechanism for framing a productive and ongoing dialogue between designer and subject matter expert. It offers a shared basis for discussions about effective ways of presenting complex dynamic subject matter more effectively. A designer can contribute expertise in techniques of visualization to such discussions that complement the content expert's contributions regarding the subject matter itself.

A further application of event unit analysis is its use by researchers to stimulate new approaches to animation design that are potentially more effective than conventional designs [19]. This is the focus of an important thread in our own research which investigates possibilities for improving the match between how animations present their information and the distinctive characteristics of human information processing. This research aims to minimize the kind of non-productive application of viewers' processing resources that typically occurs with conventionally designed animations and re-direct those capacities to activities of central importance to building high quality mental models. To this end, a recently completed experiment studied a composite approach combining aspects of conventional and compositional animation designs in order to provide greater support for crucial mental model building processes.

4   Conclusion

The prevailing conventional approach to designing animated diagrams results in the privileging of behavioural realism over viewer information processing considerations. Because insufficient attention is given to analysis of the subject matter, particularly with respect to its dynamics, the posited advantages of these comprehensive animations too often remain unfulfilled. Event unit analysis offers those who develop animations of complex subject matter a novel and potentially powerful methodological tool for improving their designs. It provides a systematic way of identifying and characterizing aspects of a system that would likely pose processing problems for viewers if the subject matter was to be presented in a dynamically veridical manner. The insights available from an appropriate event unit analysis allow possible negative consequences that can arise from behaviorally realistic animations to be avoided by incorporating spatiotemporal modifications as a legitimate part of animation design. Departures from conventional presentation regimes, such as those implemented in a compositional design, can improve the match between how animations present their information and the capacities of human information processing. Although event unit analysis tends to be more straightforward for mechanical systems such as the piano, care is needed to ensure that the level of analysis applied is appropriately fine-grained for the individual entities being considered. It seems that biological systems such as the kangaroo are inherently more complex because of the co-presence of motion and transformation dynamics. Event unit analysis offers a structured way to promote closer collaboration between designers and subject matter experts that has potential to substantially improve the effectiveness of animated diagrams. In addition, it provides a tool for researchers who wish to explore new approaches to animation design that could result in viewers developing higher quality mental models of the depicted content. If taken up by these different communities, it also offers the possibility of helping to bridge the gaps that currently exist between those who conduct research on animations and the design practitioners who are responsible for producing them [20].

Acknowledgment. The authors sincerely thank David Edmonds, Veterinarian, for his expert advice regarding the biomechanics of kangaroo locomotion.

References

1. Bernay, S., Bétrancourt, M.: Does animation enhance learning? A meta-analysis. Comput. Educ. **101**, 150–167 (2016)
2. Cutting, J.E.: Representing motion in a static image: constraints and parallels in art, science, and popular culture. Perception **31**, 1165–1193 (2002)
3. Hegarty, M., Sims, V.K.: Individual differences in mental animation during mechanical reasoning. Mem. Cogn. **22**, 411–430 (1994)
4. Lowe, R.K.: Animation and learning: Selective processing of information in dynamic graphics. Learn. Instr. **13**, 157–176 (2003)
5. Lowe, R.K., Boucheix, J.-M.: Cueing complex animations: does direction of attention foster learning processes? Learn. Instr. **5**, 650–663 (2011)
6. Boucheix, J.-M., Lowe, R.K., Putri, D.K., Groff, J.: Cueing animations: dynamic signalling aids information extraction and comprehension. Learn. Instr. **25**, 71–84 (2013)
7. Lowe, R., Boucheix, J.-M.: Learning from animated diagrams: how are mental models built? In: Stapleton, G., Howse, J., Lee, J. (eds.) Diagrams 2008. LNCS (LNAI), vol. 5223, pp. 266–281. Springer, Heidelberg (2008). https://doi.org/10.1007/978-3-540-87730-1_25
8. Rosenholtz, R.: Capacity limits and how the visual system copes with them. Electron. Imaging (Proc. Hum. Vis. Elect. Imaging) **16**, 8–23 (2017)
9. Boucheix, J.-M., Lowe, R.K.: An eye tracking comparison of external pointing cues and internal continuous cues in learning from complex animation. Learn. Instr. **20**, 123–135 (2010)
10. de Koning, B.B., Jarodzka, H.: Attention guidance strategies for supporting learning from dynamic visualizations. In: Lowe, R., Ploetzner, R. (eds.) Learning from Dynamic Visualization, pp. 255–278. Springer, Cham (2017). https://doi.org/10.1007/978-3-319-56204-9_11

11. Wolfe, J.M., Horowitz, T.S.: Five factors that guide attention in visual search. Nat. Hum. Behav. **1**, 1–8 (2017)
12. Narayanan, N.H., Hegarty, M.: Multimedia design for communication of dynamic information. Int. J. Hum Comput Stud. **57**, 279–315 (2002)
13. Lowe, R.K., Boucheix, J.-M.: Principled animation design improves comprehension of complex dynamics. Learn. Instr. **45**, 72–84 (2016)
14. Lowe, R., Boucheix, J.-M.: Dynamic diagrams: a composition alternative. In: Cox, P., Plimmer, B., Rodgers, P. (eds.) Diagrams 2012. LNCS (LNAI), vol. 7352, pp. 233–240. Springer, Heidelberg (2012). https://doi.org/10.1007/978-3-642-31223-6_24
15. O'Connor, S.M., Dawson, T.J., Kram, R., Donelan, J.M.: The kangaroo's tail propels and powers pentapedal locomotion. Biol. Let. **10**, 20140381 (2014)
16. Kriz, S., Hegarty, M.: Top-down and bottom-up influences on learning from animations. Int. J. Hum.-Comput. Stud. **65**, 911–930 (2007)
17. Boucheix, J-M., Porte, L., Lowe, R.K.: Investigating fundamental features of complexity in animation processing. Paper to be Presented at EARLI SIG 2 Meeting, Prague, August 2020
18. Zacks, J.M., Speer, N.K., Swallow, K.M., Braver, T.S., Reynolds, J.R.: Event perception: a mind/brain perspective. Psychol. Bull. **133**, 273–293 (2007)
19. Scheiter, K.: Design of effective dynamic visualizations: a struggle between the beauty and the beast? commentary on parts I and II. In: Lowe, R., Ploetzner, R. (eds.) Learning from Dynamic Visualization, pp. 233–251. Springer, Cham (2017). https://doi.org/10.1007/978-3-319-56204-9_10
20. McGill, G.G.: Designing instructional science visualizations in the trenches: where research meets production reality. In: Lowe, R., Ploetzner, R. (eds.) Learning from Dynamic Visualization, pp. 119–150. Springer, Cham (2017). https://doi.org/10.1007/978-3-319-562 04-9_6

Evaluating Visualizations of Sets and Networks that Use Euler Diagrams and Graphs

Almas Baimagambetov[1](✉)(iD), Gem Stapleton[2,3](iD), Andrew Blake[1](iD), and John Howse[1](iD)

[1] Centre for Secure, Intelligent and Usable Systems, University of Brighton, Brighton, UK
{a.baimagambetov,a.l.blake,john.howse}@brighton.ac.uk
[2] University of Cambridge, Cambridge, UK
ges55@cam.ac.uk
[3] University of Kent, Canterbury, UK
g.stapleton@kent.ac.uk

Abstract. This paper presents an empirical evaluation of state-of-the-art visualization techniques that combine Euler diagrams and graphs to visualize sets and networks. Focusing on SetNet, Bubble Sets and WebCola – techniques for which there is freely available software – our evaluation reveals that they can *inaccurately* and *ineffectively* visualize the data. Inaccuracies include placing vertices in incorrect zones, thus incorrectly conveying the sets in which the represented data items lie. Ineffective properties, which are known to hinder cognition, include drawing Euler diagrams with extra zones or graphs with large numbers of edge crossings. The results demonstrate the need for improved techniques that are more accurate and more effective for end users.

Keywords: Euler diagrams · Graphs · Sets · Networks · Visualization

1 Introduction

A major goal of set and network data visualization is to draw diagrams that are both accurate and effective for users [1]. This is significant because there is a substantial amount of set and network data available, arising in various application areas [1,18,20], including bioinformatics, social networks, cartography and software architecture. This paper focuses on the common approach of using Euler diagrams and graphs in combination [1]. Euler diagrams represent sets and the graphs represent data items and relationships between them. We evaluate state-of-the-art techniques to reveal that they can produce layouts with both *inaccurate* and *ineffective* properties, hindering comprehension. No prior evaluation has compared set and network techniques by exposing the ways in which they possess inaccurate or ineffective properties. A take-away message from our research is that improved techniques are necessary for the effective visualization of sets and networks.

© Springer Nature Switzerland AG 2020
A.-V. Pietarinen et al. (Eds.): Diagrams 2020, LNAI 12169, pp. 323–331, 2020.
https://doi.org/10.1007/978-3-030-54249-8_25

Section 2 summarises layout properties of Euler diagrams and graphs known to impact cognition, as well as existing techniques for drawing Euler diagrams and graphs in combination. A comparative evaluation of state-of-the-art techniques is given in Sect. 3. We conclude and discuss future work in Sect. 4.

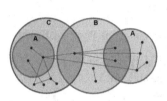

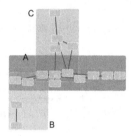

Fig. 1. SetNet.   **Fig. 2.** WebCola.

2 Background

There are various layout properties of Euler diagrams and graphs that can lead to poor comprehension. Automated visualization techniques should aim to avoid such properties whilst ensuring an accurate visualization of the underlying data.

Euler Diagram Properties. Prior research has led to the identification of properties of Euler diagrams that impact their effectiveness [3], with an important category being five *well-formedness properties* [15]:

- *Unique labels:* no two curves have the same label; curve labels that occur more than once are called *non-unique labels*. See Fig. 1, drawn using SetNet [16], where two curves labelled A represent the same set A.
- *Connected zones:* all of the zones in the diagram are connected components of the plane; a zone which is not connected is called *disconnected*.
- *Non-concurrent curves:* no parts of the curves run along the same path. In Fig. 2, drawn using WebCola [7], curves A and B share a concurrent segment.
- *Only two-points:* whenever a point is passed through by curves, it is passed through at most twice; points that fail this condition are called *triple points*.
- *Simple curves:* no curve self-intersects. Self-intersecting curves are *non-simple*.

Euler diagrams that break a well-formedness property hinder user comprehension [15] and possess one of the *ineffective properties*: non-unique labels, disconnected zones, concurrent curves, triple points, or non-simple curves. Other ineffective properties include *extra zones* and *non-circular curves*. Diagrams with extra zones are not *well-matched* to their semantics [9]. Circles were found to be a more effective curve shape than ellipses, squares or rectangles [3].

Diagrams are inaccurate when they omit zones that represent non-empty sets. Clearly, a diagram with *omitted zones* does not accurately reflect the data.

Fig. 3. Extra edge-curve crossings.

Fig. 4. No extra crossings.

Fig. 5. No extra crossings.

Fig. 6. A misplaced vertex.

In summary, automated Euler diagram layout techniques should avoid the ineffective properties of non-unique labels, disconnected zones, concurrent curves, triple points, non-simple curves, extra zones and non-circular curves, as well as the inaccurate property of omitted zones.

Graph Properties. Breaking the following properties reduces effectiveness [6]:

- *No edge crossings:* there are no points where two edges cross.
- *No edge bends:* edges are drawn as straight lines.
- *No edge-vertex intersections:* no edge passes through a non-incident vertex.
- *No vertex-vertex intersections:* there are no overlapping vertices.

That is, automated graph layout techniques should avoid the ineffective properties of edge crossings and edge bends and the inaccurate properties of edge-vertex intersections (where non-incidence is required) and vertex-vertex intersections (which could appear as a single vertex).

Further Properties. Combining Euler diagrams with graphs gives rise to further properties of interest:

- *No extra edge-curve crossings:* no graph edge passes through more curve segments than necessary.
- *Vertices in the correct zone:* no graph vertex lies on a curve or outside of the zone to which it belongs (Fig. 6).

Graph edges connect vertices placed in Euler diagram zones. When vertices are in different zones, edges that connect them necessarily pass through some Euler diagram curves. Extra crossings between graph edges and the underlying diagram can lead to visual clutter, impairing readability [5]. In Fig. 3, the edges unnecessarily pass through the curve S; Figs. 4 and 5 redraw the diagram without the extra crossings. In addition, when vertices are located in the same zone, the Gestalt principle of *common region* [11] indicates that we perceive them as being grouped together, which should assist with a correct interpretation of the diagram. Extrapolating from this insight, the more curves passed through by an edge connecting two vertices may lead to a perception of them having less in common. In particular, the sets in which the data items, represented by the two vertices, both lie could be deemed fewer in number.

Properties and Layout Quality. Summarising the above, visualization techniques should attempt to avoid properties that hinder cognition. Failure to avoid ineffective properties will give rise to diagrams that are ineffective. In addition, techniques should not produce diagrams that inaccurately represent the data from which they are derived. Such diagrams will lead to incorrect deductions being made about the underlying data.

Existing Techniques. A range of techniques draw combined Euler diagrams and graphs, including SetNet [16], WebCola [7], Bubble Sets [4], EulerView [19], Vizster [10] and KelpFusion [13]. A comprehensive overview of these and other techniques is available in [1]. Our evaluation, in Sect. 3, focuses on SetNet, Web-Cola and Bubble Sets; justification for selecting these techniques is also provided in Sect. 3.

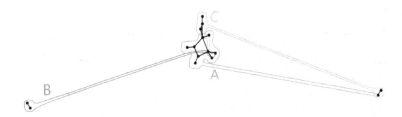

Fig. 7. Bubble sets.

SetNet [16] often produces diagrams with the ineffective property of non-unique labels, as in Fig. 1. *WebCola* [7] lays out the graph using a force-directed approach and then fits rectangles around the vertices. The rectangles attempt to have the smallest width and height needed to enclose their set members. This leads to diagrams with curve concurrency, as in Fig. 2 between A and B. *Bubble Sets* [4] routes curves around an already drawn graph. The graph is drawn first, independently of the curves, so Bubble Sets typically avoids ineffective graph properties. However, Fig. 7 allows us to observe that the graph layout can lead to convoluted curves. When routing the curves, Bubble Sets attempts to exclude non-set members within the curves, however this is not guaranteed. Hence, some visualizations are inaccurate. It is not possible for any technique to always accurately visualize the data and avoid all undesirable properties [8]. Our evaluation sets out to reveal the extent to which SetNet, Bubble Sets and WebCola produce diagrams with ineffective or inaccurate properties.

3   Evaluation: Inaccurate and Ineffective Properties

We selected techniques for our evaluation such that (a) they drew combined Euler diagrams and graphs, (b) the software was freely available, and (c) they could theoretically visualize any finite collection of sets and associated network, even though the implementation may fail. Bubble Sets [4], SetNet [16] and Web-Cola [7] were the techniques that met these criteria. All the diagrams used in our study are available at https://github.com/AlmasB/D2020 and are marked to show where property violations occurred. The software implementations use different rendering details, such as vertex sizes, and different heuristics when producing algorithms from underlying theory. Note that such implementation decisions may impact the results presented in this paper. For example, changing the graph algorithm used for Bubble Sets, or the vertex sizes in WebCola, will likely affect the occurrences of inaccurate and ineffective properties.

3.1   Data for Visualization

In order to evaluate the techniques, we needed data for visualization. We used SNAP Twitter ego-networks [12] where data sets had up to 68413 vertices, 1685163 edges and 99 sets, which is too complex for the practical evaluation of visualization tools. The size of the data sets needed to be controlled and, as such, we appealed to existing evaluations to inform us of appropriate numbers of sets, vertices and edges. Consistent with previous studies [14,15], we used a maximum of 8 sets. We selected the minimum number of sets to be two since, unlike in set-only data, a variety of combined Euler diagrams and graphs can be produced with two sets. Studies involving graphs typically had around 10 to 100 vertices and 40 to 170 edges [13,14,16,17]. We selected data sets with 2, 4, 6, or 8 sets, 10 to 100 vertices, and 40 to 170 edges, to give controlled variety.

We then identified SNAP data with required numbers of sets and reduced the number of vertices and edges within them, to manage the network complexity. Firstly, we removed vertices with degree 0 as they do not materially affect any of the properties being evaluated. Secondly, we removed any multiple edges since, when drawn, the associated edges would just be on top of each other, and we also removed loops. Thirdly, we randomly removed vertices using an iterative approach, whilst ensuring that if this created any degree 0 vertices, they would be removed also until the number of vertices was in the given bounds. This process left us with a set of reduced SNAP data sets, from which we randomly selected a sample for our evaluation.

We explain how we selected reduced-complexity data sets for the 2-set case; the other cases are similar. We computed the median numbers of zones, vertices and edges. These medians were used to sub-divide the 2-set data sets into eight groups: a low (i.e. below the median) number of zones, vertices and edges; those with a low number of zones and vertices, but a high number of edges; those with a low number of zones and edges, but a high number of vertices; and so forth. From each of these eight sub-divisions, we randomly selected one data set for visualization, giving eight 2-set data sets. As we are visualizing 2-, 4-, 6-, and 8-set data sets, this gave us 32 data sets. In one case, SetNet could not draw the selected data set. This data set had 8 sets, a high number of zones, a low number of vertices and a high number of edges. No other SNAP data set could be reduced to match the given combination of the number of sets, zones, vertices and edges. The evaluation we present is based on the remaining 31 data sets.

3.2   Statistical Analysis Results

For each technique and for each data set, we counted the number of times each undesirable property occurred in the produced visualization. Our goal is to rank the techniques, for each undesirable property, to give an indication of relative effectiveness. For each technique, each undesirable property either (a) cannot be present, since the theoretical underpinnings of the technique ensured that it would not be, or (b) can be present. In category (a), the technique is necessarily superior, for that property, than any technique in category (b). For those in category (b), statistical analysis was performed on the counts in order to derive further ranking information. Given that the counts are not normally distributed and that the same data sets were used across four techniques, a non-parametric Friedman test was applied to rank at least three techniques and a Wilcoxon test was applied to rank exactly two techniques. If significant differences were revealed in the former case, a Nemenyi post-hoc analysis was used to derive a ranking. Throughout, results are taken to be significant at the 5% level. For all counts from which the statistical analysis results were obtained, see https:// github.com/AlmasB/D2020. The techniques are abbreviated as follows: SetNet (SN), Bubble Sets (BS), and WebCola (WC).

Table 1. Means for inaccurate properties.

Property	SetNet	Bubble Sets	WebCola
Omitted zones	**0**	**0**	0.8
Edge-vertex intersections	76.2	6.9	213.0
Vertex-vertex intersections	2.2	**0**	2.5
Vertices in incorrect zone	0.9	0.5	2.6

Table 2. Means for ineffective properties.

Property	SetNet	Bubble Sets	WebCola
Non-unique labels	0.5	**0**	**0**
Disconnected zones	**0**	8.5	0.2
Concurrent curves	**0**	1.0	2.1
Triple points	**0**	0.7	0.5
Non-simple curves	**0**	**0**	**0**
Non-circular curves	**0**	4.9	4.9
Extra zones	0.1	1.9	0.5
Edge crossings	1236.8	588.4	1153.6
Extra edge-curve crossings	34.8	224.6	143.0

Evaluation of Inaccurate Properties. Table 1 summarises the mean counts of the inaccurate properties; the means for category (a) techniques are in bold and are necessarily 0. Table 3 shows which techniques participated in a statistical test, the p-value associated with the test and the derived post-hoc ranking; $A < B$ means A had significantly fewer inaccuracies, and therefore A is more accurate than B. Bubble Sets is consistently ranked as most, or jointly most, accurate. WebCola was ranked as least accurate or jointly least accurate, performing particularly badly for edge-vertex intersections with the mean of 213.0.

Evaluation of Ineffective Properties. Table 2 summarises the mean counts for the ineffective properties and Table 4 shows the technique rankings; the techniques employed straight line edges, so there were never edge bends. The results

Table 3. The p-values and technique rankings for inaccurate properties.

Property	Statistical test	p-value	Ranking
Omitted zones	–	N/A	BS = SN < WC
Edge-vert. inter.	SN, BS, WC	**<0.001**	BS < SN < WC
Vert.-vert. inter.	SN, BS, WC	**0.040**	BS = SN = WC
Vert. incorrect zone	SN, BS, WC	**0.035**	BS < WC, BS = SN, SN = WC

Table 4. The p-values and technique rankings for ineffective properties.

Property	Statistical test	p-value	Ranking
Non-unique labels	–	N/A	BS = WC < SN
Disconnected zones	BS, WC	**0.001**	SN < WC < BS
Concurrent curves	BS, WC	**0.001**	SN < BS < WC
Triple points	BS, WC	0.255	SN < BS = WC
Non-simple curves	–	N/A	SN = BS = WC
Non-circular curves	–	N/A	SN < BS = WC
Extra zones	SN, BS, WC	**0.003**	SN < BS, SN = WC, BS = WC
No edge crossings	SN, BS, WC	**<0.001**	BS < SN = WC
No extra edge-curve crossings	SN, BS, WC	**<0.001**	SN < BS = WC

here reveal there is no clear cut 'least ineffective' technique, as measured by these property counts. However, WebCola still fairs particularly poorly, being ranked worst or joint worst for seven out of the nine properties. SetNet is ranking best or joint best for seven out of the nine properties. Lastly, Bubble Sets is ranked best or joint best three times and worst or joint worst on five occasions. A further point of note is that non-unique labels and disconnected zones are particularly undesirable ineffective properties [15] and should be avoided where possible, even if that means other properties are exhibited. Bubble Sets was ranked (joint) best for non-unique labels but the worst for disconnected zones. By contrast, SetNet was ranked worst for non-unique labels and best for disconnected zones.

4   Conclusion and Future Work

A major problem when producing visualizations of data is finding an accurate and effective layout. A lot of attempts have been made to draw combined Euler diagrams and graphs but the state-of-the-art has not typically attempted to avoid properties that are empirically justified to be ineffective. Moreover, existing techniques can also produce inaccurate visualizations, thus not giving a true representation of data. There are three key take-away messages from our evaluation. Firstly, WebCola performed particularly badly: it is, compared to SetNet and Bubble Sets, particularly inaccurate and ineffective. Focusing on accuracy, Bubble Sets and SetNet were on par, except for edge-vertex intersections where Bubble Sets was superior. Regarding ineffective properties, SetNet is mostly superior to Bubble Sets. Our suggestion, based on these results, is that Bubble Sets should be the technique of choice whenever visualization accuracy is more important than effectiveness.

An important factor to consider is that the evaluated properties act as a proxy to diagram effectiveness. We should be mindful that avoiding inaccurate and ineffective properties does not necessarily ensure effectiveness. Our evaluation has focused on countable properties, yet there exist other properties, which relate to aesthetics, that can also impact effectiveness [2]. As it currently stands, the aesthetics of diagrams are not readily measurable and, so, were not part of our evaluation. In the future, empirical studies involving human participants are needed.

Acknowledgement. Gem Stapleton was partially funded by a Leverhulme Trust Research Project Grant (RPG-2016-082) for the project entitled Accessible Reasoning with Diagrams and EPSRC grant EP/T019603/1.

References

1. Alsallakh, B., Micallef, L., Aigner, W., Hauser, H., Miksch, S., Rodgers, P.: The state-of-the-art of set visualization. Comput. Graph. Forum **35**(1), 234–260 (2016)
2. Benoy, F., Rodgers, P.: Evaluating the comprehension of Euler diagrams. In: 11th International Conference on Information Visualization, pp. 771–778. IEEE (2007)
3. Blake, A., Stapleton, G., Rodgers, P., Howse, J.: The impact of topological and graphical choices on the perception of Euler diagrams. Inf. Sci. **330**, 455–482 (2016)
4. Collins, C., Penn, G., Carpendale, M.S.T.: Bubble sets: revealing set relations with isocontours over existing visualizations. IEEE Trans. Vis. Comput. Graph. **15**(6), 1009–1016 (2009)
5. Debiasi, A.: Study of visual clutter in geographic node-link diagrams. Ph.D. thesis, University of Trento (2016)
6. Dunne, C., Shneiderman, B.: Improving graph drawing readability by incorporating readability metrics: a software tool for network analysts. Uni. of Maryland, HCIL Tech Report HCIL-2009-13 (2009)
7. Dwyer, T.: Webcola: constraint-based layout in the browser. https://ialab.it. monash.edu/webcola/ (2013). Accessed 2 May 2019
8. Flower, J., Howse, J.: Generating Euler diagrams. In: Hegarty, M., Meyer, B., Narayanan, N.H. (eds.) Diagrams 2002. LNCS (LNAI), vol. 2317, pp. 61–75. Springer, Heidelberg (2002). https://doi.org/10.1007/3-540-46037-3_6
9. Gurr, C.: Effective diagrammatic communication: syntactic, semantic and pragmatic issues. J. Vis. Lang. Comput. **10**(4), 317–342 (1999)
10. Heer, J., Boyd, D.: Vizster: visualizing online social networks. In: IEEE Symposium on Information Visualization, pp. 32–39. IEEE (2005)
11. Koffka, K.: Principles of Gestalt Psychology. Lund Humphries, London (1935)
12. Leskovec, J., Krevl, A.: SNAP datasets: stanford large network dataset collection. http://snap.stanford.edu/data (2014). Accessed 9 Oct 2019
13. Meulemans, W., Henry Riche, N., Speckmann, B., Alper, B., Dwyer, T.: Kelp-Fusion: a hybrid set visualization technique. IEEE Trans. Vis. Comput. Graph. **19**(11), 1846–1858 (2013)

14. Riche, N., Dwyer, T.: Untangling Euler diagrams. IEEE Trans. Vis. Comput. Graph. **16**(6), 1090–1099 (2010)
15. Rodgers, P., Zhang, L., Purchase, H.: Wellformedness properties in Euler diagrams: which should be used? IEEE Trans. Vis. Comput. Graph. **18**(7), 1089–1100 (2012)
16. Rodgers, P., Stapleton, G., Alsallakh, B., Michallef, L., Baker, R., Thompson, S.: A task-based evaluation of combined set and network visualization. Inf. Sci. **367–368**, 58–79 (2016)
17. Saket, B., Simonetto, P., Kobourov, G., Borner, K.: Node, node-link, and node-link-group diagrams: an evaluation. IEEE Trans. Vis. Comput. Graph. **12**(20), 2231–2240 (2014)
18. Santamaría, R., Therón, R., Quintales, L.: Bicoverlapper: a tool for bicluster visualization. Bioinformatics **24**(9), 1212–1213 (2008)
19. Simonetto, P., Auber, D., Archambault, D.: Fully automatic visualisation of overlapping sets. Comput. Graph. Forum **28**(3), 967–974 (2009)
20. Wasserman, S., Faust, K.: Social network analysis. CUP (1994)

Visual Causality: Investigating Graph Layouts for Understanding Causal Processes

Dong-Bach Vo[1(✉)], Kristina Lazarova[1], Helen C. Purchase[1], and Mark McCann[2]

[1] School of Computing Science, University of Glasgow, Glasgow G128RZ, UK
{dong-bach.vo,kristina.lazarova,helen.purchase}@glasgow.ac.uk
[2] SMRC/CSO Social and Public Health Sciences Unit, University of Glasgow, Glasgow G23AX, UK
mark.mccann@glasgow.ac.uk

Abstract. Causal diagrams provide a graphical formalism indicating how statistical models can be used to study causal processes. Despite the extensive research on the efficacy of aesthetic graphic layouts, the causal inference domain has not benefited from the results of this research. In this paper, we investigate the performance of graph visualisations for supporting users' understanding of causal graphs. Two studies were conducted to compare graph visualisations for understanding causation and identifying confounding variables in a causal graph. The first study results suggest that while adjacency matrix layouts are better for understanding direct causation, node-link diagrams are better for understanding mediated causation along causal paths. The second study revealed that node-link layouts, and in particular layouts created by a radial algorithm, are more effective for identifying confounder and collider variables.

Keywords: Causal inference · Causal graph · Graph layout

1 Introduction

Causal inference, used in areas as diverse as employment discrimination and biochemical reactions, is the study of whether a putative cause is responsible for an effect [7,10]. A causal system can be expressed as a set of graphical objects: nodes, representing variables, with possible causal relationships from one to another represented by directed edges [24].

Causal diagrams provide specific graphical structures that facilitate the identification of specific causal model properties (see Fig. 1). In a causal graph, variables are represented with nodes, and statistical dependance, (i.e. causal relationships) between two variables with edges. A causal path is defined by an exposure, an outcome, and the set of all nodes and directed edges that connect the exposure to the outcome. Figure 2 shows different causal paths from the exposure node A to the outcome node D. If a node on a causal path is caused by two other nodes on that same path, it is known within the social science community as a collider; the effect of this is that the statistical dependence between

© Springer Nature Switzerland AG 2020
A.-V. Pietarinen et al. (Eds.): Diagrams 2020, LNAI 12169, pp. 332–347, 2020.
https://doi.org/10.1007/978-3-030-54249-8_26

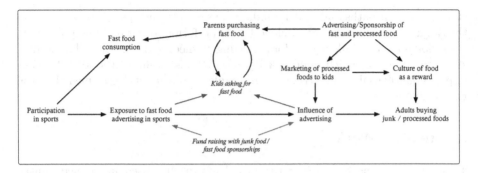

Fig. 1. A causal path from the community based systems diagram of obesity causes created by health and well being experts [1]. In the causal path between the nodes *Participation in sports* and *Adults buying junk/processed foods*, *Kids asking for food* is a collider and *Fund raising with junk food/fast food sponsorships* is a confounder.

the two other nodes may be weakened. If a node on a causal path influences multiple other nodes on the same path, it creates a confounding bias: thus "back door paths", with such nodes are called confounders. These graphical structures give information on the influence of an external intervention on an outcome: in the first case, influencing A will lead to a corresponding change in D, whereas in the latter two cases, changing A may not cause a change in D. Identifying such graphical structures on small graphs is straightforward, however causal models and their graphical representation can be sophisticated and challenging to work with [13]. Figure 1 shows an example of both a confounder and a collider.

Despite the prior extensive research on the relative usefulness of different graph layouts for a variety of tasks, the causal inference domain has not benefited from graph layout research. This avenue of research has the potential to have a significant impact on the way in which causal graphs are used in applied research and decision-making, for example in the formulation of health policy.

In this paper, we investigate how different graph visualisations can support causal reasoning. To the best of our knowledge, no other research has investigated this. In the first study, we investigate which layouts are most appropriate for

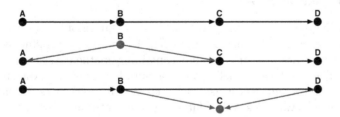

Fig. 2. Causal paths between A and D. Top: directed causal path. Center: causal backdoor path, B is a confounder on the path. Bottom: causal blocked path, C is a collider on the path.

studying causal paths and understanding causal relationships. The results show that adjacency matrix layouts yielded better performance for reasoning on direct causation and node-link layouts for reasoning on mediated causation. The second study investigated which node-link layout methods facilitate the identification of particular causal visual structures in graphs. Participants performed the best with radial layouts.

2   Related Work

This research aims to improve the visual approaches used in applied causal inference domains. It builds upon previous research in statistical causal inference using graphs and on research on visualising relationships in data.

2.1   Visualising Causal Inference

Causal graphs are networks that represent causation or the influence between properties of a domain. For example, the obesity system map represents influences such as education, stress or purchasing power over obesity [1,13]. Causation can be modelled quantitatively (the relationships between the entities are formalised in terms of conditional probability distributions derived from empirical data) or qualitatively (based on personal or expert opinion) [18].

Causal graphs formalize one's understanding of causal influences [24]. In population health, they have supported researchers to understand the associations between social policy, family characteristics, genetics, and foetal alcohol spectrum disorder [23]. While numerical statistical models can support causal inference, graphical approaches to causal problems have had a profound influence on the ways in which statistical models have been (and should correctly be) constructed [30], as well as providing a more engaging method of presenting evidence and eliciting opinions around causal questions with non-statistical audiences. Sophisticated interactive visualization applications exist to support causal inference using quantitative causal models represented as graphs [7,27,30,32], e.g. *Tetrad* [27], *Dagitty* [30], *Visual Causal Analyst* (VCA) [32].

2.2   Representing a Graph

The pioneering research in the graphical representation of causes was Wright's method in the field of animal genetics [34], formalising the influence of plausible causes on variables in a system combining mathematical and graphical modelling. The graphical model provides a causal overview as a directed acyclic graph where nodes represent causal variables and directed edges the causal relationships between variables. While later research contributed towards better and mathematically proven and graphical methodologies to measure causality [24], no empirical study has been conducted to evaluate the understandability of such graphical representations.

In contrast, the layout of directed graphs has been studied extensively in the graph drawing and information visualization research community [2,14,20], and several studies have found that the way in which a graph is laid out plays an important role in revealing the underlying meaning and structure of graphs [2]. For example, Purchase *et al.*'s study on the influence of aesthetic graphic layout criteria such as edge bending, edge crossings, or edge angle between nodes on graph readability, showed that edge crossings affect the graph reading most [25]. Another study looking at eye movements when reading graphs revealed that edge length may also affect performance [2].

The semantic domain of graphs should also be considered when designing or selecting layout [22,25]. For instance, McGrath *et al.* found that participants perceived differently the 'prominence' and the 'bridging' properties of a social network depending on the position of the nodes in undirected graphs [22], concluding that, given a specific domain, the best representation may depend on the type and the valence of the information one wants to convey. Causal diagrams are semantically rich as they can communicate probabilistic independence or show confounding biases, and no research to date has investigated the best graph layout to support the understanding of causal diagrams.

As an alternative directed graph representation, adjacency matrices show relationships between nodes in a binary matrix, with target and source nodes of each edge indicated in the matrix cells (Fig. 3).

Interaction with adjacency matrices has been found to be worse than with node-link diagrams [11,12]. Ghoniem *et al.* showed that participants performed better in several topographic graph reading tasks using matrices [12]. The task of finding paths between two nodes was better using node-link diagrams, though this performance decreased as the size of the graphs increased. Keller *et al.* generalised Ghoniem et al's finding [19], suggesting that the suitability of the representation may depend on the task performed and its semantic nature [19].

Information visualisation systems can combine adjacency matrix with node-link layouts; for example, *MatrixExplorer* offers a way to switch from matrix to node-link to take advantage of both representations [15]. Both representations can be used to depict different types of relationships. *NodeTrix* visualises social networks and performs very specific tasks relating to social sciences: the matrix layout represents intra-community relationships while node-links layout is used to depict inter-community relationships [16].

2.3   Comparing Layouts for Causal Inference

The most efficient layouts for causal inference may depend upon nature of the causal reasoning tasks. Since node-link diagrams are the most common graphical representation for causal inference, layouts implementing the best for graph reading, such as minimisation of edges crossing or orthogonality [25], could improve causal reasoning task performance. Adjacency matrices have been shown to outperform node-link diagrams for many abstract related tasks but such studies have not been conducted on a semantically-rich directed graphs like those used in causal reasoning [12]. We report on two studies which aim to compare graph

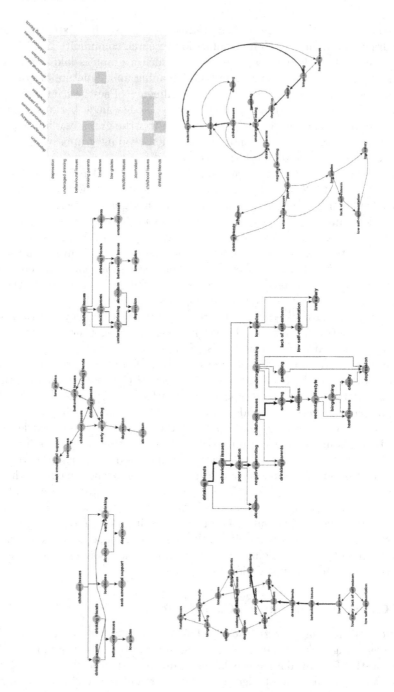

Fig. 3. Types of layout in the study. The top line shows some layouts used to investigate causation intelligibility. From left to right, the graph layouts are: parallel-series (PL), spring (SL), hierarchical (HL) and matrix out-degrees descending order (MODL). The bottom line shows some layouts to investigate the identification of causal structures. From left to right, the graph layouts are: spring (SL), hierachical (HL) and radial (RL).

layouts for causal inference. The first study investigates the best visualisation method for understanding causal paths in causal graphs; the second study compares the use of different graph layouts in identifying causal structures.

3 Investigating Causation Intelligibility

We investigated task performance when participants explore a causal graph when answering questions about its causal path relationships, looking at three common tasks related to causal inference: understanding direct causation, understanding mediated causation (i.e. indirect causation), and identifying causal structures.

Several node-link layouts have been proposed in the graph drawing community: we selected those we believed would improve participants' performance [8] (Fig. 3). The *hierarchical* layout emphasises structures in graphs by following regular patterns that can be easily followed by users' eyes [29]: including drawing direct connected nodes close to each other, limiting the number of edge crossings, and an orthogonal layout. *ReactionFlow*, a tool to support causal inference in biology, inspired the choice of the *parallel-series* directed graphs layout, popular for visualising flows in data [7]. This layout combines several graphs by merging the common roots into a single root when possible with all the paths parallel to each other, minimising edge crossings and bending, and following an orthogonal form shown to be effective for understanding abstract graphs [2,4,25]. In *spring* layouts, physical repulsive forces result in nodes with weak ties being pulled away from the others. Since as confounders and colliders on the graph are attached to a causal path by at least two edges going to the same direction (Fig. 1), this type of layout might create highly visible clusters around such highly connected nodes.

Several reordering techniques for highlighting data of interest through visual patterns in adjacency matrices have been proposed [3,21]. *Alphabetic* layouts have been found to outperform node-link layouts for tasks related to reading undirected graphs larger than 20 nodes [12], and can improve graph reading performance especially for users without prior knowledge of a domain [19]. Two other matrix layouts were added: *out-degrees* and *in-degrees* descending arrangement, with the expectation that they could help identify colliders and confounders. The *out-degrees* (resp. *in-degrees*) descending arrangement sorts the number of the edges going out from (resp. going towards) each vertex in a descending order.

4 Investigating the Effect of Causal Layouts

We designed 3 datasets each from one of these themes: drinking issues, examinations, and health related gym behaviour; for each, we created graphs of different sizes: 10, 20 and 30 nodes. Each graph contains several causal paths, where a causal path is a path through the graph from an exposure node (e.g. teenage drinking), through mediated nodes (e.g. alcohol dependency, depression, liver failure) to an outcome node (e.g. death from alcoholism). All causal paths in the graphs included 8 nodes and 7 edges. We had 6 presentation conditions, 3 node-link drawings (*spring, hierarchical, parallel*) and 3 matrix presentations (*alphabetic, in-degree, out-degree*).

Two types of question were used: direct causation on a path (e.g. "What factor is causing factor X?"), and mediated causation along longer paths ("Is this causal path correct?"). It has been shown that following mediated paths in applied causal contexts is not trivial [5]. One question of each type was associated to each possible graph (3 *sizes* × 6 *presentations*) that being 36 unique tasks.

We anticipated that node-link layouts would result in better performance for understanding causation (H1) since matrix layouts do not perform well for following paths in abstract undirected graphs of over 30 nodes [12]. In particular, *hierarchical* layout would be the best layout (H2) as it has been proven to be successful for abstract graphs [25].

4.1   Experimental Design

The yEd Graph Editor was used to create the graphs and the layouts with respect to the three chosen node-link layout algorithms [35]: *hierarchical, parallel-series*, and *spring* (yEd's organic force-directed layout). The adjacency matrices were arranged with *alphabetic, in-degrees* and *out-degrees* descending orders (Fig. 3).

4.2   Procedure

The experiment was conducted using a custom-built experimental software on a laptop computer, in the presence of the experimenter. The training materials (written documentation and video) presented to participants had been piloted with several people in advance to ensure that they adequately explained the task and did not include obvious biases. These materials used a graph of only five nodes and four edges to explain the concept of causality between variables and how it is depicted in both node-link and graphical form. They were then invited to ask for any clarification.

For each trial, the stimulus consisted in displaying a layout among the 18 available and one of the two associated questions, together with multiple choice options for answering the question. For each question, 4 potential answers were suggested to the participants. Participants were told that the correct answer could always be found in the graph and that they should not need to resort to guessing. The plausible answers were presented through a radio-button list to guarantee a unique answer from the participants. The trial was over when the participant selected an answer by clicking on a radio button.

The experiment started with 6 training questions, which were discarded from the dataset, to help them familiarise themselves with the system and the task, and to mitigate any learning effect. The experimental phase comprised 36 trials with stimuli ordered by a partial Latin square design to avoid any presentation order effect. Since we wanted to emulate a reader's process of attempting to understand a causal graph as a whole, participants had to visually scan the drawing to identify the nodes of interest before responding. At the end participants were given a questionnaire to assess subjective preferences. Each evaluation session lasted for about 60 min.

The independent variables were layout type, graph size and question type. The dependent variables were response time and answer accuracy. The response time was measured between the stimulus appearance and the validation of an answer, including the duration of the cognitive process of understanding the causal question and the localisation of the nodes of interest. Thirty volunteers took part in the study. Participants were between 20 and 29 years old (Mdn = 22.57, SD = 2.14) and 6 were male. They were all undergraduate students with no prior experience working with graphs.

4.3   Results

We collected 1080 trials (30 × 36), with success rate of 98.80%. We removed the data from 12 outlying trials, when the distance of the sample from the mean response time was three times greater than a standard deviation (i.e. greater than 86 s). To accommodate any non-parametric nature of data distribution, an aligned rank transform (ART) was performed before further analysis [17,33].

Table 1. Median response time in seconds by graph layout and size for direct and mediated causal inference. S denotes small graphs, M medium graphs and L large graphs. HL is hierarchical, SL is spring and PL is parallel layout. MAL is matrix alphabetic, MIDL is matrix in-degree and MODL matrix out-degree ordering layout.

Size		Direct causation						Mediated causation					
		HL	SL	PL	MAL	MIDL	MODL	HL	SL	PL	MAL	MIDL	MODL
S	Median	8.81	11.36	13.19	10.57	9.97	8.42	26.17	16.54	20.35	13.64	21.96	26.22
	IQR	4.75	3.20	4.95	5.20	4.88	4.01	7.83	6.99	8.6	11.56	14.95	13.33
M	Median	13.54	12.85	12.07	12.46	13.88	11.06	12.49	37.19	22.72	19.01	33.93	23.92
	IQR	8.53	5.72	6.54	10.11	5.18	4.60	6.21	12.93	11.42	10.15	24.65	17.91
L	Median	15.45	16.94	26.32	14.06	13.59	13.30	25.83	45.89	27.79	44.46	42.13	44.83
	IQR	12.39	8.13	8.73	6.7	4.59	7.23	16.84	26.70	37.37	16.46	18.10	15.13

The two questions asked (direct causation between two nodes, medicated causation along a path) are sufficiently different for separate analyses to be appropriate.

Direct Causation. The median response time was the fastest for MODL for small, medium and large graphs. The slowest response times were found for PL with small and large, and for MIDL for medium graphs (Table 1 and Fig. 4).

A two-way ANOVA on the aligned rank transformed data revealed a significant main effect with layout ($F_{5,492}$ = 20.21, $p < .0001$) and size ($F_{2,492}$ = 105.44, $p < .0001$) factors, and an interaction effect for layout × size ($F_{10,492}$ = 9.91, $p < .0001$). A *Post hoc* Tukey's HSD test found all the layouts significantly faster than PL (all $t(491) > 5.91$, $p < .0001$), and MODL significantly faster

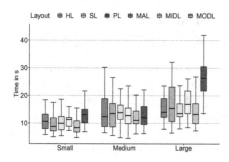

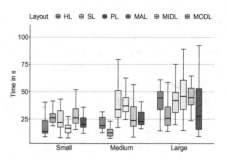

Fig. 4. Median response times for direct causation

Fig. 5. Median response times for mediated causation

than SL ($t(491) = 3.30$, $p < .001$) and MAL ($t(491) = 3.05$, $p < .05$). Exploring small graphs was significantly faster than medium ($t(493) = 5.48$, $p < .001$) and large ($t(493) = 14.39$, $p < .001$) graphs; Exploring medium faster than large graphs ($t(493) = 8.92$, $p < .001$). *Post hoc* pairwise comparisons with Holm-Bonferroni correction revealed that all the interactions of all the layouts with PL were significant for small and large (all $\chi^2 > 33.58$, $p < .0001$), and for medium and large graphs (all $\chi^2 > 26.06$, $p < .0001$).

Mediated Causation. The fastest response time was found for MAL with small graphs, for HL with medium and large graphs. It was the slowest for MODL with small graphs and for SL with medium and large graphs. The results are shown in Table 1 and in Fig. 5.

An ANOVA on the align rank transformed data showed a significant main effect for layout ($F_{5,482} = 19.07$, $p < .0001$) and size ($F_{2,482} = 82.13$, $p < .0001$) and a significant effect for interaction of both ($F_{10,482} = 12.64$, $p < .0001$). A Tukey's *Post hoc* pairwise comparison found MAL significantly faster than HL, MIDL, SL and MODL (all $t(482) > 3.37$, $p < .05$). HL was significantly faster than MIDL, SL, and MODL (all $t(482) > 7.02$, $p < .0001$) and PL faster than MIDL, SL and MODL (all $t(511) > 4.54$, $p < .001$). Exploring small graphs was significantly faster than medium ($t(482) = 4.69$, $p < .0001$) and large ($t(482) = 12.68$, $p < .0001$) graphs, and exploring medium faster than large ($t(481) = 8.08$, $p < .0001$). *Post hoc* pairwise comparison of factor interactions using Holm-Bonferroni correction showed significant differences between medium and large graphs for MAL with MIDL, SL and PL (all $\chi^2 > 12.80$, $p < .01$). It was also the case for MODL with MIDL, SL and PL (all $\chi^2 > 12.86$, $p < .01$). The differences between small and large graphs were significant for HL with MAL, MIDL, MODL and SL (all $\chi^2 > 12.22$, $p < .05$), for MAL with PL ($\chi^2 18.81$, $p < .001$), and for SL with MIDL and PL (both $\chi^2 > 9.70$, $p < .05$). There were significant differences between medium and large graphs for SL with HL, MAL, MODL and PL (all $\chi^2 > 16.54$, $p < .005$), for HL and MAL, MIDL and PL (all $\chi^2 > 18.59$, $p < .005$), and for MODL with MIDL ($\chi^2 11.53$, $p < .05$).

Participants completed a questionnaire investigating the relative easiness of working with node-link or matrix layouts on a scale from 0 to 5. A Mann-Whitney test indicated that the median score for node-link layout ($Mdn = 3$, $IQR = 2$) was significantly greater than the score for matrix layout ($Mdn = 2$, $IQR = 1.75$, $U = 234.5$, $p < 0.001$). 80% of the participants preferred to work with node-link diagrams over matrices.

4.4   Discussion

H1 was not supported: node-link diagrams were not the fastest. PL and SL exhibited the worst performance for understanding direct and mediated causation in large graphs. H2 was partially supported as HL gave the best performance for understanding mediated causation but only with medium and large graphs.

The results indicated an interesting trend when comparing layout performance with regard to graph sizes. Some layouts that were slower for small graphs were faster with medium or large graphs. MIDL became significantly faster than some node-link layouts with small and large graphs for understanding direct causation. However, the participants did not notice this performance boost with matrix layouts; subjective ratings show preference for node-link layouts.

Performance also differed for direct and mediated causal reasoning. MODL showed the best performance for direct causal reasoning whatever the graph size, outperforming all node-link layouts. Finding a direct cause was easier on matrix layouts than on node-link layouts, contradicting H2. While labels are scattered around the plane in node-link layouts, they are arranged following a single horizontal (columns) or vertical (rows) line in matrix layouts. Furthermore, the fast access to highly connected nodes supported participants in highlighting causal relationships, and arranging the row and the column headers with alphabetic order helps users to locate the target nodes and its causal predecessor or successor even faster. For small and large graphs, the *parallel-series* layout displayed the worst performance, showing that even if paths are explicitly drawn, not all the node-link layouts are appropriate for causal inference. This is an important finding as this layout is currently used in existing causal inference software [7].

For mediated causation reasoning, as graph sizes increased, the overall performance got worse, but the worsening in performance for each layout differed. HL was the fastest for medium and for large graphs, making it a good option for reasoning about mediated causation and partially validating H2. While it seems the alphabetic matrix layout was the most efficient for small graphs, node-link based layouts were faster for medium and large graphs. Because matrix layouts require users to perform saccades from row to column headers to follow paths, analysing long paths were more challenging. This was accentuated by the fact that, depending on the arrangement of the rows and the columns, two consecutive nodes' labels are unlikely to be located next to each other in the matrix headers. These results are in line with the findings for syntactic graphs [12,28] and connectivity models [19].

The results suggest MIDL may be promising for causal reasoning in even larger graphs than in this study; further research is needed to confirm this.

5 Identifying Causal Structures

The first study focused on understanding which layout best supports following directed causal paths. However, the presence of colliders or confounders can affect causal interpretation, conflicting with intuition. Highlighting these causal processes effectively is crucial for evidence-informed decision making.

5.1 Experimental Design

Two sets of questions were designed: investigating the direct identification of confounders and colliders relative to a path, and identifying these causal structures by exploring the entire graph.

After being presented with a highlighted pair of one node and one path in a graph, *direct identification* question asked whether the node was a collider or a confounder with respect to the path, or neither. For the *exploratory identification* question, a path of a graph was highlighted and participants were asked to enumerate all the colliders and confounders related to the path.

The hierarchical (HL) and spring (SL) layouts from the previous study were retained, but the parallel-series layout (PL) was discarded because of its weak performance in the first study. A radial tree layout (RL, also created by yEd, as noted in Sect. 4.1) was added to the conditions as this layout is widely used to depict relationships among diverse entities [9]. An adjacency matrix layout was also included, with rows and columns ordered by the type of the nodes: the nodes at the start of the causal paths were used as first indices, while the nodes at the end of the causal paths were used as the last indices. This was so as to gather meaningful causal information in the centre of the layout as much as possible. Only two graph sizes were used (medium: 20 nodes, large: 40 nodes). Small graphs were discarded as we thought the task would be too easy given the results of the first study. For each domain (drinking issues, exams, and health related gym behaviour), 6 new graphs were generated. Each causal path in the graphs included 8 nodes and 7 edges.

5.2 Procedure

Participants were introduced to causal relationships and their representation with node-link and matrix layouts. Then, the experimenter explained to the participants the collider and confounder concepts and what these structures look like on node-link and matrix diagrams: a collider on a causal path is a node resulting of a common effect of two other nodes on this same path; a confounder on a causal path is a node that influences multiple other variables on this same path (Fig. 1). Before starting, the participants could practice with two node-link and two matrix layout examples to ensure they had correctly understood the concepts and the instructions.

For each trial, the stimulus consisted in displaying a random question and the associated layout. For a direct identification task, participants had to select whether the node was a "collider", "confounder", or "none". For an exploration

Table 2. Mean success rate in % and median reaction time in seconds for direct identification of graphical causal structures.

		Success rate					Reaction time			
		HL	SL	RL	ML		HL	SL	RL	ML
M	Mean	92.13	92.22	87.64	65.17	Median	19.52	21.76	21.78	31.76
	SD	0.27	0.28	0.33	0.48	IQR	12.10	18.63	16.44	17.02
L	Mean	85.39	93.33	93.26	81.93	Median	21.34	17.50	20.79	33.00
	SD	0.35	0.25	0.25	0.39	IQR	16.95	0.25	18.71	18.72

task, they had to select the only four collider or confounder nodes with respect to the highlighted path among a list of 10 candidates. A partial Latin square was used to avoid any ordering effect. Each evaluation session lasted for about 60 min. The apparatus from the previous study was used.

The independent variables of this study were layout type, graph size and question type. The dependent variables were the response time, which was measured between the stimulus appearance and the validation of an answer, and the answer accuracy. A total of 540 answers were collected. Thirty volunteers took part to the study. Participants were between 20 and 27 years old ($M = 22.57$, $SD = 2.14$). All of them were students and 14 were female, and undergraduate students with no prior knowledge of graphs.

5.3   Results

The data were split according to the type of question (direct identification or exploration).

Direct identification of causal structures. We discarded 12 samples from our data for the direct identification task and 24 samples for the graph exploration task because their distance to the mean response time was greater than three times the standard deviation (i.e. greater than 224 s).

The success rate varied between 65.17% (ML) and 92.22% (SL) for medium sized graphs and between 81.93% (ML) and 93.33% (SL) for large sized graphs (Table 2). A repeated-measures ANOVA on the regression model found a significant difference for layouts ($F_{3,703} = 31.43$, $p < .001$). *Post hoc* Tukey's pairwise comparisons showed that ML was significantly worse than all the other layouts (all $p < .001$). Median response times for the direct identification task shown in ranged from 19.52 s (HL) to 31.76 s (ML) for medium graphs and from 21.34 s (HL) to 33.00 s (ML) for large graphs (Table 2). A two-way ANOVA on the ART data revealed a significant effect of the layout ($F_{3,203} = 31.75$, $p < 0.001$). *Post hoc* Tukey's pairwise comparisons found ML significantly slower than all the other layouts ($p < 0.001$).

Exploratory Identification of Causal Structures. We discarded all the matrix data, since participants' performance in this condition was extremely poor, and no meaningful comparisons could be made. The success rate for finding colliders was 87.78% for medium graphs and 87.64% for large graphs, and 90% for confounders in medium graphs and 86.04% in large graphs (Table 3). A repeated measures ANOVA on the regression model showed significant effect of the layout ($F_{2,527=6.06}$, $p < 0.05$) for finding colliders. *Post hoc* Tukey HSD pairwise comparisons found SL significantly better than HL ($p < .05$). A significant effect of the size ($F_{1,529} = 8.07$, $p < .01$) and the layout ($F = 18.95$, $p < .001$) was found for finding confounders. *Post hoc* Tukey HSD pairwise comparisons found SL and RL significantly better than HL (both $p < .01$) and medium significantly better than large graphs ($p < .01$). The median response time for finding all the colliders and the confounders was 63.40 s ($IQR = 47.28$) for SL, 72.94 s ($IQR = 39.08$) for HL, and 82.35 s ($IQR = 44.04$) for RL in medium graphs. It reached 70.19 s ($IQR = 32.40$) for RL, 84.40 s ($IQR = 50.71$) for HL and 83.11 s ($IQR = 42.60$) for SL in large graphs. A two-way ANOVA on the ART data revealed a significant effect of size ($F_{1,145} = 13.62$, $p < .001$) and of the interaction between both factors ($F_{2,145} = 13.92$, $p < .0001$). *Post hoc* Tukey's pairwise comparisons found exploring medium graphs significantly faster than large graphs ($p < 0.001$). *Post hoc* pairwise comparison using Holm-Bonferroni correction based on the interaction revealed that while RL was slower than HL ($\chi^2 = 12.30$, $p < .001$) and SL ($\chi^2 = 26.71$, $p < .0001$) for medium graphs, it became faster than both for large graphs.

5.4   Discussion

The results for the matrix layout were so poor in supporting participants' identification of collider or confounder structures in graphs that we omitted them from the data analysis for both questions. This is interesting in itself, because not only were MIDL and MODL found to be promising for reasoning causal graphs in our first study, but also previous research has advocated for the usage of matrix layouts for reading nodes' connectivity in graphs of 20 nodes and more [12]. One possible reason may be our participants' unfamiliarity with the matrix representation, or the fact that there is no obvious visual pattern that clearly highlights the existence of confounders or colliders in matrices.

When exploring the graph to find confounders and colliders, HL exhibited the worst performance, despite being one of the most praised layouts for its aesthetic characteristics [6]. While SL and RL manifested similar accuracy for finding causal structures in graphs, RL performed better as the number of nodes

Table 3. Mean success rate in % for exploratory identification of causal structures in graphs. SD values are indicated in parentheses.

Node type	HL medium	SL medium	RL medium	HL large	SL large	RL large
Colliders	81.11	87.78	82.02	74.71	87.21	87.64
	(0.39)	(0.33)	(0.39)	(0.44)	(0.33)	(0.33)
Confounders	81.11	90.00	87.64	60.92	86.04	83.14
	(0.39)	(0.30)	(0.33)	(0.49)	(0.35)	(0.38)

increased, becoming faster than both SL and HL with large graphs. This is a compelling finding as previous research on syntactic graphs has advised the use of RL over orthogonal layouts. This suggests that RL could better support users with identifying confounding and colliding processes.

6   General Discussion and Future Work

While HL was the most efficient for understanding causal paths, matrix layouts were promising. In this context, MAL can improve the understanding of causation, and in particular, localisation on the nodes of interest. Note that MIDL performance also increased with graph size. MIDL and MODL give fast access to highly connected nodes—the nodes likely to be of interest in the causal inference process. However, these matrix layouts did not support the identification of causal structures which are likely to be highly connected. This may have been caused by the lack of expertise of our participants in causal inference and information visualisation. Further research is needed to understand better the potential of such layouts with directed graphs for causal inference in applied settings and especially with expert users.

None of the matrix layouts presented here were suitable for identifying causal structures. However, since row and column permutations affect readability, more research is needed to identify further permutations that might highlight causal relationships and similarities [11].

For node-link diagrams, we find that the RL node-link layout was the most efficient layout for identifying causal structures, but following causal graphs and identifying relevant structures to identify colliders and confounders would require different layouts. Another research direction might be to investigate how hybrid methods or animation could support users for juxtaposing or switching from one layout to another [14, 31].

Finally, we only looked at a limited set of causal structures, and limited path lengths; we thus have no way of knowing how layout features will operate under more complex and diverse circumstances that are likely to arise in applied settings. This limitation makes further research based on increasingly complex causal structures all the more important.

7   Conclusion

This is the first empirical study of how visual aesthetics can influence how non-expert viewers interpret causal graphs. Our findings suggest that existing principles for general graph readability are insufficient to depict causal graphs effectively. First, causal graphs have structures with a specific interpretation that do not appear in graphs used in other domains. Second, the domain problem is a compound sequence of basic visual analytic tasks (e.g. search the plane, identify connections, infer direction of connections). It appears that different layouts are faster for each basic task, and that there are unexpected relationships between the compound tasks and features of the layout.

Our findings suggest that matrix layouts are the best layouts to investigate direct causal relationships, with matrix-out-degree the fastest, while node-link diagrams with hierarchical layout is the most promising for mediated causation. For identifying causal structures, radial was the most promising layout, with its performance increasing with the size of graphs. This suggests that causal inference could benefit from visualisation tools that provide multiple coordinated views [26], thus supporting users in a range of different tasks for understanding causation. Further investigation that considers cognitive and visual processes would help in explaining the results of our experiment, and better understanding of the principles of visual causal inference will assist in developing readable and informative causal graphs.

Note. Ethical clearance was given by the Ethics Committee of the College of Science and Engineering at the University of Glasgow (ref: 300150001). Study materials are available at http://www.dcs.gla.uk/~hcp/Diagrams2020.

References

1. Allender, S., et al.: A community based systems diagram of obesity causes. PLoS One **10**(7), e0129683 (2015)
2. Bae, J., et al.: Developing and evaluating quilts for the depiction of large layered graphs. IEEE TVCG **17**(12), 2268–2275 (2011)
3. Behrisch, M., et al.: Matrix reordering methods for table and network visualization. Comput. Graph. Forum **35**(3), 693–716 (2016)
4. Bennett, C., et al.: The aesthetics of graph visualization. In: Proceedings of the 2007 Computational Aesthetics in Graphics, Visualization, and Imaging, pp. 57–64 (2007)
5. Braveman, P., Gottlieb, L.: The social determinants of health: it's time to consider the causes of the causes. Public Health Rep. **129**(2), 19–31 (2014)
6. Burch, M., et al.: Evaluation of traditional, orthogonal, and radial tree diagrams by an eye tracking study. IEEE TVCG **17**(12), 2440–2448 (2011)
7. Dang, T., et al.: ReactionFlow: an interactive visualization tool for causality analysis in biological pathways. BMC Proc. **9**, S6 (2015)
8. Di Battista, G.: Graph Drawing: Algorithms for the Visualization of Graphs. An Alan R. Apt Book. Prentice Hall, Upper Saddle River (1999)
9. Draper, G., et al.: A survey of radial methods for information visualization. IEEE Trans. Vis. Comput. Graph. **15**(5), 759–776 (2009)
10. Elmqvist, N., Tsigas, P.: Causality visualization using animated growing polygons. In: Proceedings of IEEE Information Visualization 2003, vol. 2003, pp. 189–196. IEEE (2003)
11. Garaigordobil, M., et al.: Childhood depression: relation to adaptive, clinical and predictor variables. Front. Psychol. **8**(MAY), 1–9 (2017). https://doi.org/10.3389/fpsyg.2017.00821
12. Ghoniem, M., et al.: A comparison of the readability of graphs using node-link and matrix-based representations. In: Proceedings of IEEE Information Visualization, pp. 17–24 (2004)
13. Government, U.: Reducing obesity: obesity system map, tackling obesities: future choices – building the obesity system map (2007). https://www.gov.uk/government/publications/reducing-obesity-obesity-system-map

14. Heer, J., Robertson, G.: Animated transitions in statistical data graphics. IEEE TVCG **13**(6), 1240–1247 (2007)
15. Henry, N., Fekete, J.D.: MatrixExplorer: a dual-representation system to explore social networks. IEEE TVCG **12**(5), 677–684 (2006)
16. Henry, N., et al.: NodeTrix: a hybrid visualization of social networks. IEEE Trans. Vis. Comput. Graph. **13**(6), 1302–1309 (2007)
17. Higgins, J.J., Tashtoush, S.: An aligned rank transform test for interaction. Nonlinear World **1**(2), 201–211 (1994)
18. Keatley, D.A., et al.: Lay understanding of the causes of binge drinking in the United Kingdom and Australia: a network diagram approach. Health Educ. Res. **32**(1), cyw056 (2017)
19. Keller, R., et al.: Matrices or node-link diagrams: which visual representation is better for visualising connectivity models? Inf. Vis. **5**(1), 62–76 (2006)
20. von Landesberger, T., et al.: Visual analysis of large graphs: state-of-the-art and future research challenges. Comput. Graph. Forum **30**(6), 1719–1749 (2011)
21. Liiv, I.: Seriation and matrix reordering methods: an historical overview. Stat. Anal. Data Min. **8**(5), 70–91 (2010)
22. McGrath, C., et al.: The effect of spatial arrangement on judgments and errors in interpreting graphs. Soc. Netw. **19**(3), 223–242 (1997)
23. McQuire, C., et al.: The causal web of foetal alcohol spectrum disorders: a review and causal diagram. Eur. Child Adolesc. Psychiatr. **29**(5), 575–594 (2019). https://doi.org/10.1007/s00787-018-1264-3
24. Pearl, J.: Causal diagrams for empirical research. Biometrika **82**(4), 669–688 (1995)
25. Purchase, H.C., et al.: Empirical evaluation of aesthetics-based graph layout. Empir. Softw. Eng. **7**(3), 233–255 (2002)
26. Roberts, J.C.: State of the art: coordinated & multiple views in exploratory visualization. In: Fifth International Conference on Coordinated and Multiple Views in Exploratory Visualization (CMV 2007), pp. 61–71. IEEE (2007)
27. Scheines, R., et al.: The TETRAD project: constraint based aids to causal model specification. Multivar. Behav. Res. **33**(1), 65–117 (1998)
28. Shen, Z., Ma, K.L.: Path visualization for adjacency matrices. In: Museth, K., et al. (eds.) Eurographics/ IEEE-VGTC Symposium on Visualization. The Eurographics Association (2007)
29. Sugiyama, K., Misue, K.: Visualization of structural information: automatic drawing of compound digraphs. IEEE Trans. Syst. Man Cybern. **21**(4), 876–892 (1991)
30. Textor, J., et al.: DAGitty: a graphical tool for analyzing causal diagrams. Epidemiology (Cambridge, Mass.) **22**(5), 745 (2011)
31. Vehlow, C., Beck, F., Weiskopf, D.: The state of the art in visualizing group structures in graphs. In: Borgo, R., et al. (eds.) Eurographics Conference on Visualization (EuroVis) - STARs. The Eurographics Association (2015)
32. Wang, J., Mueller, K.: The visual causality analyst: an interactive interface for causal reasoning. IEEE TVCG **22**(1), 230–239 (2016)
33. Wobbrock, J.O., et al.: The aligned rank transform for nonparametric factorial analyses using only anova procedures. In: Proceedings of CHI 2011, p. 143. ACM Press, New York (2011)
34. Wright, S.: Correlation and causation. J. Agric. Res. **20**(7), 557–585 (1921)
35. yWorks: yEd Graph Editor. http://www.yworks.com/products/yed

Influence of Shape, Density, and Edge Crossings on the Perception of Graph Differences
An Investigation Under Time Constraints

Günter Wallner[1]([✉]), Margit Pohl[1], Cynthia Graniczkowska[1], Kathrin Ballweg[2], and Tatiana von Landesberger[2,3]

[1] TU Wien, Vienna, Austria
{guenter.wallner,margit.pohl,cynthia.graniczkowska}@tuwien.ac.at
[2] Technische Universität Darmstadt, Darmstadt, Germany
kathrin.ballweg@gris.tu-darmstadt.de
[3] Karlsruher Institut für Technologie, Karlsruhe, Germany
tatiana.antburg@kit.edu

Abstract. The perception of differences between graphs represented as node-link diagrams is an important issue in many disciplines. This paper presents results from a study with 40 participants. The goal of the study was to test whether shape, density, and edge crossings of the graph influence the perception of differences between graphs and the order in which they are perceived. The participants worked under time constraints. Our results indicate that an increase in density lowers the recognition of differences while a newly introduced edge crossing helps to spot a change. Shape did not have a significant influence on the perception of differences.

Keywords: Graph comparison · Graph differences · Perception

1 Introduction

Analysts are frequently exposed to the task of visually comparing two similar graphs [1]. In many cases, the differences can be explicitly encoded in the graph structure, e.g., through color-coding of nodes and edges [7]. This, however, is not always possible as visual variables such as color may already be used for encoding other information. In such cases, the observer needs to compare the structure of the graphs visually. Thus, better understanding which factors facilitate or impede the recognition of differences in node-link diagrams can be of great value, e.g., to help create specifically optimized layouts for comparison purposes.

In our previous work [19] we studied which factors influence the perception of changes in directed acyclic graphs (DAGs) and which strategies people adapt to compare them by relying on screen capturing and qualitative content analysis of thinking aloud protocols. As the study was exploratory and relied on people's explanations, no time limit was imposed for comparison. However, time may

© Springer Nature Switzerland AG 2020
A.-V. Pietarinen et al. (Eds.): Diagrams 2020, LNAI 12169, pp. 348–356, 2020.
https://doi.org/10.1007/978-3-030-54249-8_27

impact which changes are recognized, which factors contribute to recognition, and how people approach the comparison. Research in cognitive psychology indicates that time constraints result in a more shallow processing of information, more important features are predominantly perceived, and that the accuracy of judgements decreases [17]. Time constraints also impose a higher workload on study participants (e.g., [4,9]). Time constraints also play an important role in many practical contexts. However, to the best of our knowledge, time constraints have not been investigated systematically in usability research.

Hence we decided to find out whether time constraints also play a role for detecting differences in DAGs. In this paper, building upon our previous results, we thus present a follow-up study focusing on the influence of time on the perception of differences. Our results show that changes to the outer shape (i.e silhouette) of the graph, lower local density, and the introduction of edge crossings help to facilitate the recognition of differences also under time constraints.

2   Related Work

In cognitive psychology, the investigation of similarity perception has been an important topic. The development of categories is based on similarity perception because similar objects are placed into the same category [8]. There are different mathematical models (e.g., multidimensional or featural models) to describe similarity perception. Most models rely on the comparison of distinct features of objects, but it has been noted that similarity is a more complex phenomenon [15].

There is some research in information visualization addressing comparing processes in visualization in general. Gleicher [6] describes common challenges in comparison processes. He assumes that the main challenges are size and complexity of the visualizations being compared. He states that there are different strategies to tackle comparison processes: scan sequentially, select subsets, and summarize. Possible design solutions to support comparison processes include adding statistical/analytical measures or appropriate interaction possibilities.

Investigations concerning the perception of visual features of node-link diagrams mainly concentrate on single graphs and do not address the comparison of such representations. Li et al. [10] investigated which nodes are more salient, focusing on features such as node degree and attributes of the surroundings of a node. Marriott et al. [12] studied the influence of different layout features, including symmetry and collinearity, on the memorability of graphs. Soni et al. [16] studied whether properties like graph density influence the perception of graphs. These studies do not address graph comparison as such, but are still relevant for consideration in the design of graphs that should facilitate comparison processes.

Processes concerning the comparison of node-link diagrams have been investigated much less than the perception of single node-link diagrams. Some research addressed the perception of dynamic graphs. Making sense of dynamic graphs is partly based on comparing a number of time-slices of a node-link diagram. Archambault et al. [2] studied whether difference maps could assist users in such processes. They found out that, overall, difference maps did not help, but were useful to assess the changes in the number of edges. Bridgeman and Tamassia [5] investigated the perception of differences and similarities of graphs. Their results show that similarity perception relies more on the borders or the shape of the graphs, while detection of differences rather focuses on the interior of graphs. In cognitive psychology it is discussed whether object perception is more holistic or analytic. There is some indication that this depends on whether the features of an object depend very much on the context in which they are shown [13]. There are still many open issues in this context.

Ballweg et al. [3] investigated which factors influence similarity perception of small directed acyclic graphs (DAGs). von Landesberger et al. [18] described methodological challenges to be addressed when conducting studies on graph comparison and reported preliminary results on factors influencing the perception of similarity of very small star-shaped node-link diagrams. Wallner et al. [19] studied which factors influence the perception of changes in DAGs. Especially shape of the graph, density of links and nodes, and edge crossings were found to influence the perception of differences. The study presented here is based on this work. To the best of our knowledge, the issue of time constraints has not been investigated extensively in Human-Computer Interaction or cognitive psychology, which both concentrate on measuring reaction time but not the effect of time constraints on the achievement of participants.

3   Study Design

In previous research, Wallner et al. [19] found that the shape of graphs, their density, and edge crossings influenced the ease with which users were able to identify differences between graphs. This research was conducted without time constraints. For reasons detailed in Sect. 1 we thus decided to conduct similar research under time constraints. We formulated the following research questions:

R1:   Do the variables shape, edge crossings, and local density influence the recognition of differences under time constraints?

R2:   Do the variables shape, edge crossings, and local density affect the sequence of perceived differences? When several differences between two graphs exist, are shape changes, for example, detected earlier than other changes?

For comparability with previous studies, we used the same dataset as Wallner et al. [19]. This dataset consists of in total 16 graph pairs. These were originally created by deriving four alterations by adding up to four edges and nodes (incl. an extra edge) to four different base graphs that themselves differed in size (between about 40–100 nodes) and structure. In the study the original (base) graph was displayed below the altered version. Figure 1 gives some examples with differences marked in red for representation purposes.[1]

---

[1] For a complete overview of all graph pairs please refer to: https://figshare.com/s/27396e7451506f3e827d.

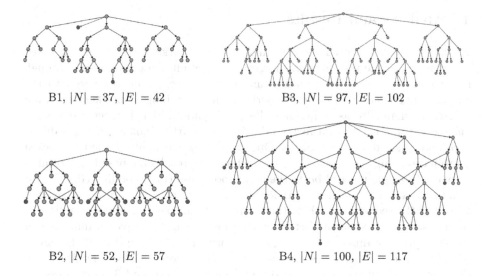

B1, $|N| = 37$, $|E| = 42$

B3, $|N| = 97$, $|E| = 102$

B2, $|N| = 52$, $|E| = 57$

B4, $|N| = 100$, $|E| = 117$

Fig. 1. The four base graphs $B1 - B4$ (blue) with the changes of one alternative graph highlighted in red (for representation purposes only). In the study alternative and base graph were displayed below each other. (Color figure online)

Procedure: For data collection we administered an online survey using LimeSurvey [11] to students at the TU Wien by advertising it in lectures. Informed consent was obtained on the first page of the survey. This was followed by basic demographic questions inquiring about the age, gender, and familiarity with graph visualization. The latter was recorded on a 5-point scale anchored by 1 = very familiar and 5 = very unfamiliar. The main part of the survey consisted of showing the 16 graph pairs in, following Wallner et al. [19], semi-random order. In other words, we counterbalanced the order of graphs while also making sure that graphs with similar changes are not displayed consecutively. For each graph pair, participants had to mark the differences in the upper graph by dragging markers to the respective locations. Once a marker was placed it could not be moved anymore. To allow subjects to familiarize themselves with this interaction we included an example before showing the actual graphs. As we were interested in how salient certain changes are, we imposed a time limit of one minute for each graph pair. Once the participant indicated to have finished marking all differences or the time limit was over, the participants were asked to indicate on 5-point scales how certain they were (1 = very certain, 5 = very uncertain) to have found all differences and how difficult it was (1 = very easy, 5 = very difficult) to find them. Afterward, the survey continued with the next graph pair.

Participants: In total, we received 40 complete responses from 29 males and 11 females. Participants were on average 25 years of age (min = 19, max = 50). Five participants indicated to be very familiar with graph visualization. The majority (24) rated their familiarity with a 2 or 3, and seven with a 4. Only five stated to be very unfamiliar. On average participants needed 21 min to complete the survey.

4 Analysis and Results

As the survey only stored the coordinates of the markers, these were exported and mapped to the positions on the graph images on a per-user basis. Through manual inspection of the resulting images these were then compared to the encoded differences. We opted to perform this matching of markers to graph differences manually as sometimes the participants did not exactly place the markers on, for instance, a newly added node. Markers not matching a difference were ignored for the analysis. One graph pair was omitted due the tracked coordinates being erroneous. That is, the following results are based on a total of 11 pairs. If people marked both, the added node and corresponding edge, it was counted only once. We then compiled if and how often a difference was spotted as well as the sequence in which they were marked. Each difference was categorized based on three 'local' factors which were revealed to have an influence on the perception of differences (cf. [19]): 1) shape (yes/no), that is, if the newly added node or edge changes the outer hull, i.e. silhouette of the graph. If no, the change was further categorized based on 2) density and 3) edge crossing. Density encoded how dense the graph is in the area of change. It was classified qualitatively into low, $medium$, and $high$. $Medium$ had approximately twice as much space surrounding the change and $high$ roughly twice as much as $medium$. Edge crossing (yes/no) encoded if the change introduced a new edge crossing. Responses to the Likert-like scales were treated as ordinal for the analysis.

Averaged certainty and difficult ratings for the four base graphs show a decrease in certainty (c) and an increase in perceived difficulty (d) with increasing graph complexity with B1 ($c = 1.44 \pm 0.68$, $d = 1.64 \pm 0.76$), B2 ($c = 1.81 \pm 0.87$, $d = 2.16 \pm 0.93$), B3 ($c = 2.11 \pm 0.89$, $d = 2.38 \pm 0.84$), and B4 ($c = 2.59 \pm 1.04$, $d = 2.99 \pm 0.92$). Spearman correlations based on the certainty and difficulty ratings of the individual pairs showed significant correlations between certainty and difficulty ($r_s = .717$, $p < .001$) and between the percentage of found differences[2] and difficulty ($r_s = -.230$, $p < .001$) and certainty ($r_s = -.313$, $p < .001$).

A chi-square test to examine if changing the shape influenced the perception of a difference was not significant ($\chi^2(1) = 2.48$, $p = .115$). To assess if density and newly introduced edge crossings influenced the perception of differences we used generalized estimating equations (GEE) with a binary logistic regression model. The encoded differences were treated as a within-subject variable. GEE model estimates are summarized in Table 1(a). No statistically significant interaction effect between density and edge crossing could be observed. The results indicate that an increase in density lowers the recognition of a difference significantly, while a newly introduced edge crossing helps to spot a change.

---

[2] Since different graph pairs had a different number of changes we expressed the number of detected differences in terms of percentages instead of raw counts.

Table 1. Results of generalized estimating equations models predicting the effect of edge crossing and density on (a) if a differences is recognized or not and the order in which they are found for graphs with (b) two, (c) three, and (d) four changes (OR = odds ratio, calculated as e^B, B = coefficient, CI = confidence interval).

Predictor	B	OR	95% CI	p	B	OR	95% CI	p
edge crossing								
no			— reference —				— reference —	
yes	1.438	4.212	[1.807, 2.820]	.001	1.421	4.141	[0.540, 2.302]	.002
density								
low			— reference —				— reference —	
medium	-0.697	0.498	[-1.172, -0.222]	.004	-0.412	0.662	[-0.628, -0.196]	< .001
high	-2.079	0.125	[-2.583, -1.576]	< .001	-1.430	0.239	[-2.237, -0.624]	.001

| (a) recognition | (b) order, two changes |

Predictor	B	OR	95% CI	p	B	OR	95% CI	p
edge crossing								
no			— reference —				— reference —	
yes	-0.749	0.473	[-1.203, -0.294]	.001	-1.810	0.164	[-2.264, -1.356]	< .001
density								
low			— reference —				— reference —	
medium	0.186	1.204	[-0.157, 0.529]	.288	1.853	6.380	[1.371, 2.336]	< .001
high	1.138	3.120	[0.618, 1.658]	< .001	3.708	40.77	[2.445, 4.972]	< .001

| (c) order, three changes | (d) order, four changes |

Since places within sequences of different length are not directly comparable, sequences in which differences were found were analyzed separately for graph pairs encoding two (6 pairs), three (5), and four differences (4). Influence of shape was again assessed using chi-square tests showing a significant influence of shape changes on how early a difference was marked for graphs with two ($\chi^2(1) = 15.41$, $p < .001$) and four ($\chi^2(3) = 12.86$, $p = .005$) changes but not for graphs with three changes ($\chi^2(2) = 0.535$, $p = .765$). Influence of density and edge crossings were assessed using GEE as above but with ordinal logistic regression models. GEE model estimates for graphs with two, three, and four changes are shown in Table 1(b-d). Interestingly, results for the three and four changes graphs are antipodal to those of graphs with two changes. In case of the former two, increased density is a factor that contributed to changes being recognized later while for graphs with only two changes, increased density surprisingly helped to spot differences early. The same applies to changes introducing edge crossings, in case of three and four changes these helped to recognize a difference before others, while for graphs with two changes it was the other way round.

5   Discussion

In summary, if graphs were perceived as more difficult, participants were less certain to have found all differences. If participants found more differences than they considered the task less difficult. Finding more changes also made participants feel more confident that they really spotted all differences.

If a change affected the shape, i.e. the hull of the graph, then it helped to spot the change before other changes in the majority of cases. However, it also showed not to be a decisive factor if a change is recognized or not. Density and introducing edge crossings, on the other hand, showed to be important if a change is recognized at all when the outer shape is not affected. Our results thus confirm the findings of our qualitative work [19] that introducing an edge crossing helps to locate a difference. While edge crossings have been considered detrimental for graph comprehension (e.g., [14]) it appears that for certain applications such as difference perception purposefully introducing a crossing can also be beneficial. Similarly, higher density areas made it more difficult to actually find a difference and also how early it was recognized, whereas placing changes in low density areas helped to spot them. However, our results also showed the inverse effect in case of graphs with only two changes. This may warrant further investigations but we suspect this to be a result of some of the changes in high density areas also being located near the boundary of the graph and were thus easier to spot.

When interpreting the results of this study it should thus be kept in mind that controlling for all kinds of confounding factors while still maintaining a certain systematic variation across the encoded differences is challenging to achieve in such a complex setting. Results may also change if the time limit is further reduced and/or the graph size increases.

In general, however, our results indicate that the influence of these factors also hold up when comparisons need to be made under time constraints. However, the importance of the outer shape – while still important – appears not to be as pronounced compared to our results without enforced time limit. There is some indication that time constraints generate a less holistic approach of participants, but there are still many open issues to be investigated in future research. Use of eye-tracking technology may shine further light on these issues. Lastly, we should highlight that we relied on a convenience sample and graphs of a certain size and complexity. As such results may not apply equally to other graphs. In future work, we will make use of these findings to inform the development of an algorithm that adjusts the layout specifically for comparison purposes.

6   Conclusions

In the study reported here, we tested how time limits affect the importance of several graph-related properties for the perception of differences in directed acyclic graphs. With respect to RQ1 – the influence of shape, edge crossings, and local density – our results indicate that edge crossings and density significantly impacted the recognition of differences, while the outer shape of the graph did not. In response to RQ2, all three factors, in general, did affect the order in which differences were perceived but the direction (beneficial or detrimental) of their influence was not entirely consistent across graph pairs with different amount of changes. Further work is required to gain more holistic insights on this matter.

References

1. Andrews, K., Wohlfahrt, M., Wurzinger, G.: Visual graph comparison. In: 13th International Conference Information Visualisation, pp. 62–67 (2009)
2. Archambault, D., Purchase, H.C., Pinaud, B.: Difference map readability for dynamic graphs. In: Brandes, U., Cornelsen, S. (eds.) GD 2010. LNCS, vol. 6502, pp. 50–61. Springer, Heidelberg (2011). https://doi.org/10.1007/978-3-642-18469-7_5
3. Ballweg, K., Pohl, M., Wallner, G., von Landesberger, T.: Visual similarity perception of directed acyclic graphs: a study on influencing factors and similarity judgment strategies. J. Graph Algorithms Appl. **22**(3), 519–553 (2018)
4. Bogunovich, P., Salvucci, D.: The effects of time constraints on user behavior for deferrable interruptions. In: Proceedings of the SIGCHI Conference on Human Factors in Computing Systems, New York, NY, USA, pp. 3123–3126. ACM (2011)
5. Bridgeman, S., Tamassia, R.: A user study in similarity measures for graph drawing. In: Marks, J. (ed.) GD 2000. LNCS, vol. 1984, pp. 19–30. Springer, Heidelberg (2001). https://doi.org/10.1007/3-540-44541-2_3
6. Gleicher, M.: Considerations for visualizing comparison. IEEE Trans. Visual Comput. Graphics **24**(1), 413–423 (2018)
7. Gleicher, M., Albers, D., Walker, R., Jusufi, I., Hansen, C.D., Roberts, J.C.: Visual comparison for information visualization. Inf. Vis. **10**(4), 289–309 (2011)
8. Goldstone, R.L., Son, J.Y.: Similarity. In: Holyoak, K.J., Morrison, R.G. (eds.) The Cambridge Handbook of Thinking and Reasoning. Oxford University Press, Oxford (2012)
9. Hertzum, M., Holmegaard, K.D.: Perceived time as a measure of mental workload: effects of time constraints and task success. Int. J. Hum. Comput. Interact. **29**(1), 26–39 (2013)
10. Li, J., Liu, Y., Wang, C.: Evaluation of graph layout methods based on visual perception. In: Proceedings of the Tenth Indian Conference on Computer Vision, Graphics and Image Processing. ICVGIP 2016, New York, NY, USA. ACM (2016)
11. Limesurvey GmbH.: Limesurvey (2020). http://www.limesurvey.org
12. Marriott, K., Purchase, H., Wybrow, M., Goncu, C.: Memorability of visual features in network diagrams. IEEE Trans. Visual Comput. Graphics **18**(12), 2477–2485 (2012)
13. Peterson, M.A., Rhodes, G. (eds.): Perception of Faces. Objects and Scenes. Analytic and Holistic Processes. Oxford University Press, Oxford (2003)
14. Purchase, H.: Which aesthetic has the greatest effect on human understanding? In: DiBattista, G. (ed.) GD 1997. LNCS, vol. 1353, pp. 248–261. Springer, Heidelberg (1997). https://doi.org/10.1007/3-540-63938-1_67
15. Reisberg, D.: Cognition: Exploring the Science of the Mind. W.W. Norton and Co, Boston (1997)
16. Soni, U., Lu, Y., Hansen, B., Purchase, H.C., Kobourov, S., Maciejewski, R.: The perception of graph properties in graph layouts. Comput. Graphics Forum **37**(3), 169–181 (2018)

17. Svenson, O., Maule, A. (eds.): Time Pressure and Stress in Human Judgement and Decision Making. Plenum Press, New York (1993)
18. von Landesberger, T., Pohl, M., Wallner, G., Distler, M., Ballweg, K.: Investigating graph similarity perception: A preliminary study and methodological challenges. In: Proceedings of the 12th International Joint Conference on Computer Vision, Imaging and Computer Graphics Theory and Applications, pp. 241–250. SCITEPRESS (2017)
19. Wallner, G., Pohl, M., von Landesberger, T., Ballweg, K.: Perception of differences in directed acyclic graphs: influence factors & cognitive strategies. In: Proceedings of the 31st European Conference on Cognitive Ergonomics, New York, NY, USA, pp. 57–64. ACM (2019)

Map or Gantt? Which Diagram Helps Viewers Best in Spatio-Temporal Data Exploration Tasks?

Leonie Bosveld-de Smet[(✉)] and Daniël Houben

University of Groningen, Groningen, The Netherlands
l.m.bosveld@rug.nl

Abstract. In this paper we investigate the effectiveness and efficiency of two two-dimensional static visual representations of spatio-temporal data, a map-based and a Gantt-based diagram, in their support of various information retrieval tasks. The map-based diagram is characterized by a natural spatial arrangement of locations on a schematic map. The Gantt-based one represents time naturally as a linearly ordered set of time intervals from left to right. A within-subject empirical experiment has been conducted, in which participants were asked to verify queries about persons, locations, and time intervals. The formulation of the queries was based on (i) Bertin's three reading levels, (ii) certain cognitive operations, and (iii) different syntactic orders of expressions denoting persons, locations and times. Response correctness and response time were recorded. With respect to response accuracy, both diagrams support viewers well in nearly all information retrieval tasks. Regarding efficiency, the map-based diagram elicited significantly faster response times than the Gantt-based one, except for queries with time in focus. The results suggest that map-based diagrams require less search and reasoning effort of viewers to retrieve the information asked for in the task types used in this study.

Keywords: Information visualization · Spatio-temporal data · Map · Gantt chart · Data exploration tasks · Reading levels · Cognitive operations

1 Introduction

This paper is about visual representations of spatio-temporal data based on two popular static two-dimensional diagrams, the geographic map and the Gantt chart. It is also about data exploration tasks to be performed with the aid of these two diagram types. Both diagram types are adapted to make them suited to the representation of the three components involved in spatio-temporal data, which are objects, locations and times. The paper has two aims. The first is to investigate to what extent the adaptations of the map and the Gantt chart facilitate the performance of certain information retrieval tasks. The second aim is to explore in what way task type and complexity of the information depicted affect task performance.

© Springer Nature Switzerland AG 2020
A.-V. Pietarinen et al. (Eds.): Diagrams 2020, LNAI 12169, pp. 357–364, 2020.
https://doi.org/10.1007/978-3-030-54249-8_28

Spatio-temporal data are data that relate to both space and time. Andrienko *et al.* classify these data according to the kind of changes occurring over time [1]. In this study, the spatio-temporal data are based on appearances of individuals, also called agents, at a certain location in a certain time interval. The pattern of appearance and disappearance of agents at certain locations may be thought of as a continuous path through space-time. The changing states can be fully known, only partially known, or unknown.

Spatio-temporal data are best represented in a way that conforms to human conceptualizations of the world in space and time [7]. For the representation of space, static maps are a popular and intuitive way to show all kinds of geographical information. Map representations use horizontal and vertical axes to encode the canonical world directions of north-south and east-west [8]. Mapping time to space is less obvious. Time is an abstract notion. Its dynamic character suggests a representation by time, rather than space. Dynamic and interactive visual representations of spatio-temporal data can add a dimension to the interpretation of geographic data. Dynamic maps allow to view temporal characteristics of change in 'world time' or 'display time' [3]. Nevertheless, we often use space to reason about time [5]. Timelines are powerful and well-understood metaphors for visualizing time. For most European people, time is naturally represented as a timeline from left to right, or from top to bottom, indicating progression of time [9]. Such a timeline is a linearly ordered set of time points or time intervals within a certain timespan. Calendars, diaries, appointment books and the like make use of this conceptualization of time.

The two diagrams used in this study are adaptations of two popular diagrams most people are familiar with, namely the geographic map and the Gantt chart. Originally neither of these diagram types are designed for the representation of spatio-temporal data. For this study, they are adapted in order to represent all three interrelated components involved in spatio-temporal data, following Kriglstein *et al.* [6]. Figures 1 and 2 illustrate how we have adapted the map and the Gantt chart. In the map adaptation, locations are visualized as circles corresponding to their geographic location. The Gantt adaptation uses the original time representation of the Gantt, as a timeline of time intervals on the x-axis at the top, from left to right, as time proceeds. In the map, time intervals are indicated by numeric annotations next to circle portions. Moreover, residence time corresponds to sizes of circle portions that are calculated relatively to the other agents' residence times at that location. In the Gantt adaptation, locations are placed on the y-axis as textual row labels, from top to bottom, in alphabetical order. Shape and color coding are used for the representation of agents. A legend associates colors to agents' names. The map adaptation represents agents as circle portions in different colors, the Gantt adaptation consists in replacing the bars that originally illustrate projects, by agents' appearances, in different colors. Note that in both adaptations, only one component gets an intuitive representation, which is location in the map and time in the Gantt, while the other components' representations are less intuitive.

For this study, we decided to differentiate agents' paths through time and space according to complexity. We consider a path and its representation as simple in case it implies at most two location changes of an agent. For complex paths the number of an agent's moves varies from two to six. Note that the complexity of a path affects its representation.

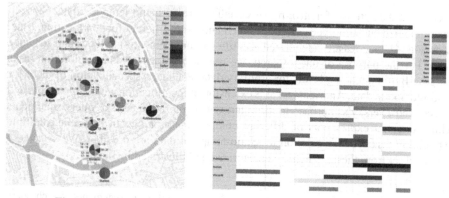

Fig. 1. Map (left) and Gantt (right) depicting the same complex scenario

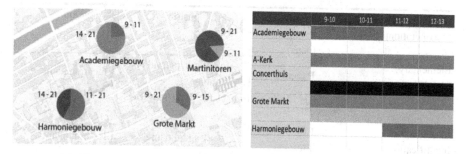

Fig. 2. Parts of Map (left) and Gantt (right) depicting simple scenarios

For the measurement of users' performance with the map-based and the Gantt-based adaptations, we have used a variety of visual data exploration tasks. There are numerous typologies of data exploration tasks [1]. One such typology is suggested by question types and reading levels, proposed by Bertin for arbitrary data [2]. There are as many question types as there are components in the data. For each question type, Bertin introduces three reading levels: elementary, intermediate, and overall. The level of reading indicates whether a question refers to a single component (elementary), to a group of components (intermediate), or to the whole phenomenon characterized by all components together (overall). Peuquet confines Bertin's notions of question type and reading levels to spatio-temporal data [7]. The notion of reading levels can be independently applied to the spatial and to the temporal dimensions of spatio-temporal data. Combinations are possible. Bertin's scheme is not fully satisfying for spatio-temporal data. While it makes explicit that exploration tasks involve identification of (sets of) single elements, it leaves implicit whether other cognitive operations are involved. Within the same question type and reading level, the exploration task may indeed require the analyst to compare or relate two or more (sets of) elements. The identification-comparison dimension should be added to the typology of data exploration tasks [1]. Comparison should be interpreted here in Blok's broad sense of determining relationships [3]. The concrete linguistic specification of data exploration tasks adds another differentiating aspect. Kessell and

Tversky, in their study of matrix-based visualizations of spatio-temporal data, chose to operationalize question types as query statements with different foci on location, time, or person [4]. Queries are categorized according to the element(s) in focus and sentence order. For the purpose of our research, we used a typology of data exploration tasks merging Bertin's reading levels for arbitrary data, Peuquet's specialization of these for spatio-temporal data, Andrienko et al.'s extension of identification with comparison, and Kessell and Tversky's approach to formulate data exploration tasks as query statements with referential expressions of different components as topic. In principle, multiple exploration task types in relation to spatio-temporal data are possible. We selected a restricted set from these, which are categorized and illustrated in Table 1.

Table 1. Query types used in the experiment and examples of query statements of each query type, translated from Dutch.

Reading level and cognitive operation(s)	1st position (component in focus)	2nd position	3rd position
Elementary; Identification	1 agent name	1 time interval (1 hour)	1 location name
	e.g.: **Julia** is from **11 to 12** at **the Pathé**		
Intermediate; Identification	1 time interval (1 hour)	>1 agent name	1 location name
	e.g.: From **13 to 14 Arie and Stefan** are on **the Martinitoren**		
Intermediate; Identification, Comparison and Counting	1 time interval (1 hour)	cardinality of group of agents	1 location name
	e.g.: From **15 to 16** there are **exactly three persons** at **the Vismarkt**		
Overall; Identification and Comparison	1 agent name	whole timeline	>1 location name
	e.g.: **Bert** visits **today the HEMA and the railway station**		
Overall; Identification, Comparison, and Counting	1 location name	whole timeline	cardinality of group of agents
	e.g.: **The A-Kerk** is visited **today** by **exactly five persons**		

In order to get more insight into the information read-off afforded by adaptations of the map and the Gantt chart, and its possible relation with query type and complexity, we have formulated the following three interrelated research questions:

RQ1: To what extent do two specific adaptations of the map and the Gantt chart facilitate naive users in the performance of spatio-temporal data exploration tasks?

RQ2: Does task type, characterized on the basis of (i) reading level, (ii) cognitive operations involved, and (iii) task wording, affect task performance?

RQ3: Does information complexity, based on number of moves of agents through space and time, affect task performance?

2 Method

To answer the research questions, we conducted an empirical experiment with a within-subject design[1]. Forty individuals with different age, gender, and educational background were recruited to take part in the experiment. The sample consisted of 18 male and 22 female participants, with a wide age range from 16 to 78. All participants were native speakers of Dutch, with normal reading proficiency. None of the participants was color blind. All participants were familiar with maps and tabular representations of timelines. Most were more or less familiar with the city center used in the scenarios represented by the diagrams.

All participants were subjected to 32 different queries in total, corresponding to the five different types of data exploration tasks as given in Table 1. Sixteen queries (4 categorized as elementary, 4 as intermediate, and 8 as overall) had to be answered with the map, 8 with the simple version, and 8 with the complex one. The same distribution of queries was used for the Gantt. The visualization types and the queries were presented to the participants in random sequence. Answer accuracy and answer completion time were recorded. Half of the queries are true, the other half false.

The map-based and the Gantt-based visualizations each represent different scenarios of people residing at different locations during certain time intervals. The locations are chosen in the center of the city of Groningen, in the north of the Netherlands. The spatio-temporal data consist of 12 different agents, 12 one-hour time intervals, ranging from 9 A.M. to 9 P.M. and 12 well distinguishable locations (church, shop, cinema, etc.) in the city of Groningen. The movement of agents differs from no movement to a maximum of six location changes. These data are visualized in the map and the Gantt format as shown in Fig. 1 for a complex scenario.

A digital survey was created in Qualtrics. The total survey consisted of (i) an introductory page, explaining shortly the experiment, (ii) the actual survey with the 32 query statements and accompanying visual representations, and (iii) post-task questions, consisting of demographic questions and questions about preference, and insightfulness and aesthetics of the diagram types used in the study.

Each participant took individually part in the experiment in a quiet environment, and used a mouse, keyboard, and display with a minimum resolution of 1600×900 px. The researcher was present in the room, with view on the display and the participant, and took notes, if there was a reason to do so.

---

[1] The materials will be available for the interested readers. Contact the authors for more information.

3 Results

There was one outlier. The results discussed below are based on 39 × 32 result data points for accuracy and for completion time, each. No effect of age, gender, educational background and preference was found. For the inferential statistics, we have used paired-samples t-tests. An overview of all response accuracy and response time results is shown in Table 2.

Table 2. Mean response accuracy (left) and mean response time (right) results per task type, diagram type, and diagram complexity degree.

Data Exploration task	Response accuracy measures (Mean accuracy in percentages)				Completion time measures (Mean completion time in seconds)			
	Simple versions		Complex versions		Simple versions		Complex versions	
	%	p	%	p	Mean	p	Mean	p
Elem. ident.								
Map	92.3	0.744	93.6	0.534	**34**	**<0.001***	**41**	**<0.001***
Gantt	91.1		91.1		**43**		**53**	
Interm. ident.								
Map	87.2	0.711	89.7	0.711	27	0.294	29	0.494
Gantt	89.7		87.2		29		27	
Interm. count.								
Map	92.3	0.570	**94.9**	**0.002***	20	0.901	28	0.918
Gantt	94.9		**64.1**		20		28	
Overall comp.								
Map	98.7	0.999	98.7	0.570	**36**	**0.005***	**38**	**<0.001***
Gantt	98.7		97.4		**42**		**47**	
Overall count.								
Map	98.7	0.103	98.7	0.999	**23**	**0.002***	**21**	**0.002***
Gantt	93.6		98.7		**30**		**40**	

Results in **Bold**, and p-values in **Bold** with asterisk indicate significant Map-Gantt differences.

Both map-based and Gantt-based representations of spatio-temporal data are nearly equally effective. Regarding overall response accuracy, there is no significant difference between the map and the Gantt $(t(38) = -1.859, p = 0.0707$ (two-tail)). Neither task type, nor complexity seems to affect accuracy performance. The only significant difference in accuracy performance we have detected is one between the complex map and the complex Gantt, for the intermediate search level task involving identification of a single time interval and a single location, and counting of number of agents visiting that location at that time. This task turned out to be more difficult to perform with the aid of the complex Gantt (only 24 of the 39 queries, 64.1%, were answered correctly) than for the complex map (37 correct answers out of 39, 94.9%). At α-level 0.05, this difference is significant $(t(38) = -3.376, p = 0.002$ (two-tail)), in favor of the map.

The efficiency results clearly show that the map-based representations are more facilitative than the Gantt-based ones. On average the participants took six minutes to verify the 16 queries with the Gantt, and took five minutes with the map to verify 16 similar queries. Overall, the participants performed the tasks significantly faster with the map than with the Gantt ($t(38) = 7.223$, $p = <0.001$ (two-tail)). The completion times per task type given in Table 2 shows much more diversity than the response accuracy results. Significant differences have been found for tasks with a component in focus other than time. The participants performed the elementary identification tasks significantly faster with both the simple and complex versions of the map (simple: $t(38) = 4.566$, $p = <0.001$ (two-tail); complex: $t(38) = 4.580$, $p = <0.001$ (two-tail)). Similar results are observed for the overall search tasks, with either agent or location in focus, and involving only comparison, or comparison and counting. Both simple and complex versions of the Gantt turned out to be significantly less supportive than their map variants (overall comp. simple: $t(38) = 2.958$, $p = 0.005$ (two-tail); overall comp. complex: $t(38) = 4.793$, $p = <0.001$ (two-tail); overall count. simple: $t(38) = 3.361$, $p = 0.002$ (two-tail); overall count. complex: $t(38) = 3.286$, $p = 0.002$ (two-tail)). We observe that complexity of scenario depicted tends to increase response times. Yet, this increase is not significant.

4 Discussion

Both map-based and Gantt-based adaptations allow naive users to answer the query statements quite accurately, without there being a significant difference between the two diagram types. There is only one exception. The participants made significantly more errors with the Gantt-based representation depicting complex information in their performance of intermediate reading level tasks, involving identification, comparison, and counting, with focus on time in wording. We suspect that this result is due to the visual delimitation of location. In the map, the locations are clearly delimited by their circular shape. The Gantt cells don't have clear contour lines for location. During the experiment some participants used their finger on the screen to make sure whether a bar was part of the row corresponding to some location. The map-based adaptation is, however, significantly more facilitative with respect to efficiency, especially in tasks which do not have time in focus (**RQ1**).

Task type has barely influence on effectiveness, but it does affect efficiency. Focus on time in task wording seems to lead to relatively faster response times in the Gantt-based diagram, but does not seem to be harmful for the map-based one, although time does not get an intuitive representation here. Task wording has an effect, but this effect seems to be rather moderate, as it did not help participants to be more accurate in the complex case (**RQ2**).

The results do not suggest any clear effects of complexity of information depicted in the diagrams, neither on effectivity, nor on efficiency of task performance. Only in one specific case participants performed significantly worse, but in this case the participants were relatively faster, due to the wording of the task. So here again, the effect is moderate. A visually clearer design of location rows in the Gantt might eliminate this significant difference (**RQ3**).

In conclusion, in their specific forms chosen for this study, maps fit cognitively better to spatio-temporal exploration tasks than Gantt charts do, at least with respect to efficient scanning. There is a limited effect of task type, and a very modest effect of complexity of information represented on task performance. Understanding of and reasoning with diagrams involve an interaction between a variety of factors: (i) a diagram's inherent structural properties, (ii) specific design options chosen, (iii) match between task requirements and ease of information retrieval afforded by the diagram, and (iv) individual user's characteristics such as age, prior knowledge, cognitive style, and preference. Inherent structural properties of the two diagram types in combination with the design options used may be responsible for the better performance of the map. Also, more familiarity with a map than with a Gantt chart, and prior knowledge of the city center depicted may have worked in favor of the map. Based on the results of this study, involving only a restricted set of task types, we are not able to separate the wheat from the chaff. The results of the current study do not provide compelling evidence about which factor has been most influential. Further research has to be performed.

References

1. Andrienko, N., Andrienko, G., Gatalsky, P.: Exploratory spatio-temporal visualization: an analytical review. J. Vis. Lang. Comput. **14**(6), 503–541 (2003)
2. Bertin, J. Sémiologie graphique: les diagrammes. Mouton, Paris (1967)
3. Blok, C.: Monitoring change: characteristics of dynamic geo-spatial phenomena for visual exploration. In: Freksa, C., Habel, C., Brauer, W., Wender, Karl F. (eds.) Spatial Cognition II. LNCS (LNAI), vol. 1849, pp. 16–30. Springer, Heidelberg (2000). https://doi.org/10.1007/3-540-45460-8_2
4. Kessell, A., Tversky, B.: Visualizing space, time, and agents: production, performance, and preference. Cogn. Process. **12**(1), 43–52 (2011)
5. Kriglstein, S., Pohl, M., Smuc, M.: Pep up your time machine: recommendations for the design of information visualizations of time-dependent data. In: Huang, W. (ed.) Handbook of Human Centric Visualization, pp. 203–225. Springer, New York (2014). https://doi.org/10.1007/978-1-4614-7485-2_8
6. Kriglstein, S., Haider, J., Wallner, G., Pohl, M.: Who, where, when and with whom? Evaluation of group meeting visualizations. In: Jamnik, M., Uesaka, Y., Elzer Schwartz, S. (eds.) Diagrams 2016. LNCS (LNAI), vol. 9781, pp. 235–249. Springer, Cham (2016). https://doi.org/10.1007/978-3-319-42333-3_19
7. Peuquet, D.J.: It's about time: A conceptual framework for the representation of temporal dynamics in geographic information systems. Ann. Assoc. Am. Geogr. **84**(3), 441–461 (1994)
8. Tversky, B.: Distortions in memory for maps. Cogn. Psychol. **13**(3), 407–433 (1981)
9. Tversky, B., Kugelmass, S., Winter, A.: Cross-cultural and developmental trends in graphic productions. Cogn. Psychol. **23**(4), 515–557 (1991)

On Effects of Changing Multi-attribute Table Design on Decision Making: An Eye-Tracking Study

Takashi Ideno[1,2](✉) , Masahiro Morii[2] , Kazuhisa Takemura[3] ,
and Mitsuhiro Okada[2]

[1] Tokuyama University, Gakuendai, Shunan-Shi, Yamaguchi, Japan
idenodei@gmail.com
[2] Keio University, 2-15-45, Mita, Minato-ku, Tokyo, Japan
[3] Waseda University, 1-6-1, Nishi-Waseda, Shinjuku-ku, Tokyo, Japan

Abstract. Information tables are often used for decision making. This study considers multi-attribute table designs from a diagrammatic perspective. We used two experiments to show how the decision-making strategies and performance are changed based on table design changes, using the eye-tracking method. We employed a multi-attribute catalog table with alternatives presented along the horizontal axis and attributes along the vertical axis in Experiment 1 and the opposite layout in Experiment 2. In each experiment, we used four different types of representations of the attribute values, and these values were restricted to two levels for comparison with previous works. The four types used were: (i) numerical representations, (ii) textual representations, (iii) black-and-white representations with black representing better values, and (iv) black-and-while representations with white representing better values. Our results suggest, among others, that (1) placing the alternatives along the vertical axis makes the table easier to decide in comparison to the opposite layout, and that (2) the two-stage decision strategy is taken with numerical representations and textual representations, while a single stage strategy is taken with the black-and-white representations. We also showed how the graphic black-and-white representations made decision-making easier, and how the order changes of alternatives and of attributes of a table influenced decision makers' decision.

Keywords: Multi-attribute table design · Decision making · Eye-tracking

1 Introduction

It has previously been reported that the presentation of information in graphical-diagrammatical form often facilitates users' information processing, compared with presentations in textual form. This is also the case in the context of decision making. For example, Savage [1] showed that changing the Allais Paradox task presentation to a "table" presentation instead of the original textual presentation increased the number of subjects making rational decisions in the sense of expected utility theory [2–4].

© The Author(s) 2020
A.-V. Pietarinen et al. (Eds.): Diagrams 2020, LNAI 12169, pp. 365–381, 2020.
https://doi.org/10.1007/978-3-030-54249-8_29

Existing studies introduced bar charts as graphical representations for multi-attribute decision making (decisions among alternatives with multiple attributes) [5, 6]. Their studies showed some advantages to presenting alternatives in the form of bar charts; however, the disadvantage of the bar-chart presentation method is that it requires multiple charts corresponding to the number of attributes, meaning that many pages of bar charts are needed for one multi-attribute decision-making process.

A table is a typical among graphical presentation showing multiple alternatives of many attributes in one view. As noted by Savage [1] in the Allais Paradox task—a typical example of decision making under uncertainty—a table representation is effective in decision making. It can be said that a table's multi-attribute presentation of many alternatives makes it easier to make a decision. A typical example of a multi-attribute table is a consumer product catalog, which is commonly used in both traditional print and e-commerce. These tables are typically a matrix in which multiple product alternatives are presented on one axis and multiple product attributes to be compared on the other axis. In many decision-making situations—such as choosing services, policies, and election candidates—a multi-attribute table presentation is often considered to have the advantage of making it easier to decide.

Tables are the most basic of graphic displays; however, incorporating additional graphic presentation techniques into this format is also expected to be effective. There is a large body of research on decision making based on multi-attribute tables. For example, Payne et al. and Takemura conducted a study on decision-making strategies by presenting a multi-attribute table [7–10]. One utility based decision-making strategy is the additive strategy, which involves examining every attribute value for each alternative and calculating the utility for each alternative. However, as the additive strategy requires high cognitive load in a multi-attribute task, decision makers often adopt a two-stage decision-making strategy. In the first stage, they compare the most important attribute value for each alternative to narrow down the range of alternatives. In the second stage, utilities of the remaining alternatives are calculated and compared to make a decision. Previous studies have proposed that in the simulation method and the information-monitoring method, the two-stage strategy is effective in actual decision making [7–10].

In a typical setting of multi-attribute table decision-making research, the product names of the alternatives are arranged on the horizontal axis at the top of the table and the attributes are arranged on the vertical axis. Considering additive strategy, the table should be viewed vertically; however, when employing the two-stage strategy to reduce the cognitive load, the alternatives are narrowed down by viewing horizontally in the first stage with a vertical shift to calculate utility in the second stage.

Russo and Rosen [11] introduced the eye-tracking method, which investigates multi-attribute decision-making strategies by considering eye-movement. In this paper, we employ the eye-tracking method and report new findings on the effect of the graphical representation of multi-attribute tables. Our experimental settings were based on a product catalogue multi-attribute table with five alternatives and five attributes of digital cameras. The attribute level is simplified to two levels.

In our study, the following graphical presentation effects were examined: displays with two levels of numerical values and displays with two levels of binary color coding (black-and-white). The experiments investigated the effect on the decision-making process of reversing the horizontal and vertical axes. These experimental settings have not been used in previous multi-attribute decision-making research, and our study is the first to do so. A cognitive experiment comparing two levels of values in a black-and-white display and in a textual display was conducted by Shimojima and Katagiri [12], where the two levels were binary (i.e., true and false) and the tasks were limited to cognitive tasks. Morii et al. [13] introduced graphical representation in multi-attribute decision-making research by showing attribute values in black-and-white squares only, based on the work of Shimojima and Katagiri [12]. In [13] their black-and-white attribute tables, the values of attributes were also limited to two (with a certain threshold for each attribute) and each cell of the table was colored either black or white on a white background. They compared two methods of systematic color assignment: "quantitatively-coherent" and "qualitatively-coherent". These methods refer to the ways in which the black-and-white distinction represented the quantitative amount distinction and the ways in which it represented the quality distinction, respectively. Their main findings were that the qualitatively-coherent tables (in which, for example, the better attribute "price" value was colored as black even if the price value itself was smaller, for the black-is-better coherent tables) made decision-making easier than quantitatively-coherent tables (in which the better attribute "price" was colored as white as the price was lower) and that participants used the two-stage strategy. In the experiments of this paper, we employed the qualitatively-coherent tables, which were known easier for decision making by this former work. We also included tables with numerical values, as those are the most usual as the merchandise product catalogs, and tables with textual values, to make the setting similar to the setting of [12], where tables with textual single-letter symbols were considered for cognitive tasks, while we used numeral and textual values in a more natural setting for decision making tasks. Furthermore, a recent study [14], analyzed the comparison between vertical and horizontal display of products from the perspective of marketing research using an eye-tracking method [14]. The results showed that horizontal display enhanced variety seeking. Horizontal (vs. vertical) displays are easier to process due to a match between the human binocular vision field. However, their study focused on product displays without relating to attribute displays. Our study examines the effect of reversing the horizontal and vertical axes from the perspective of multi-attribute decision making with tables, not just product display level. We posed the following hypotheses:

Hypothesis (1) Tables using the vertical axis for the alternatives (Fig. 1-2 type) make participants' decision-making easier than tables using the axes the other way around (Fig. 1-1 type) even if the information content is exactly the same (e.g., Fig. 1-1 and Fig. 1-2), presuming that the easier horizontal eye-movement helps the standard additive utility search along each alternative.

Hypothesis (2) Tables using the black-and-white graphic representations (e.g., Fig. 1-3 and Fig. 1-4) make decision-making easier in comparison to tables using the numerical representations (e.g., Figure 1-1 and Fig. 1-2) and to tables using the textual representations (see Method Sect. 2.2). This is partly because we use black for representing the better in Fig. 1-3 values out of the two values *coherently*, which makes the utility-based normative decision easy; this is suggested partly from our former work [13], and partly from former work on purely cognitive tasks [12].

Our main findings were as follows:

1. We found that there was an effect of switching the roles of the axes, which supported Hypothesis (1); our experiments showed that placing the product-alternatives along the vertical axis made decisions easier than did placing them along the horizontal axis.
2. Our multi-attribute decision-making tasks using color (black-and-white) tables suggested that the response latency, eye-movements, and cognitive load were lower than those of numerical and textual tables. This supported Hypothesis (2).
3. Our eye-movement data analysis showed that fixation shifts with the numerical and textual value tables, when the alternatives were placed along the horizontal axis, suggested that participants took the two-stage strategy, which supported Hypothesis (3). We also found that, even though placing the alternatives along the vertical axis made the decision easier (as stated in 1 above), the participants' fixation shifts were still consistent with the two-stage strategy, which contradicted Hypothesis (3). With the black-and-white graphic tables, the eye-movement data suggested that the participants took a single-stage strategy, which supported Hypothesis (3).
4. We found that the influence of permutations of alternatives/attributes of the tables on decision making depended on types of representations (i.e., numerical representation, textual representation, and black-and-white representation).

These results provide a basis for considering a multi-attribute table design not only for merchandise catalogs but also for a wide range of decision tables of services, administration, policy choice, and election candidates, as well as various situations in education, and so on. This is discussed in the last section of this paper.

The rest of this paper presents the methods, results, and discussion.

2 Method

2.1 Participants

Forty-eight Asian students (16 males, 19–26 years old) with normal or corrected-to-normal vision were assigned to two experiments. All participants provided written informed consent in accordance with the protocol approved by the ethics committee of Keio University. Participants were individually tested and were remunerated with JPY 1,100 (approximately USD 10) for their participation.

2.2 Apparatus and Stimuli

The eye-tracking system EyeLink 1000 (SR Research Ltd., Ontario, Canada) was used to record participants' eye-movements. The stimuli were presented at the center of a 23-in. display (Mitsubishi Electric Corp., RDT234WX, Tokyo, Japan). The display was viewed from a distance of 75 cm and the head was stabilized. The display resolution was $1,920 \times 1,080$ pixels and the visual angles were $37.5°$ horizontally and $21.6°$ vertically. A fixation was defined as velocity, acceleration, and duration of eye-movements with respective thresholds of 30 °/s, 8000 °/s^2, and 100 ms.

In the experiments, a multi-attribute table of digital cameras was presented at the center of the display and the information search process was recorded by the eye-tracking system up to selecting an alternative by pressing a key. The multi-attribute table used in Experiment 1 consisted of five alternatives and five attributes, with the alternatives arranged horizontally and the attributes arranged vertically. Figure 2 shows the samples of the four types of multi-attribute tables.

Type 1: attribute value was expressed by a numerical value
Type 2: attribute value was expressed by a value "equal to or greater than" the reference value or "less than" the reference value with these textual words
Type 3: a better-quality attribute value was indicated by a black square, and a worse white
Type 4: a better-quality attribute value was indicated by a white square, and a worse black.

Note that exactly the same information contents could be expressed among the three Types, 2, 3 and 4, and their numerical instances could be expressed by Type 1 (as shown below).

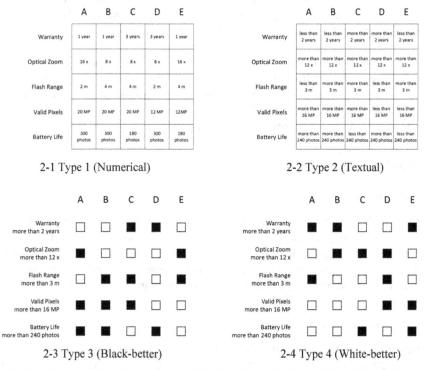

2-1 Type 1 (Numerical)　　　　　　2-2 Type 2 (Textual)

2-3 Type 3 (Black-better)　　　　　2-4 Type 4 (White-better)

Fig. 2. Sample of multi-attribute tables used in Experiment 1. Our multi-attribute tables were described in Japanese. Actually, 'more than' and 'less than' in each cell of Type 2 were expressed '以上', '未満' in Japanese two characters, respectively (e.g., 16MP 以上, 16MP未満). The exact meaning of '以上' is 'more than or equal to'. This is the case for the attribute expressions of Type 3 and Type 4.

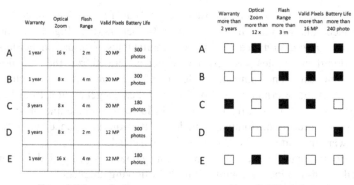

Type 1 (Numerical)   Type 3 (Black-better)

Fig. 3. Sample of multi-attribute tables in Experiment 2.

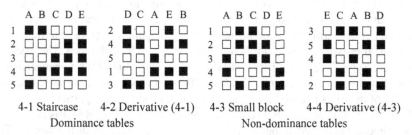

4-1 Staircase   4-2 Derivative (4-1)   4-3 Small block   4-4 Derivative (4-3)

Dominance tables   Non-dominance tables

Fig. 4. Sample tables in the dominance and the non-dominance tables in the case of Type 3. To illustrate the permutation of alternatives and attributes, the names of alternatives shown in the alphabet were indicated so that 4-2 corresponded to 4-1 and 4-4 corresponded to 4-3. In the actual experiment, the alternatives were always named A, B, C, D, and E from the left.

In Experiment 2, the arrangement of the vertical axis and the horizontal axis was switched (i.e. 5 alternatives × 5 attributes). Figure 3 shows the samples of Type 1 and Type3 in Experiment 2 that correspond to Type 1 and Type 3 in Fig. 2.

Both in Experiment 1 and Experiment 2 for each Type (Type 1 to Type 4), we used two classes of tables, the "dominance tables" class and the "non-dominance tables" class. A "dominance table" consisted of one alternative having only one better attribute, two alternatives having two better attributes, one alternative having three better attributes, and one alternative having four better attributes which was dominant over three other alternatives except one alternative which had two better attributes (e.g., Fig. 4-1 and Fig. 4-2 in the case of Type 3). We called this a "dominance table" in this paper as it had one alternative which was dominant over almost all other alternatives except one (e.g., alternative E over B, C, D, except A in Fig. 4-1 and in Fig. 4-2 in the case of Type 3). A "non-dominance table" consisted of five alternatives that having no superiority/dominance relationship to each other, with three alternatives having three better attributes and two alternatives having two better attributes (e.g., Fig. 4-3, Fig. 4-4 in the case of Type 3). A table of this class was called a "non-dominance table" because of the non-dominance relationship among all five alternatives. Our stimuli-generation procedures were as follows: we took a dominance table with a "staircase" pattern of

1-2-3-4 betters (e.g., Fig. 4-1 in the case of Type 3) as a *basic dominance table* and a non-dominance table with a "small block" of 2-3-2 betters (e.g., Fig. 4-3 in the case of type 3) as a *basic non-dominance table*. Other stimuli tables of the dominance tables class (of the non-dominance tables class resp.) were then generated from the basic dominance tables (from the basic non-dominance tables, resp.) by permutations (i.e., changing the listing orders) of the alternatives and of the attributes. A generation from Fig. 4-1 to Fig. 4-2 (from Fig. 4-3 to 4-4, resp.) of Type 3 illustrates an example of the results of generation procedures of the dominance tables (of the non-dominance tables, resp.) The procedures were the same for Type 1, Type 2, and Type 4.

Use of the dominance tables (the non-dominance tables) was called the dominance condition (the non-dominance condition) in the following chapters.

2.3 Procedure

After general information was provided and the experimental procedure described, participants sat on a chair in front of a computer screen, and the calibration procedure was completed before starting the experiment. Every participant was exposed to four blocks of 32 trials; four types of multi-attribute tables were used in each block. The first three blocks were Type 2 (Textual), Type 3 (Black-better), and Type 4 (White-better) and the three trial sequences were counter balanced. The last block was Type 1 (Numerical). The order of the trials in each block was also randomized for each participant.

At the beginning of each block, an example of the stimulus table was shown, and the experimenter provided verbal instructions. As an example, the instruction for Type 3 was as follows: "For each attribute, black cells mean TRUE and white cells mean FALSE for the attribute labels." The test block was started if there were no questions from participants.

In the test trial, after a fixation cross was presented for one second, five alternatives were presented in a multi-attribute table. Participants were asked to choose the most desirable alternative by pressing the corresponding key, without any time pressure. If the participant made their choice by pressing the key, the next trial began with no inter-trial interval. Participants' eye-movements were recorded during the experiment. In the eye-movement data analysis, we divided each trial into the first half and the second half at the median of each trial (from the stimulus onset to the key pressing). We analyzed how the decision-making processes were different between in the first and second halves.

3   Results

3.1   Response Latency

Figure 5 shows that Experiment 1 (attributes × alternatives) had a shorter response latency than Experiment 2 (alternatives × attributes). An analysis of variance (matrix arrangement × representation pattern (Type 1 to 4) × table class (dominance condition and non-dominance condition)) showed that the main effect of the matrix arrangement was significant (F [1, 46] = 4.639 < .05). This result was consistent with Hypothesis (1). The main effect of the presentation patterns was significant (F [3, 138] = 16.925 <

.001). As a result of the subtest, the response latencies in Type 3 (Black-better) and Type 4 (White-better) were shorter than those of Type 1 (Numerical) and Type 2 (Textual). This result was consistent with Hypothesis (2). Furthermore, the main effect of the table class (F [1, 46] = 55.356 < . 001) was significant. There was a significant interaction between the representation pattern and the table class (F [3, 138] = 14.469 < .001). In the dominance condition, the response latencies under Type 3 (Black-better) and Type 4 (White-better) were shorter than those in Type 1 (Numeric) and Type 2 (Textual). In the non-dominance condition, the response latencies for Type 1 (Numeric), Type 3 (Black-better), and Type 4 (White-better) were shorter than those in Type 2 (Textual). These results partially supported Hypothesis (2).

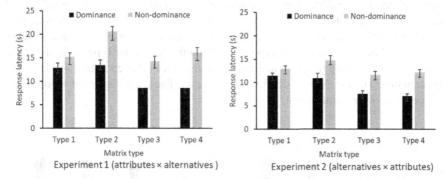

Fig. 5. The mean response latency for each type with error bars denoting standard errors of the mean.

3.2 Number of Consistent Choices

In this experiment, 32 multi-attribute tables were presented for each table type. For the breakdown of the 32 multi-attribute tables, four basic tables were arranged for the dominance-tables and the non-dominance-tables, and four multi-attribute tables with the same meaning (information content) but with different arrangements were created by changing the positions of the alternatives and attributes from each basic table. This enabled us to calculate whether all of the four choices matched for each basic table. The number of same choices among the four differently arranged tables with the same meaning/information content was called the *number of consistent choices*. This number was used as an indicator of utility-based choice, as the higher number indicated participants' better performance according to their own utility, independently of the apparent differences of looking among the same content tables. Figure 6 shows the number of consistent choices for each experiment.

The analysis of variance showed that the main effect of the table class was significant (F [1, 46] = 90.330 < .0001). The number of consistent choices in the dominance condition was higher than that in the non-dominance condition. There was also a significant interaction between the matrix arrangement and the table class (F [3, 138] = 5.615 < .001). The result of the subtest showed that in the dominance condition, the number of consistent choices for Type 3 (Black-better) and for Type 4 (White-better) was higher than that for Type 1 (Numeric). In the non-dominance condition, there was no difference by representation pattern. This result was consistent with Hypothesis (2) under the dominance condition. Furthermore, the effect of the table class for each type was examined, and the number of consistent choices was higher in the dominance condition than in the non-dominance condition for Type 2(textual), 3 (Black-better) and 4 (White-better), however no significant difference was found for type 1 (numerical). We examined the difference between the number of consistent choices among the staircase tables (the basic tables) and that among the derivative tables without staircase-like pattern in the dominance condition. We did not find any difference between the two. We predicted that the staircase-like looking tables supported participants utility-based decision making easier as stated in Hypothesis (4), but our results could be seen that all graphic dominance tables supported utility-based decision without being influenced from order change manipulations, in comparison to the numerical tables. The influence from changing the order of alternatives and attributes to decisions was the same higher level for the both two classes in Type 1. On the other hand, in Type 2, 3, and 4 the influence from changing the order to decisions in the dominance condition was less than (higher number) that in the non-dominance condition. These clarified what we expected in Hypothesis (4) to some extent.

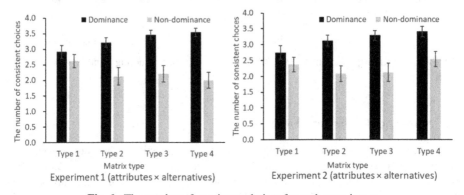

Fig. 6. The number of consistent choices for each experiment.

3.3 Fixation Shift Patterns

We omitted the eye-movement data of seven participants whose fixations were not measured (four in Experiment 1 and three in Experiment 2) and calculated the number of fixation shifts per condition for each participant. The area of interest was set to correspond to each cell of the multi-attribute table. A vertical shift was defined as a fixation shift within the same row, and a horizontal shift was defined as a fixation shift within the same column. Examples of a horizontal shift and a vertical shift are shown in Fig. 7. The average number of fixation shifts per experiment is shown on Fig. 8.

The result of the analysis of variance showed that the main effect of matrix arrangement was significant and that Experiment 2 (alternative $\times$ attribute) had fewer shifts than Experiment 1 (attribute $\times$ alternative; $F[1, 39] = 4.592 < .05$). This result supported

Hypothesis (1). The main effect of the representation pattern was significant (F [3, 117] = 36.511 < .001). As a result of the subtest, the number of fixation shifts in Type 3 (Black-better) and Type 4 (White-better) were fewer than those of Type 1 (Numerical) and Type 2 (Textual). This result supported Hypothesis (2). The main effect of shifts patterns was also significant (F [3, 117] = 20.556 < .001). Vertical shifts were fewer than horizontal shifts. Furthermore, the interaction of three factors (matrix arrangement × representation pattern × fixation shift pattern) were also significant (F [3, 117] = 2.709 < .05).

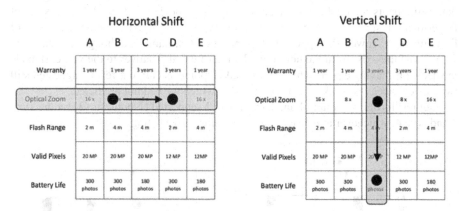

Fig. 7. Sample of a horizontal fixation shift and a vertical fixation shift.

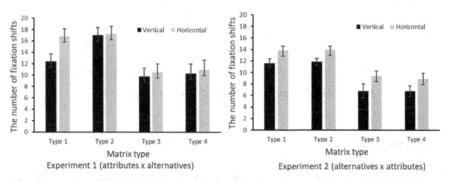

Fig. 8. The number of fixation shifts for each experiments.

To compare the shift pattern differences more accurately, we calculated the transition score based on Payne's study [7]. This score is defined as follows:

$$Transition\ Score = \frac{S_{ver} - S_{hori}}{S_{ver} + S_{hori}}$$

S_{ver} is defined as fixation shifts within the same column, whereas S_{hori} is defined as fixation shifts within the same row. This score ranges from −1.0 to +1.0, with a higher value indicating more vertical fixation shifts while a lower value indicates more horizontal fixation shifts.

The average number of transition scores per experiment is shown on Fig. 9. The analysis of variance showed that the main effect of the matrix arrangement was significant (F [1, 39] = 8.572 < . 01). Participants' fixations shifted horizontally more frequently in Experiment 2 (alternative × attribute) than in Experiment 1 (attribute × alternative). There was also a significant interaction of three factors (F [3, 117] = 11.924 < .001). The subtests showed the fixation shift patterns in Type 1 and Type 2 were changed between those in the first half and those in the second half. These results suggested that participants adopted a two-stage strategy in Type 1 and Type 2. The results of Experiment 1 supported Hypothesis (3) for Type 1 and Type 2, while the result of Experiment 2 showed the opposite of Hypothesis (3); namely, although the changing the roles of the axis (from the horizontal listing of the alternatives to the vertical) made the decision-making easier (which supported Hypothesis (1)), our result suggested still two-stage strategy was taken in Types 1 and 2, which we had not predicted.

Our results of Experiment 1 and Experiment 2 supported Hypothesis (3) for the Type 3 and type 4, whichever axis was used for the alternative listing.

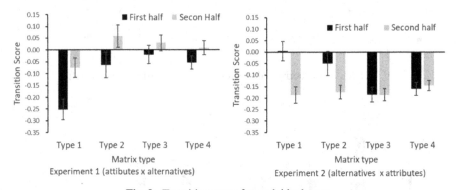

Fig. 9. Transition score for each block type.

4 Discussion

The purpose of our study was to investigate some table designing effects on individuals' decision-making processes. Our results show as follows.

1. Effect of changing the roles of the vertical and horizontal axes.

One of the major findings of this paper is the effect of switching the roles of the vertical and horizontal axes of multi-attribute tables for decision making, by Experiments 1 and 2 (see Fig. 2 and 3). Our results concerning response latencies in 3.1 (see Fig. 5) and fixation shift patterns of participants (see Fig. 8) in 3.3 revealed that, in all Types 1, 2, 3, and 4, the tables with vertical alternatives (Fig. 3) had a shorter response latency, a lower number of fixation shifts, and increased horizontal fixation shifts than a table with vertical attributes (Fig. 2). These results support Hypothesis (1). This might suggest that the table design of Fig. 3 facilitates decision makers' decisions. This was an unexpected finding in the multi-attribute decision-making studies from the 1970s, as no researchers in the field have been aware of this basic issue of the table design. In fact, using the most advanced theoretical studies with computer simulation, no theoretical difference has been assumed between the style designs from Fig. 2 and those of Fig. 3. The advantage of Fig. 3 makes sense, as our eye-movements are based on horizontal directions, and it facilitates ideal decision making based on the utility of each alternative. This finding is, in our opinion, important in the sense that it is not only concerned with commercial product catalogs but also political election candidate tables, travel scheduling choice tables, public policy tables, and others. In fact, although many former studies on multi-attribute decision making have used the Fig. 2 style, most e-commerce tables with scrolling functions use the Fig. 3 style because of the display constraints of electronic devices without knowing the basic psychological research such as this. Our results give some justification for the current prevalent style of the choice of axes in e-commerce.

2. Two-stage strategy for (Type 1, 2) and one-stage strategy for (Type 3, 4).

In particular, with the numerical tables (Type 1) in Experiment 1 and 2, we observed that the fixation shift patterns (Fig. 9) changed from the first half of the trial to the second half. Our result supports Hypothesis (3). This indicates a two-stage decision-making strategy, which means that the alternatives were narrowed down by an in-attribute search, regardless of the alternatives of the vertical axis and the horizontal axis.

We observed that even when the roles of the axes were switched (so that the alternatives were arranged along the vertical axis and the attributes were arranged along the horizontal axis), although the switching facilitated participants' decision makings as we pointed out in 1 above, the participants still followed the two-stage strategy (Fig. 9), which contradicts our Hypothesis (3); we had predicted that easier decision making (with the easier additive utility search suggested by Hypothesis (1)) would simplify the strategy. Although the two-stage strategy had often been noted in prior research by theoretical simulation results and traditional information board methods, our work relating the two-stage strategy is, as far as we know, one of only a few studies in the natural setting of decision makers' decision environment using the eye-tracking method.

We also examined the effect of color (black and white) representations of attribute values. Our results concerning a response latency (Fig. 5) and the number of shifts (Fig. 7) revealed that the black-and-white tables (Type 3 and 4) had a shorter response latency and a lower number of fixation shifts than the numerical tables (Type 1) and the textual tables (Type 2). These results support Hypotheses (2). One important finding of this study is that eye-movement patterns—which are consistent with the two-stage strategy found when numerical values (and textual values) are used for attribute values—are not found in black-and-white graphic displays of attribute values (Fig. 8 and 9). This result supports Hypothesis (3), indicating that decisions are made using a single-stage strategy in the condition of a graphic representation. Moreover, similar to the results of a previous cognitive experiment [12], reduction of cognitive load by black-and-white display was also observed in the context of our multi-attribute decision-making tasks. (Ease of utility-based decision making was suggested for the dominance table class of graphic tables, while this was not the case for the non-dominance tables, as we reported in 3.2). In [13], we used only color graphic tables in which both qualitatively-coherent color tables (i.e., smaller value, say, of price is black for the black-better table) and quantitatively-coherent color tables (i.e., small value of price is white, because of smallness, for the black-bigger table), and we found participants' tendency of two-stage strategy with the stimuli of both tables. On the other hand, in the experiments of this paper, we used the qualitatively-coherent color tables, and we found a single strategy, which suggests different ways of designing among the same black-and-white framework change decision makers' strategy.

3. Colored attribute value tables partially help utility-based decision independently of order manipulations of alternatives/attributes.

We used two classes of tables; the dominance tables class and the non-dominance tables class; a dominance table having certain strong dominance relations, in the sense of utility, among some alternatives, and a non-dominance table having no dominance relation at all among the alternatives. We examined influence of order changing of alternatives and of attributes for the same table contents to participant's decision. Our results, using the number of consistent choices in 3.2, showed that participants' decisions using graphic black-and-white tables were less influenced by changing the alternatives/attributes enumeration orders of the same table contents in comparison to that of using the numerical, for the case of dominance tables. On the other hand, no difference was found for the non-dominance tables. This suggested a positive answer to Hypothesis (4) partly. Among the different appearances of black and white shapes of the same content tables, we found no difference on the number of consistent choices, which contradicted Hypothesis (4) partly. This suggests that the graphic black-and-white tables make the utility relations in a table clearer to help decision maker's decision independently of possible order manipulation of the alternatives/attributes. We believe that further research in this direction would provide useful information as to how to design tables to assist decision maker's decision with less possible biases of listing order manipulation of alternatives/attributes. We plan to use the partial utility measure of participants for further research.

In fact, our results on the non-dominance tables (tables in which all five alternatives are competing each other without any partial dominance relation) suggest that decision makers' decisions could be easily manipulated by the layout designs of a multi-attribute table. For example, table designers or companies could put specific alternative on the top or in the center in order to manipulate or interfere with decision makers' decision. How to provide table designs that are fair for decision makers' rational decisions or their own utility-based decision is, in our opinion, an important research subject for the diagram study research community.

We would like to add one last remark regarding our main findings. As we stated above, the effect of changing the roles of the axes (see 1 above) was a characteristic finding from the five decades of research on multi-attribute decision making since the 1970s. One interpretation of this result may suggest that table designers should design tables in the Fig. 3 style (as the current e-commerce tables typically do). We emphasize this application of our main result in 1 above. However, taking into account our results in 2 above with regard to the two-stage strategy, we could consider the possibility of the opposite interpretation for fair table designs for decision makers. The results in 2 above tells us that when we use numerical (or textual) tables, even if switching the roles of the axes, decision makers still seem to take a two-stage strategy rather than a single (only utility-based) strategy. If so, decision makers' first stage of narrowing down the five alternatives to a few alternatives is an important process. Additionally, the decision maker should take time for this first stage, and use of axes in the Fig. 3 style might decrease this important process, costing too much. From this interpretation, the two-stage strategy associated with the Fig. 2 style use of axes might have its significance. Hence, there are two possible opposite interpretations of our finding 1 above.

	Product A	Product B	Product C	Product D	Product E
Valid Pixels	12 MP	20 MP	24 MP	20 MP	20 MP
Optical Zoom	5 x	8 x	4 x	5 x	4.2 x
F Number	2	2.8	2.8	1.8	1.8
Focus Distance	25mm	24mm	28mm	24mm	24mm
Touch Panel	●	●	●	●	
GPS	●		●		
Blue Tooth		●	●		
USB Charge	●	●		●	
Water Proof		●			●
Self Timer	●		●	●	●

10-1 Commonly used table

	Product A	Product B	Product C	Product D	Product E
Price	¥44,200	¥132,800	¥95,400	¥94,800	¥79,600
Valid Pixels	12 MP	20 MP	24 MP	20 MP	20 MP
Optical Zoom	5 x	8 x	4 x	5 x	4.2 x
F Number	2	2.8	2.8	1.8	1.8
Focus Distance	25mm	24mm	28mm	24mm	24mm
Shutter Speed	1/2000	1/4000	1/2000	1/1600	1/2000
Battery Life	340 photos	260 photos	200 photos	230 photos	235 photos
Weight	257g	302g	253g	340g	304g
Best Sellers	1	2	3	4	5
Customer Rating	4.0	4.0	3.5	3.0	3.0

10-2 Highlight table

Fig. 10. Sample of attribute tables in our future work.

Based on the results of this paper, in the future, we hope to run the following two natural extensions of the current study, which are both combinations between Type 1 and Type 3. (1) We could study the most commonly used catalog designs to confirm the various graphic effects that we obtained in this paper. A typical type of catalog is the type of Fig. 10-1 where the numerical attributes (Type 1 in this paper) and the graphic yes-no values (Type 3 or 4 in this paper) for function values are combined. One could add horizontal belts to support horizontal eye-movements. Hence, this sort of commonly used table design is a combined design we studied in this paper. It is plausible that we could explain why the commonly used table designs are useful and justifiable from basic psychological research from a diagrammatic viewpoint. (2) Another way to combine our basic types to make a practically useful table would be to have a "highlight table," where certain important attribute values are "fairly" highlighted, combining Type 1 (numerical values) with the colored backgrounds of some important values such as in Fig. 10-2. This is a combination of Type 1 and Type 3 and could be used to design tables with high quality features, leading to fair and easy decisions. The graphic effects of Type 3 are expected to support typical value-based tables.

Acknowledgements. This work was supported by JSPS KAKENHI Grant Numbers JP19KK0006, JP17H02265, JP17H02263, JP19K13844.

References

1. Savage, L.J.: The foundations of statistics. Courier Corporation (1972)
2. Allais, M.: Le comportement de l'homme rationnel devant le risque: critique des postulats et axiomes de l'école Américaine. [Rational behavior under risk-criticism of the postulates and axioms of the american school]. Econometrica **21**(4), 503–546 (1953). https://doi.org/10.2307/1907921
3. Yamagishi, K.: Koudou Ishikettei Ron kara Kangaeru. [Considering from the view of behavioral decision theory] In: Sakadami, T. (ed.) Ishikettei to Keizai no Shinrigaku [Psychology of Decision-making and Economics], pp. 156–168. Asakura Publishing, Tokyo (2009)
4. Harman, J.L., Gonzalez, C.: Allais from experience: choice consistency, rare events, and common consequences in repeated decisions. J. Behav. Decis. Making **28**(4), 369–381 (2015). https://doi.org/10.1002/bdm.1855
5. Jarvenpaa, S.L.: The effect of task demands and graphical format on information processing strategies. Manage. Sci. **35**(3), 285–303 (1989). https://doi.org/10.1287/mnsc.35.3.285
6. Jarvenpaa, S.L.: Graphic displays in decision making—the visual salience effect. J. Behav. Decis. Making **3**(4), 247–262 (1990). https://doi.org/10.1002/bdm.3960030403
7. Payne, J.W.: Task complexity and contingent processing in decision making: an information search and protocol analysis. Org. Behav. Hum. Perf. **16**, 366–387 (1976). https://doi.org/10.1016/0030-5073(76)90022-2
8. Payne, J.W., Bettman, J.R., Johnson, E.J.: Adaptive strategy selection in decision making. J. Exp. Psychol.: Learn. Mem. Cogn. **14**(3), 534–552 (1988). https://doi.org/10.1037/0278-7393.14.3.534
9. Payne, J.W., Bettman, J.R., Johnson, E.J.: The Adaptive Decision Maker. Cambridge University Press, Cambridge (1993)
10. Takemura, K.: Behavioral Decision Theory: Psychology and Mathematical Representations of Human Choice Behavior. Springer, New York (2014)
11. Russo, J.E., Rosen, L.D.: An eye fixation analysis of multialternative choice. Mem. Cogn. **3**(3), 267–276 (1975). https://doi.org/10.3758/BF03212910
12. Shimojima, A., Katagiri, Y.: An eye-tracking study of integrative spatial cognition over diagrammatic representations. In: Hölscher, C., Shipley, T.F., Olivetti Belardinelli, M., Bateman, J., Newcombe, N.S. (eds.) Spatial Cognition, pp. 262–278. Springer, Berlin (2010). https://doi.org/10.1007/978-3-642-14749-4_23
13. Morii, M., Ideno, T., Takemura, K., Okada, M.: Qualitatively coherent representation makes decision-making easier with binary-colored multi-attribute tables: an eye-tracking study. Front. Psychol. **8**, 1388 (2017). https://doi.org/10.3389/fpsyg.2017.01388
14. Deng, X., Kahn, B.E., Unnava, H.R., Lee, H.: A "wide" variety: effects of horizontal versus vertical display on assortment processing, perceived variety, and choice. J. Mark. Res. **53**(5), 682–698 (2016). https://doi.org/10.1509/jmr.13.0151

Logic and Diagrams

Using Multigraphs to Study the Interaction Between Opposition, Implication and Duality Relations in Logical Squares

Lorenz Demey[1]([✉])[iD] and Hans Smessaert[2][iD]

[1] Center for Logic and Philosophy of Science, KU Leuven, Leuven, Belgium
lorenz.demey@kuleuven.be
[2] Department of Linguistics, KU Leuven, Leuven, Belgium
hans.smessaert@kuleuven.be

Abstract. This paper uses multigraphs to study the interaction between opposition, implication and duality relations in classical and degenerate logical squares. We show, first of all, that opposition and implication are highly symmetrical in their interaction with each other. Secondly, opposition and implication also display a higher-order symmetry, in the sense that they fulfill highly similar roles in their respective interactions with duality. Thirdly, we show that all these symmetries hold for classical squares as well as for degenerate squares.

Keywords: Square of opposition · Logical square · Duality · Opposition · Implication · Multigraph · Logical geometry

1 Introduction

Logical geometry studies Aristotelian diagrams, such as the square of opposition and its various extensions and generalizations. These diagrams represent a number of formulas from some logical system, and the various relations holding between them. In this context, diagrammatic reasoning consists in a form of 'diagram chasing' [1]; for example, in a well-known reasoning task, one is presented with a square of opposition and the truth value of one of its formulas, and is then asked to determine the truth values of the three other formulas in the square, by making use of the Aristotelian relations that are present in the square [9, 13].

A well-known phenomenon for this type of diagrams is that multiple (types of) relations may simultaneously obtain among the formulas of a given diagram. For example, consider the well-known modal square shown in Fig. 1(a) [10]. As far as the *Aristotelian* relations are concerned, the formulas $\Box p$ and $\Box \neg p$ in this diagram are each other's *contraries*: they cannot be true together, but they can be false together. However, as far as the *duality* relations are concerned, these same two formulas are each other's *internal negation*: they result from applying

© Springer Nature Switzerland AG 2020
A.-V. Pietarinen et al. (Eds.): Diagrams 2020, LNAI 12169, pp. 385–393, 2020.
https://doi.org/10.1007/978-3-030-54249-8_30

the modal □-operator to resp. p and its negation $\neg p$. The formulas in the square in Fig. 1(a) thus simultaneously stand in Aristotelian and duality relations. By contrast, the formulas in the classical square in Fig. 1(b) [2] stand in Aristotelian relations to each other, but not in any duality relations.

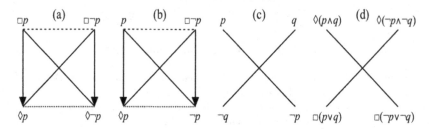

Fig. 1. (a–b) Two classical squares from resp. [10] and [2]; (c–d) two degenerate squares from resp. [4] and [11].

The two diagrams in Fig. 1(a–b) are examples of *classical* squares. It is well-known in logical geometry that next to the classical squares, there is exactly one other type of logical square, viz. the *degenerate* squares [4]. Degenerate squares often occur as subdiagrams inside a larger diagram, e.g. a Buridan octagon [11]. Apart from the contradictory relations on their diagonals, degenerate squares do not exhibit any Aristotelian relations. With regard to duality, there is again some variation. On the one hand, the degenerate square in Fig. 1(c) does not exhibit any duality relations, apart from the external negations on its diagonals. By contrast, the degenerate square in Fig. 1(d) does exhibit the full range of duality relations; for example, $\Diamond(p \wedge q)$ and $\Diamond(\neg p \wedge \neg q)$ are each other's internal negation, because these two formulas result from applying the binary operator $\Diamond(\cdot \wedge \cdot)$ to resp. p, q and their negations $\neg p$, $\neg q$.[1]

Coherent sets of logical relations are sometimes called *geometries* [15]. For example, the Aristotelian relations of contradiction, contrariety, subcontrariety and subalternation constitute the Aristotelian geometry ($\mathcal{AG}$). Similarly, one can also define the duality geometry ($\mathcal{DG}$), the opposition geometry ($\mathcal{OG}$) and the implication geometry ($\mathcal{IG}$); precise definitions will be offered later in the paper.

The interaction between these different geometries turns out to be quite subtle, which is illustrated by the fact that a single diagram (e.g. Fig. 1(a)) can simultaneously represent multiple geometries. Consequently, these geometries and their interactions have been studied extensively in recent years [3,5–7,14–16]. In particular, in [8] we proposed *multigraphs* as a new tool to investigate the interaction between $\mathcal{AG}$ and $\mathcal{DG}$ in several logical squares and octagons.

---

[1] Note that $\Diamond(\cdot \wedge \cdot)$ can be seen as the composition of the modal $\Diamond$-operator and the Boolean $\wedge$-operator, and thus also gives rise to more complex types of duality behavior [3,6–8]. However, in this paper we will simply view $\Diamond(\cdot \wedge \cdot)$ as a single operator, which exhibits the simplest type of duality behavior (cf. $\mathcal{DG}$ in Sect. 2).

The overarching goal of the present paper is to show that multigraphs are by no means limited to $\mathcal{AG}$ and $\mathcal{DG}$, but can also be used to fruitfully study the interactions between other geometries. In particular, we will investigate the interactions (i) between $\mathcal{OG}$ and $\mathcal{IG}$, (ii) between $\mathcal{OG}$ and $\mathcal{DG}$, and (iii) between $\mathcal{IG}$ and $\mathcal{DG}$, in classical and degenerate squares.[2] We will even construct multigraphs that exhibit the interactions between these three geometries ($\mathcal{OG}$, $\mathcal{IG}$ and $\mathcal{DG}$) all at once. These investigations yield three main results. First of all, $\mathcal{OG}$ and $\mathcal{IG}$ are highly symmetrical in their interaction with each other. Secondly, $\mathcal{OG}$ and $\mathcal{IG}$ also display a higher-order symmetry, in the sense that these two geometries fulfill highly similar roles in their respective interactions with $\mathcal{DG}$. Thirdly, all these symmetries hold for classical as well as degenerate squares.

The paper is organized as follows. Section 2 surveys the required theoretical background. Section 3 uses multigraphs to study the interaction between $\mathcal{OG}$, $\mathcal{IG}$ and $\mathcal{DG}$ in classical squares, and Sect. 4 does the same for degenerate squares. Section 5 wraps things up, and mentions some questions for further research.

2 Theoretical Background

We start by introducing the various logical geometries that will be studied in this paper. Logical relations can be characterized with various degrees of abstractness and generality [5,7]. For our current purposes, it will suffice to stick to the traditional, informal definitions. Two statements φ and ψ are said to be

contradictory (CD)	iff	φ and ψ cannot be true together	and
		φ and ψ cannot be false together,	
contrary (C)	iff	φ and ψ cannot be true together	and
		φ and ψ can be false together,	
subcontrary (SC)	iff	φ and ψ can be true together	and
		φ and ψ cannot be false together,	
non-contradictory (NCD)	iff	φ and ψ can be true together	and
		φ and ψ can be false together,	
in bi-implication (BI)	iff	φ entails ψ	and ψ entails φ,
in left-implication (LI)	iff	φ entails ψ	and ψ doesn't entail φ,
in right-implication (RI)	iff	φ doesn't entail ψ	and ψ entails φ,
in non-implication (NI)	iff	φ doesn't entail ψ	and ψ doesn't entail φ.

The first four of these relations constitute the *opposition geometry*, i.e. $\mathcal{OG} := \{CD, C, SC, NCD\}$. The next set of four relations is the *implication geometry*, i.e. $\mathcal{IG} := \{BI, LI, RI, NI\}$. Both of these geometries can naturally be ordered in terms of their information levels [15]: NCD and NI are the least informative relations of $\mathcal{OG}$ and $\mathcal{IG}$, respectively, CD and BI are their most informative relations, and C, SC, LI and RI occupy intermediate positions. Finally, we define the Aristotelian geometry $\mathcal{AG} := \{CD, C, SC, LI\} \subseteq \mathcal{OG} \cup \mathcal{IG}$, and note that it is 'hybrid' between $\mathcal{OG}$ and $\mathcal{IG}$ in an information-optimizing fashion [15].

---

[2] We thus use one type of diagrams (multigraphs) to study another (logical squares)!

We now turn to the duality relations. Suppose that φ and ψ are the results of applying n-ary operators O_φ and O_ψ to n propositions $\alpha_1, \ldots, \alpha_n$, i.e. $\varphi \equiv O_\varphi(\alpha_1, \ldots, \alpha_n)$ and $\psi \equiv O_\psi(\alpha_1, \ldots, \alpha_n)$. We say that φ and ψ are each other's

external negation (ENEG)	iff	$O_\varphi(\alpha_1, \ldots, \alpha_n) \equiv \neg O_\psi(\ \alpha_1, \ldots,\ \alpha_n)$,
internal negation (INEG)	iff	$O_\varphi(\alpha_1, \ldots, \alpha_n) \equiv O_\psi(\neg\alpha_1, \ldots, \neg\alpha_n)$,
dual (DUAL)	iff	$O_\varphi(\alpha_1, \ldots, \alpha_n) \equiv \neg O_\psi(\neg\alpha_1, \ldots, \neg\alpha_n)$,
identical (ID)	iff	$O_\varphi(\alpha_1, \ldots, \alpha_n) \equiv O_\psi(\ \alpha_1, \ldots,\ \alpha_n)$.

These relations constitute the *duality geometry*, i.e. $\mathcal{DG} := \{\text{ID}, \text{ENEG}, \text{INEG}, \text{DUAL}\}$, which has also been studied extensively in recent years [3,6,14,16].

In order to study the interaction between $\mathcal{AG}$ and $\mathcal{DG}$, we previously introduced the notion of an $\mathcal{AG}/\mathcal{DG}$-multigraph [8]. This notion can easily be generalized as follows. Let D be a diagram that simultaneously represents geometries $\mathcal{G}, \mathcal{G}' \in \{\mathcal{AG}, \mathcal{OG}, \mathcal{IG}, \mathcal{DG}\}$. The $\mathcal{G}/\mathcal{G}'$-*multigraph for* D is defined to be a multigraph [12] with the elements of $\mathcal{G} \cup \mathcal{G}'$ as its vertices, and precisely as many edges between vertices $R \in \mathcal{G}$ and $R' \in \mathcal{G}'$ as there are pairs of formulas in D that simultaneously stand in the relations R and R'. Informally, the $\mathcal{G}/\mathcal{G}'$-multigraph for D represents how often each combination of a $\mathcal{G}$- and a $\mathcal{G}'$-relation occurs in D, and can thus help to shed light on the interaction between $\mathcal{G}$ and $\mathcal{G}'$.

Since multigraphs are crucially concerned with *numbers* of (combinations of) logical relations in a given diagram, it is important to be explicit about how these relations will be counted. For example, a logical square has 4 formulas, and is therefore usually said to have $\binom{4}{2} = \frac{4 \times (4-1)}{2} = 6$ relations (in visual terms: the 4 sides of the square and its 2 diagonals). In this calculation, the division by 2 captures the idea that the *order* of the formulas does not matter. However, looking at the definition of $\mathcal{IG}$, it should be clear that order matters after all: $LI(\varphi, \psi)$ iff $RI(\psi, \varphi)$. Furthermore, the subtraction of 1 captures the idea that we are excluding *identical* pairs (φ, φ). However, looking at the definitions of $\mathcal{OG}$, $\mathcal{IG}$ and $\mathcal{DG}$, it should be clear that such pairs should be kept on board after all: $NCD(\varphi, \varphi)$, $BI(\varphi, \varphi)$ and $\text{ID}(\varphi, \varphi)$. Consequently, in the remainder of this paper, we will count the number of relations in a logical square as $4 \times 4 = 16$.

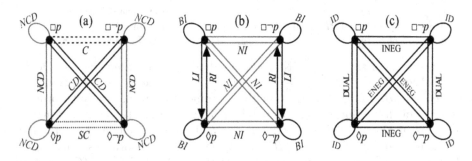

Fig. 2. (a) Opposition, (b) implication and (c) duality relations in the classical square shown in Fig. 1(a).

3   Classical Logical Squares

The classical modal square for $\{\Box p, \Box\neg p, \Diamond p, \Diamond\neg p\}$, which was already shown in Fig. 1(a), simultaneously exhibits $\mathcal{OG}$, $\mathcal{IG}$ and $\mathcal{DG}$. Consider, for example, the formulas $\Box p$ and $\Box\neg p$: we simultaneously have $C(\Box p, \Box\neg p)$, $NI(\Box p, \Box\neg p)$ and INEG($\Box p, \Box\neg p$). All $\mathcal{OG}$-, $\mathcal{IG}$- and $\mathcal{DG}$-relations among $\Box p$, $\Box\neg p$, $\Diamond p$ and $\Diamond\neg p$ are shown in Fig. 2(a), (b) and (c), respectively.

Counting the various combinations of opposition and implication relations in this square, we obtain the $\mathcal{OG}/\mathcal{IG}$-multigraph shown in Fig. 3(a). For example, this multigraph indicates that there are 4 CD/NI-combinations, viz. $(\Box p, \Diamond\neg p)$, $(\Diamond\neg p, \Box p)$, $(\Diamond p, \Box\neg p)$ and $(\Box\neg p, \Diamond p)$. Note that this multigraph exhibits perfect vertical symmetry, which means that $\mathcal{OG}$ and $\mathcal{IG}$ play very similar roles within the modal square. This vertical symmetry can be characterized in purely informational terms: the least informative relation from one geometry co-occurs precisely with the three informative relations from the other geometry. More concretely, $NCD \in \mathcal{OG}$ co-occurs with $BI, LI, RI \in \mathcal{IG}$, and vice versa, $NI \in \mathcal{IG}$ co-occurs with $CD, C, SC \in \mathcal{OG}$. This symmetry between $\mathcal{OG}$ and $\mathcal{IG}$ is explained in more detail in Theorems 2, 5 and 6 of [15].

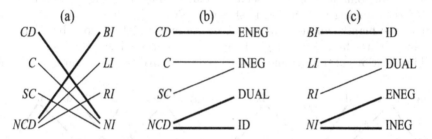

Fig. 3. (a) $\mathcal{OG}/\mathcal{IG}$-, (b) $\mathcal{OG}/\mathcal{DG}$- and (c) $\mathcal{IG}/\mathcal{DG}$-multigraphs for the classical square shown in Fig. 1(a). Thin and thick edges represent combinations of relations that co-occur resp. 2 and 4 times.

We now turn to the interaction between $\mathcal{OG}$ and $\mathcal{DG}$ in the modal square, which is summarized by the $\mathcal{OG}/\mathcal{DG}$-multigraph shown in Fig. 3(b). For example, this multigraph indicates that there are 2 $C/$INEG-combinations, viz. $(\Box p, \Box\neg p)$ and $(\Box\neg p, \Box p)$. While there is a clear correspondence between CD and ENEG, we see that INEG co-occurs with C as well as SC, and NCD co-occurs with DUAL as well as ID. This shows that the interaction between $\mathcal{OG}$ and $\mathcal{DG}$ is more subtle than is sometimes thought, especially by authors who come close to outright identifying opposition and duality relations [17].

In a similar fashion, we can also construct the $\mathcal{IG}/\mathcal{DG}$-multigraph, which is shown in Fig. 3(c). For example, this multigraph indicates that there are 2 $LI/$DUAL-combinations, viz. $(\Box p, \Diamond p)$ and $(\Box\neg p, \Diamond\neg p)$. While there is a clear correspondence between *BI* and ID, we see that DUAL co-occurs with *LI* as well as *RI*, and *NI* co-occurs with ENEG as well as INEG. Most importantly, note that the $\mathcal{IG}/\mathcal{DG}$-multigraph in Fig. 3(c) is isomorphic to the $\mathcal{OG}/\mathcal{DG}$-multigraph in Fig. 3(b), through the isomorphism $f : \mathcal{OG} \cup \mathcal{DG} \to \mathcal{IG} \cup \mathcal{DG}$:

$R \in \mathcal{OG} \cup \mathcal{DG}$	CD	C	SC	NCD	ENEG	INEG	DUAL	ID
$f(R) \in \mathcal{IG} \cup \mathcal{DG}$	BI	LI	RI	NI	ID	DUAL	ENEG	INEG

This isomorphism is logically meaningful, in that it corresponds to negating a relation's second argument: for all $R \in \mathcal{OG} \cup \mathcal{DG}$ it holds that $R(\varphi, \psi)$ iff $f(R)(\varphi, \neg\psi)$; cf. Lemma 3 of [15]. For example, we have $CD(\varphi, \psi)$ iff $BI(\varphi, \neg\psi)$, and also ENEG(φ, ψ) iff ID$(\varphi, \neg\psi)$. Now consider the 4 CD/ENEG-combinations from the $\mathcal{OG}/\mathcal{DG}$-multigraph in Fig. 3(b), viz., $(\Box p, \Diamond\neg p)$, $(\Diamond\neg p, \Box p)$, $(\Diamond p, \Box\neg p)$ and $(\Box\neg p, \Diamond p)$. Systematically negating the second argument yields $(\Box p, \neg\Diamond\neg p)$, $(\Diamond\neg p, \neg\Box p)$, $(\Diamond p, \neg\Box\neg p)$ and $(\Box\neg p, \neg\Diamond p)$, which are precisely the 4 BI/ID-combinations from the $\mathcal{IG}/\mathcal{DG}$-multigraph in Fig. 3(c).

We thus find that $\mathcal{OG}$ and $\mathcal{IG}$ are not only symmetrical in their interaction with each other (cf. Fig. 3(a)), but also in their respective interactions with $\mathcal{DG}$ (cf. the isomorphism between Figs. 3(b) and (c)). To summarize these findings, we combine the three separate multigraphs from Fig. 3 into one large $\mathcal{OG}/\mathcal{IG}/\mathcal{DG}$-multigraph, which is shown in Fig. 4(a). This multigraph clearly reveals the highly symmetrical nature of the mutual interactions between $\mathcal{OG}$, $\mathcal{IG}$ and $\mathcal{DG}$ in the classical logical square in Fig. 1(a). The underlying reasons and implications of this symmetry will need to be investigated in far more detail.

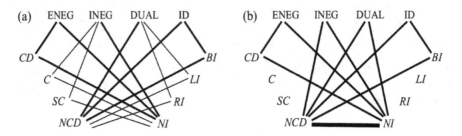

Fig. 4. $\mathcal{OG}/\mathcal{IG}/\mathcal{DG}$-multigraphs for (a) the classical square shown in Fig. 1(a) and (b) the degenerate square shown in Fig. 1(d). Thin, thick and very thick edges represent combinations of relations that co-occur resp. 2, 4 and 8 times.

We now briefly consider the modal square for $\{p, \neg p, \Diamond p, \Box\neg p\}$, which was shown in Fig. 1(b). This alternative square simultaneously exhibits $\mathcal{OG}$ and $\mathcal{IG}$, but not $\mathcal{DG}$. For example, we simultaneously have $NCD(p, \Diamond p)$ and $LI(p, \Diamond p)$, but p and $\Diamond p$ do not stand in any duality relation. The $\mathcal{OG}/\mathcal{IG}$-multigraph for this alternative square is isomorphic to the one in Fig. 3(a), since both are $\mathcal{OG}/\mathcal{IG}$-multigraphs for classical squares. Finally, since this alternative square does not exhibit any duality relations except for ENEG on its diagonals, it does not make much sense to construct $\mathcal{OG}/\mathcal{DG}$- or $\mathcal{IG}/\mathcal{DG}$-multigraphs for it.

4   Degenerate Logical Squares

We now turn to the degenerate logical squares, starting with the one shown in Fig. 1(c). This degenerate square simultaneously exhibits $\mathcal{OG}$ and $\mathcal{IG}$, but not $\mathcal{DG}$. Consider, for example, the formulas p and q: we simultaneously have $NCD(p, q)$ and $NI(p, q)$, but these two formulas do not stand in any duality relation. All $\mathcal{OG}$- and $\mathcal{IG}$-relations in this square are shown in Fig. 5(a) and (b), respectively, while its $\mathcal{OG}/\mathcal{IG}$-multigraph in shown in Fig. 5(c). Note that this multigraph again exhibits perfect vertical symmetry. In particular, the least informative relations of $\mathcal{OG}$ and $\mathcal{IG}$ (viz. NCD and NI) co-occur with each other, which explains the absence of any Aristotelian relations on the four sides of the degenerate square (cf. Theorems 7 and 8 of [15]).

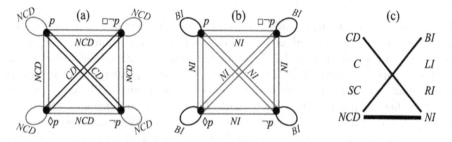

Fig. 5. (a) Opposition relations and (b) implication relations in the degenerate square shown in Fig. 1(c); (c) $\mathcal{OG}/\mathcal{IG}$-multigraph for this degenerate square. Thick and very thick edges represent combinations of relations that co-occur resp. 4 and 8 times.

Since the degenerate square in Fig. 1(c) does not exhibit any duality relations except for ENEG on its diagonals, it does not make much sense to construct $\mathcal{OG}/\mathcal{DG}$- or $\mathcal{IG}/\mathcal{DG}$-multigraphs for it. By contrast, the degenerate square in Fig. 1(d) not only exhibits opposition and implication, but also duality relations, as shown in Fig. 6. Consequently, we can now construct not only an $\mathcal{OG}/\mathcal{IG}$-, but also $\mathcal{OG}/\mathcal{DG}$- and $\mathcal{IG}/\mathcal{DG}$-multigraphs. In particular, the $\mathcal{OG}/\mathcal{IG}$-multigraph is isomorphic to the one shown in Fig. 5(c), since both are $\mathcal{OG}/\mathcal{IG}$-multigraphs for degenerate logical squares. Furthermore, the $\mathcal{OG}/\mathcal{DG}$- and $\mathcal{IG}/\mathcal{DG}$-multigraphs again turn out to be isomorphic to each other. For reasons of space, however, we only show the 'combined' $\mathcal{OG}/\mathcal{IG}/\mathcal{DG}$-multigraph; cf. Fig. 4(b). Once again, this multigraph clearly reveals the highly symmetrical nature of the mutual interactions between $\mathcal{OG}$, $\mathcal{IG}$ and $\mathcal{DG}$ in the degenerate square in Fig. 1(d).

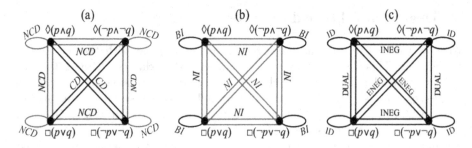

Fig. 6. (a) Opposition, (b) implication and (c) duality relations in the degenerate square shown in Fig. 1(d).

5   Conclusion

In this paper we have used multigraphs to investigate the interactions between $\mathcal{OG}$, $\mathcal{IG}$ and $\mathcal{DG}$ in classical as well as degenerate logical squares. First of all, we have shown that $\mathcal{OG}$ and $\mathcal{IG}$ are highly symmetrical in their interaction with each other—cf. Fig. 3(a). Furthermore, $\mathcal{OG}$ and $\mathcal{IG}$ also display a higher-order symmetry, in the sense that these two geometries fulfill highly similar roles in their respective interactions with $\mathcal{DG}$—cf. the isomorphic multigraphs in Figs. 3(b–c). Finally, these symmetries not only hold for classical squares, but also for degenerate squares—compare Figs. 3(a) and 4(a) with resp. Figs. 5(c) and 4(b). These results clearly illustrate the potential fruitfulness of multigraphs for studying the interactions between various logical geometries.

In future work, we will extend this research line along three complementary dimensions. First of all, we will explore alternative multigraph visualizations, which optimize different diagrammatic criteria (e.g. central symmetry, fewer edge crossings, etc.). Secondly, we will study interactions involving the Aristotelian geometry $(\mathcal{AG})$, in particular the interactions $\mathcal{AG}/\mathcal{OG}$ and $\mathcal{AG}/\mathcal{IG}$. Thirdly, we will also look at diagrams larger than squares, e.g. logical hexagons and octagons.

Acknowledgements. We would like to thank Margaux Smets for her valuable feedback on an earlier version of this paper. The research of the first author was supported by a Postdoctoral Fellowship of the Research Foundation–Flanders (FWO) and a Research Professorship (BOFZAP) from KU Leuven.

References

1. De Toffoli, S.: 'Chasing' the diagram - the use of visualizations in algebraic reasoning. Rev. Symb. Log. **10**, 158–186 (2017)
2. Dedelley, J.: Summulae Logicae (Editio Tertia). Joannes Paulus Schleig (1738)
3. Demey, L.: Algebraic aspects of duality diagrams. In: Cox, P., Plimmer, B., Rodgers, P. (eds.) Diagrams 2012. LNCS (LNAI), vol. 7352, pp. 300–302. Springer, Heidelberg (2012). https://doi.org/10.1007/978-3-642-31223-6_32
4. Demey, L.: Computing the maximal Boolean complexity of families of Aristotelian diagrams. J. Log. Comput. **28**, 1323–1339 (2018)

5. Demey, L.: Metalogic, metalanguage and logical geometry. Log. Anal. **248**, 453–478 (2019)
6. Demey, L., Smessaert, H.: Duality in logic and language. In: Fieser, J., Dowden, B. (eds.) Internet Encyclopedia of Philosophy. University of Tennessee (2016)
7. Demey, L., Smessaert, H.: Metalogical decorations of logical diagrams. Log. Univers. **10**, 233–292 (2016)
8. Demey, L., Smessaert, H.: Aristotelian and duality relations beyond the square of opposition. In: Chapman, P., Stapleton, G., Moktefi, A., Perez-Kriz, S., Bellucci, F. (eds.) Diagrams 2018. LNCS (LNAI), vol. 10871, pp. 640–656. Springer, Cham (2018). https://doi.org/10.1007/978-3-319-91376-6_57
9. Dopp, J.: Formal Logic. Joseph F. Wagner Inc., New York (1960)
10. Fitting, M., Mendelsohn, R.L.: First-Order Modal Logic. Kluwer (1998)
11. García Cruz, J.D.: Aristotelian relations in PDL: the hypercube of dynamic oppositions. South Am. J. Log. **3**, 389–414 (2017)
12. Harary, F.: Graph Theory. CRC Press, Boca Raton (1994)
13. Hurley, P.J.: A Concise Introduction to Logic. 11 edn. Wadsworth (2012)
14. Smessaert, H.: The classical Aristotelian hexagon versus the modern duality hexagon. Log. Univers. **6**, 171–199 (2012)
15. Smessaert, H., Demey, L.: Logical geometries and information in the square of opposition. J. Logic Lang. Inform. **23**, 527–565 (2014)
16. Smessaert, H., Demey, L.: Duality patterns in 2-PCD fragments. South Am. J. Log. **3**, 225–272 (2017)
17. Yao, Y.: Duality in rough set theory based on the square of opposition. Fundam. Inform. **127**, 49–64 (2013)

Opposition Relations Between Prophecies

José David García Cruz[1]([⊠])(iD) and Yessica Espinoza Ramos[2]

[1] Institute of Philosophy, Pontifical Catholic University of Chile,
Santiago de Chile, Chile
jdgarcia2@uc.cl
[2] Faculty of Philosophy, Meritorious Autonomous University of Puebla,
Puebla, Mexico
yle.morph@gmail.com

Abstract. This paper presents two versions of opposition relations for prophetical statements, the first one is an application of "Ockham's thesis" in Classical propositional Logic. The second one is a reinterpretation of that thesis in the logic MRS^P.

Keywords: Ockham's thesis · Conditional · Connexive logics · Opposition theory

1 Introduction

The aim of this paper is to compare two ways of representing oppositions of prophetic statements. We will begin presenting what we have called "Ockham's thesis". According to Ockham[1], prophecies about future contingents are conditional expressions. From a logical point of viwe that means that a prophetic sentence such as "before the cock crow twice, thou shalt deny me thrice"[2], is a conditional (say "$(A \supset B)$"). The novelty of Ockham's interpretation lies in assuming that expressions like this contain an implicit antecedent (say "A") that in making it manifest, and in connection with the consequent shows the meaning of the prophecy. Ockham's discussion in his treatise is devoted to the problem of future contingents, but assumes theory of oppositions and some intuitions about conditionals. Due to this fact we propose two alternatives for representing the opposition of prophecies. On the one hand, it is explored opposition of prophecies in Classical propositional Logic (CL), where several interesting consequences and some intuitive ideas about conditionals are considered.

Supported by Pontifical Catholic University of Chile and ANID. This work is part of the project: *The logic of prophetical conditionals: Prophetical languaje, divine communication, and human freedom* 61559-3, supported by John Templeton Foundation. We are grateful to Manuel Correia and to anonymous referees for their valuable corrections, comments and suggestions to an earlier version of this paper.

[1] [14, p. 44].
[2] (Mark, 14:72).

© Springer Nature Switzerland AG 2020
A.-V. Pietarinen et al. (Eds.): Diagrams 2020, LNAI 12169, pp. 394–401, 2020.
https://doi.org/10.1007/978-3-030-54249-8_31

Consequently, a problem is outlined concerning what we have called *auto-conditional prophecy*. This problem throws us to the study of the oppositions in the logic MRS^{P3}, in which we propose a solution to the mentioned problem. From this analysis two consequences are presented in detail: a) the inversion of oppositions in MRS^P, and b) a generalized definition of oppositions, which can be applied to multiple-valued paracomplete logics.

The plan of the paper is as follows. In section two we outline Ockham's analysis of prophetical discourse. Section three is devoted to analyze Ockham's thesis in CL with some results and an outline of the problem of *autoconditional prophecies*. Section four present a solution to the problem and a reinterpretation of the opposition relations in MRS^P.

2   A Brief Presentation of Ockham's Thesis

Ockham holds that "all prophecies regarding any future contingents [are] conditionals"[14, p. 44]; we have called this idea "Ockham's thesis". This philosopher proposed the thesis to eliminate the tension between logical omniscience and free will, this tension is eliminated maintaining that prophecies are means by which God communicates future knowledge, and this information when being in conditional form does not conflict with human freedom.

According to Ockham's thesis, the expression "before the cock crow twice, thou shalt deny me thrice" is a conditional whose antecedent is implicit, either in the scriptures or in the formulation itself. It is the task of the exegete to find this information to give coherence to the prophecy within the communicative system between God and the human being[4].

Despite being an original proposal, it has not been explored logically at present, although there are works that try to question it. In this regard, A. Edidin's work is the most notable [5]. In summary, he maintains that Ockham's example is designed to work like this, and that in other examples it is not possible to make the antecedent explicit, and therefore, a) the conditional is trivial, or b) the antecedent is very strong and therefore it is not possible to unfold it, or finally, c) that the conditional is false [5, p. 184][5].

In our view, Edidin's argument fails because he does not realize that the scriptures themselves offer evidence to extract the antecedent for more complex prophecies that are not so easily explainable in terms of conditionals[6].

What interests us is Ockham's formulation of the problem, since it establishes a direct connection with opposition theory. The problem is to question whether what is revealed by the prophets is necessary or contingent [14, p. 44]. If necessary, since what is revealed is about the future, the opposite will not be true and the prophecy is true from now on.

---

[3] See [6], [7].

[4] For a more detailed analysis you can consult [9].

[5] For more details see [9].

[6] This theme is left for a future paper dedicated exclusively to analyzing Edidin's argument and Ockham's thesis.

The problem arises when faced with the idea that revealed truths force facts to happen in such a way, and since they are revealed truths they are necessary. Ockham will argue a few lines below that these truths are not necessary but contingent, and also, conditional.

This allows him to continue affirming that the prophet state a contingent proposition, because what he says is true under a certain condition, that expressed by the antecedent, which is sometimes explicit and sometimes not [14, p. 44]. The fact that they are contingent makes interesting the question about how they oppose[7], we present in our next section our analysis of the oppositions of prophecies in terms of conditional opposition.

3   Classical Opposition of Prophecies

3.1   Classical Logic and MRS^P

By means of $\mathfrak{L}$ we will identify the propositional language that we will use, formed as usual from a non-empty collection of variables $Var = \{A, B, C, ...\}$ and a collection of logical connectives $C = \{\supset, \neg\}$. For Classical propositional Logic (CL) the semantics is composed of models of the form $\mathcal{M} = \langle \mathfrak{L}, V, D^+, v \rangle$, with $V = \{\bot, \top\}$, $D^+ = \{\top\}$, and $v : Var \longrightarrow V$. The definitions of logical consequence and logical truth are the definitions are those that are already known in a standard way. Let $\mathfrak{M}$ be a collection of models, we say that a formula φ is a logical truth (and we will write $\Vdash \varphi$) if $v(\varphi) \in D^+$, $\forall v \in \mathcal{M}$. Given a collection Σ of formulas, we say that a formula φ is a logical consequence of Σ, and we write $\Sigma \Vdash \varphi$, if $v(\beta) \in D^+$ $(\forall \beta \in \Sigma)$, then $v(\varphi) \in D^+$, $\forall v \in \mathcal{M}$. On the other hand, the logic MRS^P differs from CL because its collection of truth values is $V = \{\bot, *, \top\}$, while the collection of designated values is $D^+ = \{\top\}$, ordered as: $\bot < * < \top$. Truth tables for conditional and negation are given in Table 1.

Table 1. MRS^P tables for conditional and negation

¬	A	⊃	⊤	*	⊥
⊥	⊤	⊤	⊤	*	⊥
⊤	*	*	*	*	*
⊤	⊥	⊥	*	*	*

3.2   Prophecies in CL

To begin with the analysis consider the opposition diagram in Fig. 1. The formulas in this diagram can be divided into two groups: negative and positive. The diagram consider standard opposition relation definitions[8].

---

[7] Because if they were necessary, they would simply be contradictory.

[8] Our multiple-valued version of opposition relations are the following.

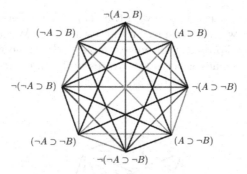

Fig. 1. Classical Octagon of Prophecies

Now, consider our example "If you are pressured by people, before the cock crow twice, thou shalt deny me thrice" as a natural language correlate of "$(A \supset B)$". In Fig. 1 are displayed the possible opposition relations between the formulas[9]. The main candidate to be an opposite of "$(A \supset B)$" is "$\neg(A \supset B)$" because external negation forms a contradictory formula.

According to truth tables for conditional we have that there are three more alternatives to be opposite of "$(A \supset B)$", which are composed of combinations of internal negations that affect "A", "B", or both. Therefore, the three opposites and "$(A \supset B)$" are subcontraries each other, that means they can be true simultaneously, but not simultaneously false. The cases in which they maintain different value are the least interesting since they only present opposite truth conditions.

Definition 1. *MV-Contradiction: Given two formulas $\varphi, \psi \in \mathfrak{L}$, we say that φ and ψ are contradictory, whenever $\forall v \in \mathcal{M}$, $v(\varphi) \in D^+$ if and only if $v(\psi) \notin D^+$.*

Definition 2. *MV-Contrariety: Given two formulas $\varphi, \psi \in \mathfrak{L}$, we say that φ and ψ are contraries, whenever $\forall v \in \mathcal{M}$, if $v(\varphi) \in D^+$ then $v(\psi) \notin D^+$, and if $v(\varphi) \notin D^+$ then $v(\psi)$ could be in D^+ and could be in D^-.*

Definition 3. *MV-Subcontrariety: Given two formulas $\varphi, \psi \in \mathfrak{L}$, we say that φ and ψ are subcontraries, whenever $\forall v \in \mathcal{M}$, if $v(\varphi) \notin D^+$ then $v(\psi) \in D^+$, and if $v(\varphi) \in D^+$ then $v(\psi)$ could be in D^+ and could be in D^-.*

Definition 4. *MV-Subalternation: Given two formulas $\varphi, \psi \in \mathfrak{L}$, we say that ψ is subaltern of φ, whenever $\forall v \in \mathcal{M}$, if $v(\varphi) \in D^+$ then $v(\psi) \in D^+$, and if $v(\psi) \in D^+$ then $v(\varphi)$ could be in D^+ and could be in D^-.*

---

[9] This diagram is one of the opposition diagrams known in the specialized literature as the octagon of opposition. See for example [12], [4], and [1], for a general revision of the most popular opposition diagrams known in the literature; and for a detailed analysis of implication and opposition relations see [4] and [8]. Red color represents contradiction, blue contrariety, green subcontrariety and black subalternation. For oppositions in the context of non-classical logics see [11] and [15].

These oppositions depend largely on the definitions of conditional and negation, in this respect we will consider an interesting case. What would happen if the antecedent of the prophecy of our example is the same as the consequent one? A prophecy becomes a necessary expression[10] and some other negations become contingent, as shown in Fig. 2.

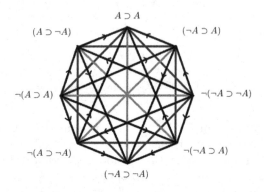

Fig. 2. Classical octagon of autoconditional prophecies

Despite forming these interesting oppositions, is it coherent to accept these type of autoconditional prophecy as genuine formulation? In this regard, we consider another logic where formulas such as the previous one are logical contingencies, preserving the contingent nature of the prophecies[11].

4   Connexive Opposition of Prophecies

As we saw in the previous section, if we accept that the prophecies can be formed with the "$(A \supset A)$" formula the prophecies become logical truths. We turn the discussion to the logic "MRS^P", in this logic other interesting formulas are also validated, two of them are in the octagon presented above, we refer to the *Aristotle's thesis* in its two versions: $\neg(A \supset \neg A)$ and $\neg(\neg A \supset A)$[12].

---

[10] And therefore, the problems reported by Ockham arise, if we consider prophecies as necessary sentences.

[11] Another question arises. In which sense prophecies of the form "$A \supset A$" are genuine prophecies? One may consider that the characteristic of a prophecy is to produce new information given some different data, in this sense, there is no justification to consider these form of conditional as a real logical correlate of prophecies. Another options is to consider autoconditional prophecies as extreme cases of prophecies. These questions remain open in this work and are left for future research. I appreciate the fruitful discussion with Manuel Correia at this respect.

[12] This logic is part of the family of logics known as connexive logics, logics that are neither subsystems nor extensions of CL and that are characterized by validating principles that, like those mentioned, are not classical theorems. For more details see [2], [3], [7], [10], [13] and [17].

In CL both are logical contingencies, while in this logic they are tautologies. This is mainly because in CL, $v(A) = v(\neg(A \supset \neg A)) = v(\neg A \supset A)$ and $v(\neg A) = v(\neg(\neg A \supset A)) = v(A \supset \neg A)$. In Table 2 it can be seen that these equalities are not satisfied, and therefore the octagon undergoes modifications and results in the diagram of Fig. 3.

Table 2. MRS^P tables for octagon of prophecies

$A \supset B$	$\neg(A \supset B)$	$\neg(A \supset \neg B)$	$(A \supset \neg B)$	$\neg(\neg A \supset B)$	$(\neg A \supset B)$	$(\neg A \supset \neg B)$	$\neg(\neg A \supset \neg B)$
⊤	⊥	⊤	⊥	⊤	*	*	⊤
*	⊤	⊥	⊤	⊤	*	*	⊤
⊥	⊤	⊥	⊤	⊤	*	*	⊤
*	⊤	⊤	*	⊥	⊤	⊥	⊤
*	⊤	⊤	*	⊤	*	⊤	⊥
*	⊤	⊤	*	⊤	⊥	⊤	⊥
*	⊤	⊤	*	⊥	⊤	⊥	⊤
*	⊤	⊤	*	⊤	*	⊤	⊥
*	⊤	⊤	*	⊤	⊥	⊤	⊥

The octagon of Fig. 3 satisfies the following properties. First, if we divide the formulas into ⊤-predominant (particular) and ⊥-predominant (universal) following C. Williamson (see [16, p. 499] and [8, p. 256]), we may propose a generalization dividing the formulas in D^+-predominant and D^--predominant. In that sense we will have multiple-valued universal and particular formulas, which form a square of contraries and subcontraries, respectively.

The interesting thing about this is that just the contrary formulas of CL are the subcontrary of MRS^P, and vice versa. For the same reason, subalterns are reversed and the only ones that remain the same are contradictory. This is due to two reasons: a) because the universal formulas of CL are the particular ones of MRS^P and viceversa; b) because of the negation of MRS^P does reverse the value * towards the value ⊤[13].

Finally, taking up the problem of autoconditional prophecies, the octagon formed in Fig. 4 satisfies more oppositional operations than that of Fig. 3, there is only an equivalence relation between the two versions of Aristotle's thesis, and the relations of contrariety and subcontrariety are distributed proportionally. All these relations are satisfied due to the generalized version of the oppositions we gave in this section, and interestingly, these definitions are not sensitive to systems in question, that is, they are fulfilled in both regardless of whether they maintain different characteristics and produce different octagons.

---

[13] To analyze this feature is interesting but it comes out of our goals.

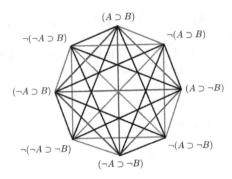

Fig. 3. Octagon of prophecies in MRS^P

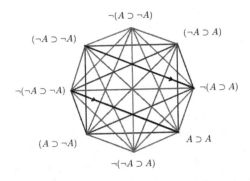

Fig. 4. MRS^P octagon of autoconditional prophecies

5   Conclusions

We have presented a brief synthesis of what we call *Ockham's thesis*. From this thesis we outline two ways of opposition of prophetic expressions, one based on CL and the other on MRS^P. As a main result, an octagon of oppositions can be constructed in CL. We have considered the option that the prophecies can be represented by formulas such as "$A \supset A$", and this led us to the construction of a second octagon. Consequently, these two octagons have been replicated in MRS^P, where another two octagons have been presented (Fig. 4). Finally, a generalized definition of opposition relations was presented to unify these two alternatives of representation.

References

1. Béziau, J.-Y.: The power of the hexagon. Log. Univers. **6**(1–2), 1–43 (2012). https://doi.org/10.1007/s11787-012-0046-9
2. Bradshaw, R.: A propositional logic with subjunctive conditionals. J. Symb. Logic **27**(3), 327–343 (1962)

3. Cantwell, J.: The logic of conditional negation. Notre Dame J. Formal Logic **49**(3), 245–260 (2008)
4. Demey, L., Smessaert, H.: Metalogical decorations of logical diagrams. Log. Univers. **10**(2), 233–292 (2016). https://doi.org/10.1007/s11787-015-0136-6
5. Edidin, A.: Ockham on prophecy. Int. J. Philos. Reli. **13**, 179–189 (1982)
6. Estrada-González, L.: Weakened semantics and the traditional square of opposition. Log. Univers. **2**(1), 155–165 (2008). https://doi.org/10.1007/s11787-007-0024-9
7. Estrada-González, L., Ramárez-Cámara, E.: A comparison of connexive logics. IfCoLog J. Logics Appl. **3**(3), 341–355 (2016)
8. García-Cruz, J.D.: From the square to octahedra. In: Béziau, J.-Y., Basti, G. (eds.) The Square of Opposition: A Cornerstone of Thought. SUL, pp. 253–272. Springer, Cham (2017). https://doi.org/10.1007/978-3-319-45062-9_15
9. García-Cruz, J.D.: Aristotle's thesis and Ockham's Conditional Analysis of Prophecy (2019, preprint)
10. McCall, S.: A history of connexivity. In: Gabbay, D., Guenthner, F. (eds.) Handbook of the History of Logic, vol. 11. Logic: A History of its Central Concepts, pp. 415–449. Elsevier, Amsterdam (2012)
11. Méles, B.: No group of opposition for constructive logics: the intuitionistic and linear cases. In: Béziau, J.-Y., Jacquette, D. (eds.) Around and Beyond the Square of Opposition. Studies in Universal Logic, pp. 201–217. Springer, Basel (2012). https://doi.org/10.1007/978-3-0348-0379-3_14
12. Moretti, A.: The Geometry of Oppositions and the Opposition of Logic to It. In: Bianchi, I., Savardi, U. (eds.) The Perception and Cognition of Contraries. McGraw-Hill, Milano (2009)
13. Mortensen, C.: Aristotle's thesis in consistent and inconsistent logics. Stud. Logica **43**(12), 107–116 (1984). https://doi.org/10.1007/BF00935744
14. Ockham, W.: Tractatus de Praedestinatione et de praescientia Dei et de futuris contingentibus. Translated, introduction, notes and appendices by Marilyn McCord Adams and Norman Kretzman. Hackett Publishing Company (1983)
15. Vidal-Rosset, J.: The exact intuitionistic meaning of the square of opposition. In: Béziau, J.-Y., Basti, G. (eds.) The Square of Opposition: A Cornerstone of Thought. SUL, pp. 291–303. Springer, Cham (2017). https://doi.org/10.1007/978-3-319-45062-9_17
16. Williamson, C.: Squares of opposition: comparisons between syllogistic and propositional logic. Notre Dame J. Formal Log. **13**, 497–500 (1972)
17. Wansing, H.: Connexive Logic, The Stanford Encyclopedia of Philosophy, Zalta, E.N. (ed.) (2016). https://plato.stanford.edu/archives/spr2016/entries/logic-connexive/

Compositional Diagrammatic First-Order Logic

Nathan Haydon and Paweł Sobociński$^{(\boxtimes)}$

Tallinn University of Technology, Tallinn, Estonia
{nathan.haydon,pawel.sobocinski}@taltech.ee

Abstract. Peirce's β variant of Existential Graphs (EGs) is a diagrammatic formalism, equivalent in expressive power to classical first-order logic. We show that the syntax of EGs can be presented as the arrows of a free symmetric monoidal category. The advantages of this approach are *(i)* that the associated string diagrams share the visual features of EGs while *(ii)* enabling a rigorous distinction between "free" and "bound" variables. Indeed, this diagrammatic language leads to a *compositional* relationship of the syntax with the *semantics* of logic: we obtain models as structure-preserving monoidal functors to the category of relations.

In addition to a diagrammatic syntax for formulas, Peirce developed a sound and complete system of diagrammatic reasoning that arose out of his study of the algebra of relations. Translated to string diagrams we show the implied algebraic structure of EGs sans negation is that of cartesian bicategories of relations: for example, lines of identity obey the laws of special Frobenius algebras. We also show how the algebra of negation can be presented, thus capturing Peirce's full calculus.

1 Introduction

Peirce's Existential Graphs (EGs) arose out of his continued study and development of the algebra of relations. As a diagrammatic calculus, EGs use lines to represent identity, conjunction and existence and nested circles (Peirce's notion of the "cut"[1]) to capture negation. These graphical elements are drawn on the sheet of assertion: the blank page upon which a graph is scribed. Our focus is on the algebra of the β variant of EGs, which we treat as string diagrams. The resulting language, which we call Dβ, shares the same visual features of EGs.

We argue that Peirce's β is closely related to the algebraic structure of cartesian bicategories of relations [7]. Indeed, lines of identity, as string diagrams, obey the laws of special Frobenius algebras, while derivations in the negation-free fragment are the 2-cells of free cartesian bicategories. We identify the additional rules needed to handle negation, which are adapted from Peirce's calculus of

---

[1] In this paper, we use "cut" in the Peircean sense to mean negation, not the standard notion of cut from proof theory.

This research was supported by the ESF funded Estonian IT Academy research measure (project 2014-2020.4.05.19-0001).

A.-V. Pietarinen et al. (Eds.): Diagrams 2020, LNAI 12169, pp. 402–418, 2020.
https://doi.org/10.1007/978-3-030-54249-8_32

diagrammatic reasoning. Throughout, we argue that Peirce's seminal studies led him to intuitions that suggest that he—at least implicitly—identified the very same algebraic structures.

While Dβ is visually similar—we joke that a diagram in Dβ looks like an EG if you squint—it is important to highlight some differences. Making the Frobenius structure explicit in Dβ imposes more rigour on lines of identity. Relations in Dβ have left and right wires corresponding to arity/co-arities of the relations. This may actually help the presentation of graphs in EGs as Peirce sometimes imposes an order on relations that is not directly read off the ligatures. An explicit Frobenius structure gives the flexibility of rearranging wires as needed, so expressivity is not lost, but also allows us to have a definite ordering, which is useful in many examples. This amendment, maintaining the visual features while being more definite/exact, may very well be a welcome addition.

Perhaps more significantly, in order to achieve compositionality, the string diagrammatic account forces us to keep track of bound and free variables in a more precise way than in Peirce's original EGs. Indeed the *existential* in the name of EGs means that scribing a graph on the sheet of assertion is to assert the existence (i.e. the quantification) of the respective predicate/variable. EGs have, as Zeman has put it, "implicit quantification" [19]. Treatment of free and bound variables in modified versions of EG (see [4,10]) equip EGs with additional structure. The string diagrammatic language Dβ makes this treatment quite natural—the result is less cumbersome than the technology of variable management (e.g. α-conversion, capture-avoiding substitution) often waved through at the start of many traditional courses on predicate logic.

Brady and Trimble have previously developed a string diagrammatic account of EGs [2,3], relying as we do on monoidal categories and in particular, the poset-enriched monoidal category of relations as a semantic universe for logic. However, their string diagrams are geometric/topological entities. Instead, we emphasize their *syntactic* nature, which allows, e.g. to define the notion of model as simple inductive procedure, not unlike Tarski's compositional semantics for predicate logic. Moreover, we work in the framework of (poset enriched) props [11], which emphasizes the algebraic structure borne by the underlying monoidal category.

In the discussion below we assume some familiarity with the reading and transformation (i.e. inference) rules of EGs. For a lengthier introduction to Peirce's EGs, and one that includes a description of Peirce's transformation rules, see [17]. Further accounts can be found in [4,9,18], and the introduction in [15]. For an introduction to Peirce's compositional/valental account of relations, see [17, p. 113–118]. A contemporary presentation can be found in [5].

Structure of the Paper. In Sect. 2 we introduce Dβ and show how to translate it to and from traditional syntax. In Sect. 3 we introduce the structure of cartesian bicategories, which informs the notion of model of the logic, introduced in Sect. 4. We identify iteration laws of this structure with the cut in Sect. 5 and conclude with a worked example of diagrammatic reasoning in Sect. 6.

2 String Diagrams as Syntax

We start with Peirce's *valental* theory of relations, inspired by the theory of valence in chemistry, where elements have open bonds that act as attachment points from which more complex compounds and molecules can be built. Relations are thus seen as having analogous open bonds that can be filled and combined with other relations to form more complex relations.

Consider the 'loves' relation, which in usual FOL syntax is written $\mathsf{loves}(x, y)$. The relation remains indefinite insofar as the objects/subjects of the relation are unspecified, i.e. the variables x and y remain free. Peirce adds "blanks" or "hooks" as graphical placeholders to represent the unspecified objects/subjects, which when filled, "complete the relation". In our example 'loves' is a dyadic relation, and we represent hooks as "dangling" wires, arriving at —[loves]— . Filling in the hooks/connecting the wires in the diagrammatic notation is an analogous operation to passing from *free* to *bound* variables in the usual FOL syntax.

Specific relations are combined by joining free hooks together with what Peirce calls a line of identity. A line of identity asserts the identity of each object/subject at its endpoints. We represent lines of identity with the generators $\{\bullet\!\!-, \, \supset\!\!\bullet\!\!-, \, -\!\!\bullet, \, -\!\!\bullet\mathsf{C}\}$ of a monoid-comonoid pair. Consider the diagrams below.

Reading from left to right, the first diagram is the conjunction of the is a pear and is ripe relations where the hooks are unfilled/wires are dangling. In usual FOL syntax, is a pear$(x) \wedge$ is ripe(y). In the second diagram the hooks are filled/wires are capped off with a unit generator. In usual FOL syntax, $\exists x.$ is a pear$(x) \wedge \exists y.$ is ripe(y). In the third, using the comultiplication generator the two wires have been equated but there is a dangling wire to the left; is a pear$(x) \wedge$ is ripe(x). In the final diagram the wire has been capped off: $\exists x.$ is a pear$(x) \wedge$ is ripe(x).

The syntax of Dβ below follows Peircean considerations. Let Σ be a monoidal signature: symbols R each with an arity $ar(R) \in \mathbb{N}$ and coarity $coar(R) \in \mathbb{N}$.

Example 1. The signature for our running example is

$$\Sigma = \{\mathsf{adores}, \mathsf{is\ a\ woman}, \mathsf{is\ a\ catholic}\}$$

with $ar(\mathsf{adores}) = coar(\mathsf{adores}) = 1$, $ar(\mathsf{is\ a\ woman}) = ar(\mathsf{is\ a\ catholic}) = 1$, $coar(\mathsf{is\ a\ woman}) = coar(\mathsf{is\ a\ catholic}) = 0$. The diagrammatic convention for an element $R \in \Sigma$ is to draw it as a box, with $ar(R)$ wires, ordered from top to bottom, "dangling" on the left and, similarly, $coar(R)$ wires on the right. Thus:

$$\Sigma = \{ \ -\!\boxed{\mathsf{adores}}\!- \ , \ -\!\boxed{\mathsf{is\ a\ woman}} \ , \ -\!\boxed{\mathsf{is\ a\ catholic}} \ \} \, .$$

Below we define our recursively defined syntax using BNF notation. These are the basic syntactical elements from which terms in $D\beta_\Sigma$ are constructed.[2]

$$c ::= \text{—•} \mid \text{—}\math{C} \mid \text{•—} \mid \text{⊃—} \mid R \in \Sigma \tag{1}$$

$$\mid \square \mid \text{——} \mid \times \tag{2}$$

$$\mid c \oplus c \mid c \,; c \mid c^- \tag{3}$$

At this point, the diagrammatic elements of the syntax in (1) and (2) ought to be considered as mere symbols that denote constants. The operations are given in (3): two binary operations ';', '$\oplus$' and one unary operation •^-. These have their own diagrammatic convention: $c \,; c'$ is drawn $\boxed{c}\boxed{c'}$, $c \oplus c'$ is drawn $\begin{smallmatrix}\boxed{c}\\\boxed{c'}\end{smallmatrix}$, and c^- is drawn $\boxed{\overline{c}}$. Roughly the operations here can again be seen in terms of our relational story from above. '$\oplus$' allows us to scribe relations adjacent to each other (i.e. in parallel) on the sheet, ';' allows us to wire relations together in series (similar to connecting relations via lines of identity), and placing a relation inside a cut expresses its negation/complement.

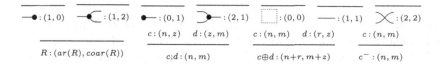

Fig. 1. Sort inference rules.

As opposed to the usual syntax of FOL, ours (1) (2) (3) does not have variables, nor variable binding. The price is an inductive discipline, given in Fig. 1. Intuitively, it keeps track of "dangling" wires—terms are associated with a *sort*, a pair of natural numbers (n, m) that counts the wires on the left and on the right—and ensures that for a term $c \,; c'$, c and c' have the right number of wires on their corresponding boundaries so that ';' as "connecting wires" to make sense. It is easy to prove that if a term has a sort, it is unique.

Example 2. The term $\text{—•} \,; \text{—•}$ has no sort and no diagrammatic depiction. On the other hand $\text{—•} \oplus \text{—•} : (2, 0)$. Given the signature of Example 1, consider the term $((\text{•—} \,; \text{—}\math{C}) \,; ((\text{adores} \,; \text{is a woman})^- \oplus \text{is a catholic}))^-$ with sort $(0, 0)$.

---

[2] Henceforward we will not write the subscript Σ, assuming a fixed ambient monoidal signature.

Using the diagrammatic conventions yields the following, where the dotted-line boxes play the role of the parentheses.

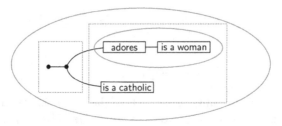

It is not difficult to see that sorted terms are in 1-1 correspondence with such diagrams, provided that enough dotted-line boxes are inserted to disambiguate the associativity of ';' and '⊕' and the priority between them.

2.1 Translating to and from Traditional Syntax

The (traditional) syntax below is expressive enough to capture first order logic, containing equality, relation symbols, existential quantification and negation.

$$\Phi ::= \top \mid \Phi \wedge \Phi \mid x_i = x_j \mid R(\overrightarrow{x}) \mid \exists x.\Phi \mid \neg\Phi \qquad \text{(FOL)}$$

To ease the translation between the diagrammatic and the traditional, we introduce a half-way formalism that constraints the syntax FOL with explicit free-variable management. This is a mild extension of a similar calculus in [1, Sec. 2] where an analogous translation is given, albeit without the presence of negation.

$$\frac{}{0 \vdash \top}\,(\top) \qquad \frac{R \in \Sigma \quad ar(R) = n}{n \vdash R(x_0, \dots, x_{n-1})}\,(\Sigma) \qquad \frac{n \vdash \Phi}{n-1 \vdash \exists x_{n-1}.\Phi}\,(\exists)$$

$$\frac{}{2 \vdash x_0 = x_1}\,(=) \qquad \frac{m \vdash \Phi \quad n \vdash \Psi}{m+n \vdash \Phi \wedge (\Psi[\overrightarrow{x}_{[m,m+n-1]}/\overrightarrow{x}_{[0,x_{n-1}]}])}\,(\wedge) \qquad \frac{n \vdash \Phi}{n \vdash \neg\Phi}\,(\neg)$$

$$\frac{n \vdash \Phi \quad (0 \le k < n-1)}{n \vdash \Phi[x_{k+1}, x_k/x_k, x_{k+1}]}\,(\mathsf{Sw}_{n,k}) \qquad \frac{n \vdash \Phi}{n-1 \vdash \Phi[x_{n-2}/x_{n-1}]}\,(\mathsf{Id}_n) \qquad \frac{n \vdash \Phi}{n+1 \vdash \Phi}\,(\mathsf{Nu}_n)$$

The idea is that a judgment $n \vdash \Phi$ expresses the fact that Φ is a formula with free variables from the set $\{x_0, x_1, \dots, x_{n-1}\}$. Indeed, we have the following:

Proposition 1. *A formula Φ with free variables in $\{x_0, x_1, \dots, x_{n-1}\}$ is derivable from (FOL) if and only if $n \vdash \Phi$.*

Using the above, we can present a translation Θ from (FOL) to Dβ by induction on the derivation of $n \vdash \Phi$. The rules are given in Fig. 2. A similar translation can be given from Dβ to (FOL). Another important fact is that the translations respect the underlying semantics of the logics—due to space restrictions we are not able to show this here. We shall introduce the semantics of Dβ in Sect. 4.

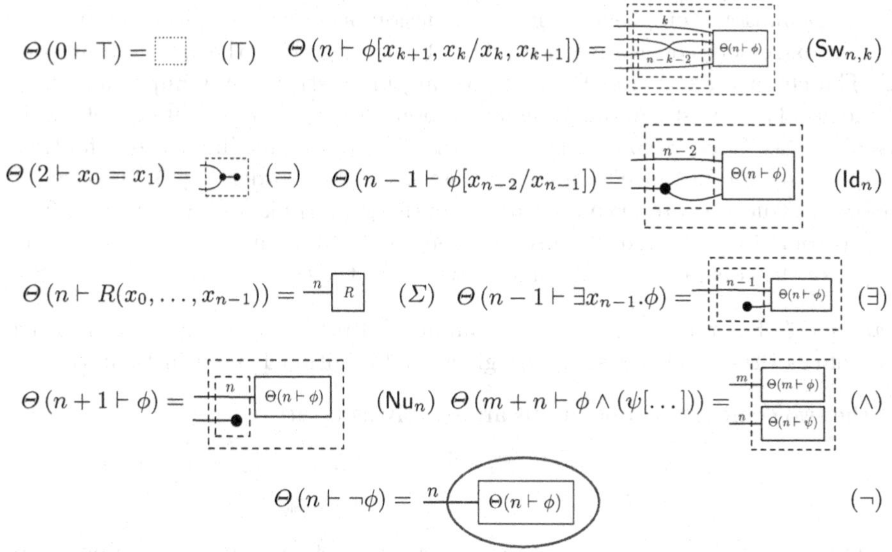

$\Theta\,(0 \vdash \top) = \boxed{}$ (⊤) $\Theta\,(n \vdash \phi[x_{k+1}, x_k/x_k, x_{k+1}]) =$ [diagram] $(\mathsf{Sw}_{n,k})$

$\Theta\,(2 \vdash x_0 = x_1) =$ [diagram] (=) $\Theta\,(n - 1 \vdash \phi[x_{n-2}/x_{n-1}]) =$ [diagram] (Id_n)

$\Theta\,(n \vdash R(x_0, \ldots, x_{n-1})) = \overset{n}{-}\boxed{R}$ (Σ) $\Theta\,(n - 1 \vdash \exists x_{n-1}.\phi) =$ [diagram] (∃)

$\Theta\,(n + 1 \vdash \phi) =$ [diagram] (Nu_n) $\Theta\,(m + n \vdash \phi \wedge (\psi[\ldots])) =$ [diagram] (∧)

$\Theta\,(n \vdash \neg\phi) = \overset{n}{-}$ [diagram containing $\Theta(n \vdash \phi)$] (¬)

Fig. 2. Translation Θ from FOL to Dβ.

Example 3. Referring to Example 2, the formula expressed by the diagram is

$\neg(\exists x.\ \text{is a catholic}(x) \wedge \neg(\exists y.\ \text{adores}(x, y) \wedge \text{is a woman}(y)))$
$\equiv \forall x.\ (\neg\text{is a catholic}(x) \vee (\exists y.\ \text{adores}(x, y) \wedge \text{is a woman}(y)))$
$\equiv \forall x.\ \text{is a catholic}(x) \rightarrow \exists y.\ \text{adores}(x, y) \wedge \text{is a woman}(y).$

2.2 String Diagrams

In order not to clutter diagrams with dotted-line boxes, we will not consider raw terms, but terms quotiented by the laws of symmetric strict monoidal categories [11,12] of a particularly simple nature: the set of objects is the natural numbers and $m \oplus n \overset{\text{def}}{=} m + n$. Such categories are called props. Some care has to be taken with the $\bullet^-$ operation, which is not standard: we introduce a simple extension to the usual definition below.

Definition 1. *A prop $\mathbb{X}$ with a unary operation on homsets (*uoh-prop*) is a prop with a family of operations $\overline{}_{m,n} : \mathbb{X}[m, n] \to \mathbb{X}[m, n]$, where $m, n \in \mathbb{N}$.*

We are ready to define the notion of syntax we will use throughout the paper.

Definition 2. (Syntax). *Let Dβ be the uoh-prop where arrows $m \to n$ are (m, n)-sorted terms, modulo the laws of symmetric monoidal categories. The additional unary operation on homsets is given by $\bullet^-$.*

While Definition 2 emphasises the construction of terms from the grammar, $D\beta$ has an extremely concise mathematical description: it is the *free* uoh-prop on Σ. The characterisation of $D\beta$ as a free algebraic structure is important: first, it means that our string diagrams are a bona fide notion of syntax, not unlike usual syntax trees. Second, just as syntax admits elegant inductive definitions (not unlike, for instance, Tarski's semantics of first order logic), in order to define a structure preserving translation (homomorphism of uoh-props) from $D\beta$ to some target semantic universe (some uoh-prop), it suffices to define the target of the constants (1). We shall use this for the concept of *model* in Sect. 4.

Example 4. For the category-theory uninitiated reader, let us give an intuitive summary of the algebraic structure given by Definition 1, used in Definition 2.

– the two composition operations are strictly associative, e.g.

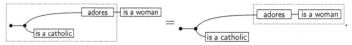

This means the result is the same irrespective of the order we compose, i.e. whether we start with the adored woman or the adoring catholic.

– the two composition operations are compatible, e.g.

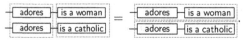

– the first two constants of (2) are *identities*; the first the identity on 0, the second the identity on 1. This means, e.g.

The combination of identity laws and the compatibility of ';' with '⊕' means that unconnected components can be "slid" past each other, e.g.

In Peirce's EGs these features are built directly into the conventions of the sheet of assertion. The identities follow from the properties of composition with a blank sheet or with a line of identity. In regards to composition and associativity on the sheet itself, Peirce writes: "If two propositions are written, detached from one another, on the sheet of assertion, both are asserted, regardless of whether one is to the right, to the left, at the top, or at the bottom of the other... If three or more propositions are all written, detached from one another, on the sheet of assertions, the logical relation of any pair of them is the same as that of any other pair" [16, p. 488].

– the last constant of (3) is a *symmetry*. This means that diagrams constructed from it and the identity "behave" as permutations, e.g.

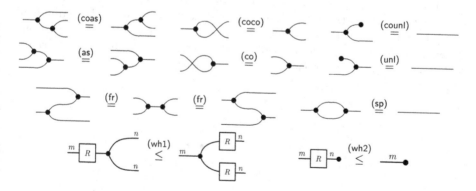

and arbitrary diagrams can "slide" across symmetries[3], e.g.

3 The Algebra of Lines of Identity

In this section we identify some of the algebraic structure of $D\beta$ that will, in Sect. 5, result in a calculus for diagrammatic reasoning. In addition, the structure introduced here will allow us to specify the correct concept of model in Sect. 4.

Figure 3 depicts the laws of cartesian bicategories (of relations) [7]. Equations (coas), (coco), (counl) say that ($\multimap\!\!\mathbf{C}$, $\multimap\bullet$) is a cocommutative comonoid, while (as), (co), (unl) say that ($\mathbf{D}\!\!\multimap$, $\bullet\!\!\multimap$) is a commutative monoid.

The three equations (fr) are the Frobenius equations. While any two of the three can be used to derive the others, all three are useful in diagrammatic reasoning. The equation (sp) is the so-called "special" law. The equations thus far define what is usually referred to as a (commutative) special Frobenius bimonoid.

It is worth reflecting on how these laws are captured in Peirce's EGs. As mentioned previously, associativity and commutativity are built into the conventions of the sheet of assertion, where the order of composition of relations on the sheet is immaterial. Each of the other rules can be seen as following from the combination of monadic, dyadic, triadic identity elements. (unl) and (counl) are equivalent to being able to add a branch to any line of identity. Peirce called

Fig. 3. The laws of cartesian bicategories of relations.

---

[3] These equations are examples of *naturality* of the symmetry.

this triadic identity element, where a branch forms a point with three extending wires, the teridentity relation. Peirce's interpretation of this rule in EGs, given in a letter to Lady Welby, is worth quoting: "every line of identity ought to be considered as bristling with microscopic points of teridentity" [14].[4]

The (fr) and (sp) equations can be seen as observations about the composition of teridentity relations. Two teridentity relations brought together by connecting two of each of the three wires is equivalent to a single (dyadic) line of identity. This yields the (sp) equation. Similarly, the various combinations of two teridentity relations connected through one wire likewise yield the (fr) equalities. Peirce is explicit about the interpretation of this rule in his EGs. He writes: "Quateridentity [Peirce's term for a point with four extending wires] is obviously composed of two teridentities; i.e. This ─┼─ is ─┬─ or ✕ or ✕" [14]. Clearly, Peirce had the topological intuitions conveyed by the Frobenius structure.[5]

Notice that (wh1) and (wh2) are not equalities and as such, in subsequent diagrammatic reasoning, derivations can only use them left-to-right. Moreover, they use the diagrammatic convention where a wire with a natural number label m stands for m wires stacked on top of each other. The inequations (wh1) and (wh2) specify that all arrows are weakly homomorphic w.r.t. the comonoid structure. In cartesian bicategories, moreover, the monoid structure is required to be right adjoint to the comonoid structure. This means the following inequalities:

In the context of Frobenius bimonoids that satisfy (wh1) and (wh2), all of (ra1)-(ra4) are redundant. As we will see, (wh1) and (wh2) (along with the redundant (ra1)-(ra4)) give rise to Peirce's transformation rules in EGs. Peirce's assertion, for example, that any graph scribed on the sheet itself (i.e. that is not scribed within a cut) can be erased can be proved as follows.

Lemma 1. $\underset{m}{}\!\!-\!\!\boxed{R}\!\!-\!\!\underset{n}{}\ \overset{(er)}{\leq}\ \multimap\ \multimapinv.$

Proof. $\underset{m}{}\!\!-\!\!\boxed{R}\!\!-\!\!\underset{n}{}\ \overset{(ra3)}{\leq}\ -\!\!\boxed{R}\!\!\multimap\ \multimapinv\ \overset{(wh2)}{\leq}\ \multimap\ \multimapinv.$

---

[4] See, also, [CP 4:583]: "the line of identity...must be understood quite differently. We must hereafter understand it to be *potentially* the graph of teridentity by which means there will virtually be at least one loose end in every graph".

[5] Elsewhere Peirce writes: "There is no need of a point from which four lines of identity proceed; for two triple points answer the same purpose ✕" [16, p. 357].

Remark 1. It is well-known that the Frobenius equations induce a self-dual compact closed structure. Roughly speaking, this allows us to "rewire" diagrams, moving wires between the boundaries. We have used this already in the first diagrams of Example 4, on the is a catholic relation.

4 Models

Recal uoh-props, introduced in Definition 1. Below we identify an important class of uoh-props, which together serve as the semantic universe for $D\beta$.

Definition 3. *Let X be a set. The uoh-prop Rel_X has, as arrows $m \to n$, relations $X^m \to X^n$ (subsets of $X^m \times X^n$), where X^m is the m-fold cartesian product of X. Given a relation $R : X^m \to X^n$, R^- is the (set-theoretical) complement of R as a subset of $X^m \times X^n$.*

Composition in Rel_X is relational composition: given $R : m \to k$ and $S : k \to n$, $R \; ; \; S = \{ (x, y) \mid \exists z \in X^k. (x, z) \in R \wedge (z, y) \in S \} \subseteq X^m \times X^n$. The monoidal product is cartesian product of relations.

It is well-known that Rel_X is a cartesian bicategory of relations, that is, it satisfies all of the equations of Fig. 3. In the setting of Rel_X, —◀ is the diagonal relation $\{(x, \binom{x}{x})) \mid x \in X\}$ while —• is the relation $\{(x, \star) \mid x \in X\}$, where $\star$ is the unique element of the singleton set X^0. The relations denoted by ▶— and •— are, respectively, the opposite relations. Henceforward we will call these four relations the *canonical Frobenius structure* of Rel_X.

The following is the central definition of this section.

Definition 4. *A model for $D\beta$ consists of a set X and a morphism of uoh-props*

$$\llbracket - \rrbracket : D\beta \to \mathsf{Rel}_X$$

that maps $\{$ —◀, —•, ▶—, •— $\}$ to the canonical Frobenius structure of Rel_X.

Referring back to the syntax definition (1), to give such a morphism is to give, for each $\sigma : (m, n) \in \Sigma$, a relation $\llbracket \sigma \rrbracket \subseteq X^m \times X^n$. The rest of the mapping is induced compositionally.

Remark 2. Note that *closed* diagrams, that is those of sort $(0, 0)$ map to relations of type $0 \to 0$, that is, subsets of $X^0 \times X^0$. Since X^0 is a singleton, there are precisely two such relations – the empty ($\varnothing$) and the full ($\{(\star, \star)\}$). We identify these with *truth values* – $\varnothing$ with $\bot$ (false) and $\{(\star, \star)\}$ with $\top$ (true).

Example 5. Take the signature of Example 1. Let $X = \{m, w\}$. To define $\llbracket - \rrbracket : D\beta \to \mathsf{Rel}_X$ we need only choose valuations of —[adores]—, —[is a woman], and —[is a catholic] as relations. Let $\llbracket$ —[is a woman] $\rrbracket \subseteq X^1 \times X^0 = \{(w, \star)\}$. Similarly, let $\llbracket$ —[is a catholic] $\rrbracket = \{(m, \star)\}$. If we set $\llbracket$ —[adores]— $\rrbracket \subseteq X^1 \times X^1 = \{(m, w)\}$

then $[\![$ 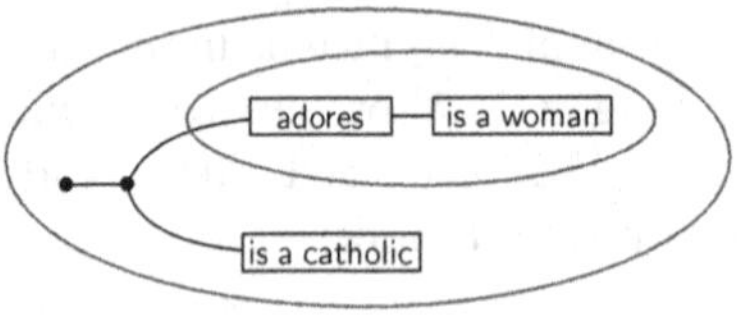

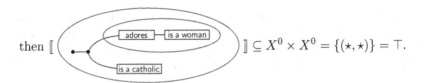

$]\!] \subseteq X^0 \times X^0 = \{(\star,\star)\} = \top$.

On the other hand, if we assign $[\![$ 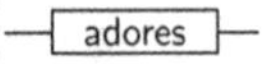

$]\!] = \{(m,m)\}$ then

$[\![$ 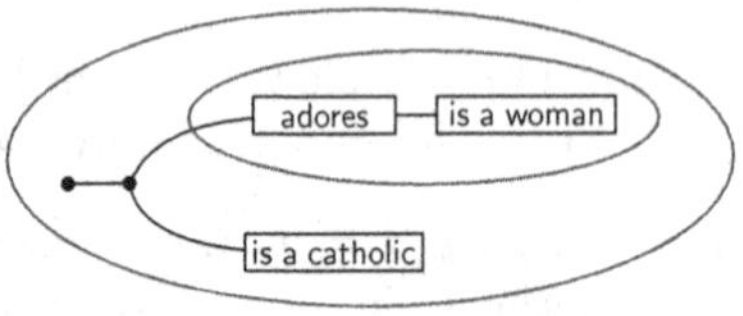

$]\!] \subseteq X^0 \times X^0 = \varnothing = \bot$.

Having established the notion of model, we introduce the notions of *soundness*, *completeness* and *logical equivalence*. Two terms t, u of $\mathsf{D}\beta$ are said to be logically equivalent if they have the same semantics in all models, $[\![t]\!] = [\![u]\!]$. An equation is *sound* if it preserves logical equivalence. A calculus is complete if it equates all logically equivalent terms. Note that the fact that Rel_X is a cartesian bicategory of relations means that all of the laws introduced in Sect. 3 are sound.

5 The Algebra of Cut

In Sect. 3 we began the process of axiomatising logical equivalence. Thus far, negation has not played a significant role in our exposition. In Fig. 4 we identify a calculus that is sound, and—taken in conjunction with the laws of Fig. 3—we conjecture to be complete. The equations of Fig. 4 describe the interactions between the algebraic structure of Fig. 3 and Peirce's cut (negation). First, we explain the jagged-line notation, which emphasizes the *local* nature of the interactions. It is shorthand for an arbitrary context inside the cut. For example, (frcut) stands for

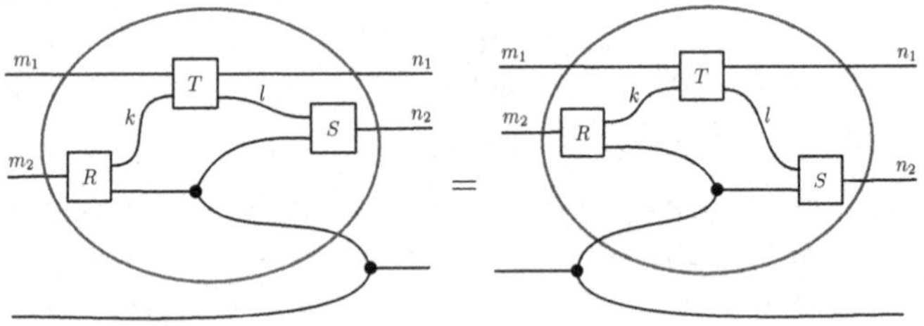

for arbitrary R, S and T. Thus with (frcut) we can, roughly speaking, "rewire" a cut to move wires between its left and right boundaries. Indeed (frcut) is a kind of Frobenius law for cuts. In short, the combination of (symcut) and (frcut) means that the cut boundary is permeable to "wiring" and the permutation structure.

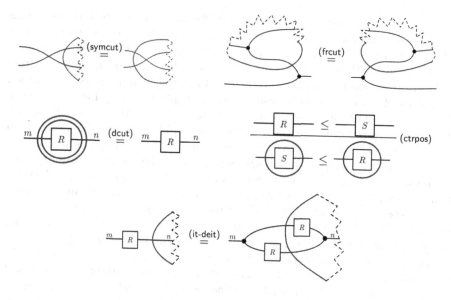

Fig. 4. The algebra of cut.

(dcut) is a diagrammatic representation of Peirce's rule for adding or erasing a double cut around any partial graph. Of course, this is a non-constructive rule; in this paper we only consider classical logic. Some progress has been made recently [13] in the study of how EGs can be used as an intuitionistic logic and we plan to investigate this in our framework in future work.

The (ctrpos) judgement single-handedly captures much of the behavior of the transformation rules within the cut. Peirce explains it as follows: "Of whatever transformation is permissible on the sheet of assertion, the reverse transformation is permissible within a single cut." [16, p. 353]. While our presentation of (ctrpos) represents this point with respect to a single cut, it is worth noting that the reversal continues within subsequent nested cuts. The result is that the same transformation rules that apply on the sheet itself (i.e. to graphs that are not within a cut) also apply to graphs within an even number of cuts.[6] As a rule the

---

[6] Following the passage quoted above, Peirce writes: "In short, whatever transformation is permissible on the sheet of assertion is permissible on the sheet of assertion within any even number of cuts while the reverse transformation is permissible within any odd number of cuts" [16, p. 353] Or alternatively: "All illative processes are subject to the apagogical principle, or principle of contraposition, which, as applied to graphs, is as follows: If any illative process is valid within an even number of enclosures, its reverse is valid within an odd number, and vice versa" [15, p. 94]. See also [16, p. 257-8, p. 478-9, & p. 539].

principle of contraposition has been markedly absent from other presentations of Peirce's transformation rules in the literature. The latter point is all the more significant in that Peirce often emphasizes the principle at the beginning of his presentations of EGs and often motivates the other transformation rules from it.[7] Our presentation situates the principle in its position of primary importance.

Intuitively, the principle of contraposition captures the symmetry between the valid twin inference rules of modus ponens and modus tollens. If we can infer the transformation from R to S then we can likewise infer from the denial of S the denial of R. In terms of Dβ and Peirce's EGs, and as stated above, the principle of contraposition allows us to perform the reverse transformations when working within a cut. Our previous proof of the erasure rule, which states that any graph written on the sheet itself (i.e. in an even area) can be erased, can be reversed using (ctrpos) to yield Peirce's insertion rule. Likewise, Peirce's rule that a line of identity can be broken on the sheet itself (ra3) can be reversed using (ctrpos) to yield his rule that a line of identity can be joined in an odd area.[8]

The rule (it-deit) is a statement of Peirce's principle of iteration/deiteration. In Peirce's own words the rule is stated as follows: "... any partial graph, detached or attached, may be iterated within the same or additional cuts provided every line or hook of the iterated graph be attached in the new replica to identically the same ligatures as in the primitive replica; and if a partial graph be already so iterated it can be deiterated by the erasure of one of the replicas which must be within every cut that the replica left standing is within" [16, p. 358]. This rule applies in the same area as the partial graph—i.e. the same rule holds in the case where no cut is present. For us, it is useful to separate the two ideas conceptually, since the latter is implied by the algebraic structure in Sect. 3.

It is worth noting that our (it-deit) rule is similar to Burch's presentation of "Doppelgänger pairs" that form when a line of identity crosses a cut (or two lines of identity abut each other at a cut) [6]. Our rule is more general, as it applies not simply to lines of identity but to relations and partial graphs. Each case is unified under the same rule here.

While the soundness of the other rules in Fig. 4 is straightforward, (it-deit) is more involved and less intuitive.

---

[7] See, for example, the passages in the previous footnote.

[8] In Peirce's words: "... it is to be noted that a line of identity may be broken within an even number of cuts or on the sheet of assertion, while two lines may be joined within an odd number of cuts" [16, p. 358].

Lemma 2. (it-deit) *is sound.*

Proof. Since we can "rewire" any cut so that it only has wires on its left boundary, without loss of generality it suffices to show that:

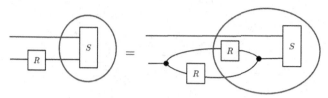

is sound for all possible valuations of R and S. Using traditional syntax, and simplifying somewhat, this is to show the following logical equivalence:

$$\exists z.\ R(x_2, z) \wedge \neg S(x_1, z)$$
$$\equiv \exists z_1.\ R(x_1, z_1) \wedge \neg(\exists z_2, z_3.\ R(x_1, z_2) \wedge z_1 = z_3 \wedge z_2 = z_3 \wedge S(x_1, z_3))$$

Instead of dealing with the complicated formulas above, we instead directly use the definition of model introduced in Sect. 4. Suppose for some model, $\begin{pmatrix} x_1 \\ x_2 \end{pmatrix}$ is on the LHS. This happens exactly when there is some y_2 s.t. $x_2 R y_2$ and $\begin{pmatrix} x_1 \\ x_2 \end{pmatrix} \notin S$.

Suppose now that $\begin{pmatrix} x_1 \\ x_2 \end{pmatrix} \in$ RHS. This happens exactly when there is some y_2 s.t. $x_2 R y_2$ and $\begin{pmatrix} x_1 \\ x_2 \\ y_2 \end{pmatrix} \notin$![R, S diagram]. This non-inclusion happens exactly when it is not the case that $x_2 R y_2$ or $\begin{pmatrix} x_1 \\ x_2 \end{pmatrix} \notin S$. Since $x_2 R y_2$ by assumption, it happens precisely when $x_2 R y_2$ and $\begin{pmatrix} x_1 \\ x_2 \end{pmatrix} \notin S$.

It follows that LHS and RHS denote the same relation in all models. $\qquad \square$

We can use (it-deit) to obtain two similar laws that are useful in diagrammatic proofs. We omit proofs for space reasons but note that Peirce can be seen using an instance of (ii) in his 1903 Lowell Lectures [16, p. 358-9].

Lemma 3.

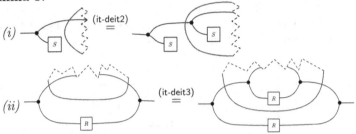

We can also use (it-deit) to extend a line of identity into a cut. Note that Lemma 4 follows from (it-deit2) when S is the counit.

Lemma 4.

Both Lemma 3 and Lemma 4 show how (it-deit) captures both iteration for a line of identity and for a relation/partial graph.

6 Diagrammatic Reasoning in Action

Example 6. We return to our running example and conclude with a complete diagrammatic derivation of the judgement

$$\frac{\text{isacatholic}(\text{Charles}) \wedge \forall x.\ \text{isacatholic}(x) \to \exists y.\ \text{adores}(x, y) \wedge \text{isawoman}(y)}{\exists y.\ \text{adores}(\text{Charles}, y) \wedge \text{isawoman}(y)}.$$

In the derivation we use the triangle notation[9] to denote a *constant* symbol of the logic, that is, a relation that is guaranteed to have singleton models. This (and similarly *function* symbols) are easily encoded in the graphical formalism and do not add expressivity; it suffices to assert that:

---

[9] Borrowed from the notation for states in categorical quantum mechanics [8].

We proceed with the derivation below:

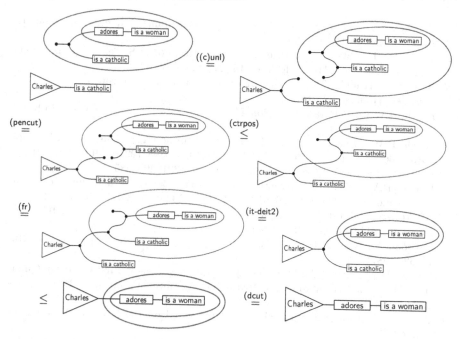

7   Conclusion

Peirce's EGs arose out of his continued study of the algebra of relations and his concern for developing an efficient graphical notation. Seen through contemporary string diagrams, Peirce's lines of identity obey the rules of special Frobenius algebras, while Peirce's inference rules for lines of identity are the axioms of cartesian bicategories of relations. Moreover, diagrammatic reasoning can be extended to cover negation in a straightforward manner.

The category theoretic account of EGs presented here yields a diagrammatic calculus that is as expressive as first-order logic. We summarize the specific benefits of the graphical logical language when we say that it is *compositional*. The syntax is string diagrams, the semantics is Rel_x, and models structure-preserving maps. In particular sub-formulas (sub-diagrams) have their own meaning as relations, with the meaning of the entire formula (diagram) obtained by composing these. In these respects our approach follows Peirce's original intentions.

In regards to Peirce scholarship, our presentation suggests new means of interpreting the transformation rules in EGs. Following Peirce, this presentation showcases contraposition as the governing duality between positive and negative contexts on the sheet. We also clarify the rule of iteration. Robert's presentation [17, pp. 57-8] includes important but fairly ad hoc clauses to the Beta rules of iteration. These clauses, as well as Burch's more recent developments in [6], are unified here with a single principle of iteration. Finally, situating Peirce's EGs in contemporary category theory [2,3] allows for further study and comparisons.

References

1. Bonchi, F., Seeber, J., Sobociński, P.: Graphical conjunctive queries. In: Computer Science Logic 2018 (CSL 2018) (2018)
2. Brady, G., Trimble, T.: A categorical interpretation of C. S. Peirce's propositional logic alpha. J. Pure Appl. Algebra **149**, 213–239 (2000)
3. Brady, G., Trimble, T.: A string diagram calculus for predicate logic and C. S. Peirce's system beta (2000)
4. Burch, R.W.: A Peircean Reduction Thesis. Texas Tech University Press, Lubbock (1991)
5. Burch, R.W.: Valental aspects of peircean algebraic logic. Comput. Math. Appl. **23**(6), 665–677 (1992). https://doi.org/10.1016/0898-1221(92)90128-5. http://www.sciencedirect.com/science/article/pii/0898122192901285
6. Burch, R.W.: The fine structure of Peircean ligatures and lines of identity. Semiotica **186**, 21 (2020–01-22T12:56:46313+01:00 2011). https://doi.org/10.1515/semi.2011.045. https://www.degruyter.com/view/j/semi.2011.2011.issue-186/semi.2011.045/semi.2011.045.xml
7. Carboni, A., Walters, R.F.C.: Cartesian bicategories I. J. Pure Appl. Algebra **49**, 11–32 (1987)
8. Coecke, B., Kissinger, A.: Picturing Quantum Processes - A First Course in Quantum Theory and Diagrammatic Reasoning. Cambridge University Press, Cambridge (2017)
9. Dau, F.: Mathematical logic with diagrams based on the Existential Graphs of Peirce (2005)
10. Hereth Correia, J., Pöschel, R.: The power of peircean algebraic logic (PAL). In: Eklund, P. (ed.) ICFCA 2004. LNCS (LNAI), vol. 2961, pp. 337–351. Springer, Heidelberg (2004). https://doi.org/10.1007/978-3-540-24651-0_29
11. Lack, S.: Composing PROPs. Theor. Appl. Categories **13**(9), 147–163 (2004)
12. Mac Lane, S.: Categorical algebra. Bull. Am. Math. Soc. **71**, 40–106 (1965)
13. Minghui, M., Pietarinen, A.: A graphical deep inference system for intuitionistic logic. Logique et Analyse **245**, 73–114 (2019). https://doi.org/10.2143/LEA.245.0.3285706
14. Peirce, C.S.: Letters to Lady Welby. MS [R] L463, from the Commens Bibliography. http://www.commens.org/bibliography/manuscript/peirce-charles-s-nd-letters-lady-welby-ms-r-l463
15. Pietarinen, A.V.: The Logic of the Future, vol. 1. De Gruyter, Berlin (2019)
16. Pietarinen, A.V.: The Logic of the Future, vol. 2 & 3. De Gruyter, Berlin (forthcoming) (cited page numbers are from a previous draft copy)
17. Roberts, D.D.: The Existential Graphs of Charles S. Peirce. Mouton, The Hague (1973)
18. Shin, S.: The Iconic Logic of Peirce's Graphs. MIT Press, Cambridge (2002)
19. Zeman, J.J.: A system of implicit quantification. J. Symb. Logic **32**(4), 480–504 (1967). http://www.jstor.org/stable/2270176

Free Rides in Logical Space Diagrams Versus Aristotelian Diagrams

Hans Smessaert[1]([✉]) [ID], Atsushi Shimojima[2][ID], and Lorenz Demey[3][ID]

[1] Department of Linguistics, KU Leuven, Blijde-Inkomststraat 21,
3000 Leuven, Belgium
hans.smessaert@kuleuven.be
[2] Faculty of Culture and Information Science, Doshisha University, 1–3
Tatara-Miyakodani, Kyotanabe 610-0394, Japan
ashimoji@mail.doshisha.ac.jp
[3] Center for Logic and Philosophy of Science, KU Leuven, Kardinaal Mercierplein 2,
3000 Leuven, Belgium
lorenz.demey@kuleuven.be
https://www.logicalgeometry.org

Abstract. In this paper we compare two types of diagrams for the representation of logical relations such as contradiction and contrariety, namely Logical Space diagrams (LSD) and Aristotelian diagrams (AD). The cognitive potential of Free Ride – defined in terms of tracking by consequence (Shimojima 2015) – is shown to hold for LSDs but not for ADs. The latter, however, do exhibit a greater inspection potential – defined in terms of tracking by correlation. The translational or informational equivalence between LSDs and ADs is contrasted to their lack of computational equivalence and their different degrees of iconicity.

Keywords: Cognitive potential · Free Ride · Logical Space Diagram · Aristotelian diagram · Translation · Informational/computational equivalence · Degrees of iconicity

1 Introduction

The overall aim of this paper is to apply the general framework for the analysis of diagrams proposed by Shimojima [6] to two different types of diagrams for Aristotelian relations (such as contradiction or contrariety). In Sect. 1 we briefly present both the general framework – with a special focus on the cognitive potential of Free Ride – and the four Aristotelian relations. In Sect. 2 we introduce a new representation system for Aristotelian relations, namely LOGI-CAL SPACE DIAGRAMS (LSDs), and study their cognitive (Free Ride) potential in terms of tracking by consequence. In Sect. 3 we observe that, although the

---

The first author acknowledges the financial support from the Research Foundation – Flanders (FWO) of his research stay at Doshisha University with the second author. The third author holds a Postdoctoral Fellowship of the Research Foundation – Flanders (FWO) and a Research Professorship (BOFZAP) from KU Leuven.

© Springer Nature Switzerland AG 2020
A.-V. Pietarinen et al. (Eds.): Diagrams 2020, LNAI 12169, pp. 419–435, 2020.
https://doi.org/10.1007/978-3-030-54249-8_33

cognitive potential of Free Ride does not hold of the standard representation of Aristotelian relations by means of ARISTOTELIAN DIAGRAMS (ADs), the latter do allow a weaker mechanism of tracking by correlation. In Sects. 4 and 5 we investigate the translation relation between LSDs and ADs, which observes informational equivalence but not computational equivalence, and which reflects differences in degree of iconicity between the two types of diagrams.

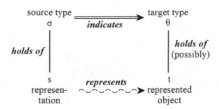

Fig. 1. General framework for the analysis of diagrams [6, Figure 21].

General Framework for the Analysis of Diagrams. In order to characterise the semantic content of a diagrammatic representation, the framework adopted in this paper [6, p. 23ff] has a two-tier semantics. It draws a distinction between a TOKEN level at the bottom of Fig. 1 – with a REPRESENTATION relation $\rightsquigarrow$ from a representation s to represented object t – and a TYPE level at the top of Fig. 1 – with an INDICATION relation $\Rightarrow$ from a source type σ to a target type θ. In the case of a street map, for instance, the representation s is a particular sheet of paper (token) and the arrangement of lines and symbols is the source type σ or property holding of (or 'being supported' by) that s. The represented object t is a particular region of a city (token) and the arrangement of streets and buildings is the target type θ or property holding of that t. A representation s represents an object or situation t as being of target type θ if s represents t and s supports a source type σ that indicates θ [6, p. 27].

Since the notions of consequence tracking and Free Ride will be defined in terms of source and target types, this paper will focus on the type level and the indication relation established by the semantic conventions for the relevant representational practice.[1] We say that a set Γ of source types COLLECTIVELY INDICATES a set Δ of target types ($\Gamma \Rightarrow \Delta$) if Γ and Δ stand in a one-to-one correspondence under the indication relation $\Rightarrow$.

Furthermore, a CONSTRAINT is a regularity governing the distribution of sets of types Γ and Δ in a particular class of tokens. There is a constraint $\Gamma \vdash \Delta$ from antecedent set Γ to consequent set Δ if *some* type in Δ must hold of a token if *all* types in Γ hold of that token [6, p. 30f]. Thus $\{\gamma_1, \gamma_2\} \vdash \{\delta_1, \delta_2\}$ means that if γ_1 *and* γ_2 hold of a token (conjunctively), then δ_1 *or* δ_2 must hold of that token

---

[1] A semantic convention is essentially arbitrary in its origin, but once people start conforming to it [...] it becomes a "self-perpetuating" constraint over the representational acts of a group of people [6, p. 26].

(disjunctively). A constraint of the form $\Gamma \vdash \{\delta\}$, with a singleton consequent set, is called a CONSEQUENTIAL CONSTRAINT (CC) and rewritten as $\Gamma \vdash \delta$: if all members of Γ hold of a token, then the definite type δ must hold of it. Constraints may hold both between sets of source types and between sets of target types. It is precisely the correspondences between constraints involving source types and those involving target types that account for many characteristic cognitive potentials of diagrammatic representation systems [6, p. 31].

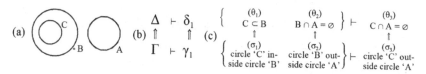

Fig. 2. (a) Free ride in Euler diagram (b–c) Consequence tracking [6, Figure 28–30].

Free Rides and CC Tracking by Consequence. Suppose we take the target types $C \subset B$ (θ_1) and $B \cap A = \varnothing$ (θ_2) as the premises of a syllogism at the top of Fig. 2(c). In order for the Euler diagram in Fig. 2(a) to express these two pieces of information, the semantic conventions require us to realise two source types at the bottom of Fig. 2(c), namely the circle labeled 'C' is inside the circle labeled 'B' (σ_1) and the circle labeled 'B' is outside the circle labeled 'A' (σ_2). By virtue of the natural spatial (geometrical and topological) constraints on the arrangements of symbols in Euler diagrams, the realisation of σ_1 and σ_2 automatically realises a third source type, namely that the circle labeled 'C' is outside the circle labeled 'A' (σ_3). Although this is a side effect of the original operation, σ_3 has an independent semantic value, namely that $C \cap A = \varnothing$ (θ_3). This target type θ_3 is a piece of information that we get 'for free'. Hence, to check the validity of the syllogism, we do not have to infer conclusion θ_3 from the premises $\{\theta_1, \theta_2\}$. The constraint governing Euler diagrams takes over the work of making the necessary inference, a mechanism called FREE RIDE [6, p. 33]. In the case of a Free Ride potential, expressing a set of information Δ in a representation automatically results in the expression of other, consequential information δ_1. This enables us to skip the mental deductive steps from Δ to δ_1, and to substitute them with the task of reading off δ_1 from the representation [6, p. 36]. Figure 2(b) represents this general constellation of CONSEQUENCE TRACKING. Vertically, Γ collectively indicates Δ ($\Gamma \Rightarrow \Delta$) and γ_1 indicates δ_1 ($\gamma_1 \Rightarrow \delta_1$). Horizontally, there is a match ('tracking') between the CC $\Gamma \vdash \gamma_1$ on the source types of the representation and the CC $\Delta \vdash \delta_1$ on the target types of the represented object. In order to distinguish it from other types of tracking between source and target type constraints, we refer to the Free Ride mechanism in Fig. 2(b–c) – rendering inference unnecessary – more explicitly as CC TRACKING BY CONSEQUENCE.

Aristotelian Relations. In the research programme of Logical Geometry [3, 7] a central object of investigation is the so-called 'Aristotelian square' or 'square of opposition', which visualises logical relations of opposition and implication. Table 1 defines these ARISTOTELIAN RELATIONS in an informal way.[2] Two propositions α and β are said to be:

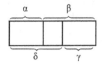

Fig. 3. Logical space diagram (LSD).

Table 1. Aristotelian relations.

a.	contradictory	$CD(\alpha,\beta)$	iff	α and β cannot be true together and α and β cannot be false together
b.	contrary	$C(\alpha,\beta)$	iff	α and β cannot be true together but α and β can be false together
c.	subcontrary	$SC(\alpha,\beta)$	iff	α and β can be true together but α and β cannot be false together
d.	in subalternation	$SA(\alpha,\beta)$	iff	α entails β but β doesn't entail α

Assuming a meaning postulate relating *dead* and *not alive*, the propositions *The fly was alive* and *the fly was dead* are contradictory (it has to be one situation or the other, but not both), whereas *The fly was alive* and *The fly was killed* are contrary (it may be neither, namely when the fly died a natural death).

2   CC Tracking by Consequence in Logical Space Diagrams

Basic Syntax and Semantics. In Fig. 3 we introduce a new type of diagram, namely the LOGICAL SPACE DIAGRAM (or LSD for short). The big rectangle represents the complete Logical Space, i.e. the set of possible situations in the world, or the set of all relevant entities of a given logical type (the 'universe of discourse'). Logical Space can then be subdivided in different parts, i.e. subsets of those possible situations, indicated by means of vertical lines inside the big rectangle.[3] Curly brackets accompanied by a small Greek letter then indicate for

---

[2] In model-theoretic semantics, these relations receive a modal definition in terms of the (non-)existence of models/possible worlds in which both formulas are true/false.

[3] Although the full 2D potential of LSD diagrams is not exploited in the present analysis, subdivisions of Logical Space can be both vertical and horizontal.

which part of Logical Space a given proposition, indicated by the Greek letter, holds, i.e. in which situations that proposition is true, or for which subset of entities of a given logical type a property holds. The LSD format could be considered a notational variant of the Linear Diagram System [1] or the Euler diagram system[4] in which an area is visually represented if and only if it is non-empty. One advantage of such LSDs is the very natural and intuitive representation of the opposition and implication relations.

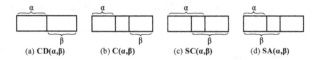

(a) CD(α,β)   (b) C(α,β)   (c) SC(α,β)   (d) SA(α,β)

Fig. 4. LSDs for Aristotelian relations.

Aristotelian Relations and LSDs. In Fig. 4 we use the Logical Space diagrams to visualise each of the Aristotelian relations defined in Table 1. Three out of the four Aristotelian relations are defined in terms of the two conditions of 'possibly being true together' and 'possibly being false together'. In terms of the LSDs, for two propositions to 'possibly be true together' means that there is an OVERLAP between their two designated areas, whereas for two propositions to 'possibly be false together' means that their is a GAP between their two designated areas. When two propositions are contradictory, the LSD in Fig. 4(a) has no gap and no overlap between their two areas. They are mutually exclusive and jointly exhaustive, and thus yield a perfect bipartition of Logical Space. With the contrary propositions in Fig. 4(b), by contrast, there is no overlap but there is a gap between the two areas. Subcontrary propositions result in the inverse constellation in Fig. 4(c), in which there is no gap but there is an overlap in the middle. Notice that the fourth Aristotelian relation, namely subalternation in Table 1(d), is the odd one out in that it is defined in terms of unidirectional (i.e. asymmetric) entailment instead of in terms of (symmetric) opposition. This hybrid nature of the set of Aristotelian relations in Table 1 is discussed in full detail in [7]. Nevertheless, the LSD for subalternation in Fig. 4(d) can be characterised by means of the same two visual ingredients as the other three relations in Fig. 4(a–c): the two areas designated to the two propositions reveal both a gap (on the right) and an overlap (on the left).

2.1   CC Tracking by Consequence with Two Premises in LSDs

Remember from the Euler diagram in Fig. 2 above that the starting point for a Free Ride mechanism is the combination of two pieces of information, namely

---

[4] The crucial ingredients are basically the same, namely a universe set U and two subsets A and B, which yield four areas to be considered, namely $A \cap B$, $A \setminus B$, $B \setminus A$ and $U \setminus (A \cup B)$ (see also [9]). Given the definition of a proposition as a class of possible worlds, relations between classes in Euler diagrams straightforwardly correspond to relations between propositions in Aristotelian diagrams.

a first relation between objects A and B, and a second relation between objects B and C. All four LSDs in Fig. 5 take as their first relation a contradiction between α and β. The gap in the middle of Fig. 5(a–b) can be characterised either in terms of a contrariety between α and γ in Fig. 5(a) or in terms of a subalternation between γ and β in Fig. 5(b). The overlaps in Fig. 5(c–d) are either due to the subcontrariety between β and δ in the middle of Fig. 5(c) or to the subalternation between α and δ at the left of Fig. 5(d). Depending on which 'perspective' is taken as the second relation – indicated by the asterisks – the four LSDs in Fig. 5 each give rise to their own Free Ride constellation.

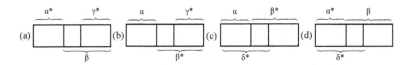

Fig. 5. LSDs for (a–b) {C, CD, SA} and (c–d) {SC, CD, SA}.

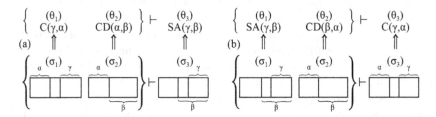

Fig. 6. CC tracking by consequence in LSDs (a) **Free Ride 1a**: {C, CD} ⊢ SA and (b) **Free Ride 1b**: {SA, CD} ⊢ C.

Let us first consider the case of Fig. 5(a), spelled out in full detail in Fig. 6(a). The target type θ_1 – the contrariety relation $C(\gamma,\alpha)$ – is indicated by the gap in the source type σ_1 LSD, whereas the θ_2 contradiction $CD(\alpha,\beta)$ is indicated by the bipartition in the σ_2 LSD. If we now combine σ_1 and σ_2, the natural spatial (geometrical and topological) constraints on the arrangements of symbols in the LSD representation format automatically yield the LSD in Fig. 5(a). The latter now also reveals both a gap and an overlap between γ and β in σ_3 of Fig. 6(a), and thus conveys a new piece of information 'for free', namely the subalternation relation $SA(\gamma,\beta)$ in θ_3. Thus, Fig. 6(a) nicely illustrates the general mechanism of CC tracking by consequence in Fig. 2(b) above between the CC on the target level – {θ_1, θ_2} ⊢ θ_3 – and that on the source level – {σ_1, σ_2} ⊢ σ_3. The physical operations of drawing a diagram let us project the premises {θ_1, θ_2} of our inference onto an external diagram {σ_1, σ_2}, exploit the spatial constraints holding there (yielding σ_3), and gain a Free Ride to the logical consequence θ_3.

Although the LSD is identical in Fig. 5(a) and Fig. 5(b), we get a shift in perspective from the gap between α and γ in the former case to the inclusion of γ in β in the latter case. The corresponding shift from Fig. 6(a) to Fig. 6(b) involves the switch of the first premise θ_1 and the conclusion θ_3. The two premises $\{SA(\gamma, \beta), CD(\beta, \alpha)\}$ in Fig. 6(b) are expressed by the inclusion of γ in β in σ_1 and the bipartition between α and β in σ_2. By spatial necessity, the combination of the latter two results in the gap between α and γ in σ_3, which expresses the valid conclusion of the inference – namely the contrariety relation $C(\gamma, \alpha)$ – as a Free Ride.

Completely analogously, the identical LSDs in Fig. 5(c) and Fig. 5(d) switch the perspective from the overlap between β and δ in the former case to the inclusion of α in δ in the latter case. The corresponding shift from Fig. 7(a) to Fig. 7(b) involves the switch of the second premise θ_2 and the conclusion θ_3. The two premises $\{CD(\alpha, \beta), SC(\beta, \delta)\}$ in Fig. 7(a) are indicated by the bipartition between α and β in σ_1 and the overlap between β and δ in σ_2. By virtue of the spatial constraints on LSDs, the combination of the latter two necessarily yields the inclusion of α in δ in σ_3. This in turn serves as a Free Ride and gets interpreted as the valid conclusion of the inference – namely the subalternation $SA(\alpha, \delta)$ in θ_3. With the two premises $\{CD(\beta, \alpha), SA(\alpha, \delta)\}$ in Fig. 7(b), the combination of the bipartition between α and β in σ_1 and the inclusion of α in δ in σ_2 automatically results in the overlap between β and δ in σ_3. This Free Ride yields the valid conclusion in θ_3 of the subcontrariety relation $SC(\beta, \delta)$.

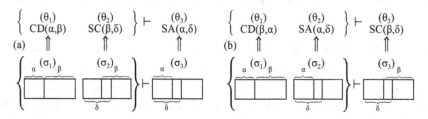

Fig. 7. CC tracking by consequence in LSDs (a) **Free Ride 2a**: $\{CD, SC\} \vdash SA$ and (b) **Free Ride 2b**: $\{CD, SA\} \vdash SC$.

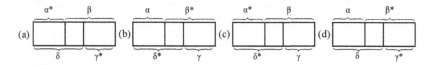

Fig. 8. LSDs for $\{CD, C, SC, SA\}$.

In both LSD constellations in Fig. 5(a–b) and Fig. 5(c–d) three Aristotelian relations are involved, namely {C, CD, SA} and {SC, CD, SA} respectively. Both these sets gave rise to two valid syllogisms each, namely Free Ride 1a {C, CD} ⊢ SA in Fig. 6(a), Free Ride 1b {SA, CD} ⊢ C in Fig. 6(b), Free Ride 2a {CD, SC} ⊢ SA in Fig. 7(a) and Free Ride 2b {CD, SA} ⊢ SC in Fig. 7(b). What all these valid patterns have in common is that the CD relation is always one of the premises, whereas the other two relations may serve both as premise and as conclusion. In other words, the third logical combination – with CD in the conclusion and the other two relations as the premises – turns out to be excluded in both cases: {C, SA} ⊬ CD and {SC, SA} ⊬ CD respectively. What is more, these two pairs of premises are compatible with any possible Aristotelian relation. Although this situation can be related to the notions of OVER-SPECIFICITY and INDETERMINACY in [6, p. 60ff], more research is needed to clarify the special status of the CD relation.[5]

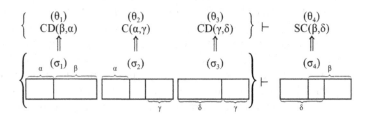

Fig. 9. CC tracking by consequence in LSDs: **Free Ride 3a** {CD, C, CD} ⊢ SC.

2.2   CC Tracking by Consequence with Three Premises in LSDs

Let us now move from CCs with two premises to the constellations in Fig. 8 with three premises. All four LSDs contain two contradiction relations, namely between α and β as well as between γ and δ. Depending on which 'perspective' is taken as the third relation, these LSDs each give rise to their own Free Ride mechanism.

Taking the gap between α and γ in Fig. 8(a) as the second premise in Fig. 9 yields the Free Ride 3a. If you combine the two bipartitions α-β (σ_1) and γ-δ (σ_3) with the α-γ gap (σ_2), the spatial constraints of LSDs automatically give you the β-δ overlap (σ_4), which expresses the conclusion θ_4 of the valid syllogism {CD, C, CD} ⊢ SC. Focusing on the overlap between β and δ in Fig. 8(b), by contrast, would yield a variation of the pattern in Fig. 9 in which the second premise σ_2/θ_2 and the conclusion σ_4/θ_4 are switched around. In other words, whenever you observe a β-δ overlap in combination with the two bipartitions (α-β and γ-δ), you get an α-γ gap as a Free Ride. This modification of the original Free Ride 3a in Fig. 9 thus results in the Free Ride 3b for the valid

---

[5] In particular in terms of the tracking of the two disjunctive constraints {C, SA} ⊢ {CD, C, SC, SA, Un} and {SC, SA} ⊢ {CD, C, SC, SA, Un}, where Un stands for UNCONNECTEDNESS, the absence of any Aristotelian relation [7].

syllogism {CD, SC, CD} ⊢ C. If we take the inclusion of α in δ in Fig. 8(c) as our perspective, we get the Free Ride 4a in Fig. 10. The combined observation of the two bipartitions α-β (σ_1) and γ-δ (σ_3) with the gap plus overlap between α and δ (σ_2) by spatial necessity results in the gap plus overlap between γ and β (σ_4), which expresses the conclusion θ_4 of the valid syllogism {CD, SA, CD} ⊢ SA. And finally, focusing on the inclusion of γ in β in Fig. 8(d) would yield a variation of the pattern in Fig. 10 in which the second premise σ_2/θ_2 and the conclusion σ_4/θ_4 are again switched around. This modification of the original Free Ride 4a in Fig. 10 thus results in the Free Ride 4b for the same valid syllogism {CD, SA, CD} ⊢ SA. The observation made at the end of the previous subsection concerning the particular status of the CD relation turns out to generalise to the patterns with three premises: both in Fig. 9 and Fig. 10 the two CD relations have to be among the premises. Notice, finally, that the combination of Free Rides 4a and 4b in Fig. 8(c–d) and Fig. 10 serves as an elegant visualisation of the Law of Contraposition: $\neg\alpha = \beta$ (CD), $\neg\delta = \gamma$ (CD), $(\alpha \to \delta)$ (SA) $\Leftrightarrow (\neg\delta \to \neg\alpha) \Leftrightarrow (\gamma \to \beta)$ (SA).

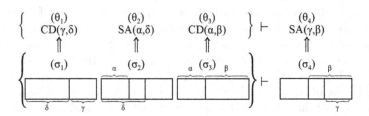

Fig. 10. CC tracking by consequence in LSDs: **Free Ride 4a** {CD, SA, CD} ⊢ SA.

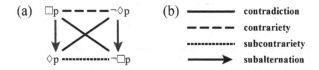

Fig. 11. (a) Aristotelian diagram (AD) and (b) coding conventions.

3   CC Tracking by Correlation in Aristotelian Diagrams

Basic Syntax and Semantics. In order to draw an ARISTOTELIAN DIAGRAM (AD for short), we first of all need a (non-empty) fragment F of a language L, i.e. a subset of formulas of that language. The formulas in the fragment F must be contingent and pairwise non-equivalent, and the fragment has to be closed under negation: if formula φ belongs to F, then its negation $\neg\varphi$ also belongs to F. For the language S5 of Modal Logic (with operators $\Box$ for necessity and $\Diamond$ for possibility), for instance, such a fragment F could be $\{\Box p, \neg\Box p, \Diamond p, \neg\Diamond p\}$.

An Aristotelian diagram for F is then defined as a diagram that visualizes an edge-labeled graph G. Figure 11(a) presents the AD for the modal fragment $\{\Box p, \neg\Box p, \Diamond p, \neg\Diamond p\}$. The vertices of G are the elements of F, whereas the edges of G are labeled by all the Aristotelian relations holding between those elements, using the coding conventions in Fig. 11(b): full line for CD, dashed line for C, dotted line for SC, and arrow for SA.

Subdiagrams in ADs. From a diagrammatic point of view there are (at least) two ways of looking at a standard square AD. First of all, an AD can be seen as consisting of two triangular subdiagrams: the 'right triangle' in Fig. 12(a) and the 'left triangle' in Fig. 12(b).[6] Secondly, the AD contains two X-shaped subdiagrams: the 'hour glass' in Fig. 12(c) and the 'bow tie' in Fig. 12(d).

It is important to stress here that these four ARISTOTELIAN SUBDIAGRAMS (henceforth AsDs) are not ADs themselves. Since ADs always consist of an even number of vertices, triangles are excluded in principle.[7] The hour glass and the bow tie in Fig. 12(c–d), by contrast, do contain an even number of vertices, and do respect the constraint of closure under negation. However, that still does not make them ADs, because the latter have to represent *all* Aristotelian relations holding between the vertices.[8] Nevertheless, in spite of the four AsD shapes in Fig. 12 not being ADs themselves, they play a crucial role as the elementary building blocks of such ADs. In the second part of this paper we will precisely demonstrate how these four AsD shapes relate to the different types of Free Ride that were distinguished for the Logical Space diagrams in the first part.

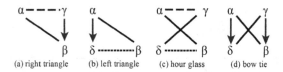

Fig. 12. Triangular and X-shaped Aristotelian subdiagrams (AsDs).

3.1   CC Tracking by Correlation with Two Premises in ADs

Observe, first of all, that the 'right triangle' in Fig. 12(a) and Fig. 13(a) represents the same $\{C, CD, SA\}$-constellation as the LSDs in Fig. 5(a–b). Hence,

---

[6] We ignore the fact that both triangles have a mirror image along the vertical axis.

[7] The right and left triangle in Fig. 12(a–b) are not closed under negation, since the negations of γ and δ are absent from the respective triangles.

[8] The hour glass in Fig. 12(c) does not visualise the two vertical SA relations, whereas the bow tie in Fig. 12(d) does not visualise the horizontal C and SC relations.

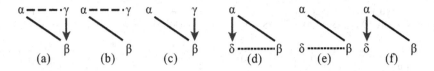

Fig. 13. AsDs for (a-b-c) {C, CD, SA} and (d-e-f) {SC, CD, SA}.

Fig. 13(b–c) each represent the two premises of the valid syllogisms {C, CD} ⊢ SA and {SA, CD} ⊢ C, given in detail in Fig. 14(a) and Fig. 14(b) respectively.

Let us first consider Fig. 14(a) in some detail. Due to the semantic constraints on ADs, we know for sure that – whenever we get from γ to α by means of a dashed C-line in σ_1', and from α to β by means of a full CD-line in σ_2' – there will be an SA-arrow from γ to β in σ_3'. This is a typical constellation of 'diagram chasing' [2] or 'transitive closure': if you first get from A to B and then from B to C, then you also get from A to C directly. On the target type level, Fig. 6(a) and Fig. 14(a) have exactly the same CC (for the valid syllogism). On the source type level of the actual LSD and AD, however, the two are fundamentally different. With the Free Ride 1a in the LSD, there is a matching CC: the σ_3 conclusion from the $\{\sigma_1,\sigma_2\}$ premises is a matter of inevitable spatial constraints. Although the σ_3' source type in Fig. 14(a) is equally inevitable, it is not a matter of spatial necessity. There is nothing in the act of drawing the dashed line and the full line for the $\{\sigma_1',\sigma_2'\}$ 'premises' which would force you to draw the arrow of the σ_3' as a 'conclusion'. Hence, the bottom part of Fig. 14(a) does *not* constitute a source type level CC, and the overall constellation is *not* an instance of the Free Ride mechanism.

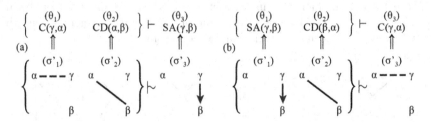

Fig. 14. CC tracking by correlation in ADs (a) {C, CD} ⊢ SA and (b) {SA, CD} ⊢ C.

Nevertheless, when we inspect a well-formed AD, the combined observation of the two source types $\{\sigma_1',\sigma_2'\}$ systematically correlates with the observation of σ_3', by virtue of their correspondence (through the indication relation ⇑) with the premises and the conclusion of the CC on the target type level. In order to reflect this fundamental difference between ADs and LSDs, we replace the turnstile symbol ⊢ between the $\{\sigma_1,\sigma_2\}$ premises and the σ_3 conclusion in the LSDs with the CORRELATION symbol ∼ between the $\{\sigma_1',\sigma_2'\}$ and the σ_3' source types in the AD. The overall constellation – which is manifestly weaker than that

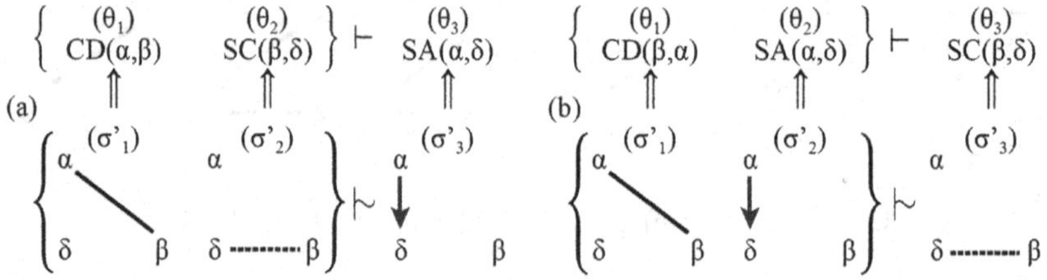

$$\left\{ \begin{array}{cc} (\theta_1) & (\theta_2) \\ CD(\alpha,\beta) & SC(\beta,\delta) \end{array} \right\} \vdash \begin{array}{c} (\theta_3) \\ SA(\alpha,\delta) \end{array} \qquad \left\{ \begin{array}{cc} (\theta_1) & (\theta_2) \\ CD(\beta,\alpha) & SA(\alpha,\delta) \end{array} \right\} \vdash \begin{array}{c} (\theta_3) \\ SC(\beta,\delta) \end{array}$$

(a) ⇑ ⇑ ⇑ (b) ⇑ ⇑ ⇑

$$\left\{ \begin{array}{cc} \alpha\,(\sigma'_1) & \alpha\,(\sigma'_2) \\ \diagdown & \downarrow \\ \delta \quad \beta & \delta \cdots \beta \end{array} \right\} \sim \begin{array}{c} \alpha\,(\sigma'_3) \\ \downarrow \\ \delta \quad \beta \end{array} \qquad \left\{ \begin{array}{cc} \alpha\,(\sigma'_1) & \alpha\,(\sigma'_2) \\ \diagdown & \downarrow \\ \delta \quad \beta & \delta \quad \beta \end{array} \right\} \sim \begin{array}{c} \alpha\,(\sigma'_3) \\ \\ \delta \cdots \beta \end{array}$$

Fig. 15. CC tracking by correlation in ADs (a) {CD,SC}⊢SA and (b) {CD,SA}⊢SC.

of CC tracking by consequence with the Free Rides in LSDs – will accordingly be referred to as CC TRACKING BY CORRELATION in ADs.

As we observed in connection with the move from Fig. 6(a) to Fig. 6(b), the first premise and the conclusion are switched going from Fig. 14(a) to Fig. 14(b) to yield the second valid inference, i.e. {SA, CD} ⊢ C. Visually speaking, the combined observation of the SA-arrow from γ to β in σ'_1 and the full CD-line from β to α in σ'_2 by semantic convention correlates with the observation of the dashed C-line from γ to α in σ'_3. The overall constellation of CC tracking by correlation in Fig. 14(b) thus counts as the weaker counterpart of the Free Ride 1b in Fig. 6(b).

Completely analogously, the 'left triangle' in Fig. 12(b) and Fig. 13(d) represents the same {SC, CD, SA}-constellation as the LSDs in Fig. 5(c–d). Hence, Fig. 13(e–f) each represent the two premises of the respective valid syllogisms {CD, SC} ⊢ SA and {CD, SA} ⊢ SC. Thus, the CC trackings by correlation in Fig. 15(a–b) count as the weaker versions of the CC trackings by consequence with Free Rides 2a and 2b in Fig. 7(a–b), respectively. As we observed above with the Free Rides in LSDs, in all four valid syllogisms in Fig. 14(a–b) and Fig. 15(a–b) the CD relation is always one of the premises, whereas the other two relations serve both as premise and as conclusion.[9]

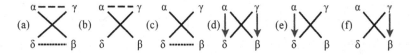

Fig. 16. AsDs for (a–c) {CD, C, CD, SC} and (d-f) {CD, SA, CD, SA}.

3.2 CC Tracking by Correlation with Three Premises in ADs

At the end of the previous section we moved from the CC tracking by consequence with two premises to that with three premises. In this subsection we make

---

[9] An analysis in terms of OVER-SPECIFICITY or INDETERMINACY [6, p. 60ff] remains a topic for further research.

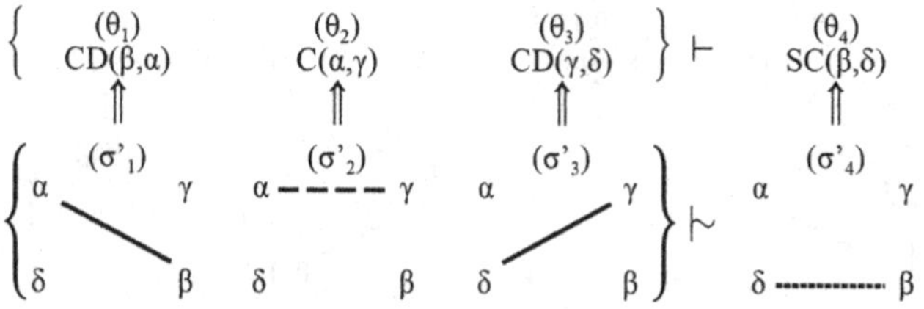

$$\left\{ \begin{array}{cccc} (\theta_1) & (\theta_2) & (\theta_3) \\ CD(\beta,\alpha) & C(\alpha,\gamma) & CD(\gamma,\delta) \end{array} \right\} \vdash \begin{array}{c} (\theta_4) \\ SC(\beta,\delta) \end{array}$$

Fig. 17. CC tracking by correlation in ADs: {CD, C, CD} ⊢ SC.

the corresponding move for CC tracking by correlation. The hour glass pattern in Fig. 12(c) and Fig. 16(a) first of all allows the perspective in Fig. 16(b), which is elaborated in Fig. 17, and which can be seen as the AD counterpart of the LSD Free Ride 3a in Fig. 9. The 'diagram chasing' now consists of three steps from start to finish (instead of two in the previous subsection). By virtue of the semantic constraints on ADs, we know for sure that – whenever we get from β to α by means of a full CD-line in σ'_1, from α to γ by means of a dashed C-line in σ'_2, and from γ to δ by means of a full CD-line in σ'_3 – there will be a dotted SC-line from β to δ in σ'_4. By means of the indication relation, this correlation on the source level is mapped onto the CC on the target level which captures the valid syllogism {CD, C, CD} ⊢ SC.

Moving to the second perspective on the hour glass in Fig. 16(c), we get a modification of the configuration in Fig. 17 in which the second 'premise' σ'_2/θ'_2 and the 'conclusion' σ'_4/θ'_4 are interchanged. In other words, moving from α to β (CD) in σ'_1, from β to δ (SC) in σ'_2, and from δ to γ (CD) in σ'_3 would be equivalent to moving in one big step from α to γ (C) in σ'_4. This source level correlation is then again mapped onto the target level CC capturing the valid syllogism {CD, SC, CD} ⊢ C from the Free Ride 3b discussed with Fig. 9.

The two perspectives on the bow tie pattern in Fig. 12(d) and Fig. 16(d), namely Fig. 16(e–f), together yield another visual representation of the Law of Contraposition. Figure 16(e) and Fig. 18 can be seen as the AD counterpart of the LSD Free Ride 4a in Fig. 10. The joint observation of moving from γ to δ (CD) in σ'_1, from δ to α (SA) in σ'_2, and from α to β (CD) in σ'_3 systematically correlates with the observation of the SA move from γ to β. This correlation matches the target level CC capturing the valid {CD, SA, CD} ⊢ SA syllogism. Figure 16(f) then corresponds to the LSD Free Ride 4b, discussed in connection with in Fig. 10, and requires a modification of Fig. 18 in which σ'_2/θ'_2 and σ'_4/θ'_4 are again interchanged. Notice, to conclude, that both in Fig. 17 and Fig. 18, the two CD relations once again have to be among the 'premises' of the correlation.

4 The Translation Relation Between LSDs and ADs

From an informational point of view, the Logical Space diagrams introduced in Sect. 2 and the Aristotelian diagrams introduced in Sect. 3 are by and large equivalent to one another. The two diagonals for contradiction in Fig. 19(b)

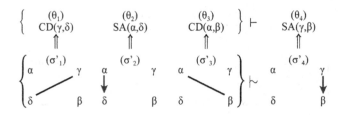

Fig. 18. CC tracking by correlation in ADs: {CD, SA, CD} ⊢ SA.

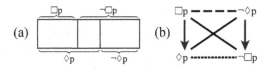

Fig. 19. (a) Logical space diagram versus (b) Aristotelian diagram.

correspond to the two bipartitions at the top and the bottom of Fig. 19(a), whereas the two subalternation arrows in Fig. 19(b) correspond to the fact that in Fig. 19(a) the areas for both $\Box p$ and $\Diamond p$ at the left and those for $\neg\Box p$, and $\neg\Diamond p$ at the right exhibit both a gap and an overlap. The dashed line for contrariety at the top of Fig. 19(b) reflects the gap between the areas for $\Box p$ and $\neg\Diamond p$ in Fig. 19(a), while the dotted line for subcontrariety at the bottom of Fig. 19(b) reflects the overlap between the areas for $\neg\Box p$ and $\Diamond p$ in Fig. 19(a).

In order to capture these systematic correspondences between the two types of representations, we introduce the notion of a translation relation between visual representations. Figure 20 demonstrates how such a relation fits into an extension of the general framework for the semantic analysis of diagrams introduced in Fig. 1. Remember that the latter's two-tier semantics draws a distinction between the token level and the type level. Hence, at the bottom of Fig. 20, we first of all define a TRANSFORMATION relation – indicated with the dashed double arrow – between the two material (token level) representations s (i.e. the LSD) and s' (i.e. the AD). The actual TRANSLATION relation – indicated with the full line double arrow – holds on the type level between the source types σ and σ'. The translational equivalence between the latter is then expressed by the fact they both stand in an indication relation with the same target type θ.

The source of the natural language metaphor of translation is straightforward: two natural language expressions (source types σ and σ') stand in a relation of translational or informational equivalence with one another if they are mapped onto the same meaning, i.e. the same target type θ.[10] Furthermore, the analogy with natural language nicely announces the distinction between informational and computational equivalence [4] to be discussed in the next section.

---

[10] Both with the diagrams in Fig. 20 and with natural languages, we want to emphasize the bidirectionality of the transformation and translation relations, as opposed to the (basic) unidirectionality of the indication and representation relations.

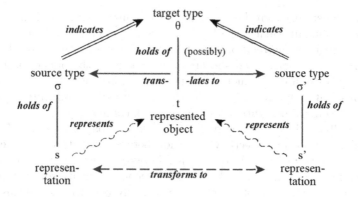

Fig. 20. General framework for the analysis of diagrams in translation.

Consider, for instance, the translation relation between a Dutch sentence written in the phonographic Roman alphabet and a Japanese sentence written in kanji and kana signs. Although the sentences may be perfectly equivalent from an informational point of view, there are huge computational or cognitive differences between the two writing system in terms of production, perception and learnability. In the next section, a similar discrepancy will be shown to hold for the two visual representation systems of LSDs and ADs under scrutiny.

5   Different Degrees of Iconicity with LSDs and ADs

The overall constellation of CC tracking by consequence that gives rise to the Free Ride potential of the LSDs is first and foremost a matter of CONSTRUCTING the diagrams step by step. The weaker constellation of CC tracking by correlation with the ADs, by contrast, is primarily a matter of INSPECTING complete diagrams, i.e. of eye-tracking steps through the diagram. The cognitive utility of the regularities in ADs thus lies in the fact that the transitivity from origin to goal allows you to read off in one big step the effect of two or three small steps. In other words, what you see as 'conclusion' is the logical consequence of what you have read off during the initial inspection of the first two or three steps. Hence, ADs can be considered as convenient pedagogical tools for learning about consequential relationships. Although this inspection value perspective is still there with the LSDs, it is less perspicuous. Since the visual components are more intertwined, more effort is needed, often involving so-called perspective or aspect shifting [6, p. 149ff]. Furthermore, when the structures get more complex – representing Aristotelian relations holding between six or more entities – the greater spatial independence or separation of the relations in the hexagonal (or bigger) ADs results in greater visual clarity and transparency.

The manifest differences between LSDs and ADs in terms of cognitive potentials (or the lack of computational equivalence [4]) can also be related to the semiotic notion of ICONICITY. On the standard view, iconicity is defined in terms of an isomorphism between the structure of the source domain and the structure of the target domain. Hence, the LSDs in this paper would be iconic representations, by virtue of the relationship of similarity between the constellations of surface areas in 2D space and subsets of situations in the outside world. The ADs, by contrast, are – semiotically speaking – no iconic but symbolic representations, without any such relationship of similarity, and purely based on visualisation conventions within a given research community.

On the alternative view proposed in the present paper (see also [5]), however, iconicity is not an object-level relation between structures of objects but rather a meta-level relation of isomorphism between constraints on source types and constraints on target types.[11] As a consequence, iconicity comes in degrees, depending on the strength of the constraints involved in the isomorphism. The strongest form of iconicity is obviously the one based on CC tracking with Free Rides, as illustrated with the LSDs. Diametrically opposed to the Free Rides with certain diagrammatical representation systems is the total absence of Free Rides in the case of linguistic representation systems [8]. The latter can thus be considered as exhibiting a zero degree of iconicity. The main advantage of this alternative approach to iconicity, however, is that it allows a much more fine-grained analysis in terms of various intermediate degrees of iconicity.[12] Rather than simply dismissing the ADs as symbolic representations, i.e. as non-iconic, they can now be argued to exhibit a weaker, intermediate degree of iconicity. In particular, the overall constellation of CC tracking by correlation in ADs may be 'weaker' than the CC tracking by consequence with the Free Rides in LSDs, it nevertheless counts as a (partial) isomorphism between sequences of source types and sequences of target types. Finally, also the fact that neither LSDs nor ADs are completely commutative – in the sense that you always need the contradiction relation(s) among the premises – may eventually be accounted for in terms of weaker constraints or intermediate degrees of iconicity.

6   Conclusion

In Sect. 2 we introduced LOGICAL SPACE DIAGRAMS (LSDs) as a new representation system for Aristotelian relations of opposition and implication, and defined their cognitive (Free Ride) potential in terms of consequential constraint (CC) tracking by consequence. In Sect. 3 we argued that, although the Free Ride mechanism does not hold of the standard representation by means of ARIS-TOTELIAN DIAGRAMS (ADs), the latter do allow a weaker mechanism of CC tracking by correlation. In Sects. 4 and 5 we investigated the translation relation between LSDs and ADs, which observes informational equivalence but not

---

[11] The possible connection with the so-called 'operational' conception of similarity and iconicity in Peirce, as elaborated by Stjernfelt [10, chapter 4] constitutes an intriguing topic of further research.

[12] For example, on this account, Euler diagrams are more iconic than Venn diagrams because they exhibit more constraint trackings. Similarly, the Euler system 2 is stronger and thus more iconic than system 1 since it generates more Free Rides [9].

computational equivalence. CC tracking by consequence with LSDs is crucially a matter of constructing the diagrams step by step, whereas CC tracking by correlation with ADs is primarily a matter of inspecting complete diagrams. This difference relates to differences in degree of iconicity between LSDs and ADs.

References

1. Bellucci, F., Moktefi, A., Pietarinen, A.V.: Diagrammatic autarchy. Linear diagrams in the 17th and 18th centuries. In: CEUR workshops proceedings, vol. 1132, pp. 23–30 (2014)
2. De Toffoli, S.: 'Chasing' the diagram - the use of visualizations in algebraic reasoning. Rev. Symbolic Logic **10**, 158–186 (2017)
3. Demey, L., Smessaert, H.: Combinatorial bitstring semantics for arbitrary logical fragments. J. Philos. Logic **47**(2), 325–363 (2017). https://doi.org/10.1007/s10992-017-9430-5
4. Larkin, J., Simon, H.: Why a diagram is (sometimes) worth ten thousand words. Cogn. Sci. **11**, 65–99 (1987)
5. Shimojima, A.: The graphic-linguistic distinction exploring alternatives. Artif. Intell. Rev. **15**, 5–27 (2001). https://doi.org/10.1023/A:1006752931044
6. Shimojima, A.: Semantic Properties of Diagrams and Their Cognitive Potentials. CSLI Publications, Stanford (2015)
7. Smessaert, H., Demey, L.: Logical geometries and information in the square of oppositions. J. Logic Lang. Inf. **23**(4), 527–565 (2014). https://doi.org/10.1007/s10849-014-9207-y
8. Stapleton, G., Jamnik, M., Shimojima, A.: What makes an effective representation of information: a formal account of observational advantages. J. Logic Lang. Inf. **26**(2), 143–177 (2017). https://doi.org/10.1007/s10849-017-9250-6
9. Stapleton, G., Shimojima, A., Jamnik, M.: The observational advantages of Euler diagrams with existential import. In: Chapman, P., Stapleton, G., Moktefi, A., Perez-Kriz, S., Bellucci, F. (eds.) Diagrams 2018. LNCS (LNAI), vol. 10871, pp. 313–329. Springer, Cham (2018). https://doi.org/10.1007/978-3-319-91376-6_29
10. Stjernfelt, F.: Diagrammatology: An Investigation on the Borderlines of Phenomenology, Ontology and Semiotics. Springer, Dordrecht (2007). https://doi.org/10.1007/978-1-4020-5652-9

Fregean Logical Graphs

Francesco Bellucci[(✉)]

Department of Philosophy and Communication, University of Bologna, Via Azzo Gardino 23, 40122 Bologna, Italy
francesco.bellucci4@unibo.it

Abstract. In "Gedankengefüge" Frege says that any two sentences of the form "*A* and *B*" and "*B* and *A*" have the same sense. In a 1906 letter to Husserl he says that sentences with the same sense should be represented in a perfect notation by one and the same formula. Frege's own notation, just like any linear notation for sentential logic, is not perfect in this sense, because in it "*A* and *B*" and "*B* and *A*" are represented by distinct formulas, as is any pair of logically equivalent compound conditionals. A notation for the sentential calculus that meets Frege's worries about conjunction, and indeed about any symmetric relation that there may be occasion to symbolize, is Peirce's Alpha graphs.

Keywords: Frege · Peirce · Logical graphs · Notations

1 Frege

In "Gedankengefüge", the last of his published essays, Frege says that any two sentences of the form of (1) and (2) have the same sense, i.e. express the same thought.

(1) *A* and *B*
(2) *B* and *A*

He explains that "this divergence of expressive symbol and expressed thought is an inevitable consequence of the divergence between spatio-temporal phenomena and the world of thoughts" (Frege 1984, 393). Let us assume that sameness of sense can be explained in terms of logical equivalence.[1] Then, since (1) and (2) have, according to Frege, the same sense, they are logically equivalent. In order to *prove* their logical equivalence one would need to apply to them some form of commutation rule for logical conjunction like the following, where "=" is the sign of logical equivalence:

(CR) ξ and $\zeta = \zeta$ and ξ

---

[1] It is debatable that this is how Frege would have explained sameness of sense. In a famous 1906 letter to Husserl he seems to be saying that logical equivalence is a sufficient criterion for sameness of sense. But this is in neat contrast with his principle of sense composition; see Dummett (1981, ch. 17). However, whether or not Frege did in fact think that logical equivalent sentences express the same sense does not affect in the least my argument. But see Bellucci (2020) for a discussion.

© Springer Nature Switzerland AG 2020
A.-V. Pietarinen et al. (Eds.): Diagrams 2020, LNAI 12169, pp. 436–444, 2020.
https://doi.org/10.1007/978-3-030-54249-8_34

But in order for (CR) to be applicable to sentences of the form of (1) and (2), these have to be in fact distinct sentences. With this is meant that (1) and (2) have to be distinct sentence *types*. It would make no sense to apply (CR) to two distinct sentence *tokens* of the same sentence type.

In a 1906 letter to Husserl, Frege toys with the idea that in a perfect system of logical representation, sentences with the same sense (here called, following Husserl, "equipollent") should be expressed by one and the same formula: "all that would be needed would be a single standard proposition for each system of equipollent propositions" (Frege 1980, 67). It is clear that Frege's own "Begriffsschrift" is not, in this sense, a perfect system of logical representation. In the "Begriffsschrift" (1) and (2) are expressed by distinct formula types (Fig. 1).

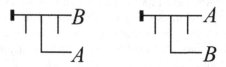

Fig. 1. Two logically equivalent sentences in Frege's "Begriffsschrift"

It could be objected that since Frege's "Begriffsschrift" has no primitive for conjunction (or, for that matter, for any other symmetric sentential operator), the claim that Frege's "Begriffsschrift" is not a perfect system of logical representation cannot rest upon its inability to cancel the divergence between the symbol for conjunction and the thought of conjunction. This is of course true. However, a parallel case could be made for the manner in which the "Begriffsschrift" represents compound conditionals. Conditionals of the form of (3) and (4) are logically equivalent:

(3) $A \supset (B \supset C)$
(4) $B \supset (A \supset C)$

In the "Begriffsschrift" (3) and (4) are represented respectively as the formulas (a) and (b) in Fig. 2. The logical equivalence of Fig. 2a and Fig. 2b is guaranteed in the *Begriffsschrift* by Axiom 8 (Frege 1879, §16), and in *Grundgesetze* is proved as a theorem (Frege 2013, §12).

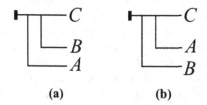

(a)   (b)

Fig. 2. Two logically equivalent sentences in Frege's "Begriffsschrift"

Now, there is a tendency in Frege's own presentations of the "Begriffsschrift" to consider the "transposition of the antecedents" more as a convention of the notation than as an axiom of the system (that is, as a rule of syntactical equivalence rather than as a rule of logical equivalence). For example, in *Grundgesetze*, just after having recalled the necessity of proving the theorem of the transposition of the antecedents, Frege adds: "as not to become tied up in excessive complexity, I here wish to assume this interchangeability generally granted, and to make use of it in future without further explicit mention" (Frege 2013, §12). Likewise, in the notes from the lectures held in 1910–1911 and 1913 taken by Carnap, Frege considers coordinate conditions to be interchangeable without treating this convention as an axiom of the system (see Reck and Awodey 2004, 52, 56, 71).

Macbeth (2005) and Schlimm (2018) seem to suggest that this is a peculiar feature of the "Begriffsschrift". Angelelli (2008) objects that it is not clear in what sense the application of the principle of transposition of the antecedents in the "Begriffsschrift" is different from the application in standard linear notations of an axiom like "$A \supset (B \supset C) = B \supset (A \supset C)$". In order for the "Begriffsschrift" principle of transposition of the antecedents to be applicable to formulas of the form of those in Fig. 2a and 2b, these have to be in fact distinct formulas, i.e. distinct formulas *types*, for it would make no sense to apply the "Begriffsschrift" principle of transposition of the antecedents to two distinct formula *tokens* of the same formula type. Since Frege does introduce in his systems this principle (even if in some presentations of the "Begriffsschrift" he tends to consider its application obvious), then the formulas in Fig. 2a and Fig. 2b are in fact distinct formula types. And since the formulas in Fig. 2a and Fig. 2b are logically equivalent, then the "Begriffsschrift", though it has no primitive for conjunction, yet fails to cancel the divergence of expressive symbol and expressed thought in the case of logically equivalent sentences of this form.

It is important to notice that the two cases under consideration—conjunctive sentences and compound conditional sentences—manifest a divergence between expressive symbol and expressed thought which derives from the necessity of linearly ordering the sentential variables—the conjuncts in conjunctive sentences like (1) and (2), and the antecedents in compound conditional sentences as those in Fig. 2a and 2b. I will come to this in the next sections. There are, of course, other kinds of cases. For example, "$A \supset B$" and "$\sim(A \& \sim B)$" are logically equivalent but notationally distinct sentences. But in this case the divergence between expressive symbol and expressed thought has nothing to do with a specific character of the notation: in *any* notation whatever that has implication, conjunction, and negation as primitives such divergence is inescapable. The same is true of logically equivalent sentences like "A" and "$\sim \sim A$" – of which Frege also says, in "Gedankengefüge", that they have the same sense (Frege 1984, 399). But this, again, has nothing to do with the specifics of the notation: in *any* notation whatever that has negation as a primitive (as contrasted, for example, with pure implicational systems) such divergence is inescapable. In what follows I will focus exclusively on divergences that can be imputed to the specific character of a notation, which, I shall show, is its *linearity*.

2   Dummett and Geach

How should we devise a notation, then, in order for (1) and (2) to be formalized by one and the same formula? Michael Dummett made a proposal: "an ideal representation of the connective 'and' would involve writing the sub-sentences on top of one another, as in a monogram, but each only half as bold as their unconjoined counterparts. In such notation, '*A* and *B*' would really be indistinguishable from '*B* and *A*'" (Dummett 1981, 332). The monogram that Dummett has in mind would appear roughly as the one in Fig. 3:

Fig. 3. "*A* and *B*" in Dummett's monogrammatic notation

But to what use can Dummett's monogrammatic notation for conjunction be really put? It could not be made part of a notation for the sentential calculus. For how could we represent a sentence like "*A* & *B* & *C* & *D*" in such a notation? The overlapping of the sentential variables in the monogram would render it unreadable. But even supposing actual readability not to be an issue, how could we represent a sentence like "$((A \supset B) \supset C)$ & D" in this notation? Can we write the conjuncts "$(A \supset B) \supset C$" and "D" on top of one another as in Fig. 4? How should we then distinguish the monogram for "$((A \supset B) \supset C)$ & D" from the monogram for "$((A \ \& \ D) \supset B) \supset C$"? Dummett's monogrammatic notation is plainly inconsistent. The proposal has to be taken as a *metaphor* of a notation that complies with the commutative spirit of conjunction, not as a principle for the building of one.

Fig. 4. "$((A \supset B) \supset C)$ & D" in Dummett's monogrammatic notation

Peter Geach made a different proposal: "The necessity of uttering or writing α before β, or β before α, is merely physical necessity, not logical, and one can imagine a two-mouthed race that could first sing the connective with both mouths in unison and then sing the notes for α and β simultaneously" (Geach 1976, 442). We *can* no doubt imagine such a race, but such an image is hardly sufficient for the construction of a notation that could meet Frege's worries about the representation of logical conjunction.

However unworkable they may be, Dummett's and Geach's proposals sufficiently evidence that the "perfect" notation that Frege has contemplated has to abandon linearity. Linearity is a feature of natural languages and of many formalized languages alike, but while in the case of natural languages linearity is a direct consequence of its reproducing oral speech, in the case of formalized languages linearity is only a consequence of their imitating natural languages. This point was clearly made by Herbert Enderton: "Natural languages are spoken. We speak in real time, and real time progresses linearly. Consequently formal languages were constructed with linear expressions. But formal languages are not spoken (at least not easily). So there is no reason to be influenced by the linearity of time into being narrow minded about formulas. And linearity is the ultimate in narrowness" (Enderton 1970, 393). As Frege clearly saw, linearity is the reason why in most formal languages the representation of symmetric relations manifests a divergence between expressive symbol and expressed thought. In order to overcome this divergence and meet Frege's worries, we have to abandon linearity, and with it the convenience of the typesetter. This should scarcely be problematic in such a domain as the philosophy of logic, where "the convenience of the typesetter is certainly not the *summum bonum*" (Frege 1984, 236).

3 Peirce

A notation for the sentential calculus that meets Frege's worries about the divergence between symbol and thought in the representation of conjunction, and indeed of any symmetric relation that there may be occasion to symbolize in a logical notation— a notation which is neither a metaphor nor an image, but a demonstrably complete and coherent system of sentential logic (Hammer 1996)—is Peirce's system of Alpha graphs. In this system it is impossible to express the logical equivalence expressed by (CR), because no such things as two distinct sentences as (1) and (2) can be written in this system and *a fortiori* can flank the "=" in (CR).

The Alpha system, corresponding to sentential logic, is based on two primitives: conjunction and negation.[2] The sheet on which the graphs are written is called the "sheet of assertion", and is in itself a well-formed Alpha graph. Topologically, the sheet of assertion is a two-dimensional ambient space with no direction. Conjunction is represented as the unordered juxtaposition of sentential variables on the sheet of assertion. Negation is represented by an oval that encircles the sentential variables that are negated. By means of conjunction and negation, any Alpha graphs can be constructed. The sheet of assertion and any portion of it enclosed within an oval is called an "area".

For example, Fig. 5 is the Alpha graph for "*P* & *Q*", and Fig. 6 is the Alpha graph for "*P* & *Q* & *R*".

$$P\ Q$$

Fig. 5. "*P* & *Q*" in Peirce's Alpha graphs

---

[2] Peirce sometimes considers the Alpha graphs to be based on the scroll, corresponding to the material implication, as the sole primitive, from which the meaning of the single cut (negation) is derived as the implication of the false. If so considered, the only symmetric relation that Alpha graphs represent is that between the antecedents of conditionals of the form of (3) and (4). The comparison between the "Begriffsschrift" and such scroll-based Alpha graphs awaits investigation.

$$P \ Q \ R$$

Fig. 6. "*P* & *Q* & *R*" in Peirce's Alpha graphs

Since the sheet of assertion has no direction, the position of the sentential variables on it is not a representing fact; therefore, all the possible dispositions of the propositional variables "*P*", "*Q*", and "*R*" within the same area—of which those in Fig. 7 below are but a small sample—must count as different graph tokens of the same Alpha graph type. In like manner, each formula in Fig. 8 is a graph token of the graph type that in linear notation can be written as "*P* & *Q* & ~ *R*". In a linear notation, permutation always produces different sentence types: (1) and (2) are indeed distinct sentence types obtained by permutation of the conjuncts. In Alpha graphs, by contrast, any movement of sub-graphs within any one and the same area will not produce distinct graph types but only distinct graph tokens of the same graph type. For this reason, Alpha graphs dispense with the standard rules of commutation and associativity.[3]

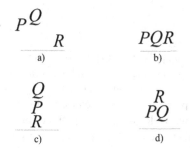

a)   b)

c)   d)

Fig. 7. Distinct tokens of the Alpha graph type for "*P* & *Q* & *R*"

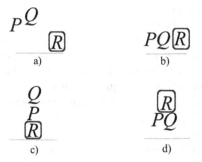

a)   b)

c)   d)

Fig. 8. Distinct tokens of the Alpha graph type for "*P* & *Q* & ~ *R*"

---

[3] This is admitted by the finest students of the graphs, cf. Hammer (1996) and Dipert (2006).

Each of the formulas in Fig. 7 is a distinct graph token of the same graph type. A graph type is, in other words, a *class of equivalence* of graph tokens. To the Alpha graph type in Fig. 7 there correspond in linear notation six distinct sentence types:

(7.1) $P \& Q \& R$
(7.2) $P \& R \& Q$
(7.3) $R \& Q \& P$
(7.4) $R \& P \& Q$
(7.5) $Q \& P \& R$
(7.6) $Q \& R \& P$

In like manner, to the Alpha graph type in Fig. 8 there correspond in linear notation six distinct sentence types:

(8.1) $P \& Q \& \sim R$
(8.2) $P \& \sim R \& Q$
(8.3) $\sim R \& Q \& P$
(8.4) $\sim R \& P \& Q$
(8.5) $Q \& P \& \sim R$
(8.6) $Q \& \sim R \& P$

In linear notation, one can apply (CR) to pairs of sentences, because in this language the permutation of elements in a string always yields distinct sentence types; and (CR) is only applicable if two distinct sentence types flank the "=". In Alpha graphs, by contrast, one cannot apply (CR) to pairs of graphs, because in this language no rearranging of graphs lying on the same area yields distinct graph types but only distinct graph tokens of the same graph type (which is a class of equivalence of graph tokens).

As far as conjunction is concerned (but the proposal is extendible to any representation of symmetric connectives that exploits a two-dimensional ambient space with no direction, as the sheet of assertion of the Alpha graphs), no "divergence of expressive symbol and expressed thought" is present. Linear languages force us to write a conjunct before or after the other, while no such ordering belongs to the thought of the conjunction. One may also put the matter thus: the commutativity (and associativity) of conjunction (or, for that matter, of any symmetric relation there may be occasion to express) is so fundamental that it should be reflected at the level of syntax. Think of the usual treatment of the disjunctive (or conjunctive) normal forms in propositional logic: when a normal form is expressed in standard syntax, one has to choose an ordering of the conjuncts and the disjuncts. These choices are somehow not *in rebus*, but only reflect the linearity of the notation.

Is Frege's own "Begriffsschrift" linear? If the principle of transposition of the antecedents is a special rule of the "Begriffsschrift", which Frege in some sense "took for granted", then the horizontal in a "Begriffsschrift" formula is not linearly ordered, but only partially ordered, i.e. partially ordered by the signs of negation. But if the principle of transposition of the antecedents is no specific rule of the "Begriffsschrift", because it does for the "Begriffsschrift" compound conditionals what the rule "$A \supset (B \supset C) = B \supset (A \supset C)$" does in linear notation, then the horizontal in a "Begriffsschrift" formula is linearly ordered. In the one case, we could describe the "Begriffsschrift" as a two-dimensional notation in which one axis, the vertical, is linearly ordered, while the other, the horizontal, is partially ordered: in this case, interchanging the conditions attached to a portion of the horizontal in which no sign of negation occurs would not yield distinct formula types, but distinct tokens of the same type. In the other case, we should describe the "Begriffsschrift" as a two-dimensional notation in which both axes are linearly ordered, so that switching elements on either dimension yields not distinct formula tokens of the same formula type, but distinct formula types (whether logically equivalent or not). As I argued above, the fact that the principle of transposition of the antecedents is assumed as an axiom in the *Begriffsschrift* and proved as a theorem in *Grundgesetze* should lead us to conclude that for Frege Fig. 2a and 2b contain distinct formula types (which are logically equivalent). And if these formulas are distinct formula types, then the horizontal is linearly, and not partially, ordered. And thus Frege's notation, though two-dimensional, suffers from the same limitations with respect to the representation of symmetric logical relations as standard linear notations.

The limitation in question, and the divergence that derives from it, only concerns linear languages, or languages which, like the "Begriffsschrift", can be assimilated to linear ones with respect to the representation of symmetric logical relations. Of course, linear languages are more effectively written and typeset than non-linear ones. But if we agree with Frege that the convenience of the typesetter cannot be the *summum bonum*— not, at least, in the philosophy of logic—then there should be in principle no reason not to consider Peirce's Alpha graphs as a better notation for the representation of the sentential calculus than any other equivalently expressive linear notation—and, in a very precise sense, the embodiment of Frege's worries about the divergence between symbol and thought in the representation of symmetric logical relations.

References

Angelelli, I.: Macbeth's 'Hitherto unimaginable' Frege. Rev. Modern Logic **11**, 127–131 (2008)

Bellucci, F.: Frege on Compound Thoughts. A Wittgensteinian Diagnosis. Rivista di filosofia **111**, 55–80 (2020)

Dipert, R.: Peirce's Deductive Logic. In: Misak, C. (ed.) The Cambridge Companion to Peirce, pp. 287–324. Cambridge University Press, Cambridge (2006)

Dummett, M.: The Interpretation of Frege's Philosophy. Duckworth, London (1981)

Enderton, H.B.: Finite partially ordered quantifiers. Zeitschrift für Mathematische Logik und Grundlagen der Mathematik **16**, 393–397 (1970)

Frege, G.: Begriffsschrift. Nebert, Halle (1879)

Frege, G.: Basic Laws of Arithmetic. vols. I–II. Edited by Ebert, P.A., Rossberg, M. (2013). Oxford University Press, Oxford (ed. or. 1893–1903, Jena: Verlag Herrman Pohle)

Frege, G.: Philosophical and Mathematical Correspondence. Edited by Gabriel, G. et al (1980). Blackwell, Oxford

Frege, G.: Collected Papers on Mathematics, Logic, and Philosophy. Edited by McGuinness, B. (1984). Blackwell, Oxford

Geach, P.T.: Critical Notice of M. Dummett, "Frege. Philosophy of Language". Mind **85**, 436–449 (1976)

Hammer, E.: Peircean Graphs for Propositional Logic. In: Allwein, G., Barwise, J. (eds.) Logical Reasoning with Diagrams, pp. 130–147. Oxford University Press, Oxford (1996)

Calculus *CL* as a Formal System

Jens Lemanski[1]([✉])[ID] and Ludger Jansen[2,3][ID]

[1] Institute of Philosophy, FernUniversität in Hagen, Hagen, Germany
jens.lemanski@fernuni-hagen.de
[2] Institute of Philosophy, Universität Rostock, Rostock, Germany
ludger.jansen@uni-rostock.de
[3] Chair for Philosophy, University of Passau, Passau, Germany

Abstract. In recent years *CL* diagrams inspired by Lange's *C*ubus *L*ogicus have been used in various contexts of diagrammatic reasoning. However, whether *CL* diagrams can also be used as a formal system seemed questionable. We present a *CL* diagram as a formal system, which is a fragment of propositional logic. Syntax and semantics are presented separately and a variant of bitstring semantics is applied to prove soundness and completeness of the system.

1 Introduction

Calculus *CL* is a new interpretation of a *C*ubus *L*ogicus described by Johann Christian Lange in 1714 [8]. *CL* is a logic diagram that combines features of Euler-Venn diagrams, line diagrams, tree diagrams and squares of opposition. It can be used for various logics and thus the original idea of Lange has been called a 'logica universalis' and an 'algebra universalis' by Leibniz [9, vol. V, 405]. Today, there are three views on logic diagrams: (1) a 'suspicious' one, viewing diagrams only as a heuristic means; (2) a 'practical view', according to which diagrams can present theorems or solve problems in a certain context; and (3) a 'formal one' viewing diagrams as a formal language [14]. Since the paradigmatic work of Sun-Joo Shin in 1994, many logicians have discarded the 'suspicious view' on diagrams and elaborated Leibniz's and Lange's 'practical' or 'formal view' on diagrams: Shin demonstrated that logic diagrams can have a syntax on their own which can be clearly distinguished from their semantics. Furthermore, she proved that Venn-type diagram systems can be constructed as a formal system that is sound and complete.

Shin's work has been extended in the last decades for many other diagram systems using different kinds of logic: Hammer applied Shin's method to Euler diagrams and expanded her completeness theorem [5]; inspired by Shin's work, Howse et al. developed so-called 'Spider' and 'Concept Diagrams' which can be applied in ontology engineering, artificial intelligence and computer science in general [7]; an Euler diagrammatic inference system in Gentzen-style was introduced by Takemura et al. [13]; and diagrams for non-classical logic were recently elaborated by Bhattacharjee et al. [2] and Castro-Manzano [3].

© Springer Nature Switzerland AG 2020
A.-V. Pietarinen et al. (Eds.): Diagrams 2020, LNAI 12169, pp. 445–460, 2020.
https://doi.org/10.1007/978-3-030-54249-8_35

Lange's diagrams are new to the debate, and they have been discussed from a 'practical view', i.e. in the context of extended syllogistics [12], of analogical reasoning [1], of oppositional geometry [11], of bitstring semantics [15] and ontological reasoning [10]. In this paper, it is our main goal to demonstrate that also a formal view on *CL* diagrams is possible. Thus we will develop a *CL* calculus for a fragment of propositional logic. This formal system follows Shin and Hammer in many ways. In contrast to logic systems based on Euler-Venn-Peirce diagrams, *CL* is strictly hierarchical in structure. This can be interpreted such that *CL* follows ontological structures, for example based on jointly exhaustive and pairwise disjoint (JEPD) classifications and can therefore be applied particularly well in disciplines such as knowledge representation, artificial intelligence, medicine, biology, and philosophy, to name but a few [6].

The system we are presenting here is a specific and simple case that demonstrates how to use such a hierarchically ordered diagram type. Since it is a specific case of many other possible interpretations of *CL*, we simply call it $\mathcal{CL}_\mathcal{I}$. Our overall motivation is that showing how a formal system of *CL* can be proven to be sound and complete will convince other researchers to work on further and more complex forms and uses of Lange-type diagrams.

In Sect. 2, we will present the syntax of the diagrams, Sect. 3 introduces a non-exhaustive bitstring semantics which allows one to use Boolean Algebra in the proofs for soundness (Sect. 4) and completeness (Sect. 5). In Sect. 6, we conclude by comparing $\mathcal{CL}_\mathcal{I}$ to standard propositional logic.

2   Syntax

In normal symbolic logic, a calculus consists of axioms and inference rules. In diagrammatic reasoning systems, transformation rules are included instead of inference rules [16]. In this section, we will present the syntax of $\mathcal{CL}_\mathcal{I}$ by defining what a diagram is (2.1) and by giving examples of diagrams (2.2). Transformation rules (2.3) show how to manipulate diagrams, so that all and only diagrams are consequences of given diagrams.

2.1   Diagrams of $\mathcal{CL}_\mathcal{I}$

CL diagrams consist of two kinds of diagrammatic objects: structural and content elements. Structural elements are the same in all *CL* diagrams. The content elements may differ from system to system.

Definition 1 (Diagrammatic objects). $\mathcal{CL}_\mathcal{I}$ *consists of the following diagrammatic objects:*

(a) Structural elements of $\mathcal{CL}_\mathcal{I}$ *are basics and classes:*

Solid boxes	□	Solid boxes containing no dotted lines are called 'basics'.
Dotted lines	⬚	Solid boxes containing dotted lines are called 'classes'.

(b) Content elements of $C\mathcal{L}_I$ are shadings, tensors, and lines:

Shadings	▰	Solid boxes may be shaded completely.
Tensors	⊗	Solid boxes may have a tensor inside.
Lines	——	Tensors may be connected to other tensors using lines to form a tensor sequence.

Definition 2 (Minimal $C\mathcal{L}_I$ diagram). *A diagram is a minimal $C\mathcal{L}_I$ diagram iff it is a diagram such that it consists only of structural elements (basics and classes), such that*

(a) there are only basics in the lowest row,

(b) in no row there is any class that is smaller than the classes or basics in the row below,

(c) every vertical line is a continuation of a vertical delineation of the basics in the lowest row,

(d) every vertical delineation of the basics in the lowest row is continued through the upper rows,

(e) vertical lines may be solid or dotted, but once they have started to be dotted (looking from the bottom to the top) they do not become solid again, and

(f) every box or class is completely contained in exactly one row.

Definition 3 (Comprisal). *A class comprises a solid box below iff all vertical lines of the box lead to vertical lines of the class.*

Definition 4 ($C\mathcal{L}_I$ diagram). *Every minimal $C\mathcal{L}_I$ diagram is a $C\mathcal{L}_I$ diagram. If a $C\mathcal{L}_I$ diagram can be drawn by adding a shading of a complete solid box to a $C\mathcal{L}_I$ diagram, then it is a $C\mathcal{L}_I$ diagram. If a $C\mathcal{L}_I$ diagram can be drawn by putting a tensor into a solid box of a $C\mathcal{L}_I$ diagram, then it is a $C\mathcal{L}_I$ diagram. If a $C\mathcal{L}_I$ diagram can be drawn by adding a line between two tensors of a $C\mathcal{L}_I$ diagram, then it is a $C\mathcal{L}_I$ diagram. Nothing else is a $C\mathcal{L}_I$ diagram.*

A regular CL diagram is based on 2^n basics in the lowest row. All other CL diagrams are irregular [15]. In the following, we make extensive use of regular CL diagrams with four basics in the bottom row. The use of four basics in our examples is without loss of generality of $C\mathcal{L}_I$ diagrams. What is a limitation of our discussion here is that we discuss diagrams of the same size only.

We use the Roman alphabet to denote boxes and classes: The lower case letters $\{d, e, f, g\}$ indicate the four basics in our examples; uppercase letters $\{A, B, C\}$ denote classes. Letters are not themselves diagrammatic objects, but only names of structural elements.

2.2 Examples of $C\mathcal{L}_I$ Diagrams

The diagrams 1.1–1.6 are $C\mathcal{L}_I$ diagrams: $D_{1.1}$ is a minimal diagram without any information. In all other diagrams content elements are represented.

$D_{1.2}$ shows exactly one ■ in one solid box which is called B; $D_{1.3}$ demonstrates that a $\mathcal{CL_I}$ diagram can also have more than one shading; $D_{1.4}$ depicts two $\otimes$'s at C and d, and $D_{1.5}$ a $\otimes$-sequence with links in e and g; in $D_{1.6}$ all content elements are involved and combined with each other.

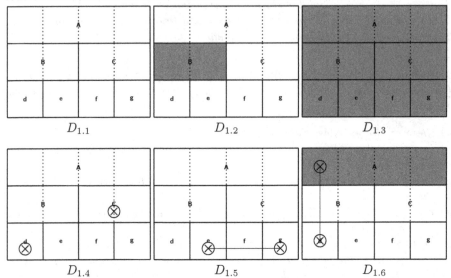

$D_{2.1-2.6}$ are not $\mathcal{CL_I}$ diagrams: In $D_{2.1}$, the two basics d, e are not distinguished by solid boxes. In $D_{2.2}$ we find two solid, instead of dotted lines within the box of A. In $D_{2.3}$, ■ does not fill the whole solid boxes of B or C. In $D_{2.4}$, both $\otimes$ are not located inside a solid box. In $D_{2.5}$, the line does not connect two $\otimes$'s to $\otimes$-sequence. $D_{2.6}$ is a well-formed diagram in another CL system, but not in $\mathcal{CL_I}$ [10].

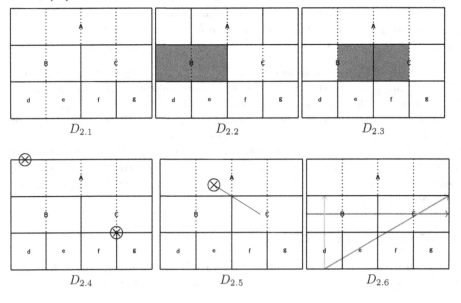

2.3   Rules of Transformation

In this section, we introduce seven rules of transformation which can be classified into four types of manipulations, i.e. (I) erasure, (II) addition, (III) unification, and (IV) inconsistency.

Definition 5 (Obtainability). *Let D be a diagram and Δ be a set of diagrams, $\Delta \vdash D$ iff D is an element of Δ or is obtainable from elements of Δ by means of the transformation rules.*

In general, rules of transformation allow us to manipulate diagrams, and thus are similar to rules of inferences in algebraic deduction systems which allow us to manipulate algebraic formulas. The rules of transformation are as follows:

I **Erasure**
 I.1 We may erase a ▬, a whole ⊗-sequence or an isolated ⊗.
 I.2 We may erase any ⊗ of a ⊗-sequence if that ⊗ is in ▰.
 II **Addition/Replacement**
 II.1 We may add any number of ⊗'s to an existing ⊗-sequence or to an isolated ⊗ such that they build a new ⊗-sequence.
 II.2 A ⊗ in a solid box can be replaced by a ⊗-sequence in exactly the solid boxes in the row below that are comprised by the original box, such that this sequence is connected with the remainder of the original ⊗-sequence if the replaced ⊗ was part of a ⊗-sequence.
 A ⊗-sequence in a row of solid boxes can be replaced by a ⊗ in the solid box that comprises exactly these boxes, such that this new ⊗ is connected with the remaining ⊗-sequence if it replaces a part of ⊗-sequence only.
 III **Unification**
 Given two diagrams D_1 and D_2, we can obtain a unified diagram D_{1+2} iff any content element of D_{1+2} is contained in D_1 or D_2.
 IV **Inconsistency**
 IV.1 For any diagram that includes ▰ and ⊗ in the same box, any other diagram can follow.
 IV.2 For any diagram in which all ⊗ of a ⊗-sequence are also ▬, any other diagram can follow.

Most of the above given rules are similar to the rules of transformation which are to be found in the systems of Shin, Hammer etc., mentioned above in Sect. 1. Therefore, we will not explain them in detail, but illustrate them by giving examples. However, RII.2 is unique to $\mathcal{CL_I}$ and does not correspond to any of the above mentioned systems. We will therefore insert a short explanation at the appropriate place.

The following are three examples of RI:

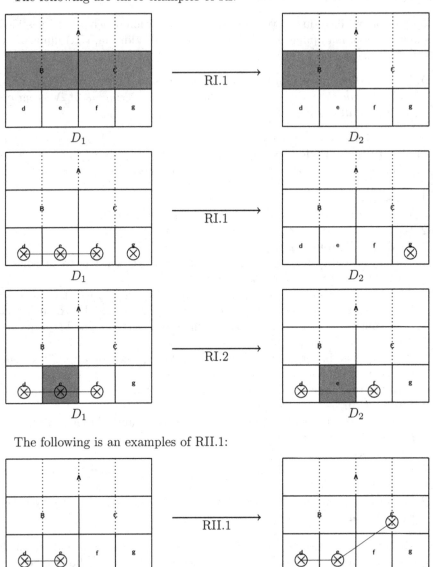

The following is an examples of RII.1:

The following illustrates RII.2:

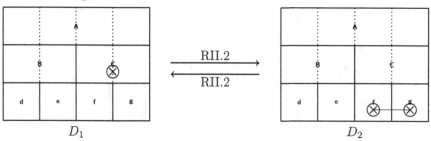

$$D_1 \qquad\qquad\qquad D_2$$

Using RII.2, diagram D_1 with a single $\otimes$ in C is transformed into diagram D_2 with a $\otimes$-sequence in the two basics f and g immediately below the class C. The second arrow, going from D_2 to D_1 indicates that RII.2 also allows to replace the $\otimes$-sequence connecting f and g in D_2 with a single $\otimes$ in C in D_1.

If a $\otimes$-sequence is given in two basics or classes which are not comprised in the same class by Definition 3, RII.2 cannot be applied. For example, if e is comprised by B and f by C, RII.2 cannot be applied to a $\otimes$-sequence of e and f.

If RII.2 is applied to a $\otimes$-sequence in which not all $\otimes$ have been replaced, then the remaining $\otimes$'s must be linked with the replaced $\otimes$ or $\otimes$-sequence. For example, take diagram D_2 from the example of RII.1 given above, in which we find a $\otimes$-sequence in d, e, and C. Here, it is also possible to replace the single $\otimes$ in C with a $\otimes$-sequence in f and g by using RII.2. Let D_3 be the result of this process of manipulating, then D_3 has a $\otimes$-sequence in d, e, f, and g. Furthermore, it is possible to replace the $\otimes$-sequence in d and e with a single $\otimes$ in B by using RII.2. Let D_3 be the result of this process of manipulating, then D_3 has a $\otimes$-sequence in $B\,C$.

The following are two examples of RIII. Due to lack of space, we do not draw arrows leading from D_1 and D_2 to D_{1+2}:

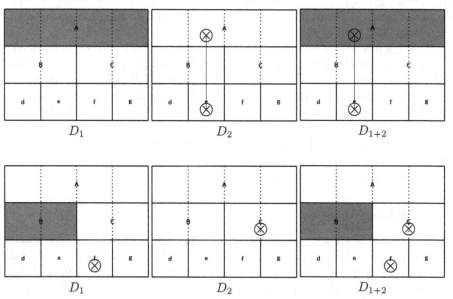

The following are two examples of RIV:

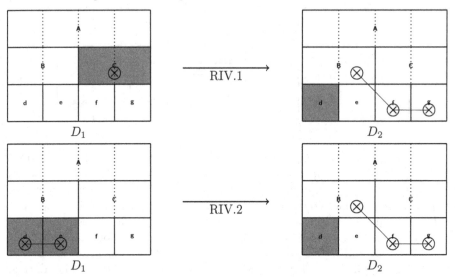

3 Bitstring Semantics

In this section a variant of bitstring semantics for $\mathcal{CL_I}$ diagrams is given. A bitstring is a finite sequence of characters consisting of the bit-alphabet $\Sigma = \{0, 1\}$. Normally, bitstring semantics is used to study logical relations between formulas in a fragment [4]. In contrast, we here use bitstrings to study the relations between fragments of diagrams, using them as a device to systematically describe $\mathcal{CL_I}$ diagrams. The bitstring semantics we use here is one possible variant of many. A detailed description of this specific bitstring semantic for CL is given in [15].

By using a bitstring semantics for $\mathcal{CL_I}$, we raise two questions as follows: (1) If a $\mathcal{CL_I}$ diagram D is obtainable from a set of $\mathcal{CL_I}$ diagrams Δ ($\Delta \vdash D$) is it the case that D follows from Δ ($\Delta \models D$)? (2) Whenever D follows from the diagrams in Δ, is it the case that D can be transformed on the basis of Δ? Question (1) asks for the soundness of the system, question (2) asks for the completeness. With the help of a bitstring semantics, we will answer both questions in Sect. 4 and 5. But before, we will focus on what a bitstring model for $\mathcal{CL_I}$ is (Sect. 3.1) and show the connection between diagrammatic and bitstring representations in $\mathcal{CL_I}$ by giving an example (Sect. 3.2).

3.1 Bitstring Models

In $\mathcal{CL_I}$, we use bitstrings to systematically name basics and classes. The length of each bitstring is determined by the number of basics. As said in Sect. 2, we will use only $\mathcal{CL_I}$ diagrams with four basics as examples here. The n-th bit-position in a bitstring represents the n-th basic in the $\mathcal{CL_I}$ diagram. In the bitstring of a solid box, exactly the positions of those basics are flagged '1' which are comprised by the box. Since basics are just one single solid box in one of the columns of the bottom row, they always have a Hamming weight $w = 1$, i.e. there occurs exactly one '1' in the bitstring. Two higher classes in the middle row, each comprising the two basics below them, have a $w = 2$. The class A given in the highest row has the maximum $w = 4$ since it overarches all four basics (see Fig. 1).

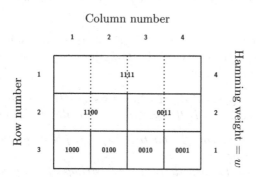

Fig. 1. Interpretation of basics and classes

We adopt bitstring semantics to interpret information given in a CL_I diagram and to perform a limited set of bitwise operations (similar to Boolean operations) with these information:

Definition 6 (Bitstring terms). *A term b is a bitstring term iff one of the following holds:*

(a) b is a bitstring,
(b) b is the negation of a bitstring term ($\neg b$),
(c) b is the conjunction of two bitstring terms ($b_1 \wedge b_2$),
(d) b is the disjunction of two bitstring terms ($b_1 \vee b_2$).

Normally, Boolean operations on bitstrings are well-defined operations that lead to well-defined resulting bitstrings. Some of these results, however, would not match to well-defined CL_I diagrams since there are bitstrings with length of 4 that do not name any solid boxes. In the system presented here, for example, it is not intended that the negation inverts all bits of the bitstring.

As an interpretation of a CL_I diagram we define the bitstring function β. β is a function that interprets diagrammatic elements, diagrams, as well as whole sets of diagrams.

Definition 7 (Interpretation of basics). *If x is a basic, $\beta(x)$ is a bitstring such that exactly one position is '1' and the length of the bitstring equals the number of basics in that diagram.*

Without loss of generality, we will fix the convention to flag the first bit as '1' for the outmost left basic, and then move the flag one position to the right for the next neighbour on the right side of a basic in such a way that the second basic has a '1' at the second bit position and '0' at all other. This procedure is repeated for all basics until the '1' appears at the last bit position of the bitstring of the last basic in the diagram, so that all basics have a Hamming distance of 2.

Definition 8 (Interpretation of classes). *If x is a class, $\beta(x)$ is a bitstring such that a position in the string is flagged '1' iff it is flagged '1' in one of the basics comprised by x.*

Figure 1 shows a minimal diagram in which bitstrings are substituted for lower case and uppercase letters of $\mathcal{CL_I}$. It shows how bitstrings are systematically assigned to basics and classes.

Definition 9 (Interpretation of diagrams). *If D is a diagram, then $\beta(D)$ is the set of bitstring terms B that consists of exactly the following elements:*

(a) for every isolated tensor, the bitstrings of every basic or class that contains that isolated tensor,

(b) for every shading, the negations of the bitstrings of every basic or class that is shaded, and

(c) for every sequence, the disjunctions of the bitstrings of the classes or basics connected through the tensor sequence.

As indicated in the discussion of Definition 6, we will treat negation and disjunction of bitstrings here as mere syntactic operations and will not make use of the underlying semantics with the exception of what we state in Definition 11.

Definition 10 (Interpretation of sets of diagrams). *If Δ is a set of diagrams, $\beta(\Delta)$ is the union of all sets of bitstrings terms that are interpretations of the elements of Δ.*

Definition 11 (Satisfiability of bitstring terms). *A bitstring term b is satisfiable given a set of bitstring terms B (or B-satisfiable, for short) iff one of the following is the case:*

(a) b is an element of B;

(b) b is the result of deleting a conjunct from a B-satisfiable conjunction of bitstrings or negated bitstrings;

(c) b is the result of replacing a B-satisfiable disjunction of bitstrings $b_1, b_2, \ldots$ such that the n-th bit-position of b is '1' iff there is some b_i such that the n-th position of b_i is '1', or vice versa;

(d) b is the result of combining two B-satisfiable bitstring terms satisfiable in B into a conjunction;

(e) b is the result of combining a bitstring term that is B-satisfiable with any other bitstring term in a disjunction;

(f) b is the result of deleting a bitstring term from a disjunction if that disjunction and the negation of bitstring are B-satisfiable;

(g) *b* *is any bitstring term if, for some bitstring term, both this term and its negation are B-satisfiable.*

Note that bitstring terms correspond to single content elements in a diagram (i.e. ⊗, ■, or ⊗-sequence). Whole diagrams thus correspond to sets of bitstring terms; a minimal diagram corresponds to the empty set of bitstring terms. We thus have also to define the satisfiability of whole sets of bitstring terms.

Definition 12 (Satisfiability of sets of bitstring terms). *A set of bitstring terms B_2 is satisfiable given a set of bitstring terms B_1 (or B_1-satisfiable, for short) iff every element of B_2 is B_1-satisfiable.*

Corollary 1. *The empty set is trivially B_1-satisfiable for any B_1.*

Corollary 2. *Any subset of a B_1-satisfiable set is B_1-satisfiable.*

Definition 13 (Satisfiability). $\Delta \models D$ *iff $\beta(D)$ is satisfiable in $\beta(\Delta)$, i.e. iff the set of bitstring terms B_2 corresponding to D is B_1-satisfiable, whereby B_1 is the union of all those sets of bitstring terms which correspond to the elements of Δ.*

3.2   Correspondance between Syntax and Semantics

The correspondence between syntax and semantics can be illustrated by an example. The example shows at first how to obtain a conclusion diagram D from a set of premise diagrams Δ ($\Delta \vdash D$) and then the translation of Δ and D into a common prooftree by using bitstrings. For better comparison we have inserted the bitstrings directly into the diagrams (as explained in Sect. 3.1).

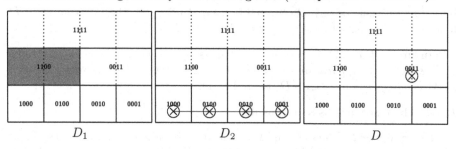

$$D_1 \qquad\qquad\qquad D_2 \qquad\qquad\qquad D$$

There is no rule to go directly from D_1 and D_2 to D. For this reason, there must be intermediate steps. First, RII.2 is applied twice, starting from D_2, so that the ⊗-sequence is shifted from the basics in the lowest row 3 to the classes in the middle row. This leads us from D_2 via D_3 to D_4. In the next step, D_1 is combined with D_4 with the help of RIII. The result is D_5. RI.2 is now applied to D_5, whereby D is obtainable.

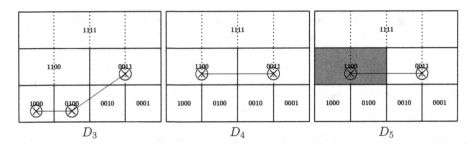

$$D_3 \qquad\qquad D_4 \qquad\qquad D_5$$

By using Definition 6, the following prooftree shows the analogues reasoning on the semantic bitstring level corresponding to the above example. For a better comparison we have added the diagrammatic rules at each step as a label.

$$
\cfrac{
D_1\{\neg 1100\} \quad
\cfrac{
\cfrac{
\cfrac{D_2\{1000 \vee 0100 \vee 0010 \vee 0001\}}{D_3\{1000 \vee 0100 \vee 0011\}} \text{ (RII.2)}
}{D_4\{1100 \vee 0011\}} \text{ (RII.2)}
}{D_5\{\neg 1100 \;\wedge\; (1100 \vee 0011)\}} \text{ (RIII)}
}{D\{0011\}} \text{ (RI.2)}
$$

4 Soundness

In this section, we prove that the transformation rules are stated correctly given the bitstring semantics outlined in Sect. 3. In other words, we prove, that if D is obtainable from a set of diagrams Δ ($\Delta \vdash D$), then it is the case that $\beta(D)$ is satisfied given $\beta(\Delta)$, i.e. $\Delta \models D$. We are proving this hypothesis in two steps: First, we prove that all transformation rules are valid; second, we show by induction that for any D obtainable from Δ ($\Delta \vdash D$), the bitstring term D follows from the set of bitstring terms Δ, $\Delta \models D$.

Theorem 1 (RI–RIV). *For every D that is obtainable from a set of diagrams Δ by exactly one application of RI–IV, it is the case that $\beta(D)$ is satisfied given $\beta(\Delta)$ is satisfied, i.e.: If $\Delta \vdash D$, then $\Delta \models D$.*

Proof. The following cases are possible:

(RI.1) Suppose D follows from Δ by erasing a ■, a $\otimes$ or a $\otimes$-sequence. Then there is a negated bitstring, a bitstring sequence or a single bitstring in $\beta(\Delta)$ that is not an element of $\beta(D)$. If content information is erased, $\beta(D)$ is obviously a subset of $\beta(\Delta)$ and by Definition 12 and 11 (a), $\Delta \models D$.

(RI.2) Suppose D follows from Δ by erasing a $\otimes$ in a box x of a $\otimes$-sequence, which is also ■. If $\beta(x)$ is erased from a disjunction of bitstring terms, we have $\beta(\Delta)$ by Definition 11 (f), so that $\Delta \models D$.

(RII.1) Suppose D follows from Δ by adding a link x to a $\otimes$-sequence. If $\beta(x)$ is added to a conjunction of bitstring terms, we have $\Delta \models D$ by Definition 11 (e).

(RII.2) Suppose D is obtained from Δ by replacing a $\otimes$ in a solid box x by a $\otimes$-sequence in exactly the solid boxes y and z in the row below that are comprised by x. According to Definition 8, $\beta(x)$ is flagged '1' iff the bitstring of one of the boxes comprised by x. There are two cases: (a) If the replaced $\otimes$ in x was not part of a $\otimes$-sequence, then $\beta(y \vee z)$ is satisfiable iff $\beta(x)$ is, according to Definition 11 (c). (b) If the replaced $\otimes$ in x was part of a $\otimes$-sequence continuing in $x_1, x_2, \ldots$, then $\beta(y \vee z \vee x_1 \vee x_2 \vee \ldots)$ is satisfiable iff $\beta(x \vee x_1 \vee x_2 \vee \ldots)$ is, according to Definition 11 (c). Hence, for both cases $\Delta \models D$.

(RIII) Suppose D follows from Δ by unification. Then D contains content elements from various diagrams in Δ, but in any case each bitstring in $\beta(D)$ is also an element of $\beta(\Delta)$. Hence $\Delta \models D$.

(RIV.1) Suppose D follows from Δ by inconsistency. Then in one $D' \in \Delta$ there is a box x that is both shaded and contains a $\otimes$. Thus, $\beta(\Delta)$ contains both $\beta(x)$ and its negation. Then by Definition 11 (g), any bitstring term is Δ-satisfiable, including D. Hence $\Delta \models D$.

(RIV.2) Suppose D follows from Δ by inconsistency. Then in one $D' \in \Delta$ there is a set of boxes x that is both shaded and contains a $\otimes$. Thus, $\beta(\Delta)$ contains both $\beta(x)$ and its negation. Then by Definition 11 (g), any bitstring term is Δ-satisfiable, including D. Hence $\Delta \models D$.   □

The soundness theorem that follows assures us that reasoning with RI–IV can never lead to a false conclusion from true premises:

Theorem 2 (Soundness). *Every D that is obtainable in $\mathcal{CL_I}$ from a set of diagrams Δ is such that its corresponding set of bitstring terms $\beta(D)$ is satisfiable given the set of bitstring terms $\beta(\Delta)$ corresponding to Δ, i.e.: If $\Delta \vdash D$, then $\Delta \models D$.*

Proof. We prove this by induction over length of derivation L of D from Δ:
Induction basis: $L = 0$, i.e. $D \in \Delta$. Then trivially every element of $\beta(D)$ is an element of $\beta(\Delta)$ by Definition 10.

Induction step: If we suppose that D is directly derived from a satisfiable set of diagrams Δ' by exactly one transformation rule, Theorem 2 follows immediately from Theorem 1.   □

5 Completeness

Theorem 3 (Completeness). *For every bitstring term b that is satisfiable in B there is a diagram D matching to b that can be derived from the set of diagrams Δ matching to B, i.e.: If $\Delta \models D$, then $\Delta \vdash D$.*

Proof. We prove this by induction over length of derivation L of the bitstring term in question:
Induction basis: $L = 0$, i.e. b is an element of B. Then d is an element of Δ and, trivially, d is derivable from Δ.

Induction step: Assume that the theorem holds for $L = n$, show that it also holds for $L = n + 1$. The last step of the derivation of satisfiable bitstring terms can be any of (a) to (f).

(a) b is the result of combining two bitstrings terms satisfiable in B in a conjunction. If we have a diagram for the two bitstrings to be combined, we get a diagram for the conjunction with RIII.

(b) b is the result of deleting a conjunct from a B-satisfiable conjunction. Diagram derivable with RI.1 or RI.2, depending on whether the conjunct is a bitstring or a negated bitstring.

(c) b is the result of replacing a B-satisfiable disjunction of bitstrings $b_1, b_1, \ldots$ such that the n-th position of b is '1' iff one of b_1 or b_2 has there is some b_i such that the n-th position of b_i is '1' or vice versa.
Diagram derivable with RII.2.

(d) b is the result of combining a bitstring term that is satisfiable in B with any other bitstring term in a disjunction. If we have a diagram for the original satisfiable bitstring term, we get a diagram for b with RII.1.

(e) b is the result of deleting a bitstring term from a disjunction if that disjunction and the negation of the bitstring are satisfiable. The diagram can be derived by RIV.

(f) b is any bitstring term if, for some bitstring, both this bitstring and its negation are satisfiable in B. If we have a diagram for a bitstring and its negation, we have a diagram with $\otimes$ in a certain box and another diagram with ▬ in that very box. With RIII, we get a diagram that contains $\otimes$ and ▬ in the same box. But then we can get a diagram for any arbitrary b with RIV.
As these are all possible cases, Theorem 3 follows.   □

6   Discussion and Conclusion

Our aim was to show that it is possible to have not only a practical view on CL, but also a formal one. For this purpose we designed a system called $C\mathcal{L_I}$, which can be interpreted as a fragment of propositional logic applied to a hierarchical structure. The structural elements of CL, such as basics and classes, represent hierarchically structured propositions to which content elements such as tensors, shading and lines can be applied. The intepretation of structural and content elements of $C\mathcal{L_I}$ in terms of propositional logic can be illustrated by the following table:

Structural elements	$\square$, $\boxed{\,:\,}$	Propositions
Content elements	▬	Negation
	$\otimes$	Affirmation
	$\otimes$-sequence	Disjunction
	Co-occurrence of unconnected content elements in the same diagram	Conjunction

Four types of rules allow transformations of diagrams with respect to these content elements. The transformation rules can also be seen as equivalents to deduction rules in propositional logic. These equivalences are shown in the following table:

RI.1	Conjunction elimination
RI.2	Disjunctive modus tollendo ponens
RII.1	Disjunction introduction
RII.2	$p \leftrightarrow (q \lor r), q \lor r \vdash p$ or $p \leftrightarrow (q \lor r), p \vdash q \lor r$
RIII	Conjunction introduction
RIV.1, RIV.2	Ex falso quodlibet

Using a specific bitstring semantics we have shown that this system is sound and complete.

It is, however, only a fragment of propositional logic. For example, there is no obvious way to express a material conditional, and there are only very restricted possibilities to translate complex expressions from propositional logic into $\mathcal{CL_I}$. In particular, only boxes can be shaded, i.e. only atomic propositions and disjunctions of these can be negated.

Throughout the paper we have used regular CL diagrams with the same very small number of basics. This was an example to show how $\mathcal{CL_I}$ actually works. As mentioned before, this limitation to four basics was not a limitation of the generality of the system. The definitions, rules and proofs of $\mathcal{CL_I}$ apply to any regular CL diagram, regardless of size.

However, unlike many diagram systems mentioned in the introduction, $\mathcal{CL_I}$ is a static system in which there is no transformation rule that allows the structural elements of the diagram to be changed. Instead, all transformation rules describe transformation between CL diagrams of the same size. This indeed limits the applicability of $\mathcal{CL_I}$. However, it is conceivable that this disadvantage could be remedied in future dynamic CL systems including CL diagrams of different size.

After all, our aim here was simply to show that CL can be systematized at all. But achieving this goal is important for several reasons. Not only does it show that it will soon be possible to build more complex systems with the structural elements of CL, in which dynamic principles represent a larger fragment of propositional logic. It also is a motivation to test CL systems for other parts of logic. Since there is already a practical view on CL in areas such as extended syllogistics, it should also be possible to create different formal systems that correspond to predicate logic. And since Lange already described possible applications of the structural elements for modal logic 300 years ago, there is reason to suspect that CL can be extended in the above mentioned directions.

In addition, other extensions of CL can be envisaged: Similar to diagrams used in areas such as ontology engineering, content elements in CL do not have to be restricted to only one structure. If one wants to represent relations between several CL diagrams, representing various ontologies, it is also conceivable that

CL is not only understood as a two-dimensional structure, but that the system can be extended to n-dimensional objects. If these ideas were to be realised at some point, Leibniz's assessment that Lange's calculus is an 'algebra universalis' might become plausible to us.

References

1. Barbot, N., Miclet, L., Prade, H., Richard, G.: A new perspective on analogical proportions. In: Kern-Isberner, G., Ognjanović, Z. (eds.) ECSQARU 2019. LNCS (LNAI), vol. 11726, pp. 163–174. Springer, Cham (2019). https://doi.org/10.1007/978-3-030-29765-7_14
2. Bhattacharjee, R., Chakraborty, M.K., Choudhury, L.: Venn diagram with names of individuals and their absence: a non-classical diagram logic. Log. Univers. **12**(1), 141–206 (2018). https://doi.org/10.1007/s11787-018-0186-7
3. Castro Manzano, J.M.: Remarks on the idea of non-monotonic (diagrammatic) inference. Open Insight **8**(14), 243–263 (2017)
4. Demey, L., Smessaert, H.: Combinatorial bitstring semantics for arbitrary logical fragments. J. Philos. Logic **47**(2), 325–363 (2017). https://doi.org/10.1007/s10992-017-9430-5
5. Hammer, E.M.: Logic and Visual Information. CSLI Publ, Stanford (1995)
6. Neher, E.: Jordan Triple Systems by the Grid Approach. LNM, vol. 1280. Springer, Heidelberg (1987). https://doi.org/10.1007/BFb0078217
7. Stapleton, G., Howse, J., Bonnington, A., Burton, J.: A vision for diagrammatic ontology engineering. In: Proceedings of the International Workshop on Visualizations and User Interfaces for Knowledge Engineering and Linked Data Analytics (VISUAL 2014), pp. 1–13 (2014). http://ceur-ws.org/Vol-1299/
8. Lange, J.C.: Inventum novum quadrati logici universalis, Müller, Giessen (1714)
9. Leibniz, G.W.: Opera omnia, nunc primum collecta, ed. by L. Dutens, Fratres de Tournes, Geneva (1768)
10. Lemanski, J.: Automated reasoning and ontology editing with calculus CL. In: Chapman, P., et al. (eds.) Diagrams 2018, LNAI, vol. 10871, pp. 752–756. Springer, Heidelberg (2018)
11. Lemanski, J.: Oppositional geometry in the diagrammatic calculus CL. S. Am. J. Logic **3**(2), 517–531 (2017)
12. Lemanski, J.: Euler-type diagrams and the quantification of the predicate. J. Philos. Logic **49**(2), 401–416 (2019). https://doi.org/10.1007/s10992-019-09522-y
13. Mineshima, K., Okada, M., Takemura, R.: A diagrammatic inference system with Euler circles. J. Logic Lang. Inf. **21**(3), 365–391 (2012). https://doi.org/10.1007/s10849-012-9160-6
14. Moktefi, A.: Diagrams as scientific instruments. In: Benedek, A., Veszelszki, A. (eds.) Virtual Reality - Real Visuality. Visual, Virtual, Veridical, pp. 81–89. Peter Lang, Frankfurt am Main (2017)
15. Schang, F., Lemanski, J.: A bitstring semantics for calculus CL. In: Vandoulakis, I., Beziau, J.-Y.: Studies in Universal Logic. Birkhäuser, Basel (2020)
16. Shin, S.-J.: The Logical Status of Diagrams. Cambridge University Press, Cambridge (1994)

Truth Graph: A Novel Method for Minimizing Boolean Algebra Expressions by Using Graphs

Eisa Alharbi[(✉)]

Kuwait Oil Company, Ahmadi, Kuwait
ealharbi@kockw.com

Abstract. Boolean algebra expressions are used by stakeholders from a range of disciplines, such as engineers, to build logic circuits. To reduce the cost and transaction numbers of logic circuits, engineers minimize Boolean expressions by reducing the number of terms or arithmetic operations. A well-known pictorial method applied for minimizing Boolean expressions is the Karnaugh map. However, a drawback is that these maps are not effective for minimizing Boolean expressions involving more than four variables. We introduce a novel method for minimizing Boolean expressions by using graphs, which we call a "Truth Graph" that can be effectively applied when many variables exist.

Keywords: Boolean algebra · Minimizing Boolean expressions

1 Introduction

Stakeholders, such as engineers, use Boolean algebra expressions for building logic circuits. To reduce the cost of these circuits, they must reduce (or minimize) the original Boolean expressions to an equivalent expression that includes fewer terms or arithmetic operations. The process of minimizing Boolean expressions is not straightforward, and understanding circuits and the connections between its components is challenging for engineering students [13]. Geoffrey et al., who studied students' misconceptions of circuits, revealed that " these misconceptions result from the need to manage a lot of information that has not been properly organized in the students' minds." [9].

Tools, such as truth tables and the Karnaugh map (K-map), were introduced to help simplify minimizing Boolean expressions [14]. However, these tools have drawbacks. Truth tables grow very fast as the number of rows for an n-variable function is 2^n. Therefore, having more than five variables, for example, will make the construction of the table laborious and prone to error.

The K-map is another form of the truth table that facilitates the minimization of Boolean algebra expressions without requiring the use of Boolean algebra theorems. However, the K-map becomes highly confusing when minimizing expressions that involve more than four variables. For example, a 4-variable K-Map will include $2^4 = 16$ cells, each having a value of either 0 or 1. These 16 cells consist of four rows and four columns, each labelled with two binary numbers

A.-V. Pietarinen et al. (Eds.): Diagrams 2020, LNAI 12169, pp. 461–469, 2020.
https://doi.org/10.1007/978-3-030-54249-8_36

that bring the total binary number in a 4-variable K-Map to 32. Analyzing the relations between these binary numbers by grouping adjacent cells that contain the one values to determine a minimum expression can also be arduous and prone to error. Studies demonstrated that students find K-maps difficult to use, such as Zilles et al. who interviewed students taking a logic course that incorporated using K-maps, and reported, "because Karnaugh maps are a major topic in both ECE 290 and CS 231, we were surprised to find that students were generally reluctant to use them." [15]. Considering that both truth tables and the K-map are utilized as pedagogical tools, having an enhanced teaching approach that supports many variables and reduced visual complexity would be valuable.

Learning with an appropriate representation can enhance learners' performance [1]. Cromley investigated if different representations led learners to use different strategies and reported that "students verbalize more inferences when reading diagrams compared to text" [8]. The superiority of visual notations over textual and symbolic versions has been reported by Larkin and Simon [10], Cheng [7], and many others, including Ainsworth and Loizou [2], Alharbi [3], and Butcher [5].

By considering the superiority of visual notations, especially in logic with their support for observational advantages and reasoning [11,12], in terms of visual complexity and drawability [4,6], visual notations can be effective representations for minimizing Boolean expressions. This paper introduces a new method for minimizing Boolean algebra expressions that takes advantage of the benefits of visual representations to overcome the limitations of truth tables and the K-Map approaches.

2   Truth Graph Expressions

A truth table is a simple tool for showing the truth-value of all possible combinations of the variables within an expression. Combinations leading to false outputs are not involved in the minimization process. Therefore, truth graphs only represent combinations that lead to truth outputs. Figure 1 and Table 1 illustrate how a truth graph and truth table represent the Boolean expression $(A + B) * C$ with values. In Fig. 1, each variable can have one of two values, 1 or

Table 1. Truth values.

A	B	C	Output
0	0	0	0
0	0	1	0
0	1	0	0
0	1	1	1
1	0	0	0
1	0	1	1
1	1	0	0
1	1	1	1

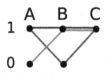

Fig. 1. Truth graph. (Color figure online)

0. The upper nodes represent the 1 values, and lower nodes represent 0. Values not included in the graph do not lead to truth outputs, such as the value 0 for variable C is not included in the graph.

Values (or nodes) are connected by edges that represent truth paths. In Fig. 1, there exist three truth paths highlighted in green, red, and blue. These truth paths represent the truth outputs of the combinations of the values. For example, in the green path, the value 0 from A is linked with the value 1 of B, which is linked with the value 1 of C. This truth path is read as 011 or FTT, which is equivalent to the fourth row in Table 1. The red path represents the values 1 A, 0 B, and 1 C, and the blue path represents the values 1 A, 1 B, and 1 C. If there exists no edge (link) between two values, then the combination of these values is false. For example, no link exists between 0 A, 0 B, and 0 C.

In the graph, we include nodes with written values of 1 and 0 to illustrate the idea. These elements can be eliminated to make the graph simpler without impacting the semantics. Figure 2 shows the same graph after removing the nodes and written values, which reduces the visual complexity and transforms the graph into a representation similar to electrical signals that can be read easily and matched to its meaning, where high waves represent 1 values and low waves represent 0. This version of the graph appears more straightforward and easier to draw compared to a truth table, especially with many variables.

Fig. 2. Truth graph after removing nodes and written values.

3   Truth Graph Minimization Method

Reducing the number of variables or connections corresponds to minimizing Boolean expressions. The truth graph method minimizes Boolean expressions by following two rules:

If two paths pass through the same variables and values, except for one variable where one path passes through 1 and the other passes through 0, then this variable can be eliminated from the two paths. For example, $ABC + \overline{A}BC = BC$.

If one path passes through fewer variables than another path, and the shortest path passes through the same variables and values, except for one variable, then the value can be eliminated only from the path that has more variables. For example, $AB + \overline{A}BC = AB + BC$.

Regardless of the values, in the first rule, two expressions must have the same variable, and in the second rule, one expression is subsumed by another. In Fig. 2, the green and blue paths pass through the same values, except the values of variable A. Therefore, these two paths can be minimized to BC. In Fig. 3, the black path represents the combined result of the green and blue paths. Next, we combine this result with the red path. Both black and red paths pass through the values 1 and 0 of variable B, and the red path passes by more values. Therefore, we eliminate the value of variable B from the red path. The result of the red path becomes AC.

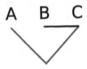

Fig. 3. The result of minimizing the green and blue paths. (Color figure online)

The final minimization result of the truth graph in Fig. 2 becomes AC + BC, as shown in Fig. 4. The dashed line is used instead of a solid line to avoid visual complexity and illustrates that A is linked to C without B. The solid line links all variables it passes through, where the dashed line skips some variables. In this example, the dashed line passes through AB and C, and the small black dots below the variables A and C represent that A is linked to C without B.

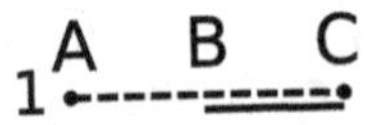

Fig. 4. The result of minimizing the three paths. (Color figure online)

The final minimization result is not affected by the order of the combinations because combining any two paths first will lead to the same result. For example, we can start by combining the red and blue paths by eliminating the variable B. The result is AC, as shown in Fig. 5. The black dotted line represents the result of minimizing the red and blue paths. Then, the black dotted and green paths can be minimized by eliminating the value 0 of variable A from the green path. The reason for eliminating the value of A from the green path only is because the green path passes through more variables than the black path, which passes through only two variables. The result is the same as the previous result, as shown in Fig. 4.

Fig. 5. The result of minimizing the green and blue paths. (Color figure online)

The minimization rule cannot be applied to the combination of the green and red paths because the two paths pass through three values and share only one value. Figure 6 shows several examples of combining truth paths that cannot be minimized. The truth paths in graphs a and b do not share any values, and the truth paths in graphs c, d, e, and f share only one value as they pass through three values. The truth paths in graphs g and h share two values as they pass through four values.

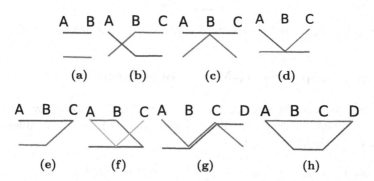

Fig. 6. Examples of graphs that cannot be minimize. (Color figure online)

4   Truth graph and K-Map (Three Variables)

K-map cells filled with either 1s or 0s, where the 1 values indicate that the true values of the combination and 0 values indicate the falsity. To find the minimum logic function, these 1 values must be grouped in a specific way for determining the function F of the K-Map. Tables 2 and 3 show how both the K-map and truth graph, respectively, represent $000 + 001 + 110$. Figure 7 presents the result of combining the two truth paths in the first row of Table 3. The red and green paths share the same values, except for the one variable C, which is eliminated. Figure 8 shows the results of combining the two paths. Then, we add the third path from the second row of Table 3 into the results of the combination of the two previous paths. Figure 9 illustrates the results of this combination that includes no common value for the black and blue paths to share. Therefore, this represents the simplest expression of $00 + 110$ ($\overline{AB} + AB\overline{C}$).

Table 2. K-Map with truth values.

BC

A		00	01	11	10
	0	1	1	0	0
	1	0	0	0	1

Table 3. K-Map with truth paths.

BC

A		00	01	11	10
	0	—	⟋		
	1				⟍

Fig. 7. Graph 1 and 2   **Fig. 8.** Results of Graph 1 and 2 (Color figure online)

Fig. 9. Graph 3 and the results of Graph 1 and 2 (Color figure online)

5   Truth Graph and K-Map (Four Variables)

The same process is followed with four variables. Table 4 shows how the K-map represents all possible combinations, and Table 5 includes the same information represented by the truth graph.

Table 4. K-Map with values.   **Table 5.** K-Map with truth paths.

CD

AB	00	01	11	10
00	0000	0001	0011	0010
01	0100	0101	0111	0110
11	1100	1101	1111	1110
10	1000	1001	1011	1010

CD

AB	00	01	11	10

Let us assume that four combinations lead to true values, including $\overline{AB}CD + \overline{A}BCD + ABCD + A\overline{B}C\overline{D}$. Figure 10 illustrates how the K-map and truth graph represent this information. Table 6 shows step-by-step how the combination of these values is minimized using our method. Step 1 combines the red and green paths so that we can eliminate variable B with the result shown in Step 2. Step 3 combines the result of step 1 with the blue path, and the value of variable A is eliminated from the blue path only because it passes through more variables (ABCD) compared to the black path (ACD). Step 4 shows the results of step 3, and step 5 combines the result of step 3 with the yellow path. The yellow path shares only one variable with the other paths, which means no further minimization may occur. So, step 5 represents the final minimization of the truth graph in Fig. 10. As discussed above, we can select any two paths to begin the minimization process because any combination order leads to the same results. Moreover, the method is not affected by increasing the number of variables, which is a drawback of other methods.

CD

AB   00 01 11 10

	00	01	11	10
00	0	0	1	0
01	0	0	1	0
11	0	0	1	0
10	0	0	0	1

Fig. 10. Truth graph and K-map (4 variables).

Table 6. An example of minimzation process.

Step	Symbolic Representation	Graphical Representation
1	$\overline{A}BCD + \overline{A}BCD$	A B C D
2	$\overline{A}CD$	A B C D
3	$\overline{A}CD + ABCD$	A B C D
4	$\overline{A}CD + BCD$	A B C D
5	$\overline{A}CD + BCD + A\overline{B}C\overline{D}$	A B C D

6   Truth Graph (Six Variables)

The truth graph method can be effectively applied to Boolean expressions with many variables. Figure 11 shows a truth graph representing an $ABC\overline{D}EF + AB\overline{C}\overline{D}EF + \overline{A}B\overline{C}DF$ expression. The blue and yellow paths pass through the same variables and values, except for variable B. Therefore, B is eliminated from the two paths, as shown in Fig. 12. The black path represents the result of the combination of the blue and yellow paths. The black dotted line indicates that variable B is not included in the path. The red path passes through more than one value from the blue and yellow paths. Therefore, this represents the minimum expression as $AC\overline{D}EF + \overline{A}B\overline{C}DEF$.

A B C D E F

A B C D E F

Fig. 11. Truth graph (6 variables).   **Fig. 12.** Truth graph minimization result.

7   Conclusion

We introduced a novel method for minimizing Boolean expressions with graphs by considering the advantages of visual representations, including their simplicity, to overcome the limitations of truth tables and K-maps. Our next step will perform student tests to determine if an advantage exists for using these graph when minimizing Boolean algebra expressions compared to other representations, such as the K-map. Additional future work will be the implementation of tool support, as developing a tool that can automatically minimize drawn sketches will be valuable.

References

1. Ainsworth, S.: Deft: a conceptual framework for considering learning with multiple representations. Learn. Instr. **16**(3), 183–198 (2006)
2. Ainsworth, S., Th Loizou, A.: The effects of self-explaining when learning with text or diagrams. Cogn. Sci. **27**(4), 669–681 (2003)
3. Alharbi, E., Howse, J., Stapleton, G., Hamie, A., Touloumis, A.: Visual logics help people: an evaluation of diagrammatic, textual and symbolic notations. In: 2017 IEEE Symposium on Visual Languages and Human-Centric Computing (VL/HCC), pp. 255–259. IEEE (2017)
4. Alsallakh, B., Micallef, L., Aigner, W., Hauser, H., Miksch, S., Rodgers, P.: Visualizing sets and set-typed data: State-of-the-art and future challenges (2014)
5. Butcher, K.R.: Learning from text with diagrams: Promoting mental model development and inference generation. J. Educ. Psychol. **98**(1), 182 (2006)
6. Chapman, P., Stapleton, G., Rodgers, P., Micallef, L., Blake, A.: Visualizing sets: an empirical comparison of diagram types. In: Dwyer, T., Purchase, H., Delaney, A. (eds.) Diagrams 2014. LNCS (LNAI), vol. 8578, pp. 146–160. Springer, Heidelberg (2014). https://doi.org/10.1007/978-3-662-44043-8_18
7. Cheng, P.C.-H.: Why diagrams are (sometimes) six times easier than words: benefits beyond locational indexing. In: Blackwell, A.F., Marriott, K., Shimojima, A. (eds.) Diagrams 2004. LNCS (LNAI), vol. 2980, pp. 242–254. Springer, Heidelberg (2004). https://doi.org/10.1007/978-3-540-25931-2_25
8. Cromley, J.G., Snyder-Hogan, L.E., Luciw-Dubas, U.A.: Cognitive activities in complex science text and diagrams. Contemp. Educ. Psychol. **35**(1), 59–74 (2010)
9. Herman, G.L., Loui, M.C., Zilles, C.: Students' misconceptions about medium-scale integrated circuits. IEEE Trans. Educ. **54**(4), 637–645 (2011)
10. Larkin, J.H., Simon, H.A.: Why a diagram is (sometimes) worth ten thousand words. Cogn. Sci. **11**(1), 65–100 (1987)
11. Shimojima, A.: Semantic properties of diagrams and their cognitive potentials. In: Shimojima, A. (ed.) Center for the Study of Language and Information. CSLI Publications, California (2015)

12. Stapleton, G., Jamnik, M., Shimojima, A.: Effective representation of information: generalizing free rides. In: Jamnik, M., Uesaka, Y., Elzer Schwartz, S. (eds.) Diagrams 2016. LNCS (LNAI), vol. 9781, pp. 296–299. Springer, Cham (2016). https://doi.org/10.1007/978-3-319-42333-3_28
13. Trotskovsky, E., Waks, S., Sabag, N., Hazzan, O.: Students' misunderstandings and misconceptions in engineering thinking. Int. J. Eng. Educ. **29**(1), 107–118 (2013)
14. Veitch, E.W.: A chart method for simplifying truth functions. In: Proceedings of the 1952 ACM national meeting (Pittsburgh), pp. 127–133 (1952)
15. Zilles, C., Longino, J., Loui, M.: Student misconcfptions in an introductory digital logic design course. In: ASEE Annual Conference and Exposition, Conference Proceedings (2006)

Posters

Syllogisms with Intermediate Quantifiers Solved in Marlo Logic Diagrams

Marcos Bautista López Aznar$^{(\boxtimes)}$ (iD)

University of Huelva, Huelva, Spain
marlodiagram@gmail.com

Abstract. In this article we propose diagrams with the ability to represent syllogisms that, in addition to the traditional quantifiers "all", "some" and "none", can represent the so-called intermediate quantifiers or probabilistic quantifiers "most", "a few", "half", etc. The graphs contained in this paper have been developed based on the Marlo diagram, a tool for teaching logical reasoning that operates with propositional models that are constructed by quantifying the predicate in a way similar to Hamilton or Jevons in the 19th century. The quantification of the predicate allows us to represent the possibilities implicit in the premises, so that when the synthesis of the propositions is made later, the working memory can take these possibilities into account. In this way, we prevent our students from committing the persistent fallacies of denying the antecedent and affirming the consequent.

Keywords: Logic diagrams · Visual reasoning · Diagrammatic reasoning · Intermediate quantifiers · Syllogism

1 Propositional Models Beyond Traditional Quantifiers

Traditionally, the syllogism propositions have been divided into universal and particular, affirmative and negative. However, as Valiña [8] indicates, this choice is arbitrary and does not take into account other quantifiers, such as Most (M) and Few (F), with which people reason naturally [4–7]. With the intention of representing the logic of probability, some of the first modern logicians developed linear diagrams in which it was important to represent the relative extent of class B compared to class A. However, Venn [9] stated that any introduction of considerations such as these should be avoided as they tend to confuse the domains of logic and mathematics, and because ambiguous representations also occur. In fact, to solve certain ambiguities in the graphs, we ourselves have had to match the graphic representation of "Some A", "A few A" and "At least one A" in the propositional models. To interpret Fig. 1, what must be remembered is that we place the name of the variable that works as a subject in the center of the propositional models. A explanation of Marlo diagram is available on Youtube [1]. The universal models are not divided, and the areas that remain undetermined in particular models are left blank or labeled with a question mark (see Fig. 3 now). On the other hand, when the variable that functions as a predicate is taken universally, it only appears within the subject's model, but when it is considered in a particular way, it is also indicated

© Springer Nature Switzerland AG 2020
A.-V. Pietarinen et al. (Eds.): Diagrams 2020, LNAI 12169, pp. 473–476, 2020.
https://doi.org/10.1007/978-3-030-54249-8_37

outside the model with a question mark. The exterior of the A model is interpreted as ¬A. Only combinations incompatible with the explicit and necessary associations are prohibited. The rest are possibilities neither confirmed nor refuted by the models [2, 3]. For example, in the conditional model *All A is B*, it is no longer possible to include ¬B in any region of *A*, because in the entire extension of *A* we have *B*, but it is still possible to suppose ¬B associated with ¬A and that's why we write "¬b?" outside the model of A. The subscript *x* indicates "whole" and can be interpreted as the conditional "→". The subscript *m* indicates "most".

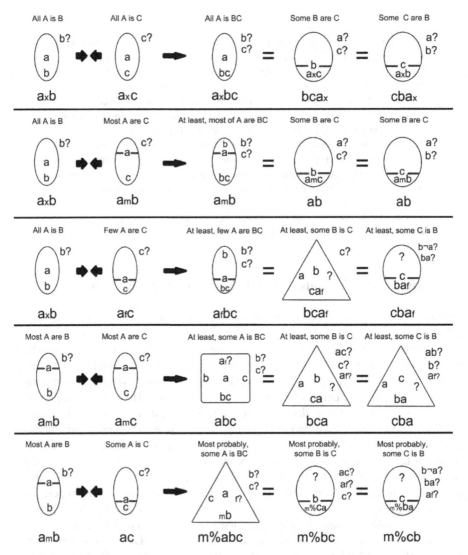

Fig. 1. Syllogisms with intermediate quantifiers and conversion of their conclusions.

1 No bird is a mammal. 2 Most quadrupeds are mammals. 3 Only birds fly. 4 Anything that does not fly is terrestrial or aquatic. 5 Quadrupeds are not aquatic. Therefore, most quadrupeds are terrestrial.

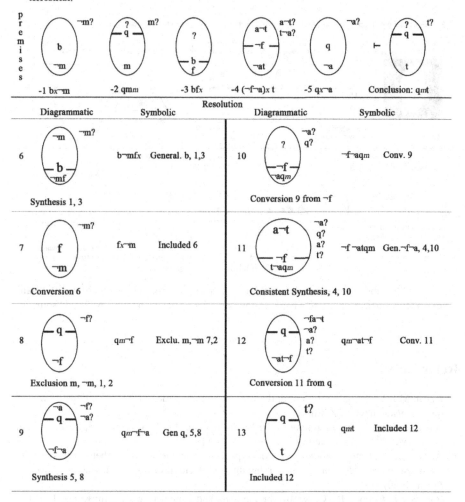

Fig. 2. Syllogism solved with intermediate quantifiers in Marlo diagram.

The subscript *f* indicates "A few" and in this work it is equivalent to no subscript, which indicates "some", "at least one" or "part". If we interpret the expression "*A few A are B*" as "*Only a few A are B and the rest are ¬B*", then we would write ¬B without question mark in the larger region of *A*. All variables located on the sides of triangles or squares are potentially combinable. For example, in the square model of "*At least some A are BC*", all *A* could finally be *BC*, but there is a possibility that a small part of *A* is ¬B¬C. In this square, the possibilities of AB¬C and AC¬B are represented on the sides labeled B and C respectively, although finally both sides could be ABC. Figure 2 represents a syllogism with five dichotomous variables that are quantified with All, Most and Few.

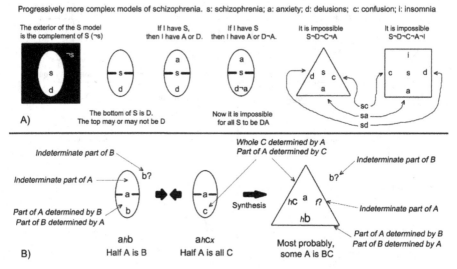

Fig. 3. A) Meaning of the model regions. B) Explanation of propositional models with "Half". (The divided models mean *some* when we limit ourselves to the quantifiers "All" and "some").

References

1. Aznar, M.B.L.: Visual reasoning in the Marlo diagram [Video file] (2018). https://www.you tube.com/watch?v=ivEZ4Pfr6tQ
2. Aznar, M.B.L.: Visual reasoning in the Marlo diagram. In: Sato, Y., Shams, Z. (eds.) Ceur-ws.org, vol. 2116 (2018). http://ceur-ws.org/Vol-2116
3. Aznar, M.B.L.: Diagramas lógicos de Marlo para el razonamiento visual y heterogéneo: válidos en lógica matemática y aristotélica. (Unpublished doctoral dissertation). Huelva University, Spain (2020)
4. Barwise, J., Cooper, R.: Generalized quantifiers and natural language. In: Kulas, J., Fetzer, J.H., Rankin, T.L. (eds.) Philosophy, Language, and Artificial Intelligence. Studies in Cognitive Systems, vol. 2. Springer, Dordrecht (1981). https://doi.org/10.1007/978-94-009-2727-8_10
5. Chater, N., Oaksford, M.: The probability heuristics model of syllogistic reasoning. Cogn. Psychol. **38**(2), 191–258 (1999). https://doi.org/10.1006/cogp.1998.0696
6. Thompson, B.: Syllogisms using "few", "many", and "most". Notre Dame J. Formal Logic **23**(1), 75–84 (1982). https://doi.org/10.1305/ndjfl/1093883568. https://projecteuclid.org/euc lid.ndjfl/1093883568
7. Peterson, P.L.: On the logic of "few", "many", and "most". Notre Dame J. Formal Logic **20**(1), 155–179 (1979). https://doi.org/10.1305/ndjfl/1093882414. https://projecteuclid.org/ euclid.ndjfl/1093882414
8. Valiña, M.D.: Efecto del contenido y microgénesis de la tarea en razonamiento silogístico con cuantificadores probabilísticos: un estudio cronométrico. Cognitiva **1**, 199–212 (1988)
9. Venn, J.: Symbolic Logic. MacMillan, London (1881). https://doi.org/10.1037/14127-000

The Indemonstrables of Chrysippus of Soli in Marlo Logical Diagrams. Could Propositional Calculus Be Nothing but Syllogisms?

Marcos Bautista López Aznar$^{(\boxtimes)}$ (ID)

Huelva University, Huelva, Spain
marlodiagram@gmail.com

Abstract. It has traditionally been considered that, while Aristotelian syllogism was limited to justifying a logic of terms, the indemonstrables established by the Stoics and Chrysippus of Soli (280–206 BC) laid the foundation for the validity of the logic of sentences. However, and thanks to the quantification of the predicate postulated by Hamilton and Jevons among others, we do not apply different principles when representing propositional calculus or Aristotelian syllogisms in our diagrams. The differences we find depend on what diagram we use, but not on what kind of logic we represent. Peirce claimed that reasoning is subject to the general laws of nervous action. In this regard, when representing the indemonstrables in Marlo expectations networks, which try to emulate the parallel processing related to the excitatory and inhibitory synapses of our neurons, it seems sufficient to appeal to the fact that by eliminating certain combinations their alternatives become necessary. However, in Marlo diagram, serial processes related to reasoning using verbal propositions take center stage: we reach conclusions by linking the middle term of the premises in the same way that we do in the syllogism, and in this case, reasoning is also subject to the general laws of communication.

Keywords: Logic diagrams · Indemonstrables · Visual reasoning · Syllogism

1 Could Propositional Calculus Be Nothing but Syllogisms?

All logical connectives ($\leftrightarrow$, $\rightarrow$, $\veebar$, etc.) can be expressed in networks by eliminating nodes forever ($\nexists$), except the conjunction of two variables, which we express by activating the node that represents said association. In figure number one we can see tree diagrams that contain the four combinations that we obtain from two variables considered dichotomously. The node $\underline{d}$, which is underlined, is a criterion node from which the branches "d" and "¬d" arise. The first premise always removes a combination from the universe of discourse and, sometimes, categorically affirms that there is "something" that is present here and now. The second premise only affirms or temporarily denies some of the combinations that still remain. The conclusion is obtained by spreading truth and falsehood through the network nodes [3]. For example, if "D node" is true and "d¬l" is impossible ($\nexists$), then "DL node" is true. And if "¬DN node" is false and "¬d¬n" is impossible, then "¬D node" is false [2] (Fig. 1).

© Springer Nature Switzerland AG 2020
A.-V. Pietarinen et al. (Eds.): Diagrams 2020, LNAI 12169, pp. 477–480, 2020.
https://doi.org/10.1007/978-3-030-54249-8_38

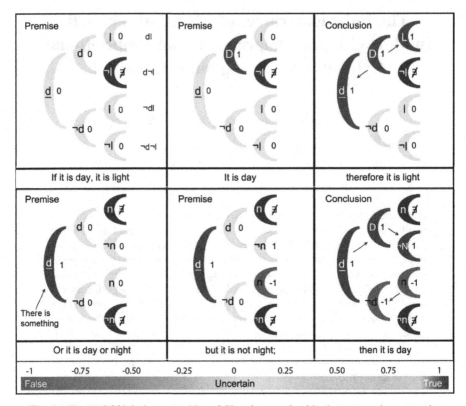

Fig. 1. First and fifth indemonstrables of Chrysippus solved in the expectation networks.

The representation of inferences in Marlo diagrams seems to show different cognitive processes than networks (see Fig. 2). Only relevant regions of the universe of discourse are explicitly represented in Marlo diagrams. Anything outside the "a region" of a model must be considered as "¬a". Any combination that does not contradict what was already indicated as necessary within the models is considered as possible. Variables with a question mark, as well as the blank regions in the models, represent possible combinations, which can be removed without denying the proposition. For instance, in Fig. 2(2), in the diagram number one, the variable "b?" represents the combination "b¬a", which is neither asserted nor denied in a conditional statement; the blank region within model number two means "b¬a" and the one in number three means "¬b¬a". The subject and the predicate of a proposition can be considered universal or particular. Particular subject: divided model. Universal subject: undivided model. Universal predicate: it only appears within the model. Particular predicate: it is written inside and outside the model. As we can see in Fig. 2(3), models whose subjects are identical can be synthesized into one. Necessary conclusions are only drawn when superimposing the models of the middle term we cannot avoid associating the variables that now act as predicates within the same region (all or part of one with all or part of the other).

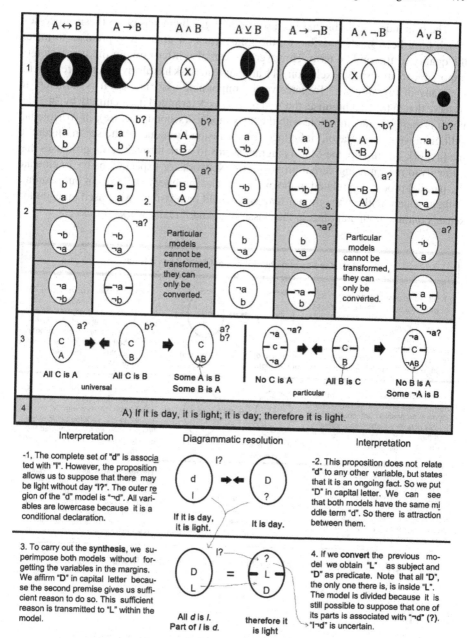

Fig. 2. 1. Elementary propositions in Venn. 2. Elementary propositions in Marlo models: conversion and transformation are based on networks of expectations. 3. Example of universal and particular synthesis: at least one universal model. 4. First indemonstrable of Chrysippus solved by synthesis in a syllogistic way.

The fifth indemonstrable has been solved in Fig. 3 by means of synthesis processes, which have been made possible by the transformation of the first premise to match the quality of the middle term. However, we can also infer through the perception of impossible relationships (exclusion) [1], although this task has always been more difficult for many of my students. To perceive the impossible associations, it is sufficient to observe that in the first premise, the "¬d model" is determined in its entirety by "n", and that it is therefore incompatible with the "¬N model" (second premise). In Aristotelian syllogism we can also avoid inferences by exclusion by reducing the second figure to the first [4]. To sum up, the Marlo diagram seems to work through serial processes that allow us to reason using verbal propositions. Networks of expectations try to emulate the parallel processing related to the excitatory and inhibitory synapses of our neurons, without which neither thought nor language would be possible. We, based on common sense, combine both diagrams in the classroom. And it really works for us.

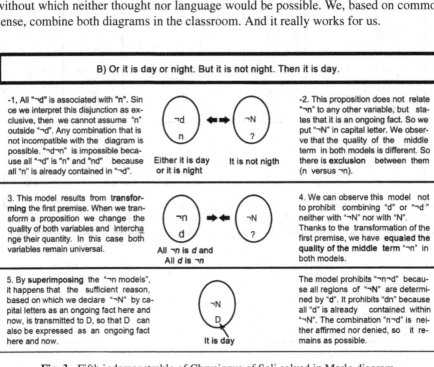

Fig. 3. Fifth indemonstrable of Chrysippus of Soli solved in Marlo diagram.

References

1. Aznar, M.B.L.: Visual reasoning in the Marlo diagram. In: Sato, Y., Shams, Z. (eds.) Ceur-ws.org, vol. 2116 (2018). http://ceur-ws.org/Vol-2116
2. Aznar, M.B.L.: Diagramas lógicos de Marlo para el razonamiento visual y heterogéneo: válidos en lógica matemática y aristotélica. (Unpublished doctoral dissertation). Huelva University, Spain (2020)
3. Bochenski, J.M.: History of Formal Logic. University of Notre Dame, Notre Dame (1961)
4. Peirce, C.S.: On the algebra of logic. Am. J. Math. 3(1), 15–57 (1880). https://doi.org/10.2307/2369442

'Tokenized' Dynamic Diagrams: An Approach for Improving Mental Model Construction?

Jean-Michel Boucheix[1] and Richard Lowe[1,2](✉)

[1] Université Bourgogne Franche-Comté (LEAD-CNRS), Dijon, France
[2] Curtin University, Perth, Australia
r.k.lowe@curtin.edu.au

Abstract. Novel 'Compositional' designs based on the Animation processing Model (APM) allow learners to build mental models of referent content that are superior to those acquired from conventionally-designed animations. Additional gains in the effectiveness of APM-based designs appear feasible if the animation's external depiction of content was to be better aligned with characteristics of the internal tokens by excising parts of the animation's constituent graphic entities not central to their functional role. Dynamic inferences would let learners mentally elaborate the resulting fragmentary depiction to produce the required tokens. Implementation of this tokenized design approach are discussed.

Keywords: Animated diagrams · Mental models · Tokens · Information processing · Comprehension

1 Introduction

The Animation Processing Model (APM) is concerned with perceptual and cognitive processes that are central to constructing a high quality mental model from a dynamic depiction of complex subject matter [1]. Mental model theory [2, 3] posits that *tokens* are fundamental to how the mind represents knowledge – they are the raw material from which mental models are composed. Conventionally-designed 'comprehensive' animations depict their subject matter in an essentially literal manner with characteristics that have little in common with hypothesized properties of tokens [4]. One possible approach for optimizing the effectiveness of animations would be to design them so that internal 'tokenization' of the externally presented information is facilitated.

2 Animation Design and Tokens

Using the APM, failures of traditionally-designed comprehensive animations to produce anticipated learning benefits [e.g., 5, 6] can be accounted for in terms of the barriers they present to (i) successful *decomposition* of these demanding external representations into *event units* (entities plus their associated dynamics), and (ii) *composition* of such event units into adequate higher order knowledge structures that internally represent the target

A.-V. Pietarinen et al. (Eds.): Diagrams 2020, LNAI 12169, pp. 481–484, 2020.
https://doi.org/10.1007/978-3-030-54249-8_39

subject matter. The failures can be substantially ameliorated by an alternative 'Composition Approach' design regime [7]. Recent research on animated piano mechanism diagrams indicated a key reason for the benefits of a compositional design is that its pre-decomposed chunks of information ('Relation Sets') result in far more targeted learner processing behavior [8]. In particular, learners' foveal visual attention tended to be primarily devoted to causally-relevant contact interactions between adjacent functional components.

Learner processing of compositional animations could perhaps be facilitated further if the design of the presentation treated 'less crucial' aspects of information differently from more functionally important aspects. In particular, instead of indiscriminately incorporating all the detail of each component in the depiction, they could be 'tokenized' by omitting details that are functionally non-crucial. The presence of dynamics would allow the discontinuities in such tokenized depictions to be mentally 'filled-in' by the learner using domain general knowledge about real-world dynamics and related Gestalt ideas. For example, apparently separate graphic fragments that move together in a regular fashion are likely to in fact be connected, even if the connection is invisible (Common Fate). Figure 1 illustrates an implementation of such modification for a dynamic diagram of how an upright piano mechanism functions.

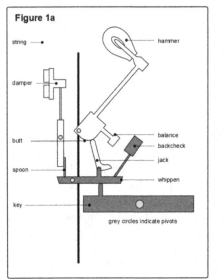
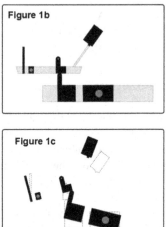

Fig. 1. (a) Piano mechanism with key-whippen relation set (grey). (b) Key-whippen pair showing fragments retained in tokenized version (black). (c) Tokenized key-whippen pair after movement, plus original positions (dotted lines). Coordinated displacements allow inferences to be made about which fragments are parts of the same wholes and how they are connected.

According to the APM, successful animation processing relies on interplay between bottom-up information (as provided by the externally presented animation) and information that is available top-down (as provided internally by the viewer's existing background knowledge). Appropriate elaboration of sets of fragments in a tokenized animation in order to generate functionally effective mental tokens requires inferences that rely on both these types of information. A pilot study assessed viewers' capacity to make such inferences.

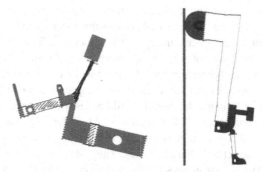

Fig. 2. Example completions of entity fragments drawn by pilot study participants after having viewed a tokenized version of the piano mechanism animation.

Participants were presented with tokenized versions of various animated relation set pairs from the piano mechanism in which only 50% of the entity (by area) was retained and asked to draw in what would be required to complete each of the entities involved. In all instances, the fundamental connections existing between fragments were correctly indicated in the drawings (Fig. 2).

3   Conclusion

An implicit goal of educational animations that portray complex content is to help learners to acquire a high quality metal model of the depicted referent material. However at first sight, changing from standard depictions of the content to tokenized representations could appear potentially counterproductive. Converting standard depictions of the entities in an animation into sets of fragments as suggested involves introducing a high level of abstraction that severely reduces the amount of information available to the viewer. In the piano example given here, we removed 50% of what was present in the original. Nevertheless, there is a compelling threefold rationale for this seemingly drastic surgery:

1. Research on learners' processing of a Compositional animation found that foveal attention was dedicated primarily to small, functionally-crucial aspects (i.e., contact interactions between entities) rather than to entities' non-functional details.
2. Tokenized entities are highly consistent with the form of representation posited to be fundamental to mental models (so that learners need to carry out less representational conversion in order to internalize externally presented information)

3. Patterns of coordinated motion amongst the fragments of entities remaining after tokenization of a dynamic display allow the fundamental connections and overall configuration to be reconstituted through everyday inference processes.

Tokenized animations involve a radical departure from the prevailing design approaches used to develop conventional comprehensive animations. However, in principle the disparity between the actual appearance of the referent content and the highly abstracted version depicted in the animation is not dissimilar to that between a photograph of an electronic device and its formal circuit diagram. In the case of an electronic diagram, it is assumed that the viewer will possess the specialized knowledge and skills required to carry out the necessary interpretative processes. Training to develop these capacities is an accepted part of science education, even for high school students. An important potential advantage we envisage for this tokenized approach is that the learner will likely acquire a more generalizable and flexible representation of the target content. This is because the resulting mental model should be less tied to specific surface features of the system being represented. The learner would thus be able to apply this representational framework to a wider range of superficially diverse examples that nevertheless share common deep structural characteristics. This robust underpinning of fundamentals would have particular advantages for more demanding high level activities such as transfer and problem solving.

References

1. Lowe, R., Boucheix, J.-M.: Learning from animated diagrams: how are mental models built? In: Stapleton, G., Howse, J., Lee, J. (eds.) Diagrams 2008. LNCS (LNAI), vol. 5223, pp. 266–281. Springer, Heidelberg (2008). https://doi.org/10.1007/978-3-540-87730-1_25
2. Johnson-Laird, P.N.: Mental Models. Towards a Cognitive Science of Language, Inference, and Consciousness. Cambridge University Press, Cambridge (1983)
3. Tversky, B.: Cognitive maps, cognitive collages, and spatial mental models. In: Frank, A.U., Campari, I. (eds.) COSIT 1993. LNCS, vol. 716, pp. 14–24. Springer, Heidelberg (1993). https://doi.org/10.1007/3-540-57207-4_2
4. Ploetzner, R., Lowe, R.K.: A systematic characterisation of expository animations. Comput. Hum. Behav. **28**, 781–794 (2012)
5. De Koning, B.B., Tabbers, H.K., Rikers, R.M.J.P., Paas, F.: Animation guidance in learning from a complex animation - seeing is understanding? Learn. Instr. **20**, 111–122 (2010)
6. Bernay, S., Bétrancourt, M.: Does animation enhance learning? A meta-analysis. Comput. Educ. **10**, 150–167 (2016)
7. Lowe, R.K., Boucheix, J.-M.: Principled animation design improves comprehension of complex dynamics. Learn. Instr. **45**, 72–84 (2016)
8. Lowe, R., Boucheix, J.-M., Menant, M.: Perceptual processing and the comprehension of relational information in dynamic diagrams. In: Chapman, P., Stapleton, G., Moktefi, A., Perez-Kriz, S., Bellucci, F. (eds.) Diagrams 2018. LNCS (LNAI), vol. 10871, pp. 470–483. Springer, Cham (2018). https://doi.org/10.1007/978-3-319-91376-6_42

Depicting Negative Information in Photographs, Videos, and Comics: A Preliminary Analysis

Yuri Sato[1]([✉])[ID] and Koji Mineshima[2]([✉])

[1] The University of Tokyo, Tokyo, Japan
satoyuri0@gmail.com
[2] Keio University, Tokyo, Japan
minesima@abelard.flet.keio.ac.jp

Abstract. It is often claimed that pictures are not well suited to representing negative information. Against this widely held view, we argue that a close look at how ordinary people use visual representations will show that negative information can be depicted in various interesting ways. We focus on three types of representations, namely, photographs, videos, and comics, and discuss design varieties for depicting negation.

Keywords: Negation · Image · Comics · Semantics · Information design

1 Introduction

Negation plays a substantial role in conveying information in human thinking and communication. Although negation in natural language has been a major research topic in logic, philosophy, and linguistics (cf. [9]), it is often claimed that negation is not well suited to visual thinking and communication [2,5,12].

Against this widely held view, we argue that a close look at how people use visual representations in the real world will show that negative information can be depicted in various interesting ways. Among them, we focus on three types of visual representations: photograph, video (film), and comics (manga). These three types of visual representations can be roughly classified in the following way. Videos and comics are distinguished from photographs in that they consist of *temporal sequences*, which typically represent sequences of multiple events or scenes. Comics are similar to linguistic representations in that they have a variety of *conventional devices* for expressing thoughts, emotions and other non-visual properties and attitudes. By contrast, photographs and videos typically do not involve conventional devices, though they can be enriched with symbols or linguistic materials such as subtitles.

In recent years, semantic analyses of these visual representations have been developed, including those for photographs [8], films [6], and comics [1]. To our knowledge, however, the question of how such visual representations can express

© Springer Nature Switzerland AG 2020
A.-V. Pietarinen et al. (Eds.): Diagrams 2020, LNAI 12169, pp. 485–489, 2020.
https://doi.org/10.1007/978-3-030-54249-8_40

negation has been largely unexplored. As a first step towards an analysis of negation in visual representations, this paper presents a preliminary sketch of design varieties for depicting negation in the three types of visual representations.

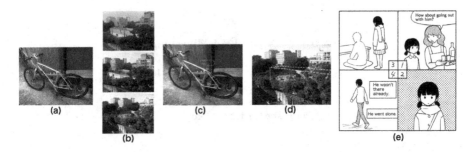

Fig. 1. (a) a photograph of bicycle; (b) a video on buildings; (c) an augmented picture of 1a; (d) an augmented picture of 1b; (e) a comic page with a dotted line convention

2   Photographs

Of the three type of visual representations, we begin with photographs or pictures. What information can we extract from a photograph? Fig. 1a shows a photograph of a bicycle. Here one could easily extract conjunctive information; e.g., there are tires, wheels, pedals, and a handle. Furthermore, if you look at the photograph carefully, you would notice something strange: there is *no* saddle in this orange-colored bicycle. This in turn suggests that, in contrast to the case of conjunctive information, extracting negative information from photographs is more involved in that it usually requires background knowledge; in the case of Fig. 1a, it requires the prior knowledge that a bicycle usually has a saddle. For those who do not know what bicycles are and what they are composed of, it would be much difficult to extract negative information from Fig. 1a.

To see the difficulty involved in extracting negative information from photographs, it is illustrative to consider the case of AI researches on the automation of image description as machine learning tasks (see [3] for a survey). Here one of the goals is to generate a description or a caption for a given image in terms of objects, attributes, and relationships appearing in it using machine learning techniques. This usually requires collecting training data by means of human annotation. In many cases, however, images referring to objects that are not directly depicted and hence requiring background knowledge are outside of the scope (see p. 412 of [3]).

These observations enable us to consider the question of what type of picture or photograph is well suited to expressing negative information. Our conjecture is that a photograph can deliver a negative proposition (e.g. "the bicycle does not have a saddle") if it easily evokes an alternative context in which a positive counterpart (e.g. "the bicycle has a saddle") holds. The psychological findings on sentence verification by picture could be supportive for this conjecture. In cognitive psychology, it has been widely observed that negative sentences (e.g., the door is not open) take a longer time to verify the meaning in a picture than positive sentences (e.g., the door is closed). More specifically, in the typical experiments, participants were asked to judge whether sentences were true of pictures. Interestingly, it is reported that, given an appropriate context (e.g., looking for something, lifting something, playing something), the time differences between positives and negatives were not found in cognitive outcomes [7].

3 Videos

As analyzed in the previous section, photographs, which are typically given as one sheet, can convey negative information with the aid of some background knowledge or context. Such background knowledge or context can be naturally realized in multiple pictures presented in a temporal sequential manner; i.e., videos. Consider the case of Fig. 1b. This is a video (sequential images) of the renovation of a building. Here the temporal order is from top to bottom; the top side image is earlier in time than the bottom side image. Compared to the top side image, we can extract the negative information that "there is no building" from the bottom side image. Note here that it would be difficult to derive the above negative information only from the bottom side image, while it could be easily derived from the comparison of temporal-sequential multiple sheets.

Note that not only the negative information that there is no building but also the action event of "the building was demolished" can be described in the video in Fig. 1b. In contrast to our focus, prior work in psychology [13] and AI on video description [11] has focused on the latter aspect. They have dealt with the problem of how we give temporal sequential and multiple simultaneous events (especially, actions such as jump) in video segmentation and annotation.

4 Comics

As discussed in the previous section, even the content of a video (multiple photographs) is ambiguous in that it can be interpreted either as conveying negative information or as the action relation across multiple frames. In order to *selectively* express negative information, we can add conventional devices into images. The idea is similar to the one in augmented reality [10]; so we call it "augmented picture". Figure 1c is an augmented picture of Fig. 1a. Here the negative information that there is no saddle is expressed by dotted lines, without using background knowledge. Likewise, by using the dotted lines, Fig. 1d depicts the negative information that there is no building as one-sheet representation, in contrast to the video in Fig. 1b where temporal-sequential multiple frames are used.

In the real world, the technique of enclosing by dotted lines can be frequently found in comics (manga), as emphasized in Cohn's [4] visual narrative grammar of comics. Here comics are illustrations having temporal-sequential multiple frames. Figure 1e is an example of comics, which expresses that "a character is not there" by using a dotted line (written based on the original comic[1]). In addition, we can find various designs using conventional devices to represent negative information in comics. In Osamu Tezuka's *Phoenix: Resurrection*[2], a boy was dead, then "everything returned to *nothing*", which is depicted by what the frame is filled with black. In Tezuka's *Budda*[3], a fox can find some food but a rabbit can *not* find any food. Here, the fact that the rabbit could not find food is expressed by placing just a cross in a balloon. In Tezuka's *Phoenix: Civil War*[4], a monkey says to a dog, "Do not walk in large numbers!", by putting a cross on a herd of dogs in a balloon. Note here that the negation here is not the negative form of a verb but a speech act of prohibition. Interestingly, the above conventional devices are used not only in comics but also in other complex visual representations. For example, unknown and unexplored regions in a map was represented by filling a portion of an area with gray color. In pictograms of laundry symbols, which is standardized as ISO 3758, a cross notation expressing prohibition is also used. For instance, when a cross is put on an iron mark, it is designed to mean *Do not iron*.

Our next step is to run some experiments to test whether ordinary people interpret the meaning of visual representations as designers intended. Through the experiments, we would try to shed light on the factors affecting people's interpretation of visual representations. It is expected that the experiments and analyses would provide some evidence for the naturalness of conventional devices in diagrammatic representations (e.g., shading in Venn diagrams), and the design guide of information visualization.

References

1. Abusch, D.: Applying discourse semantics and pragmatics to co-reference in picture sequences. In: Sinn und Bedeutung, vol. 17, pp. 9–25 (2013)
2. Barwise, J., Etchemendy, J.: Hyperproof: logical reasoning with diagrams. In: Reasoning with Diagrammatic Representations, pp. 77–81. AAAI Press (1992)
3. Bernardi, R., Cakici, R., Elliott, D., et al.: Automatic description generation from images: a survey of models, datasets, and evaluation measures. J. Artif. Intell. Res. **55**, 409–442 (2016). https://doi.org/10.1613/jair.4900
4. Cohn, N.: The Visual Language of Comics: Introduction to the Structure and Cognition of Sequential Images. Bloomsbury, London (2013)
5. Crane, T.: Is perception a propositional attitude? Philos. Q. **59**, 452–469 (2009). https://doi.org/10.1111/j.1467-9213.2008.608.x

---

[1] Page 7, Jun Sakura. "Yugami-kun ni wa Tomodachi ga Inai" vol.9, Shogakukan. Free online page: https://csbs.shogakukan.co.jp/book?book_group_id=7148.

[2] Pages 8–9, Osamu Tezuka "Phoenix" vol.7, Kodansha. Free online page: https://tezukaosamu.net/jp/manga/396.html.

[3] Page 21, Osamu Tezuka "Budda", vol.1, Kodansha. Free online page: https://tezukaosamu.net/jp/manga/434.html.

[4] Page 275, Osamu Tezuka "Phoenix", vol.12, Kodansha. https://tezukaosamu.net/jp/manga/401.html.

6. Cumming, S., Greenberg, G., Kelly, R.: Conventions of viewpoint coherence in film. Philos.' Impr. **17**, 1–29 (2017)
7. Dale, R., Duran, N.D.: The cognitive dynamics of negated sentence verification. Cogn. Sci. **35**, 983–996 (2011). https://doi.org/10.1111/j.1551-6709.2010.01164.x
8. Greenberg, G. J.: The semiotic spectrum. Ph.D thesis. Rutgers University (2011)
9. Horn, L.R.: A Natural History of Negation. University of Chicago Press, Chicago (1989)
10. Sato, Y., Sugimoto, Y., Ueda, K.: Real objects can impede conditional reasoning but augmented objects do not. Cogn. Sci. **42**, 691–707 (2018). https://doi.org/10.1111/cogs.12553
11. Yeung, S., Russakovsky, O., Jin, N., Andriluka, M., Mori, G., Fei-Fei, L.: Every moment counts: dense detailed labeling of actions in complex videos. Int. J. Comput. Vis. **126**(2), 375–389 (2017). https://doi.org/10.1007/s11263-017-1013-y
12. Wittgenstein, L.: Notebooks 1914–1916. Anscombe, G.E.M., von Wright, G.H. (eds.). University of Chicago Press (1914/1984)
13. Zacks, J.M., Tversky, B., Iyer, G.: Perceiving, remembering, and communicating structure in events. J. Exp. Psychol. Gen. **130**, 29–58 (2001). https://doi.org/10.1037/0096-3445.130.1.29

The Marlo Diagram in the Classroom

Marcos Bautista López Aznar$^{(\boxtimes)}$ ⓘD

Huelva University, Huelva, Spain
marlodiagram@gmail.com

Abstract. In this paper we present some results obtained using the Marlo diagram for the didactic of logic in a High School in Huelva, Spain, between 2014 and 2019. This tool was created by the author to improve the bad results obtained with traditional methods of propositional calculus, excessively complex, abstract and far from common sense. To avoid the most frequent fallacies in the classroom, we developed a simple and intuitive diagrammatic deduction system that allows us to decompose and visualize the simplest and most elementary steps of reasoning. Our goal was reinforcing valid inference patterns by synchronizing natural, formal and diagrammatic languages. Although in 2014 we could only solve syllogisms in our diagram, since 2016 we can also solve propositional logic exercises. This is possible by expressing all logical connectives by quantifying the predicate. Proceeding this way allows us to solve any inference of the propositional calculus in our diagrams through the same processes of analysis and synthesis that take place in the syllogism. The fact of recovering the middle term as the basis for any inference allows us to teach logic from common sense and, consequently, obtain better results in performance tests. The first comparisons we have made of our teaching method with the conventional method encourage us to continue developing a tool that, according to our experience, allows us to improve abstract thinking from an earlier age than conventional methods.

Keywords: Critical thinking · Diagrammatic reasoning · Didactics of logic

1 The Marlo Diagram Results

Disappointed by the low performance of our logic students, we try to develop a system of diagrammatic representation that allows us to visualize each of the steps that the mind must follow when it passes from the premises of an argument to its conclusion. In 2013, we began to systematically observe our students solving logical problems in the classroom. They were asked to "think aloud" and, meanwhile, we analyzed their eye movements on the chalkboard: do they look, point and name the elements of the exercise in a coordinated manner? Where is the difficulty for them? Where have they gone out of the way? Finally, we generated diagrams that quantify the predicate and allow us to explicitly indicate which combinations of variables should be considered in the conclusions. Thus, we avoid the fallacies of the affirmation of the consequent and the denial of the antecedent. The initial version of Marlo diagram was tested with sixteen-year-old students of the I.E.S. Pablo Neruda de Huelva in 2014 [1] (Fig. 1).

© Springer Nature Switzerland AG 2020
A.-V. Pietarinen et al. (Eds.): Diagrams 2020, LNAI 12169, pp. 490–493, 2020.
https://doi.org/10.1007/978-3-030-54249-8_41

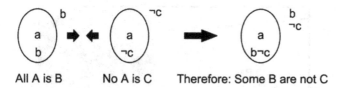

Fig. 1. Example of syllogism solved in the Marlo diagram in 2014.

Students received theoretical instruction on the diagram through the teacher's explanations on the chalkboard for seven hours and then received a workbook with thirty solved exercises in which they spent an average of three hours according to them. The subsequent examination consisted in solving, step by step, six syllogisms of varying difficulty. 88.3% of students passed the exam. And there were 36.6% perfect exams, without a single mistake. The bar graph shows the results in number of students and points obtained in the exam. The maximum score was 10 (Fig. 2).

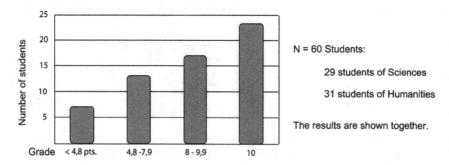

Fig. 2. Results of the 2014 test on syllogism with the Marlo diagram [1].

These results persuaded us to work with a group of eleven and twelve year old students and we were able to verify that 90% of them understood the principles of the method (Fig. 3).

In 2016, we developed a formal notation system that quantifies the variables with a subscript x which means "all" and that has allowed us to represent the logical connectives [3]. Thus, we begin to solve the propositional logic exercises as if they were syllogisms. And now, when our students solve these types of problems, they look for the variables that act as a middle term by linking the premises with the conclusion.

We compared academic achievement of four groups of students in a logic test in 2018. The traditional method was applied by a teacher, with more than twenty-five years of experience, in a group of Humanities (30 students) and another of Sciences (35 students). The first had an average equal to 5.9 in the final grade of June considering the grades of all students in all subjects. The second got a 7.1. The author, with twenty years of experience, applied Marlo diagram in two groups, one of Humanities (32 students) and another of Sciences (28 students). The first had an average in the final grade of June equal to 6.7 and the second 7.6. Here we limit ourselves to offering data on the performance of each group in the execution of the most complex exercise of the logical test we did. The study sample contained 125 people (Fig. 4).

Fig. 3. Eleven and twelve-year-old children solving syllogisms [2, 7].

Conventional	Marlo	▨ Conventional ▧ Marlo	
-1 p → q ⊢ ¬p	-1 $p_x q$ ⊢ ¬P		
-2 r → ¬q	-2 r_x¬q		
-3 s ∨ r	-3 s, r		
-4 t → ¬s	-4 t_x¬s		
-5 t	-5 T		

Fig. 4. Exercise solved with conventional formal notation and Marlo diagram notation quantifying the predicate. The bars show the percentage of students who successfully completed the exercise.

We apply the same correction criteria to all students. In the Science groups, the exercise was solved by 40% of the students who used the traditional method and by 50% of the students who were instructed in the Marlo diagram. In the Humanities groups, the exercise was solved only by 3% of the students who used the traditional method. However, 34% of the students who were instructed in the Marlo diagram did the exercise well. The fact that some of our students benefit more than others from the Marlo diagram is consistent with the results in cognitive research [4]. However, we believe that it is necessary to go beyond the classic distinction between visual and non-visual students who do not need to use any type of visual support to work with abstract schemes [6, 8]. From our point of view, diagrams improve logical competence insofar as they allow us to integrate the linguistic, formal and visual processes that take place during inference. And in this sense, the perspective of the quantification of the predicate [5] will allow us to benefit from common sense, because it allows the return of the middle term as the basis of the inference. Although our research can only be considered a pilot study, it allows us to open new lines of research on how to improve the logical competence of our students. It would be very difficult to carry out an experimental design that would determine with certainty in which sense the improvement has depended on the specific use of our diagrams, on solving the propositional calculus in a syllogistic way or on the integration between natural language, formal languages and Marlo diagrams. However, in 2014 we obtained our best results without using any formal notation. Because of this, we believe that Marlo diagrams improve understanding of the logical form of propositions, as well as understanding the exact conditions under which argument patterns are valid or invalid. Since 2013, around 500 students have worked with these diagrams (Fig. 5).

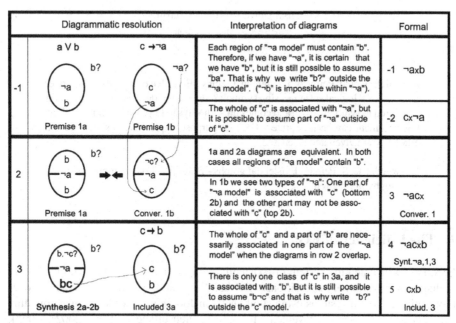

Fig. 5. $[(a \vee b) \wedge (c \rightarrow \neg a)] \rightarrow (c \rightarrow b)]$ solved in the Marlo diagram by recovering the middle term as the basis of the inference. Subscript x works like a conditional, but it means "totality"; his absence means "part".

References

1. Aznar, M.B.L.: Adiós a bArbArA y Venn. Lógica de predicados en el diagrama. Paideia Revista de Filosofía y didáctica filosófica **35**(102), 35–52 (2015)
2. Aznar, M.B.L.: Niños resolviendo silogismos con el Diagrama de Marlo [video file]. https://www.youtube.com/watch?v=6blBu1EN_EM
3. Aznar, M.B.L.: Visual reasoning in the Marlo diagram. In: Sato, Y., Shams, Z. (eds.) Ceur-ws.org, vol. 2116 (2018). http://ceur-ws.org/Vol-2116
4. González, G., Castro Solano, A., González, F.: Perfiles aptitudinales, estilos de pensamiento y rendimiento académico. Anuario de Investigaciones **15**, 33–41 (2008)
5. Jevons, W.: Pure Logic or the Logic of Quality. Stanford, London (1864)
6. Krutetskii, V.: A the Psychology of Mathematical Abilities in Schoolchildren. University of Chicago Press, Chicago (1976)
7. Marlo diagram Homepage. http://www.diagramademarlo.com. Accessed 11 Jan 2020
8. Meavilla Seguí, V.: Razonamiento visual y matemáticas. Sigma: revista de matemáti-cas=matematika aldizkaria **27**, 109–116 (2005)

Typical Cases Showing the Efficiency
of Existential Graphs

Takashi Sasaki$^{(\boxtimes)}$

Kansai University, Osaka, Japan
7sasaki@gmail.com

Abstract. Could Peirce?s Existential Graphs (EGs) have any advantage over propositional logical systems using symbols? Shin concludes that EGs are efficient compared to symbolic logic and comes up with ways to improve it. I consider how this argument can be interpreted. For that purpose, typical cases showing such efficiency are given and discussed.

Keywords: C. S. Peirce · Existential graphs · Diagram · Logical representation · Philosophy of notation

1 The Efficiency of EGs

C. S. Peirce invented the system of Existential Graphs (EGs) as ?a very simple system of diagrammatization of propositions? (CP 4.354). Could EGs have any advantage over propositional logical systems using symbols? Sun-Joo Shin answers this question affirmatively and proposes improvements to increase their efficiency (Shin 2002). I think that two-dimensional representation of EGs plays important role in its efficiency.

By utilizing such representations that are effectively realized by two-dimensional grouping, it is easy to regard diagrams within a flexible range as ?one diagram?. Such representations are examples of the multiple readings that Shin has discovered. Of particular importance in such cases are disjunction, conditional, and double cuts shown in Fig. 1.

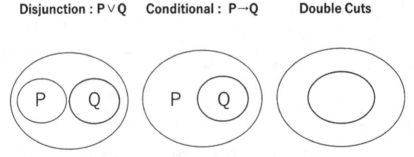

Fig. 1. The representation of disjunction, conditional, and double cuts using EGs

© Springer Nature Switzerland AG 2020
A.-V. Pietarinen et al. (Eds.): Diagrams 2020, LNAI 12169, pp. 494–497, 2020.
https://doi.org/10.1007/978-3-030-54249-8_42

2 Cases and Considerations

In this section, we will confirm the efficiency that can be achieved in the various stages of constructing proofs using EGs. In the proof, the following efficiency is realized.
Efficiency by being free from the order of the arrangement of signs.
(**Proof 1**) P?Q? Q?P

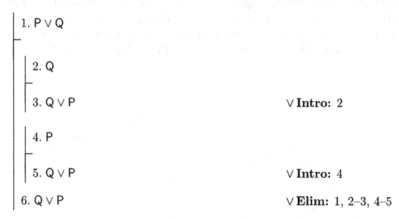

1. P ∨ Q

   2. Q

   3. Q ∨ P   ∨ **Intro:** 2

   4. P

   5. Q ∨ P   ∨ **Intro:** 4

6. Q ∨ P   ∨ **Elim:** 1, 2–3, 4–5

This proof related to the commutative law of disjunction is completed in six steps, including the rules of inference of the disjunction elimination and the disjunction introduction, and two sub-proofs related to disjunction introduction. The same proof using EGs is shown below.

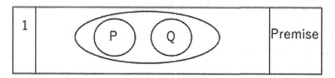

Fig. 2. Proof 1 using EGs

In this case, EGs complete the proof just by drawing the premise of inference. In other words, by drawing the premise of this inference with EGs, we can see the conclusion in the diagram. This is one of the things I call Free-Ride in EGs, whereby we automatically grasp the conclusion without inference. This Free-Ride in EGs leads to efficiencies, especially in proofs using ?Intro, ?Elim, and part of proofs using ?Elim in Fitch proof.

The reason why the Free-Ride in EGs is realised in these cases is that EGs are free from the restriction of the order of signs when they are arranged on a sheet. For example, in symbolic notation where symbols are arranged in a line, P?Q must be regarded as a different notation from Q?P, which is the conclusion. However, in EGs, they are just two ways in which P and Q can be juxtaposed and are considered the same. In Fig. 2, P and Q are side by side for convenience, but, as long as the two are juxtaposed, in EGs they are considered the same in principle, whether they are arranged horizontally, vertically, or diagonally.

Especially for proofs involving negation, such as Proof 1 and Fig. 1, it is important to realise this is the transition from parentheses to cuts (Sasaki 2018). This is because the transition realises a cut as a logical connective of negation and designation of the scope of negation in one notation, and also frees us of the restriction of arranging the signs in a line.

Utilizing logical connectives as figures. This is the efficiency realised by recognising some diagrams as a single figure in units of the area surrounded by the outermost cut and applying the transformation rules. In the following, examples are shown for some of the five transformation rules of the Alpha part of EGs (Figs. 3, 4 and 5).

$$A \rightarrow B \ \vdash A \rightarrow (B \lor C)$$

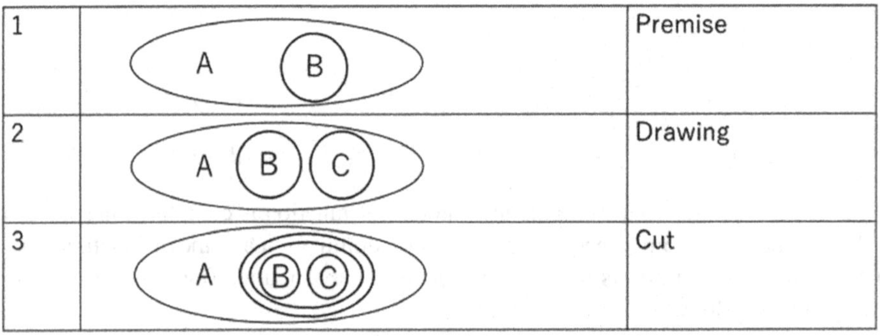

1		Premise
2		Drawing
3		Cut

Fig. 3. Drawing

$$A \leftrightarrow B, B \leftrightarrow C \ \vdash A \leftrightarrow C$$

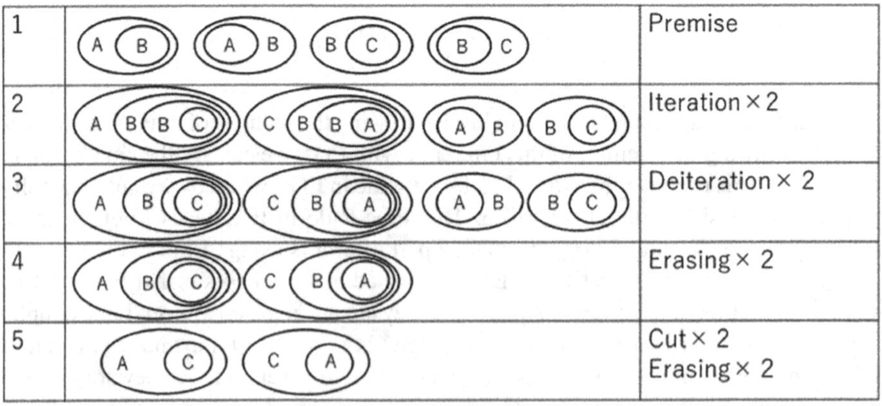

1		Premise
2		Iteration × 2
3		Deiteration × 2
4		Erasing × 2
5		Cut × 2 Erasing × 2

Fig. 4. Erasing

$\vdash (P \rightarrow (Q \rightarrow R)) \leftrightarrow ((P \wedge Q) \rightarrow R)$

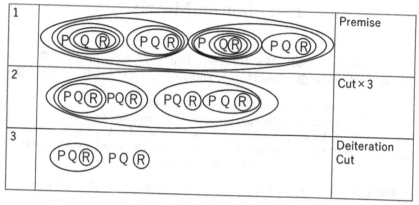

Fig. 5. De-iteration

In order to realize these transformations efficiently, it is necessary to draw or delete the entire diagram at once using a logical connective as a figure. Thus, in the practice of proofs using EGs, it is possible to obtain an efficiency that is difficult to realize with symbolic logic systems by effectively utilizing the two-dimensional grouping. In addition, it is speculated that EGs have their own advantages, such as the efficiency of making proofs including sub-proofs unnecessary. Many of the EGs? strengths are still awaiting elucidation, and I think they will continue to be of value for further research.

References

Shin, S.: The Iconic Logic of Peirce's Graphs. The MIT Press, Cambridge (2002)

Sasaki, T.: Multiple readings of existential graphs. In: Chapman, P., Stapleton, G., Moktefi, A., Perez-Kriz, S., Bellucci, F. (eds.) Diagrams 2018. LNCS (LNAI), vol. 10871, pp. 598–604. Springer, Cham (2018). https://doi.org/10.1007/978-3-319-91376-6_54

The Sung Diagram: Revitalizing the Eisenhower Matrix

Hannah Bratterud[1], Mac Burgess[2], Brittany Terese Fasy[2(✉)] [ID],
David L. Millman[2] [ID], Troy Oster[2], and Eunyoung (Christine) Sung[2] [ID]

[1] Purpose & Performance Group, Tulsa, OK, USA
hbratterud@purposeandperformancegroup.com
[2] Montana State University, Bozean, MT, USA
{mburgess,brittany.fasy,david.millman,christinesung}@montana.edu,
toster1011@me.com

Abstract. The Eisenhower Decision Matrix, credited to the task management system of US President Dwight Eisenhower, is a graphical diagram used in strategy and planning for tasks. This matrix, however, only provides four types of priorities. We identify a collection of scenarios in which the traditional matrix provides misleading suggestions and propose an extension to the matrix that addresses the misleading suggestions illustrated with examples and implementation in a web application.

Keywords: Eisenhower matrix · Prioritization

1 Introduction

I have two kinds of problems, the urgent and the important. The urgent are not important, and the important are never urgent.

– Dwight D. Eisenhower [5]

The Eisenhower matrix is a graphical diagram used in strategy and planning. The diagram contains four quadrants: important/urgent, important/non-urgent, non-important/urgent, and non-important/non-urgent; see Fig. 1a. The user of the matrix places their tasks into one of the four quadrants. In practice, the diagram is a useful tool to avoid the trap of spending time on urgent but unimportant tasks and not enough time on important and not urgent tasks.

Indeed, Covey [4] suggested marking the urgent/important tasks the highest priority, making time for the important/not urgent tasks and delegating urgent/important tasks. But, we believe that the simple matrix is missing a key detail: *the fit*. For example, consider the important/urgent task in which Christine is packing for a move in two days. The Eisenhower matrix would suggest that she start packing for the move. But, if Christine has the resources to hire a moving company, it does not require Christine's time and therefore should be delegated. We propose an extension of the Eisenhower matrix, called the *Sung Diagram*[1] that incorporates the fit for the agent that will perform the task.

---

[1] The diagram is named in honor of the coauthor who's upcoming move inspired the extension of the diagram.

© Springer Nature Switzerland AG 2020
A.-V. Pietarinen et al. (Eds.): Diagrams 2020, LNAI 12169, pp. 498–502, 2020.
https://doi.org/10.1007/978-3-030-54249-8_43

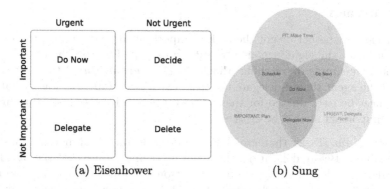

Fig. 1. Comparison of the Eisenhower decision matrix and the Sung Diagram.

2 Methods

We extend the Eisenhower Matrix to The Sung Diagram by adding *fit*. That is, if the agent (e.g., person, company, or group) is required for the task. By adding a third binary variable, a Venn diagram is a suitable representation; see Fig. 1.

First Dimension: Importance Important means "of great significance or value; likely to have a profound effect on success" [9]. How one defines importance, therefore, potentially affects success. Tasks can be important for various reasons: societal (e.g., curing cancer), individual (e.g., exercising regularly), organizational (e.g., marketing product), etc. Importance is about the *impact* of accomplishing the task; bringing intrinsic benefit to someone or some group.

Second Dimension: Urgency Urgency is defined as promptly requiring attention [11,13]. Often, task order is based on the urgency. In both the Eisenhower Matrix and the Sung Diagram, however, task order is not dictated by urgency alone. In the Sung Diagram, we require that no urgent task has a blocker; that is, any urgent task can begin immediately.

Forgotten Third Dimension: Fitness From the moving example, recall that packing is urgent and important yet she has the resources to hire help, which implies *she* does not need to do the packing. The example highlights the missing element of the Eisenhower Matrix: the fitness for the agent to complete the task. The decision for fitness has two components: (1) *Capability:* is the agent the most capable to accomplish this task? Certain tasks require training (e.g., home electrical work) or practice (e.g., a piano recital). In fact, evidence shows that aligning tasks with strengths or capabilities increases productivity and satisfaction [8,12]. In addition, the agent must not have the ability to delegate to someone else who is more trained or practiced. (2) *Ipseity:* does completing this task contribute to the agent's ipseity (sense of self)? The agent has values, be it explicitly stated in a mission statement or informally as goals. We ask the agent to assess: Does this task contribute to a "Big Hairy Audacious Goal" [3]?

2.1 Outcomes

After deciding whether or not the task is important, urgent, and fit, the task is assigned one of the eight regions (or *outcomes*); see Fig. 1b. The rules for the outcome have simple overarching principles: (1) *Delegation:* If the task is not fit, then the agent should delegate the task. (2) *Re-evaluation:* Tasks that are urgent must be re-evaluated for their importance and fitness. Tasks that are fit but not important should be critically evaluated.

Delegate Now. Tasks that are urgent and important, but not fit, must be delegated now. Before delegating, the agent must first ensure that the task is fit for the delegate. For example, suppose a person is notified that their renal unit has recently been sold, and that they have 14 days to move out. They walk into Joe the real estate agent's office, but Joe specializes in house commercial sales, not in rentals. He immediately calls his colleague who does specialize in rentals in order to make a referral for the person.

Do Now. Tasks that are urgent, important, and fit must be done now, by the agent. Consistent application of the Sung Diagram will limit the number of tasks that appear in this region at the same time. For example, a pre-med college student who has an exam tomorrow in their microbiology class will have to study. Studying is urgent, important, and fit (as no one can do it for them).

Delegate Next. Tasks that are urgent, but not important nor fit, must be delegated next. First, you need to assess: do you know the right person to accomplish this task? If not, this task should be deleted. For example, if you are a researcher and asked to review a research paper in a field only tangentially related to your own, this task is neither important nor fit *for you*, but is usually urgent. You can decline to review the paper, or you can assign this to your graduate student as a learning experience to prepare for being an independent scholar.

Do Next. Tasks that are urgent and fit, but not important, must be done next, by the agent. An effort should be made to get all of the tasks in both the 'Do Now' and 'Do Next' regions as soon as possible. For example, the pre-med student may want to respond to phone notifications. The task is urgent and fit. However, we include a caveat: these tasks are not important, so the fitness much be re-evaluated first. If re-evaluation finds that they are not fit (such as the phone notifications [1,10]), then these tasks should be deleted.

Schedule. Tasks that are important and fit, but not urgent, must be scheduled. Tasks in this region are discussed exhaustively by Covey [4]. For example, if your life goal is to write a novel, but your job is a computer programmer at a start-up company, you must block-off time to work on the novel.

Plan. For tasks that are important, but not fit nor urgent, you must create a plan for how they should be accomplished. The first step of this planning is to decide who is the best person to accomplish this task? If the task is an easy one to accomplish and your current set of 'Do Now' and 'Do Next' tasks are short, you can be the one to do this. However, most of the tasks in the 'Plan' region can be delegated. For example, if you often travel to meet donors for your institution and have an assistant that knows your travel preferences and calendar, then booking your trips takes a few minutes for them to plan.

Delete. Tasks that are not urgent, important, nor fit should be deleted. The hours in the day are limited, and some things must be let go. For example, suppose a friend recommends that you ride on a roller coaster at a local amusement park, but you are afraid of heights.

2.2 Interactive Diagram

We created an application[2] implementing the Sung Diagram. To use the application, enter the task name, select appropriate check boxes (important/urgent/fit), and click "Submit". The task name will be added to a visualization. The application was written in JavaScript and using the React framework [14]. React was chosen as it is an industry standard tool for front end web development and it supports continued feature development. The application was initialized with Create React App [6], which removes boilerplate setup in a React application. The visualization is implemented using libraries Venn.js [7] and D3.js [2]. The libraries enable the rendering and layout of area proportional Venn diagrams.

Acknowledgements. We thank Luke Freeman and Chris Province for their thoughtful discussions. We also thank our friends and family who have provided inspiration for the numerous examples scattered throughout this paper.

References

1. Alter, A.: Irresistible: The Rise of Addictive Technology and the Business of Keeping us Hooked. Penguin Books, New York (2018)
2. Bostock, M., Davies, J., Heer, J., Ogievetsky, V.: D3.js. https://d3js.org
3. Collins, J., Porras, J.I.: Built to Last: Successful Habits of Visionary Companies. Random House, London (2005)
4. Covey, S.R.: The 7 Habits of Highly Effective People: Powerful Lessons in Personal Change, 25th anniversary edn. Simon & Schuster (2013)
5. Eisenhower, D.D.: Address at the Second Assembly of the World Council of Churches (1954). Eisenhower attributes this to a former college president
6. Facebook: Create React App. https://github.com/facebook/create-react-app
7. Frederickson, B.: Venn.js. https://github.com/benfred/venn.js/
8. Strengths meta-analysis report (2015). https://www.gallup.com/cliftonstrengths/en/269615/strengths-meta-analysis-2015.aspx, clifton Strengths by Gallup
9. Importance: Lexico, powered by Oxford (2002). https://www.lexico.com/
10. Lanier, J.: Ten Arguments for Deleting Your Social Media Accounts Right Now (2018)

---

[2] The app is hosted at https://sungdiagram.herokuapp.com/. The code is available at https://github.com/TostySSB/sungdiagram and is released under the MIT license.

11. Reddi, B.A.J., Carpenter, R.H.S.: The influence of urgency on decision time. Nat. Neurosci. **3**(8), 827–830 (2000)
12. Rigoni, B., Asplund, J.: Global study: ROI for strengths-based development. In: Workplace. Gallup, September 2016
13. Urgent: Merriam-Webster Dictionary (2002). http://www.merriam-webster.com
14. Walke, J., Facebook, Community: React. https://reactjs.org

Marlo's Networks of Expectations in the Classroom: A Tool for Heterogeneous Reasoning

Marcos Bautista López Aznar(✉) ⓘ

Huelva University, Huelva, Spain
marlodiagram@gmail.com

Abstract. In this article we present some results obtained between 2016 and 2019 using Marlo's expectations networks (M.E.N.) as a tool in the teaching of logic in a secondary school in Huelva, Spain. M.E.N is a Bayesian tree structure implemented with logical nodes in which the propositions can be encoded as true, false, probable or uncertain. These networks have been used with students be-tween the ages of 14 and 18 to solve problems of first-order logic and mathematical probability. The networks, which have been developed in parallel with the Marlo diagram, represent in an exhaustive and heterogeneous manner all combinations of variables that can take place in the universe of discourse. Students make inferences by interpreting, on the one hand, the spatial information offered by the coordinates of the variables within the system, and on the other hand, the labels of natural and formal languages. But in addition, the truth values of each of these nodes can be expressed by perfectly synchronized numerical and chromatic scales. From these heterogeneous forms of graphic representation, we have created digital infographics that can be used on laptops and mobile phones in the classroom. From daily practice with these tools, we verify that some students with mathematical learning disabilities can reason in a surprisingly fluid and rigorous manner using colors. It is also notable that some of the best mathematical students cannot reason using colors. In any case, all students (chromatic, based on numbers and mixed) benefit from the diagrams.

Keywords: Logic diagrams · Diagrammatic reasoning · Visual reasoning

1 Marlo's Expectation Networks (M.E.N.)

Marlo Expectations networks [2] allow visualizing how truth (activation) and falsehood (inhibition) propagate through the nodes of a network structure configured as a tree diagram. They are inspired by neural networks that process information in parallel and accept uncertainty as part of the argumentative processes. Because of this, it is easy to use abductive reasoning with them. The sets formed by associations of *Or* nodes, *Object* nodes and *And* nodes are the basis of inferences in the more complex versions of the network. An *Object* node represents a unique and distinct combination of variables that may be present (True) or absent (False) here and now. An *Or* node represents a more

© Springer Nature Switzerland AG 2020
A.-V. Pietarinen et al. (Eds.): Diagrams 2020, LNAI 12169, pp. 503–506, 2020.
https://doi.org/10.1007/978-3-030-54249-8_44

general and less specific combination of variables than those represented in the *Object* nodes. For instance, if it is true that there are cheap pencils (*Object* node A = +1 = blue) and expensive pencils (*Object* node B = +1 = blue), then it is true that there are pencils (*Or* node = +1 = blue). Moreover, if it is false that there are pencils (Or node = −1 = red), then it will be false that there are cheap pencils (*Object* node A = −1 = red) and it will also be false that there are expensive pencils (Object node B = −1 = red). When the *And* node is false, we can infer that we don't have *Object A* or we don't have *Object B*. And in this case, all we know about A and B is that both are probably false (−0,5 = orange), despite the fact that one of them may finally be true. All the propagation laws of activation and inhibition by network nodes can be easily deduced from Fig. 1.

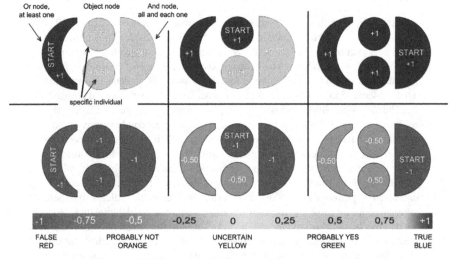

Fig. 1. Laws of inference within a set.

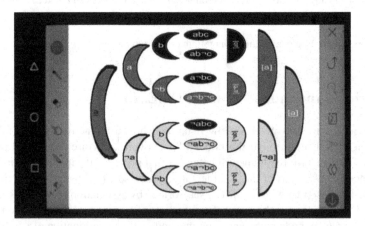

Fig. 2. Syllogism in the Alpha system solved on a mobile phone.

As we can see in Fig. 2, the objects are grouped together into sets and, in turn, the groups are grouped together into the system we call Alpha. We developed these networks in the classroom as a tool that allowed fifteen-year-olds to solve syllogisms on computing devices using colors in 2016. Later we code the colors using numbers.

In 2017 we created a simpler version of the networks in which the logical connectives are represented by eliminating certain nodes from the network: in the exercise of Fig. 3, the network numbers indicate which premises eliminate the black nodes).

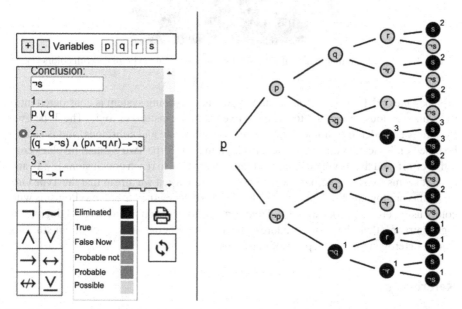

Fig. 3. Exercise of propositional logic solved in a logical tree diagram of Marlo. Pepe Amoedo infographic design.

Based on our experience of the past four years using networks of expectations in the classroom, students can be classified as chromatic, mathematician and mixed, depending on the way they solve the problems. Remember that the use of colors in the teaching of logic is not something new. It goes back at least to Ramon Lull [5] and was used by Lewis Carroll, Charles Sanders Peirce and, more recently, Barwise and Etchemendy's Tarski's world [3], and Ferdinando Cavaliere [4], among others (Fig. 4).

Krutetskii [6] has already made a classification of students in "visual" and "non-visual": Visual students have a marked inclination towards the visual aspects of Mathematics and, consequently, make use of visual reasoning; Non-visual students do not need to use any type of visual support to work with abstract schemes. The intermediate or harmonic group would be formed by students who make a balanced use of visual and analytical reasoning [7]. Perhaps our chromatic students correspond to the so-called visual students, while the ones we call mathematicians are the analytical ones. However, the speed with which some chromatic students make inferences, as opposed to the precision of those who use numbers, reminds us of the old classification of reasoning systems

Fig. 4. Student with mathematical learning disabilities solving syllogisms with colors [1].

in Type One and Two. Traditionally, the Type One reasoning system is considered intuitive, unconscious and is said to use cognitive shortcuts instead of logic. The Type Two System is considered biologically more recent, deliberate and conscious, and is said to be based on logic. Cognitive researchers claim that the Type Two System involves cognitive effort, and that is why it is slower than System One to reach conclusions [8]. In any case, it seems to us that perhaps we are not quite fair when we affirm that the Type One System is not logical. Students with acalculia who have learned to solve syllogisms with colors using our networks are logical and force us to question the traditional dogmas of logocentrism. It will be easier to address the diversity of cognitive styles of our students from a heterogeneous conception of reasoning.

References

1. Aznar, M.B.L.: Visual reasoning with colors in tree diagrams [video file] (2018). https://www.youtube.com/watch?v=Bk4uFzhVYqk
2. Aznar, M.B.L.: Redes de expectativas lógico-matemáticas, una herramienta para el desarrollo del razonamiento. In: Libro de actas VIII Congreso Iberoamericano de Educación Matemática, CIBEM, pp. 283–293. FESPM, Madrid (2018). http://cibem.org/images/site/LibroActasCI BEM/ComunicacionesLibroActas_Posters.pdf
3. Barwise, J., & Etchemendy, J.: The Language of First Order Logic: Including the Program Tarski's World 3.0 CSLI Lecture notes, vol. 23 (1991)
4. Cavaliere, F.A.: Diagrammatic bridge between standard and non-standard logics: the numerical segment. In: Moktefi, A., Shin, S.-J. (eds.) Visual Reasoning with Diagrams, pp. 105–116. Springer, Basel (2013). https://doi.org/10.1007/978-3-0348-0600-8_5
5. de la Torre Gómez, A.: El método cartesiano y la geometría analítica. Matemáticas enseñanza universitaria **14**, 75–87 (2006)
6. Krutetskii, V.A.: The Psychology of Mathematical Abilities in Schoolchildren. University of Chicago Press, Chicago (1976)
7. Meavilla Seguí, V.: Razonamiento visual y matemáticas. Sigma: revista de matemáticas = matematika aldizkaria **27**, 109–116 (2005)
8. Payá Santos, C., Delgado Morán, J.J.: Uncertainty of dimensional analysis of intelligence. URVIO Revista Latinoamericana de Estudios de Seguridad **21**, 225–239 (2017). https://doi.org/10.17141/urvio.21.2017.2962

Experimenting with Diagrams in Mathematics

Michał Sochański[✉] [ID]

Adam Mickiewicz University, Poznań, Poland
michal.sochanski@amu.edu.pl

Abstract. In this paper a way of understanding differences between diagrams is proposed, based on how their spatial properties relate to conceptual content they refer to and on how this content is assigned to diagrams. It is also argued that some uses of one of the distinguished classes of diagrams can be construed as a specific kind of experiment.

Keywords: Philosophy of mathematics · Diagrammatic reasoning

1 Introduction

Literature on mathematical diagrams points at various properties that characterize diagrammatic representation on epistemological, semiotic and methodological levels. In this paper, a way of understanding differences among diagrams themselves is proposed, based on how spatial properties of diagrams relate to conceptual content they refer to and on how this content is assigned to them. Focus will be put on the distinct characteristics of one class of diagrams that can be called "conventional", in particular it is argued that some of their uses can be construed as a specific kind of experiment. Being aware of an ongoing discussion concerning diagrammatic (or spatial) aspects of mathematical notation, I will focus on diagrams only, and assume a "working" definition of a diagram as a representation in which meaning is assigned not only to symbols but to such physical marks as lines, points or colors and two-dimensional relations between them.

2 Two Classes of Mathematical Diagrams

The distinction to be introduced attempts to explain how diagrams of branches of mathematics like geometry and topology, that originate in analysis of inherently spatial concepts, differ from diagrams that are constructed in an arbitrary way in order to represent concepts that are not spatial. Mathematical concepts represented by diagrams of the first type evolve as idealization of spatial properties of physical objects – topological properties and relations ("X lies left of Y", "X is inside Y", "X and Y cross"), geometric properties of metric character (length, measure of an angle) or other characteristics of shapes or processes that occur in space. Those diagrams are characterized by the fact that topological relations between their elements denote actual topological properties of the represented mathematical objects. This is not intended to mean that spatial language

© Springer Nature Switzerland AG 2020
A.-V. Pietarinen et al. (Eds.): Diagrams 2020, LNAI 12169, pp. 507–510, 2020.
https://doi.org/10.1007/978-3-030-54249-8_45

actually refers to physical objects, but rather to precise formulations or idealizations of spatial concepts, such as point, surface or distance. Whether a diagram belongs to this class or not is a matter of degree, as various mathematical concepts idealize physical properties in different ways and to a different degree (e.g. topology studies properties that do not change under continuous transformation and disregard metric properties). In case of diagrams of plane geometry and knot theory this reference to spatial properties is perhaps most direct. Topological properties are also directly referred to when diagrams are used to study e.g. planar graphs or wallpaper groups. In turn, diagrams used in non-Euclidean geometry or general topology may refer to spatial concepts in a less direct way (via further conceptualization and idealization).

Diagrams of the second kind, which I propose to call "conventional" diagrams, are constructed in order to study mathematical concepts that are not spatial, but which the mathematician attempts to investigate with use of a suitable diagrammatic representation. For that purpose, selected properties of those concepts are translated into a spatial language in order to gain insight into them with help of the known advantages of diagrammatic representation, such as its ability to grant free rides, aspect shift or provide simultaneous display of information [7, 8]. In this way, and in contrast to the diagrams of the first class, the direction in which mathematical practice proceeds is from concepts to visualization. In this case diagrams are used as a tool and the choice of spatial language is arbitrary, in the sense that it may be constructed or chosen in any way the mathematician wants, as long as it adequately represents the investigated mathematical properties and as long as it is fruitful. In that sense diagrams are used in a conventional way. Examples include Euler and Venn diagrams, diagrams used in mathematical analysis or graph theory, as well as various computer-generated images (examples are discussed in more depth in the next section).

The distinction sketched above can be juxtaposed with the issue of iconicity of mathematical diagrams, that is the question whether they somehow resemble the represented mathematical object. One could consider such resemblance to be either a direct, pictorial one or structural resemblance understood as homomorphism between elements of the diagram and appropriate properties of mathematical objects. It is a matter of dispute, what could be resembled by the topological properties of diagrams of the first type discussed. On the other hand, both types of diagrams can be argued to structurally resemble their subject matter (see e.g. discussion in [1] and [6]). However, diagrams of the second type are also conventional in the sense that choice of the spatial language is arbitrary and in that sense shapes and topological relations relate to the represented object by convention. This issue has been discussed in [5] where it is distinguished between *resemblance diagrams*, which "have a direct likeness to the physical objects that the corresponding mathematical concepts are supposed to model" and *abstract diagrams* which are "only meaningful if the mathematical content they represent is understood through a particular conceptual map"[1]. In [4] Marcus Giaquinto suggests in turn that mathematical diagrams "belong to a spectrum, depending on the extent to which they depend on resemblance on the one hand and on conventions of representation on the other hand" [4]. This interesting debate will not be taken further in this paper, I believe that it would require a more in-depth discussion of particular viewpoints on the nature of mathematical objects.

---

[1] In [5] it is proposed to take Cartesian diagrams as the third subclass of mathematical diagrams.

3   Experimental Nature of "Conventional" Diagrams

In the remaining part of the paper I will focus on an aspect of mathematical practice which involves creation of a "conventional" diagram in order to investigate properties of non-spatial mathematical concepts. Examples of several types of "conventional" diagrams will be discussed, followed by comments on experimental nature of such practice.

Firstly, "conventional" diagrams can be simple arrangements of "traditional" symbolic marks in space in a way that may make it possible to notice patterns and discover new facts about the investigated objects. Patterns or subsets of the arranged elements can then be marked by colors or other visual means, in order to make it easier for the eye to notice them. The experimental element in this case is just the simple act of arranging or coloring elements of the diagram. Examples include dot diagrams in number theory, noticing patterns in Pascal's triangle or the construction of Ulam spiral which led to the discovery that primes often occur on diagonals of the diagram[2]. Secondly, properties of the investigated object may be translated into a well-known type of "conventional" diagram. In this way sets can be represented by Euler or Venn diagrams, relations by diagrams of graph theory and functions by Cartesian diagrams[3], to name the most common examples. In all those cases selected topological properties of the diagram represent properties of non-spatial concepts[4]. Thirdly, a new spatial language may be created or "tried out". Such situation often takes place in case of computer visualizations which are used to explore large amounts of "mathematical data". Examples include number theory, where various colored diagrams are used to investigate distributions of digits in expansions or finite and infinite series and summations [3] as well as fractal theory, in which visual techniques are used to study the behavior of iterations (one famous example is the visualization of Mandelbrot's set which is in fact an example of creative use a Cartesian diagram). In order to investigate large amounts of such data, e.g. large body of examples that may serve to confirm (or falsify) conjectures like Riemann hypothesis or Goldbach's conjecture, computational mathematics also uses standard charts used in data analysis like scatterplots or bar charts, as well as other novel visualization techniques.

The experimental nature of all the above mentioned uses of "conventional" diagrams consists firstly in the freedom of "trying out" new types of spatial language and assigning mathematical meaning to its elements, in order to gain best insight into the investigated object. Other aspects of such practice also have an experimental flavour: it is not known in advance what the effect of the translation of mathematical properties into spatial ones will be; further, some spatial properties of the diagram may strike the mathematician

---

[2] It should be noted that Stanisław Ulam came up with this way of representing the set of natural numbers while playing around with a pencil and sheet of paper. This fits well the described practice of "experimenting with representation".

[3] Cartesian diagrams are various visualizations that make use of the Cartesian coordinate system to represent objects that can be characterized by two numeric values such as a function with single real argument and value, two numeric properties of an object or a set of pairs of real numbers which satisfy a certain property $P(x,y)$.

[4] It may also happen that the translation is made into a geometric language, e.g. when properties of numbers are investigated after representing them as line segments or areas. In this case the geometric diagram should also be treated as "conventional" diagram.

as surprising, inspire further research and gain new interpretation (those could be unexpected patterns in the visualization of Mandelbrot's set, decimal expansions or Ulam spiral). This understanding of a "mathematical experiment" differs from experimentation understood as manipulation of representations that was present, among other, in writings of Peirce. It is also different from the concept of mathematical experimentation as the use of computation to analyse examples, test new ideas and search for patterns as described in [2]. However, visual investigations that are aspects of experiments in that sense are often also experiments in the sense described in this paper. The practice of "trying out spatial representations" can be called experimental on a broad understanding of the term "experiment". In particular, this does not have to mean that such practices are not *a priori*, no specific analogies with experiments in the natural sciences also need to be involved. However, it seems that it is possible to consider creation of new diagrams as a specific kind of mathematical practice that requires skills in semiotics and good acquaintance with different types of visual languages and available spatial properties.

References

1. Barceló Aspeitia, A.A.: Mathematical pictures. In: Chapman, P., Stapleton, G., Moktefi, A., Perez-Kriz, S., Bellucci, F. (eds.) Diagrams 2018. LNCS (LNAI), vol. 10871, pp. 137–147. Springer, Cham (2018). https://doi.org/10.1007/978-3-319-91376-6_15
2. Borwein, J., Bailey, D.: Mathematics by Experiment. Plausible Reasoning in the 21St Century. A K Peters Ltd., Natick (2004)
3. Borwein, P., Jörgenson, L.: Visible structures in number theory. Am. Math. Mon. **108**(10), 897–910 (2001)
4. Giaquinto, M.: Visual Thinking in Mathematics. Oxford University Press, Oxford (2007)
5. Johansen, M.W., Misfeldt, M., Pallavicini, J.L.: A typology of mathematical diagrams. In: Chapman, P., Stapleton, G., Moktefi, A., Perez-Kriz, S., Bellucci, F. (eds.) Diagrams 2018. LNCS (LNAI), vol. 10871, pp. 105–119. Springer, Cham (2018). https://doi.org/10.1007/978-3-319-91376-6_13
6. Macbeth, D.: Seeing how it goes: paper-and-pencil reasoning in mathematical practice. Philosophia Mathematica (III) **20**, 58–85 (2012)
7. Shimojima, A.: Semantic Properties of Diagrams and Their Cognitive Potentials. CSLI Publications, Stanford (2015)
8. Stenning, K.: Seeing Reason: Image and Language in Learning to Think. Oxford University Press, Oxford (2002)

Historio-Graphy

Amirouche Moktefi[(⊠)]

Tallinn University of Technology, Tallinn, Estonia
amirouche.moktefi@taltech.ee

Abstract. It is common to meet with timelines in popular history books. Yet, historians seldom acknowledge the usage of such diagrams in their practice. Rather than a general prejudice against diagrams, we argue that timelines suffer from their embodiment of biases that do not match with widespread standards of historical writing. For instance, the linearity of timelines suggests continuity between events that might actually be disconnected. Timelines visualise a specific narrative and hide historian's act of selection. To exhibit this hidden face, one needs to depict the events that have not been selected in the narrative. For the purpose, we introduce a scheme that can be used to visualise the narrative's construction. An application to the historiography of modern logic is provided.

Keywords: Timeline · Historiography · Chronology · History of logic

1 The Historian's Timelines

Recent literature shows how timelines may be used in historical research both for discovery and exposition [2, 3]. Timelines are scientific instruments at the disposal of historians [8]. Yet, the latter tend to dismiss timelines in their actual practices:

Strangely, despite the "spatial turn" in the humanities […], this recent wave of research on diagrams has not yet reached the shores of history. No one objects to using timelines as pedagogical aids […] But, outside the classroom, we find resistance to the idea that manipulating diagrams might yield genuine historical insight. Timelines, it seems, are meant for history teachers, not historians. [2, p. 19]

We argue that there are good reasons for this dismissal. Indeed, timelines suffer from an overspecification that carries misconceptions about historical research.

Timelines commonly consist of a directed line on which historical events are attributed spots. It is easy to understand their force when it comes to visualizing sequences of discrete events. Indeed, the spots do not merely represent the relations between the events; they *have* those relations [7, p. 610]. For instance, a spot *A precedes* a spot *B* on the timeline the same way event *A precedes* event *B* in time (Fig. 1). This *matchedness* make it possible to visually obtain new information: from the fact that *A* precedes *B* and *B* precedes *C*, one may observe that *A* precedes *C*.

© Springer Nature Switzerland AG 2020
A.-V. Pietarinen et al. (Eds.): Diagrams 2020, LNAI 12169, pp. 511–514, 2020.
https://doi.org/10.1007/978-3-030-54249-8_46

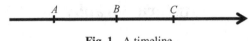

Fig. 1. A timeline

2 Fallacies

Timelines are appropriate for the representation of ordered discrete events, such as genealogies, lists of Queens and Kings, chronologies of life events, etc. However, the discipline of history does not merely order events of the past, it also attempts to connect and explain them. In this respect, timelines suggest more than there is and may lead the historian to fallacious conclusions.

A fallacy, that we may name the 'continuity fallacy', consists in connecting historical events A and B merely on the ground that A precedes B, as suggested by the positions of their spots on the timeline (Fig. 2). Another fallacy that we may call the 'direction fallacy', results from the assumption that historical events are directed towards us. This is shown by the arrow in the timelines (Fig. 3) and may be interpreted in terms of determinism or progress. Yet, in both fallacies, other paths may exist.

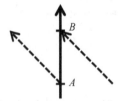

Fig. 2. The continuity fallacy

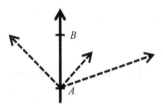

Fig. 3. The direction fallacy

These fallacies are often committed in intellectual histories that select past events from a modern standpoint and favor logical over historical connections between past events. As such, they produce a distorted image of science as a cumulative enterprise. Thomas Kuhn famously opened his seminal *The Structure of Scientific Revolutions* with a discussion of the role of history in the shaping of the image of science and praised the ongoing historiographical revolution among historians of science:

> The result of all these doubts and difficulties is a historiographic revolution in the study of science, though one that is still in its early stages. Gradually, and often without entirely realizing they are doing so, historians of science have begun to ask new sorts of questions and to trace different, and often less than cumulative, developmental lines for the sciences. Rather than seeking the permanent contributions of an older science to our present vantage, they attempt to display the historical integrity of that science in its own time [...] Seen through the works that result, [...] science does not seem altogether the same enterprise as the one discussed by writers in the old historiographic tradition. By implication, these historical studies suggest the possibility of a new image of science. [4, p. 3]

This new historiographic tradition does not aim at recording the advancements of science. It rather accounts for scientific activity in its context. The timeline's overspecification does not match well with this agenda. Yet, it can be used with benefit to exhibit the historian's selected narrative.

3   Visualizing the Narrative

Timelines order the events they depict and, hence, suggest that those events were steps directed towards us rather than mere historical moments. They cannot be blamed for visualizing a specific narrative which is constructed by the historian himself. However, timelines hide that construction process and the historian's act of selection. To exhibit this hidden face, one needs to visualize the historical moments that have not been selected as part of the narrative and which, hence, are kept "out of the line". For the purpose, we introduce a scheme that can be employed in historiography to visualize the narrative and its construction (first used in [6]).

Let there be a historical narrative that accounts for the development of ideas in a specific area of knowledge. Imagine two periods separated by an event B that produces the shift from one tradition to another (Fig. 4). To exhibit the construction of the narrative, we spread historical moments on two-dimensions as shown in (Fig. 5). The two traditions are exhibited on parallel dotted lines. The red line indicates the historian's narrative. It goes on the first tradition before moving to the second at the occurrence of event B. The points outside the red line are not selected by the historian.

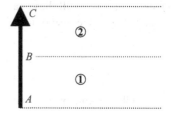

Fig. 4. 1D timeline

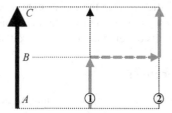

Fig. 5. 2D timeline

In particular, the red line which denotes the historical narrative divides the space into two parts. Above the line, one meets with teachers, popularisers and conservatives who work on outdated ideas while their colleagues moved to a more 'advanced' tradition. Under the line, we find the land of precursors cherished by intellectual historians [5]. It contains actors, ideas and events that anticipate the standard narrative.

This scheme clearly shows how the historian selects a narrative and keeps out events that are not within his purpose. If history cannot be written without a narrative, then these schemes are useful to convey to the eye the narrative and its cost. Let us consider, for illustration, the historiography of modern logic.

4   Towards Modern Logic

Two periods are commonly distinguished in the 'mathematization' of logic: first, George Boole introduced a mathematical theory of logic in 1847. Then, Gottlob Frege's 1879 ideography opened the way to the logic of mathematics (Fig. 6). This account (and its timeline) invites priority disputes on the paternity of modern logic [10].

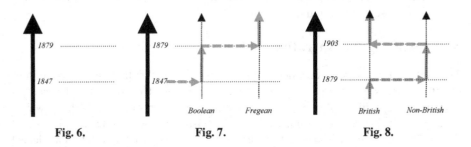

Fig. 6.   Fig. 7.   Fig. 8.

To visualise the construction of this narrative, we appeal to our 2D timeline. The two traditions are on parallel dotted lines and the narrative is in red. It opens with the advent of the Boole, 'jumps' to Frege in 1879 and stays there (Fig. 7). It suggests the end of the Boolean tradition with the advent of Frege while it actually continued well beyond. A variation is obtained by making the lines stand for geographical areas (Fig. 8). The traditional narrative indicates work by British Booleans, then leaves in 1879 to mark research abroad. It comes back to Britain in the early 1900s with the arrival of Bertrand Russell. We observe a gap that falsely suggests a decline of British logic in that period. It is, hence, unsurprising that post-1879 logicians, who were both Boolean and British (such as Lewis Carroll and Hugh MacColl [1]), lacked exposition in literature since they suffered from the biases exhibited by (Fig. 7) and (Fig. 8). To fill these gaps, it is necessary to pay attention to the social dimensions that shaped the discipline of logic, both in its development and its circulation [9].

References

1. Abeles, F.F., Moktefi, A.: Hugh MacColl and Lewis Carroll: crosscurrents in geometry and logic. Philosophia Scientiae **15**(1), 55–76 (2011)
2. Champagne, M.: Diagrams of the past: how timelines can aid the growth of historical knowledge. Cogn. Semiot. **9**(1), 11–44 (2016)
3. Ciric, D.: Design-data intelligence: Microhistories and diagrammatic reasoning. In: Scale of Design: From Micro to Macro Conference Proceedings, Belgrade: Strand - Sustainable Urban Society Association, pp. 155–171 (2016)
4. Kuhn, T.: The Structure of Scientific Revolutions, 3rd edn. Chicago University Press, Chicago (1996)
5. May, K.O.: Historiographic vices II Priority chasing. Historia Math. **2**, 316 (1975)
6. Moktefi, A.: Lewis carroll and the British nineteenth-century logicians on the barber shop problem. In: Proceedings of the CSHPM, vol. 20, pp. 189–199 (2007)
7. Moktefi, A.: Is Euler's circle a symbol or an icon? Sign Syst. Stud. **43**(4), 597–615 (2015)
8. Moktefi, A.: Diagrams as scientific instruments. In: Benedek, A., Veszelszki, A. (eds.) Virtual Reality – Real Visuality, pp. 81–89. Peter Lang, Frankfurt am Main (2017)
9. Moktefi, A.: The social shaping of modern logic. In: Gabbay, D., et al. (eds.) Natural Arguments: A Tribute to John Woods, pp. 503–520. College Publications, London (2019)
10. Peckhaus, V.: Was George Boole really the 'father' of modern logic? In: Gasser, J. (ed.) A Boole anthology, pp. 271–285. Kluwer, Dordrecht (2000)

A Semiotic-Conceptual Analysis of Euler and Hasse Diagrams

Uta Priss$^{(\boxtimes)}$

Zentrum für erfolgreiches Lehren und Lernen,
Ostfalia University, Wolfenbüttel, Germany
www.upriss.org.uk

Abstract. Semiotic-Conceptual Analysis (SCA) considers diagrams (and in general any signs) as consisting of representamens, denotations and interpretations which supports investigating these three components individually and jointly. A core notion for diagram research is "observability" which refers to logically valid statements that can be visually extracted from diagrams. This notion is included into the SCA vocabulary and discussed with respect to Euler and Hasse diagrams.

1 Introduction

Semiotic-Conceptual Analysis (SCA) is inspired by the theory of semiotics of the American philosopher Charles S. Peirce and uses some of his terminology [2]. SCA notions, however, are mathematically defined and thus, in some sense, more abstract than their philosophical counterparts. The purpose of SCA is to investigate questions of what and how something is represented and why certain representations have advantages over others under some circumstances. As an example, SCA is applied to Euler and Hasse diagrams in this short paper. Definition 1 summarises the core definitions of SCA. Further detail cannot be provided here and is presented by Priss [2].

Definition 1. For a set R (called *representamens*), a set D (called *denotations*) and a set I of partial functions $i : R \twoheadrightarrow D$ (called *interpretations*) a *semiotic relation* S is a relation $S \subseteq I \times R \times D$. A triple $(i, r, d) \in S$ with $i(r) = d$ is called a *sign*.

For a semiotic relation S with a tolerance relation $\sim_D$, a tolerance relation $\sim_{D \cap R}$, an equivalence relation $\approx_R$ and a partial function $f : R \twoheadrightarrow D$:

- (i_1, r_1, d_1) and (i_2, r_2, d_2) are *synonyms* $\iff d_1 \sim_D d_2$;
- (i_1, r_1, d_1) and (i_2, r_2, d_2) are *polysemous* $\iff r_1 \approx_R r_2$ and $d_1 \sim_D d_2$;
- $(i, r, d) \in S$ is an *icon* $\iff r \sim_{D \cap R} d$ (i.e., describable by a unary relation)
- $(i, r, d) \in S$ is an *index* $\iff f(r) = d$ (i.e., describable by a binary relation)
- $(i, r, d) \in S$ is a *symbol* $\Leftrightarrow (i, r, d)$ is neither icon nor index.

© Springer Nature Switzerland AG 2020
A.-V. Pietarinen et al. (Eds.): Diagrams 2020, LNAI 12169, pp. 515–519, 2020.
https://doi.org/10.1007/978-3-030-54249-8_47

Representamens are physical representations of signs. Denotations are meanings of signs and in SCA presented as formalised concepts. Interpretations usually encode a context (time and place) of when a sign is used and possibly further information about a sign producer. A tolerance relation is a mathematical expression of similarity. An example of f would be an algorithm for calculating d from r, instead of a relationship between representamens and denotations that changes with every interpretation.

Several (partial ordering) relations can be defined for signs, for example, *implications* (based on logical implications amongst denotations) and *observations* (derived from compound representamens). For a sign a to be observable from a sign b, the representamen of a has to be derivable from the representamen of b by using some kind of visual algorithm or visual moves. Observability was motivated by Stapleton et al.'s definition [4]. Ideally, only logically true statements should be observed, thus if a sign a is an observation from a sign b then $b \implies a$ should hold. *Translations* amongst signs are morphisms that should preserve meaning in some form. They can lead to *translational loss* or *gain* because, for example, denotations can be modelled using different conceptual models and signs with equivalent denotations can produce different observations.

SCA starts with a qualitative framework (as in Sect. 2) that roughly characterises how these notions apply to an example. It then continues with more detailed formal analyses, in particular with respect to observations and translations. Both of which are only sketched in this short paper.

2   Applying the SCA Framework to Venn and Euler Diagrams

Venn and Euler diagrams are a means for graphically representing sets and their intersections and unions. A more detailed introduction is, for example, provided by Rodgers [3]. Venn diagrams show all possible intersections for a set of sets. Euler diagrams are similar to Venn diagrams but exclude zones which are known to be empty. The following terminology applies to Venn and Euler diagrams in this paper: Venn and Euler diagrams consist of closed *curves* which have *labels*. *Minimal regions* are the smallest areas in a diagram which are surrounded by edges and are not divided further. *Regions* are sets of minimal regions. *Zones* are maximal regions that are within a set of curves and outwith the remaining curves. *Existential import* means that zones must correspond to non-empty sets.

The reason for distinguishing minimal regions and zones is that zones are the smallest set-theoretically meaningful areas in a diagram whereas minimal regions are the smallest visible areas in a diagram. In a *well-formed* Euler diagram, zones correspond to minimal regions. Further conditions for well-formed Euler diagrams are, for example, prohibiting more than 2 curves to cross in a point and curves to intersect themselves. Formalising and characterising well-formed Euler diagrams is not trivial. Flower, Fish & Howse [1] present an algorithm for well-formed Euler diagrams and provide a formalisation as *dual graphs* (with zones as sets of labels and edges between adjacent zones) and *superdual graphs* (with edges between any two sets of labels that differ by a single element).

Applying (a very brief) SCA Framework yields the following initial analysis:

Interpretations: relevant choices for types of interpretations are whether existential import is required (X+) or not (X−) and whether the names of the labels are important (L+) or the labels can be renamed arbitrarily (L−). Other interpretations are possible, for example, non-standard interpretations if someone misreads a diagram or sees a diagram but does not know what it is.

Denotations: a general conceptual model is presented by standard mathematical set theory and anything that is potentially known about it. A more concrete model for Euler diagrams might be a mathematical characterisation of well-formed diagrams.

Representamens: a Venn or Euler diagram is a compound sign. Diagrams can be considered equivalent representamens if a reversible visual translation exists between them. In particular, a translation must preserve existential import conditions in the case of X+ and labels in the case of L+.

Synonymy: one can investigate whether one synonym is "better" than another because it provides more observations or is well-formed or calculate how many synonyms are possible under certain conditions.

Polysemy: one can investigate how diagrams are affected by changing the interpretation, for example, from X+ to X− or by assigning actual elements to the sets.

Icons: depend on personal preferences and historical, cultural background. Presumably, the containment and intersection of circles is considered similar to set operations.

Indices: for example, dual graphs can be considered closely indexically related to Venn and Euler diagrams because they can be easily algorithmically determined.

Translations: Many translations are possible, for example using set-theoretic expressions with labels and $\{\cap, \cup, \subseteq, =\}$; dual or superdual graphs, partially ordered sets of zones, or conjunctive normal forms.

Translational Loss and Gain: for example, the actual positions and shapes of the curves are not considered relevant and omitted in translations. Different translations invoke different conceptual models which may add background information.

3 Observability of Euler and Hasse Diagrams

Stapleton et al. [4] argue that while many expressions may be implied by a set-theoretic expression, only the expression itself is observable from a set-theoretic expression. They conclude that Euler diagrams have a maximal observational advantage over set-theoretic expressions because all logically valid statements can be observed from them. An example is presented by D1 in Fig. 1 which shows that $A \cap B = \emptyset \implies C \cap B = \emptyset$. An alternative to Euler diagrams is provided by Hasse diagrams[1] of partially ordered sets, such as D2 in Fig. 1. The filled nodes in D2 correspond to the zones in D1 (including the top node which corresponds to the outer zone). The empty nodes correspond to empty sets. In many cases the Hasse diagram without the empty nodes and ignoring the ordering is isomorphic to the superdual graph of an Euler diagram. They are not isomorphic if the Hasse diagram contains edges between nodes that differ in more than one label, which implies a non-well-formed Euler diagram.

In D2, the highest shared node below a set of nodes presents an intersection (e.g. $A \cap B$). Containment amongst sets corresponds to following upwards edges (e.g. $C \subseteq A$) whereas implications amongst empty sets corresponds to following downwards edges (e.g. $A \cap B = \emptyset \implies C \cap B = \emptyset$). One can argue that D2 has an observational advantage over D1 because one can additionally count how many implications are possible. Users, however, will most likely find D1 more intuitive to read, and more iconic for set containment, than D2. D1 also conveys a feeling of understanding of why an implication exists: it is physically impossible in a 2-dimensional space for C to get out of its container A and anywhere near B. Because of the physical constraints, changing D1 so that $(A \backslash C) \cap B = \emptyset$ but $C \cap B \neq \emptyset$ cannot be presented as a well-formed Euler diagram. In D2, however, it would be possible to fill in the bottom node. In that case empty nodes would only indicate that the set at that node is empty. Thus, Hasse diagrams can express any constellation of sets (the same as Venn diagrams with shading) whereas well-formed Euler diagrams with existential import cannot.

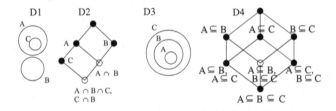

Fig. 1. Euler and Hasse Diagrams

We are proposing that even some mathematical expressions can lead to more than one observation. For example, we would argue that the mathematical expression $A \subseteq B \subseteq C$ allows the same observations as D3 if one knows the convention of abbreviating transitive operations in that manner. D4 displays logical statements and their conjunctions instead of sets and intersections as in D3. It contains an empty node because of $A \subseteq B, B \subseteq C \iff A \subseteq B \subseteq C$. We would argue that while these two statements are logically equivalent, with respect to observations they are different.

---

[1] SCA normally uses Hasse diagrams of lattices in the sense of Formal Concept Analysis but because of space limitations only partially ordered sets are discussed here.

The purpose of SCA is to provide a vocabulary that facilitates, for example, an investigation of why and how mathematically equivalent signs provide different observations. Apart from the basic definitions of SCA, it is not intended to develop new formalisms but, instead, to incorporate existing ones and combine them with a semiotic perspective. SCA is not restricted to mathematical applications because it can also be used for analysing natural or other formal languages [2]. This paper gives rise to questions about further relationships between well-formed Euler diagrams and partially ordered sets (or lattices) which will be addressed in a future publication.

References

1. Flower, J., Fish, A., Howse, J.: Euler diagram generation. J. Vis. Lang. Comput. **19**(6), 675–694 (2008)
2. Priss, U.: Semiotic-conceptual analysis: a proposal. Int. J. Gen. Syst. **46**(5), 569–585 (2017)
3. Rodgers, P.: A survey of Euler diagrams. J. Vis. Lang. Comput. **25**(3), 134–155 (2014)
4. Stapleton, G., Jamnik, M., Shimojima, A.: What makes an effective representation of information: a formal account of observational advantages. J. Logic Lang. Inform. **26**(2), 143–177 (2017)

On the Shoulders of Giants: Colourful Argument Trees for Academic Writing

Maarja Kruusmaa, Amirouche Moktefi[✉], and Jeffrey Tuhtan

Tallinn University of Technology, Tallinn, Estonia
{maarja.kruusmaa,amirouche.moktefi,jeffrey.tuhtan}@taltech.ee

Abstract. Academic writing courses tend to focus on rhetorical and linguistic components rather than on argument making. This is unfortunate since it is precisely the purpose of scientific writing to expose arguments. We present an attempt to overcome this divide. For the purpose, we introduce colourful argument trees that do not merely exhibit the structure of a complex argument but also the state of our confidence in its statements and its inferences. The visualisation of the argument and the integration of the sources into its structure provide students with a better understanding of scientific writing.

Keywords: Argument · Tree · Academic writing · Logic teaching · Bibliography

1 Arguments in Academic Writing

Academic work involves a literary activity since a significant part it consists in reading and writing. It is thus unsurprising that academic writing courses are found in most curricula for early career scientists. However, such courses tend to focus on rhetorical and linguistic components through a set of writing guidelines while the argumentative components are separately taught within philosophy or 'critical thinking' courses. A consequence of this divide is that students are seldom taught argument making in the specific context of scientific writing. This is unfortunate since it is precisely the purpose of a successful scientific text to expose an argument:

> "[T]he quality of the academic essay depends on the development of an argument. It is therefore problematic when writing instruction is not focused on argumentation, but refers to it fleetingly, inconsistently, and under the guise of related aspects, such as structure or style.

> Currently, the teaching of writing tends to focus on linguistic or 'surface' features [....] without making explicit that developing an argument is the over-reaching requirement. Instead, academic writing instruction should start from this requirement and treat related aspects as subordinated." [6, p. 153]

Ursula Wingate states that developing an argument consists of three components: "(1) the analysis and evaluation of content knowledge, (2) the writer's development of a position, and (3) the presentation of that position in a coherent manner" [6, p. 146]. She

© Springer Nature Switzerland AG 2020
A.-V. Pietarinen et al. (Eds.): Diagrams 2020, LNAI 12169, pp. 520–524, 2020.
https://doi.org/10.1007/978-3-030-54249-8_48

proposes an 'essay writing framework' in which these components are interlinked, since the selection and use of sources is crucial to establish the writer's position which needs to be clearly presented. Although this (linear) framework captures traditional formats of scientific articles, it does not suffice to account for the writing process itself. Indeed, the latter often requires moving forth and back between these components (Fig. 1), through an interplay of reading, revising and editing [1].

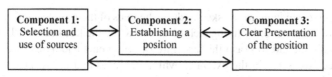

Fig. 1. (Based on [6, p. 153])

In this paper, we present an attempt to bring together argument making and academic writing in a course jointly delivered by philosophers and engineering scientists. The course was taught within a doctoral engineering curriculum at Tallinn University of Technology (Estonia). For the purpose, we introduce diagrams that do not merely exhibit the structure of a complex argument that is displayed but also the state of our confidence in its constituents. The writing activity is then directed towards increasing this confidence. This dynamic process is oriented and visualized through a progressive colouring of the tree. We present the trees in Sect. 2 and their use in Sect. 3.

2   Argument Trees

An argument is commonly understood as a set of interconnected statements, so that some of them (*i.e.* premises), give support some others (*i.e.* conclusions). An argument is valid when the inferential link between its premise(s) and its conclusion(s) holds. A valid argument is, then, said to be sound if, additionally, its premise(s) are true. In scientific literature, one faces complex arguments. It is useful to convey their structure to the eye with the help of argumentative graphs, known as argument trees. The construction of these trees is not an objective in itself: they are rather understood as instruments to manipulate the argument that is displayed [5].

Fig. 2.   **Fig. 3.**   **Fig. 4.**

Three main devices are needed: a (labelled) circle stands for a statement (Fig. 2), an arrow indicates inference (Fig. 3), and a bracket gathers joint statements (Fig. 4). A tree consists of interconnected nodes (statements) that lead from premise(s) to conclusion(s). It is observed that *linked* nodes stand for *linked* statements. Hence, the force of these diagrams springs from their high iconicity: they do not merely *represent* relations between statements; they *have* those relations [4, p. 610]. Argument trees are commonly found in logic and critical thinking textbooks [2, 3]:

'An argument tree is a device that can be used for representing arguments in the form of a diagram. They are helpful when we are reconstructing arguments, particularly complex ones, because they provide a means of showing the ways in which the different parts of an argument are related to each other. They show how the premises support the conclusion. Constructing argument trees is a very valuable tool and you will find it helpful to use them in your own analyses of real-world arguments.' [2, p. 73]

In our course, students were asked to draw the trees of their prospected article (based on pre-existing abstract or by fixing a claim and drawing the tree backward). Completed trees offer valuable aid to grasp the structure of arguments and assess their strengths. Yet, one needs to ascertain the extent to which premises and inferences hold in order to ascertain the conclusion(s). For the purpose, we conventionally colour in red what is supported by literature and in blue what is taken to be (self-) evident (*i.e.* does not require justification). To some extent, the latter group gathers statements that are accepted within the student's community but may need to be justified (and hence become red) for a wider readership. The colouring of the tree allows students to identify weaknesses in their arguments and work on their improvement. This requires amending them to justify what was hitherto unsubstantiated (uncoloured). This process is tracked through the progressive colouring of the tree. Two trees obtained by students are reproduced (Fig. 5 and Fig. 6) with students' permission.

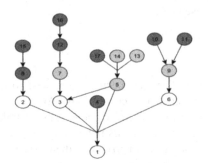   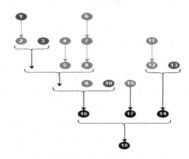

Fig. 5. (Color figure online)   Fig. 6. (Color figure online)

3   On the Shoulders of Giants

The introduction of colours helps differentiating the stances that students may hold towards their arguments. Since complex arguments may be reduced to series or combinations of simpler ones, let us conveniently consider a unitary argument formed of a premise, an inference and a conclusion. We get a typology of 8 postures, depending on how substantiated (in red) the constituents of the argument are (Fig. 7):

1) The student infers a previously unknown statement from a fact.
2) The student attempts to demonstrate a connection between two facts.
3) The premise and the inference are known. The student deduces the conclusion.

4) All components are known. The student gathers them to form the argument
5) Nothing is known. The student conjectures a statement that would yield another.
6) The student searches for what would produce a statement that is already known.
7) Two unknown statements are linked. The student proves one to deduce the other.
8) A fact follows from an unknown statement. The student proves the latter.

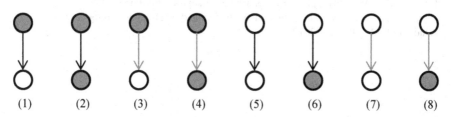

(1)   (2)   (3)   (4)   (5)   (6)   (7)   (8)

Fig. 7. (Color figure online)

In each stance, the coloured diagram exhibits what is yet to be achieved and what is needed to achieve it. For instance, an uncoloured premise is unsubstantiated. To evidence it, the student may provide an appropriate bibliographic reference to back it up. When such reference is not found, he may demonstrate that the premise follows logically from another statement that is substantiated. Otherwise, the student may justify that statement empirically (*i.e.* through observation or experiment). The ensuing amendment of the tree strengthens the argument. This example points to the role of references in academic writing. Students commonly wonder "how many references" to include in their essays and often over-refer to display "how much" they read:

Inexperienced writers often express doubt as to what to cite, where, and how. As a rule of thumb, you should focus only on literature that you have actually read and cite only those works that are *necessary* and *sufficient* to provide your reader with a comprehensive overview of your research project and how it fits within the broader context of your discipline. [1, p. 94].

It is disputable to strictly limit to *sufficient* sources since multiple (independent) sources increase confidence in a given statement. This is exhibited in the tree with independent premises supporting a conclusion. Yet, it is true that over-reference is undesired. As to necessity, uncoloured arrows and nodes at the top of the tree make clear where references are missing. In complex arguments, a tree can also be improved by cutting branches that do not contribute to the conclusion. This eliminates irrelevant or unnecessary sources. Most importantly, the visualisation of the argument provides the student with a better understanding of the role of sources in the making of arguments. As such, it increases his awareness of both what a scientific text is and how it stands within a tradition of research shaped by the student's predecessors.

References

1. Aliotta, M.: Mastering Academic Writing in the Sciences. CRC Press, Boca Raton (2018)
2. Bowell, T., Kemp, G.: Critical Thinking: A Concise Guide. Routledge, London (2010)
3. Hurley, P.J.: A Concise Introduction to Logic. Cengage Learning, Stamford (2015)
4. Moktefi, A.: Is Euler's circle a symbol or an icon? Sign Syst. Stud. **43**(4), 597–615 (2015)
5. Moktefi, A.: Diagrams as scientific instruments. In: Benedek, A., Veszelszki, A. (eds.) Virtual Reality – Real Visuality, pp. 81–89. Peter Lang, Frankfurt am Main (2017)
6. Wingate, U.: 'Argument!' helping students understand what essay writing is about. J. Engl. Acad. Purp. **11**, 145–154 (2012)

Beta Assertive Graphs

Francesco Bellucci[1], Daniele Chiffi[2], and Ahti-Veikko Pietarinen[3,4(✉)]

[1] University of Bologna, Bologna, Italy
francesco.bellucci4@unibo.it
[2] Politecnico di Milano, Milan, Italy
chiffidaniele@gmail.com
[3] Tallinn University of Technology, Tallinn, Estonia
ahti.pietarinen@gmail.com
[4] HSE University, Moscow, Russia

Abstract. Assertive graphs (AGs) modify Peirce's Alpha part of Existential Graphs (EGs) and are used to reason about assertions without any *ad hoc* sign of assertion. This paper presents an extension of propositional AGs to Beta by lines. Absence of polarities necessitate Beta-AGs to resort to two kinds of lines: standard lines (a certain method of asserting), and barbed lines (a general method of asserting). A new set of rules of transformations for Beta-AGs is presented that derive theorems of quantificational intuitionistic logic. Beta-AGs offer a new system to analyse assertions through quantificational diagrams.

Keywords: Existential/Assertive graphs · Quantifier · Intuitionistic logic

1 Introduction

In many logical systems, an *ad hoc* sign of assertion is commonly used [1,4,6]. In contrast, some systems have no *ad hoc* sign for assertions, although assertions would have a major inferential role, as in Existential Graphs (EGs), which have an *embedded* sign of assertion in *the sheet of assertion* [1,5,8–10].

Using the resources of diagrammatic reasoning of Peirce's EGs, we propose an intended interpretation for acts of logical assertions involving quantification, represented in the system of *Beta Assertive Graphs* (Beta-AGs). It is an extension of Alpha-AGs introduced in [3], formalising a class of (intuitionistic) quantificational linguistic acts that are *assertive*.

2 Beta-AGs: Two Kinds of Lines

Beta-AGs is a conservative extension of propositional AGs to first-order quantification. Since it maintains the constructive nature of AGs, we need two independent signs for quantification that are both primitive. The *universal quantifier*

The paper was prepared within the framework of the HSE University Basic Research Program and funded by the Russian Academic Excellence Project '5–100'.

A.-V. Pietarinen et al. (Eds.): Diagrams 2020, LNAI 12169, pp. 525–529, 2020.
https://doi.org/10.1007/978-3-030-54249-8_49

is expressed as a line crossed by two *barbs* (*barbed line*) (Fig. 1a). The *particular (existential) quantifier* is expressed by a *standard line* (Fig. 1b).[1]

The intended meaning of the line is "a general method to justifiably assert something" (Fig. 1a), and of the barbed line "a specific or a certain method to justifiably assert something" (Fig. 1b). We may call both of these lines *lines of assertion*.

Figure 1:   (a)   (b)

Boxes have a key role in Beta-AGs just as they do in AGs. The box in Fig. 4a means that "a content is asserted". The blank sheet (space of all assertions) means that a logical truth is asserted (Fig. 2b).

Figure 2a: ☐   Fig. 2b:

In Beta AGs, boxes are used as graphical devices to disambiguate logical order of quantifiers and scopes. Boxes and lines may be combined as in Fig. 3a, which expresses "anything is asserted of F" ("anything that is asserted means asserting F of it"). The graph of Fig. 3b states that "something is asserted of F".

Figure 3: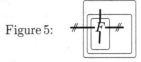
             (a)   (b)

Figure 4 indicates the FOL formula $\forall x \exists y F(x, y)$. This is consistent with Peirce's "endoporeutic" interpretation of graphs.

Figure 4:   ⊬──F──

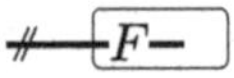

Nested quantifiers are expressed as in Fig. 5, corresponding to the formula $\forall x \exists y \forall u \exists z F(x, y, u, z)$.

Figure 5:

The diagrams above are examples of how quantificational lines interact with boxes in AGs in the composition of complex formulas. The definition of well-formed Beta-AGs is easily construed. But the graph in Fig. 6, despite its apparent simplicity, is not a well-formed graph of the language since it does not disambiguate between the logical priority scopes of the two different lines of assertion.

Figure 6:   ──F⤫

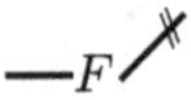

An important feature of AGs is that the boxes can be *cornered*. From a simple box containing any graph inside (including the blank graph), a cornering can be

[1] Symbolizing two quantifiers separately derives from Peirce's 1882 notation [2,7].

inferred, which contains the original graph in the inner area (consequent) of the cornering, and conversely. That is:

(CR)   From ☐ we may infer ☐☐ , and back.

This reversible transformation is a *Cornering Rule* (CR). Cornered graphs are conditional assertions, with antecedent (the outer) and consequent (the inner) areas [3]. The other logical connectives are, just as in Alpha-AGs, *juxtaposition* of graphs on the sheet of assertion that stands for conjunction, the connector "+" for *disjunctions*, and the *blot* "•" for *absurdum*.

3   Rules of Transformation of Beta-AGs

The two major irreversible rules of transformations, *insertions* and *erasures*, are as in AGs. They are not expressed in terms of the polarities of the areas (negative and positive) as in EGs but take into account what is permissible within the antecedent and the consequent areas of cornerings.

The reversible *Beta-iteration* and its converse *Beta-deiteration* behave just as they would when manipulating standard lines of identity in Beta-EGs [10]. In addition, several new rules need to be added to the rules of Alpha-AGs to handle inferences with assertive quantificational lines:[2]

Insertion

(1.1) Any two loose ends of a simple line may be connected on the antecedent of cornering:

From ⊏⊐ we may infer ⊏⊐ .

(1.2) Any two loose ends of a barbed line can be connected on the antecedent of cornering:

From ⊏⊐ we may infer ⊏⊐ .

(1.2.1) A barb '//' can be inserted on a loose end of a simple line on antecedent areas:

From ⊏⊐ we may infer ⊏⊐ .

(1.2.2) A box can be added to a barbed line on a consequent area:

From ⊏ #— ⊐ we may infer ⊏ #—□ ⊐ .

Erasure

(2.1) Any simple line can be cut on a consequent area of a cornering (and on the sheet of assertion):

From ⊏ —⊐ we may infer ⊏ — — ⊐ .

(2.2) Any barbed line can be cut on an antecedent area of a cornering:

From #—⊐ we may infer #—⊐ .

---

[2] Any line depicted on antecedent areas as loose may be continuous, branching or connected, just as ligatures may be in Beta-EGs.

(2.2.1) A barb can be erased from the barbed line whose outermost loose end rests on a consequent area of a cornering (or on the sheet of assertion):

From $\boxed{\;\;/\!\!\!-\;\;}$ we may infer $\boxed{\;\;-\;\;}$.

(2.2.2) On an antecedent area of a cornering, a box can be removed from a barbed line that penetrates into it, thus:

From $/\!\!\!-\!\!\square\,\sqcap$ we may infer $/\!\!\!-\!\!\sqcap$.

Axioms

(Ax.1) An unattached simple line ——, a simple loop $\bigcirc$, and a simple dot **0** (atrophied loop, not to be confused with the blot of absurdity) can be inserted and erased anywhere on the sheet (including within boxes and cornerings).

(Ax.2) An unattached barbed line $/\!\!\!-$, barbed loop $\overset{\prime\prime}{\bigcirc}$, and a barbed dot $\oplus$ can be inserted and erased anywhere on the sheet.

Remark. As is intutitionistic logic, the graph of the formula $\neg\forall x\neg Fx \rightarrow \exists x Fx$ is not a theorem of Beta-AGs: Asserting that $\forall x\neg Fx$ is not asserted does not produce something that is asserted. Notice also that $\neg\forall x Fx \rightarrow \exists x\neg Fx$ is not a theorem of the system—semantically, "absence of an assertion is not an assertion of an absence".

4   Conclusion

Beta-AGs extend the system of propositional assertive graphs (AGs) to accommodate quantification. Two distinct notations for quantification—the lines of assertion—are needed, and they are not interdefinable. Beta-AGs maintain all the constructive features of AGs and result in a diagrammatic system for intuitionistic quantificational logic, represented by logical graphs with assertion-based interpretation of the main logical constants. There are no polarities in the language, and consequently the insertion and erasure rules are more bountiful than in the classical case.

Further research is devoted to a more comprehensive presentation of the main logical properties of the system of Beta-AGs, including discussion of their relevance to philosophy of logic, philosophy of notation, and the logic of assertions.

References

1. Bellucci, F., Pietarinen, A.-V.: Assertion and denial: a contribution from logical notations. J. Appl. Logic **25**, 1–22 (2017)
2. Bellucci, F., Pietarinen, A.-V.: From Mitchell to Carus: fourteen years of logical graphs in the making. Trans Peirce Soc. **52**, 539–575 (2016)
3. Bellucci, F., Chiffi, D., Pietarinen, A.-V.: Assertive graphs. J. Appl. Non Classical Logic **28**(1), 72–91 (2018)
4. Carrara, M., Chiffi, D., De Florio, C.: Assertions and hypotheses: a logical framework for their opposition relations. Logic J. IGPL **25**(2), 131–144 (2017)

5. Chiffi, D., Pietarinen, A.-V.: On the logical philosophy of assertive graphs. J. Logic Lang. Inf. (2020). https://doi.org/10.1007/s10849-020-09315-6
6. Frege, G.: Begriffsschrift. L. Nebert, Halle (1879)
7. Peirce, C.S.: Writings of Charles S. Peirce. Vol. 4. Peirce Edition Project (ed.). Indiana University Press, Bloomington (1989)
8. Peirce, C.S.: Logic of the Future: Writings on Existential Graphs. Volume 1: History and Applications. Pietarinen, A.-V. (ed.). De Gruyter, Berlin (2019)
9. Pietarinen, A.-V., Chiffi, D.: Assertive and existential graphs: a comparison. In: Chapman, P., Stapleton, G., Moktefi, A., Perez-Kriz, S., Bellucci, F. (eds.) Diagrams 2018. LNCS (LNAI), vol. 10871, pp. 565–581. Springer, Cham (2018). https://doi.org/10.1007/978-3-319-91376-6_51
10. Roberts, D.D.: The Existential Graphs of CS. Peirce. The Hague: Mouton, Paris (1973)

Peirce's Inclusion Diagrams, with Application to Syllogisms

Reetu Bhattacharjee[1] and Amirouche Moktefi[2(✉)]

[1] Jadavpur University, Kolkata, India
reetub588@gmail.com
[2] Tallinn University of Technology, Tallinn, Estonia
amirouche.moktefi@taltech.ee

Abstract. While developing his system of Existential graphs which he viewed as the logic of the future, Charles S. Peirce continued working on variations of past diagrams. In particular, he introduced in the period 1896–1901 an original variation of Eulerian diagrams where the shape of the curves indicated the sign of the classes that were contained in them. These diagrams recently attracted attention for their ability to represent negative terms more directly than earlier schemes. Yet, we offer here a more general rationale: we argue that Peirce conceived these diagrams by making inclusion the main operator, a practice that is found in his other logical systems, both algebraic and diagrammatic. This is achieved by expressing universal propositions in an inclusional form. This shift allows him to classify syllogisms under just three diagrammatic forms in a style that is found in some of his contemporaries.

Keywords: Peirce · Euler diagram · Inclusion · Syllogism

1 Inclusion Diagrams

It is well known that Charles S. Peirce invented a system of Existential Graphs (EG) which he viewed as the logic of the future. Yet, he also developed variations of Eulerian diagrams. This antiquarian interest in the diagrams of the past might seem anomalous. Yet, we argue that Peirce's variation, where the shape of the curve embodies a logical meaning, corroborates his notational concerns.

Peirce introduced this special Eulerian scheme in two manuscripts: Ms 481 (dated 1896-7) and Ms 1147 (dated 1901) [11]. Instead of adopting the traditional Eulerian circles where the shape has no logical meaning [5], Peirce admits a variety of figures that are interpreted as follows: the term on the concave side of a curve is positive and its complement is found on the convex side. For instance, the positive term *A* is found inside the curve in (Fig. 1) but outside the curve in (Fig. 2). This convention eases the representation of negative terms and propositions involving them [9]. To represent existence, Peirce introduces a dot. For instance, (Fig. 3) asserts that 'Some A exists' while (Fig. 4) states that "Some non-A exists".

© Springer Nature Switzerland AG 2020
A.-V. Pietarinen et al. (Eds.): Diagrams 2020, LNAI 12169, pp. 530–533, 2020.
https://doi.org/10.1007/978-3-030-54249-8_50

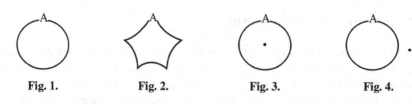

Fig. 1.   **Fig. 2.**   **Fig. 3.**   **Fig. 4.**

It is tempting to name these diagrams in reference to their unusual shapes. However, we consider them here rather from the standpoint of their use and acknowledge their embodiment of the primacy of inclusion. Indeed, unlike Boole's immediate followers who claimed equation to be the cornerstone of logic, Peirce and some other logicians favoured inclusion (in class calculus, and hence implication in propositional calculus). This divide in the choice of the copula led to rivalry between logical systems [3]. In this period, Peirce developed several notations for logic but maintained a regular concern about the reduction of the number of connectives and the primacy of inclusion (or implication), a line of thought that led to his system of Existential graphs [1, 2].

These concerns are also found in Peirce's modification of Euler diagrams. Indeed, he systematically reduced relations of exclusion in his diagrams into inclusions (a practice that anticipates [12]). For instance, to express the fact that "No *A* is *B*", it suffices to state that "All *A* are non-*B*". Actually, each universal proposition can be expressed as an inclusion in two possible forms, depending on which term is said to be included in the other (Fig. 5). It is of no logical matter which term is included in the other, as Christine Ladd-Franklin, Peirce's student, has noted: "When an exclusion is to be made into an inclusion, it is a matter of indifference which of its terms is regarded as predicate; every exclusion contains within itself two inclusions, of which each is the converse by contraposition of the other" [4, p. 27]. Yet, for the purpose of diagrammatic representation, the choice of the subject and predicate is conveniently made and proves important to ease the merging of the premises in syllogisms. This is made possible thanks to Peirce's innovation regarding the shape of the curves.

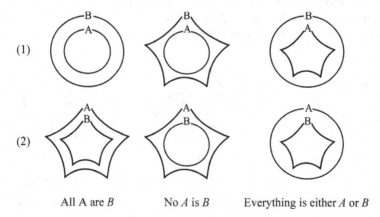

(1)

(2)

All A are *B*   No *A* is *B*   Everything is either *A* or *B*

Fig. 5. Representation of universal propositions with Peirce's inclusion diagrams

2   A Classification of Syllogisms

Peirce's innovation is used with benefit in his treatment of syllogisms. Indeed, although he does not explicitly describe the three forms that we expose below, Peirce clearly distinguishes three groups of syllogisms: universal, particular and spurious. The particular syllogisms are slightly refined in the second manuscript [11]. Peirce's classification is based on the determination of three patterns (Fig. 6) in which the dotted lines indicate uncertainty as to the shape of the curve:

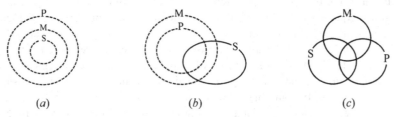

(a)   (b)   (c)

Fig. 6. Peirce's three forms of syllogisms

(a) For a universal syllogism (i.e. has two universal premises), a curve S is inside a curve M which is itself inside a curve P. The shape of the curves depends on the types of propositions and are chosen in such a way as to make the three terms include each other in that order. The conclusion is necessarily a universal proposition.

(b) For a particular syllogism (i.e. has one universal and one particular premise), a curve P is inside a curve M. A concave curve S intersects with both P and M. The shape of curves P and M depends on the propositions and are chosen in such a way as to maintain the existential import (marked with a dot) outside the curve M. The conclusion is necessarily a particular proposition.

(c) For a spurious syllogism (i.e. has two particular premises), three concave curves S, M, and P intersect with each other. Existential import is marked with dots. The conclusion is necessarily a particular proposition.

An example of each case is provided in (Fig. 7).

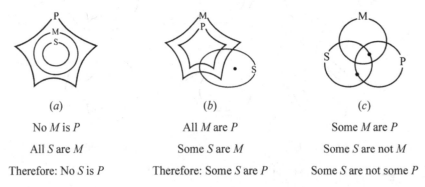

(a)   (b)   (c)

No M is P   All M are P   Some M are P

All S are M   Some S are M   Some S are not M

Therefore: No S is P   Therefore: Some S are P   Some S are not some P

Fig. 7. Examples of each form of syllogism

Peirce's classification resembles those made by some of his contemporaries, in particular that of Lewis Carroll. The latter also distinguished three patterns of syllogisms [8]. His first two figures correspond to Peirce's patterns (*a*) and (*b*). Carroll's and Peirce's third patterns differ. Carroll's is consequent to his admission of existential import in universal affirmative propositions to conform to the 'facts of life' [6]. Peirce held a different view but introduced a third pattern to account for syllogisms with two particular premises even though they yield non-standard propositional forms. Interestingly, Ladd-Franklin identified earlier, in 1883, just two forms of syllogisms in line with Peirce's and Carroll's first two forms [4]. Both Peirce and Carroll were familiar with Ladd-Franklin's work [7, 10]. Peirce's classification of syllogisms, hence, connects well with similar work in his time. However, his approach differs from those of Ladd-Franklin and Carroll, in two main aspects. First, he presented his forms diagrammatically while the others formulated them algebraically. Second, he adopted an inclusional notation while the others rather used exclusional notations. These specificities are precisely embodied in Peirce's inclusion diagrams.

References

1. Bellucci, F., Moktefi, M., Pietarinen, A.-V.: Simplex sigillum veri: Peano, Frege and Peirce on the primitives of logic. History and Philosophy of Logic **39**(1), 80–95 (2018)
2. Bellucci, F., Pietarinen, A.-V.: From Mitchell to carus: fourteen years of logical graphs in the making. Trans. Charles S Peirce Soc. **52**(4), 539–575 (2016)
3. Durand-Richard, M.-J., Moktefi, A.: Algèbre et logique symboliques: arbitraire du signe et langage formel. In: Béziau, J.-Y. (ed.) La Pointure du Symbole, pp. 295–328. Pétra, Paris (2014)
4. Ladd-Franklin, C.: On the algebra of logic. In: Peirce, C.S., (ed.) Studies in Logic, pp. 17–71. Little Brown, and company, Boston (1883)
5. Moktefi, A.: Is Euler's circle a symbol or an icon? Sign Syst. Stud. **43**(4), 597–615 (2015)
6. Moktefi, A.: On the social utility of symbolic logic: Lewis Carroll against 'The Logicians. Studia Metodologiczne **35**, 133–150 (2015)
7. Moktefi, A.: Are other people's books difficult to read? The logic books in Lewis Carroll's private library. Acta Baltica Historiae et Philosophiae Scientiarum **5**(1), 28–49 (2017)
8. Moktefi, A.: Logic. In: Wilson, R.J., Moktefi, A. (eds.) The Mathematical World of Charles L. Dodgson (Lewis Carroll), pp. 87–119. Oxford University Press, Oxford (2019)
9. Moktefi, A., Pietarinen, A.-V.: Negative terms in Euler diagrams: peirce's solution. In: Jamnik, M., Uesaka, Y., Elzer Schwartz, S. (eds.) Diagrams 2016. LNCS (LNAI), vol. 9781, pp. 286–288. Springer, Cham (2016). https://doi.org/10.1007/978-3-319-42333-3_25
10. Pietarinen, A.-V.: Christine Ladd-franklin's and victoria Welby's correspondence with Charles peirce. Semiotica **2013**(196), 139–161 (2013)
11. Pietarinen, A.-V.: Extensions of Euler diagrams in peirce's four manuscripts on logical graphs. In: Jamnik, M., Uesaka, Y., Elzer Schwartz, S. (eds.) Diagrams 2016. LNCS (LNAI), vol. 9781, pp. 139–154. Springer, Cham (2016). https://doi.org/10.1007/978-3-319-42333-3_11
12. Skliar, O., Monge, R.E., Gapper, S.: Using inclusion diagrams as an alternative to Venn diagrams to determine the validity of categorical syllogisms. arXiv:1509.00926 (2018). https://arxiv.org/abs/1509.00926

The DNA Framework of Visualization

Yuri Engelhardt[1]([✉]) [iD] and Clive Richards[2] [iD]

[1] University of Twente, Enschede, The Netherlands
yuri.engelhardt@utwente.nl
[2] Birmingham City University, Birmingham, UK
clive.j.richards@me.com

Abstract. A comprehensive framework is presented for analyzing and specifying an extensive range of visualizations in terms of their fundamental 'DNA' building blocks of visual encoding and (de)composition.

1 Introduction

In their "Tour through the Visualization Zoo", Heer et al. (2010) say that "all visualizations share a common 'DNA' – a set of mappings between data properties and visual attributes" (p. 60). We use this metaphorical idea of the 'DNA of visualization' in a similar vein, taking it to the extent of identifying a comprehensive set of individual DNA building blocks of visualizations and the rules for combining them. This allows for the construction of a broad range of different types of visualizations.

Numerous authors have written about analysing visualizations and various visualization grammars have been developed (e.g. *Vega-Lite* www.vega.github.io). We have reviewed this work and we have identified gaps in what is covered (see Engelhardt and Richards 2018). The framework we present here fills these gaps. It:

1. provides a comprehensive system for exploring and checking design possibilities for visualization.
2. offers a system of tree diagrams for representing (de)composition and visual encoding in visualizations (constructed from their 'DNA').
3. presents a way of describing visualizations with rigorously systematic natural language sentences, which specify (de)composition and visual encoding.
4. covers a very broad design space of visualization, not only including visual representations that involve numerical information, but also visualizations such as family trees, Venn diagrams, flow charts, texts using indenting, technical drawings and scientific illustrations.

The above characteristics of the framework enable the analysis and comparison of visualization types, and potentially provide a design method for exploring visualization options. Like academic work in linguistics, the work presented here is primarily not prescriptive but descriptive, in the sense that it enables the understanding and modelling of (graphic) language.

Y. Engelhardt and C. Richards—both authors contributed equally to the work

© The Author(s) 2020
A.-V. Pietarinen et al. (Eds.): Diagrams 2020, LNAI 12169, pp. 534–538, 2020.
https://doi.org/10.1007/978-3-030-54249-8_51

2   The Building Blocks and How They Relate to Each Other

The process diagram in Fig. 1 shows all our DNA building blocks and their possible relationships for expressing information visually. For ease of use we have given each DNA building block a three letter abbreviation. The DNA building blocks fall into several main groups: *types of information* to be represented, *visual encodings* to represent them, *visual components* that make up the visualization, and any *directions* or *layout principles* that may be involved. *Visual encodings* can be used for *arranging*, *varying* or *linking* visual components. *Arranging* visual components into meaningful configurations is how visualizations are *constructed*.

Our *visual encodings* include the use of Bertin's 'visual variables', some Gestalt principles of perception (e.g. grouping by proximity) and other fundamental ways of expressing information visually. A visual component can be involved in several different visual encodings, simultaneously representing different types of information.

We refer to a 'well-formed' combination of DNA building blocks as a *visualization pattern*. Many common *visualization patterns* have been given a name (e.g. 'pie chart') and are generally referred to as 'chart types', while novel or rare patterns often do not have a name (yet). A visualization pattern can be transformed into another pattern by adding, replacing or removing one or more DNA building blocks. A large number of patterns has been analyzed using this system. Some examples can be found in Fig. 2. Many more analyses are on our accompanying website: www.VisDNA.com.

3   Discussion and Conclusions

The framework offers a potential research tool for exploring various kinds of commonalities, family resemblances and differences between visualization patterns within collections of graphic representations. The DNA building blocks and the precisely defined methods by which they can be combined (see www.VisDNA.com) offer the potential for machine readable specifications. This may serve as a basis for a system providing computer generated visualization advice, which could be linked to a rendering engine in order to produce actual visualizations and variants of them.

Because of its flexible building block structure, additional DNA elements may be added to the framework to accommodate any new constructions that one may want to describe and that cannot be fully analysed using the current scheme. An example may be the addition of DNA building blocks for interactivity in visualizations.

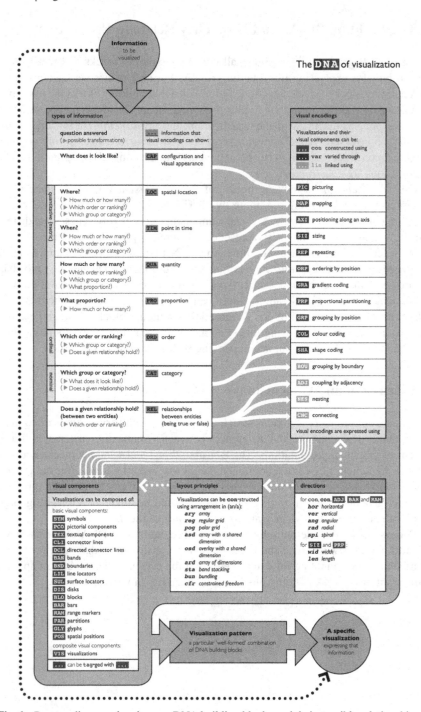

Fig. 1. Process diagram showing our DNA building blocks and their possible relationships.

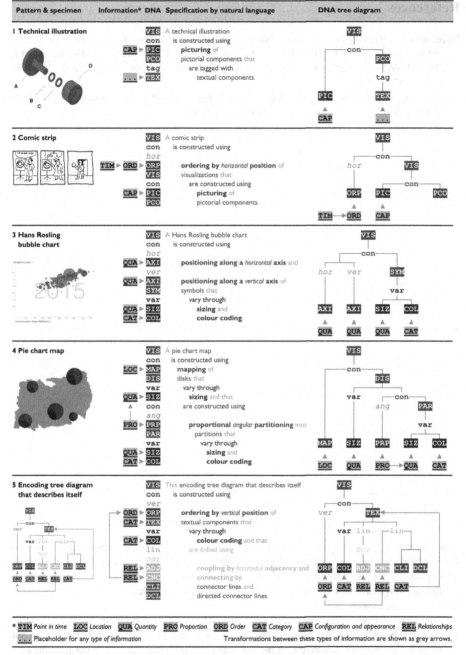

Fig. 2. Example DNA analyses. See www.VisDNA.com for analyses of many more types of visualizations. *Images at 1 and 4 courtesy of the DataVizProject by Ferdio, Creative Commons Attribution-NonCommercial-NoDerivatives 4.0 International License:* www.datavizproject.com

References

Engelhardt, Y., Richards, C.: A framework for analyzing and designing diagrams and graphics. In: Chapman, P., Stapleton, G., Moktefi, A., Perez-Kriz, S., Bellucci, F. (eds.) Diagrams 2018. LNCS (LNAI), vol. 10871, pp. 201–209. Springer, Cham (2018). https://doi.org/10.1007/978-3-319-91376-6_20

Heer, J., Bostock, M., Ogievetsky, V.: A tour through the visualization zoo. Commun. ACM **53**(6), 59–67 (2010). https://doi.org/10.1145/1743546.1743567

Imagine a Round Square

Amirouche Moktefi[⊠] and Jelena Družinina

Tallinn University of Technology, Tallinn, Estonia
amirouche.moktefi@taltech.ee, jelena.issajeva@gmail.com

Abstract. There is growing interest in the logic of imagination. A widespread position holds that all that is imagined is conceived and all that is conceived is possible. Hence, (logical) impossibilities such as 'round squares' cannot be imagined. Yet, during a tutorial at the *Diagrams 2018 conference*, we asked participants to undertake this impossible task: to imagine a round square, and we collected their drawings. Should we then dismiss the collected round squares on the ground that they cannot *be*? We present the outcomes of this experiment and explore what it teaches us on imagination, impossible objects and diagrams. In particular, we argue that there is no need to draw an object that is *actually* round and square in order to visualise an object that is round and square. All that is needed is to visualise the possession of those properties of round-ness and square-ness. Diagrams help considerably.

Keywords: Imagination · Round square · Impossible objects

1 Imagine

Although it can be traced back at least to Leibniz [14], there has recently been growing interest in the logic of imagination [13]. Based on earlier views held by Descartes and Hume, it is held that all that is imagined is conceived and all that is conceived is possible [6]. Consequently, (logical) impossibilities such as 'round squares' cannot be imagined. We argue that round squares can be imagined.

We first note that recent attempts focus on *propositional* imagination and reduce the imagination of objects into a propositional form:

"[An object] can be viewed as a collection of properties and can be defined, therefore, as a collection of properties. So, each object corresponds in some sense to a given proposition. Give any object, for instance, *Manhattan*, we can associate to it a proposition: *There exists Manhattan*. This leads us to the view according to which all kinds of imagination can be reduced to propositional imagination." [6, pp. 106–107]

This is unsatisfactory since to imagine an object is different from imagining the existence of the object. The act of imagining is directed towards different targets.

Also, it is disputable to assess the *actuality* of imagination by the *accuracy* of the imagined objects. Descartes' *chiliagon* (a polygon with a thousand sides) is commonly offered as an illustration of an object that can be conceived but cannot be imagined:

© Springer Nature Switzerland AG 2020
A.-V. Pietarinen et al. (Eds.): Diagrams 2020, LNAI 12169, pp. 539–543, 2020.
https://doi.org/10.1007/978-3-030-54249-8_52

"It is not easy for us to concretely draw a chiliagon on a piece of paper, however this is not technically impossible. But it is clear that we cannot have a mental image of it just closing our eyes." [4, p. 71]

We argue that one may well be said to have imagined a chiliagon even though she fails to *actually* picture a polygon with a thousand sides. Indeed, imagined objects are mere approximations, even when we imagine existing objects such as monuments or celebrities. Imagining *Manhattan*, for instance, can only be approximate since it probably is more difficult to achieve than to imagine a *chiliagon*. Even imagining a simple geometrical figure would be impossible if one is required to deliver a flawless figure. That imagination produces incorrect objects does not entail that imagination is absent or unworkable. It is simply incorrect to confuse the act of imagination with its object, and to transfer impossibility from one to another.

Finally, drawing from Voltaire's distinction, imagination does not need to be 'passive' as would be the case when we represent perceived objects. It can also be 'active' by combining them to produce new objects [2]. This creativity has throughout history produced objects that might at first look contradictory, but that are commonly used today (*e.g.* virtual reality, American Indian, science fiction, civil war, etc.). Hence, even though 'round squares' might not exist yet, one could well direct her imagination to it and produce them, as Hugh MacColl observed a century ago:

"We have all seen and drawn triangles; but a "round square" is at present meaning-less. In the course of the future evolution of English, our descendants may some day apply the term to some reality, and then it will cease to be unreal; just as a *horseman* does not now mean an unreal combination of *horse* and *man*, like a centaur, but a real man riding on a real horse". [9, p. 471]

MacColl had a dispute with Bertrand Russell about the nature of such objects [15]. Russell also debated the subject with Alexius Meinong [17]. In both disputes, 'round squares' were discussed, and Russell objected to their existence because they violate the law of contradiction: "the round square is round, and also not round" [16, p. 483].

2   Seven Round Squares

How would a round square look like if we were asked to imagine it? At the *Diagrams 2018 conference*, we asked about 30 participants in a tutorial to imagine and draw a round square. This task is held to be impossible since whatever participants imagine, it can-not be both round and square [4]. Yet, seven distinct 'round squares' were collected (Fig. 1). Other configurations are obviously possible. Skepticism about the imaginabil-ity of 'round squares' springs from the opposition between Square-ness and Round-ness ([3] rightly argued that this is not a matter of contradiction but of mere contrariety). The difficulty consists in combining these incompatible properties. Yet, the collected 'round squares' show various tricks to achieve this impossible mission. Each figure instantiates square-ness and round-ness in a specific way: either by (1) drawing the associated figure (square, circle), or (2) part of the figure (edge, dot) or (3) naming it (label). The com-bination of the properties is expressed either by: (1) merging the *instantiations* of the properties, (2) introducing a device (line of identity), or (3) standpoint (projections).

(*a*) A square with round edges.

(*b*) A circle inside a square.

(*c*) A circle with dots standing for the edges of a square that is not drawn.

(*d*) A circle disrupted by the four edges of a square that is not drawn.

(*e*) A circle and a square connected with a line to indicate their identity.

(*f*) A circle labelled 'Square'.

(*g*) A cylinder that appears as a square from one side and as a circle from another.

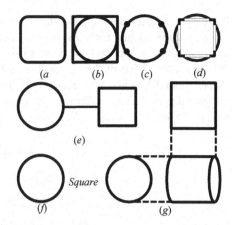

Fig. 1. Seven imagined 'round squares'

We see that to imagine an object that has a property, the *imagined object* does not need to *have* that property. We just need to *show* that possession. For instance, if we wish to imagine a hot tea, our imagined object does not need to be hot itself! We may just indicate the heat with steam. Similarly, it is not necessary to produce an object that *is* round and square in order to imagine a 'round square'. We merely need to depict the joint *possession* of round-ness and square-ness. Diagrams help.

3   Diagrams Help

Figure 1 depicted some strategies that are used to imagine a 'round square'. The recipe may be generalized to all impossible (and also possible) objects: instantiate the properties of the object, then express their joint possession. This design suggests an easy method of visualization that we will introduce after a short historical digression. We alluded earlier to MacColl's treatment of impossible objects. Lewis Carroll also considered imaginary objects and classes, the latter containing only imaginary objects [5, p. 2]. An imaginary class is not empty since it does contain objects, even if they are imaginary. MacColl, possibly under Carroll's influence [1], extended the idea:

> Let e1, e2, e3, etc. [...] denote the universe of *real existences.* Let 01, 02, 03, etc., denote our universe of *non-existences,* that is to say, of unrealities, such as *centaurs, nectar, ambrosia, fairies,* with self-contradictions, such as *round squares, square circles, flat spheres,* etc. [...] Finally, let S1, S2, S3, etc., denote our *Symbolic Universe,* or "Universe of Discourse," composed of all things real or unreal that are named or expressed by words or other symbols in our argument or investigation. By this definition we assume our Symbolic Universe [...] to consist of our Universe of realities, e1, e2, e3, etc., together with our universe of unrealities, 01, 02, 03, etc., *when both these enter into our argument.* [8, p. 74]

In the symbolic universe, *non-existences* (including Round squares) and *existences* are on the same footing. Hence, one does not need to differentiate their visualisations.

It is easy to employ diagrams for the purpose. For instance, we draw a circle for the set of squares and another for round objects. The intersection contains objects that are both round and square. We mark the intersection to denote a specific 'round square' (Fig. 2). Of course, the shape of the curves does not logically matter [10], and we could have shaped them differently to increase suggestiveness. Yet, what matters is that the marked individual possesses the properties of round-ness and square-ness and, thus, stands for a round square [12, p. 181].

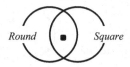

Fig. 2. Visualization of a round square.

It is easy to imagine the disappointment that this scheme may generate among the readers who had higher expectations in terms of *naturalness*. Yet, such demands are unjustified since diagrams are not 'pictorial images' of the objects they stand for. They are rather instrument that are shaped in such a way as to achieve a specific function in a specific context and that may be manipulated with imagination [7, 11]. There are no more *natural* diagrams than there are round squares, so far.

References

1. Abeles, F.F., Moktefi, A.: Hugh MacColl and Lewis Carroll: crosscurrents in geometry and logic. Philosophia Scientiae **15**(1), 55–76 (2011)
2. Arana, A.: Imagination in mathematics. In: Kind, A. (ed.) The Routledge Handbook of Philosophy of Imagination, pp. 463–477. Routledge, London (2016)
3. Beziau, J.-Y.: Round squares are no contradictions (Tutorial on negation contradiction and opposition). In: Beziau, J.-Y., Chakraborty, M., Dutta, S. (eds.) New Directions in Paraconsistent Logic. SPMS, vol. 152, pp. 39–55. Springer, New Delhi (2015). https://doi.org/10.1007/978-81-322-2719-9_2
4. Béziau, J.-Y.: Possibility, imagination and conception. Princípios **23**(40), 59–95 (2016)
5. Carroll, L.: Symbolic Logic. Macmillan, London (1897)
6. Costa-Leite, A.: Logical properties of imagination. Abstracta **6**(1), 103–116 (2010)
7. Giardino, V.: Manipulative imagination: how to move things around in mathematics. Theoria **33**(2), 345–360 (2018)
8. MacColl, H.: Symbolic reasoning (VI). Mind **14**(53), 74–81 (1905)
9. MacColl, H.: Symbolic logic (a reply). Mind **16**, 470–473 (1907)
10. Moktefi, A.: Is Euler's circle a symbol or an icon? Sign Systems Stud. **43**(4), 597–615 (2015)
11. Moktefi, A.: Diagrams as scientific instruments. In: Benedek, A., Veszelszki, A. (eds.) Virtual Reality – Real Visuality, pp. 81–89. Peter Lang, Frankfurt am Main (2017)
12. Moktefi, A.: Diagrammatic reasoning: the end of scepticism? In: Benedek, A., Nyiri, K. (eds.) Vision Fulfilled: The Victory of the Pictorial Turn, pp. 177–186. Hungarian Academy of Sciences – Budapest University of Technology and Economics, Budapest (2019)
13. Niiniluoto, I.: Imagination and fiction. J. Semant. **4**, 209–222 (1985)

14. Rabouin, D.: Les mathématiques comme logique de l'imagination: Une proposition leibnizienne et son actualité. Bulletin d'analyse phénoménologique **13**(2), 222–251 (2017)
15. Radford, C.: MacColl, Russell, the existential import of propositions, and the null-class. Philos. Q. **45**(180), 316–331 (1995)
16. Russell, B.: On denoting. Mind **14**(56), 479–493 (1905)
17. Smith, J.F.: The Russell-Meinong debate. Philos. Phenomenological Res. **45**(3), 305–350 (1985)

Visualizing Curricula

Jacklynn Niemiec(✉) (iD)

Drexel University, Philadelphia, PA 19104, USA
jnn33@drexel.edu

Abstract. The poster presents an approach for curriculum mapping through the use of data visualization techniques. A sample set of six courses is selected to study the potential of this method. Primary course data is mined from syllabi and assignments and then organized in a database format. The structure leverages course content as data to visualize information about learning objectives, competencies, and sequencing. Course content and sequence-based mapping examples provide evidence of this approach.

Keywords: Mapping · Visualization · Data · Education · Curriculum

1 Introduction

Curriculum mapping is a widely accepted practice in education: a curriculum map cross-references course or program level outcomes against course content to reveal gaps or redundancies. Curriculum maps follow a schedule to locate where and when the learning of specific topics will occur. This format maps curricula linearly, as a path to follow, and presumes that each student will follow that particular route and learn at the same rate. These maps separate knowledge and abilities into individual cells, taking stock of the learning outcomes in a binary way. However, to cross-reference outcomes, such as concepts and skills, within a course requires more nuance. Visualizing connections across a curriculum, whether in or out of sequence, is essential. This type of assessment is especially useful for faculty teaching in architectural education, where skills, concepts, standards, and critical thinking support the integration of knowledge in comprehensive design outcomes.

The poster presents an approach for curriculum mapping through the use of data visualization techniques. Generating visualizations from data reveals unknown patterns and potential connections through "mapping" rather than "tracing" or documenting expected outcomes [1]. Tracing course outcomes defines points in time when all students realize a specific skill or concept—traditional curriculum maps present course information as a matrix, reinforcing a binary visual language and linear structure. Organizing course content as a database allows for filtering and sorting per metadata, supporting a myriad of visualization types. For instance, sorting curriculum data by learning outcome and then by course assignment yields information about which assignments build on one another over time. A different strategy may look at learning outcomes over time to identify which patterns or rhythms emerge in the repetition of topics.

A.-V. Pietarinen et al. (Eds.): Diagrams 2020, LNAI 12169, pp. 544–547, 2020.
https://doi.org/10.1007/978-3-030-54249-8_53

2 Method

A sample set curriculum of six courses is selected. The classes are sequential and taught over two years of a Bachelor of Architecture program. The courses cover a range of learning outcomes for architecture students, including skills, concepts, standards, and processes [2]. These range from freehand drawing to three-dimensional digital modeling. The complexity of the course content is especially relevant to this study because it provides a rich set of data to explore. Each assignment is multifaceted and teaches students fundamental concepts along with the necessary skills to execute the work. Primary course data is mined from syllabi and assignments and then organized in a database format.

Three categories organize the data: information, outcome, and structure. Information data defines vital information such as the title, date, and course number. Outcome data lists information related to learning outcomes such as outcome topics, level of difficulty, and cognitive processes. Structure data lists specific considerations of the assignment or learning outcome, such as the format or medium used. Each course and assignment are input with a unique ID in a stacked format (Table 1). This format lists each incidence of a learning outcome topic as a unique component of the course sequence. This arrangement allows for sorting the content in various ways, such as isolating the sequencing of concepts versus skills in the curriculum.

Table 1. Abbreviated database sample

Information		Outcome					Structure	
ID	#	Topic	Level	Type	Process	x	Tool	Source
001	211	Composition	1	Concept	Reproduce	1.1	Model	Analog
002	211	Modeling	1	Skill	Produce	1.3	Model	Analog
003	212	Photography	1	Skill	Translate	1.2	Camera	Digital
004	211	Hierarchy	1	Concept	Identify	1.4	Model	Analog
005	213	Lineweight	2	Standard	Reproduce	1.1	Drafting	Analog

Some qualitative categories included in the database are assigned numeric values. The category "level" applies a number based on the incidence of that topic occurring in the course sequence. Because most outcomes recur in the sequence, their level increases over time. A multiplier *(x)* weights the incidence of each topic by the process applied within the cognitive learning levels [3].

The database structure leverages course content for visualizing information about learning objectives, competencies, and sequencing [2]. Functions such as comparison, distribution, flow, and patterns are possible to generate using this method. Once the data is stacked, visualization tools such as RAWGraphs, an opensource software, facilitates the translation of data into visual form. Subsequent graphic refinement and composition in Adobe Illustrator highlight the information presented.

3 Results

The poster presents the curriculum in two visualization forms, content and sequence-based mapping [4]. Curricular content visualizations examine the learning objectives and their distribution. Curricular content is presented here as an alluvial diagram [Fig. 1]. This visualization type sorts the four primary learning objectives (skill, standard, concept, and process) by course, then by topic and again by analog versus digital medium. Density in particular areas tracks emphasis on a topic or medium in the curriculum as a whole. Color tracks the incidence of digital tools within the connections.

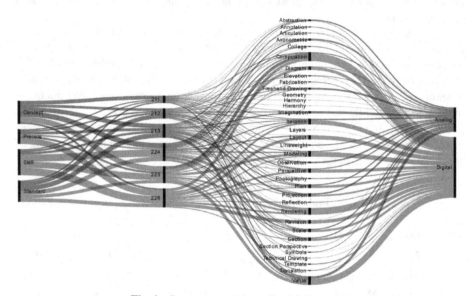

Fig. 1. Content mapping as alluvial diagram.

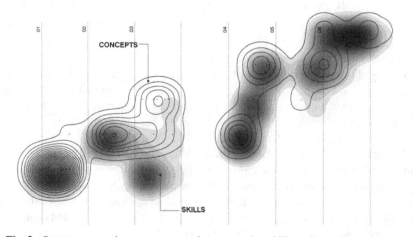

Fig. 2. Sequence mapping as a contour plot, comparing skills and concepts over time.

Sequence visualizations document the courses over time, considering them as a series. Mapping flow in curricula provides insight into connections across various categories; a contour plot is presented here as a sequence-based mapping [Fig. 2]. The contour plot assesses individual assignment difficulty (y-axis) over time (x-axis) and displays density through the distance between contours. This visualization type provides evidence of course content and anomalies within each course. The density of points in a particular area reveals a consistency in the level of difficulty and cognitive processes required in each course.

4 Conclusions

The results support the potential of data visualization in curriculum mapping. Future work may examine best-fit visualization types, corresponding student assessments, and use of a database to support curriculum mapping as an ongoing, internally motivated process rather than a singular exercise [5].

Acknowledgments. I wish to thank the faculty and administrators who have contributed to the creation of the courses and curriculum studied in the poster.

References

1. Wang, C.-L.: Mapping or tracing? Rethinking curriculum mapping in higher education. Stud. High. Educ. **40**, 1550–1559 (2015)
2. Aldowah, H., Al-Samarraie, H., Fauzy, W.M.: Educational data mining and learning analytics for 21st century higher education: a review and synthesis. Telemat. Inform. **37**, 13–49 (2019)
3. Krathwohl, D.R., Anderson, L.W.: A Taxonomy for Learning, Teaching, and Assessing: A Revision of Bloom's Taxonomy of Educational Objectives. Longman, New York (2009)
4. Arafeh, S.: Curriculum mapping in higher education: a case study and proposed content scope and sequence mapping tool. J. Furth. High. Educ. **40**, 585–611 (2016)
5. Maki, P.L.: Developing an assessment plan to learn about student learning. J. Acad. Librariansh. **28**, 8–13 (2002)

Elucidating the Effects of Diagram Use Training for Math Word Problem Solving

Hiroaki Ayabe[1]([✉]), Emmanuel Manalo[1], and Noriko Hanaki[2]

[1] Graduate School of Education, Kyoto University, Kyoto, Japan
ayabe@nips.ac.jp, manalo.emmanuel.3z@kyoto-u.ac.jp
[2] Faculty of Liberal Arts, The Open University of Japan, Chiba, Japan
noriko.hanaki@academion.com

Abstract. In solving math word problems, diagram use is generally considered effective [1]. However, although teachers often demonstrate diagram use, students do not use them spontaneously, and when they do, they tend to use them ineffectively. The prevalence of student difficulties in problem solving can at least in part be attributed to these problems [2]. Recently, we demonstrated that both knowledge about diagram use and practice are necessary to promote spontaneous use [3], and result in improvements in correct answer rates [4]. However, the components of instruction necessary for diagram use mastery, and the corresponding physiological consequences (brain activity) remain unclear. Thus, we clarified these issues in the present study. Sixteen participants (aged 15.7 ± 2.9 years) were given math word problems for which the use of tables was deemed effective for generating a solution. Data collection was in three phases: No-Instruction-or-Training, Asked-to-Use-a-Table, and After-Table-Use-Training. We measured their math word problem solving performance, and frontal brain/cerebral blood flow using fNIRS (Functional near-infrared spectroscopy). Only after the Table-Use-Training did participants show improvements in correct answer rates (pre- and post-training comparison, $t_{(15)} = 2.54, p = .022$), corresponding with an increase in table use ($t_{(15)} = 7.93, p < .001$). Furthermore, following training, participants showed blood flow increase in the left frontal area of the brain (dorsolateral- and ventrolateral-prefrontal cortex) while solving the problems. These results indicate that simply asking students to use diagrams is not adequate: appropriate training is necessary for effective use. They also provide evidence for physiological/brain consequences of successful learning/skills acquisition.

Keywords: Math education · Diagrams · Tables · Skills training · Brain measurements of learning

1 Introduction

It is necessary for us to use mathematics in various facets of everyday life. Developing skills in solving math word problems are particularly important because such problems contextualize the need to apply math knowledge and skills, rendering them as useful

© Springer Nature Switzerland AG 2020
A.-V. Pietarinen et al. (Eds.): Diagrams 2020, LNAI 12169, pp. 548–552, 2020.
https://doi.org/10.1007/978-3-030-54249-8_54

practice for real life situations. However, the correct answer rates tend to be low. Generally, students do not use diagrams spontaneously when solving such problems even though diagrams are considered effective tools for solving them [1]. Furthermore, even when they use diagrams, they do not always succeed in solving the problems [2]. Recent studies suggest that the reduction of cognitive load following instruction and development of diagram knowledge (knowing *what, when,* and *how* to use them) encouraged spontaneous use [3]. They also suggest that knowledge about diagram use is domain specific, meaning that knowledge about using particular diagrams (e.g., tables) for solving particular kinds of problems (e.g., rate of change) are not generalizable to solving other kinds of problems (e.g., point of intersection) [4].

However, the components of instruction necessary for diagram use mastery, and the corresponding physiological consequences (brain activity) remained unclear. Thus, the present study was aimed at clarifying them in math word problem solving. We hypothesized that instructions that encourage students to construct the appropriate diagram would promote its use but that such use would not always result in improving the correct answer rates as they might lack domain specific skills. Another aim was to elucidate the physiological mechanism of acquiring diagram use skills by considering cerebral blood flow as a measure/indicator of such mastery.

2 Method

This research was approved by the ethics committee of the lead researchers' university. Participants were 16 students from elementary school level to undergraduate university level (female $= 6$; mean age $= 15.7 \pm 2.9$ years). We employed a pre- and post-test design within participants, with intervention phases (Pre-intervention 1: "No-Instruction-or-Training"; Pre-intervention 2: "Asked-to-Use-a-Table", during which the participants were asked to use a table but not given any training; Intervention: during which "Table-Use-Training" instruction was provided; and Post-intervention: which only comprised problem solving assessment). Participants were randomly divided into three groups to verify the isomorphism of the problems (see Table 1).

Table 1. Implementation schedule

Sess.	Phase	Instruction	Group A (N = 6)	Group B (N = 5)	Group C (N = 5)
1	Pre-int. 1	No-Instruction-or-Training	Game	Sweets	Factory
	Pre-int. 2	Asked-to-Use-a-Table	Sweets	Factory	Game
2	Intervention	Table-Use-Training instruction provided			
3	Post-int.	Only given problems to solve	Factory	Game	Sweets

The study was conducted in three sessions: session 1 (Pre-int. 1 and Pre-int. 2 tests), session 2 (intervention of teaching of diagram knowledge of tables), and session 3 (Post-int. test). The test sessions were conducted in the laboratory to measure frontal brain activity (using fNIRS; Functional near-infrared spectroscopy) of the participants during solving of the problems given (15–25 min each, including the time for attaching and detaching the fNIRS equipment); only the intervention session was carried out in another room to provide diagram knowledge about Tables (30 min). Tables were deemed to be helpful for solving the problems used (see Table 2). Preliminary analysis confirmed their isomorphism in terms of difficulty, as no significant differences between problems occurred in all phases. In the present study, isomorphic problems refer to problems that have different cover stories but have equivalent solving structures. Here, the solving structure is one in which the answer to the problem can be calculated by focusing on the number sequence in the table or array that is constructed.

Table 2. Problems used

Prob	Isomorphic problems
Game	Studying and Playing Time: A boy spends a total of 150 min every day studying and playing games. If his study time is longer than that of playing games, he will play games 30 min longer the next day. Otherwise, he will study 45 min longer than the time spent on playing games on the previous day. He studied for 50 min on day 1. On day 365, how many minutes will he study for?
Sweets	Sweets Tree: There is a sweets tree which bears a total of 111 macaroons and eclairs every day. If eclairs are more than macaroons, it will bear 33 more macaroons the next day than the number of eclairs on the previous day. Otherwise, it will bear 22 less macaroons than those on the previous day. It bore 99 macaroons on day 1. How many macaroons will the tree bear on day 365?
Factory	Automobile Factory: A factory manufactures automobile parts, packing 150 parts in each box and carries as many boxes as possible to the assembly plant every day. If the number of the parts left are more than 75, the factory will produce 180 parts the next day. Otherwise, it will produce 220 parts. The number of the parts left was 130 on day 1. How many parts will be left on day 365?

In the test sessions for the three groups, the three kinds of problem were provided in a counterbalanced order (see Table 1). A questionnaire was given immediately after each task. In the intervention sessions, instructions to develop semantic and procedural knowledge for use of tables were provided. Equivalent math word problems (isomorphic in structure and requirements), in which tables were required to efficiently arrive at their solutions, were created and used in the instructions and tests (different problems were used in instructions and tests). All the problems were presented in sentences only, and contained no expressions to explicitly induce diagram use. The diagrams and answers included on answer sheets were scored by two undergraduate students with no vested interested in the outcomes, using rubrics that allocated 0–8/0–5 points (diagram score/problem score) depending on appropriateness, correctness, and detail [4].

3   Results and Discussion

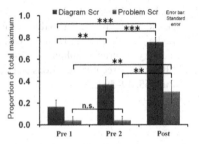

Comparisons of scores at Pre-int. 1 and Pre-int. 2 phases revealed that diagram use scores increased ($p < .01$) but correct answer rates did not (n.s.; see Fig. 1). This suggests that asking students to use a table increased their diagram use but did not improve their ability to solve the problems. Comparing Pre-int. 2 and Post-int. phases revealed that correct answer rates also increased ($p < .01$).

Fig. 1. Changes in diagram score and problem score in all phases ($N = 16$)

This suggests that, after providing instruction, not only diagram use but also correct answer rates increased. Comparisons of brain activities at Pre-int. 1 and Pre-int. 2 revealed that cerebral blood flow did not change (n.s.). However, comparisons at Pre-int. 1 and Post-int. revealed that cerebral blood flow increased around the left frontal area (DLPFC and VLPFC, $p < .05$ for both; see Fig. 2).

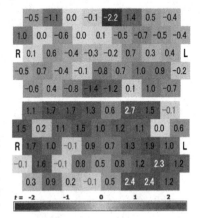

These results of the present study demonstrate that interventions of simply asking students to use diagrams are not adequate, but providing instruction and practice improves correct answer rates. These results also suggest that students were given new knowledge about tables through instruction, not based on their original knowledge, and acquired the skills of use through practice. That is, activation in the left-VLPFC is considered as reflecting memory retention [5], while that in the left-DLPFC is indicative of cognitive control by reconstruction due to new memories [6].

Fig. 2. Changes in cerebral blood flow at points of measurement in the frontal lobe from right (R) to left (L) (numerical values are *t-test* scores; upper = Pre-int. 2, lower = Post-int., both compared to Pre-int. 1 as baseline; $N = 16$)

The findings of this study reveal objective evidence by linking behavioral and physiological methods. Though it has previously been difficult to distinguish the components of instruction necessary for diagram use mastery, this integrated method helped to identify the effects of instruction and practice on diagram use skills acquisition.

References

1. Uesaka, Y., Manalo, E., Ichikawa, S.: What kinds of perceptions and daily learning behaviors promote students' use of diagrams in mathematics problem solving? Learn. Instr. **17**, 322–335 (2007)
2. Uesaka, Y., Manalo, E.: Peer instruction as a way of promoting spontaneous use of diagrams when solving math word problems. In: Proceedings of the 29th Annual Cognitive Science Society, pp. 677–682. Cognitive Science Society, Austin (2007)
3. Ayabe, H., Manalo, E.: Can spontaneous diagram use be promoted in math word problem solving? Lect. Not. Artif. Intell. **10871**, 817–820 (2018)

4. Ayabe, H., Manalo, E., Hanaki, N.: Teaching diagram knowledge that is useful for math word problem solving. In: EAPRIL 2019 Proceedings, pp. 388–399 (2020). ISSN: 2406-4653
5. Badre, D., Wagner, A.D.: Left ventrolateral prefrontal cortex and the cognitive control of memory. Neuropsychologia **45**, 2883–2901 (2007)
6. Elliott, R.: Executive functions and their disorders: imaging in clinical neuroscience. Br. Med. Bull. **65**, 49–59 (2003)

Author Index

Printed in the United States
By Bookmasters